SYRIA BETRAYED

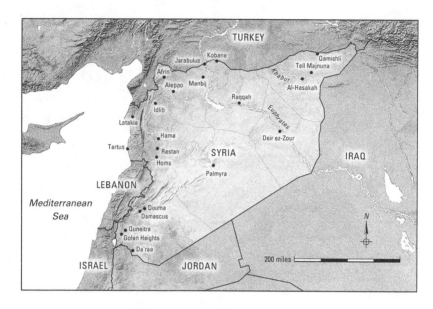

Syria

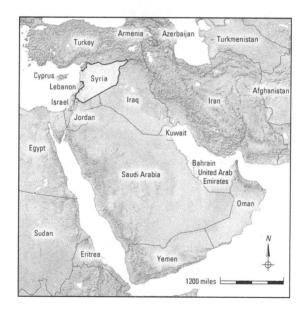

Syria and Its Neighbors

ALEX J. BELLAMY

SYRIA BETRAYED

Atrocities, War, and the Failure
of International Diplomacy

COLUMBIA UNIVERSITY PRESS

NEW YORK

Columbia University Press
Publishers Since 1893
New York   Chichester, West Sussex
cup.columbia.edu

Library of Congress Cataloging-in-Publication Data
Names: Bellamy, Alex J., 1975– author.
Title: Syria betrayed : atrocities, war, and the failure of
international diplomacy / Alex J. Bellamy.
Description: New York : Columbia University Press, [2022] |
Includes bibliographical references and index.
Identifiers: LCCN 2021058087 (print) | LCCN 2021058088 (ebook) |
ISBN 9780231192965 (hardback) | ISBN 9780231550086 (ebook)
Subjects: LCSH: Syria—History—Civil War, 2011—Atrocities. |
War crimes—Syria—History—21st century. | Political violence—Syria—
History—21st century. | Civilian war casualties—Syria. |
War victims—Syria.
Classification: LCC DS98.6 .B443 2022 (print) | LCC DS98.6 (ebook) |
DDC 956.9104/23—dc23/eng/20220105
LC record available at https://lccn.loc.gov/2021058087
LC ebook record available at https://lccn.loc.gov/2021058088

Cover design: Julia Kushnirsky
Cover photo: © William Daniels/Panos Pictures

CONTENTS

ACKNOWLEDGMENTS

I T TAKES a village to write a book, and in the writing of this book I have incurred many debts of gratitude. I am grateful to all those busy people who gave up their time to answer my questions and reflect on their memories and experience of Syria's war. I am especially grateful to my mentor, guide, occasional coauthor, and friend, Edward C. Luck, who helped so much in getting this project off the ground and guiding me through the labyrinth that is politics at the United Nations but sadly passed away before I could finish. This book is in essence a testimony to the aspirations that drove Professor Luck through his long career of service to the UN and the academy and a reminder that much more needs to be done to fulfill those aspirations. I am also immensely grateful to Ivan Simonovic for his help and guidance inside and outside the UN and to Simon Adams and Savita Pawnday at the Global Centre for the Responsibility to Protect for their help and sage advice on all things related to UN politics and R2P.

Particular thanks, as always, are owed to Paul D. Williams. Paul played a role in every part of this project, not least by reading the whole manuscript, and his influence can be seen on every page.

Mareen Brosinsky provided research assistance on Syria before this particular project was conceived, and Diogo Quental de Sousa assisted in its final stages. Kyle Beardsley, Richard Caplan, Liz Carmichael,

Allard Duursma, Rosemary Foot, Jamie Gaskarth, Luke Glanville, John Gledhill, Lisa Hultman, Sabrina Karim, Jonathan Leader Maynard, Richard Lock-Pullan, Stephen Mcloughlin, Keith Porter, Andrea Ruggeri, Jennifer Welsh, and Nick Wheeler read, discussed, and otherwise supported the research and writing, including by engaging with earlier iterations of the text and ideas. Noura Aljiwazi helped me better understand the roots of the crisis and its opening phases. Thanks to OxPeace, New College Oxford, the University of Uppsala, the University of Birmingham, and the Stanley Institute for allowing opportunities to share aspects of this work in talks and to learn from the insightful feedback. Thanks also to the Department of Politics and International Relations at the University of Oxford for the opportunity to be a visiting fellow there, time used to complete the first draft. I owe a debt of thanks to my colleagues at the Asia Pacific Centre for the Responsibility to Protect, especially Arna Chancellor, Sarah Teitt, Noel Morada, Nikki Marczak, and Kirril Shields.

I am immensely grateful to Caelyn Cobb at Columbia University Press for her unfailing enthusiasm, support, and assistance and to Anita O'Brien, whose edits improved my prose no end.

This was a difficult book to write, and I could not have done it, or anything else, without the relentless love, care, support, joy, and wisdom of my wife, Sara Davies, and our son, Isaac. To them, I owe the biggest debt of all.

Brisbane, October 2021

TERMS AND ABBREVIATIONS

SYRIAN GOVERNMENT SIDE

Mukhabarat, Military Intelligence Directorate. Responsible for state security, intelligence gathering, interrogation, prisons, and other armed security activities. Also contains at least four paramilitary units.

NDF, National Defense Forces, 2012–. Pro-regime paramilitary forces formed with Iranian assistance and paid salaries by the government. Size: ca. 50,000–100,000.

shabiha, Pro-regime militia and organized crime groups.

OPPOSITION SIDE

Ahrar al-Sham, 2011–. Islamist and Salafist coalition of armed groups. In 2012–2013 it was the second largest coalition after the FSA. Operating mainly around Idlib, it was a member of the Islamic Front. Has evolved since 2018 and allied with the SNA. Size: 10,000–20,000.

Ansar al-Sham, 2012–. Latakia-based Islamist armed group that joined the Islamic Front in 2013. Remnants largely in the Idlib district, cooperating with HTS. Size: < 2,000.

Farouq Brigades, 2011–2014. FSA-aligned, moderately Islamic armed group operating in Homs. Dissolved as a result of military reverses and rise of more hard-line groups. Size: 7,000–10,000.

FSA, Free Syrian Army, 2011–2017. Loose organization of allied armed groups established by officers defecting from the Syrian Army. Remnants were folded into the Turkish-backed Syrian National Army (SNA) in 2017. Size: ca. 25,000–50,000.

Harakat Hazzm, Hazzm Movement, 2014–2015. U.S.-backed alliance of secular and moderate armed groups operating mainly in Idlib and Aleppo. Size: ca. 400.

HNC, Higher Negotiations Committee, 2015–. Umbrella body created to represent the opposition in the Geneva peace talks.

HTS, Hay'at Tahrir al Sham, 2017–. Salafist Jihadist armed group operating in Idlib. Formerly known as al-Nusra. Size: 12,000–20,000.

ISIS, Islamic State in Iraq and al-Sham [greater Syria]. In Syria, principally active 2014–2019. Also known as Islamic State (IS) and Islamic State in Iraq and the Levant (ISIL). Extreme radical Islamist group that emerged from Al-Qaeda in Iraq (AQI) and the Islamic State in Iraq (ISI). Began taking territory in Syria in 2014; largely defeated there in 2019. Size: 30,000–50,000, around half of which operated in Syria.

Islamic Front, 2013–2015. Coalition of Sunni Islamist groups operating in Aleppo Governate. Members included Liwa al-Tawhid, Jaish al-Islam, and Ahrar al-Sham. Always a loose coalition, it crumbled in 2015. Size: ca. 40,000–70,000.

Jabhat al-Nusra (al-Nusra), 2012–2017. Salafist Jihadist group founded by Al-Qaeda in Iraq and affiliated with Al-Qaeda. Broke with ISIS in 2014. Joined with other Islamist Salafist groups to become HTS in 2017. Size: 12,000–30,000.

Jaysh al-Fatah, 2015–2017. Coalition of Salafist Jihadist groups led by al-Nusra and supported by Saudi Arabia, Qatar, and Turkey. Defections, starting with Ahrar al-Sham, led the coalition to dissolve. Size: 30,000–50,000.

Jaysh al-Islam, 2011–2018. Originally known as Liwa al-Islam. Moderately Islamist and sectarian group whose formal position became more secular and democratic. Allied with the FSA until 2013. Operated mainly in Damascus area. Its fighters were bused out of Douma in 2018 as part of the surrender agreement and many joined the SNA. Size: 12,000–15,000.

KNC, Kurdish National Council, 2011–. Coalition of Kurdish political groups opposed to the PYD.

Liwa al-Asifa, Storm Brigade, ca. 2012–2015. Small FSA-aligned Palestinian armed group. Size: < 500.

Liwa al-Tawhid, Al-Tawhid Brigade, 2012–2014. Operating mainly in the North around Aleppo, linked to Muslim Brotherhood and allied with the FSA. Some units operated alongside Kurdish YPG and were later integrated into the SDF. Size: ca. 5,000–10,000.

National Unity Brigades, 2012–2014. Armed opposition alliance composed mainly of national and religious minorities (Alawites, Christians, Druze) allied to the FSA. Size: ca. < 500–2,000.

NLF, National Liberation Front, 2018–2021. Armed group backed by Turkey operating principally in Idlib and elsewhere in the North. Folded into the SNA in 2021. Size: ca. 25,000.

Northern Brigade, Northern Democratic Brigade, formerly Liwa Hursan al-Haqq, 2012–. Secular Sunni armed group operating in northern Syria. Initially under the FSA umbrella, it later allied with the Kurdish YPG and joined the SDF. Recipient of U.S. military assistance. Size: 1,200–1,500.

PYD, Partiya Yetikiya Demokrat, Democratic Union Party. Principal Kurdish political party.

SDF, Syrian Democratic Forces, 2015–. Combined Kurdish-Arab force led militarily by the YPG. Size: ca. 150,000 (including YPG).

SNA, Syrian National Army, 2017–. Also known as the Turkish-backed Free Syrian Army. Coalition of armed opposition groups orchestrated and backed by Turkey. Participated in Turkish military interventions in Syria and reportedly also in Turkish-backed operations in Libya and Azerbaijan. Incorporated the NLF in 2021, significantly increasing its size. Size: 20,000–30,000.

SNC, Syrian National Council, 2011–. Political coalition of opposition groups established in Turkey.

SOC, National Coalition for Syrian Revolution and Opposition Forces, 2012–. Political coalition of opposition groups established in Qatar.

Southern Front, 2014–2018. Alliance of fifty to sixty secular and moderate religious opposition armed groups based in southern Syria, supported by the Military Operations Centre in Amman, Jordan. Dissolved after the defeat of the southern de-escalation zone. Size: 20,000–30,000.

Syrian Revolutionary Front, 2013–2015 in the North, 2013–2018 in the South. Coalition of secular and moderately Islamist armed groups fighting under the banner of the FSA. Established in response to the Islamic Front. Size: 7,000–15,000.

YPG, Yekineyen Parastina Gel, People's Defense Units, 2011–. Principal Kurdish armed group and principal group within the SDF. Size: ca. 100,000–135,000.

OTHER ABBREVIATIONS

AKP	Justice and Development Party
AQI	Al-Qaeda in Iraq
AU	African Union
AVLB	Armored Vehicle Launched Bridge
CDS	Council for Democratic Syria
CENTCOM	Central Command
GCC	Gulf Cooperation Council
IBSA	India, Brazil, and South Africa
ICC	International Criminal Court
ICRC	International Committee of the Red Cross
IDF	Israeli Defence Force
ISSG	International Support Group for Syria
JIM	Joint Investigative Mechanism
JOG	Joint Operational Group
LAS	League of Arab States, Arab League
LCC	Local Coordination Committee
MOC	Military Operations Center
NCB	National Coordination Body for Democratic Change
NSC	National Security Council
OIC	Organization of the Islamic Conference
OPCW	Organization for the Prevention of Chemical Weapons
R2P	responsibility to protect
RCC	Revolutionary Command Council
TOWs	Tube-launched, optically tracked, wireless-guided missiles
UNAMI	UN Assistance Mission in Iraq
UNSMIS	UN Supervision Mission in Syria

SYRIA BETRAYED

PROLOGUE

Humanity's Orphans

Everybody had their agenda and the interests of the
Syrian people came second, third, or not at all.

—Lakhdar Brahimi, UN special envoy for Syria, August 31, 2015

N EARLY 2011 the world was stunned as the Arab Spring tore through Tunisia, then Egypt, and then Libya, Bahrain, Oman, Yemen, and Jordan. Syria stood at the precipice. As diplomats at the United Nations argued about what to do in Libya and the deteriorating situation in Côte d'Ivoire, few understood that Syria was descending into a hell of civil war that would consume more than half a million lives, displace more than half the country's population, host the brutally genocidal Islamic State, and draw in the militaries of Iran, Hezbollah, Russia, the United States, Turkey, and others. As Syria's tragedy unfolded, not one foreign government consistently prioritized the protection of Syrians from atrocity crimes. Not only did they do little to alleviate suffering, much of what they did made matters worse. They betrayed Syria's civilians by breaking the trust between peoples, states, and global institutions exemplified by the responsibility to protect.

It is difficult to convey the extent of the brutality inflicted on Syria's tormented civilians since the uprising began in 2011, since raw numbers have a numbing effect. Syrians have been shot in the streets as they protested. Tens of thousands were hauled into prisons and tortured until dead. Tens of thousands more live on in those conditions. Barrel bombs packed with high explosives, nails, and other makeshift shrapnel have been hurled indiscriminately by the dozen into civilian neighborhoods. Men, women, and children have been gassed to death with sarin and chlorine. Civilians have been shot, knifed, beheaded, and even crucified. They have been denied food, water, and medicine to the point of malnutrition. Children have had their homes brought down on top of them and have been raped, shot, tortured, and forcibly recruited into armed groups. Women and girls have been kidnapped, trafficked, and sold as sex slaves. Schools have been systematically targeted and destroyed. Hospitals and medical centers suffered the same fate. The government and its allies were not responsible for all Syria's atrocities, but they were responsible for the overwhelming majority. Syrian civilians found themselves trapped between ISIS extremism and its deranged ideology enforced by beheading, immolation, and slavery and the indiscriminate barrel bombs, artillery fire, rockets, missiles, and militia of the government and its allies. Yet even at the peak of ISIS's power in Syria, jihadists killed Syrian civilians at a lower rate than the government. Different datasets record the number of civilians killed by the government and its allies in the decade between 2011 and 2021 as being between 175,000 and 207,000. In comparison, those same datasets record that ISIS was responsible for the deaths of between 5,000 and 6,500 Syrian civilians. The number of civilians killed by other opposition groups ranges between 6,000 and 11,000. Put another way, the Syrian government and its allies are likely responsible for between 86 and 94 percent of all civilian deaths directly caused by the war. These stark discrepancies show that while opposition groups certainly perpetrated atrocities, they did not do so on anything like the scale perpetrated by the government and its allies. There is no place for moral equivalency in the story of Syria's war.

More than sixty years earlier, the newly established United Nations General Assembly adopted a convention to prohibit genocide and establish a legal duty to prevent it. Two years later the four Geneva Conventions established what we today call International Humanitarian Law. Additional protocols agreed to in 1977 stipulated that "the civilian population as such, as well as individual civilians, shall not be the object of attack. Acts or threats of violence the primary purpose of which is to spread terror among the civilian population are prohibited" (article 13, protocol II). The protocols required that any use of force be strictly confined to military goals and established the legal principle of discrimination—the rule that soldiers are *obliged* to discriminate between soldiers and civilians and should refrain from violence if they cannot tell the difference. Violations of these laws have become known as "war crimes" and "crimes against humanity." New laws restricted the use of "Certain Conventional Weapons" (1980, 1995, 1996, 2008). The Chemical Weapons Convention in 1997 prohibited possession, manufacture, and use of chemical weapons, and the Organization for the Prohibition of Chemical Weapons was established to oversee it. In the same year, the Ottawa Treaty banned the manufacture, stockpiling, and use of antipersonnel land mines. In 2008 cluster munitions were also prohibited, by a treaty that garnered the support of more than a hundred states. The scope of legal obligations doesn't end with the prohibition of genocide, war crimes, and crimes against humanity, however. States have legal obligations to prevent these crimes, protect their victims, and promote compliance with the law. These laws reshaped expectations about how war ought to be conducted and civilians protected from its worst ravages. They established legal limits to what a government can lawfully do to its people. They codified the notion that sovereignty entails legal responsibilities as well as rights.

But these laws always stood in tension with two harsh political realities: First, that in war power tends to matter more than justice, since when the fighting starts actors rarely yield to law and justice alone. Indeed, it is precisely because they disagree about what justice is and what it entails that they fight. Second, that for all the talk of the rights of individuals and groups to protection from atrocity crimes, governments have tended to privilege sovereignty—especially their own—over the protection of basic human rights. There is a good reason for that, for sovereignty and its attendant right to noninterference protects postcolonial and small states from the coercive interference of the powerful and helps maintain a basic condition of orderly conduct among states. The awkward juxtaposition of the humanitarian aspirations expressed in international humanitarian law and a sovereignty-based international order raised difficult practical and ethical questions about what to do when states themselves committed atrocities against sections of their own population. The result was an acute gap between what the law said about how states should behave and how they actually behaved. Genocide, war crimes, and crimes against humanity persisted, often untroubled by outside interference. This became a matter of global concern after the Cold War and high-profile failures to stem genocide in Rwanda and Srebrenica; mass killing and ethnic cleansing in Angola, Bosnia, Burundi, Croatia, East Timor, Kosovo, Liberia, Sierra Leone, Zaire/Democratic Republic of Congo; and state repression in Iraq. Time and again, international society proved unwilling or unable to uphold its own laws in the face of such disasters. The principle of the "responsibility to protect"—or R2P as it has become known—was devised as a way of navigating these dilemmas. Unanimously endorsed by the UN General Assembly in 2005, the principle meant that governments recognized they have a responsibility to protect their populations from genocide, war crimes, ethnic cleansing, and crimes against humanity. They agreed to encourage and help one another fulfill their responsibility. They also pledged to use diplomatic, humanitarian, and other peaceful means to protect populations and decided that when a state is manifestly failing to protect its population from atrocities, the international community has a responsibility to take "timely and decisive action" to do so, using all necessary means through the United Nations Security Council. This commitment was made unanimously by the largest ever gathering of Heads of State and Government at the United Nations in 2005. It was reaffirmed by the General Assembly in 2009 and 2021. At the time of this writing, R2P had featured in ninety-two UN Security Council resolutions and statements and fifty-eight resolutions of the UN Human Rights Council. All this counted for little in Syria.

This book explains how and why the world failed to fulfill its responsibility to protect Syrians. Ultimately, it is a story of priorities, of how other things came to be seen as being more important than protecting Syrians from their government. So-called realists might say that this is inevitable; that we live in a brutal and illiberal world where power matters more than justice and where even trying to stop atrocities in other countries invariably makes things worse. But this takes too much for granted. It ignores evidence that determined action *can* mitigate and end atrocities.[1] And, like all structural theories, it absolves individuals of responsibility for their choices. As I will show, political leaders were presented time and again with choices, and almost every time they chose not to make alleviation of Syria's suffering their priority. These choices had direct, sometimes immediate, consequences for the lives of Syrians, usually for the worse. Things could have been different. Steps could have been taken to save lives, perhaps even lots of lives. I will show how decision making was guided by shibboleths; false assumptions that were exposed one by one. Chief among them was the conviction that Syria's president, Bashar al-Assad, could be persuaded to reform or agree to share power through a political settlement. Foreign actors clung to that belief despite its evident faults even as their peace processes zombified. There were other shibboleths too, about the impossibility of using force to good effect, about the opposition's inherent extremism, and about Russian good faith.

There are innumerable ways of telling this tragic story, but however one tells it, the central point remains the same: that despite moral imperatives, legal obligations, and our knowledge of what happens when the world turns a blind eye to atrocities, governments and international organizations chose not to prioritize the protection of Syrians because they thought other things were more important. First, Syria's civilians were betrayed by their own government. To Assad, killing civilians was always a price worth paying for regime survival. Then, they were betrayed by the government's foreign allies who blocked any meaningful multilateral approach to the crisis. Almost from the start, Assad's tottering government depended for its survival on foreign allies, principally Iran, Russia, and Hezbollah, cheered on from the sidelines by China and to a lesser extent, at the beginning at least, India, Brazil, and South Africa. Then those who claimed to be the friends of Syria's people, their most immediate neighbors, betrayed them. For all their posturing, Syria's Arab neighbors also had other priorities and were often more concerned with their own survival and legitimacy and their regional competition for hegemony, status, and influence, than they were with the plight of Syrians. They competed against one another as much as with Damascus and fostered the fragmentation and radicalism that doomed Syria's opposition. Turkey stayed the course longer than the others but mainly because it had a Kurdish problem and a refugee crisis to resolve. And then, those states most vociferous in their support for R2P and the principles of protection betrayed Syria's civilians. The West stridently condemned the violence, demanded reform, and agonized over what to do. Admittedly, the actions of others presented concerned Westerners with few appealing options. But protecting Syria's civilians was never their main priority either. For the United States at different times, priorities included military withdrawal from the Middle East, combatting Islamist terrorism, rapprochement with Iran, and protecting itself and its allies from the perceived threat posed by refugees fleeing for their lives. For Europeans, distracted by economic crisis and disunity, fear of terrorism and refugees always loomed larger than humanitarian concerns. Priorities shifted, but the protection of Syrian civilians was rarely even close to being at the top of the list. Even the United Nations—the institution entrusted to implement R2P—succumbed. As earnest efforts to negotiate peace crumbled, the organization propped up a zombie peace process that helped Assad while its humanitarian agencies funneled millions of dollars to the government and hundreds of millions of dollars worth of aid to government-controlled areas, despite that same government prohibiting the flow of aid to opposition areas it was besieging, bombarding, and starving. Thus did the United Nations aid and abet a government strategy based on atrocities.

Each betrayal made it more difficult for others to make a positive difference. Assad's refusal to compromise closed off any chance that dialogue and persuasion might reconcile the demands of most of Syria's people with the interests of Syria's government. The regime's determination to cling to power no matter the cost made the politics of coercion inevitable. By backing Assad, Russia and Iran raised the stakes and the potential costs of coercion, while Russia and China ensured little could be achieved multilaterally through the United Nations. At the beginning of the crisis, when a determined and united UN might have achieved a better result, Assad's allies were fortified by states like India, Brazil, and South Africa, who intentionally diluted and delayed the UN's response at precisely the time it needed strengthening and quickening. Though their influence was limited, these states must share some of the blame for the horrific results of their actions. Some regional actors tried and failed to change the military situation; the United States dabbled half-heartedly in supporting Syria's armed opposition but had little enthusiasm for it and no appetite at all for anything more direct. Undoubtedly there was sympathy for the plight of Syria's unfortunate civilians both in the region and in the wider world, but there were no political leaders willing to pay any sort of cost to help them.

This is a painful story about how governments and institutions vested with the responsibility to protect abandoned Syrian civilians to their fate. It is both a reminder that the rights of civilians to not be tortured, gassed, bombed, and shot by their government have yet to override the rights and interests of states and an explanation of how that fact came to be.

1

ARAB SPRING

SYRIA'S REVOLUTION began with a whimper. Inspired by the dramatic events in Tunisia and Egypt, a handful of activists called for a "Day of Rage" on February 4–5, 2011, to express discontent toward their corrupt and authoritarian government and demand reform.[1] A week or so later, as Hosni Mubarak resigned his presidency in Cairo, a larger demonstration erupted in Damascus after police beat up a stall holder in the al-Hamidiya Souq.[2] France's ambassador, Eric Chevallier, cabled that while there were some commonalities between the recent revolutions in Egypt and Tunisia and the situation in Syria, the latter had a more complex sectarian mix, a more brutal and deeply embedded security state, and an alliance with Hezbollah that made it unclear how things would proceed.[3] U.S. ambassador Robert Ford reported that "this tinder is dry."[4]

The tinder was lit by events in the southern city of Daraa. There, five teenagers scrawled an impromptu rebuke to the country's authoritarian leader, Bashar al-Assad, on a school wall. The Political Security Directorate promptly arrested the alleged offenders and twenty other teenagers. They were beaten and tortured. Some had their fingernails extracted; some were forced to sleep naked on wet cold floors; some were left in stress positions for hours; some were electrocuted.[5] Daraa was a conservative, tight-knit community. Most of the arrested teenagers were members of the Abezaid clan, whose elders sought out Atef Najib, head of one of the local branches of the feared Mukhabarat, the secret police, and the president's cousin, to plead for the boys' release. "Forget you have children," Najib told them. "And if you want new children in their place, then send your wives over and we'll impregnate them for you."[6] It is hard to think of a greater insult. The protests grew, with hundreds joining the families marching through Daraa after Friday prayers on March 18. The Mukhabarat opened fire on the protestors, killing four. The killings only angered the people more. The protests grew. Thousands attended the funerals of these first victims. Security forces used tear gas and live bullets on them. Six more protestors were killed, and the situation spiraled quickly out of control. Assad tried to quell the unrest by offering condolences to the families of those killed, but his security forces delivered a different message. Protestors responded by setting Daraa's Ba'ath Party headquarters and the Syriatel building alight. They established a makeshift field hospital in the Omari Mosque to treat protestors targeted by the security forces. Worried the mosque might become a rallying point for dissent, as Tahrir Square had in Cairo, Assad ordered it be closed. Elite Mukhabarat units from Damascus led an assault on the mosque which left more than thirty-five people dead. "We had no choice but to nip this whole thing in the bud," Assad explained to one of his top aides.[7] A dragnet fell on Daraa, and hundreds of protestors and sympathizers were imprisoned.[8]

The attack on the Omari Mosque triggered demonstrations across the country, including in Homs, Baniyas, Latakia, Tartus, Idlib, Qamishli, Deir ez-Zor, al-Hasakah, Raqqa, Hama, Aleppo, and several Damascus suburbs. Around seventy protestors were killed in the marches after Friday prayers on March 25.[9] These were genuinely spontaneous, locally organized uprisings, inspired by the Arab Spring but driven by the deep resentments caused by decades of misrule, corruption, and brutal abuse by the government. Hollowed out by years of state repression, the opposition had no effective leadership and few means of coordination—something that proved fatal in the coming years. Protestors in different parts of the country demanded different things. In Daraa they wanted justice and an end to the decades of emergency rule that allowed the Mukhabarat to act with impunity. In

Latakia and Tartus, religious conservatives railed against legislation prohibiting teachers from wearing the *niqab*. In Homs, they complained about the privileges enjoyed by Alawites, the minority Shi'ite sect of the Assads. All wanted an end to unaccountable, abusive, and corrupt government. Local Coordination Committees (LCCs) sprang up to organize Friday protests and coordinate social media messages, making use of whatever people and resources came to hand.

The government seemed unsure of how to react. The attack on the Omari Mosque had not cowed the protests as Assad had expected, and he was uncertain about whether to offer concessions or crack down even harder.[10] Hard-liners advocated repression, arguing the governments in Tunisia and Egypt had brought disaster on themselves by not fighting to survive. Others, including Manaf Tlass, counseled restraint, arguing that repression might inflame the situation further and attract foreign intervention. On that, the global context was especially difficult to read. As things escalated in Syria, Muammar Gaddafi's brutal crackdown in Libya pushed NATO to intervene. That didn't augur well for Syria's hard-liners. But, just three days before, Saudi Arabia had led the Gulf Cooperation Council (GCC) in a military intervention in Bahrain to *support* government repression of protestors, at the cost of nearly a hundred lives.[11]

Could Assad replicate Bahrain's apparent success while avoiding Gaddafi's fate? That seems to have been his initial calculation: to use force slowly and gradually to avoid excessive international opprobrium.[12] Plain-clothed members of the Mukhabarat and Alawite criminal gangs known as *shabiha* routinely fired on demonstrators, but the daily toll rarely exceeded a dozen. Far more extensive was the rounding up, intimidating, imprisoning, and torturing of people suspected of participating in protests or having ties to those who were. But when protestors threatened to overrun whole suburbs, towns, or villages, the government's response became devastating. The security forces hit centers of opposition, such as Deraa, Homs, and Rastan, particularly hard.[13] Each time, the escalation of violence proved counterproductive, so Assad tried to sweeten the deal with concessions. He sacked the governor of Daraa, overturned the *niqab* ban, lifted "emergency rule," increased subsidies on heating fuel and other essentials, increased public service pay, promised to prosecute those responsible for killing protestors, and ended formal discrimination against the Kurds. Most Syrians still feared the chaos of revolution and retained some faith in Assad, hoping he would prove to be a reformer at heart by offering concessions to his opponents. They were sorely disappointed when the president used his March 30 address to the nation to vilify them instead. The following day, government snipers again fired on unarmed protestors. Emergency rule may have been lifted, but the Mukhabarat continued to arrest, detain, and torture people in their thousands and use live bullets on unarmed protestors, all with complete impunity.

With one hand appearing to conciliate, Assad used his other hand to stoke the flames of sectarianism to rally his base of Alawite support and sow discord among the opposition's growing ranks. Damascus portrayed the opposition as a front for jihadism and between March and June helped build this reality by releasing Islamist extremists—many of them hardened veterans of the Iraq insurgency—from the notorious Sednaya prison. Presented as a concession to the opposition (one it hadn't asked for), this was evidently intended to spread chaos by fracturing and radicalizing the opposition while strengthening the government's claim to be the victim of jihadist terrorism.[14] This was a highly cynical and carefully calibrated strategy, not an impulsive reflex. It proved successful, but only by exacting a terrible toll on human life.

A TONE OF RETICENCE

The initial international response to Syria's crisis was reticent. One Western diplomat described the situation as an "irritant."[15] There were three main reasons why. First, few understood how vulnerable to an uprising Assad's government was since most foreign governments believed Syria's government more stable and popular than Egypt's or Libya's.[16] Second, since the whole Middle East was in chaos in March 2011, only limited attention could be paid to Syria. The uprising in Daraa occurred almost simultaneously with a Saudi-led intervention in Bahrain, the eruption of armed conflict in Yemen, and the beginning of NATO-led military intervention in Libya. Arab governments were preoccupied with crises at home and in Egypt, Bahrain, and Libya; the United States was focused on Egypt (a key regional ally), Libya, and extricating itself from Iraq and Afghanistan (via a temporary surge initiated in 2009 with the aim of creating conditions for withdrawal); the UK and France were heavily invested in Libya. Third, what governments did know about Syria was that the risks of instability and conflict likely outweighed any possible good that might come of it. Most believed instability in Syria could provoke other disasters, such as war in Lebanon and Iraq, a new conflagration between Israel and Palestine, and a jihadist resurgence. The United States worried it could complicate withdrawal from Iraq.[17] Turkey worried that chaos in Syria might embolden its own Kurds. No one was eager to do anything that might destabilize Syria further.

The U.S. administration banked on Assad weathering the storm. Barack Obama had become U.S. president in 2008, promising to extract the United States from Iraq and Afghanistan. He pledged retrenchment and accommodation abroad, political transformation at home. This meant shifting resources from defense and foreign affairs toward social and economic programs, evading partisan struggles over foreign policy, and avoiding new international entanglements, especially in the Middle East.[18] "I'm not opposed to all wars," Obama once said, "I'm opposed to dumb wars."[19] He had always thought Iraq a dumb war and saw the urge to intervene in Syria in similar terms. The president understood the risks of region-wide instability and jihadist revanchism posed by growing chaos in Syria but saw it as a "wicked problem" to which there was no good solution. As Secretary of State Hillary Clinton later explained, "Do nothing, and a humanitarian disaster envelops the region. Intervene militarily, and risk opening Pandora's box and wading into another quagmire, like Iraq. Send aid to the rebels and watch it end up in the hands of extremists. Continue with diplomacy and run head-first into a Russian veto." None of these approaches "offered much hope of success."[20] All were laden with risks.

Obama wanted a new way of doing foreign policy, one that placed less emphasis on military force and more on the virtues of restraint, diplomacy, and accommodation. His approach hinged on the view that seemingly intractable problems could be resolved by constructive engagement and compromise. Since 2009, the new administration had tried to do just that with the government in Damascus, hoping a combination of diplomacy, soft power, and offers of sanctions relief might prize it away from Iran and encourage it to play positive roles in Iraq and Palestine. Assistant Secretary of State Jeffrey Feltman found Syria's foreign minister, Walid al-Moualem, "constructive" when the two met.[21] Under Secretary of State William Burns met Assad the following year but gave a more cautious report: "They will evade and obfuscate."[22] Undeterred, the administration had normalized diplomatic relations and dispatched Robert Ford to serve there as ambassador.[23]

When the protests erupted, Ford reported that "Assad is no Qaddafi. There is little likelihood of mass atrocities. The Syrian regime will answer challenges aggressively but will try to minimize the use of lethal force."[24] This view was widely shared in foreign policy circles. The chair of the Senate's Foreign Relations Committee, John Kerry, told an audience in Washington, D.C., that Assad was committed to maintaining a secular state in Syria.[25] Clinton described Assad as a reformer.[26] These comments reflected the administration's view that Assad could be relied on to manage Syria's crisis. U.S. officials privately urged Damascus to show restraint, hold those responsible for violence accountable, and introduce reforms, but they also made clear that the United States had no intention of interfering directly.[27]

Most Western governments hewed a similar line. European embassies in Damascus counseled both sides on the need for political dialogue, and the European Union explored how it might assist Syrian reform.[28] France was the most outspoken, but even it judged it would be best if Assad dealt with things himself. As one of Syria's former colonial rulers, France was far from a disinterested power, and its nationalist president, Nicolas Sarkozy, was eager to restore waning French influence there. The French government's Arab Spring had got off to a poor start when protests erupted in Tunisia. Paris had instinctively backed its longtime ally, the country's corrupt and authoritarian Ben Ali, only to find itself backing the wrong side when he fled into exile. Sarkozy tried to correct things by leading calls for military action against Gaddafi when the Libyan leader turned his guns on protestors.[29] The United States was initially skeptical about intervening in Libya, but when the UK and, surprisingly, the League of Arab States (LAS) called for the imposition of a no-fly zone to prevent a massacre should the rebel stronghold of Benghazi fall to Gaddafi, Obama reluctantly agreed on the condition that the intervention be authorized by the UN Security Council and the Europeans do the heavy lifting.[30] Emboldened by diplomatic success on Libya, Sarkozy was the most vociferous of the Western leaders on Syria, but even he confined himself to merely criticizing Assad at the outset.[31] In Damascus, French ambassador Chevallier urged Assadists to lead the reform movement.[32] Like other Western governments, Paris did not consider initiating direct talks between the government and opposition and instead placed their faith in Damascus.[33] Sarkozy's patience soon wore thin, however, and by the end of the year the French were among the first to raise the prospect of using force to create humanitarian corridors and buffer zones.[34]

The government closest to Assad was Iran. After testy beginnings, political ties between Syria and the Islamic Republic had flourished in the late 1980s when Hafez al-Assad, Bashar's predecessor and father, stood alone among Arab leaders in backing Tehran in its war with Saddam Hussein's Iraq.[35] The two governments learned to set aside their ideological differences (the Ba'athists are nominally secular; Iran is an Islamic Republic), theological disputes (the Alawites were considered heretical Shi'ites by Iran's religious leadership), and rivalry in Lebanon, as Damascus joined Tehran in supporting Hezbollah. But Iran's initial response to the Arab Spring was complicated by the fact that it was a revolutionary government brought to power by a popular struggle against a hated dictator and which had for decades waged hot and cold war on Sunni dictatorships. Tehran's instinct, therefore, was to support the Arab Spring uprisings and welcome revolts in Tunisia, Egypt, and the Gulf as revolutions against illegitimate Western-backed autocracies.[36] Syria posed a problem to this self-identity, so Tehran initially tried to balance these competing imperatives by assisting Assad, dispatching elite Revolutionary Guard (Quds force) officers to advise Syria's security forces, while simultaneously urging him to exhibit restraint and offer political concessions.[37]

Iran's traditional rivals Qatar, Saudi Arabia, and Turkey were initially concerned about the possible contagious effects the instability unleashed by the Arab Spring might have on them. They were therefore reluctant to add momentum to the protests by heaping pressure on Assad. With a population of only 300,000 citizens and 2.3 million migrant workers, tiny Qatar is an absolutist monarchy that uses its immense oil wealth to buy regional influence. Under the leadership of Emir Sheikh Hamad bin Khalifa al-Thani (1995–2013) and ambitious foreign minister Sheikh Hamad bin Jassim al-Thani (1992–2013), who also served as prime minister between 2007 and 2013, Qatar wanted to carve out a reputation as an international mediator, leading efforts—with differing degrees of success—in Lebanon, Darfur, Afghanistan, and Yemen. It developed an activist independent foreign policy prefaced on two contradictory pillars: strong support for conservative Islamism and groups like Hamas and the Muslim Brotherhood, and allegiance to the United States, who's Central Command (CENTCOM) was based in Doha. Its ties with the Muslim Brotherhood ran deep despite ideological differences, and Qatar provided sanctuary to Brothers fleeing persecution in Egypt in the 1950s and 1960s and to Syrians fleeing persecution in the 1980s.[38] Qatar was an enthusiastic supporter of military intervention in Libya and looked to use this to position itself on the right side of the Arab Spring and leverage influence. But Syria presented an altogether more difficult challenge. Qatar's relationship with Damascus had warmed in the years preceding 2011, and the emirate had invested heavily there.[39] The two governments held similar positions on Palestine and shared a deep distrust of Saudi Arabia.[40] Consequently, Qatar was in less of a hurry to condemn Damascus than it had been Tripoli. Not until late March did its cable news channel Al Jazeera begin extensive coverage of Syria's protests. The emir called Assad in March to counsel restraint but also signaled his continuing support.[41]

The Arab Spring came as an unwelcome shock to Saudi king Abdullah bin Abadulaziz Al Saud. An absolutist and highly conservative monarchy with its own disenfranchised Shi'ite population, the kingdom had good reason to fear popular revolution. In 1979 armed Sunni radicals demanding an end to Saudi Arabia's pro-Western foreign policy had seized the Grand Mosque in Mecca and held it for nearly two weeks before security forces retook it, at the cost of some 250 lives. To shore up their domestic legitimacy, the al-Sauds had become more conservative, deepening the sectarian dimension of its rivalry with Iran, a contest that played out in the bloody Iran-Iraq and Lebanon wars of the 1980s and in both Syria and Yemen in the 2010s. More pressing for Riyadh than sectarian rivalry in early 2011, though, were fears for its own future. These were stoked by the rise of the Muslim Brotherhood, one of its principal rivals for leadership in the Sunni world, in Egypt. The Brothers had long spearheaded popular opposition to the Gulf monarchies; now the revolution in Egypt looked certain to catapult them to power in one of the region's most important states. Stunned and terrified by Washington's abandonment of its long-standing Egyptian ally, Hosni Mubarak, Riyadh blamed the United States for mismanaging the Cairo crisis. The monarchy looked on in horror as small protests erupted in Jeddah, Qatif, and Riyadh and Saudi dissidents planned their own "Days of Rage." Its overwhelming urge to protect itself by countering popular uprisings wherever they happened outweighed whatever interest it may have had in weakening sectarian rivals like Assad. As Riyadh saw it, what Assad was doing in Syria was no different from what it was doing in Bahrain, where it had spearheaded an armed intervention at the request of the emirate to suppress a Shi'ite Arab Spring uprising.[42] Indeed, the two issues seemed connected, since Riyadh hoped Damascus and Tehran could be persuaded to restrain restive Shi'ites in Bahrain. Thus, between March and May 2011, Saudi Arabia conveyed support, including financial assistance, to Assad.[43] The emir of Kuwait did likewise. Like Iran, Saudi Arabia urged Damascus to restrain its security forces and introduce reforms to calm the situation. Saudi Arabia and Qatar used their influence to keep Syria off the Arab League's agenda and ensure there was no concerted move from the Gulf Cooperation Council.[44]

Syria's northern neighbor, Turkey, also reacted cautiously to the events of early 2011. The region's only Muslim majority democracy, Turkey was in the throes of its own revolution of sorts. At home, the ambitious and charismatic prime minister, Recep Tayyip Erdogan, whose Islamic-leaning Justice and Development Party (AKP) came to power in 2002, had overseen a period of unprecedented growth that had transformed the country's economic landscape. The Kurdish question loomed over Turkey's relationship with Syria, but things were changing there, too. Around 20 percent of Turkey's population is Kurdish, a group with its own language, history, and traditions. Conflict over language, land rights, and self-government had exploded into violence in the late 1970s when a leftist revolutionary, Abdullah Ocalan, launched a bloody armed rebellion. Pursued by the Turkish authorities, Ocalan fled to Syria and received sanctuary from Hafez al-Assad. From there, Ocalan's Kurdistan Worker's Party (PKK) waged a brutal campaign of terrorism and insurgency to which Turkey responded in kind, exacting a terrible toll. Over three decades of war, more than 40,000 soldiers and fighters were killed. The PKK killed more than 6,500 civilians in terrorist and other attacks, and the Turkish military killed more than 18,000 Kurdish civilians. Turkey's position improved with Syria's decision in 1998 to expel the PKK's leadership. Erdogan came to power determined to resolve the conflict and secure Turkish membership of the European Union. In 2005 he introduced reforms awarding better representation as well as language and cultural rights to the Kurds. A ceasefire was declared and, though broken periodically by both sides, generally held. Turkey's Kemalist nationalists were aghast at this, as were PKK hard-liners, since each opposed granting any concessions to the other. But despite sporadic upsurges of violence, between 2006 and 2011 the Turkish government and PKK sent delegates to Oslo for secret talks that came agonizingly close to a peace accord in 2012–2014 before breaking down, thanks largely to events in Syria. Within that context, at the start of 2011, Ankara was principally worried that instability in Syria might embolden the Kurdish Democratic Union Party (Partiya Yeti-kiya Demokrat, PYD), the PKK's principal Syrian ally, and unsettle the fragile negotiations.[45]

In foreign affairs, Erdogan's early Europeanism had gradually given way to a radical new approach. Convinced that Turkey had the material power to exert greater influence in the world, Foreign Minister Ahmet Davutoglu proposed a new, independent—some called it "neo-Ottoman"—foreign policy to replace its previously pro-NATO orientation. His vision emphasized Turkey's position as a bridge between West and East. Where Turkey had been treated as a second-class citizen by the West, Davutoglu saw that it could become a leader in the Middle East. A Sunni Muslim majority society with a democratic government, secular state, and thriving market economy, Turkey offered a model the region's Sunnis could emulate. This could be translated into regional influence by reaching out to neighboring states and groups like the Muslim Brotherhood.[46] Within this context, relations between Turkey and Syria improved strikingly in the 2000s.[47] In keeping with Davutoglu's "no problems with neighbors" idiom, Erdogan cultivated a personal friendship with Assad and seemed to think the Syrian leader might look to Turkey as a model. Visa restrictions were eased, and commercial ties grew steadily. Thus, when Syria's crisis erupted in March 2011, Erdogan believed he was uniquely well placed to influence Syria's leader.[48] He called Damascus at least twice in late March to encourage Assad to initiate reform, lift restrictions on the Muslim Brotherhood, and restrain violence, and to offer reassurance that Turkey would oppose sanctions and military intervention.[49]

THE SECURITY COUNCIL BLOCKED

The protests became larger, better organized (thanks to the creation of Local Coordination Committees), and more violent (thanks to the government) through April and May 2011.[50] Protests following Friday prayers on April 22—the day Assad formally ended the state of emergency—were the largest and bloodiest yet, as security forces killed around a hundred people.[51] Three days later, tanks rolled into the center of Daraa, intending to break the protests at their core. The city was effectively placed under siege, and more than two hundred people were killed in just two weeks.[52] Water and electricity were cut off, and the nearby Jordanian border closed. Soldiers fired indiscriminately at protestors, and snipers targeted ambulances ferrying the injured to hospitals. Thousands were seized and taken to schools and fields, where many were tortured and several killed.[53] The following Friday, April 29, people from the surrounding area poured out of the mosques after prayers and marched on Daraa to break the siege. Among them was a thirteen-year-old boy, Hamza Ali al-Khateeb. When snipers opened fire, killing more than thirty, Hamza disappeared, likely snatched by the Air Force Intelligence Directorate. His tortured and mutilated body was returned to his family a month later. He had been shot three times and beaten, his jaw and both knee caps smashed. He had been whipped, electrocuted, and burnt dozens of times with cigarettes. His penis had been severed.[54] A moment of clarity had been reached: Assad's reforms were proving meaningless. The protests, and violence, escalated.

The increasing violence forced governments to begin rethinking their initial responses. Faith in Assad receded, but most still believed it best to persuade the Syrian government to restrain its security forces and reform. Turkey and Qatar dispatched a string of senior envoys to Damascus, among them Sheikh Tamim bin Hamad al Thani, Qatar's crown prince. Tamim suggested Syria's problems lay in chronic under-development and promised financial help if Assad restrained the security forces and shared power. Assad reassured the prince that the situation was not as bad as portrayed in the media.[55] Other emissaries followed, repeating the same message. They advised Assad to call multiparty elections and pledged to support his candidacy if he did. Turkish officials proposed elections to establish a new government headed by Assad, to which Syria's president reportedly responded favorably.[56] In truth, Assad had no intention of going further in reforms than he already had, a reality underscored by the increasing violence each Friday.[57] Inevitably, relations between Damascus and its Arab and Turkish neighbors grew testier as entreaties were rebuffed, not helped by the Syrian media's increasingly shrill claims that Saudi Arabia and Qatar were conspiring against the government. In response, Al Jazeera's coverage became more critical and Erdogan's messages more pointed.[58] The Gulf states flexed their diplomatic muscle in early May by forcing Syria to abandon its bid for election to the UN's Human Rights Council in favor of Kuwait.[59] Yet neither Qatar nor Saudi Arabia was prepared yet to break from Assad: the former was concerned to protect its investment; the latter, about containing popular uprisings.

Chevallier cabled a more somber assessment of the situation to Paris: "This will be very tough, bloody, and long."[60] U.S. rhetoric grew sharper, too, and officials canvassed support for imposing sanctions should the pressure need to be ratcheted up further.[61] The Europeans were receptive; the Arabs and Turks less so. In a telephone conversation, the UN's secretary-general, Ban Ki-moon, urged Assad to restrain the security forces and restore order, begin an inclusive political dialogue, and commit to reform.[62] At the UN Security Council, diplomats from the council's two permanent European members, the UK and France, teamed up with German diplomats to propose a press statement—one of the council's least formal and least binding outputs—to "unreservedly condemn" government violence, call for restraint and an end to bloodshed, appeal for meaningful reform, and support the secretary-general's call for an independent investigation. But the initiative ran aground almost immediately. The United States, Britain, France, Germany, Bosnia, Portugal, Gabon, and Nigeria agreed that the council should criticize government violence, support the secretary-general's call for an independent investigation, and apply pressure on the regime by warning of sanctions if the violence continued unabated. But Russia made it clear it opposed *any* statement or resolution critical of Assad, as did Lebanon, an elected nonpermanent member of council that worried Syria's instability could spread across its border. That much was anticipated; the antipathy of other council members, including China, Brazil, India, and South Africa, was not. These four powers expressed concern at the violence but argued the council should not get involved. India alleged that "extremist elements" were attacking security forces, its ambassador Hardeep Singh Puri observing that "it is for States to decide on the best course of action to maintain internal law and order." Brazil expressed "solidarity" with the protestors but insisted this be balanced against the need for stability. South Africa "regretted" the loss of life but "welcomed" Assad's reforms, as did China.[63] This outpouring of faith in Assad made it relatively easy for Russia to rebuff efforts to use Security Council multilateralism to ratchet up pressure on the Syrian leader. The council was thus blocked from the very start, and Assad and his allies knew it. Russia was primarily responsible for that, but Brazil, China, India, and South Africa all played their part in preventing the Security Council from responding early to Syria's spiraling crisis.

THE VIEW FROM MOSCOW

Syria was important to Moscow, but it was not Russia's only regional concern. The Russian government had worked hard in the 2000s to improve relations with Saudi Arabia, Qatar, Jordan, the UAE, and—above all—Turkey, establishing commercial and military ties with all of them as well as strengthening ties with Israel. The Kremlin hoped to avoid having to choose between Damascus and these hard-won relationships and, like everyone else, believed Assad could be persuaded to restrain his security forces and provide just enough reform to mollify the protestors. Its diplomats conveyed this message throughout March and April, with no more success than anyone else. Irritated by Assad's recklessness, Russian officials sometimes revealed frustrations in public, making it difficult to tell just how far Russia would go to coerce or support Assad.[64]

The Kremlin saw Syria's crisis as a national security problem, not a human rights issue. From the first, Moscow viewed the Arab Spring as a worrying extension of the "color revolutions" that had upended allies in Belgrade (2000), Georgia (2003), Ukraine (2004–2005), and Kyrgyzstan (2005) and threatened friendly governments in Lebanon (2006) and Iran (2009).[65] Some in the Kremlin saw Western hands beneath all this and feared the ultimate goal was a "Russian spring."[66] Thus the Kremlin was instinctively hostile to regime change from below and in early 2011 saw what it believed to be a worrying pattern of Western-backed activism in that direction. Within that context, it was also concerned about the rising tide of Security Council interventionism epitomized by the NATO-led intervention in Libya. It is not that Russia was a principled defender of state sovereignty: it was quite relaxed about violating sovereignty when it suited its own interests to do so, as it had in Georgia (2008) and would go on to do in Ukraine (2014). What worried the Kremlin was the West abrogating for itself the right to determine which regimes to change.[67] Loose talk of pressuring governments to do the right thing or of regime change encouraged instability and violence, Foreign Minister Sergei Lavrov argued with increasing frequency in the spring and summer of 2011. The real danger, he warned, lay not in government repression but in the prospect that the idea that "the foreigners will help us" overthrow unpopular regimes was becoming "contagious." This would invite a "whole array of civil wars."[68]

Where the West saw the Arab Spring as a set of spontaneous prodemocracy uprisings, the Kremlin saw violent revolutions driven by radical Islamism that threatened to spread chaos, extremism, and terrorism. It worried that if Assad went the way of Mubarak, the result would be an unstable failed state on its southern flank that could act as an incubator for projecting Islamist terrorism into Russia's own southern Caucasus, reigniting jihadist wars that had claimed tens of thousands of lives in Chechnya and Dagestan in the 1990s.[69] These fears were exaggerated but not entirely unfounded: a significant proportion of the Islamist foreign fighters who flocked to Syria in 2012 were Russian speakers, commonly referred to as "Chechens." Within that frame, Syria held an especially important place in the Kremlin's view of the Middle East. Damascus was a longstanding Soviet and Russian ally—in fact Russia's last reliable regional ally. The two governments had deep links. Cooperation with Syrian intelligence was critical to Soviet and Russian knowledge and influence in the region. The Soviets/Russians maintained listening stations in Syria to keep tabs on Israel and Lebanon. There were military links, too, though these should not be overstated—the links in 2011 were nothing compared to those of a decade later. In 2011 Russia retained a decrepit naval resupply base at Tartus (refurbished after 2012), its only base in the Mediterranean. The two countries were trading partners, and Syria was a major client for Russian arms, but by no means one of the largest. There were strong domestic imperatives behind the relationship, though. Appeals to Russian nationalism and vocal opposition to the West were popular among Russians. So, too, was the idea of defending Syria's Orthodox Christians and other minorities against Islamic extremism. The government's purported defense of Syria's Christians won particularly enthusiastic support from the Russian Orthodox Church.

Libya certainly cast a shadow over Russian thinking, but the idea that the Kremlin's objections to NATO's role in Libya *caused* Russian obduracy on Syria is overstated. For one thing, we need to be careful about chronology since Russia's obduracy on Syria predated its sharp antagonism with the West over Libya. Certainly, Lavrov described "attempts to reproduce the Libyan experience in other countries and regions" as "very dangerous."[70] But this was *after* Gaddafi's violent death at the hands of his Libyan enemies on October 20, 2011, five months *before* Russia blocked the Security Council on Syria. In late April 2011, when Russia began to block the council, Gaddafi was still president of Libya and still in Tripoli. Although Lavrov complained from mid-April about the risk of NATO widening its Libya campaign, those concerns had not yet been realized. Barack Obama, David Cameron, and Nicolas Sarkozy had published an open letter calling on Gaddafi to step aside, but they emphasized their goal was "not to remove Gaddafi by force."[71] In fact, this position was not very different from the Kremlin's. In late April Russia formally supported a G8 declaration that stated unequivocally that Gaddafi "must go."[72] Through the spring and summer of 2011, Russia held different positions on Libya and Syria, Lavrov repeatedly insisting Libya was an exceptional case and that Syria (and Yemen for that matter) would not be treated the same way, a point underscored by Dmitry Medvedev.[73] "Syria is a more complex issue," Medvedev explained in early August. "Gaddafi, for one, had issued unequivocal orders to slaughter opposition activists. By contrast, Syria's president never ordered anything like that."[74]

Behind everything lurked arguably the most important factor of all: Vladimir Putin. Forced by Russia's constitution to hand the presidency to Medvedev in 2008, Putin remained a dominant figure in Russian politics from his position as prime minister. Medvedev, though, led the government on foreign policy and Putin disapproved of how he was handling it. More apprehensive about the "color revolutions" and suspicious of the West than his president, Putin saw the Arab Spring as the latest in a long line of U.S.-backed conspiracies to topple unfriendly governments, a "dress rehearsal" for what might one day happen in Moscow. In Assad, Putin saw someone not unlike himself, a leader resistant to the West and someone the Kremlin should back.[75]

Russia's view in the spring of 2011 was that diplomatic pressure on Assad could inflame an already volatile situation by encouraging protestors and weakening the government. Worried about the rising tide of popular revolution, Islamism, and instability, the Kremlin feared Assad's fall might create a dangerous political vacuum. This became a recurring theme in Russian diplomacy, along with calls for the opposition to stop using violence and outsiders to stop giving arms to nonstate groups. But Moscow also believed Assad was courting disaster by soft-pedalling on reform and using excessive force. With one hand the Russians tried to prevent the imposition of diplomatic or economic sanctions that might hurt Assad; with the other, they tried to persuade him to change course. The Kremlin wanted to give Assad time to reform and banked on Damascus stemming the crisis. But this strategy was self-defeating since the more Russia objected to international action, the more it encouraged Assad to use force, not reform, to prevail.

An associated question was just how much influence Moscow exercised over Damascus anyway. Russia's record during this early phase was mixed: its calls for restraint and reform enjoyed no more success than anybody else's. Influence is not a one-way street, of course, and just as the Kremlin could apply pressure on Damascus, so Damascus had leverage over the Kremlin given the latter's view that its own interests depended on the Syrian state's survival. Pushing Assad too hard, or allowing others to do so, could precipitate the very thing Russia wanted to avoid most of all: state collapse. Over time, Assad and his advisors came to understand their leverage over Russia, which they employed to good effect.[76] Moscow's ability to influence Assad was therefore limited: it had a sledgehammer to crack a walnut but desperately wanted the walnut kept intact.

THE CRISIS ESCALATES

With the Security Council already in deadlock, Western governments looked for alternative ways to apply pressure on Assad. In an impressive display of diplomatic coordination, Syria's ambassadors in London, Paris, Berlin, Rome, and Madrid were summoned to receive a simultaneous demarche, warning that unless violence ended immediately, the EU would impose an arms embargo, asset freezes, and travel restrictions.[77] Syria rejected the ultimatum, so the EU followed through on May 6 with targeted sanctions against six high-ranking officials, though not Assad because the EU wanted to retain that option as future leverage. When Damascus once again rejected European demands, sanctions were extended to Assad and thirteen close aides. Over the coming months, European sanctions were extended more than twenty times, until by the end of 2012 they covered 180 individuals and 54 institutions. The EU also imposed an arms embargo in May, which had more of a symbolic than a practical effect since most of the country's arms came from Russia. The United States imposed targeted sanctions against Assad and other senior regime figures on April 29 and May 18.

Saudi Arabia, Qatar, and Turkey were in a more difficult position. Each had its own reasons for wanting to avoid a breach with Assad, so they continued to resist the urge to impose sanctions. Yet they also knew that Assad was not heeding their pleas and feared that continuing to stand aside in the face of such extreme brutality would damage their standing with their own restive populations. On May 22 the Organization of the Islamic Conference (OIC) expressed concern and joined calls for the government to show restraint. The Arab League broke out of its torpor, too, condemning the violence in Syria on June 14. Saudi Arabia and Qatar were behind both moves. Meanwhile, divisions in the UN Security Council did not prevent other arms of the United Nations adding to the pressure for change. The Human Rights Council held a special session and decided to dispatch an investigative mission. The secretary-general called again on May 4 for an end to violence and an independent inquiry into the killings. He also sought permission for a UN team to enter to assess the humanitarian situation. The UN's top humanitarian official, Valerie Amos, expressed her "concern" to the Security Council and noted that the deployment of tanks into cities was "alarming."[78] The Office of the UN High Commissioner for Refugees announced it was working with Lebanon to assist people fleeing the violence in ever greater numbers. None of this made much difference. By mid-May, credible reports estimated that 1,100 people had been killed and another 8,000 detained. The media reported mass graves in Daraa.[79] The regime's supporters responded by doubling down. On May 25 Hezbollah's Hassan Nasrallah issued a strongly worded statement of support for Assad.

Efforts to bridge the Security Council's divides persisted. The UK and France raised the idea of a statement or resolution once again but found Russia, China, and India still opposed and insistent that Syria posed no immediate threat to international peace and security.[80] The United States was also ambivalent, worried that precipitate council action could inflame the situation or that Russian and Chinese vetoes might embolden Assad and diminish the council's leverage. The Europeans were confident that they had the nine affirmative votes needed for a resolution, since they thought both Brazil and South Africa could be persuaded now that the situation had deteriorated, and some thought it might be wise to force a vote. The Europeans circulated a draft resolution on May 25 that condemned government violence and called for restraint, "comprehensive and credible" reforms, the lifting of the siege on Daraa, a credible investigation of human rights abuses by the UN Human Rights Council's investigative mission, and tangible measures to prevent the sale of arms and ammunition. The response from Russia and China was cool at best.

Meanwhile, Syria lurched toward civil war. In early June, protests in Jisr al-Shughur, a largely conservative and Sunni town close to the Turkish border in Idlib governate in the country's Northwest, escalated into a pitched battle. Many families in Jisr al-Shughur bore the scars of Hafez al-Assad's war on the Muslim Brotherhood in the 1980s. Protests there had become increasingly violent until, on June 4, a day when twenty thousand people took to the streets, Basil al-Masry took his gun and attacked a security outpost. He was killed in the act, but the perception that he was another unarmed victim of the government led things to boil over. Armed men fired at security forces and government snipers fired on the protestors, killing five. Protestors and armed men stormed the Military Security Directorate, killing at least eight officers inside. Attack helicopters raked the town with bullets, and the government dispatched security officers to reinforce its position. It claimed that 120 officers were ambushed and killed, a number confirmed by the opposition. The inevitable response was massive. The government attacked the town with helicopters, tanks, and armored personnel carriers. More than 150 people were killed and more than 1,000 arrested during "mopping up" operations.[81] Most of town's population fled across the border into Turkey, provoking a burst of outrage from Erdogan, who described the Syrian commander leading the operation, Assad's younger brother, Maher al-Assad, as "brutish and inhuman." Syrian officials, accustomed to Turkish quiescence, reacted bitterly, but Erdogan intimated Turkey might in future support tougher measures through the United Nations if things did not soon improve.[82]

At the United Nations, the number of states prepared to simply accept Russia's argument that Assad be given more time was dwindling, but Brazil, India, and South Africa still felt the European draft text too prescriptive, and the Russians warned that any resolution might become a pretext for Western military intervention. The Europeans toned down the language on political reform by calling instead for "Syrian-led" dialogue—an ill-defined process rather than endpoint, which nevertheless became a central component of diplomatic efforts. But still consensus proved elusive.

Assad was unswayed, unwilling to even consider negotiating with the opposition. Syria's security forces used force systematically to prevent the opposition establishing territorial footholds by subjecting Homs, Baniyas, Douma, Talkalakh, Tafas, and Rastan to the treatment meted out in Daraa. By mid-July the number of civilian casualties had grown to 1,900, and the UN's human rights mission and humanitarian organizations found their route into Daraa blocked.[83] But the more the security forces pushed, the more regime soldiers began to defect and the more the opposition pushed back, inflicting losses. The crisis reached Hama in full force at the beginning of July. Protests there escalated in the first week of July when demonstrators occupied the city's central Asi Square and proclaimed it liberated. Government forces, including tanks and artillery, encircled the city, killing more than a dozen people. Barricades were thrown up to prevent the army and Mukhabarat advancing, and the demonstrations continued. Viewing all this from Damascus, Robert Ford and Eric Chevallier decided they should visit Hama to demonstrate their solidarity with the protestors and find out more about them.[84] They were greeted as heroes by the protestors, who took their visit as a sign of Western support. The visit won the city temporary respite as Damascus clambered to figure out whether it portended a change in Western policy. But it also gave the opposition false expectations of foreign help since Ford and Chevallier were acting on their own initiative, not signaling a change in Western policy.[85] The visit also played into Assad's hands as evidence that the demonstrations were indeed orchestrated by foreigners. The response in Damascus was predictably bitter and the government complained of foreign interference.[86] Angry crowds attacked the American and French embassies with bombs.

Whatever the merits and problems with the ambassadorial visit to Hama, it was clear that quiet diplomacy backed by modest targeted sanctions was not proving effective at persuading Damascus to end the violence. Since the June violence in Jisr al-Shughur, some ten thousand refugees had fled into Turkey. There were mounting calls in the United States for tougher action.[87] Some inside the administration agreed. "If Assad views this as life or death for him, and it is," one of Obama's top advisors confided after Ford's mission to Hama, "then no amount of diplomacy is likely to persuade him."[88] But most governments remained unsure of how to bring additional pressure to bear, especially as the Security Council was blocked.[89] Britain's foreign secretary, William Hague, spoke for many when he explained that "the levers we have are relatively limited." Military intervention was not "even a remote possibility" due to the risks involved.[90] The options short of force seemed limited too. Michael Posner, the State Department's top human rights official, told a congressional committee that since the United States was so unpopular in the Middle East, it lacked the diplomatic leverage needed to exert meaningful pressure for reform. The United States also had little economic leverage since decades of Western sanctions had served to limit the Syrian economy's exposure to the West.[91]

Things escalated still further at the end of July. Damascus worried that the approaching Ramadan, which usually swelled the numbers attending mosques, would propel a surge in demonstrations. These fears were compounded when, on July 29, a group of disaffected officers led by Colonel Riad al-Asaad of the air force proclaimed the founding of a Free Syrian Army (FSA) to protect the people from their government. Government forces launched an orchestrated countrywide crackdown, hitting Hama especially hard. More than 150 people were killed in a single day, including more than 100 in Hama and nearly 30 in Deir ez-Zor.[92] Shocked at this rapid escalation of violence, Ban Ki-moon telephoned Assad to demand its end.[93] Navi Pillay, the UN's high commissioner for human rights, was equally blunt in her assessment.[94] France led strident European condemnation, closely followed by the UK, Germany, Italy, and others.[95] The EU imposed a new round of travel bans and financial sanctions on Assad's inner circle, and its Security Council members decided to try again with another draft resolution.[96] There were some grounds for optimism. The Ramadan violence seemed to provoke a softening of Moscow's support for Assad when Medvedev labeled it "unacceptable" and called for its immediate end.[97] Sergei Vershinin, the diplomat responsible for Russia's Middle East policy, indicated that the Kremlin was not "categorically" opposed to a UN resolution, though it must be balanced and not threaten sanctions.[98] Encouraged, American, British, and French diplomats approached their Russian counterparts and Ban Ki-moon to explore the potential for a new draft resolution. The UN's Oscar Taranco tried to underscore its urgency by briefing council members on the escalating violence. In addition to the increasing death toll, he told them, some three thousand people were missing and some twelve thousand had been arrested.

Yet the West and Russia still disagreed about what should be criticized and what demanded. They even disagreed on the form the council's demarche should take, with the Russians wanting a nonbinding statement, not a resolution, and the Europeans insisting the time for a mere statement had passed. The Europeans wanted to reference the fact that the violence might amount to crimes against humanity, something Russia, China, and India opposed. Instead, these three countries wanted to criticize violence by the opposition as well as the government. Some wanted to back the UN's human rights investigation and a call for the secretary-general to report on progress; others opposed these measures. In the end, almost all the European demands were revised downward. The Security Council's first response to the crisis in Syria was thus a statement that condemned "the use of force against civilians by the Syrian authorities" and called for an immediate end to violence by all parties, full respect for human rights, steps to ensure perpetrators were held accountable, implementation of the government's promised reforms, alleviation of the humanitarian situation, and full cooperation with the UN's human rights investigation. It also requested that the secretary-general report back on developments.[99] Perhaps worried the statement indicated a wavering of Russian support, Assad called Ban Ki-moon, promising to end the violence.[100] But it was neither the first nor the last time that Assad made such a promise. And it made no practical difference. The crackdown continued unabated, especially in Hama.

SHIFTING SANDS

The rare display of Security Council unity inspired others to intensify their diplomatic efforts, some because they sensed an opportunity to persuade Syria to change course, but others—who knew Assad better—because they were growing exasperated at his duplicity. In the first camp was the IBSA grouping of emerging powers (India, Brazil, and South Africa). United by confidence in their global standing and the coincidence they were all serving terms as elected security council members, on August 10 a delegation from the three countries arrived in Damascus to urge the government to end its crackdown and expedite reforms.[101] They left satisfied, believing they had found the basis for, in the words of India's ambassador to the United Nations, "a genuine peace process."[102] They had achieved nothing of the sort. All they had done was deliver a message almost identical to those already conveyed by Ban Ki-moon, the Americans, Europeans, Saudis, Qataris, Turks, and even Russians. And they had received the same hollow response.

IBSA was a sideshow; the shifting of attitudes in the Middle East was not. The leaders of Turkey, Saudi Arabia, and Qatar had all been rebuffed by Assad, causing deep personal offense and prompting them to rethink their strategies. Events outside Syria also encouraged them to rethink their earlier reticence about challenging Damascus directly. Riyadh's situation had changed markedly since the spring: the protests in Bahrain had been quashed, NATO had seriously weakened Gaddafi's Libya, protests in Oman and Jordan had dissipated with the help of Saudi funds and limited political reform, and its own domestic position looked stronger thanks to a multibillion-dollar welfare package. The tidal wave of democracy, seemingly inexorable in March and April, had been contained. Meanwhile, Damascus had proven itself unreceptive to the kingdom's diplomacy and Syria's opposition quite resilient. At home, King Abdullah's quiescence was becoming a political liability as popular outrage at Syria's violence grew. Moreover, far from reciprocating Saudi reticence, Iran was evidently increasing its support to Assad. These changing circumstances prompted Riyadh to adopt a more assertive approach. On August 8 King Abdullah became the first Arab head of state to publicly criticize Assad and impose diplomatic sanctions.[103] Bahrain and Kuwait quickly followed suit.[104]

Qatar had closed its Damascus embassy two weeks earlier.[105] Like both Saudi Arabia and Turkey, it had invested faith and cash in its attempt to influence Damascus but had achieved little. With the situation in Syria seemingly spiraling out of control, Doha's belief that it could protect its investment by shielding Assad dissipated. So it too changed its strategy, by looking for ways to increase pressure on Syria's leadership. Qatar reached out to Syria's Muslim Brotherhood, seeing its ally as the potential motor for change in Syria that it had proven to be in Egypt and looked to use its assumption of the Arab League's rotating presidency. Having earlier conspired with Riyadh to keep Syria off the league's agenda, Qatar now used its position to do the opposite.

Turkey was also exasperated by Assad's obstinacy and alarmed at the spiraling crisis, especially the growing number of Syrians fleeing northward. Turkey's public messages sharpened, but Ankara was not yet ready to abandon its initial approach and so persisted with attempts to influence Assad without alienating him. Thus Erdogan resisted U.S. calls for sanctions. It was a tightrope Ankara would be unable to walk much longer, and Erdogan banked on a more concerted diplomatic effort delivering better results. After conferring with Clinton, he dispatched Davutoglu for talks with the Syrian government, including Assad. Turkey could not "remain indifferent" to the violence, Davutoglu explained as he implored the Syrians to end it. But just what Turkey would do if Assad demurred remained unclear: Davutoglu had already ruled out buffer zones and Erdogan sanctions.[106] True to form, Assad explained he had introduced reforms but needed more time to implement them, and that his security forces were combatting foreign-backed "terrorists." He agreed, though, that Turkey's ambassador be permitted to visit Hama to verify the situation there for himself. Like others before him, Davutoglu left satisfied, thinking he had achieved what no one else had. But that wasn't how Syria's media reported the meeting. It claimed Assad had rebuffed Turkey's demands.[107]

The next day, Turkey's ambassador, Omer Onhon, visited Hama, chaperoned by government officials. He met the governor, walked the streets, and prayed at the mosque. Then he reported that the tanks were withdrawing and the heavy weapons being removed.[108] Delighted, Erdogan publicly boasted about his successful diplomacy and told AKP colleagues he expected the Syrian government to begin reforms within fifteen days.[109] But he was about the discover that he didn't have the influence he thought he had, as there was in fact no let-up at all in the violence. In Latakia, two gunboats joined in the shelling of a seafront district that had seen increasingly large demonstrations, killing more than twenty people. In Damascus, thousands were rounded up over the weekend of August 13.[110] Tanks were back on the streets of Hama within days. Erdogan was enraged by Assad's duplicity. Davutoglu demanded an immediate and unconditional end to violence and intimated that Turkey would consider additional measures to protect civilians, including intervention, should Damascus refuse to budge.[111] Messages flowed between Ankara and Damascus, but nothing changed. A UN human rights report that fall identified in Syria "a pattern of human rights violations that constitutes widespread or systematic attacks against the civilian population, which may amount to crimes against humanity."[112]

ASSAD MUST GO

Pressure for action was building in the West, too. Obama conferred by telephone with Cameron, Sarkozy, and King Abdullah, the four leaders agreeing the patient approach had not worked, though they were unsure of precisely what to do next.[113] Few now believed Assad could be simply persuaded to alter course. Something would need to happen to change Assad's calculations. Russian and Chinese obstinacy blocked off multilateral options such as comprehensive sanctions, a legally enforceable arms embargo, or judicial accountability through the International Criminal Court (ICC). Unilateral embargoes and targeted sanctions could be expanded, but the West's economic leverage was limited. Military options were squarely off the table. Even were anyone willing to countenance them (which nobody was), Syria's opposition held no defensible territory that could be turned into a safe haven and had no military capacity on the ground, there was no chance of a UN mandate to make it legal, and no one had good answers about what an intervention would hope to achieve. Meanwhile, military intervention in Libya was dragging on inconclusively, prompting Obama to doubt whether the West had *any* capacity to shape the Arab Spring.

Most governments in the West and Middle East believed that one way or another, Assad would fall. But how, and at what cost, remained unclear. As Jeffrey Feltman explained to the Senate Foreign Affairs Committee in March 2012, "the demise of the Assad regime is inevitable," but "we do not know for sure when the tipping point, the breaking point, will come in Syria but it will come." Timing was crucial. "It is important that the tipping point for the regime be reached quickly because the longer the regime assaults the Syrian people, the greater the chances of all-out war and a failed state." Without decisive international action, a quick end to Syria's struggle was unlikely and a prolonged conflict laden with dangers more probable: "I do not know when the tipping point is going to come. . . . But I hope I did not make it sound as if it is coming tomorrow. I wish it were, but we do not have any magic bullets. . . . The longer this goes on, the deeper the sectarian divisions, the higher the risks of long-term sectarian conflict, the higher the risk of extremism."[114] The world could sit back and wait for Assad to fall, but that might take a long time, a lot of blood, and much regional instability. Since Assad could not be simply persuaded, a better option seemed to be that he be coerced to reform. This basic Western strategy of coercing Assad to reform or agree to a political settlement was set in August 2011 and did not fundamentally change through all the years of war that followed, despite its all too obvious flaws.

What could be done quickly to increase the coercive pressure? Call for Assad to step aside. During the more hopeful days of the Egyptian and Libyan uprisings, the U.S. and other Western governments had demonstrated solidarity with the protesters by calling on Mubarak and Gaddafi to step down. Yet, five months into Syria's crisis, they had still not done the same with Assad. The inconsistency was obvious. There were reasons to think this might push Assad into a corner he would have to negotiate his way out of, but it was always a long shot, and no one expected the move would have much effect in isolation from other initiatives.[115] By August 2011 U.S. intelligence reports were painting a bleak assessment of Assad's future. Assad was "a dead man walking," Fred Hof, the State Department's senior advisor on Syria, told a congressional committee toward the end of the year.[116] Obama still had his doubts and was not alone in that: similar debates about Assad's future played out in capitals across Europe and the Middle East as governments tried to make sense of the increasingly troubled situation.[117] Abu Dhabi's Crown Prince Mohamed bin Zayed thought Syria's president imperiled but judged he "could hang on for a long time." Saudi Arabia's King Abdullah thought Assad "finished."[118]

The question of whether the United States should call on Assad to step down first arose in the spring when Hillary Clinton, U.S. ambassador to the United Nations Susan Rice, and special assistant to the president Samantha Power had all strongly supported it. Obama was more skeptical and cautioned that while calling for Mubarak to step down had yielded almost instant results, the situation in Syria were very different. For one thing, while the United States was a major donor to Egypt, it had little popularity and few financial or other ties it could use to influence Syria. This view was shared by Ambassador Robert Ford, who cautioned against calling for Assad to step aside on the grounds it would create expectations of outside help the administration had no intention of fulfilling.[119] The British and French ambassadors meanwhile warned their capitals that Assad's regime was neither frail nor likely to soon become so.[120] In early August Erdogan expressed his own doubts, asking the United States to hold off so as not to jeopardize Davutoglu's mission to Damascus.[121] Yet with multilateral channels blocked and bilateral avenues so limited, there seemed little else the United States could do to apply the pressure it thought necessary to move the Syrian government toward reform.[122] It was that lack of options that finally persuaded Obama in August to call on Assad to step aside, a move quickly followed by the UK, France, Germany, Canada, and others.[123]

Turkey initially stopped short, but Erdogan relented a month later and agreed with Obama on the need to "increase pressure" on Damascus. Turkey severed diplomatic relations, imposed an arms embargo, and warned of further sanctions if the violence continued.[124] It also invited the Syrian National Council (SNC) to establish itself in Istanbul. This new body, led by secular intellectual Burhan Ghalioun, comprised political exiles, the Muslim Brotherhood, and representatives of the LCCs and the Kurdish Future Movement. It established itself as the peak coordinating and negotiating body of the opposition. By this move, Ankara hoped to position itself as the group's principal partner and influencer. Not until November, though, did Erdogan call publicly for Assad to step down. By then, Ankara was confident Assad would fall and that a government led by the SNC and Turkey's ally the Muslim Brotherhood would arise in its place. It was not alone. Egypt's new government stated Syria was heading toward "the point of no return."[125] Jordan's King Abdullah II bin Al-Hussein called for Assad to step aside.[126] The Gulf Cooperation Council issued a statement calling on Assad to end violence and initiate reforms, and the Arab League's secretary-general, Amr Moussa, called for an end to violence.

Obama doubted that merely calling on Assad to step aside would make much of a difference but was reluctant to do anything that might draw the United States back into the Middle East. Thus when the State Department's Frederick Hof delivered memos on options for practical steps to help achieve regime change, he found the White House uninterested. This was not because Obama believed Assad's fall inevitable or imminent, but because he was reluctant to embroil the United States in events he thought it could not control and did not affect the country's vital interests.[127] Obama called on Assad to step aside in the forlorn hope that the call itself might have some effect, not because he intended it as a statement of American objectives that would be backed by more tangible measures. The statement *was* the instrument of coercion. Hof resigned in September 2012, protesting what he saw as the administration's failure to back its words with deeds.[128]

As Robert Ford feared, the U.S. call raised expectations among the Syrian opposition such that no matter how often Western governments ruled out a Libya-style intervention, Syrian activists and neighboring governments (especially Turkey, Saudi Arabia, and Qatar) became convinced it was inevitable and acted accordingly. Neighboring states encouraged and supported the opposition, believing victory was now inevitable. Assad's prospects certainly looked grim, but, if anything, the call to step aside only further discouraged Damascus from the path of reform by removing already weak incentives to compromise and vindicating Assad's claim to be defending the country from Western conspiracies and jihadists. The U.S. call also forced the hand of Assad's allies in Tehran and Moscow, and they decided to back the government. The key problem in all this—something both Ford and Hof recognized—was the chasm between ends and means. The West wanted Assad to negotiate a political settlement but had no intention of compelling him to do so or of forcing regime change if he did not accept a settlement. Its strategy, therefore, was simply incapable of achieving its stated goal.

Two days after Obama called on Assad to step aside, Libya's capital, Tripoli, fell to Qatari-backed rebels, catching Western capitals and the Kremlin alike by surprise.[129] A month later, Vladimir Putin announced he would succeed Dmitry Medvedev as Russia's president.

DEADLOCK

Calling for Assad to step aside proved a catalyst for moves to increase pressure on the Syrian government. In early September the EU joined the United States in banning the import of Syrian oil. Australia and Canada followed suit. Turkey imposed an arms embargo on September 23 and froze Syrian government assets. The Arab League froze trade with Syria's government and central bank, imposed travel bans on government officials, suspended infrastructure investment, and banned private and commercial flights to Syria.[130] Economic sanctions, intended to ramp up coercive pressure, certainly troubled Assad, his family, and his inner circle but failed to prompt a change of heart in the government or economic elite. That was in part because Syria's economic elite was so closely tied to the regime and in part because the government insulated itself and its allies from the worst effects.[131] This mounting pressure yielded some results. Iran, its regional standing damaged by its support for Damascus, urged Syrians to "sit down together to reach a solution, away from violence."[132] On August 20 Damascus finally granted the UN human rights team access to some of the worst-affected areas, including Hama, Homs, Idlib, and Latakia.[133] But these moves were countered by Russia, which forcefully restated its commitment to Syria's president and demanded he be granted more time to reform.[134] On August 22 it was joined by

China in voting against a UN Human Rights Council resolution that condemned human rights abuse in Syria and established a Commission of Inquiry, a resolution backed by thirty-three states, including Chile, Botswana, Indonesia, Thailand, and Senegal, and rejected by just two others—Cuba and Ecuador.[135] A few days later Russia and China issued a joint statement urging foreign powers to stay out of Syria's "internal affairs." The following week, Russia's foreign minister, Mikhail Bogdanov, visited Damascus to convey his government's solidarity.[136]

Given the West's limited bilateral leverage, the UN's multilateral channels offered one of the few available options for applying pressure. With that in mind, Western governments proposed a draft Security Council resolution imposing targeted asset freezes and an arms embargo and warning of further measures, including referring the situation to the International Criminal Court should the violence continue. Russian and Chinese diplomats were unsurprisingly hostile and flatly ruled out sanctions, the ICC, or any other coercive measure. India and South Africa were also unconvinced. But having secured a large majority in the Human Rights Council, some Western diplomats hoped they could secure enough votes in the Security Council resolution to isolate Russia and China and coax them into not using their veto. Negotiations continued through September. To satisfy Russia and China, the threat of sanctions was dropped in favor of a looser promise to consider them should violence continue. References to the ICC and other accountability measures were dropped for the same reason, while, at Brazil's insistence, language was added criticizing violence by both sides. These revisions, and the increasing activism of the LAS and GCC, seemed to persuade Brazil and South Africa, but Russia, China, and India were unmoved, objecting to the merest hint of potential future sanctions. Negotiations intensified in October, and almost everything of substance was stripped out in the interests of consensus. Still Russia and China objected.[137] After more than two months of negotiation and a host of compromises, European patience expired and the draft resolution was put to a vote in the first week of October. It condemned "grave and systematic human rights" abuses by the government, demanded an immediate end to violence and human rights violations, called for an inclusive Syrian-led peace process, encouraged Arab League mediation, invited the UN secretary-general to continue his diplomatic efforts, called on states to exercise restraint in supplying arms, and expressed its intention to consider future measures under article 41 (measures short of force) of the charter.[138] Yet despite all the concessions, Russia and China cast their vetoes and Brazil, India, South Africa, and Lebanon abstained.

Russia's veto was unsurprising. Its ambassador, Vitaly Churkin, complained the draft resolution took a "confrontational approach" reminiscent of what had been attempted in Libya. There, the "demand for a quick ceasefire turned into a full-fledged civil war . . . the no-fly zone has morphed into the bombing of oil refineries, television stations and other civilian sites. . . . The arms embargo has morphed into a naval blockade in western Libya, including a blockade of humanitarian goods." Though the language threatening sanctions or other measures had been omitted at his insistence, Churkin still denounced "the threat of an ultimatum and sanctions" as "unacceptable" since it would be taken as mandates for regime change by the mendacious West. At the heart of Russia's objections, though, was concern the Security Council might weaken Assad's grip on power.[139] Equally unsurprising, China's veto disappointed Western diplomats, who had hoped their concessions might have persuaded Beijing to abstain. Its statement to the council revealed little about its thinking, Li Baodong arguing only that "sanctions and the threat thereof" would not help resolve the crisis. Lebanon's abstention was widely expected and understood. India's betrayed a view of the crisis almost identical to Russia's. Its ambassador, Hardeep Singh Puri, believed radical Islamism "a greater threat than Assad."[140] Brazil refused to accept that consensus was impossible and believed that with more time it could have found some common ground. South Africa's abstention also had little to do with Syria and everything to do with its sense of having been sidelined during the crises in Libya and Côte d'Ivoire.[141]

At the heart of the problem lay fundamental disagreements about the nature of Syria's crisis, the degree to which human rights protection should be prioritized, and the best way of restoring stability. For the West, most Middle Eastern states, and clear majorities of the UN's Security and Human Rights Councils, Syria's crisis stemmed from the government's brutal repression of peaceful protests and its refusal to reform. Syria's was a humanitarian and human rights crisis brought on by an authoritarian government resistant to reform and willing to commit crimes against humanity on its own civilians to keep itself in power. Even for these states, however, the protection of human rights had to be balanced against concerns about regional stability, Islamic extremism, and the costs, risks, and escalatory potential of interventions military or otherwise. Most followed the United States in believing the best strategy was to use political rhetoric, bilateral sanctions, and multilateral avenues to coerce Damascus into restraining violence and political reform. But because there was no plan B and the West only had limited economic leverage over Syria, the UN Security Council assumed center stage. Western governments invested in months of negotiation and compromised on almost everything in the hope of achieving what proved to be an elusive resolution. Russia, Iran, and to a lesser extent China saw the crisis very differently from how the West saw it. For them, Syria was a strategic, not human rights, problem, a crisis caused by the opposition, not the government. At stake were vital interests imperiled by any weakening of the Syrian state or change in its political orientation. Protecting Syria's government was simply more important to them than protecting Syria's people. While diplomats bickered, the United Nations reported that more than 2,700 Syrians had been killed since the start of the uprising and more than 10,000 forced to flee the country. A year later, the number of dead would be 50,000; by 2020, it was 500,000.

2

REGIONAL SOLUTIONS?

O **NE OF** the first major armed encounters between government forces and the fledgling Free Syrian Army began in the central Homs district of Baba Amr in late October 2011. There, the FSA's Khalid bin Walid brigade, led by defectors from the Syrian Army, threw up barricades and conducted ambushes targeting security forces. By early November, they had established control over the district.[1] The government countered by sending in tanks and troops to reclaim the streets, using indiscriminate artillery and sniper fire to punish rebellious districts and mass detentions, torture, and killing to eliminate opposition supporters. With the UN Security Council already blocked, the Arab League took the diplomatic initiative, poked into action by Qatar. The rest of the world was only too happy to let it.

ARAB LEAGUE

Established in 1945, the League of Arab States (LAS) has a poor track record on peace and security. Its initial response to Syria's crisis was cautious, and it took until June 2011 to even condemn the violent crackdown.[2] In truth, the league was an organization divided. Saudi Arabia, Qatar, and the United Arab Emirates (UAE) saw the body as a potential vehicle for coercing Assad, but others, such as Algeria, thought Syria's president deserved more time and claimed the organization's noninterference principle precluded its involvement. Most governments in the region, however, felt some public pressure to act. Indeed, popular sentiment in some parts of the region even extended to contemplating humanitarian intervention by the United States.[3] Demands for action grew as government violence escalated through the summer, and as the league became more engaged, UN officials consciously stepped back and allowed it to take the lead. Few believed the league could resolve Syria's crisis, but with viable alternatives in short supply, they clung to whatever they had.[4]

Led by the organization's rotating president, Qatar, a special meeting of foreign ministers in Cairo (excluding Syria) urged an immediate end to violence and agreed on a peace plan, which called for the army's withdrawal from city streets, the release of political prisoners and those apprehended during the protests, establishment of a national unity government that included opposition members, and presidential elections.[5] Assad was sufficiently receptive to leave the league's secretary-general, Nabil El-Araby (an Egyptian), believing they had a deal, though Assad had not in fact made a commitment.[6] Syria's president had no intention of sharing power, but since international pressure was mounting, political allies counseled that he accept the league's entreaties in order to relieve immediate stress, divide international opinion, undermine demands for tougher measures, and take the whole matter out of the UN's hands. Moscow in particular hoped the normally conservative league could engineer a reform package the opposition could accept but that left Assad at the helm.

Outwardly, the Syrian government accepted this friendly advice but dragged its heels on implementation. When the league's foreign ministers met in again in Cairo on October 16, an impatient Qatar successfully pressed them to accelerate matters by insisting the government start talking to the opposition within fifteen days. They also agreed to create a committee, chaired by Qatar and comprising Secretary-General Nabil El-Araby and the governments of Egypt, Algeria, Sudan, and Oman, to mediate the intra-Syrian talks.[7] The new committee traveled to Damascus to call for an immediate ceasefire, the withdrawal of soldiers from civilian areas, the release of political prisoners, and the start of a national dialogue. Again, Assad was receptive but non-committal. The committee met Syrian officials four days later in Doha. This time, the Syrians—presumably influenced by their allies—accepted the league's terms.[8] International opinion in the West as well as Russia quickly united behind the initiative.

It was clear almost immediately, though, that Damascus was not complying with its undertakings: tanks remained visible on the streets of Homs, where the shelling of the Baba Amr district continued unabated. As the league's fifteen-day deadline for talks approached, it also became clear no steps were being taken toward meaningful dialogue. Damascus blamed the opposition and insisted the security forces would return to barracks only once order was restored. To do otherwise would be to turn the streets over to the opposition, it claimed.[9] The deeper problem, though, was that the government was committed to holding on to power, while the opposition distrusted any process or deal that left the Assadists in control of the state's levers of terror.

Chastened by the noncompliance, the league threatened to suspend Syria, but violence erupted again and at least thirty protestors were killed, most in Homs, after Friday prayers on November 11. Still Damascus refused to yield, so the league carried out its threat and suspended Syria. It also recommended that its members impose their own diplomatic sanctions and initiated talks with the opposition. The league was less united than it seemed, however, and it took strident Qatari diplomacy to secure these measures.[10] Qatar's cause was helped by the region's political chaos, which had plunged three of the League's normally more influential members—Egypt, Libya, and Syria itself—into disarray. Some complained Qatar stifled debate with closed-door meetings to press its case without proper consultation.[11] When Algeria raised doubts, Qatari prime minister Hamad Bin Jassim al-Thani allegedly yelled, "Your turn will come"—an undiplomatic warning that Algeria would face its own uprising unless it put itself on the right (i.e., Qatar's) side of the debate.[12] Syria's ambassador, Youssef Ahmed, claimed Qatar's proposals "illegal" since they were not unanimously supported.[13] He had a point. Article 8 of the league's charter requires that member states respect one another's system of government, while article 18 demands that membership suspensions "go into effect upon a unanimous decision of the states, not counting the state concerned." Though several governments doubted the direction Qatar was taking the league, they were even warier of handing their own people another reason to take to the streets. Iraq, whose divided Shi'ite-led government headed by Nouri al-Malaki was sympathetic to Iran, abstained. Algeria was cowed; Lebanon and Syria voted against. Unanimity minus one was not quite achieved, but the decision was carried anyway. It was a major blow to Damascus, which had counted on the votes of Algeria, Sudan, Iraq, and Oman to stall the league indefinitely.[14] The league imposed asset freezes and travel bans on senior regime figures, limits on dealing with Syria's central bank, and a ban on Arab funding for development projects.[15] These decisions weakened Syria's already fragile economy but didn't cripple the government since Iran and Russia filled some of the gaps.[16] Coming soon after Barack Obama's call for Assad to step aside, these measures did, however, encourage the opposition and a new wave of defections from the army, which by late 2011 numbered around ten thousand.[17]

Much hinged on how Assad's allies responded. Moscow and Tehran wanted the crisis resolved and saw in the Arab League plan a way of achieving that without sacrificing Assad. Having already cast one veto in the UN Security Council, the Kremlin wanted to avoid having to cast more and was worried that should the Arab League fail because of Assad, the pressure on the Security Council to act would become difficult to resist. Besides, Russia had often found common cause with the league and did not want a political breach with it. China too wanted to avoid a dispute if possible. Yet these concerns were set against the Kremlin's enduring interests in Syria and its suspicion that any internationally brokered peace process would be a thinly veiled means of easing Assad from power.[18] One Russian official told London-based academic Christopher Phillips that the Kremlin adopted a deliberately ambiguous posture so as to retain influence over both Damascus and the West, but that it had already resolved to not concede anything that might lead to regime change.[19] Forced to choose, the Kremlin would always back Assad. It is striking just how early Russia came to this view, one from which it never wavered. It is equally striking that the West and the United Nations didn't realize that this was Russia's position until the war entered its final phase.

Toward the end of 2011, though, Russia encouraged Assad to accommodate the Arab League plan, but it didn't threaten to abandon him if he chose not to comply.[20]

Negotiations in Doha dragged on into December. On December 12 the Syrian government finally accepted a revised deal that called for a general cessation of violence and withdrawal of security forces from contested areas, monitored by Arab League observers, and the release of political prisoners. Within two weeks, the league would facilitate direct talks between government and opposition. Few harbored much hope it would succeed, however, especially when Assad publicly admitted he was not taking the process seriously.[21] Analysts worried he had accepted a deal he could not—and would not—implement since withdrawing the military would hand the streets to the protestors, loosening his grip on power. Having been locked out of the process thus far, the opposition was also skeptical. The opposition Syrian National Council accepted the league's terms, but its leader, Burhan Ghalioun, worried they would prove "worthless" in the face of government violence. Nonetheless, he welcomed the observer mission and suggested it be enlarged and given unfettered freedom of movement.[22] Ultimately, he wanted an Arab military intervention to protect civilians, establish a safety zone and humanitarian corridors, and impose a no-fly zone.[23] He also asked that the SNC be recognized as the opposition's legitimate representative. Despite the reservations, the plan secured widespread international backing.

Under the arrangement, the league was to deploy 170 monitors on a one-month renewable mandate agreed to by Damascus (in the event, the mission reached a maximum size of 144). Monitors were placed under the Syrian government's protection and not permitted to access "sensitive military sites"—in practice, anywhere experiencing active government operations. The Arab League's Nabil El-Araby advised that the monitors would include legal, administrative, human rights, and financial experts and would be deployed across the country in teams of ten.[24] The UN General Assembly endorsed the deal (133 to 11) on December 19, calling on Damascus to implement it.[25] China's abstention gave cause for guarded optimism, but, ominously, Assad's closest allies, Russia and Iran, were among those voting no. The first Arab League monitors arrived three days later, followed two days later by its head of mission, Sudanese general Mohammed Ahmed Mustafa al-Dabi. By the end of the year, around one hundred monitors were in place. Appointed at the behest of Qatar, where he had served as ambassador, and to the great annoyance of Saudi Arabia, who had wanted a leader more inclined to listed to Riyadh than Doha, al-Dabi was an unpromising choice as mission head. As head of Sudanese military intelligence in the 1990s, he had overseen several violent crackdowns on government opponents and had been a senior officer in the Sudanese Army during its campaign of mass atrocities in Darfur, for which his president, Omar al-Bashir, had been indicted by the International Criminal Court for crimes against humanity and war crimes. Some accused al-Dabi himself of helping establish the infamous *Janjaweed* militia responsible for the most shockingly brutal atrocities.[26] Concerns about his suitability were not helped by his performance. On a visit to Daraa on December 31, he told BBC reporters his monitors had not observed snipers firing on protestors, despite amateur video footage showing a monitor telling activists he had.[27] After visiting Homs, where dozens of civilians had been killed, he commented that "some places looked a bit of a mess but there was nothing frightening."[28] Demands that he be removed were aired within days of his arrival.

The mission was bedeviled with problems from the beginning. The league had never undertaken anything like this before, and it lacked the personnel, infrastructure, and experience necessary. The mission was too small, too inexperienced, and insufficiently equipped for the task. According its own report, some observers "were not capable of taking on their responsibility and did not have prior experience in this field." "Some of the observers, unfortunately, believed that their journey to Syria was for amusement, and were therefore surprised by the reality of the situation. They did not expect to be assigned to teams or to have to remain at stations outside the capital or to face the difficulties that they encountered." Some "did not grasp the amount of responsibility that was being placed on them and the importance of giving priority to Arab interests over personal interests." Several monitors were too old or unable to perform their duties owing to ill-health. Twenty-two observers declined to even join the mission, citing personal reasons. Others tried leaving early but were denied because their reasons were "unfounded" or stemmed from "a personal agenda."

Some allegedly broke their oath of allegiance to the mission and sent exaggerated informal reports to their own capitals.[29] The lack of basic equipment such as armored vehicles and protective vests damaged morale and inhibited observers from going about their work. Those who did found themselves blocked by government obstacles, violence, and intimidation.

The mission did enjoy some success. The government released three thousand political prisoners, permitted the delivery of humanitarian aid to some of the worst-affected areas, and withdrew tanks from the center of Homs. Wherever the monitors were physically present, government violence was much reduced, but monitors were kept away from the main battlegrounds. With their attention focused elsewhere, government forces killed more than two hundred people on December 19–20, 2011, alone.[30] Monitors frequently found their paths blocked and were sometimes deliberately misdirected by their government minders. While some monitors complained at being expected to leave their comfortable Damascus lodgings, others saw through the charade. Anwar Malek, an Algerian monitor, resigned in disgust, calling the mission a "farce." The mission was being "orchestrated" by Damascus, he complained, and the Syrian government "fabricated most of what we saw to stop the Arab League from taking action against the regime." "The observers have been fooled. What I saw was a humanitarian disaster. The regime isn't committing one war crime but a series of crimes against its people."[31]

Yet things were not going well for the regime, thanks to increasing protests and an FSA emboldened by new desertions.[32] By the end of January the number of desertions was estimated to be at twenty thousand, double that of a few weeks earlier. Desertions continued at a steady rate, and by June 2014, a hundred thousand soldiers had deserted the Syrian Army—a figure that does not include those who simply failed to show up for duty. This figure amounts to just less than half of the total fighting force of the army by mid-2014.[33] The violent battle for Al-Zabadani, thirty kilometers northwest of Damascus and close to the Lebanese border, demonstrated just how fragile the situation had become. In early January 2012 tens of thousands of protestors had taken to the streets to voice support for the FSA. In response, government tanks rolled into the suburbs and artillery and sniper fire rained down on protestors, killing at least twelve.[34] Soldiers, supported by the Mukhabarat and *shabiha*, moved in on January 12–13 but were repelled by the FSA. A local ceasefire was arranged, but the city was besieged. On February 4 government tanks and armored personnel carriers attacked once again, this time supported by sustained artillery fire. After a week of shelling, the FSA withdrew, and the government retook control. By then, more than 120 civilians and a similar number of soldiers (on both sides) were dead.[35]

Unabated violence like this sapped the monitoring mission of its international support. Qatar—which had invested heavily in the process but now feared a loss of political momentum—led the charge, arguing that ongoing violence showed the mission was failing.[36] Mustafa al-Dabi and El-Araby defended the mission's utility and persuaded the league to extend its mandate on January 8, and then again on January 19. Qatar complained that the mission was clearly inadequate and should be upgraded to an Arab peacekeeping mission under a UN mandate, a proposal angrily rejected by Damascus as well as Algeria and Egypt.[37] The league's thin veneer of unity was shattering. Things came to a head on January 22 when al-Dabi presented the observer mission's initial report to the league. The report bore little resemblance to reality as al-Dabi claimed that while the government had used force in Homs and Hama, the overall situation had improved, thanks to monitors. He also reported attacks on government forces in Homs, Idlib, and Hama and observed that "the media exaggerated the nature of the incidents and numbers of persons killed in the incidents." Despite clear evidence military vehicles were still being used in Al-Zabadani and elsewhere, al-Dabi claimed "that all military vehicles, tanks and heavy weapons had been withdrawn from cities and residential neighbourhoods." He also asserted that peaceful protests were "unhindered" by government forces and claimed credit for the release of detainees (though he did note discrepancies about the number of people detained).[38] Since the mission had helped quell violence, its mandate should be extended and numbers increased. But there was little chance of that. The Gulf states sharply criticized the report as biased and inaccurate. They had no faith in the mission or its head and intended to withdraw their monitors and their funding.[39] Still, al-Dabi defended the mission and repeated his insistence that the violence was declining in the face of mounting evidence to the contrary. Bleeding support and immobilized by the increasingly precarious security situation, the mission's political masters pulled the plug at the end of January.[40] Tacitly rejecting al-Dabi's assessment, El-Araby explained that "the critical deterioration of the situation in Syria and the continued use of violence" had forced his hand. The deterioration was caused, he said, by the Syrian government's decision "to escalate the military option."[41]

The Arab Monitoring Mission had quickly collapsed, for three main reasons. First, neither government nor opposition was fully committed to it. Assad negotiated to buy time and forestall more coercive interference while simultaneously using violence to press his case on the ground. Syria's president had no intention of making meaningful concessions, and since he believed the whole process was being orchestrated by his enemies in the Gulf, he saw it as a pretext for regime change. The league's increasingly obvious disunity, meanwhile, encouraged Damascus to doubt the body's resolve. The opposition never had much faith in the process or Assad's promises. Ghalioun wanted more forceful intervention, while the FSA—which felt no compunction to abide by an agreement it had played no part in negotiating—employed force where it could.[42] Continuing defections from the army raised hopes that perhaps the regime's days were numbered.

Second, international support was limited, too. While the main foreign actors hoped for success, few (if any) believed it likely, and so none except Qatar, which then quickly lost faith, invested much in it. Arab support proved wafer thin and was withdrawn inside the first month. Having invested significant diplomatic capital in the initiative, Qatar became quickly disenchanted and convinced of the need to draw in the UN Security Council; it hoped the league's failure might force the council's hand. Riyadh never threw its weight behind the plan, since it expected it would fail.[43] Neither felt any inclination to pressure the opposition to comply, but it would have made little difference even if they had. The United States, Britain, and France all doubted the LAS could succeed since they judged it unlikely that Damascus would honor its commitments.[44] While Russia welcomed the initiative and had encouraged Damascus to participate, it applied little pressure on Assad and certainly never intimated it might withdraw support should Syria's leader not keep his word. As the situation unraveled, Russia expressed mounting sympathy for the regime.

Third, the Arab League was divided and its monitoring mission inept. Algeria, Lebanon, and Iraq all had serious reservations about a plan they believed was already too assertive. The monitoring mission failed to meet basic standards of competence and was unable to manage, much less meet, expectations inside Syria. Protestors had initially welcomed the mission with enthusiasm but grew exasperated when it proved unable to protect them from regime violence. In Homs when security forces opened fire on them, protestors chanted, "Where are the Arab League monitors?"[45]

With their first plan on the rocks, the league's more activist states searched for an alternative. Events in Yemen offered an appealing model. There, another popular uprising against an autocratic leader, Ali Abdullah Saleh, had threatened to escalate into civil war. Much like Assad, Saleh had offered limited concessions while his security forces cracked down violently. By June the crisis had escalated into open fighting. The Gulf Cooperation Council led a concerted regional response, backed by Saudi and Qatari economic clout, which in November 2011 produced an agreement for a managed transfer of power. In return for immunity from prosecution, Saleh agreed to hand over power to a national unity government. Elections held in February 2012 brought a new caretaker president, Abdrabbuh Mansour Hadi, into office for a two-year term before another round of elections would determine the new government. As it transpired, things didn't work out that way. By 2013 Hadi had developed a taste for governing and decided to extend his term of office, prompting the Houthis into an open revolt, which by 2015 had plunged Yemen into civil war. But that all lay ahead. At the beginning of 2012, Yemen seemed to all the world to offer a model for managing Syria.

Qatar and Saudi Arabia proposed that the Arab League apply the Yemen model to Syria. Qatar drafted a plan calling on Damascus to establish a transitional government of national unity, overseen by Assad's vice president Farouq al-Sharaa, within two months. The transitional government should include opposition figures and assume responsibility for organizing parliamentary and presidential elections.[46] The new plan was ambivalent about Assad's fate, but its sponsors hoped to negotiate a deal like that offered Saleh—immunity from prosecution in return for a graceful exit. Qatar's Hamad Bin-Jassim al-Thani added his own embellishments later, including an Arab League peacekeeping force, modeled on the Syrian-led Arab Deterrent Force deployed to Lebanon in 1976. That idea morphed into a proposal for a joint Arab-UN peacekeeping mission but was never a serious proposition. What was serious, though, was Qatar's determination that the new plan—like the GCC's for Yemen—have teeth. Saudi Arabia had leant heavily on Saleh to push him to accept the plan, which had in turn won unanimous UN Security Council support.[47] To stand any chance, the Syria plan needed something similar. Algeria confessed it had "reservations," but the league swung behind the new initiative. Even Iraq and Lebanon gave tacit support.[48]

Damascus rejected it out of hand, though, and Assad declared he would not step aside.[49] Al-Sharaa, the man nominated by the league to replace the Syrian president, was placed under house arrest. This, the Qataris expected; the reaction reinforced their belief that the Security Council's support was needed. They were encouraged by the SNC, which welcomed the initiative but insisted Assad step down in advance of a transitional government, as Saleh had in Yemen, something Qatar was confident it could deliver should the initiative win international backing. Qatar pressed the league to seek the Security Council's endorsement, and all but Algeria, which wanted to keep the Arab League in the driving seat, and Lebanon agreed. Qatar had a harder time persuading them to impose tougher sanctions in the meantime. Saudi Arabia, UAE, and Kuwait supported that move, but Algeria, Egypt, Lebanon, and Iraq resisted. To preserve a veneer of unity, Qatar suggested they leave the question of further sanctions to the Security Council.

RETURN TO TURTLE BAY

At the end of January, Hamad Bin-Jassim al-Thani fronted the Security Council to press for a resolution supporting the new LAS initiative. A new approach was needed, he said, since "the Syrian government has failed to implement major provisions." This involved establishing a government of national unity, led by a mutually acceptable figure (Assad's deputy) and including members of the opposition, within two months. This new government would prepare for parliamentary and presidential elections "under Arab and international supervision." There should also be an independent commission to investigate human rights violations. With "the security situation . . . increasingly grave and urgent," el-Araby added, their proposal aimed to end the violence, avoid foreign interference, and facilitate a political solution. The Arab League's secretary-general underscored that the proposals "can in no way be interpreted as calling upon the Syrian President to renounce power."[50] They would prefer Assad leave, as Saleh had done, but the proposed text did not require it.

The British took the lead drafting a resolution to support the league by endorsing its plan and threatening sanctions in the event of noncompliance. There was broad support among the council's Western and Latin American members and most of its African members. But as Hillary Clinton recalls, it soon "ran into the same trouble as previous attempts." Russia was "implacably opposed to anything that might constitute pressure on Assad."[51] In fact, there may have been a fleeting sign Russia might be prepared to negotiate something along the lines the Arab League was proposing. It wanted a way out of the crisis that could preserve Assad's state intact without torpedoing hard-won relationships across the Arab world. Sources claim that during the negotiations, Vitaly Churkin tentatively floated the idea that the Russians might be open to a Yemen-like arrangement and were looking for "an elegant way for Assad to step aside." The idea came to naught, with Finland's former prime minister, the Nobel Prize–winning Martti Ahtisaari, later blaming the West, saying he presented Churkin's proposals to them but that they were uninterested because they believed the regime would soon collapse and that Russian entreaties were unserious.[52] Western officials counter there was never a serious approach from Russia. They recalled Churkin proposing the idea but no one more senior, such as Lavrov, Medvedev, or Putin, ever so much as alluded to it over many hours of discussion on Syria. During the Security Council's private deliberations, Russian diplomats consistently rejected any political transition. It seems most likely, then, that what Ahtisaari thought was a political opening was nothing more than a Churkin thought bubble.[53] The Kremlin had supported transition in Yemen only because Saleh himself had been persuaded to endorse it. Russia would support a similar deal were it backed by Assad and might tolerate the Arab League's initiative so long as it left Syria's president with a free hand, but beyond that it would not go. Meanwhile, China, India, and Pakistan, and to some extent South Africa, also remained cautious especially about the idea of imposing sanctions should Assad reject the deal.[54]

Still, the resolution's backers hoped to find a form of words acceptable to the doubters. Clinton spoke directly with Lavrov multiple times, urging him to support the resolution and deliver a united message to Assad. Lavrov complained the Arab League's proposal was one-sided since it placed all the demands on the government and made too few of the rebels. He pressed Clinton on what would happen should Assad not comply; whether the West would use the resolution to justify a Libya-style intervention. "No," Clinton responded, the goal was to persuade Assad to reform, not head toward armed intervention. "But what is the endgame?," Lavrov wondered. Clinton acknowledged she had no clear answer but argued that unless the council acted decisively, the conflict would escalate toward a civil war likely to destabilize the region and be a lightning rod for jihadism.[55] To outsiders, it was unclear which way Russia would go. Publicly, Lavrov distanced Russia from Assad, claiming, "We don't approve of what it [the Syrian government] is doing, using force against demonstrators." But he defended the regime too.[56] He also repeated what he'd told Clinton in private, that a new resolution could lead to a "disastrous" Libya-style intervention. The United States, meanwhile, sent mixed signals of its own. While Clinton reassured the Kremlin, the White House tried to exploit growing apprehensions about Assad's long-term viability.[57] This likely succeeded only in confirming Russian suspicions about what the Americans were after.

The Arab League's plan clearly commanded widespread international support, but less certain was the support of the fifteen states on the Security Council that mattered most. The British team counting likely votes knew they had support from the P3, the council's two other European members, Portugal and Germany, as well as Azerbaijan, Guatemala (replacing Brazil), Colombia, Morocco, and Togo. Togo even proposed that the council itself call on Assad to step down.[58] That was ten—more than the nine needed to carry a resolution if the veto could be avoided. Pakistan hedged, welcoming the league's efforts but refusing to be drawn on the specifics while expressing dislike toward foreign-imposed regime change. South Africa, which had abstained on the previous draft resolution, was now a cautious supporter. India was more cautious still. Hardeep Singh Puri hewed closely to the line he had adopted the previous summer, pointing to violence on both sides and preferring that political dialogue be guided by the Syrian government. China had voiced support for the Arab League and did not outright reject the resolution, but it drew red lines with respect to sanctions and regime change. The British thought they could accommodate those concerns and thus induce Beijing to abstain, isolating Russia, which might then opt to abstain too.

It all rested on Russia. Ominously, Churkin criticized the Arab League for imposing sanctions, suspending Syria, and withdrawing the monitoring mission prematurely. He also expressed doubts about the new plan, saying the Security Council could not impose a political settlement and rejecting sanctions as a slippery slope to regime change. While Arab League and Western states argued the resolution should refer to chapter 7 of the UN Charter, which relates to enforcement measures should they be necessary, Russia (and China) insisted it be limited to chapter 6, which refers to the peaceful resolution of disputes. NATO might abuse a chapter 7 resolution of any kind as tacit authorization for armed intervention, they complained. Morocco, which had taken over drafting from the British, tried to reflect these concerns in a new draft that endorsed the Arab League plan to establish a government of national unity with executive powers ahead of internationally supervised elections, called on states to restrict the flow of arms and ammunition into Syria, and committed the council to reviewing the situation within fifteen days and "to adopt further measures" should it determine that the government was not complying.[59] Assad indicated he would not accept these demands, so Russia dug in its heels and insisted that references to political transition and consideration of "further action" be removed. Russia also opposed restricting the flow of arms to the government as well as opposition, complained the draft placed excessive blame on the government relative to the opposition, and demanded a clause explicitly prohibiting future military intervention. Assad's intransigence also made China, India, Pakistan, and South Africa more skeptical. Morocco watered down the text still further to a more general statement of support for the Arab League plan, which made no mention of political transition. The resolution's supporters drew a line on the issue of potential further measures, insisting that it must be retained for the resolution to have any resonance at all. El-Araby suggested a way around the chapter 6 or 7 problem by proposing the resolution refer to chapter 8—on regional arrangements—instead. Morocco conceded the point to the Russians and Chinese and revised the text to note that the council would be acting under chapter 6. This was too much for the United States, Britain, and France, who argued that Assad's record of promise breaking showed that only a chapter 7 resolution would have the desired effect. In the end, the drafters removed references to either chapter but added a clause distancing the resolution from chapter 7's article 42 on military enforcement.[60]

Combined with the deteriorating situation in Syria and the strong advocacy of the Arab League, these concessions persuaded India and South Africa to support the resolution.[61] Its sponsors believed they had done enough to address Russian concerns and, by persuading the key swing states, had isolated the Kremlin politically. On the evening before the council was due to meet to vote on the resolution, the five permanent ambassadors gathered at Churkin's New York residence and signed off on the text, the Russian ambassador seemingly happy his conditions had been satisfied. They agreed to consult with their capitals overnight and reconvene to vote the next day. They parted believing a deal done. But it wasn't. The next morning, Britain's ambassador, Mark Lyall Grant, was called and told that the Kremlin had rejected the draft, that Churkin was raising a raft of new objections he hadn't presented the previous night: that the draft was biased, did not reflect realities on the ground, must demand that the opposition distance itself from violent extremists, and call on states to stop violence by extremist groups. He was also insisting that any withdrawal of government troops from cities be contingent on the opposition ceasing violence first.[62] We cannot know for sure what had happened overnight, but the most likely explanation is that the Kremlin had overridden Churkin and the negotiation points previously agreed to by Lavrov and Medvedev. It was well known that Lavrov had his eye on Putin's job, and that Churkin wanted Lavrov's, so neither was likely to push back against the past and future president. The British ambassador's team certainly believed that the Russian change of heart came from Putin himself. Churkin was not negotiating the text but rejecting the resolution; there were no concessions they could offer that would change Putin's mind. Thirteen of the council's fifteen members—including India, Pakistan, and South Africa—voted yes. Russia and China alone voted no, casting their vetoes.

China's veto was especially disappointing since it had previously indicated its support for the text and was now clearly following Russia's lead and allowing interests beyond Syria to determine its policy toward the country. China's vote not only contradicted what its ambassador had told his colleagues just a day earlier, it was also out of step with China's longstanding tradition of supporting regional initiatives beyond the West and set it apart from three of its BRICS partners as well as from the Arab League. Tellingly, on February 16 the Arab League tabled a draft resolution in the General Assembly that mirrored the vetoed Security Council text. A total of 137 states voted in favor, only 12 against (including China, Russia, North Korea, Zimbabwe, and Syria itself). Why, then, did China cast its veto? Principally, it seems, because it judged that stability was best served by protecting the Syrian government and its territorial integrity and feared the draft resolution might erode both. Like Russia, China was wary of rising Islamism and worried about the implications for its own Muslim Uighur population. Emerging "P2" solidarity also played a role, with China backing Russia against the West on Syria in return for similar Russian favors on questions that mattered more to Beijing.[63]

This second round of Security Council vetoes dealt a huge blow to the Arab League and to Syrians hoping the UN might do more to support a peace process. It came as a genuine shock to Western and Arab diplomats too, who had thought they were close to a deal that may have nudged the crisis toward resolution. In the final analysis, it all boiled down to the fact that Vladimir Putin opposed any political process for Syria not approved by Assad himself (something Churkin, Lavrov, and Medvedev had all expressed openness to, in the right conditions, over the previous weeks). Governments in the region and in the West were unsure of what to do next. But three effects were immediate.

First, Damascus was emboldened. The Syrian government stepped up its assault on Homs, driving Syria headlong toward civil war. The scene of much fighting in late 2011, the Baba Amr district of Homs remained in FSA hands in early February 2012. As diplomats in New York bickered, in the early hours of February 3 the FSA attacked Syrian Army checkpoints close to the frontline, killing ten and taking nineteen prisoners. Government forces retaliated with a massive and brutal response. Baba Amr was pummeled with artillery fire over the next forty-eight hours. The district's hospital was hit multiple times—a sign of things to come. Between 200 and 337 civilians were killed.[64] The shelling continued between February 9 and 11, though the FSA repelled a series of ground assaults. On February 22 veteran American war correspondent Marie Colvin and French photographer Remi Ochlik were intentionally killed by government rocket fire as they chronicled the systematic assault on civilians.[65] Reports of atrocities by both sides became more common.[66] Mass graves were discovered with the bodies of more than sixty civilians allegedly killed by the *shabiha*.[67] Intense bombardment forced the FSA to withdraw from Baba Amr at the beginning of March, though only after exacting a heavy toll on the Syrian Army.[68] The army had exacted a far heavier toll on the district's civilians, though, killing between seven hundred and a thousand.[69] The fighting in Baba Amr pushed Syria's conflict to a new level. The month following the Russian and Chinese vetoes was the most violent since the beginning of the crisis.

Second, the vetoes and the dramatic escalation of violence in Homs shocked Western and Arab governments into increasing political and material support to the opposition.[70] With American support, France's president Nicolas Sarkozy convened a "Friends of the Syrian People" group to coordinate international support for the SNC, which they recognized as the principal opposition grouping, and ramp up pressure on Assad.[71] The group comprised eleven states (including the P3, Saudi Arabia, Qatar, Jordan, Turkey, UAE, Germany, and Italy), and the UN,

Arab League, Organization of the Islamic Conference, EU, and GCC participated as observers. The new group had two ambitions: to isolate and delegitimize Assad and to lay the groundwork for a cohesive and nonextremist opposition capable of negotiating with the government and contributing to a transitional government.[72] At their first meeting, held in Tunis on February 24, the friends agreed to support the Arab League initiative, coordinate targeted sanctions against the Syrian government, and step up humanitarian assistance.

Some saw the initiative as a vehicle for marshaling more robust opposition to Assad. Saudi Arabia's foreign minister, Prince Saud al-Faisal, suggested they arm the rebels and establish a fund to pay salaries to FSA fighters. Foreign arms, ammunition, and funds had begun to flow to the Syrian opposition in greater numbers in late 2011 and early 2012.[73] Until the vetoes, most of the funding had come from private donors facilitated by the Syrian diaspora, but governments had started to become involved.[74] That now accelerated since the vetoes convinced donors Assad would have to be forcibly prized from power. The Turkish and Qatari governments used allies connected with the Muslim Brotherhood to smuggle in arms, while Saudi Arabia funneled arms through Islamist allies as well as non-Islamist intermediaries in Lebanon.[75] The volume of support remained modest, though. For instance, there is no evidence that the armed opposition had access to heavy weapons or armored vehicles before mid-2012, and estimates suggest that by September 2012 no more than 15 percent of the opposition's arms came from foreign sources. On the battlefield, opposition forces frequently suffered critical shortages of ammunition.[76]

But it was not just Assad that the region was worried about. Saudi Arabia was concerned about Iran's increasing military support for the regime (in the form of the Revolutionary Guards Quds force) as well as by signs of jihadism among Syria's armed opposition. Their principal concern on that front was the rise of Jabhat al-Nusra, a small Salafist group established in August 2011 by Abu Bakr al-Baghdadi, head of al-Qaeda in Iraq. Led by Abu Mohammed al-Jolani, al-Nusra's leadership came mainly from outside Syria.[77] The extremists had launched their first major attack in late December, using two suicide bombers to target military intelligence buildings in Damascus. On January 6 another suicide bomber killed twenty-six people when he detonated a bomb near buses carrying riot police, and on February 10 Jabhat al-Nusra detonated suicide bombs outside government buildings in Aleppo. The Saudis hoped to counter not just Assad but the jihadists too by channeling arms and cash to the mainstream opposition.

Prince al-Faisal found little enthusiasm in the West for arming Syria's opposition. Where the rise of al-Nusra encouraged Riyadh to arm FSA-aligned groups, it fueled Western doubts about the armed opposition's character and fears any arms they provided might find their way to extremists. Martin Dempsey, chair of the U.S. Joint Chiefs of Staff, voiced these concerns on February 19, just two weeks after the second vetoed resolution, expressing doubt about "who the opposition movement in Syria is at this moment" and warning that "there are indications that al-Qaeda is involved and that they're interested in supporting the opposition." It would be "premature to talk about arming" Syria's opposition, he maintained, until the United States had a clearer understanding of who they were.[78] Director of National Intelligence James Clapper aired similar concerns, as did John Kerry, chair of the powerful Senate Foreign Relations Committee.[79] The United States was also wary of placing too much emphasis on the SNC's expatriate leadership at the expense of the Local Coordination Committees and others inside Syria. Yet despite its professed support for the LCCs, relatively little aid reached them, and the SNC's international elevation via the "Friends" group made it more difficult for the local committees to establish their own international voice. Arguments against arming the opposition became less persuasive with every failed diplomatic initiative, and as the opposition militarized, the LCCs were pushed aside as foreign funding swung massively toward armed groups.[80]

The third immediate effect of the February 4 veto was a new diplomatic enterprise. Where the Arab League had looked to Yemen as a possible model, UN officials proposed an alternative based on a model used with some success in Kenya. In late 2007 the UN and African Union (AU) had appointed former UN secretary-general Kofi Annan as their joint envoy charged with brokering an agreement to stop spiraling communal violence. The situation Syria confronted in early 2012 was far worse than that faced by Kenya four years earlier, but with few other options available UN and Arab officials agreed to pursue this route and to recruit Annan himself to lead the effort. The General Assembly approved the idea in its February 16 resolution, and a few days later Annan was appointed as the joint UN-LAS envoy for Syria. It was widely understood to be Syria's last chance for peace.

3

LAST CHANCE FOR PEACE

AS SECRETARY-GENERAL until 2006, Kofi Annan had led the United Nations through difficult reforms after the organization's miserable failures while he had overseen its peacekeeping operations in Rwanda and Bosnia and the disastrous oil-for-food corruption scandal over Iraq. These reforms, which included the "Responsibility to Protect" principle as well as the creation of the UN's Human Rights Council and Peacebuilding Commission, left the organization seemingly better placed to protect civilians from atrocities. A skilled mediator, Annan had also amassed an enviable track record of resolving conflict. In 2007–2008 he had helped mediate an end to Kenya's slide toward violence, and when Secretary-General (2007–2016) Ban Ki-moon asked him to repeat the feat in Syria, he agreed despite knowing the situation was bleak and chances of success low, since he also knew failure would be catastrophic.[1] Before accepting Ban's invitation, he had called some key foreign ministries and found them encouraging. He also believed Assad's position was not wholly implacable. As UN secretary-general, Annan had spent considerable time with the Syrian president and helped persuade him to withdraw the Syrian Army from Lebanon in 2005.[2] International acceptance of Annan's mission involved a compromise between those who hoped it would facilitate political transition and those who hoped it would buy

Assad more time.[3] As Damascus saw it, the Arab League had lost legiti-macy by backing a transition and choosing sides. The fact that, as joint UN and Arab League envoy, Annan inherited the league's plan worked against him in their eyes. The opposition was distrustful, too, since it believed there could be no meaningful reform while Assad con-trolled the levers of power. Growing in confidence, it was also deeply divided since its exiled political leadership in Turkey had little author-ity over the highly fragmented opposition taking root on the ground. There were rifts inside the SNC, dominated as it was by the Muslim Brotherhood (backed by Turkey and Qatar), and lacking Kurdish, Alawite, Druze, or Christian representation. It faced accusations of favoring the Brotherhood's allies at the expense of others. It was also proving incapable of meeting the expectations inside Syria created by its pretensions to be a government-in-exile. The council raised only $40 million in 2012, most of which was spent on humanitarian relief.[4]

UN officials told Annan that Western governments had underesti-mated Assad's resilience. Annan agreed but also thought it unlikely the opposition would accept a deal that left Assad in power.[5] A man-aged transition was needed, but how could that be achieved? The strategy he hit on was to build international support for an entirely new process, independent of what had gone before. This would involve immediate steps to reduce violence, deescalate tensions, and build trust, all overseen by UN observers. Once that was achieved, talks could begin to establish a political process, and Annan would then leverage international momentum to persuade both parties to nego-tiate a deal. Annan hoped that while the parties talked, the reduction of violence would ease tensions and thus give the process irresistible legitimacy on Syria's streets. As a first step, Annan wanted a set of proposals that were short and easily digestible but contained the essential elements they needed, framed in such a way that no reason-able person could object. That meant taking political transition off the table for now. The proposals should focus on ending violence, building trust, and establishing a political process and should give no hint of prejudging the outcome. This was not about finding a solu-tion but about starting a process that key regional players and the Security Council's five permanent members (China, France, UK, United States, and Russia) could support, thus creating a "pressure point" that would compel Assad to take concrete steps and "change the dynamics of the crisis."[6] The result was a brief, six-point plan that called for the Syrian government to:

1. Commit to working with the envoy on an inclusive "Syrian-led" political process addressing the legitimate aspirations and concerns of the Syrian people.
2. Commit to stop fighting and achieve a UN-supervised cessation of all violence by all parties. Specifically, the Syrian government was asked to "immediately cease troop movements toward, and end the use of heavy weapons in, population centers, and begin pullback of military concentrations in and around population centers." It was also asked to work with Annan to bring about a "sustained cessation of armed violence in all its forms." Similar commitments would be sought from the opposition.
3. Ensure timely provision of humanitarian assistance to all areas affected by the fighting and immediately implement a daily two-hour "humanitarian pause."
4. Intensify the scale and pace of the release of arbitrarily detained prisoners.
5. Ensure freedom of movement for journalists.
6. Respect the freedom of association and right to demonstrate peacefully.[7]

   Annan hoped this could create a positive chain reaction: that international support for the plan would establish pressure on the government and armed opposition, enable a durable ceasefire, and, in turn, create space for the peaceful opposition to reclaim the streets from the army and armed groups and, finally, force the parties to agree a political settlement. Annan believed that if the regime could be persuaded to release the thousands of political prisoners it had seized over the previous eighteen months, the flower of the March 2011 revolution, this whole process could be sped up.[8]

   He arrived in Damascus on March 10, 2012, for talks with Assad, which he later described as "difficult." Annan set out the six-point plan and proposed that UN observers monitor and verify the ceasefire. He also proposed measures to alleviate suffering, protect media access to troubled areas, permit peaceful protests, and secure the release of detainees. Assad replied he would not negotiate with "terrorists" or withdraw security forces from the streets until the opposition stopped using violence and foreign governments stopped supporting them.[9] Annan knew this would be unacceptable to the opposition and thought Assad was trying to find a blanket justification for violating future ceasefires. An official response from Damascus arrived soon afterward, stating that, in keeping with the government's previous responses to diplomatic initiatives, it neither accepted nor rejected the plan but sought clarification and invited more talks. Concerned the government was either stalling or trying to derail the process by bogging it down in details, Annan declined. Banking on Russia to change the government's mind, Annan told the government it could either accept the plan or reject it and warned that the next set of proposals would be less generous. Not used to this kind of pressure, Assad tried to sidestep by offering a different concession. On March 13 Damascus granted permission for the UN's humanitarian chief, the British peer Dame Valerie Amos, to visit the country. This seemed a significant step—and in some quarters it was taken as evidence of Russian pressure on Assad—since Damascus had rejected earlier requests, drawing a critical response from the Security Council in the form of a press statement.[10] Though not much in itself, the fact that Moscow agreed to the statement seemed to suggest some disquiet with its Syrian ally and was perhaps intended as a signal that Assad should not take Russian support for granted. That Assad relented so quickly encouraged Annan to think he could be persuaded to do other things, too, if it was Russia doing the asking. Beneath the rhetoric, the government's main concerns were that withdrawing security forces would hand the streets to the opposition and that the proposed political process was simply a political transition rebadged. Annan believed both these issues could be handled.

After Damascus, Annan traveled to Doha to line up Qatar's support and then to Ankara to do the same with the Turkish government and the SNC. The opposition and its allies had expressed deep distrust of Assad and believed that meaningful reform would be possible only if the president stepped aside.[11] If that didn't happen, they thought, nothing agreed to in international negotiations would make any difference in Syria itself. Annan's team repeatedly pressed the opposition to drop its demand that Assad step down as a prerequisite for negotiations. But how could talks be free and inclusive, they replied, while Assad controlled the instruments of state terror? Annan realized this was likely true. Real reform would happen only once Assad was gone. Annan now worked on the assumption, unspoken in public, that this would be the inevitable outcome of the process he envisioned. But he also knew that establishing regime change as a prerequisite would derail that process before it began. The SNC reluctantly accepted Annan's plan, albeit more to please its foreign backers and because it had no other options than because it believed it to be a good plan. It expected that while Assad remained, ceasefires would not hold, and talks would not progress.

Annan urged the UN Security Council to issue a presidential statement endorsing his plan, judging—rightly—that going for a statement rather than a resolution would make it easier for Russia to support. Resolutions could come later, he calculated. What mattered most was applying pressure on Damascus by getting the Security Council's, and especially Moscow's, support for the six-point plan placed on the record. The Europeans and Americans welcomed the idea and suggested the council also condemn ongoing violence, refer to the need for political transition, and promise to consider further actions should the government not comply. From the Kremlin's perspective, Annan's plan held promise precisely because it made no mention of political transition and made demands that both sides end violence. To Russia, this meant that the opposition was just as likely to violate the plan as the government; it doubted that the SNC and FSA could deliver a ceasefire since both lacked control over the proliferating opposition-armed groups. Indeed, Assad's whole strategy for dealing with Annan seemed to depend on this very expectation. It was for that reason that the sequencing of a ceasefire and withdrawal became such a bone of contention. Annan's plan called for government forces to cease firing and withdraw to barracks *before* the opposition reciprocated. That was symbolically important to signal the government's commitment to the plan but was also a practical necessity since opposition fighters would not stand down while government tanks and armored vehicles remained on the streets lest the government renege on its promise and use the opportunity to crush them. Moscow preferred that the sequence run in the other direction but was content to go along with it for the time being to keep the process alive. Damascus, though, was never wholly convinced. In the end, the Security Council's statement of support offered less than the United States and Europeans had hoped for but put the Security Council on record supporting Annan's six-point plan.[12] Soon after, Russia's foreign minister Sergei Lavrov emerged from a meeting with the International Committee of the Red Cross to propose that Syrians also agree to a daily humanitarian ceasefire.

Thinking it crucial to make quick use of the positive momentum, Annan lost no time sending an assessment team, led by Major-General Robert Mood of Norway, to Damascus to prepare the details of a ceasefire and arrange the deployment of UN observers to monitor it. Having served in peacekeeping missions in the Balkans and as chief of the UN's truce supervision mission in the Golan Heights (UNTSO), Mood had an impeccable military record and was a good pick for the job. But his reception in Damascus was less than warm. Members of the advance team ran into a not-very-spontaneous pro-Assad rally, which quickly turned ugly as demonstrators attacked the monitors' vehicles. Things were not much warmer in the meeting room. The government delegation, led by Foreign Minister Walid Al-Moualem, complained that Annan's plan favored the opposition and insisted that the government have the final say on the appointment and nationality of the UN's staff in Syria, as well as control over their movements and communications. This left Mood in no doubt that the authorities intended to control every aspect of the UN's activities in Syria, as they had the Arab League's.[13] The opposition must end violence first, they insisted, and to ensure this there should be a moratorium on protests. They also insisted that Annan provide personal written assurance that the opposition would respect the ceasefire, something he obviously could not do. Annan needed Moscow's help, so he met Lavrov and Medvedev there on March 24, and both promised to encourage Assad to relent. It worked. From Moscow, Annan traveled to Beijing to shore up Chinese support, and while there he received a letter from Damascus confirming its acceptance of the six-point plan—a rapid turn-about and clear evidence of Russian influence. Though still wary of Annan, Damascus judged his terms better than the Arab League's and, at Russia's urging, thought it could tolerate the process for a while without conceding anything significant.

The next challenge, Annan thought, was to quickly negotiate and implement the ceasefire to capitalize on the gathering momentum. Not everyone agreed. Some UN officials and some diplomats thought a ceasefire premature and that more political progress was needed first. Some doubted the opposition's ability to comply and asked pointed questions about who would take responsibility for them. Annan, though, thought a reduction of violence crucial, since ongoing violence would make it more difficult for the parties to negotiate and would undermine faith in the process itself.[14] He also hoped the momentum created by international acceptance of his six-point plan would prove sufficient to coax the parties to agree to a ceasefire, creating the firebreak he was looking for. Even an imperfect ceasefire could reduce violence, reinforce positive momentum, and build public confidence, Annan thought. From the outset, his strategy had banked on shifting the locus of the crisis away from armed conflict and back toward peaceful protest. Reduced violence would give the streets back to the civilian protestors and stem the militarization, sectarianization, and radicalization of the opposition. All this, Annan hoped, would add impetus to local mobilization for reform, to which the government would be obliged to respond. Syria's future could thus be shaped by a peaceful dialogue between government and protest movement. In that context, the ceasefire was both the beginning and the tripwire, for if a ceasefire couldn't be agreed on, then nothing else would be either. Meanwhile, ceasefire violations would allow world leaders to draw their own conclusions about who was most responsible and respond accordingly.

The Security Council broadly accepted Annan's approach. To navigate the sequencing problem, Annan suggested a phased implementation beginning with the Syrian government halting troop movements toward populated areas, ceasing all use of heavy weapons around such areas, and commencing a pullback of military concentrations by April 10. That would be followed by a complete cessation of violence by all sides, beginning forty-eight hours after completion of those first steps. It was an ambitious timeframe, but as mentioned before, Annan believed momentum was key. On April 5 the Security Council issued a statement that endorsed the ceasefire, committed to considering the deployment of UN monitors should the ceasefire take hold, and reiterated its "full support" for the six-point plan.[15]

The Security Council may have backed the plan, but whether Syria's parties would implement it was another matter entirely. On the ground, armed forces tried to strengthen their position before a ceasefire came into effect. When the government's efforts proved more successful than they had anticipated, Syrian officials tried to delay the ceasefire so they could take full advantage. Walid al-Moualem reinstated the plea that the opposition be made to cease firing first since the government had no confidence in its disorderly opponents. Annan countered that as the stronger party, it made sense for the government to take the first step and that, besides, the plan had already been agreed to. The FSA's leaders, meanwhile, were adamant they had no intention of ceasing operations unless the government did first. Besides, everyone knew the SNC and FSA were unable to control the opposition's fragmented and fractious armed groups. Surrounded by doubt and mistrust, Annan worried any delay or attempt to renegotiate would bring the whole process crashing down.

With the ceasefire in doubt, Annan turned to Russia once again, which once again persuaded the Syrian government to relent—though only partially.[16] Damascus advised that although it would *begin* to withdraw its forces from contested areas on April 10, withdrawal would be completed only after the opposition's ceasefire came into effect and "normal life" was resumed. It also reserved the right to respond forcibly to opposition ceasefire violations, in effect a blanket justification for its own violations. The government also demanded international action to stem the flow of arms and money to the opposition and insisted that the United States, France, Turkey, Qatar, and Saudi Arabia stop aiding the opposition. Annan, though, refused even to contemplate reopening negotiations. The parties could comply or not. True, the edifice he had built had gaps. The withdrawal of soldiers from populated areas would be difficult to verify, not least because barracks were commonly located in populated areas. Moreover, the agreement called only for the government to "begin" to pull back military concentrations from population centers, leaving open the question of how much of a beginning was needed and what constituted "military concentrations" or "population centers."[17] But he firmly believed even an imperfect ceasefire could put downward pressure on violence and establish a tripwire on commitment to the peace process and that the government was simply trying to stall and derail the process.

When the ceasefire deadline passed, there was a discernible reduction of violence across the country, though in practice the cessation was never full or comprehensive. Accepting, though, that the ceasefire was established, the Security Council unanimously adopted Resolution 2042 (April 14) to formally endorse the six-point plan and commit itself to deploying a UN monitoring mission. In yet another sign that Moscow was distancing itself from Assad, the resolution committed the council to considering "further steps" should they be needed—a vague promise that had nonetheless been a major bone of contention for over a year. Plans for the monitoring mission were drawn up quickly, and a week later, with the ceasefire still imperfect but broadly on course, the council unanimously adopted Resolution 2043, establishing the UN Supervision Mission in Syria (UNSMIS). The new mission comprised three hundred unarmed observers, mandated for a renewable period of ninety days to monitor and report on ceasefire compliance. Teams of monitors were deployed to eight critical posts across the country (Damascus, Aleppo, Deir-ez-Zor, Hama, Homs, Idlib, Daraa, and Tartus), and a small human rights office was established in Damascus. UN observers arrived quickly, and violence abated further. Exchanges of small-arms fire continued, but government forces stopped using heavy weapons (for a period of six weeks), and there were few major military engagements.[18] In contrast to the treatment meted out to Arab League observers, the UN's monitors appeared initially to enjoy freedom of movement. Journalists, too, were granted more freedom. As the guns quieted, peaceful protests reclaimed the streets, just as Annan had hoped they would.[19]

This progress was testament, Annan later argued, to what could be achieved when the region and the Security Council were united. Deadlocked on February 4, the Security Council had now adopted a string of unanimous statements and resolutions endorsing the six-point plan, calling on the parties to comply, mandating a UN field mission, and warning of further measures should progress not be sustained. The next step was to prepare ground for a political settlement by persuading Russia and Iran to endorse the idea of a transitional government, by far the most difficult political ravine to bridge since that meant persuading them to accept that Assad would not be part of Syria's long-term future. As the ceasefire had approached, Annan had angered some Western governments by visiting Iran to, as he put it, "plant seeds." Since Iran was a potential major spoiler, he tried to convince it to accept that some form of transition in Syria was inevitable and to provide reassurance that its interests were best served by constructively participating in and influencing the peace process. Annan banked on the Iranians sharing everyone else's view that, one way or another, Assad's days were numbered, and indeed he found Tehran less hostile than he had expected. It indicated it could accept a transition at the end of Assad's term of office in 2014.[20] A start at least.

But as Annan planned his next moves, things began to unravel on the ground. After the initial reduction of violence, ceasefire violations steadily increased toward the end of April 2012. UNSMIS helped negotiate local agreements in places where government forces had still not yet withdrawn. Predictably, however, when government forces withdrew, armed opposition elements sometimes moved in to fill the void left behind. To manage the process, UN monitors sometimes drew up maps to show who should withdraw and to where, thus for the first time marking out "opposition-held" territory. This apparent loss of territory alarmed the government and brought its withdrawal to a halt. On May 1 the UN reported ceasefire violations by both sides and noted that heavy weapons, including tanks, artillery pieces, and armored personnel carriers, were still deployed in civilian areas.[21] As violence increased, UN monitors faced more government obstacles to their freedom of movement and confronted an increasingly disenchanted civilian population that expected the UN to protect them from attack, something for which they had neither the mandate nor capability.[22]

UNSMIS reported that the government increased military activities in the first weeks of May 2012, targeting Homs, Houla, Rastan, Talbisa, Al-Qusayr, and villages in Aleppo governate. It detected a "rise of coordinated [g]overnment forces' assaults as part of an offensive on population centres, using both infantry and heavy weapons, in an apparent campaign to clear territories of opposition and armed opposition groups."[23] Opposition violence also increased—most worryingly a spate of suicide bomb attacks targeting government installations in Damascus and Aleppo. Speaking on May 16, Mood noted that while violence had "significantly reduced" when UNSMIS first arrived, he "share[d] the worries of everyone who is concerned that we are seeing more violence in the last days."[24] Progress stalled on other fronts, too. Annan made no progress on the release of detainees and little obvious headway on the political front.[25] The regime refused to even meet the people leading Annan's political team, while the opposition struggled to clarify who would represent it and what political positions they would adopt. International support waned, too. An increasing number of Western governments joined Turkey and Gulf Arab governments in complaining about the government's incomplete withdrawal and the slow pace of talks and in arguing that sanctions be used to punish Assad's noncompliance, raising hackles in Moscow and Tehran. Things came to a head on May 25, when government soldiers opened fire on protestors leaving Friday prayers in Taldou. Opposition fighters fired back, and the army retaliated by shelling the town. After dusk *shabiha* militia moved in, killing indiscriminately. A total of 108 people, including 34 women and 49 children, were killed: 20 by shelling; the rest slaughtered by the militia. UNSMIS entered Taldou the following day and confirmed the massacre, identifying the culprits as pro-Assad forces.[26]

The massacre seemed a clear sign Annan's consensual approach was floundering. The world's initial response was surprisingly swift and resolute. Annan and Ban Ki-moon issued a joint statement of condemnation, joined by Western governments who also pledged to respond through the United Nations.[27] Even Russia and China condemned the massacre. Lavrov expressed "deep alarm" and took the unusual step of admitting government complicity.[28] Russia and China quickly agreed to a Security Council press statement that condemned the killing "in the strongest possible terms," requested that UNSMIS investigate and report its findings, and "demanded" that the government immediately cease use of heavy weapons near population centers and pull troops and heavy weapons back.[29] The Arab League also joined this chorus of condemnation. Perhaps taken aback by the vociferous response, the government released five hundred detainees and agreed to relax restrictions on humanitarian agencies entering the most troubled areas.

Did this new assertiveness indicate a change of heart in Russia? Certainly, Moscow judged Annan's six-point plan the most promising way of managing Syria's crisis and of avoiding the complete collapse of the state. It had grown anxious about the regime's prospects, and analysts there feared Assad's days were numbered. Especially disconcerting was the fact that opposition forces had taken several border crossings.[30] These anxieties weren't helped by the situation in Russia itself, where Putin's third inauguration as president—which had a noticeably chilling effect on U.S.-Russian relations—had been met with unprecedented public demonstrations, which Putin claimed were orchestrated by Washington.[31] Members of Annan's team recall the Russians commenting that Assad had little chance of survival and that the question of "how he quits and when" needed settling.[32] Given that the likeliest scenarios were negotiated settlement (via the Annan plan), forced transition (via a coup, opposition victory, or external intervention), or complete state collapse, the Kremlin was beginning to think that as much as it would have liked to hang on to Assad, it might have to accept a negotiated transition to prevent the emergence of a less favorable solution imposed by others.[33] For a moment, therefore, it seemed as if an international consensus was developing on two crucial points: that Assad's days in power were numbered, and that an agreement would have to be reached to manage Syria's political transition.

The day after the Security Council's press statement, Lavrov told Clinton he was eager to keep the Annan process alive. Indeed, the last thing Russia wanted was for the West to declare Assad responsible for killing the six-point plan and then move on to more coercive action that might lock it out of the deliberations or, worse, cause the state to collapse. Lavrov acknowledged the need for a political transition and conceded that Russia would not insist on Assad remaining in power if foreign-imposed regime change, likely to cause chaos and help jihadism, could be avoided. Clinton agreed that should be their approach, but how would such a transition be achieved? Clinton proposed tougher sanctions to coerce Assad into changing course, but Lavrov refused, since the Kremlin worried sanctions would compound the pressure already on the regime and might push it toward collapse. Instead, he suggested they form a "Contact Group" of key states to drive the political process—a model used with some success by the United States and Russia in Bosnia more than a decade earlier. Clinton was cool to the idea, since the two governments remained poles apart, but agreed it was worth considering.

Meanwhile, what was left of the ceasefire quickly unraveled. With fighting erupting countrywide, on June 4 the FSA suspended its ceasefire commitment and resumed "defensive operations." More reports of massacres emerged, including the killing of at least fifty-five (and maybe as many as seventy-eight) civilians by the *shabiha* in al-Qubeir—an almost copybook repeat of what had happened at Taldou that bore the hallmark of increasingly grisly sectarianism. UNSMIS monitors came under small arms fire when they tried to enter the village.[34] These were not isolated incidents. The UN identified a pattern of "intermittent artillery shelling and mortar fire followed by limited deployments of mechanized infantry and tanks into town centres, followed by the arrest or detention of suspected opposition supporters." Inevitably, these offensives triggered armed responses from the opposition.[35] Attacks on UN monitors became more frequent, too, with monitors attacked by indirect fire from heavy weapons (most likely government) and small arms fire (origins unknown). On June 12 a crowd angry at the UN's failure to protect civilians attacked an UNSMIS convoy outside al-Haffah.

Escalating violence fractured Annan's carefully constructed international consensus. The West, Gulf Arab states, and Turkey argued the massacres and lack of progress on the six-point plan exposed the futility of Annan's noncoercive method in the face of flagrant government noncompliance. It was time for real coercion, they argued. Russia and China disagreed and insisted the six-point plan remained the only viable political option. They pleaded that Assad be given more time, at least until expiry of the UNSMIS mandate in July. To save the process, Lavrov pressed his case for the "Contact Group" and proposed an international conference to develop a roadmap for implementing the six-point plan. Clinton remained "lukewarm," thinking a conference was premature when there was so little agreement on the fundamentals. To have any hope of success, a new track would have to spell out steps toward political transition supported by serious consequences for noncompliance, something she knew the Russians would not tolerate.[36] Annan, though, welcomed the idea, hoping it might help him bridge international divisions.[37]

As it was, things were brought to a head by UNSMIS itself when Mood announced its immediate suspension, citing risks to the monitors' safety and "the lack of willingness by the parties to seek a peaceful transition."[38] Behind this lay a determination that UN peacekeepers not be blamed for failing to protect civilians as they had in Rwanda and Bosnia in the 1990s.[39] To avoid the mistakes of the past, the peacekeepers intended to speak bluntly to the Security Council about what they were witnessing and not pretend they could perform tasks for which they were neither mandated nor equipped. Mood explained to the Security Council that UNSMIS could resume operations only once conditions improved but found the council divided about how to end killing and begin a political transition.[40] He was right. Whatever change of heart the Kremlin may have had, it still opposed the very notion of coercing compliance from Assad, just as many in the West and Middle East were coming to the opposite conclusion: that coercion would be necessary.[41] Conscious there was no plan B, council members fashioned a temporary fix and agreed to keep UNSMIS alive another thirty days (Resolution 2059, July 20, 2012), with extensions beyond that conditional on progress toward implementing the six-point plan. Unwilling to go on, Mood stepped down and was replaced by Senegalese general Babacar Gaye, an inauspicious choice. Gaye was later removed from his post as UN force commander in the Central African Republic for failing to prevent the sexual abuse of children by his personnel and gross mishandling of abuse allegations.[42]

Annan's first attempt at peacemaking had failed for many of the same reasons as the Arab League's. True, UNSMIS was much better led, more competent, and more effective than the Arab League's mission. True too, UNSMIS and the six-point plan enjoyed more international support than the league ever garnered. Yet failure was to be expected since the ceasefire hinged on deferring difficult political questions for another day in the hope they might be more easily addressed later. Without a political process in place to address these issues, however, the ceasefire was always highly vulnerable. The problem was that although outside parties agreed there should be a political transition, there was no consensus on what that should like look, much less how it would be achieved, and Annan soon ran up against the fact that Assad had no intention of sharing power. Annan had anticipated this roadblock and banked on the power of international political momentum and Russian influence to overcome it. But since there remained wide disagreements, there was almost no common ground on which to forge an international consensus on what to do next. Annan's strategy had always relied on Russia's willingness and ability to influence Assad. By late July it was becoming apparent, including to Moscow itself, that Russian influence was wearing thin. Annan's team recall the Russians becoming increasingly exasperated by Assad's refusal to comply and their inability to persuade him to. Russian officials privately admitted "that they might not be able to 'deliver' Assad," since it was not them propping him up, but Iran. Nonetheless, the Russian government also worried that breaking ranks with its ally by agreeing to sanctions or other modes of coercion could reveal just how limited its influence was, sacrifice its leverage, and expose the regime to external pressure that might precipitate its disorderly collapse—the worst possible outcome.[43] The Kremlin wanted a political process to manage the situation with Assad inside the tent, but it had insufficient influence to keep him there.

Meanwhile, to many in the West and the Middle East, the situation warranted a new and more coercive approach. At a meeting in Riyadh in early April, Clinton asked her Saudi counterpart, Prince Saud al-Faisal, whether Assad would agree to the Arab League's plan for a political transition if the Russians could be persuaded to support it. He thought not, explaining that Assad was under immense pressure to protect the government at any cost.[44] Not even Russian influence could change that reality. Since Assad would never willingly give up political power, al-Faisal argued, they should increase their military and financial support to the opposition. Clinton had replied at the time that the United States opposed arming the opposition, but she understood that pressure to take that path would increase if Annan failed. Prince Faisal agreed to hold off for as long as the Annan plan survived, which he expected would not be long.[45] Should Annan fail, though, the opposition's foreign backers would increase the flow of arms and cash to combat Assad. Annan, though, still had one more idea up his sleeve.

ANNAN'S LAST GAMBLE:
THE GENEVA CONFERENCE

That the Security Council had endorsed the six-point plan and mandated UNSMIS gave Annan hope it might still be possible to leverage international pressure to achieve a political settlement. But the main problem with the six-point plan—the fact it made no reference to a political settlement—had also been key to its success. He had succeeded only in pushing the Security Council onto nominally common ground in the hope that political momentum might "re-energize the drive for unity" and carry it the rest of the way.[46] Annan's new strategy turned that logic on its head. Instead of a ceasefire creating space for politics, why not use politics to force a cessation of violence? Why not, in other words, persuade the key foreign powers to agree on a vision for Syria's future and then use their influence to persuade Syria's parties, too? It is hard to exaggerate the difficulty of the task Annan set for himself, for however nervous the Kremlin was about Assad's prospects, it had given little indication it was prepared to coerce Syria's government to accept an unfavorable deal, and however hard pressed the opposition, it still had no faith in any deal that left Assad at the helm.

Moreover, there was little to suggest the necessary rapprochement between Russia and the United States might be achievable. In mid-June Obama and Putin held face-to-face talks on the sidelines of the G20 summit in Mexico. They had a full program—including bilateral relations, missile defense, nuclear issues, and Iran—but Syria was top of the agenda. Putin arrived nearly an hour late and launched into a lengthy monologue insisting that the modernization of traditional societies like Syria's be gradual and top-down. He argued that U.S. policy in the Middle East had only made things worse, and he blamed the CIA for inciting regime change and sowing instability.[47] Obama

replied that since Syria's descent into civil war risked inflaming jihadism, they should work together to resolve the conflict by implementing the six-point plan. That was no idle worry. Earlier that month, the
White House had received a memo written for Clinton by Frederic Hof
that claimed Al Qaeda was growing stronger in eastern Syria, that the
FSA lacked sufficient supplies and money to hold them off, and that,
should the extremists succeed in eastern Syria, they would likely team
up with their allies in Iraq.[48] Success, though, depended on Putin,
since only he could apply sufficient pressure on Assad and free up multilateral options by withdrawing the veto blocking the Security Council. Putin answered that he had no "particular love" for Assad but that
Syria's president was the man best placed to maintain stability.[49] The
two presidents were poles apart. They understood the situation very
differently and wanted different things. Yet since Obama was uninterested in options that might take him outside the UN's multilateral
framework, the United States had little choice but to take Putin at his
word and continue along a diplomatic track it had little faith in.

Building on Lavrov's Contact Group idea, Annan envisaged an
"Action Group for Syria" comprising the foreign ministers of the five
permanent members of the Security Council (China, France, Russia,
UK, United States), as well as Turkey, Kuwait, and Qatar. The envoy
wanted to include Iran, too, hoping it might represent the views of
Damascus and then exert positive influence over it, but the UK and
United States objected strongly, and Annan shelved the idea. To maintain balance, Saudi Arabia was also left out. The Action Group also
included the secretaries-general of the LAS and UN, as well as the EU's
high representative for foreign and security policy. Chaired by Annan,
it would agree on a blueprint for Syria's future and then use its power
and influence to persuade the parties to accept and implement it.
That, at least, was the theory. Annan proposed that the centerpiece
of the new blueprint be a transitional government of national unity,
comprising government and opposition representatives. The transitional government would exercise full executive powers, bringing the
armed forces and Mukhabarat under its control. It would be inclusive
but "exclude those whose continued presence and participation would
undermine the credibility of the transition and jeopardize stability
and reconciliation"—an implicit reference to Assad and evidence

Annan hoped Alawite leaders might be persuaded (by Moscow, mainly) to urge Assad to step aside so that they could have a seat at the table negotiating Syria's future. But this clause also meant excluding extremist armed groups and elevating the civilian protest leaders, reflecting Annan's view that Syria's brightest future lay in their hands. By this, Annan tried to accommodate both the demand that Assad be excluded from Syria's future and the counterinsistence that he not be. The transitional government would administer the country while a new constitution was devised and elections held to select a new government.

The first opportunity for the Americans and Russians to discuss the plan came a few days before they were due to convene in Geneva to formally consider it. Lavrov used a face-to-face meeting with Clinton on the fringes of the APEC Summit in St. Petersburg to urge his counterpart to make concessions. Clinton retorted in kind, "I knew the Russians would never be comfortable explicitly calling for Assad to leave office," she recalls, but she thought "Kofi had crafted an elegant solution"—a way in which Assad could be maneuvered out of office as part of a Syrian-led process that fully included the Alawites. Lavrov replied that while Russia accepted the need for political transition, its form and timing should be decided by Syrians. In other words, Russia would not accept a plan that Assad himself did not endorse. Clinton warned that failing to back Annan risked plunging Syria into civil war and turning over the initiative to Saudi Arabia, Qatar, Turkey, and Iran, who would flood the country with arms and sow chronic disorder.[50] Indeed, at a subsequent meeting of the "Friends" group, Qatar's Hamad bin Jassim and Turkey's Davutoglu pressed Clinton and British foreign secretary William Hague to agree to them supplying arms to the opposition. Clinton and Hague objected but left the meeting in no doubt about what would happen should Annan fail. Clinton suggested that if Lavrov helped the Annan process, the United States would respect Russia's interests and its military presence at the Tartus naval base should Syria's government change. Lavrov was unmoved: transition could not be imposed from the outside, he insisted. The prospects for Geneva looked bleak.

Annan opened the main meeting by presenting a written blueprint of his plan for a transitional government and imploring the Action

Group to endorse it and use its influence to bring Syria's parties onboard. Clinton welcomed the proposal, which she saw as a blueprint for a "post-Assad Syria" that maintained Syria's territorial and institutional integrity. While it would have preferred a clearer statement demanding Assad step aside, the United States was happy to support Annan's text in the interests of consensus, since by excluding those that might "jeopardize stability" from the transitional government the plan clearly ruled out the prospect of Assad remaining in power. The Security Council should formally embrace the plan too, Clinton argued, and be prepared to impose "real and immediate consequences" should Syria's parties not comply. Russia would need to use its "clout" to bring Damascus into line, she maintained.[51]

Things quickly became acrimonious once the serious bargaining began, ministers literally yelling across the table at one another. If the Russians, concerned Assad might soon fall, were contemplating an elegant transition of power, they were doing a good job of hiding it. In fact, Lavrov made no reference at all to the proposal Churkin had floated four months earlier, instead returning repeatedly to three central points: that Assad led a legitimate government, that he was combatting Islamist terrorism, and that outside powers should not compel his exit. What Lavrov was saying in Geneva was very different from what Churkin had said in New York, Robert Ford recalled.[52] Outside the room, Lavrov was overheard joking with European delegates that "it is not possible for us to host him [Assad] in Russia—we have too many of them already," and French foreign minister Laurent Fabius recalls Lavrov told him, "I am sure we can find a country in South America or Africa to take him."[53] From that, Fabius sensed the Russians were worried Assad might soon be deposed. That was likely true, but in the talks themselves Lavrov refused to concede ground. He accepted there should be a transitional government with full executive powers but drew a red line through Annan's "exclusion" clause, complaining it was tantamount to regime change. Instead, he argued, there should be a "Syrian-led" process with no predetermined outcome as to who might be admitted or excluded. Naturally, Lavrov and everybody else knew the opposition would never accept an arrangement that left Assad at the helm of the security state, and with good reason. A deal without an exclusion clause would effectively legitimize

Assad's continuation in government not just for the time being but maybe indefinitely (since he could serve in the transitional government, then seek reelection), allow his government and the Kremlin to present themselves as peacemakers, and leave the opposition blamed for collapsing the peace process when it inevitably rejected the terms. Lavrov dangled a superficially tantalizing prospect to the assembled leaders but one that threatened to undermine the whole process: they could have agreement on Annan's blueprint in return for losing that one clause.

The Americans nevertheless took the bait, at least partly. With few options, they were desperate for a deal, but since they couldn't altogether abandon the exclusion clause without changing U.S. policy and alienating Syria's opposition, they proposed a hasty compromise. Instead of the exclusion clause, they suggested the transitional government be selected by government and opposition on the basis of "mutual consent." The Americans believed this still effectively excluded Assad, since the opposition would never consent to his inclusion, but it lacked the normative quality of Annan's formulation, avoided specific reference to Assad, and left the matter entirely in Syrian hands. Therein lay a fatal problem apparent even before the day was done. Since "mutual consent" relied on reciprocity, it awarded Assad a veto over the transitional government for as long as the opposition vetoed his participation in it. It was a recipe for stalemate in perpetuity, which Lavrov seemed to understand immediately as he quickly accepted Clinton's proposal. The Americans had made a serious tactical error that effectively hamstrung the UN's peace efforts thereafter (to be fair to the United States, neither the UN, British, or French delegates in the room seemed to notice the obvious trap). In their eagerness for a deal, they also agreed to omit a reference to the UN Security Council passing a resolution to give the arrangements legal and political weight.

The agreed text, which became known as the Geneva Communiqué, clustered its objectives into three baskets: (1) full implementation of the six-point plan, (2) guidelines and principles for a political transition, and (3) actions to implement the objectives. On the first, it called for an immediate and sustained cessation of violence, the redeployment of UNSMIS and guarantees of its security and freedom of movement, progress on the release of detainees, press freedom, and respect for the right of peaceful protest. On the second, the communiqué called for a "Syrian-led" transition toward "genuinely democratic and pluralistic" government compliant with international standards on human rights. A transitional government with full executive powers, comprising members of the present government, opposition, and others, should be formed "on the basis of mutual consent." The transitional government would establish a new constitutional order, subject to popular approved, paving the way to free and fair multiparty elections that would select the new government. Crucially, "governmental institutions and qualified staff" would remain in place during the transition. Security forces would continue to perform their duties but under the control of the transitional government and, for the first time ever, with full respect for human rights. The transition would include a process of national reconciliation and transitional justice, establishing accountability for crimes committed during the conflict. On the third, the Action Group agreed to apply "joint and sustained" pressure on Syria's parties to secure compliance.[54]

It was immediately clear that the Russians and Americans had very different ideas about what had just been agreed. Lavrov emphasized that "there is no attempt to impose any kind of transition process" and that "there are no prior conditions to the transfer process and no attempt to exclude any group from the process." The agreed communiqué called for a "Syrian-led transition" and said nothing about Assad stepping aside. China's foreign minister, Yang Jiechi, agreed: the deal left Syria's political future squarely in the hands of Syrians themselves.[55] Clinton offered a very different interpretation. "Assad will still have to go. He will never pass the mutual consent test, given the blood on his hands." The communiqué was thus a "blueprint for Assad's departure."[56] The text "makes clear that the power to govern is vested fully in the transitional governing body, which strips him and his regime of all authority if he and they refuse to step down and leave."[57] Hague and Fabius agreed and demanded the Security Council begin work on a new resolution to support the arrangement and threaten sanctions on those who refused to comply.[58]

Both interpretations of the Geneva Communiqué carried a grain of truth since the communiqué had fudged the main issue, not resolved it. Lavrov was right that the text did not call on Assad to step aside or—as Annan's draft had—require the exclusion of those with blood on their hands. Nothing in the communiqué prevented the government insisting Assad be included in the transitional government and withholding its own consent unless he was. Clinton was right, too, since the text made plain that Assad could participate in the transitional government only if the opposition consented, which it would not. Yet some of her comments betrayed that maybe the United States had conceded too much. "It is incumbent upon" Russia and China, she explained, "to show Assad the writing on the wall."[59] But what if they didn't? Annan's view sat somewhere in between but closer to the West's position than Russia's. The communiqué did not spell out that Assad must step down, but there was no way of implementing the deal if he did not. "Assad will have to go," Annan wrote later.[60] "You cannot remain in power when so many people have been killed and are dying. No leader can retain legitimacy after this. The question is how he goes, and when he goes."[61] After Geneva, Annan took to scribbling a diagram of the transition process during meetings with Western governments, showing disagreement only about *when* Assad would step down, not *whether*.[62] He hoped that Geneva provided a decent blueprint for ending violence and moving toward political transition, one that took account of the different views around the table. But Annan's hopes, just like Clinton's, hinged on Russia doing precisely what it had repeatedly said it would *not* do, something it had expunged from the text: apply pressure to ease Assad from power. It was a formula doomed from the start.

TAKING GENEVA TO DAMASCUS

The holes in the arrangements were exposed surprisingly quickly. Annan wanted the Security Council to ratify the communiqué and establish a framework for implementation, something he assumed would be straightforward given the agreement at Geneva. He was wrong. The Americans, British, and French wanted a resolution with teeth, one that ramped up the pressure to implement the six-point plan and Geneva communiqué. They wanted a chapter 7 resolution that imposed consequences for noncompliance.[63] It should be "abundantly clear" to Assad's supporters, Clinton insisted, that the regime's "days are numbered." Political transition was needed to save the Syrian state from an imminent "catastrophic assault."[64] The Russians and Chinese, however, cautioned they could not support a chapter 7 resolution since that might be a slippery slope to regime change.

Things were no better in Syria. Damascus bridled at the communiqué and submitted fourteen substantive reservations. Meanwhile, angered by the communiqué's failure to call on Assad to step aside, the SNC's Bassma Kodmani lamented that "the regime is not going to cooperate on anything," reiterating the opposition's "non-negotiable" demand that Assad step aside.[65] The SNC was facing its own challenges. One problem was its lack of authority over opposition armed groups. Another was its subservience to the Muslim Brotherhood. After the Arab League peace initiative collapsed, Qatar had stepped up support for the Muslim Brotherhood in Syria, believing it offered the best way of challenging Assad and advancing its own interests.[66] Turkey joined Qatar in supporting the Brotherhood, but not all the opposition's foreign allies were happy. Saudi Arabia, the UAE, and Kuwait had their own reasons for hostility toward the Brothers.[67] They preferred to channel support to handpicked Islamists rather than the Brothers or the umbrella SNC. The West was also unwilling to support the Muslim Brotherhood, owing to its Islamist credentials, terrorism connections, and staunch anti-Semitism. The Brotherhood's dominance of the SNC deterred Alawites, Kurds, Christians, and other minorities from joining and reinforced doubts about the group's suitability to be the opposition's diplomatic vanguard. This, in turn, reinforced Western doubts about both the opposition's ability to overthrow Assad and what would happen if it did. A declassified U.S. intelligence report, dated July 30, 2012, predicted the regime could survive and hold territory for the foreseeable future and confirmed what others already suspected: that Salafists, the Muslim Brotherhood, and Al-Qaeda in Iraq (AQI) were becoming increasingly powerful and might join forces to destabilize Iraq, too.[68]

Annan presented his case to Assad on July 10. The first step should be a new ceasefire, but rather than a general nationwide ceasefire, Annan proposed "a mechanism for a ceasefire starting with any one of the (Syrian) hotspots. We can then duplicate it in another." A local ceasefire had more chance of succeeding than a national one and posed a more concentrated test since international attention would zero in on a particular locale, making violations easier to verify. Assad replied positively, posing questions about who the UN team would negotiate with on the opposition side, and how they would ensure compliance. The Syrian president complained that previous ceasefires demanded an end to the foreign financing and supply of arms to the opposition, which had never been implemented, but he accepted Annan's proposal and gave an undertaking that his forces would not use heavy weapons.[69] A successful ceasefire would allow political negotiations to begin, Annan explained, and he invited Assad to name someone to represent the government. Assad nominated Ali Haidar, minister for national reconciliation and a member of the so-called loyal opposition. Annan worried that Haidar, who was neither Ba'athist or Alawite, was not a serious negotiator. "We would have preferred the nomination of someone closer to you—someone who would be in direct contact with you to bring the dialogue process to completion." Assad tried to reassure Annan but observed, "I think your greater difficulty will be on the other side, not on ours. Will you be able to get a name to represent the opposition?" Annan was aware of that problem. He left Damascus without a deal.

The question all this presented the three Western powers on the Security Council was whether to push for a chapter 7 resolution giving teeth to what had been agreed in Geneva or settle for a chapter 6 resolution. The former would position the council to support implementation but would likely draw a Russian veto; the latter was more likely to pass but was unlikely to make any difference on the ground inside Syria. They agreed that only a bold approach would do. Things were spiraling out of control, and Syria risked total implosion unless meaningful steps were taken. In that context, it was better to try to make a difference and fail than pass hollow resolutions everyone knew would make no difference, they reasoned. In a high-stakes game of diplomatic chicken, they hoped to isolate Russia and China and use the widespread international support for Geneva to compel them to at least abstain and allow the resolution to pass. Lavrov had made it clear in Geneva that a chapter 7 resolution was out of the question, and Russian diplomats in New York lost no time underscoring that position. They would support a chapter 6 resolution endorsing Geneva, but nothing more. Annan felt "blindsided" by the American and British push for a chapter 7 resolution and initially counseled against it.[70] His strategy relied on keeping Russia inside the tent, using its influence on Assad. Questions about what should happen in the event of noncompliance should come later and, he thought, would be more easily addressed once the council had signaled its support for the overall direction. Western governments, however, doubted that momentum could be maintained and worried that events in Syria would outpace the more relaxed pace of world diplomacy.

The situation inside Syria was indeed fluid. The government was losing ground, forced even to withdraw from some parts of Damascus as the capital's center came under concerted attack. To the north, FSA-affiliated units, including the radical al-Tawhid brigade (initially affiliated with the Muslim Brotherhood), succeeded in taking most of eastern Aleppo. Meanwhile, "Chechens" and other foreign fighters helped seize the northern border crossing at Bab al-Hawa, opening the door to the inflow of foreign fighters. The rebels seized crossings into Iraq, too.[71] Two Western journalists were kidnapped by British foreign fighters. They escaped a week later, but it was a portent of things to come. The government, its forces stretched fighting fires on multiple fronts, responded with indiscriminate force. Eighty civilians were killed across the country during protests following Friday prayers on July 6. On July 12, just two days after Annan's visit to Damascus, Syrian forces attacked Tremseh, near Idlib, with helicopters and mechanized units, which were followed by *shabiha* from neighboring villages, who massacred around fifty civilians. UN observers reported evidence of heavy weapons use and confirmed victims killed at close range.[72] Territorial loss was not the regime's only problem. It was seriously bleeding from within, too. In addition to the military defections described in the previous chapter (which amounted to nearly half of its soldiers serving in 2011), nine senior government officials, including General Manaf Tlass from the Republican Guard, defected in July alone.

At its most perilous moment thus far, however, Damascus found a friend in Iran and its notorious Major General Qassem Soleimani, head of the Republican Guard's elite Quds force and mastermind of political violence from Lebanon to Yemen. The Soleimani effect was almost immediate. The Iranian advised the Syrian Army to concentrate forces on what mattered most to the regime: its cities and the routes between them. He proposed they withdraw from predominantly Kurdish areas even at the expense of turning control over to Kurdish armed groups.[73] It was not the Kurds threatening to topple Assad, and since there was no love lost between the Kurds and the Sunnis, why not let them protect their own lands rather than have Damascus do it for them? The government could reassert control once the more immediate threat had been crushed. As government forces withdrew, the Kurdish Yekineyen Parastina Gel (YPG, People's Defense Units) quickly stepped in to assume control preventing the FSA and Salafist militia from moving into these territories.[74] With hindsight, we know that withdrawal from the Northeast helped consolidate Assad's position by concentrating forces, but to those watching at the time it conveyed a sense of a regime in crisis, giving up land at a bewildering pace. The Syrian Army simply handed over swathes of territory to the YPG without a shot being fired.

Soleimani may have also moved quickly to snuff out potential weak spots inside the government. On July 18 a huge bomb at the government's national security headquarters in central Damascus killed four senior government ministers, including defense minister Dawoud Rajiha, a Christian in office since August 2011, and Deputy Defense Minister Assef Shawkat, Assad's brother-in-law. Several opposition groups claimed responsibility, including the FSA (which later retracted the claim) and Liwa al-Islam, and the government insisted al-Qaeda was responsible. Another possibility is that the regime itself, under Soleimani's tutelage, killed the four. Rajiha had known ties to the West, while Shawkat, one of the initial architects of government's crackdown strategy, had become critical of Assad's leadership and had spoken to foreign intelligence agencies about removing the president.

With Russia seemingly open to political transition from within and central Damascus under attack, nerves were frayed and suspicions rampant.[75] Whether or not it was an inside job, the bombing was certainly fortuitous for Assad since with one stroke it permanently ended murmurs of an internal putsch. Iran's hand, too, was greatly strengthened, and with it Assad's determination not be to "transitioned" from government.

Negotiations about a Security Council resolution endorsing the Geneva Communiqué gathered pace as the deadline for renewing UNSMIS (July 19) approached. With the Tremseh massacre, which he described as "another grim reminder that the Council's resolutions continue to be flouted," at the fore of his mind, Annan urged the council "to insist on implementation of its decisions and send a message to all that there will be consequences for noncompliance. This is imperative and could not be more urgent in light of unfolding events."[76] This strongly implied he now thought a chapter 7 resolution necessary, since this was the only way of sending the clear warning he envisaged. The UK, backed by the council's other Western members, circulated a draft chapter 7 resolution that aimed to extend the mission by forty-five days and impose sanctions on the Syrian government if a ceasefire was not in place and heavy weapons withdrawn from populated areas within ten days. Russia's deputy permanent representative, Igor Pankin, reiterated Lavrov's view that chapter 7 was a "red line" and offered an alternative text that simply extended UNSMIS, which won little support since it was out of step with Annan's call for urgent action. To address Russian concerns, the UK reworked its draft to explicitly require a further resolution to impose sanctions should they be necessary and provide explicit assurance that potential enforcement would be limited to the nonmilitary measures prescribed by article 41 of the charter (as distinct from article 42, which refers to military measures). But it was imperative, they thought, that the council show itself willing to back demands with action. The draft text offered the Syrian government ten days to comply, after which the council would impose sanctions under article 41 of the charter.

Reports confirming the Tremseh massacre and strident advocacy by Annan and Ban Ki-moon raised faint hopes Russia and China might in the end be dissuaded from using their veto. Indeed, Chinese diplomats appeared open to a chapter 7 resolution so long as it also made demands of the armed opposition, something the West was happy to include if it didn't contradict the six-point plan or Geneva Communiqué. While diplomats haggled in New York, Annan headed to Moscow on July 16 to speak directly with Putin. Though what was said and agreed to remains off the public record, Annan left the Kremlin apparently satisfied that Putin would help implement the agreement and quietly maneuver Assad from office.[77] In public, Lavrov reiterated Russia's support for the Geneva plan but refused to budge on the chapter 7 issue. Ban Ki-moon meanwhile visited Beijing, hoping to move China toward supporting the draft resolution. Whatever was said to Annan in Moscow and Ban in Beijing, there was no letup in New York, where both the Russians and the resolution's backers held their line and the veto remained likely.[78] To the latter, Assad's track record offered little hope of progress unless the council showed itself willing to impose consequences—that is, sanctions. Though he had stopped short of specifically referencing chapter 7, Kofi Annan had made the "consequences" point himself. As Guatemala's Gert Rosenthal told the council the next day, "The potential application of sanctions on the grounds of non-compliance was the least we could do, given the sequence of broken commitments on the part of the Government of Syria."[79]

It was no good. Thirteen of the Security Council's fifteen members, including Azerbaijan, Colombia, Guatemala, India, Morocco, and Togo, voted yes. Russia and China alone voted no and cast their vetoes. In the angry session that followed, Russia's Vitaly Churkin claimed it was fear of Western military intervention that had prompted Russia's veto. Guatemala's Rosenthal rebutted that, pointing out that the draft explicitly referred to measures under article 41, those "not including the use of armed force."[80] Even India—whose ambassador, Hardeep Singh Puri, had a year earlier sided with Russia—supported the resolution, its concerns about regime change and intervention apparently allayed. China's explanation was formulaic: the proposed draft threatened measures only against the government (untrue), undermined the principle of noninterference (also untrue since that principle, set out in article 2(7) of the UN Charter, explicitly excludes chapter 7 measures), and created disunity in the council (more plausible, though disunity was not caused by the draft resolution; it existed beyond that).

Why, though, did the West bring the draft resolution to a vote, knowing it would be vetoed? It has become popular in some quarters to blame the United States, Britain, and France by suggesting that, convinced Assad's days were numbered and determined to press ahead with regime change, they deliberately undermined Annan by insisting on a chapter 7 resolution they knew would be vetoed. But that overlooks the fact that a transition of power (a.k.a. regime change) *had* been agreed to in Geneva. What the West and Russia disagreed on was not the need for political transition but rather the mechanism. It also overlooks what Annan said to the council prior to the vote. Certainly, the envoy later criticized "finger pointing and name calling"—a sign he thought Western diplomacy could have been more tactful—and expressed frustration that the conversation became bogged down on chapter 7 while substantive questions about implementing the agreed framework remained unanswered.[81] Yet he saw the root of the problem as being the fact Russia and China were walking away from the agreement they had reached in Geneva. In Annan's words, "I thought we were making progress when all the five permanent members agreed on the need for transition. A transition meant there was going to be a change in government, the transition meant President Assad would have to leave sooner or later. And once you have that broad understanding, you should be able to build on it. But things felt apart in New York."[82]

Later, he was even more explicit in his criticism of Russia and China: "We had a difficult but a constructive meeting in Geneva to discuss a political transition," Annan said in an interview in early September 2012. "They agreed on a communiqué, but on the 19th of July when the council eventually acted the resolution was vetoed by Russia and China." "You felt undercut?" his interviewer asked. "I felt undercut," Annan replied. As if to underscore just how different his position was from Russia's, Annan continued, "Assad will have to go. You cannot remain in power when so many people have been killed and are dying. No leader can retain legitimacy after this. The question is how he goes, and when he goes."[83] Like the three Western governments, Annan had come away from Geneva thinking a transitional government required that Assad step aside and that, to use his words, it was "imperative" that the "Security Council send a message to all that there will be consequences for non-compliance."

The real problem was that Russian commitment to the political transition that they had agreed to in Geneva was always less complete than either the West or Annan realized. Lavrov, recall, had lost no time in explaining that the communiqué took Assad's exit off the table. In other words, Annan had never actually achieved the consensus on a political transition he believed he had. But there was another problem, accentuated by events after Geneva. Iran's growing influence in Damascus, typified by Qassem Soleimani's intervention, weakened the Kremlin's. Emboldened, Assad refused the terms on offer at Geneva, the terms Russia had negotiated. He would not countenance stepping aside or relinquishing Alawite control of government, and with the hard-liners now firmly in the ascendancy, nor could Russia find an artful way of shuffling Syria's president aside. Annan's strategy had always hinged on Moscow's capacity to deliver Assad's compliance. But, for all its pretensions, Russia simply did not have that sort of leverage over the Syrian government.[84] It could cajole it to participate in talks but could not persuade it to sign up to its own transition from power. What leverage Moscow enjoyed declined through July as Iranian influence increased. That presented Putin with a stark choice between, on the one hand, abandoning Assad and permitting multilateral sanctions that might either cripple the regime or hand it to the Iranians or, on the other, backing Syria's leader by blocking the Security Council. Not for the last time, Putin chose Assad.

Western governments, meanwhile, had grown exasperated by Assad's intransigence, the collapse of the April ceasefire, and continuing massacres. They had no faith that diplomacy alone could affect a shift and were finding it increasingly difficult to hold back demands that they support opposition elements more directly. Most judged that Assad was using the diplomatic process as a smokescreen to buy time while his forces pursued a military solution. But as justified as these frustrations were, there was no viable plan B. It is here that Western governments miscalculated again—allowing the Annan process to collapse without any clear idea about what would replace it.

Syria's last hope for peace was gone. UNSMIS limped on for another month before being terminated in late August. Exasperated, Annan resigned on August 2, citing government intransigence as the principal reason for the continuing bloodshed.[85] On August 3 the UN's General Assembly issued a resolution "deploring" the Security Council's failure to act on Syria by a large majority—133 states to just 12. The assembly called for implementation of the six-point plan and the Geneva Communiqué.[86] But it was howling into the wind.

Annan's initiative was almost certainly doomed from the start. Neither the government nor the opposition was wholly committed. The major powers were deeply divided.[87] Annan believed that "without serious, purposeful and united international pressure, including from the powers in the region, it is impossible for me, or anyone, to compel the Syrian government in the first place, and also the opposition, to take the steps necessary to begin a political process."[88] Some, though, criticized Annan's strategy, suggesting he conceded too much and allowed Assad to buy time by persisting too long with diplomacy.[89] Certainly, in hindsight, a strategy dependent on Russia seems seriously flawed. A leading analyst of the Security Council, Richard Gowan, suggested that Annan should have leveraged Assad's uncertainty about future military intervention to persuade the Syrian leader his interests were best served by negotiating a transition.[90] But this high-risk strategy was unlikely to have succeeded. Whatever Lavrov and Putin said about fearing the slippery slope to Western intervention, the fact was that Western governments had made it abundantly clear they had no appetite for military intervention to effect regime change in Syria. Suggestions to the contrary from Annan would have carried little credibility. What is more, Assad was confident Russia would never permit the Security Council to authorize intervention, as it had in Libya, and Iran's intervention gave Assad grounds for thinking he could hold on to power. And that ultimately was the issue. Assad's strategy, from the start, was to hold on to power. "Assad or we burn the country" was a threat, a promise, and a strategy. Others argue the opposite: that Annan should have conceded more to Damascus. He could have done more to accommodate the regime's fourteen reservations and tackle the transfer of arms to the opposition, and he could have included Damascus in the Geneva talks so that it could not have so easily dismissed the communiqué.[91] But there is no reason to think any of these measures would have produced a different result: concessions would have only encouraged the regime's hard-liners.

The principal reasons for failure were similar to those that foiled the Arab League's initiative. First and foremost, the government never intended to entertain a political process that could result in it having to share power or lose it altogether. Russian support for the April 12 ceasefire persuaded Damascus to accept the six-point plan and restrain its use of heavy weapons, but, Annan argues, "sustained international support did not follow." As the ceasefire unraveled, "the government, realizing that there would be no consequences if it returned to an overt military campaign, reverted to using heavy weapons in towns."[92] Then, with countries having tried to reinvigorate the process by securing an agreement in Geneva on the need for a political transition, no pressure was brought to bear on Assad to accept it. The Russians found Assad bolstered by the Iranians and in no mood to compromise and so chose to fall in behind Syria's leader.

Second, Syria's armed opposition—emboldened by international support and convinced Assad's days were numbered—saw the initiative as a means of removing Assad. Success on the battlefield, increasing defections from the regime, and international support made the opposition think victory was inevitable. It therefore had few incentives to compromise. To further complicate things, since the SNC lacked unity and had no authority over the armed groups on the ground, it was unable to hold the ceasefire together. This was not the reason the process failed, but it did make things more difficult.

Third, Annan could paper over deep international fissures only for so long. It was immediately clear that members of the Action Group interpreted the Geneva Communiqué very differently. What the United States and Annan thought it meant and what Putin thought were poles apart. So, while the Kremlin certainly encouraged Damascus to accept Annan's six-point plan and may have considered persuading him to support the Geneva Communiqué, it never demurred from its determination to protect Assad from material pressure. During the July crisis, its willingness even to encourage Assad evaporated almost entirely. Annan observed that "one of my biggest disappointments was on the 30th June. We had a difficult but constructive meeting in Geneva, to discuss a political transition. They agreed on a communiqué, but on the 19th of July, when the Council eventually acted, the resolution was vetoed by Russia and China."[93] On the other side, Turkey, Qatar, and Saudi Arabia had always been skeptical about the process, and all three continued supplying or facilitating the supply of arms to the opposition. None used their influence to compel the opposition to comply with the ceasefire.

Fourth, the process was plagued with logistical problems. Albeit an improvement on the Arab League's efforts, the UN's three hundred monitors on a tightly defined and temporally limited mandate were never likely to be sufficient to change things on the ground. There was always a pronounced gap between the glacial pace of international negotiations and the rapidly evolving situation on the ground. Many in the West worried that the process itself was being used as cover for the continuation of violence and that the Russians were deliberately stalling to buy time for Damascus.

The Russian and Chinese vetoes drew a line under the Annan peace process and fired the starting pistol for the escalation of conflict into a devastating country-wide civil war. Everyone knew that this would be the consequence of failure. Yet, concerned more with protecting Assad than protecting Syrians, Moscow and Beijing pulled the trigger anyway. Violence increased dramatically, and with it the civilian death toll, as emboldened Syrian government forces stepped up the aerial bombing and shelling of civilian areas. Qatar, Saudi Arabia, and Turkey responded by opening the floodgates to pour in arms, ammunition, and cash to armed opposition groups. The United States and Europe, however, had no plan B. Unwilling to act themselves, they had placed their hopes in the power of multilateralism. That had failed, and there was little sense of what, if anything, might replace it. The Security Council paralyzed, Syria's war entered a new and more deadly phase, thanks mainly to the perfidious work of Russia and China, supported on the ground by Iran.

4

SYRIAN WINTER

THE HUMANITARIAN situation in Syria deteriorated sharply following the collapse of Kofi Annan's peace process. In late 2012 the UN Commission of Inquiry reported "unrelenting violence" resulting "in thousands of deaths, untold thousands of wounded, detained and disappeared, and physical destruction on a massive scale."[1] Atrocity crimes had "continued unabated," with civilians bearing the brunt of escalating armed confrontations" that forced hundreds of thousands to flee in search of safety. Assad's foreign opponents had no clear idea what to do next. The West was hesitant about supporting the opposition, concerned it might fuel Islamism, but gave little thought to the likely consequences of dashing hopes for change—that the faltering of the mainstream opposition's fortunes might propel extremists to the fore.[2] Meanwhile, Assad had weathered the initial storm, and the July 2012 crisis had fortified the hard-liners. Growing sectarianism had helped him, too. Defections from the army were significant and increasing, but the defectors were almost exclusively Sunni. The Alawite core, which also happened to be the military elite, had held firm. The opposition's fragmentation and lack of leadership also helped Damascus. Instead of a unified opposition, the regime confronted dozens of small armed groups, none of which individually posed more than a localized threat. This allowed the regime to concentrate forces on cities and strategic centers, bringing its comparative strengths to bear on the conflict. What it lacked in manpower, the regime's arsenal made up for in artillery and airpower. External support had helped there: Russia protected the regime from international censure and sanctions, while Qassem Soleimani orchestrated military assistance from Iran. From mid-2012 the Islamic Republic poured money, arms, ammunition, and manpower into Syria to prop up the regime. Without this help, Assad would have likely fallen despite the opposition's failings.

By the end of August 2012, FSA-aligned groups led by the Islamist al-Tawhid Brigades had seized control of eastern Aleppo. The opposition controlled approximately 80 percent of the towns lining Syria's border with Turkey, securing crucial logistical routes but also opening pathways for foreign jihadists, of which there were approximately three thousand by February 2013, to enter.[3] Thus, though they had survived the immediate July crisis, the Assadists were still in trouble, and some recall the winter and spring of 2012–2013 as their most perilous.[4] The FSA struck the heart of Damascus with increasing regularity. Protests in the city's Yarmouk Palestinian refugee camp later turned into a siege, when FSA-aligned Palestinian rebels, Liwa al-Asifa, seized control of the streets there. The regime responded in December 2012 with aerial bombing. By the following July, the state had Yarmouk besieged.[5] The district soon became "the worst place in Syria," enduring months with no electricity, clean water, or food, humanitarian access denied by the government.[6] By the end of 2014, people there were dying of malnutrition. This element of regime strategy, the use of fixed-wing aircraft, helicopters, and (from December 2012 in Aleppo) even Scud missiles to indiscriminately terrorize opposition held areas, became more apparent across the country.[7] Its ground forces depleted and overstretched, the regime became increasingly dependent on air power and artillery to plug the gaps. August 2012 saw the first deployment of the crude but lethal barrel bomb: an oil barrel stuffed with explosives and metal shrapnel. Barrel bombs were tossed from helicopters without discrimination. Dropped first on Aleppo, these weapons of mass civilian destruction wreaked havoc, becoming a central element of the regime's emerging strategy of siege and starvation. Yet in the immediate term, the regime's brutal tactics slowed but did not stop the opposition's advance. Beyond Aleppo and Damascus, the rebels enjoyed successes in Idlib and Homs, too.

On closer inspection, the battle for Aleppo also exposed the opposition's fragility. Uncoordinated offensives damaged the city itself as much as they hurt government forces. The opposition was soon forced back by government counteroffensives in September and October, and in December its offensive ended entirely as some brigades ran out of ammunition.[8] Opposition fighters committed atrocities, too. In one incident, Jabhat al-Nusra and an FSA-aligned group captured and executed twenty Syrian soldiers.[9] Their administration of "liberated" areas ranged from the chaotic to the violently predatory. Different armed groups assumed control over different areas and regularly clashed as commanders squabbled over resources and fought to control Aleppo's precious assets. FSA-aligned fighters earned a reputation for crime and corruption, doing enormous damage to their reputation.[10] By contrast, al-Nusra fighters proved themselves stern in their application of Islamic law but also fearless opponents of Assad and less corruptible than the FSA. Over the winter of 2012–2013, they emerged as one of the more powerful armed groups.[11] Aleppo's Kurds, meanwhile, established armed control of their own areas.[12]

The jihadists' rise to prominence worried the West. To counter it, the United States played one of the few cards it had by designating al-Nusra a front for al-Qaeda in Iraq and thus a proscribed terrorist organization.[13] But since the United States had little presence or influence inside Syria, the designation had no practical effect beyond alienating parts of the opposition and complicating the West's relationship with it. Many moderates in the opposition thought that although it had a problematic ideology, al-Nusra was committed to combatting Assad, something that could not be said of the United States.[14] But an unvirtuous cycle was emerging in the West's attitude toward jihadism in the Syrian opposition: the more that Westerners learned about Syrian extremists, the more hesitant to involve themselves in Syria's war they became. The less involved the West became, the more reliant opponents and victims of Assad became on Islamists and the more attractive their ideology appeared to be.

THE OPPOSITION'S DESTRUCTIVE MARKETPLACE

Assad's enemies took the collapse of the Annan process as the starting gun for war. The money, arms, ammunition, and manpower they now poured into Syria increased the opposition's firepower, but at the cost of aggravating its fragmentation. Among those sending arms to Syria's opposition, there was no common goal but ousting Assad, and little coordination.[15] For example, Qatar and Turkey promoted the Muslim Brotherhood; the Saudis opposed the Brothers stoutly.[16] Divisions like that sprang up across the opposition landscape, fueled by the fact that for none of these foreign backers was the well-being or wishes of Syrians a top priority. Those were routinely overridden by the interests of those doing the donating.

Between 2012 and 2013 alone, Qatar supplied between $1 billion and $3 billion worth of arms and funds.[17] Most of this was funneled through the Muslim Brotherhood and covered the Syrian National Congress's (SNC) finances almost entirely.[18] Qatar orchestrated a "rat line" conveying weapons, including sophisticated TOW (Tube-launched, Optically-tracked, Wire-guided) antitank missiles, from Qaddafi's abandoned stores in Libya through Turkey and into Syria. Beginning as early as March 2012, approximately $100 million worth of arms was transferred via this route.[19] But transfers were poorly coordinated, and arms frequently found their way to extremists, including al-Nusra. Qatar had little experience overseeing a program of this scale and almost no intelligence network inside Syria to guide it, so the groundwork devolved to local allies. Distribution was haphazard. Some FSA-affiliated brigades received support while other nearby brigades did not, breeding disunity and fragmentation. To make matters worse, Saudi Arabia tried to counter Muslim Brotherhood influence by establishing a rival pipeline in late 2012, buying surplus weapons and ammunition from Croatia and transporting them to its own Syrian allies, mainly through Jordan.[20] Much of this went to sustaining the armed campaign around Daraa. Thus separate Qatari and Saudi networks evolved, each competing with the other for allies, while a rapidly proliferating number of armed groups competed for arms and funds.[21] Meanwhile, private Islamic donors sent cash in amounts rivaling that provided by governments through Kuwait to Salafist groups in an emerging Islamist network with close links to extremists in Iraq.[22] Aware of these problems, the CIA tried steering money and arms away from jihadists and preventing the supply of anti-aircraft and shoulder-fired missiles that could be used against the West.[23]

Turkey also changed its strategy by more directly supporting the FSA's efforts, allowing Syrian army defectors to transfer into the FSA through sanctuaries and bases in Turkey and trying to unite the army under the SNC umbrella—and thus Turkish influence.[24] Ankara wooed fighters by confidently advising that sooner or later the West would intervene to ensure their victory, but in mid-2012 the FSA had still not developed into a coherent fighting force and the chances of U.S. intervention looked slim—though Turkish officials predicted an Obama reelected in November 2012 would be more assertive.[25] In truth, publicly committed now to removing Assad, Turkey was reaching the limits of what it could achieve through the Brotherhood and SNC. Unilateral military intervention, however, was not considered a realistic option. Erdogan was unsure whether Turkey could defeat Assad, given his Iranian backing, and the Turkish leader's bombastic Syria policy enjoyed limited support at home.[26] So while Ankara publicly advocated military intervention, there was little prospect of it acting unilaterally. Instead, its strategy was much like the West's: using whatever indirect measures it could to apply pressure on Damascus in the hope that the regime would either collapse under the weight or be forced to negotiate a political transition.

In practice this meant turning a blind eye to the increasing number foreign jihadist fighters transiting through Turkey into Syria, something that drew criticism from a nervous West. The same open-border policy also allowed refugees to move in the other direction to find sanctuary, unofficial humanitarians to bring relief to civilians still inside Syria, and the opposition to maintain supply lines. By contrast, Jordan maintained much tighter control of its border, resulting in the inflow of fewer foreign fighters but also the outflow of far fewer refugees by that route. Things were further complicated by the fact that many of those involved in the smuggling networks that sustained the opposition were also connected to organized crime and jihadist networks. The distinctions between ISIS, al-Nusra, and others were not always clear-cut. Turkey thus found itself simultaneously praised for welcoming refugees and condemned for allowing the transit of jihadists—both by-products of the same open border policy. When it moved to stem the flow of jihadists by sealing its border in the fall of 2014, this also impeded the flight of refugees and others. Turkey then found itself praised for combatting jihadists but condemned for not accepting refugees.[27]

The approaches adopted by the region's principal anti-Assadists proved a recipe for disaster. By channeling support directly to their preferred armed groups, whether inside or outside the FSA, they unintentionally created a marketplace for loyalty in which the principal currency was a group's capacity to attract foreign support to supply its fighters with arms, ammunition, equipment, wages, and food.[28] To compete in that marketplace, armed groups needed a distinct brand, identity, and reputation. Those that succeeded attracted fighters and grew. Those that did not succeed withered. The movement of fighters and sometimes whole units from one group to another became commonplace, switches usually driven not by strategic necessity or ideological belief but by who offered the best terms. The largest donors— both state and private—were themselves Islamists and preferred to direct their money toward those who shared their views. Thus the stronger a group's Islamist credentials, the more likely it would be to attract foreign patronage. This skewed the whole marketplace in the Islamists' favor.

More immediately, the competitive marketplace limited the opposition's fighting capacity. Broken into small and uncoordinated units, opposition forces were incapable of conducting operations larger than localized tactical engagements and frequently refused to help one another.[29] To make matters worse, relative to the funds now pouring in to these armed groups, the SNC and the FSA were starved of resources. As a result these coordinating bodies struggled to assert their authority over better-resourced armed groups.[30] Groups split away from them to improve their own standing in the marketplace by enhancing their visibility and profile. By mid-2012 there were more than a thousand armed groups in Syria's opposition (compared with around thirty at the height of the civil war in Lebanon), of which only around half were affiliated with the FSA.[31] Different factions dominated different parts of the country: Liwa al-Tawhid in Aleppo, the

Syrian Revolutionary Front in Idlib, Jaysh al-Islam in Douma, and the Farouq Brigades in Homs.[32] The FSA exerted no direct control and only limited influence over its own affiliates. Neither did the SNC, which had only a small footprint inside Syria. Many groups complained about its domination by the Muslim Brotherhood, which, thanks to backing from Turkey and Qatar, enjoyed more influence than its numbers warranted.[33]

The SNC's problems were compounded by its inability to bring Syria's Kurds into the fold. At heart, they wanted different things: the SNC wanted Assad gone; the Kurds wanted self-rule and beyond that cared little about who governed in Damascus. Kurds wanted a state not defined by the majority Sunnis' Arab identity; the Sunnis wanted an Arab state. Animosity between Kurds and Islamists was especially deep, since the former espoused secular government and the latter Sharia law, such that to most Kurdish leaders an Assad-led government was less fear-inducing than the prospect of an Islamist government. Syria's Kurds were therefore slow to join the uprising in 2011, but as it gathered momentum, many Kurds sensed an opportunity for change and took to the streets. Yet relations with Sunnis remained uneasy, efforts to improve them not helped by divisions with the Kurdish community, especially between the Kurdish National Council (KNC), a coalition of seventeen Syrian Kurdish organizations, and the Democratic Union Party (PYD), the Syrian affiliate to the powerful Turkish Kurdistan Workers Party (PKK).[34] When Syrian forces withdrew from Kurdish areas to concentrate on defending major cities in July 2012, the PYD's militia, the People's Protection Units (YPG), stepped in and took control of swathes of territory. Almost overnight, the Kurds lost their most powerful incentive for cooperating with the mainstream opposition—common cause against Assad. At the same time, many Sunnis became suspicious of Kurdish loyalties, believing—not wholly incorrectly—the PYD/YPG had colluded with Assad during the Syrian army's withdrawal from Kurdish areas.[35] To further complicate things, the SNC—housed in Istanbul—saw Turkey as a major ally, while to the PKK-aligned PYD/YPG, Turkey posed an existential threat. Even as they talked about peace in Turkey, the PYD/YPG knew Ankara was never likely to support Kurdish self-rule in Syria. So while the United States and Europe pressed the SNC for a rapprochement with the KNC and PYD, it never got beyond some KNC members agreeing to cooperate with the SNC principally to counter PYD dominance, and even those ties never amounted to formal cooperation.[36] Turkey, naturally, adamantly opposed the very idea of bringing the Kurds into the SNC. Although its secret peace talks with the PKK continued, their ceasefire was becoming more brittle.[37]

To address these challenges, something was needed to unify the opposition, connect its leadership with groups doing the administering and fighting on the ground, and diminish the influence of the Muslim Brotherhood and the extremists. As many in the West saw it, the opposition had to get its house in order before further support could be provided to it. But in the absence of material support from the West, there was little to counter the centrifugal and radicalizing forces being unleashed by the marketplace. Unless donors changed their behavior, no amount of tinkering with umbrella bodies would change the fact that it was those with the people, money, and arms who would wield the influence.

There was a moment where the opposition might have got its house in order. In September 2012 Hillary Clinton floated the idea of replacing the SNC with a more inclusive body that would draw in the civilian-led Local Coordination Committees and Kurds and might act as a transitional government in waiting. Following up, the U.S. (withdrawn) ambassador to Syria, Robert Ford, joined forces with the well-respected Syrian dissident Riad Seif to propose just such an arrangement. What became known as the Seif-Ford plan envisaged a new representative body governed by an inclusive council of fifty, comprising twenty representatives from inside Syria, fifteen from the SNC, and fifteen from other opposition groups, including the Kurds. A technical team of eight to ten people separate from the council would establish an executive committee to manage the body's day-to-day business. Within the confines of the West's overall approach to the problem, the plan's merits were clear and Seif an ideal partner, but the combined weight of the opposition's toxic internal politics and the jealous jockeying of its regional backers meant it never got off the ground.

Ironically, the first blow was struck by Washington itself. The White House was lukewarm about the initiative and, convinced it would fail, refused to throw its weight behind it by hosting the next meeting. This had two shattering effects: it signaled Washington's disinterest, destroying whatever authority the Ford-Seif proposal might have enjoyed, and created a leadership void that Qatar was only too happy to fill. Hassam bin Jassem al-Thani offered himself as cochair with Clinton, and Doha as a venue. As the host, Qatar immediately assumed responsibility for the agenda and the all-important invitation list. What had begun as an exercise in building a more inclusive opposition became something quite different. Although some representatives from the LCCs and other grassroots bodies were invited at American insistence, their numbers were limited. Most delegates were the old crowd of Syria's exiled opposition—those backed by Qatar and Turkey. Predictably, the SNC leadership objected to the whole thing, anticipating that the plan intended to weaken its grip.[38] Turkey was equally wary, but a combination of U.S. pressure and the reassurance of Qatar's growing role brought it onboard. Qatar shared Ankara's concerns but hoped to maneuver a favorable outcome from the inside. It cajoled the SNC with the promise that reform would open up more assistance. But a storm erupted on the eve of the Doha summit when the Seif-Ford plan was presented with no mention of military assistance and only conditional financial offers amounting to far less than had been expected. Seif was ousted from the SNC executive committee (he later returned as deputy leader of the new opposition coalition), and only intense pressure from the United States, Qatar, and Turkey got the group to Doha at all.

Things were little better once there. Ford recalls that Western diplomats were excluded from some of the meetings as the Qataris took control.[39] Agreement was reached to establish a National Coalition for Syrian Revolution and Opposition Forces (SOC), but it was not the breakthrough the West had been looking for. The PYD rejected the new arrangement, and while the KNC was more positively inclined, it was so divided that it took months to formalize its participation.[40] Allocated just one-third of the seats in the body's new assembly, the influence of the SNC and Muslim Brotherhood was reduced on paper but not reality. Doha failed to establish a more representative leadership with authority and left the old guard of Syrian exiles tied to foreign patrons largely intact but with their numbers slightly reduced.

The Saudis acquiesced because the new arrangements marginally lessened the influence of Qatar and the Brotherhood, Qatar and Turkey acquiesced to keep the United States in the tent, but Western governments were the SOC's only genuine supporters, and even they were deeply dissatisfied.

Unsurprisingly, the new arrangements were insufficient to encourage Western governments to match Qatar, Saudi Arabia, Turkey, and private sources and materially shape the opposition marketplace.[41] Unwilling to offer more cash, let alone arms, the United States reverted to coercion to influence the new body by withholding recognition until it had demonstrated its capacity to represent Syrians in opposition areas. It called on EU governments to do the same. But this was a plan flawed by the unvirtuous cycle mentioned earlier, since without material resources or capabilities to compete effectively in the opposition marketplace, the SOC was no better placed to exert authority than the SNC had been. Some recognized this immediately. On November 13 France broke ranks with the United States and recognized the new body, hoping to at least grant it international legitimacy. This forced the UK, the rest of the European Union, and ultimately the United States to follow suit.[42] But while this did afford the SOC some legitimacy, it did nothing to redress its material and financial shortcomings.

More should have been done to build up the SNC and FSA and the ties between them and the armed groups, and to control the opposition marketplace. Neither group established a functioning and capable core. Nor did they help each other. By November 2012 a mere $2.8 million had been transferred from the SNC to the FSA, miniscule compared to the funding flowing directly from foreign patrons to armed groups.[43] These structural problems were understood in some quarters, but limited information and different priorities inhibited the development of a more cohesive approach to address it. Western intelligence agencies still did not have a clear picture of just who the different armed groups were and how they related to one another.[44] For the United States, the main priority remained keeping weapons out of extremist hands. It established offices in Adana (Turkey) and Jordan to monitor and coordinate arms transfers.[45] But these were partial measures that failed to address the problems at their source: that without more capable and better-integrated command and control, and functional civilian administration in opposition territory, foreign suppliers had no control over what happened to their weapons and fighters once inside Syria.[46]

The civilian administration of opposition territory was crucial yet undervalued. The need to tackle the lawlessness and chaos of rule-by-militia by supporting the LCCs to govern and administer opposition areas was well understood, but since there was little appetite for direct involvement on the ground, it was difficult to build policies to achieve that. U.S. uncertainty, for example, resulted in a funding system that required high-level approval for every project destined to support the LCCs, no matter how small.[47] As a result, the opposition's foreign backers never coalesced around a strategy of supporting civilian governance, and only small amounts of aid reached the LCCs or other civilian bodies in opposition areas. Unsurprisingly, these bodies fought a long defeat against the anarchy, militarization, and extremism wrought by the much better funded armed groups. In the immediate term, however, the SOC did create a small window of opportunity to address some of the opposition's weaknesses.

MILITARY OPTIONS

Russian and Iranian support meant Assad's regime could hang on for the time being, but the government was still losing ground, and the combination of defections and casualties was propelling the Syrian Army toward a manpower crisis. Soleimani's reforms had stopped the immediate rot but only by conceding swathes of territory, especially in the North. This presented a dilemma for the West and for Syria's neighbors: Do nothing and the conflict would likely escalate under its own steam, enveloping the region and exacting a terrible toll on Syria's civilians. Step up coercive pressure on the government and military assistance to the opposition, though, and that might also escalate the conflict and inadvertently help jihadists. In the United States, State Department analysts like Fred Hof detected the opposition's drift toward extremism and warned that the slide would continue unless more was done to buttress moderates.[48] But if Washington wanted to exert influence, it would have to become more directly involved, and one of the most obvious ways of applying pressure on Assad more directly was using military force. Two military options came to the force in public debates after the collapse of the Annan process: impose a no-fly zone to deny the regime its capacity to terrorize civilians from the air, and/or supply carefully vetted opposition groups with arms. Secretary of State Hillary Clinton proposed both. Neither was accepted.

The no-fly zone idea was first mooted seriously by Senator John McCain in March 2012. McCain argued in the Senate Foreign Relations Committee that diplomacy was failing and should therefore be bolstered by military coercion—specifically a no-fly zone—to degrade Assad's advantages and coerce him to compromise. Chairman of the Joint Chiefs of Staff Martin Dempsey briefed the White House situation room—though not the president—on contingency planning for military scenarios, including a no-fly zone, limited air strikes, opening humanitarian corridors, and maritime interdiction. Establishing a pattern of thought that chimed well with the president's own thinking, Dempsey warned a no-fly zone would require the engagement of seventy thousand service personnel to dismantle Syria's air defenses, which, he reported, posed a significant threat.[49] Speaking for the administration, Secretary of Defense Leon Panetta poured more cold water on the idea, arguing there was no legal basis for military action and that U.S. unilateralism would "make the situation worse."[50] McCain never relented, however, and when the Annan process collapsed, calls for the administration to reconsider grew.

Among those leading the charge were Turkey and France. In conversations with Clinton in mid-August 2012, Turkish ministers proposed a no-fly zone be imposed over Idlib and Aleppo.[51] Clinton found the idea attractive: a way of relieving civilian suffering and building pressure on Assad that also seemed doable with Turkish support. She agreed they should begin joint contingency planning and gauging allied support.[52] Laurent Fabius was especially enthusiastic and promised France would certainly contribute to enforcing the zone. But the trail went cold almost as soon as the secretary of state landed back in Washington. Panetta insisted military options were not "on the front burner" and would require a significant shift in the president's thinking. Fabius recalls the Americans informed him they were cool on the idea because it required a "significant military commitment" and Russian acquiescence—grounds he thought were outweighed by the potential advantages. He suspected the truth was that Obama was reluctant to get on the slippery slope toward another military engagement in the Middle East.[53]

In fact, the White House, Defense Department, and Joint Chiefs were all adamantly opposed.[54] Dempsey repeated his earlier claim that imposing a no-fly zone would be a costly and risky undertaking, requiring "hundreds of ground- and sea-based aircraft, intelligence and electronic warfare support, and enablers for refueling and communications. Estimated costs are $500 million initially, averaging as much as a billion dollars per month."[55] Not everyone in the Department of Defense saw things that way, however. According to one insider, "from DOD's vantage point, it was doable, but we really didn't want to do it. We could have worked it as we did with Northern Watch in Iraq, but that was a long-term effort."[56] Yet the leadership was hostile, and as a result realistic assessments were never conducted or presented to the president, and no consideration was given to alternatives such as imposing a no-fly zone only in the North or using stand-off weapons based in Turkey and the eastern Mediterranean to enforce the zone. White House lawyers complained there was no legal basis for a no-fly zone without a mandate from the UN Security Council. All this chimed well with the president's own view.

A second military option raised by Clinton was to arm the rebels. Once again, Turkey's Davutoglu was enthusiastic. Once again, he helped Clinton sound out allies. Once again, the French—and this time the British—were enthusiastic; the Germans less so. A plan to arm the rebels got further than the no-fly zone but ended with the same initial result. Clinton approached CIA director David Petraeus about it, and after some initial wariness he agreed to consider it more seriously because there were so few other options. With Clinton he worked up a proposal to vet, train, and equip moderate rebels, principally those operating under the banner of the FSA, whose core comprised officers who had defected from the Syrian Army, and aligned groups such as the Farouq Brigades (numbering seven to ten thousand), Liwa al-Tawhid (similarly sized), and the National Unity Brigades, as well as Kurdish forces not aligned to the Sunni opposition. They proposed that the United States could achieve three things this way: (1) give a psychological boost to the opposition and weaken the morale of Assad's allies, coercing Damascus back to the negotiating table by forestalling the possibility of military victory; (2) increase U.S. influence over the opposition by building material leverage; and (3) establish groundwork for the administration of liberated territories. Though they shared Petraeus's initial concerns, Panetta and Dempsey endorsed this plan.

President Obama was unconvinced. He doubted that arming the rebels would be sufficient to drive Assad from power and worried about potential blowback. Obama commissioned a study into the effectiveness of past U.S. programs that found only a small handful of successes and a longer list of mixed results and abject failure. Why would this plan succeed where so many others had failed? The plan wasn't to defeat Assad, Petraeus replied—that would be militarily difficult and could cause a dangerous vacuum likely filled by jihadists.[57] Instead, the aim was to *coerce* Assad into negotiating by increasing the costs of fighting. Still the president was unconvinced. He doubted a limited program could increase U.S. influence sufficiently, given the resources flowing into Syria from elsewhere. On this, he agreed with former CIA analyst Nada Bakos, who argued that Iraq had demonstrated that the United States had far less agency than it thought when it came to shaping political outcomes in the Middle East. But above all, Obama worried about blowback and the slippery slope. In the 1980s the United States had trained and equipped Afghan mujahedeen to combat the Soviets but inadvertently helped the Taliban and al-Qaeda. Could Petraeus guarantee there would be no repeat of that? Of course, there could be no guarantees, though the United States would carefully vet those it worked with. But what of the slippery slope? A limited arms program might start an inexorable slide into direct U.S. military involvement in Syria, something the president was determined to avoid above all else.[58] It was "magical thinking," Obama argued, to believe arming the rebels alone would make a difference.[59] Susan Rice, ambassador the UN and, later, national security advisor, and Ben Rhodes, senior adviser to the president, agreed with the president. Rice felt that arming the rebels would make little difference and would risk drawing the United States into Syria—and might derail the president's second term.[60] Rhodes believed the United States didn't have a good track record when it came to arming proxies. Blowback was a real threat, he argued: U.S.-backed rebels would have to fight alongside jihadists, and some brigades that had begun life as moderates had become Islamist. If the United States wanted a military solution in Syria, it should intervene directly. If it wasn't prepared to do that, then it should step back altogether.[61] The plan was rejected.

The president believed that diplomacy backed by sanctions and whatever multilateral leverage could be negotiated offered the only viable way forward—that through negotiation with adversaries and the patient application of the Obama doctrine, a political solution could be found. "We have looked at this from every angle," Obama explained in early 2014, "and the truth is that the challenge there has been, and continues to be, that you have an authoritarian, brutal government who is willing to do anything to hang on to power, and you have an opposition that is disorganized, ill-equipped, ill-trained, and is self-divided. All of that is on top of some of the sectarian divisions." In that context, "our best chance of seeing a decent outcome . . . is to work the state actors who have invested so much in keeping Assad in power—mainly the Iranians and the Russians—as well as working with those who have been financing the opposition to make sure that they're not creating the kind of extremist force that we saw emerge out of Afghanistan."[62] The United States would try bringing the parties to the negotiating table, but it would not use military means to coerce a settlement or protect civilians. Both the overall objective (persuade the Syrians to negotiate a deal) and the tools (peaceful and multilateral) would remain as they had been since early 2011.

Obama's critics point to these decisions as key turning points. The inadequate assistance the moderate opposition received made it more difficult for it to maintain military pressure on the government, dented the FSA's credibility in the opposition's political marketplace, left regional influence unchecked, and strengthened extremists relative to the opposition's moderates. Thus it directly undermined the West's stated political objectives of strengthening the moderate opposition (SNC/SOC and FSA-aligned armed groups). Starved of support, the FSA's fighting capabilities and political legitimacy were gradually stripped away, as those of the extremists strengthened.[63] The West expected much from the moderates but did little to help them. Instead, the gap between its lofty rhetoric and meager support sowed the seeds of despair. Obama later derided criticism of his Syria policy as "horse-shit."[64] He explained, "This idea that we could provide some light arms or even more sophisticated arms to what was essentially an opposition made up of former doctors, farmers, pharmacists and so forth, and that they were going to be able to battle not only a well-armed state but also a well-armed state backed by Russia, backed by Iran, a battle-hardened Hezbollah, that was never in the cards."[65] There are reasons to think the president could have been right. Arming nonstate groups did not have a good track record of success. There was little immediate prospect of Assad stepping down. Iran and Russia would simply coun-terescalate their support to Assad. Without political and organizational reform, arming the FSA would not have made it a stronger fighting force—its incompetence, corruption, and other abuses also explained its waning popularity. Qatar would have continued to back more radi-cal groups. Blowback was inevitable since Western arms would find their way to extremists. Last, there was no automatic relationship between the supply of arms and political influence.[66]

But none of these problems was insurmountable, and this may have been a case of the better being crowded out by the perfect. There were still viable allies in Syria; Ambassador Robert Ford identified several still operating in 2014. "The idea that there's no moderate opposition," Ford maintained, "is said by people who don't speak Arabic, have never been to Syria and don't know what the fuck they're talking about."[67] It is certainly true that in 2012 the most powerful part of the armed opposition was the moderate FSA and its allies. They were often corrupt, ineffective, and poorly coordinated, but they were moderate. Both military options (arming the opposition and the no-fly zone) were designed to militarily coerce Assad by denying him an expecta-tion of military victory and thus support the strategy of negotiating a political transition. Neither looked to achieve forcible regime change. Either would have increased the level of coercion, and both together may well have tipped the balance. True, Iran and Russia would have likely counterescalated, but they were doing that anyway. These military measures would have increased the costs and risks that counterescalation presented to Tehran and Moscow and may have deterred them from backing Assad so heavily by convincing them his government was ultimately doomed. Certainly, some blowback was inevitable, and arming the rebels created no silver bullet for the influence problem, but U.S. backing would have strengthened the hands of the moderates, giving them a better chance of beating the jihadists in the political marketplace.

There are especially good reasons for thinking a no-fly zone would have made a difference, not just by easing the suffering of besieged Syrian civilians but by fundamentally altering the balance of forces. It would have degraded the regime's ability to drop barrel bombs, regular bombs, and gas-filled bombs on civilians and saved tens of thousands of lives. Denying the regime access to the air would have made it more difficult for Damascus to prosecute its war strategy and made a negotiated settlement more appealing. A no-fly zone would have denied Russian access to Syrian skies. A partial or complete no-fly zone would not have ended the killing—the regime could still use artillery and siege warfare, though not as effectively—but it would have constrained it. It is for that reason that the U.S. Holocaust Memorial Museum's study of "critical junctures" in U.S. policy on Syria concluded that a no-fly zone "might have saved significant civilian lives without necessarily increasing the risk of large-scale escalation. . . . Given the level of atrocities and killing perpetrated by the regime's use of indiscriminate aerial bombing of civilian targets, particularly in northern Syria, an option to neutralize the regime's airpower over at least a portion of Syria deserved greater consideration."[68] More than seven years later, Turkey demonstrated the wisdom of this assessment in Idlib. Risky and costly as it might have been, curbing the regime's ability to rain down terror from the skies would have undoubtedly saved lives and altered the military balance, perhaps—combined with other measures—to the point of changing the regime's position on a negotiated political transition. What mattered most to the U.S. administration at the time, however, was that military options involved accepting some degree of risk. On balance, the president and his team judged the potential risks to them outweighed the potential advantages to Syrians.

BRAHIMI'S LONELY SEARCH FOR PEACE

With Kofi Annan gone, Secretary-General Ban Ki-moon approached the experienced Algerian Lakhdar Brahimi—broker of the Taif agreement that ended Lebanon's civil war and chief of the UN's diplomatic efforts in Afghanistan—as a replacement. Aware that Annan had struggled for international support, Brahimi assumed the Security Council's obvious divisions over Assad's future would make it impossible to mediate a political settlement. Before accepting the job, he asked council members to endorse his appointment and allow him freedom to negotiate without preconditions—code for the freedom to negotiate something that might leave Assad at the helm. Russia and China were unsurprisingly receptive to this new approach, which they saw as a welcome departure from Annan, but the United States, Britain, and France objected: the mediator's job was to implement the Geneva Communiqué, not rewrite it. Accordingly, Assad could participate in transitional government only if the opposition consented. With that understood, all five assured Brahimi of their support, and, in his own words, moved by "a bit of vanity and an excessive sense of duty," he accepted the role.[69]

Brahimi thought there was little hope of negotiating the sort of top-down settlement his predecessor had attempted, so he began instead with a bottom-up approach. With more than a touch of tone-deafness, he initially wanted to base himself in Damascus, until it was pointed out that this would make him beholden to the government and appear biased against the opposition, so he chose Cairo instead, meeting Egypt's newly elected Muslim Brotherhood president, Mohamed Morsi, in Cairo on September 9 and the Arab League's Nabil el-Araby the following day, before traveling to Damascus to meet Syria's foreign minister Walid al-Moualem and "loyal" opposition groups—those approved by the regime. Brahimi met Assad on September 15 and found the president "more aware than me of the scope and seriousness of this crisis." "The common ground does exist," Brahimi told reporters afterwards: "These are Syrians, they love their country and want peace for their country."[70] Precisely what that common ground was, however, was anybody's guess. Clearly, Brahimi's thoughts were turning toward a power-sharing deal that might bring Assad and the opposition together into a transitional government. But if that was the plan, it was never likely to succeed. Assad had no intention of sharing power, and the opposition feared that any arrangement that left him in charge of the security forces would not be worth the paper it was written on.

The UN envoy found Morsi willing to help. Egypt's first democratically elected president, Morsi wanted to demonstrate it was possible for Islamists to win at the ballot box and govern responsibly. At home he faced fierce opposition from Egypt's secular elite and made a series of poor decisions, including trying to appropriate more power for himself and inflict vengeance on past enemies, moves that brought protestors back onto the streets. In foreign affairs, Morsi wanted to support Sunni causes such as the Syrian revolution and Palestinian liberation through lawful means. At the OIC in Mecca, held in mid-August, he proposed an "Islamic Quartet" comprising Egypt, Iran, Saudi Arabia, and Turkey to lead mediation efforts in Syria. The four then gathered in Cairo to hash out a new approach, but despite a public show of unity, the divisions among them were unbridgeable. Three of the four demanded Assad step down; Iran rejected that out of hand, complained the quartet was unbalanced, and insisted Iraq be brought in.[71] The talks limped on inconclusively until June 2013, when Morsi finally gave up, recalled Egypt's ambassador from Damascus, and joined Saudi Arabia and Turkey in demanding a no-fly zone.[72] A month later, Morsi himself was overthrown by violent military coup. Thrown into jail and sentenced to death, he was denied medical treatment and died there in 2019.

Brahimi meanwhile focused on chalking up an early win—a temporary ceasefire to establish some trust and catapult further deals. He concentrated his efforts on negotiating a ceasefire to coincide with the three-day Muslim holiday of Eid al-Adha in late October and returned to Damascus on October 21 to press Assad and gauge his views. As before, Assad said he wanted a political solution but stressed it must be based on ending terrorism and stemming the flow of arms into the country.[73] The president agreed to a temporary ceasefire and to the delivery of humanitarian relief into besieged Homs, but the ceasefire never took hold and, after fourteen hours of trying, a UN humanitarian convoy had to turn back because the FSA could not guarantee its safety since there were twenty-one separate armed groups to negotiate with and little to indicate either side was complying with the ceasefire.[74]

The experiment in building peace from the bottom up had quickly failed, so Brahimi reverted to more traditional arm-wrangling. He needed somehow to rebuild momentum around the Geneva Communiqué and so proposed revisiting the question of a Security Council resolution. In Beijing, Foreign Minister Yang Jiechi expressed support, explaining they supported a "political transition" agreed to by Syrians.[75] Yang presented a Chinese four-point plan that echoed the communiqué's core points. Russia's Lavrov, though, was skeptical. Sensing a thinly veiled attempt to put regime change back on the agenda by reviving Geneva, Lavrov argued there was no need for a Security Council resolution and that the council should focus instead on humanitarian and counterterrorism issues.[76] Undeterred, Brahimi brought the Americans and Russians together for a series of trilateral meetings. The first, held in Dublin on December 7, included Clinton and Lavrov and seemed to go well. Having failed to persuade Obama down a more coercive path, Clinton reckoned diplomatic bargaining was all she had and was eager to pursue whatever opportunities arose. The three clarified issues around timelines and the transitional government's executive powers but made no progress on the core question of Assad. Two more trilaterals were held in Geneva on December 9 and January 11 between Brahimi and the respective deputies, William Burns and Mikhail Bogdanov. These also seemed to go well, though they again left the Assad issue unresolved. Burns tried breaking the impasse by initiating a conversation about who would serve in the transitional government, but the Russians objected that that this was a matter for the Syrians.[77] Nonetheless, Brahimi thought they had made enough progress to move forward with broader talks on the communiqué.

But if the trilateral dialogue gave grounds for hope, the situation inside Syria afforded only despair. The UN's Commission of Inquiry reported that violence increased significantly in the final months of 2012. In late August government forces shelled Daraya for four days, before *shabiha* militia entered the town. Around one hundred men threw down their weapons and sought refuge in a place known as "the gardens" but were tracked down by the progovernment militia and killed. The UN reported widespread evidence of other killings in Daraya, including of women and children. Aleppo, Daraa, Damascus, Idlib, Deir ez-Zor, Hama, Homs, Al-Hasakah, and Latakia received similarly brutal treatment. Entire neighborhoods in suburban Damascus were shelled and destroyed. Northeast of Idlib, the town of Taftanaz was reduced to ruins. Opposition forces sometimes responded in kind, sometimes torturing, and killing prisoners, killing Alawite and Christian civilians, and positioning weapons in civilian areas. These opposition abuses, the UN was quick to stress, "did not reach the intensity or scale of those committed by government forces and affiliated militia."[78]

Violence escalated further on multiple fronts in December. Deir Beelbah in Homs, for example, was subjected to days of indiscriminate artillery shelling. In the late afternoon of December 23, a queue at the Baladi bakery in Halfaya, Hama, was hit by four rockets, killing two hundred civilians and injuring many. Halfaya's was the worst but not the only deadly attack on bread lines and bakeries. Bakeries in Aleppo, Deir ez-Zor, and elsewhere in Hama suffered the same fate, atrocities designed to kill and terrorize civilians. The UN reported that "indiscriminate and widespread shelling, the regular bombardment of cities, mass killing, indiscriminate firing on civilian targets, firing on civilian gatherings and a protracted campaign of shelling and sniping on civilian areas have characterized the conduct of the Government. . . . The attacks amount to war crimes and appear to constitute a campaign against civilians in anti-Government armed group-controlled areas, which may amount to crimes against humanity."[79]

With Damascus's airport closed by the fighting, Brahimi drove into Syria's capital from Beirut on Christmas Eve 2012, hopeful that progress in the trilateral dialogue could be translated into something tangible. If he was alarmed by the growing violence, the UN's envoy didn't show it as he greeted Assad in the presidential palace atop Mount Mezzeh. Things grew tense in their private conversation when Brahimi broached whether Assad would consider relinquishing executive powers to the transitional government. Syria's president listened politely but replied that he intended to run for the presidency again at the end of his term in 2014 and that these elections, not the Geneva

Communiqué, would determine Syria's political future.[80] Syria's news agency called the talks "constructive," but in truth the government was on a collision course with a second UN envoy. Assad was reminding Brahimi that he had never accepted the communiqué, telling him the government had no intention of doing so, and announcing an alternative pathway to transition—national elections that Assad would surely win—that would undercut Geneva entirely.

The contrast between the marble-encrusted opulence of Assad's palace and Syria's grim realities could not have been starker. At the foot of Mount Mezzeh, less than a mile from the palace, sits a military hospital known as Hospital 601. Earlier in the year, UN officials had tried and failed to access it. Now, as Brahimi conversed with Assad, the president's intelligence officers in Hospital 601 were busy torturing and killing prisoners there. A survivor recalls being sent there in the winter of 2012. Severely malnourished and manacled to their beds, prisoners were left blindfolded for days, defecating where they sat.[81] Prisoners were beaten with iron bars. Some had their eyes gouged. Some were burned. Children as young as eleven had holes drilled into their bones. Thousands were killed. To relieve an administrative logjam, in December 2012 Syria's military intelligence ordered that all the bodies be taken to a military hospital for logging before being disposed of. They quickly ran out of space at Hospital 601 and were forced to use a parking garage. There, a military photographer was tasked with recording the dead. At great risk to himself, "Caesar" as he became known, was determined to expose the regime's crimes.

BATTLE LINES TAKE SHAPE

Assad's public response to Brahimi's probing Christmas Eve question came in the first week of January 2013. In a rare address to the nation, he vowed never to talk to terrorists and warned there could be no political solution until the opposition laid down their arms, but he promised to reconcile with those who had not "betrayed Syria." In an attempt to undercut Brahimi, he proposed a national dialogue with the "loyal" opposition to draft a national charter that would be put to a referendum, paving the way to parliamentary elections and a general amnesty for opposition supporters not implicated in violence.[82] The Kremlin welcomed Assad's initiative, but a frustrated Brahimi lost no time firing back, abandoning the cautious diplomacy of the past few months to insist that Assad would have to step aside before a transitional government was established—"surely he would not be a member of that government."[83] Damascus issued a stern rebuke, claiming Brahimi was biased and interfering in Syria's internal affairs. He was not invited back for months.

The newly formed National Coalition for Syrian Revolution and Opposition Forces (SOC), meanwhile, had set itself four main goals: obtain recognition as the legitimate representative of the Syrian people, unify the opposition, establish a transitional government in exile capable of administering opposition held territory, and reassure Syria's national and religious minorities.[84] The man chosen to lead the new coalition, Ahmed Moaz al-Khatib, seemed a good fit for the role. A well-respected imam, he had been an outspoken critic of the government during the 2011 uprising, for which he was imprisoned several times before escaping to Egypt. A traditionalist Sunni with a reputation for fair-mindedness, he advocated a pluralist constitution and criticized the extremists. For a moment, al-Khatib brought a new and refreshing energy to the opposition as he traveled extensively inside opposition-held Syria, trying to establish popular legitimacy and build authority with the armed groups. In early January 2013 he told Brahimi he would negotiate with Assad without preconditions based on the Geneva Communiqué. The offer, Brahimi recalled, left Damascus "surprised and embarrassed," its response "slow and confused."[85] But it also annoyed other opposition figures, especially the old guard in the Syrian National Committee leadership and their Qatari and Saudi patrons. The regime firmly rejected the offer, so the SOC leader repeated it publicly, offering to meet regime representatives if it released detainees.[86] Damascus held firm, so al-Khatib issued a direct appeal to Hezbollah's leader, Hassan Nasrallah, calling on him to stand with Syria's people just as he had stood with the Palestinians. Nasrallah's response was blunt—and should have been given more attention by foreign powers: Hezbollah would never abandon Assad.[87] Al-Khatib's energy wasn't limited to international diplomacy; it also propelled frenetic efforts to reorganize the opposition's inner functioning. He brought legal scholars together to devise a way of replacing the ad hoc systems of local justice that had sprung up in opposition-held areas with a uniform legal code. They developed a moderate Islamist code designed to win local legitimacy and head off the more extreme brands of Sharia law being imposed by some Islamists, but some Islamists rejected this challenge to their local authority.[88]

On both international and domestic fronts, the new coalition led by al-Khatib breathed fresh air into the opposition. But precisely because of that, it ran into trouble with some of its more powerful members and their foreign patrons. Things came to a head over two issues. First, the SOC was locked out of negotiations to establish a Higher Military Council to oversee and coordinate military efforts, while Qatari and Saudi representatives were admitted. Second, the opposition came to loggerheads over the establishment of a government-in-exile. No one in the region thought the SOC itself could become a stand-in government, and Qatar and Saudi squabbled over appointments, each demanding its candidates be given the key jobs. The result was a weak and divided nominal government presided over by the Qatari and SNC-backed Syrian Ghassan Hitto. American insistence that defectors from the Syrian government be given prominent roles because of their experience in governing fueled distrust.[89] Al-Khatib despaired. He was opposed to the very idea of a paper government, rightly arguing that an executive authority was needed to create a financial base and support system. But as with the military council, Qatar and Saudi Arabia got their way on the interim government, hard-wiring their own disunity into Syria's opposition and crippling the SOC.[90]

The problems were all too evident at a UN-organized conference for humanitarian donors, held in Kuwait on January 30, 2013. Al-Khatib explained that the SOC needed $3 billion to achieve its goals. That was always an unrealistic ask but not outlandish given the volume of funds going to the armed groups. The conference received impressive pledges of $1.5 billion, most of which came from the $300 million each pledged by Kuwait, Saudi Arabia, and the UAE. But these regional patrons insisted their aid be directed to their preferred groups rather than being routed through the SOC.[91] Western governments followed suit. The United States increased its supply of nonlethal aid, including body armor and "foods, medicines, meals ready to eat," promising $123 million worth.[92] The UK and France also joined in. The UK supplied $20 million of nonlethal aid to the rebels in 2013. In May 2013 the UK and France persuaded the EU to exempt the opposition from its arms embargo. But these were tiny gestures compared to the money flowing in from the region and did nothing to address the imbalance between the sorely underfunded SOC and the relatively well-endowed armed groups.

Frustrated by all this, and especially by Qatari and Saudi influence, Moaz al-Khatib—arguably the opposition's most promising potential leader—resigned in late April 2013. Their policies driven more by their own interests than concern for Syrians, the Qataris and Saudis hobbled Syria's opposition by sowing discord and fragmentation, denying Syrians the ability to speak for themselves. The two Gulf states had been allowed to play this inflated role because the United States and other Western powers had no realistic strategy for achieving their objectives, a result of their ambivalence born of other priorities.[93]

The contrast between the opposition's foreign "friends" and the regime's could not have been greater. While the former pulled themselves and their allies apart, Iran and Hezbollah pulled together.[94] The regime's support was more united and coherent and grew to outmatch the support that flowed to the rebels. Hezbollah had been initially cautious about assisting the Syrian government, its leader Hassan Nasrullah concerned it might damage its reputation as a popular Arab vanguard. But as pressure mounted on Damascus, Hezbollah began secretly funneling support, and by the summer of 2012 dozens of Hezbollah lined up alongside the government and its allies. The United States responded with targeted sanctions, but that couldn't stem the flow, and in late 2012 a UN official commented that the bodies of Hezbollah fighters killed in Syria were regularly being returned to Lebanon.[95] As the government's position worsened through 2012, Damascus and Tehran urged Hezbollah to contribute more, and, realizing Assad's defeat would spell disaster for it, Nasrallah agreed. That drew a sharp reaction from Israel, which was understandably nervous about the penetration of Hezbollah and Iranian fighters into Syrian areas close to the Golan Heights. In late January 2013 Israeli jets attacked a convoy in Syria carrying SA-17 anti-aircraft missile launchers destined for Hezbollah. The steady escalation of Hezbollah's intervention became apparent in June 2013, when around two thousand fighters led a successful offensive on al-Qusayr in the Beqaa valley. This secured a vital route for the regime and afforded a psychological boost. The opposition and its backers were shocked—the latter having wrongly assumed that Hezbollah would keep Syria's war at arms-length. Hezbollah's efforts were augmented by Iranian-organized brigades of Iraqi Shi'ites.[96] Intervention was not cost-free, however. It sustained relatively heavy casualties in Syria, losing approximately two thousand fighters in the first couple of years, damaged its legitimacy among Sunnis, and strained its relationship Hamas—which, it later emerged, assisted the rebels in Aleppo.[97]

Iranian support also increased as Tehran feared Assad's demise might cause it some existential problems. The world looked a dangerous place to Tehran in 2013, with Iran embroiled with the United States in a high-stakes game of chicken over its nuclear program. After the collapse of talks in 2009, the White House had succeeded in persuading Russia and China to impose tough economic sanctions on Iran, to which Iran had responded by expanding its enrichment program, hoping to break international will before its economy was broken by sanctions. But the gamble didn't bear fruit, and Iran's economy was crippled. Meanwhile, Israel took matters into its own hands and conducted a clandestine campaign of assassination against Iranian scientists connected to the nuclear program. In retaliation, Iranian proxies bombed a busload of young Israeli tourists, killing seven and injuring more than thirty, elevating the risk of war with Israel.[98] Within that context, Tehran simply could not countenance losing its Syrian ally. Iranian transfers of arms, ammunition, and Quds force fighters were facilitated by Iraq, whose Tehran-aligned Shi'ite government had retaken control of its airspace in late 2011. Iran also organized a pipeline for thousands of Afghani refugees and ex-Taliban fighters to receive $500 a month fighting for Assad.[99] Having helped stabilize the regime in 2012, Iran's Qassem Soleimani oversaw a restructuring of its fighting capabilities in 2013. Unreliable Sunni brigades were held back from the front line, while Alawite units were resupplied with Iranian arms and equipment. To supplement the notorious *shabiha*, Soleimani oversaw the creation of a new volunteer militia—the National Defense Forces (NDF). Iranian Revolutionary Guards recruited Alawites especially to the force, which by the end of 2013 was fifty thousand strong (comparable in size to the FSA core). The Quds force led their training, and each brigade was assigned an Iranian Republican Guard officer.[100] The NDF was soon implicated in civilian massacres, including the killing of up to 450 civilians in Al-Bayda and Baniyas on May 2–3.[101] By 2015, the UN estimated, Iran was spending $6 billion per year propping up Assad.[102]

All this equated to bloody war on multiple fronts. Approximately six thousand people, including three hundred children, were killed in April 2013, making it the war's bloodiest month yet.[103] The opposition scored some major victories, including in March 2013 when it seized its first provincial capital, Raqqa, a host of towns on the Homs-Aleppo highway, and the main hydroelectric dams on the Euphrates, victories made possible by the active participation of jihadist groups like Jabhat al-Nusra and Ahrar al-Sham. This growing influence of extremists created tensions countrywide. Twenty-one Filipino UN peacekeepers policing the contested Golan Heights were taken hostage by the jihadist Yarmouk Martyrs Brigade but were released shortly afterward.[104] North of Raqqa, al-Nusra and the FSA-aligned Farouq Brigades clashed for control of the Tal Abyad border crossing in March.[105]

Behind all this, Syria's jihadist politics were undergoing their own transformation. The same day Raqqa fell (March 4, 2013), al-Nusra's parent organization, the Islamic State of Iraq (ISI), took control of the al-Yaarubiya border crossing between Iraq and Syria. Seventy Syrian soldiers fled into Iraq but were ambushed, with forty-nine killed. This was the first time Iraq's ISI extremists had intervened directly in Syria's war. It would not be the last. In April the group's mysterious leader Abu Bakr al-Baghdadi issued a statement confirming al-Nusra was part of his organization and announcing it would be subsumed back into its parent body. The new Islamic State in Iraq and al-Sham (ISIS) would expand operations directly into Syria.[106] Jihadi politics were thrown into disarray. Al-Nusra's leader, Abu Muhammed al-Jolani, rejected Baghdadi's attempts to subsume it. To build popular support in Syria, al-Nusra had concealed its Iraqi heritage and defined its goal as ousting Assad, not establishing a regional caliphate. Al Qaeda leadership tried to mediate between the two former partners but to no avail. Conflict erupted between them, but al-Nusra lost many fighters, who defected to ISIS. Despite these deep divisions, by June 2013 ISIS had established presences in Raqqa, Deir ez-Zor, and Aleppo.[107]

Not for the first, or last, time, conflict within the opposition helped the government. Despite suffering reverses, it succeeded in stabilizing the front line by forcing the opposition to stalemates in Aleppo and Damascus, defending its lines in Daraa, consolidating its hold on the Alawite heartland around Latakia and Tartous, and isolating opposition held districts around Homs.

STALEMATE

Brahimi's peace efforts had stalemated too. The promise of al-Khatib evaporated quickly and the trilateral dialogue stumbled on but delivered nothing of substance. In late April an exasperated Brahimi briefed Security Council diplomats privately that with Assad at the helm, a negotiated settlement would be impossible. The presidential elections scheduled for 2014 presented one potential opening to orchestrate a Syrian-led transition, but only if Assad could be persuaded not to stand himself. The briefing was immediately leaked to the press, crushing any hope Brahimi had of maneuvering Russia and the United States into a common position. Predictably, Damascus denounced the envoy and his proposal.[108]

In early May Obama's new secretary of state, John Kerry—an experienced political figure initially more in tune than Clinton had been with the president's cautious view on Syria—discussed Syria with his Russian counterpart, Sergei Lavrov. To Kerry, the Russian seemed less wary about the Geneva Communiqué than he had expected, and the pair agreed on a joint statement supporting a political settlement to the conflict. Kerry said that he and Lavrov agreed that as soon as possible they would "seek to convene an international conference as a follow-on to last summer's Geneva conference."[109] U.S. and Russian officials followed up with Brahimi, this time in Geneva on June 5 to discuss arrangements for what was now being labeled "Geneva II."

They agreed the government and opposition should have direct talks but were in truth still poles apart on the central political question of whether Assad would play a part in the transitional government. There was also uncertainty about who would represent the opposition, and which other governments would be invited to participate. Brahimi thought it especially important that Iran participate—something Kerry was open to, but which could be expected to arouse opposition in the United States as well as from Saudi Arabia and Israel. Nonetheless, they agreed the talks could happen as early as June 2013.

Hopes were therefore high going into a G8 summit in Lough Erne, Northern Ireland. The host, British prime minister David Cameron, organized a leaders-only dinner to give Putin and Obama an opportunity to speak frankly about Syria, hoping it might produce "a moment of clarity." Obama, Cameron, and France's socialist president Francois Hollande all pressed Putin to persuade Assad to step down in advance of a transitional government. It was the only way a government could be formed "by mutual consent." Putin refused: the Syrian government had a right to decide for itself who would represent it in any transitional government, he argued. Cameron pressed further the following day, turning a session on counterterrorism into another discussion about Syria. Still Putin refused to budge; Lavrov subsequently blamed the three Western leaders for demolishing hopes of a Geneva II conference by insisting on Assad stepping aside as a precondition.[110] In the end, the G8 leaders agreed to "strongly support" Geneva II and left it at that, but their pretensions of support couldn't hide the fact that they bitterly disagreed about what Geneva II was meant to achieve.[111] Two months later, however, the largest single massacre of the twenty-first century thus far threatened, briefly, to smash the deepening stalemate. That it ultimately didn't, helped seal Syria's fate.

5

RED LINE

A FEW WEEKS after Kofi Annan's resignation as envoy for the United Nations and Arab League, in August 2012 President Barack Obama gave a White House press conference, during which he was asked about Syria's chemical and biological weapons stockpiles. "A red line for us," he explained, "is we start seeing a whole bunch of chemical weapons moving around or being utilized. That would change my calculus."[1] That the administration had concerns was well known. From the beginning, foreign governments worried about the safety of Syria's vast stockpiles of chemical and biological weapons, concerned they might fall into jihadist hands. Israel and the United States feared the government might be tempted to transfer the weapons to Hezbollah. Syria's opposition feared Assad's forces might use them.[2] State Department officials tasked with contingency planning for a post-Assad Syria were asked to prioritize plans to ensure no chemical weapons fell into terrorist hands. This planning helped generate military preparations, and the U.S. Navy moved five destroyers, equipped collectively with around two hundred Tomahawk missiles, into the eastern Mediterranean, ready to support efforts to neutralize the weapons should that be needed.[3] Disquiet had grown when, in July 2012, Damascus sent a veiled threat by admitting for the first time that it had chemical weapons.[4] Obama replied with a warning, giving notice the regime would be "held accountable" should it use them.[5] Obama's "red line" was not entirely out of the blue, therefore, though it did catch people by surprise. Although the president hadn't intended his words to be taken as threatening to use force should Syria use chemical weapons, that is precisely how everybody interpreted them.

CHEMICAL WEAPONS

The Syrian government likely began using chemical weapons just two months later, in October 2012. French intelligence reported their use in Salqin, west of Aleppo, and in Harasta in eastern Ghouta a month later.[6] A gas attack killing seven civilians was reported in Homs on December 22, a report later confirmed by Major-General Abdul Aziz Jassim al-Shallal after his defection.[7] We do not know why regime forces took this dangerous step, but chemical weapons did offer some advantages, specifically by providing another means of plugging gaps caused by the army's chronic manpower shortage. The weapons inflicted harm without the need for more troops and terrified the opposition's ill-disciplined fighters and civilians, demolishing their morale. Their use also signaled resolve to government supporters at a time when many were fearing the worst.[8] We cannot be sure whether Assad personally ordered every chemical attack. Western intelligence thought that unlikely. But he evidently knew chemical weapons were being used, and it is difficult to see how usage could have persisted without his general approval.[9] Chemical weapons use gathered pace in the first half of 2013. Between January and August there were at least fourteen separate incidents, resulting in 100–150 deaths.[10] As they had with previous escalations in the use of artillery and aircraft against civilians, government forces employed the weapons in limited ways to test the international reaction. British diplomats recalled seeing "dozens" of reports in April, while U.S. defense secretary Chuck Hagel confirmed evidence that chemical weapons, including the nerve agent sarin, were being used in "small amounts."[11] These were all clear signs that Obama's warning was being ignored.

One of the most intriguing cases was a sarin attack on government-held Khan al-Assal, in Aleppo governate, on March 19, which killed around twenty civilians and one soldier. Damascus and Moscow immediately claimed the opposition was responsible and demanded that the UN and Organization for the Prevention of Chemical Weapons (OPCW) investigate. The United Nations appointed Ake Sellstrom, a Swedish chemical weapons expert and veteran of the UN's disarmament verification efforts in Iraq, to lead an investigation. Sellstrom's team was delayed by bickering over his mandate: the United States insisting it include all alleged uses of chemical weapons; the Russians and Syrians, that it be limited to Khan al-Assal. In the end, they agreed Sellstrom should investigate two additional incidents—alleged chemical attacks on the Sheik Maqsood district of Aleppo on April 13 and Saraqib on April 29.[12] But they disagreed about what the team should investigate: the West wanted to know who committed the attacks; the Russians, only whether chemical weapons had been used. Moscow won that battle. In the end, the UN/OPCW investigators did not arrive in Syria until August 18, five months after the attack, and they were never granted direct access to the Khan al-Assal site. What the UN investigators found, though, was instructive. A rocket containing sarin had been fired from either a surface-to-surface launcher or, more likely, an aircraft. The chemical used was an identical match to that held in government stockpiles (and used in a later attack on Ghouta, outside Damascus). They found no evidence opposition forces had access to government stockpiles, delivery systems, or the capabilities to mix chemicals in the way used. Yet they accepted the Syrian government's claim that it had not fired the weapon, based on the fact it had landed on government-controlled territory. Sellstrom concluded it was most likely a "friendly fire" incident but was uncertain whether it was accidental (i.e., the intention had been to target an opposition area) or a parting shot from a defecting pilot (the pilot of an aircraft reported by witnesses was never identified).[13] Denied access, the team was unable to verify or deny allegations about Sheik Maqsood. In Saraqib, tissue samples from victims displayed signs of exposure to sarin. Thus, despite the delays and obstacles, the UN's investigators confirmed what Western intelligence agencies already knew: the chemical weapons genie was out of the bottle.

President Obama was becoming trapped by his own "red line": a warning having been issued, it would seriously undermine U.S.

credibility to not now respond firmly to the confirmed use of chemical weapons. Inaction would also damage the global taboo against these weapons. Yet everywhere he looked, the president saw more reasons to avoid direct military involvement. Things were falling apart in Libya, where the United States *had* intervened. On September 11, 2012, the eleventh anniversary of the 9/11 atrocities, the U.S. Embassy in Benghazi was attacked by the jihadist Ansar al-Sharia, and the U.S. ambassador, Christopher Stephens, and three other officials were killed. The Benghazi murders caused bitter recriminations on Capitol Hill as the administration's opponents blamed the White House for failing to protect the ambassador and castigated Obama's Libya policy for creating the problem in the first place. Things were not helped by Libya's descent into chaos as its divided parliament failed to establish its authority while on the streets armed factions and jihadists jostled for control. Terrorists were striking at home, too. The April 15 Boston marathon bombings and subsequent bomb scare in New York's Times Square were unrelated to Syria, but they compounded the fear that wading into Syria's war would make the United States more of a target. Meanwhile, a coup in Egypt underscored the president's suspicion that hard-won gains in the Middle East were ephemeral. In early July 2013 the Egyptian Army, encouraged and backed by Saudi Arabia and the UAE, overthrew Mohammed Morsi's elected government, arresting Morsi and other senior Muslim Brothers in the process. Headed by Abdel Fatteh el-Sisi—the former head of military intelligence now serving as defense minister—the new military government conducted a violent crackdown. When the Brotherhood responded by occupying al-Nahda and Rabaa al-Adiwiya Squares, the army moved to clear them in a massive display of force. Between 800 and 2,500 unarmed protestors were killed in the ensuing massacre. Morsi's government had certainly proven itself incompetent and overly eager to impose Islamic law and wind back democratic freedoms, but its ousting from power chilled the democratic hopes of 2011.

Moscow welcomed Morsi's demise. Pleased to see the back of his Islamist and anti-Assadist government, the Kremlin showed itself to be far from the principled opponent of regime change it claimed to be. Washington's response was confused. The administration was uncomfortable about the violent overthrow of an elected government so could not welcome Morsi's demise as the Russians did. Yet the Muslim Brotherhood was no friend, and its imposition of Islamic law, winding back of human rights, and bellicose anti-Israeli foreign policy were sources of grave concern. So the U.S. government could not bring itself to condemn the coup either. Instead, the administration opted to obfuscate on whether a coup had taken place at all.[14] America's regional allies were torn apart by events in Cairo. Qatar and Turkey had welcomed and invested heavily in Morsi's government and felt betrayed by Washington's apparent acquiescence in its downfall. They especially resented the $1.5 billion of U.S. aid that continued to flow to Egypt's military each year. Saudi Arabia and the UAE meanwhile delighted in the Brothers' demise and the blow it struck to Qatari pretensions. They poured cash in to shore up the new government and joined the new military dictator in declaring the Muslim Brotherhood a terrorist organization. The fragile coalition of Arab allies of the Syrian opposition effectively was shattered by events in Egypt.

To an already wary U.S. president, events in Libya, Boston, and Egypt confirmed his sense that the risks of involvement in Syria outweighed any transitory benefits, that there were real limits to what the U.S. could achieve internationally—using force to achieve lasting positive change chief among them. When intervention in Syria was broached, the president would ask, "Tell me how this ends?" Since no one could, military options remained firmly off the table, irrespective of the "red line" threat.[15] The president made a virtue of his caution during the 2012 election campaign, contrasting it with the disastrous adventurism of his predecessor George W. Bush and Republican opponent Mitt Romney, whose approach to the Middle East the president described as "reckless."[16] To be fair, Romney also opposed military intervention in Syria.

It was in this context that, in May 2013, Turkey's Recep Tayyip Erdogan arrived in Washington, D.C., to press the United States to show leadership on Syria. Not only was the continuing arrival of refugees a problem for Turkey, so too were the growing power of Syria's PKK-aligned Kurds and the influx of foreign jihadists. Having been browbeaten by Obama into calling for Assad to step aside, Erdogan expected the American president to lead efforts to achieve that goal and specifically hoped to persuade Obama to permit arming of the rebels and a no-fly zone over northern Syria. He was sorely disappointed. Erdogan found an American president preoccupied with Islamist terrorism and espousing a long list of other regional priorities, including Palestine, Libya, and Iran. Obama dismissed Erdogan's proposals and instead insisted Turkey do more to stem the flow of extremists into Syria.[17]

The administration's first response to the reported use of chemical weapons was equally underwhelming. It tried to buy time and legitimacy by awaiting the UN's findings, reasoning that few others would accept the veracity of U.S. intelligence alone and that a UN report would be harder for others to ignore and might create opportunities for a multilateral response that allowed the United States to enforce its "red line" without unilateral intervention.[18] But there was little chance Assad would give Sellstrom the freedom he needed to assess evidence of wider chemical weapons usage. Besides, the UN's writ was so heavily circumscribed it was unlikely Sellstrom would find much compelling evidence. Even if he did, Russia would never agree to punitive measures.

The U.S. secretary of state, John Kerry, was dispatched to Moscow to convey that the administration was aware the Syrian government was using chemical weapons and gauge the reaction. Moscow had never publicly admitted that Syria had chemical weapons. Now it strenuously denied their use. Kerry set out to Putin what the United States knew and suggested it would be in Russia's interest to rein in Assad. Putin lamented America's abandonment of "reliable" leaders in Egypt and Libya and insisted the chaos and rising extremism in Libya were testament to what happened when regimes were deposed without a plan for what would replace them. Kerry urged Putin to cooperate to secure an orderly transition in Syria. With no sense of irony (given his own government's interference in the constitutions of Georgia, Belarus, and—later—Ukraine), Putin replied that while he feared Syria's implosion and Assad's miscalculations, he also doubted the wisdom of "social engineering" in other countries. He agreed, though, that Syria's chemical weapons were a mutual problem since they might fall into jihadist hands and that there might be scope for them to cooperate on their safe removal.[19]

Plainly, handing the matter off to the UN was inadequate. The United States had issued a clear warning. Political allies, especially Jordan and Israel, demanded the administration do more.[20] If the United States didn't act, Israel probably would at some point, potentially inflaming the whole region. Kerry suggested to the president that the previously rejected Petraeus plan, which called for the arming of vetted moderate opposition groups, offered one way of increasing pressure on Assad and establishing political leverage without using force directly. He argued that since the president had demanded that Assad step aside, the United States "risked looking weak if we didn't increase support to the opposition" and made the administration look "feckless."[21] The president reluctantly agreed to an initially small CIA program to train and supply small arms and some larger weapons such as antitank weapons to carefully selected and vetted opposition groups (initially the FSA and aligned groups, expanding to non-Islamist groups in the South trained by Jordan, non-Islamists in the North acting independently of the FSA, and Kurdish groups). More advanced weapons, such as anti-aircraft missiles to combat Assad's air force, would be kept off the table to prevent them falling into the wrong hands. Codenamed Timber Sycamore, this CIA program eventually grew over a period of four years to a cost of $1 billion (a program dwarfed by Iranian aid to the government, estimated at $6 billion *annually*).[22] But whatever the merits of the Petraeus plan, this was an unfitting response to chemical weapons usage, since any cost it imposed was deferred and clandestine, not direct and open, and thus of limited value as a deterrent.[23] Some senior officials urged air strikes against government airbases used to conduct chemical attacks, but President Obama remained unwilling to even consider direct military action.[24]

MASSACRE IN GHOUTA

In the early hours of the morning on August 21, 2013, the Syrian Army opened a fusillade of shelling on the Damascus suburbs of Ein Tarma and Zamalka, in the opposition-held region known as eastern Ghouta. Ein Tarma sits around six kilometers east of the famous Al-Hamidiyah

Souq, a little more than double that from Assad's presidential palace. Zamalka is immediately to the north, the two suburbs divided by a single street. Among the conventional shells were between eight and twelve surface-to-surface rockets, each carrying a deadly payload of at least fifty liters of sarin. Many families did what they always did during air and artillery attacks and raced to the safety of their basements. But sarin is heavier than air, and the toxic gas found its way through doors, floors, and walls and into these poorly ventilated hiding places, sometimes killing whole families. Some slept through the mayhem, either inured to the constant shelling or too frail to flee. Many who did, died in their beds. Meanwhile, thousands raced to beleaguered medical centers, the panic and chaos worsened by continued shelling. Before sunrise that morning, three such centers supported by the French medical NGO Médecins sans Frontières had received more than 3,600 casualties. Survivors found it hard to breathe and suffered convulsions and spasms. Some foamed at the mouth; some experienced headaches and sickness; some red raw skin and agonized eyes. Some 355 of those that made it to these three centers alone died. What little outdated animal Atropine medics had to treat the symptoms soon ran out. At around 5 A.M., and hour before dawn, eight more rockets were fired into Moadamiya, an opposition-held suburb southwest of Damascus, in western Ghouta. The scale of the attacks and the sheer terrified chaos it sparked make it difficult to ascertain precisely how many people were killed and injured. In the hours and days that followed, hundreds of harrowing videos and photographs seeped out of the affected areas, documenting the slaughter. Taken at different places and showing different scenes, they conveyed the same story: one of massacre by chemical weapons. In total, approximately fourteen hundred people were killed, and four times that number injured. More than four hundred victims were children, many of them babies and toddlers.[25]

International outrage spread far and wide. In Washington, the normally cool-headed Barack Obama was furious.[26] The national security team was summoned to the White House situation room, where intelligence officials advised that they believed the rockets had been fired from government territory and that only the government had access to the chemicals, expertise, and launchers needed. The United

States also had phone-tap recordings of Syrian defense officials and soldiers discussing the attack.[27] "It was pretty evident to everybody in that meeting that something significant had happened," Ben Rhodes recalled.[28] For Obama, this was a potential game changer—a blatant atrocity and a direct challenge to his credibility. Gone—temporarily—was the cerebral contemplation of options and consequences. "Normally, I would want you to know what comes next," Obama told the gathered national security team, "but this is not one of those times." Still wary of military intervention, Obama was committed to that course. "When I said that using chemical weapons was a red line, this is what I meant."[29] A military response was the only way Assad would get the message.[30] Almost all his senior advisers agreed such a response was necessary. Kerry thought the Syrian Army had acted out of weakness, not strength. A forceful U.S. response would send an unequivocal message about the red line, uphold international norms, and create much-needed leverage over Assad. It would also show Damascus, Moscow, and Tehran that they had misjudged U.S. resolve and compel Moscow to change its position on Assad and perhaps help him jump before he was pushed. Chairman of the Joint Chiefs Martin Dempsey, until then an opponent of intervention in Syria, added his support to the call for a military response. Among senior White House officials, only Denis McDonough, the president's chief of staff, opposed using force, concerned the president had paid a high political price for intervention in Libya. Syria, he reasoned, would likely be worse. Even a limited intervention could put the United States on a slippery slope to greater involvement, he warned.[31]

U.S. allies urged a swift response. British prime minister David Cameron voiced his support for military action, and Britain's Joint Intelligence Committee shared the U.S. assessment of the regime's culpability.[32] The Royal Navy readied ships in the Mediterranean to participate, including the helicopter carrier HMS *Illustrious*.[33] French president Francois Hollande was equally definitive in his support for a swift military response, pledging France would also contribute. Paris sensed an opportunity to do more than just punish Assad by inflicting a blow that would force the regime to the negotiating table.[34] Of the key U.S. allies, only German chancellor Angela Merkel demurred, suggesting military action be deferred until the UN investigators issued their report. In the Middle East, Jordan, Saudi Arabia, Qatar, Turkey, and Israel all demanded a swift military response.[35] Saudi Arabia offered to submit a draft resolution in the UN General Assembly supporting military action and offered its air force to support U.S. operations, for example, by countering potential retaliation by Iran.[36] Naturally, Russia opposed military action and flatly denied the Syrian government was responsible for the attack. Vladimir Putin took the unusual step of expressing his opposition in an op-ed for the *New York Times*.[37] The UN inspection team had arrived in Syria just three days earlier, and though they had no mandate to investigate what had happened, Sellstrom felt a moral obligation to do just that. He immediately requested access to the Ghouta sites. Damascus said no.

In the days that followed, McDonough's reservations seemed to resonate more with the president. Obama's doubts were amplified by advice from the director of national intelligence, James Clapper, that the case against Assad was strong but not "slam dunk."[38] Obama also worried about the legality of using force without a Security Council mandate and was nervous that others might exploit an expansive reading of the law.[39] Then there was the question of Iran. Secret bilateral meetings on Iran's nuclear program had begun in Muscat, Oman.[40] A U.S. intervention in Syria might jeopardize those talks. But his main concern, "as usual," Susan Rice recalled, involved "thinking several plays down the field." The president assumed any use of force to disable Syria's chemical weapons capabilities would not be a one-off event, since capabilities could be not destroyed in a single hit and whatever was destroyed could be rebuilt and used again—not least because Damascus could count on Tehran and Moscow for help. Using force once would establish pressure to use it again and again to maintain the red line. With every use came a risk of countermeasures requiring an even more forceful response. Target lists would expand to taking out Syria's air defenses and air force, drawing the United States into a war it didn't want.[41] This was the slippery slope he talked so much about—the very thing that, in his view, had led to disastrous wars in Vietnam and Afghanistan. The recent painful experience in Libya seemed to confirm in his mind that military force could be effective only if followed through with maximum effort and commitment. It had been neither in Libya, and the situation had spiraled out of control. If the United States was not prepared to make a major military commitment in Syria, he believed, it should avoid taking the first step.

Meanwhile, military preparations stepped up a gear. The U.S. Navy moved a sixth ship, the USS *San Antonio*, carrying several hundred Marines, into the eastern Mediterranean. Paris assigned Rafale fighter jets based in Djibouti carrying payloads of Scalp missiles to the task. The RAF deployed six typhoon jets to Cyprus in preparation. In Washington, Dempsey presented a surprisingly comprehensive plan for extensive strikes to degrade Syria's air defenses, air force, and chemical weapons supply chain—the stockpiles themselves off-limits to avoid creating a vast toxic cloud. The plan went much further than the president was prepared to go. Obama complained it put him on the slippery slope and asked the chairman to scale it back, which it was, over several iterations. His resolve ebbing away, insiders describe Obama as being "deeply ambivalent" and "conflicted" about what to do next.[42] The president told visiting Baltic leaders on August 28 that he had become "war weary." It was imperative the UN inspection team withdraw before any air strikes since they might be detained and used as bargaining chips or human shields. Samantha Power met the UN's Ban Ki-moon on August 24 and implored the secretary-general to withdraw Sellstrom and his team, but Ban refused since it would make the UN complicit in the air strikes. Besides, he reasoned, they were doing important investigatory work. Power was not the only one lobbying the secretary-general. Russia's Vitaly Churkin was doing the same, demanding UN inspectors remain in the country to complete their work. Each day the inspectors remained inside Syria was another day that Obama delayed the strikes. And with each day that passed, the president's unease grew.[43]

Believing that the impetus for a military response was growing, on August 25 Damascus granted Sellstrom access to Ghouta, a move undoubtedly calculated to keep the inspectors in the country.[44] In the intervening days, the Syrian Army had destroyed as much evidence as it could, mainly by pummeling affected areas with shells. But despite those efforts, the UN team found overwhelming evidence of a sarin attack. Its final report pointed to "clear and convincing evidence" of sarin delivered by surface-to-surface rockets. Chemical weapons had been used "on a relatively large scale" against civilians, including children.[45] Fourteen of the seventeen environmental samples taken from Ein Tarma and Zamalka showed traces of sarin, and four of those samples exhibited high readings. These findings were later confirmed by the UN Human Rights Council's Commission of Inquiry on Syria, which concluded that "significant quantities of sarin were used in a well-planned indiscriminate attack targeting civilian-inhabited areas, causing mass casualties."[46] Sellstrom's mandate didn't extend to apportioning blame, but he told Ban that only the government had the wherewithal to commit such an attack. There was no other plausible explanation.

On August 30, a Friday fully nine days after the Ghouta massacre, Secretary-General Ban Ki-moon telephoned Samantha Power to confirm that the UN team had discovered convincing evidence that sarin gas had been used. The next morning, Sellstrom and his team would leave for Lebanon with a collection of tissue and hair samples, weapons fragments, and soil samples proving their case.[47] With the UN inspectors heading out of the country, evidence in hand, the way seemed open at last for military action. The Pentagon presented final plans that morning for what were now limited missile strikes against Syrian facilities related to air defense and chemical weapons using standoff weapons. No U.S. aircraft would overfly Syria. Naval assets were in place, the missiles primed, and targets set. That afternoon, the president approved the target list at a National Security Council (NSC) meeting.[48] All that was needed now was the final green light. As dusk fell in Damascus, people awaited what they thought would be a display of American shock and awe—some cowering in fear, others looking to the skies in hope.[49] What neither they nor those gathered in the NSC meeting that afternoon knew was that a vote in the British House of Commons in London the previous night had pushed the president's growing doubts over the edge.

The British government is not obligated to seek approval from Parliament for the use of force. But in the heated debates surrounding the march to war with Iraq in 2003, Prime Minister Tony Blair had allowed a debate and vote on whether Britain should go to war. With support from the opposition Conservatives, he had prevailed easily, by 412 to 149, but in the process established a new parliamentary custom. Eight years later Cameron won even more emphatically—557 to 13—on the question of British participation in the Libyan intervention. A leader today renowned for his overconfidence, Cameron assumed Parliament would support military action against Syria, too, and on August 27 recalled MPs from their summer recess to get their approval. The prime minister had reason to be confident. He had already met with opposition leader, Labour's Ed Miliband, and believed he had secured Miliband's backing. The balance of evidence suggests Miliband had indeed assented, though Douglas Alexander, Labour's foreign affairs spokesman and a participant at the meeting, later claimed that while Miliband had expressed openness to the proposal, he had not given the government a "blank cheque."[50] It seems Miliband may have omitted explicitly mentioning the blank check part during his meeting with Cameron.

The prime minister was therefore on less sure ground than he assumed. Given only two days to round up support, he knew some of his own Conservative MPs and Irish Unionist allies thought military action premature but was unsure just how many MPs held that view and how many would vote accordingly. Reluctant to repeat the mistake of Iraq, when the UK had joined an invasion based on faulty intelligence about weapons of mass destruction, many Labour MPs and rebel government backbenchers believed military action should be delayed until the UN completed its investigation. On the far left of the Labour Party, figures like Jeremy Corbyn were motivated by an ideology that rejected all Western intervention and contained an instinctive sympathy toward Assad. Across the West, the far left embraced outrageous Syrian, Russian, and Iranian claims that chemical weapons attacks were "false flag" operations orchestrated to provoke NATO into war. Indeed, Corbyn chaired an activist coalition—"Stop the War"—which not only opposed Western military intervention in Syria (though not Iranian or Russian intervention) but also hosted speakers who claimed the dead children of Ghouta were merely asleep, props in an elaborate stage show.[51]

Wavering in the face of opposition from their own backbenchers, Miliband and Alexander proposed that the government seek a mandate to use force from the UN Security Council. If that failed, Parliament should be given a second vote on whether to approve the use of force. Cameron agreed, and the government amended its motion to require that the Security Council meet, receive a briefing, and take a vote prior to any British involvement in strikes on Syria. Should Russia and China use their veto as expected, the motion required that the House of Commons vote again before British forces joined the fray.[52] As far as Cameron was concerned, that was that. Miliband had accepted the case for military action and had then asked for, and received, procedural concessions. But that was not the end. The vote was scheduled for the evening of Thursday, August 29. At quarter past five that afternoon, Miliband telephoned Cameron to say he had changed his mind and would not support the motion unless a string of new conditions were fulfilled.[53] These included that "compelling evidence" be provided to demonstrate the Syrian regime's responsibility—though precisely what additional evidence was needed was unclear; that the government provide a "clear legal basis" for "collective action on humanitarian grounds"—seemingly ignoring the paper issued earlier that day which did just that;[54] and that the government study the consequences of using force, though again what exactly that meant was unclear.[55] Miliband's defenders claim this was an act of principled multilateralism. It clearly wasn't. The government motion explicitly required that the Security Council vote on a resolution authorizing the use of force and that Parliament be given a second vote should a draft resolution be vetoed. In the House, Deputy Prime Minister Nick Clegg repeatedly reassured MPs that the government would not take parliamentary approval of its motion as authorization for war. Given all this, it seems the proposed amendments were intended to throttle the government's position, and that Miliband's move was driven by party political calculations, specifically divisions among his own MPs and polling that showed a distinct lack of popular enthusiasm. This was most likely an opportunistic gambit to embarrass the government and shore up left-wing support for the Labour leader. One thing is crystal clear, though. Miliband's decision making owed little to concern about what would be best for Syrians. The government defeated Miliband's amendment by more than a hundred votes (322–220), but then the government's own motion was also defeated, albeit much more narrowly by 285 to 272. Chastened, Cameron conceded the UK would not get involved in military action.[56]

The British government's position was so precarious because it had made two tactical errors. First, believing it had sufficient votes, it had allowed some MPs to return to their constituencies that afternoon. As a result, more than fifty, including ten ministers—two of whom were in the parliament building at another meeting, did not attend the vote. Had even a quarter of the government's missing MPs been in the House that night, Cameron would have carried the vote. Miliband's eleventh-hour change of heart came only after he was made aware of the government's tactical vulnerability. Second, had he understood he was heading toward defeat, Cameron could have simply pulled the motion and used his executive authority to commit Britain to participating in the military action. He could also have summoned MPs back for a new vote. That he chose not to do either demonstrated that, for all his bluster, the British prime minister was not prepared to pay a political cost to achieve what he claimed were his goals in Syria.

French commitment, though, was undiminished by events in London.[57] The French thought it imperative the response come quickly. The greater the delay, the more time Assad had to prepare his defenses and move his hardware to safety. The Elysée also expected a Russian backlash, so it was vital the strikes occur before September 5, the date of a forthcoming G20 summit—to be hosted by Putin in St. Petersburg. A call between the French and American presidents was scheduled, Hollande assumed to finalize the target list and initiate strikes.[58] He was mistaken.

As Syrians slept, the U.S. president took an early evening stroll with his chief of staff. Obama was unsure what to do. He was angered by the sarin attack, felt concerned by the need to respond, certain that failing to do so would hurt America's credibility, but worried he was stepping onto a slippery slope. What if the strikes did not deter Assad? What if Assad responded with more violence? Was he prepared to escalate? Did he have political support for that? Would Congress turn on him as it had over Benghazi? Would that undermine his domestic agenda? Always the most skeptical of the president's senior advisers on the use of force, McDonough suggested the president pause and consult Congress. If Congress agreed to support military action, Obama could proceed confident in his political backing; if it didn't, the president would have clarity about the political stakes. Obama agreed. To his team, he explained that the proposed strikes did not have a clear legal basis and could drag on indefinitely. The War Powers Act required that anything longer than sixty days have congressional approval. He also reminded them that as a candidate he had said that he would not authorize force without congressional support unless under imminent threat.[59] Most agreed with the president, but Susan Rice warned that backing down would undermine U.S. credibility and make it harder to exert influence on Syria. She alone also doubted that Congress would support the president.[60] Rice's fears were well founded—the White House congressional affairs team was confident the president would *not* get the support he wanted.[61] Kerry agreed that delaying the strikes would weaken their position in Syria but hoped that congressional support would strengthen their hand in the longer term.[62] With most of his team in agreement, the president announced he would seek congressional approval for air strikes. The immediate threat had passed; Assad and his allies breathed a sigh of relief.

The White House proposal arrived first at the powerful Senate Foreign Relations Committee. Its chair, Democrat Bob Menendez, supported the resolution, as did Republican senator John McCain. A vocal critic of the administration's tepid response to atrocities in Syria, McCain complained the president's plan did not go far enough and inserted an amendment requiring that any U.S. action "change momentum on the battlefield."[63] Only two other Republicans, Bob Corker and Jeff Flake, joined McCain. More worryingly for the White House, three Democrats (Tom Udall, Chris Murphy, and Ed Markey) opposed the motion. The committee endorsed the bill 10–7 but only after inserting additional limitations, including a time limit, a requirement that no troops be deployed into Syria, and stringent vetting for anyone receiving U.S. assistance.[64] The White House could live with the amendments, but the narrowness of the vote and the defecting Democrats doomed the resolution. Senate majority leader Harry Reid introduced the amended resolution on September 6. The numbers were tight. Fifty-one votes were needed for a simple majority and 66 for the two-thirds required to convey strong support, but projections put support for the president at between 23 and 26 votes, opposition at between 20 and 35, with between 42 and 54 votes undecided.[65] Even assuming the White House could secure most of the undecideds, success looked unlikely. Things were even worse in the House of Representatives. There, projections suggested the president could count only on 39 votes. While 151 remained undecided, even if the White House scooped them all (unlikely), it would still fall well short of a simple majority (217). The president would even struggle to carry most Democrats. Only 27 Democrats declared their support for military action, compared to 59 who voiced opposition.[66] The lawmakers' views reflected public opinion. Pew found 48 percent opposed compared to just 29 percent in favor, more of whom were Republicans. Nearly three quarters feared strikes would provoke a backlash, and nearly two-thirds that they would lead to a long-term commitment. Only one-third believed military action would discourage chemical weapons use.[67] This is not surprising given that for the past two years the administration had been arguing the case against military intervention and that, except for Syrian Americans, there was no concerted activism for Syria. As Samantha Power observed, "The student activists, civic groups, churches, mosques, and synagogues that had come out en masse to demand help for the people of Darfur were largely silent."[68] Led by "Code Pink," a leftist activist group, demonstrators took to the streets demanding "no more war" and "peace for Syria," as if preventing U.S. intervention would do that.[69] One banner claimed the case for strikes was "built on lies." None had much to say about the gassing of 1,400 people or the Syrian government's other atrocities, but then the protection of Syrians was not at the forefront of their minds.

There was no way for the president to win congressional support. Military action was taken off the table.

DISARMAMENT DEAL

Through all this, John Kerry had kept in regular contact with his Russian counterpart, Sergei Lavrov. In one of those conversations, he repeated what he had asked the previous May: whether Assad might be persuaded to allow the peaceful removal and destruction of his chemical weapons. American and Russian experts had frequently talked about cooperating to prevent terrorists obtaining Syria's chemical and biological weapons, but talk of dismantling the stockpile had always been off-limits. Lavrov, of course, wanted to prevent U.S. military intervention, which he assumed was imminent. The Kremlin feared that U.S. strikes might have such a debilitating effect on the regime that it might push the government toward collapse (as NATO had, recently, in Libya). A deal on peaceful disarmament might take the momentum away from military action. He expressed his openness to the idea but cautioned it would be risky, since the transportation of chemicals could not be secured. Kerry asked whether the UN might be asked to develop a plan for safe passage. Lavrov said he wouldn't rule it out but since there was no firm commitment on the table remained noncommittal.

The U.S. president traveled to St. Petersburg on September 5 for a long-planned G20 summit. Syria was not on the G20's agenda and neither was Obama scheduled to have a bilateral meeting with Putin—the White House having canceled in August to retaliate against Moscow's decision to grant asylum to Edward Snowdon, wanted in the United States for leaking classified information.[70] Obama quickly raised the situation in Syria and suggested the group issue a statement condemning Assad's use of chemical weapons and demanding a strong response. Putin replied there was no evidence that the Syrian government was responsible, a position backed by leaders from Brazil, China, India, and South Africa. The issue was raised again at a side meeting of foreign ministers. France's Laurent Fabius pressed the case, but Lavrov was unmoved.[71] Later, the American and Russian presidents found time for an informal face-to-face conversation. Obama urged Putin to play a more positive role in Syria. He repeated Kerry's question to Lavrov, asking whether Russia would consider cooperating to peacefully disarm Syria's chemical weapons. Catching Obama's team by surprise, Putin replied that he would.[72] That evening, Lavrov called Kerry to explore the plan further.

Visiting London on his return from St. Petersburg, Kerry gave a press conference at which he was asked whether there was anything that might avert U.S. air strikes. Seemingly off the cuff, he replied: "Sure. He could turn over every single bit of his chemical weapons to the international community in the next week—turn it over, all of it, without delay and allow the full and total accounting, but it can't be done."[73] Kerry's remarks caught the Kremlin's attention, and Lavrov called with the news that Putin had instructed him to do a deal to disarm Syria's chemical weapons, a decision the Russians quickly went public with. Russian diplomats pressed Damascus to accept the initiative, explaining the alternative would be U.S. military intervention. Syria's foreign minister, Walid al-Moualem, agreed immediately.

American and Russian officials gathered in Geneva to hash out the details. Given both their presidents supported the deal, while there was some disagreement on details, there were no fundamental obstacles. The Americans did not trust Assad to keep his word and wanted an intrusive inspection regime; the Russians wanted a more cooperative process. They agreed that the arrangement should be mandated by the UN Security Council but disagreed on whether the authorizing resolution would be passed under chapter 7. There were questions about how to determine the extent of Syria's stockpile; the Americans wanted the OPCW empowered to investigate, but the Russians wanted it limited to Syria's declared stockpile. There were questions about who would supervise and destroy the stockpiles and agreement that this was a job for the OPCW. And there were questions about where the stockpile would be destroyed. Several countries were approached. Jordan declined. Albania offered and then declined. Finally, it was agreed that the OPCW would destroy the stockpile at sea. After three days of talks, on September 14 a deal was reached to establish an internationally supervised process to remove and destroy Syria's declared chemical weapons stockpile.

Under the deal, Syria agreed to join the Chemical Weapons Convention, which prohibits the production, stockpiling, and use of chemical weapons. That, it was hoped, would ensure ongoing monitoring of its chemical weapons production. Attention now turned to the UN Security Council. There, despite French posturing, the real action happened bilaterally between Russia and the United States based on what had just been agreed to in Geneva. Sticking points remained, however. Aware that, once a deal was done, any leverage created by the threat of force would evaporate, Kerry wanted a tough resolution with legally binding demands, a robust oversight regime, clear timeframe, and measures to compel compliance should that be necessary. He also wanted explicit reference to the Geneva Communiqué, to signal that the chemical weapons deal did not supplant the broader political question. The Russians had a different view. They wanted a simple resolution endorsing the Lavrov–Kerry deal. But in truth, both sets of diplomats knew their heads of government wanted the deal—Putin because he believed it would prevent U.S. military action, Obama because he knew it would not. The diplomats would have to compromise, and that is what they did.

On September 27 the UN Security Council unanimously adopted Resolution 2118. It condemned the chemical weapons attacks on eastern Ghouta, endorsed the OPCW plan for the "expeditious destruction" of Syria's chemical weapons program and "stringent verification thereof," and called for immediate implementation.[74] On the chapter 7 issue, it settled on a single reference warning it would "impose measures under Chapter VII" in the event of noncompliance. There was no automaticity here—another resolution would be needed to authorize enforcement measures if that was deemed necessary. The resolution also endorsed the Geneva Communiqué and lent the Security Council's support to the proposed Geneva II summit. Indeed, Lavrov told the council he saw no reason to delay the conference.[75] Assad took only two days to accept the arrangement, and the process began on October 6. It would be implemented in three stages: stockpiles were declared, identified, and secured, then transported to Latakia, from where they were transferred to the OPCW's ship for destruction. The Syrian authorities made a great show of cooperating—thanks, apparently, to ongoing pressure from Russia. Some of the deal's more enthusiastic American supporters claimed it was implemented in full, with "no evidence of systematic deception on the part of the Syrian government."[76]

MISSION ACCOMPLISHED OR OPPORTUNITY LOST?

The U.S. decision not to use force in 2013 was a critical moment in Syria's civil war. Obama defended it stoutly. Asked in early 2014 whether he was "haunted" by Syria, he replied: "I am not haunted by my decision not to engage in another Middle Eastern war. It is very difficult to imagine a scenario in which our involvement in Syria would have led to a better outcome, short of us being willing to undertake an effort in size and scope similar to what we did in Iraq. And when I hear people suggesting that somehow if we had just financed and armed the opposition earlier, that somehow Assad would be gone by now and we'd have a peaceful transition, it's magical thinking."[77] Was he right?

The chemical weapons deal did do some short-term good, and it seemed for a time that it had succeeded in disarming Syria of its chemical weapons and deterring their use without drawing the United States into a military confrontation. Thus one of the deal's main architects, John Kerry, argues emphatically that it achieved precisely what the United States wanted to achieve. "Make no mistake," he claimed, "diplomacy backed by a threat of force is achieving something the use of force by definition couldn't do. Military strikes couldn't get the weapons out of Syria, period. Effective diplomacy is doing that today."[78] Within seven months, five hundred metric tons of chemicals had been removed and destroyed, and twelve months after that Syria's *declared* chemical weapons stockpile—around 1,300 metric tons from forty-five sites—had been dismantled. When ISIS later seized former chemical weapons facilities, it found them empty. The deal also created a window for further U.S.-Russian cooperation on Syria by building personal rapport between Kerry and Lavrov. It thus restored some of Geneva II's flagging momentum. In that light, it seemed significant at the time that Russia agreed to include references to both the Geneva Communiqué and chapter 7 in Resolution 2118—things it had opposed to the point of veto in the past. Finally, the deal gave the United States an artful way of addressing Syria's chemical weapons without undermining parallel negotiations with Iran over its nuclear program.

But the arrangement neither disarmed Syria of its chemical weapons nor deterred their use. Implementation problems were evident immediately. OPCW inspectors reported that beneath its veneer of cooperation, the government stalled and hampered their activities, provided incomplete and misleading information, and developed new chemical weapons capabilities.[79] By these methods, the Syrian government retained its chemical weapons capability, which it soon began using once again. Switching to chlorine, government forces recommenced chemical weapons attacks just 195 days after the passage of

Resolution 2118.[80] That is, while the disarmament process was still underway. It was using sarin again perhaps as soon as 2015, and certainly by early 2017. Thus any positives were partial and short-lived. Violence against Syrian civilians increased again once the threat of force was lifted.

Everything, in fact, had hinged on that threat of force. Moscow and Damascus relented only because they believed the alternative was American military intervention and feared this might precipitate Assad's defeat. We now know, of course, that the package of strikes Obama approved was modest, but Russia and Syria did not know that at the time and, like Obama himself, anticipated that a first round of strikes would be followed by more and morph into a campaign to degrade Assad's military capabilities. Recall that Dempsey's initial proposal was for far-reaching strikes. We now know that Obama's turn to Congress was the start of a climb-down, but that was not the only interpretation possible at the time. There was every reason for Damascus and Moscow to worry that a president emboldened by congressional support would pursue things to their bitter end. Thus the threat of force created genuine leverage, but once the threat receded, so too did the leverage. Once it became clear the United States had no intention of using force, the Syrian government's interest in complying with the chemical weapons deal evaporated. Ultimately, nonintervention taught Assad and his allies that there was nothing they could do that would provoke U.S. intervention. Any lingering uncertainty about Western military intervention disappeared.

The regime benefited directly from the deal, too. The arrangement started to relegitimize the Assad regime by making it an indispensable partner of the UN and OPCW. The government assumed responsibility for securing access to chemical weapons sites and protecting inspectors. For this, it had to launch offensives to take and secure key roads—many of which, like the crucial Homs-Damascus highway, also happened to be important strategic routes. A government offensive to retake control of the highway in November and December 2013—a strategic priority for Damascus—was tacitly welcomed by governments engaged in the chemical weapons process. Opposition movements close to that were frowned upon. Just how far the Assad regime succeeded in rehabilitating itself was revealed in 2018 when Syria

assumed the monthly presidency of the UN's disarmament committee.[81] Putin was also a winner, for he had turned a potentially disastrous moment for his Syria policy into a major triumph. In one swoop
he had saved Assad from U.S. military intervention and made Syria's
leader beholden to him. But it was not just Assad that Putin had gotten
off the hook. He had also helped Obama out of a difficult situation.
What is more, the success of American policy on Syria's chemical
weapons was now entirely dependent on Russia. The Kremlin was well
on its way to primacy on Syria, the indispensable partner anyone
would have to work through in order to achieve anything there.

The decision not to use force undermined moderate opposition
groups associated with the West—especially the umbrella FSA and
SOC, which still at this point represented the vast majority of Sunni
armed and political groups—and legitimized and emboldened the
extremists, whose rise to prominence was swift in the two years after
the Ghouta attacks. Moderates expected the United States to intervene
when Assad used chemical weapons. When that didn't happen, they
stood humiliated in the opposition's political marketplace, the
extremists conversely vindicated. The new reality came as a bitter
shock.[82] Armed groups broke away from the FSA in droves, sending it
on a long, inexorable decline. The extremists, meanwhile, were
emboldened. Obama's "red line" had worried Syria's jihadists, who
feared a U.S. intervention might target them as well the regime and
would certainly empower their moderate rivals. The jihadists loudly
opposed U.S. intervention and prepared to take shelter from attack.[83]
When the intervention failed to materialize, they reemerged emboldened. Having long insisted that the West spoke with a forked tongue
and that only the jihadists had the interests of Syrians at heart, now
they stood vindicated amid a "swelling cynicism about the Western
rhetoric on human rights" Syrians "had once believed was sincere."[84]
This cynicism nurtured the opposition's drift toward extremism. In
late September a group of Islamist militia based mainly in the North,
including al-Nusra and the al-Tawhid Brigade, rejected the SOC and
created a new opposition coalition under the framework of Sharia law.
ISIS expanded territorial control in northern and eastern Syria and
consolidated itself in Raqqa, imposing its own radical interpretation of
the law and, arresting, torturing, and executing those who opposed it.

The decision also alienated U.S. allies and friends. The French government, its strategy set and aircraft ready to fly, was deeply disappointed by Obama's climb-down. Riyadh complained bitterly that it had not been consulted. Frustrated, the Saudi government decided to strike out alone and craft a new strategy to topple Syria's government.[85] Dubbed "reckless" by some Europeans, the new Saudi strategy orchestrated by intelligence chief Prince Bandar bin Sultan had three main elements: reorganizing and unifying pro-Saudi Islamist militias, funneling arms and money to the new group, and facilitating training. The result, announced in November, was Jaysh al-Islam, a new Salafist front produced by the Saudi-orchestrated merger of more than forty Islamist groups mainly based in and around Damascus. The new army was intended to take the fight directly to Assad and his Iranian allies and counter the growing influence of al-Qaeda and ISIS. It broke from the FSA's Supreme Military Council in December. The Saudis reportedly allowed dozens of experienced jihadists to leave the country and head to Syria, even releasing some from jail.[86] They also recruited battle-hardened Pakistani veterans of Afghanistan's long wars to fortify its new training regime.

Ankara had been convinced the United States would eventually intervene and believed Obama's "red line" would be the tripwire, expecting that Turkey would join the fray when the United States did intervene. Turkish officials repeatedly reassured the opposition that intervention was coming.[87] Those expectations now shattered, Turkey's leader, Recep Tayyip Erdogan, felt betrayed and scrambled for a new strategy. Ankara doubted Assad could be defeated without foreign intervention since it could draw on its own foreign support, so it began to narrow its goals to Turkey's own immediate interests, namely, preventing Syria's Kurds from establishing a contiguous territory across its southern borders and creating pathways for the safe return of some of the by then more than two million Syrian refugees sheltering in Turkey. These two goals shaped Turkish policy for the remainder of the war. In the immediate term, though, Ankara continued turning a blind eye to the transit of foreign jihadists across its border—a source of opposition to Assad and a nuisance to the Kurds.[88]

Obama's decision permanently weakened U.S. influence over events in Syria. The threat of force had created leverage over Russia and Syria, forcing both to make concessions they had earlier resisted. John Kerry worried at the time that the chemical deal had made insufficient use of the leverage.[89] Chuck Hagel, the Republican secretary of defense at the time, later reflected that there is "no question in my mind" that the decision to step back "hurt the credibility of the president's word."[90] By rejecting the use of force, Washington sacrificed potential leverage without creating significant change. It also effectively dealt itself out of leadership of international efforts to end Syria's bloodshed, creating a political vacuum into which Russia inserted itself. Although nobody could have known this at the time, comprehensive strikes that degraded Syrian air defenses and secured the U.S. control of Syria's skies would have denied those skies to Russia. It may have also stymied the rise of ISIS. By backing down, the United States handed the initiative to the Kremlin and with it the capacity to shape Syria's future. And it was not just the president's critics who drew a direct line between events in Syria and Putin's decision six months later to occupy and then annex Crimea and support a secessionist war in Ukraine's Donbass. American allies did too. Laurent Fabius, for example, was convinced that Putin's new assertiveness was a product of his rival's display of weakness.[91]

But would the proposed strikes have made a difference? Much of this criticism and disillusion stemmed from misplaced hopes that the limited strikes proposed would precede a more sustained campaign, targeting Syria's air defenses, air force, and artillery, as well as its chemical weapons capabilities, and perhaps establishing a no-fly over all or part of the country. That is precisely what Obama feared most— the slippery slope—and what Dempsey's original package looked to set up by degrading air defenses and air capabilities. A comprehensive package like this could have significantly changed the situation on the ground. While air strikes cannot prevent close-range massacres, a comprehensive campaign could have seriously degraded the regime's capacity to indiscriminately bombard opposition cities, towns, and villagers. This would have saved thousands if not tens of thousands of civilian lives by making it much more difficult, if not impossible, for Damascus to execute its war strategy successfully. In this scenario, Assad would have had little choice but to negotiate a political transition or risk defeat. This was precisely what John McCain had in mind when he added his amendment to the president's motion. The strike package Obama approved was far more modest and focused exclusively on chemical weapons–related sites. That may have deterred chemical weapons use for a time and would have underscored the "red line" for a while. But Obama was surely right that the deterrent effect would need sustaining by repeated waves of military action. Eventually, either the red line's credibility would be eroded or the United States would be drawn more deeply into Syria's war. An administration determined to avoid doing the latter would always also achieve the former. That was the trap Obama created for himself.

There is always a price to pay when governments intervene to protect civilians in other countries. When they choose not to intervene in the face of atrocity crimes, that price is multiplied but paid by somebody else. That is what happened in Syria; the price was paid by Syrian civilians.

6

DEATH AND DIPLOMACY

WHATEVER ITS faults, the U.S.-Russian chemical weapons agreement seemed to create a window of opportunity for renewed diplomacy on Syria's political future. In late September 2013 UN secretary-general Ban Ki-moon hosted a working lunch for the foreign ministers of the "permanent five" (P5) members of the Security Council (China, France, the United Kingdom, the United States, and Russia) where they agreed to support what was at that point being called the Geneva II conference, scheduled for November, and to use their influence to persuade Syria's parties to support the process.[1] But there was little reason to think Syrians were any readier to negotiate than before and, despite their enthusiasm, no sign the West and Russia were prepared to resolve their own differences on the Geneva Communiqué. To stem the opposition's remorseless fragmentation, a prerequisite for meaningful talks, Lakhdar Brahimi recommended that the "Friends of Syria" group be downsized and refocused. Britain's foreign secretary, William Hague, agreed and facilitated a new "core group" of friends—the "London 11" (Egypt, France, Germany, Italy, Jordan, Qatar, Saudi Arabia, Turkey, the United Arab Emirates, the United Kingdom, and the United States).[2] But even within this streamlined grouping, there remained deep differences about what to do next. The United States and most of its European allies still hoped they could gently coerce both sides to accept a transitional government. Saudi Arabia, Qatar, Turkey, and Hollande's France thought this unlikely; they doubted Assad was persuadable, given his Iranian and Russian support, and urged a concerted push for regime change instead. Saudi Arabia broke ranks publicly, arguing Assad's atrocities disbarred him from a future government. Some of these governments also complained the Geneva II organizers had no plan for overcoming differences on the Geneva Communiqué—a concern shared by the SOC. Hague and John Kerry tried to reassure the skeptics by emphasizing that they all agreed Assad would have to resign when the transitional government was established because of the "mutual consent" requirement and that the only question was how he would be maneuvered from power. But in truth neither had any idea how they would persuade the Russians—let alone Assad—to accept that.[3]

This problem was debated extensively at the National Security Council in Washington, D.C., where it was agreed the goal must be a negotiated settlement, but there was little agreement on how to get there. Susan Rice recalls they fought more over this than anything else. Kerry argued more should be done to coerce Damascus without plunging the United States "irretrievably" into Syria's war. John Brennan, who had replaced David Petraeus as CIA director, and Samantha Power agreed. Options included increasing the arming and training of opposition fighters, targeted air strikes to degrade Assad's air and artillery capabilities, and establishing a safe zone or no-fly zone. Denis McDonough, Martin Dempsey, Secretary of Defense Chuck Hagel, and Susan Rice herself disagreed. A vocal if chastened advocate of intervention in Libya and a military response to the Ghouta chemical attack, Rice now thought military action in Syria would pitch the United States into war with Assad and potentially Iran and Russia, too. Safe zones and no-fly zones would require large and extended commitments of force for an uncertain payoff.[4] President Obama judged there was little the United States could do short of dragging itself into a war it didn't want to fight, didn't need to fight, and didn't know how to win.[5] The United States would stick with its strategy of gently coercing the parties to negotiate a transitional arrangement, through economic sanctions, a limited program of support to the rebels, and whatever could be agreed on by the UN Security Council.

However unpropitious, therefore, there seemed to be no political alternative to Geneva II. Getting the parties to the table, though, was not easy. Having survived the "red line" scare, Assad saw little need to talk, much less compromise. For the first time in a while, he was growing confident he could win the war. In contrast, the opposition tied itself in knots, the SOC unsure whether to participate. On the one hand, it wanted to preserve whatever international support it had and knew it risked losing sympathy if it refused to talk. On the other hand, it saw little point in further talks while the government refused to accept the Geneva Communiqué and continued using force.[6] France's Laurent Fabius spearheaded Western efforts to persuade the SOC, chairing a meeting for the "Friends of Syria" to urge its president, Ahmad Jarba, to commit to Geneva II. Jarba relented when his own backers, Saudi Arabia, joined the chorus, but only half-heartedly. Several coalition members demanded concessions be extracted in return for their participation. Specifically they wanted a precommitment that Assad would resign and guarantee that Iran would be kept out of the talks. Underlying this was a concern the talks would become a vehicle for watering down the communiqué and desire to lock in its key elements beforehand. Brahimi rejected out of hand the idea of preconditions, a rule he also applied to Damascus, which objected to negotiating with those it dubbed "terrorists."[7] But the SOC was finding it difficult to sell that message to Syria's increasingly disenchanted and fragmented armed opposition. In the South, up to seventy FSA-aligned groups renounced their affiliation with pro-Geneva II factions.[8] Things got worse when, in late October, Abu Eissa al-Sheikh, leader of a coalition of Islamic factions that included the powerful Ahrar al-Sham, Jaysh al-Islam, and Liwa al-Tawhid and comprised some forty thousand to seventy thousand soldiers, not only rejected the talks but warned that any who did not follow suit risked committing "treason."[9]

In early November Arab League foreign ministers met Syrian opposition leaders in Cairo to encourage them to participate and help them hash out a joint position to take to Geneva. The SOC leadership expressed openness so long as there was no change to the communiqué. The ministers agreed that the communiqué was non-negotiable and that the purpose of Geneva II was to establish modalities for its implementation. They also agreed to lobby the UN Security Council for a resolution demanding humanitarian access and threatening sanctions and other punitive measures if the government refused. The message was reinforced by Qatar, Saudi Arabia, Turkey, and others over the course of a two-day meeting in Istanbul a few days later. Ahmad Jarba, president of the SOC, confirmed the opposition council would participate but reiterated that he would never consent to Assad joining the transitional government.[10]

It proved no easier to persuade Assad to send a delegation. Damascus still refused to acknowledge the Geneva Communiqué as a framework for a political settlement, and with the threat of U.S. intervention now past and the battlefield situation improving, Syria's president saw little need to compromise. Back in Damascus for the first time in months, Brahimi held four days of talks with Assad and his foreign minister Walid al-Moualem. They insisted the government would not negotiate with "terrorists," that the SOC could not claim to represent the Syrian people, and that Assad's future was not up for negotiation. Assad himself told Brahimi he rejected the political transition envisaged by the Geneva Communiqué and saw no reason why he should not run for another seven-year term in elections scheduled for May 2014.[11] This worried Brahimi immensely since the elections threatened the very idea of political transition. In the end, it took direct intervention from Vladimir Putin to persuade Assad to send a delegation to Geneva. Russia's leader told Assad that since his success on the battlefield would have to be translated into a sustainable and internationally legitimate political settlement, the government should participate in the talks and present itself as a peacemaker. Putin reassured Assad there was no need to stop military operations and that he would not be forced to accept anything he didn't want to.

Brahimi meanwhile traveled on to Cairo and Tehran, where he met President Rouhani, before returning to Geneva for the first of a new series of trilateral meetings with the Americans and Russians to shore up their support prior to Geneva II. It was abundantly clear, however, that sharp differences remained on the purpose of the talks and desired outcome. Besides disagreement on Assad's future, Kerry wanted Geneva II to focus on implementing the political transition agreed to in 2012, whereas Lavrov cautioned the talks should focus on countering terrorism, local ceasefires, and humanitarian measures, not regime change—that is, on managing the war, not resolving it. They also disagreed about the composition of the opposition's negotiating team—the United States arguing it be spearheaded by the SOC, Russia insisting the coalition was unrepresentative. They did find common ground on Iran, however. With the U.S.-Iran nuclear deal nearly complete (the deal was announced on November 24, 2013, a day before the second of the trilateral meetings), Kerry signaled that the United States was prepared to allow Iran to participate so long as it formally accepted the Geneva Communiqué—something it had not yet done. Rouhani had seemed open to that possibility, Brahimi happily reported.

Not everyone shared Kerry's faith that momentum built on chemical weapons could be translated to the larger humanitarian and political issues. Saudi Arabia remained the most prominent dissident. Riyadh had no faith in the Geneva process and continued to argue that more be done to unseat Assad. The Saudi government refused Brahimi's request for a meeting and took its protest to unprecedented heights by refusing to take its seat as an elected member of the Security Council.[12] The move was a direct snub to the United States, a protest at Washington's nonintervention in Syria and nuclear deal with Iran. It was also likely an attempt to preserve Riyadh's room for maneuver outside the council.[13] Though most others were not as overt as the Saudis, several governments shared their skepticism about Geneva II and the UN's position on Syria.

Some governments, meanwhile, believed it important to refocus attention onto the deteriorating humanitarian situation and wanted to do more to address indiscriminate attacks on civilians, the besieging of opposition areas, and denial of humanitarian access. The United States, the UK, and France (the so-called P3) were wary of this approach since they knew the Russians would seize an opportunity to make short-term local humanitarian concessions to avoid having to deal with the larger political issues. But several of the council's nonpermanent members, notably Australia, Luxembourg, and Jordan, disagreed and pressed for the council to address the humanitarian crisis more directly. As the P3 feared, they were prepared to make significant compromises to get this. The Russians indicated they had little objection to a humanitarian resolution in principle so long as the text not single out the Syrian government for criticism. But they were in no hurry, so Russian diplomats proposed a symbolic presidential statement instead. Eager to achieve something, Australia and Luxembourg agreed and drafted a text that condemned violence by all parties rather than singling out the government and offered a lengthy paragraph condemning al-Qaeda-linked terrorism. The proposed text urged the Syrian authorities to speed up approvals for humanitarian workers and facilitate safe and unhindered humanitarian access. It called on all parties to respect the neutrality of schools and hospitals—sidestepping the awkward fact that only one of the parties was systematically destroying them.[14] The statement was adopted without dissent on October 2 but had no discernible effect on the conduct of the war or humanitarian access. Meanwhile, the UN's Human Rights Council instigated an investigation into the massacre as al-Qusayr (Resolution 23/1) and commissioned a report on the treatment of internally displaced people (Resolution 23/26). The UN's high commissioner for human rights, Navi Pillay, detailed the deliberate targeting of hospitals and medical personnel by government forces.[15] The Geneva-based council resolved to condemn these and other violations of international humanitarian law and demand humanitarian access. Laudable as they were, these efforts, too, made little difference.

THE BATTLE ROLLS ON

While the talking continued, inside Syria the government and its allies launched new offensives in the autumn and early winter of 2013. In Aleppo, intense bombardment and offensive operations (dubbed "Operation Northern Storm") helped government forces, backed by NDF and Hezbollah fighters, take a string of towns to the east and southeast of the city. By the end of the month, they had the airport, too, encircling two-thirds of opposition-held eastern Aleppo.[16] In December regime forces began an intensive campaign of indiscriminate barrel bombing of Aleppo, killing more than five hundred people in the final two weeks of the year.[17] The United States drafted a UN Security Council statement condemning the bombardment, but Russia objected and the text was withdrawn. The bombing continued into the new year, the death toll climbing beyond seven hundred (the number of injured beyond three thousand). With evidence the government was using not just barrel bombs but Scud missiles too indiscriminately, the UK presented a new draft statement expressing concern. The Russians again objected, and the draft was withdrawn.

To make matters worse, the government and its allies were not the only ones threatening Syria's mainstream opposition. The increasingly powerful jihadists were on the offensive, too. Reports suggest the number of foreign fighters entering Syria across Turkey's border tripled in the months following the Ghouta chemical weapons attacks.[18] Their growing presence was visible in rebel-held areas in the North, their bloody methods openly paraded. One extremist group was feared above all others: ISIS. By the fall of 2013, ISIS had around eight thousand fighters in Syria—most of them foreign. ISIS fighters distinguished themselves by their ultraradical ideology and extreme brutality. Opponents and the ideologically impure alike were gunned down or captured, tortured, and beheaded. Syrians in the North learned to fear the new arrivals. Travel became perilous, kidnappings common. In early August 2013, for example, an ISIS leader known as Abu Ayman al-Iraqi incited and led a bloody storm through a string of Alawite villages in the Latakia Mountains, killing 190 people, including 57 women and 18 children, and kidnapping 200 women and children.[19] Elsewhere, extremists inserted themselves into Syria's decrepit displacement camps.

The situation in Atimeh offers a good example of the problems arising across opposition-held territory.[20] Northwest of Aleppo, Atimeh camp—named after the closest town—started life in mid-2012 as a small and ad hoc collection of tents and temporary shelters situated on a slope abutting the barbed wire of the Turkish border. Relatively far from government-controlled territory, the camp had grown steadily as people fled violence in other parts of Syria. By the winter of 2012–2013 around fifteen thousand people lived there. Families cut down olive trees for fuel and did whatever they could to scratch out a living.

Within earshot of Turkey, the displaced of Atimeh sat on the Syrian side of the border, beyond the reach of Turkey and the UN's humanitarian agencies and essentially left to fend for themselves. For a time they did so quite successfully. Camp residents, Syrian activists, and expatriates rallied to organize supplies and establish makeshift schools. But they couldn't keep pace with growing demand. By early 2013 the population had reached thirty thousand and was growing rapidly. In March UNHCR used satellite technology to estimate there were two thousand shelters there. Two months later the figure had grown to three thousand. The ad hoc networks of support were unable to cope. Supplies became sporadic. Well-meaning but small and inexperienced NGOs failed to assess needs properly, coordinate, or supply what was needed. Some of the aid they delivered was useless; some made things worse. Conflicts erupted between camp residents and local farmers, whose own livelihoods were devastated by the loss of olive trees and farming lands, and the crime, disorder, and economic crises the displaced brought with them. So close to Turkey, Atimeh town became a haven for smugglers and organized criminals. Inside the camp, disputes over basic necessities sometimes grew violent. FSA fighters charged with protecting the camp—many of whose families also lived there—squabbled with one another and extorted money and goods from the displaced. Conditions deteriorated. By the middle of 2013, residents lived in abject squalor. The camp was divided into different sections, each managed by a different group, each competing with the other. Meanwhile, an Islamist brigade—later identified with ISIS—set up nearby and established itself in the camp. With better arms than the FSA and foreign money to distribute, the Islamists became dominant inside the camp, taking control of a large proportion of the organized crime, smuggling, and distribution of aid. In November 2013 ISIS established a reception center for foreign fighters in Atimeh.[21]

The story of Atimeh was replayed in some form across opposition-held Syria. Populations swollen by displacement, infrastructure devastated by war and the government's incessant bombardments, left local civilian authorities who were starved of resources and denied outside assistance utterly swamped. Despite valiant efforts, they buckled under the immense strain. In 2011 U.S. ambassador Robert

Ford had spoken passionately about the need to support civilian governance and the Local Coordination Committees in opposition-held areas. But very little was done as living conditions decayed, creating vacuums of hopelessness filled by the Islamists.

The emergence of ISIS represented not just a military threat to the opposition but a political one, too. These extremists were deeply divisive, horrifically violent, utterly self-serving, and largely disinterested in the struggle against Assad, their objectives extending well beyond Syria's revolution. Between mid-2013 and mid-2014, ISIS barely targeted the regime, though they openly threatened genocide against the Alawites.[22] Its military efforts were concentrated on other opposition groups, especially the FSA. Meanwhile, Assad barely touched the extremists, since he knew they posed a more immediate threat to the opposition than to him. To confront this dual challenge, seven of the largest Islamist groups opposed to Geneva II—including Jaysh al-Islam, Ahrar al-Sham, Liwa al-Tawhid, and Ansar al-Sham—joined forces to form the Islamic Front hoping to counter the growing influence of ISIS and other al-Qaeda allies in Islamist circles and take better advantage of foreign patronage.[23] Since Islamists looked basically alike to Western governments, this initiative only seemed to confirm the opposition's drift toward extremism.

The inflow of foreign jihadists was a particular problem. By spring 2013 there were as many as six thousand foreign fighters inside Syria, not including those serving with Hezbollah, the regime's other allies, and the Kurds. Most came from other parts of the Middle East, the Caucasus, and Afghanistan, but a growing number (around a thousand by the end of the year) came from Western Europe.[24] This raised fears that returning jihadists would spearhead home-grown terrorism and prompted calls for tighter restrictions on travel to the Middle East.[25] Though security agencies found little evidence to substantiate the risk, the perceived threat came to dominate European public debate about Syria, superseding concerns about Assad's atrocities.[26] Syria's president eagerly stoked these fears, inviting some of Europe's own extremist politicians on carefully stage-managed tours to see the Islamist threat for themselves. Both the extreme right and left duly became vanguards of Assadism in European debates about Syria.

The specter of home-grown terrorism reinforced the U.S. administration's determination to avoid being drawn in. In the autumn of
2013, it replaced its ad hoc approach to distributing material support,
coordinated, if at all, by the local military councils and the SNC with
a new system managed by Military Operations Centers (MOC) in Jordan (Amman) and Turkey (known by their Turkish acronym MOM).
The centers brought together military personnel and intelligence personnel from the United States, Turkey, Jordan, the UK, France, Saudi
Arabia, UAE, and Qatar with the aim of better coordinating military
planning and assistance.[27] Some suspected the initiative more focused
on monitoring and limiting what U.S. allies supplied to the rebels
than streamlining and improving U.S. support. That was a little unfair
since the MOCs played a crucial role in helping opposition factions
better prepare and coordinate their operations. But the accusation
was not entirely without merit; the centers positioned the CIA to keep
a close watch on what was supplied and to whom. The United States
remained implacably opposed to supplying anti-aircraft missiles, antitank missiles, and other sophisticated weapons to the opposition
and determined to ensure that others didn't as well.[28] Even the supply of light weapons was carefully limited. Ammunition was provided
in only small amounts, with the intention of exercising control on
dependent groups by forcing them to the MOC for ammunition and
direction.[29] By these restrictions, especially the refusal to allow the
supply of anti-aircraft weapons or impose a no-fly zone, the United
States inhibited the opposition from wearing down the Syrian Army's
military advantages, since Assad could stave off defeat for as long as
he controlled the skies. But that was precisely the point. The opposition may have wanted to depose Syria's president, but the United
States wanted to coerce him to accept a political transition. Their
goals were different.

The United States also demanded that Qatar and Saudi Arabia sort
out the manifest problems in their support programs and ensure
weapons were kept out of extremist hands, which to the Americans—
but not the Saudis, Qataris, and Turks—included the Islamic Front.
But the FSA was hardly distinguishing itself on the battlefield, nor was
it doing a good job of maintaining order in the areas it nominally

controlled, as the Atimeh experience shows. In early December 2013, fearing an imminent ISIS attack, FSA fighters fled from an important storage base near the Bab al-Hawa border crossing, abandoning radios, Kevlar jackets, medicine, trucks, and laptops provided by the United States. The ISIS attack never materialized, but the Islamic Front seized the booty instead. The United States and United Kingdom responded by suspending assistance through that route.[30] Things became even more complicated when the FSA and Islamic Front patched up their differences and began joint operations—a sensible move to enhance the opposition's operational capacity, but one that challenged the neat separation of opposition forces into moderates and extremists in the minds of Western governments.

The United States leaned heavily on Qatar's new emir, Tamim bin Hamad al-Thani, demanding he restrain the emirate's backing for Islamic Front members Ahrar al-Sham and the al-Tawhid Brigade—by then arguably the two most significant military formations in the North (operating in Idlib and Aleppo, respectively). It pressed the Saudis to do the same, efforts that enjoyed some success, evidenced by declining financial support for the Islamic Front and an increase in support for FSA-aligned factions. But things were complicated by the simmering dispute between Saudi Arabia and Qatar over the latter's links to the Muslim Brotherhood. Occasionally tensions boiled to the surface, as when Saudi Arabia and the UAE recalled their ambassadors from Doha in protest in March 2014.[31] In Syria, these tensions ensured the Saudis and Qataris tended still to funnel support to their preferred armed groups rather than the Islamic Front as a whole.

American officials also tried steering the opposition toward combatting ISIS and Al Qaeda rather than Assad. In late 2013 U.S. and Saudi officials met senior opposition fighters, including Islamic Front fighters, to encourage them to attack ISIS and promise further support if they did.[32] The opposition was receptive. ISIS posed an immediate threat, and they were keen to burnish their antiterrorist credentials in Western eyes. In early January 2014 the FSA and Islamic Front, joined later by al-Nusra, conducted an offensive to expel ISIS from their territory. Over four months of bloody fighting, they pushed the group out of Latakia, Hama, Idlib, and parts of Aleppo. In full retreat, ISIS committed bloody massacres of prisoners in Aleppo (January 6 and 8), Raqqa (January 9), and Kantari (January 13).[33] Rather than join the campaign against ISIS, the Syrian Air Force conducted operations against advancing FSA and Islamic Front forces, slowing their advance by concentrating firepower on areas from which the extremists had recently withdrawn.[34] This slowed the collapse of ISIS and allowed the extremists to withdraw from Aleppo in relatively good order and establish themselves in the countryside east of the city. In another sign that, beneath their mutually hostile rhetoric, Damascus and ISIS had shared interests: ISIS helped Damascus by sowing chaos in the opposition and focusing its military activities in areas judged less important by the regime; Damascus helped ISIS meanwhile by leaving it alone except when directly attacked.[35] To ISIS, the Alawites were enemies of the true religion destined for extermination, but for as long as the caliphate could grow by attacking others, it made sense for it to do so. An ISIS counteroffensive was defeated despite frequent use of suicide attacks, and in early February al-Nusra and allies drove it from its stronghold in Deir ez-Zor, seizing control of a swath of territory and oil and gas facilities in Syria's East. ISIS was in full retreat, but another counteroffensive took a greater toll of al-Nusra fighters than Assad's forces had ever managed to do.[36] Jolani demanded the group accept mediation or face destruction, but ISIS refused. Put on the retreat again in Deir ez-Zor and western Syria, the militants strengthened their hold over Raqqa.[37] ISIS may have suffered a reverse, but it exacted a heavy toll on its foes, killing around two thousand opposition fighters.[38] Alarmingly, few in the West seemed to notice Syrian opposition mobilization against ISIS. Almost nothing was done was support them, and it did little to correct the Western view that the opposition was tainted by association with extremism.

Meanwhile, FSA-aligned units, Islamic Front's Ahrar al-Sham, and al-Nusra launched a combined offensive against government positions around Hama, briefly capturing Murak. In the South, the FSA (which remained dominant), Ahrar al-Sham, and al-Nusra launched an offensive on Quneitra, while a group calling itself "Jabhat al-Nusra in Lebanon" targeted Hezbollah inside its Lebanese stronghold in the Beqaa valley.[39] In March al-Nusra and Ahrar al-Sham led an offensive near Latakia to capture the border town of Kessab in the far Northwest. During intense fighting, the Turkish military shot down a Syrian fighter jet it said had crossed the border into Turkish airspace.[40] At the beginning of April, a new and wider offensive was launched in the area. Damascus was on the back foot on several fronts, but elsewhere it too went on the offensive, especially in Aleppo, where indiscriminate bombardment was followed by a land offensive. Government forces and Hezbollah tried to weaken the opposition's hold on areas abutting Lebanon, enjoying a string of victories in the mountains of Qalamun.

GENEVA II

As battles raged, preparations for Geneva II stepped up in winter 2013. Since it was obvious neither side was positioned to negotiate before the end of November, as Brahimi, Kerry, and Lavrov had hoped, the talks were delayed until late February 2014. In the meantime, Syrians faced a bitter winter. The United Nations requested $13 billion to cover global humanitarian needs—the largest call in its history. Half of that was earmarked for Syria.[41] The UN's High Commission for Human Rights uncovered "massive evidence" of war crimes and crimes against humanity, and evidence of criminal culpability at the very highest levels of government. "The scale and viciousness of the abuses," Navi Pillay, the high commissioner, reported, "almost defies belief."[42] The UN's Commission of Inquiry reported widespread enforced disappearances by the Mukhabarat, finding that this, too, constituted crimes against humanity.[43] The armed opposition also committed war crimes, the UN investigators reported, the massacre in the Latakia hills chief among them, but, as before, on a much smaller scale. France's Laurent Fabius thought the prospects for peace at Geneva II grim.[44] Yet with the Security Council deadlocked and the opposition's international "friends" filled with inertia, it was the only game in town.

A new year brought new headaches about the agenda and invitation list. The SOC's commitment remained shaky, not helped by contradictory messages from the "London 11," which in public remained committed to political transition while in private some of its Western members advised the opposition it would have to accept an ongoing role for Assad or his close associates in government. Getting a deal—any sort of deal—and countering terrorism were increasingly the West's priorities now. Opposition delegates sensed that Western governments were shifting toward greater convergence with Moscow on these points.[45] Further signs of convergence were evident in Brahimi's final trilateral meeting of the conference's cosponsors, held in Paris. The Americans and Russians agreed Geneva II should first focus on confidence-building measures such as humanitarian access, local ceasefires, and prisoner exchanges. For Brahimi and the Americans, agreement on these practical issues could create the trust needed to facilitate progress on more difficult questions. But as Moscow saw things, local ceasefires and humanitarian access deals were an alternative to, not pathway toward, political transition. Over time, they became critical parts of Russian—and Syrian—political strategy, a way of distracting the United States and United Nations while also helping extend the government's territorial authority. For now, though, the cosponsors were just happy to find some common ground on which to stand.

The invitation list also proved contentious. The main question here was whether Saudi Arabia and Iran should be invited. John Kerry thought they should be since they held sway over Syria's parties. Including the Saudis would also help repair their strained relationship with Washington. Kerry pressed King Abdullah to support Geneva II, and though still deeply annoyed at Obama's volte-face on the use of force after the chemical attack on eastern Ghouta, he agreed but warned negotiations must not go on indefinitely and that "partial solutions" would "just not do."[46] Iran was more difficult. American openness to including Iran was driven in part by a belief it would help get a deal and in part by overconfidence in the power of U.S. diplomacy. In the spirit of the Obama doctrine, Kerry believed Tehran could be reasoned with to support a peace deal. Contrasting Annan's failure with their own success with Iran in negotiating a nuclear deal, Kerry and his team believed patient U.S. diplomacy could succeed where others had failed. To their minds, this was nothing short of a revolution in U.S. diplomatic affairs, a new doctrine guided by restraint, willingness to see things from other perspectives, and compromise. Brahimi and his UN boss, Ban Ki-moon, agreed it was important to have Iran at the table, as did the Arab League's Nabil El-Araby—though the league was divided since American rapprochement with Iran was a source of great alarm to Saudi Arabia, Qatar, Kuwait, and UAE.[47]

In early January, a couple of days after an interim Joint Plan of Action was concluded with Iran to manage its nuclear program, Kerry hinted publicly that the United States might be willing to include the Islamic Republic in Geneva II. France and Saudi Arabia reacted sharply, insisting Tehran be allowed to participate only if it endorsed the Geneva Communiqué—something it had refused to do.[48] Kerry responded that Iranian participation held the key to diplomatic success and suggested the United States could be flexible on the communiqué. This unleashed a predictable diplomatic storm. Already concerned the ground was being cut away from beneath its feet by Assad's plans to seek reelection in 2014, the SOC threatened to pull out if Iran was admitted without approving the communiqué. Kerry tried to finesse a compromise, suggesting Iran might attend "on the sidelines," something the Iranians found "profoundly insulting."[49] Ban Ki-moon claimed he had persuaded Iran's foreign minister, Javad Zarif, to give informal support to the communiqué and proceeded to invite Iran.[50] This drew a storm of protest from the SOC, Saudi Arabia, and France, who complained (rightly) that Tehran had still not formally endorsed the communiqué. The Saudis and SOC threatened to boycott the talks if Iran attended, forcing Kerry to request that the UN chief rescind Tehran's invitation. Thus it was the United States—which actually supported Iran's inclusion—that was publicly blamed for Iran's exclusion. The whole embarrassing affair exposed not just how fragile Geneva II was but how deep fissures were beginning to emerge among the opposition's "friends" about the future of the Geneva Communiqué. Tehran was incensed and, instead of endorsing the communiqué, pledged support to Syria's presidential election in 2014—nothing short of a full-frontal rebuttal of the whole Geneva process.[51]

Geneva II started badly and got worse from there. It began, on January 22, with a high-level segment in Montreux attended by forty governments. The organizers hoped that by letting so many governments have their say, they could underscore international support for Geneva and persuade the parties to negotiate.[52] But this assumed the forty spectators were themselves united behind the process. In fact, they were not. It was evident from the moment they stepped off the plane that the Syrian government had no intention of negotiating a deal. Its delegation, led by Foreign Minister Walid al-Moualem, was relatively junior, composed mainly of career diplomats and not one of Assad's inner circle (al-Moualem, a Sunni, was not among the almost exclusively Alawite inner circle). This was a team sent to dissemble and delay, not one empowered to do a deal. The foreign minister's opening remarks descended into a bizarre rant that irritated even the usually unflappable Ban Ki-moon.[53] Brahimi recalls, "The Syrian regime only came to Geneva to please the Russians, thinking that they were winning militarily. I told them 'I'm sure that your instructions were: "Go to Geneva. But not only don't make any concessions, don't discuss anything seriously." ' "[54] The SOC's opening remarks, given by its president, Ahmad Jarba, emphasized the regime's litany of atrocity crimes, including the mass torture and killings, and accused it of terrorism and of harboring foreign terrorists like Hezbollah and the Iranian Republican Guards. Kerry, Britain's William Hague, and Turkey's Ahmed Davutoglu hit back at al-Moualem. Lavrov defended the government.[55]

It was an inauspicious start, but Kerry and others hinted that behind the scenes progress was being made on humanitarian issues and local ceasefires. True, on the eve of the summit, Damascus had finally agreed to allow essential aid into Yarmouk, the besieged refugee camp in Damascus that still housed some eighteen thousand people and had been entirely cut off since the previous July. It didn't last, though. In March Yarmouk was sealed off once again—the regime employing malnourishment, deprivation, and aid manipulation as tactics of war. There was also progress around a proposal the United Nations and American Red Cross had been working on for a humanitarian convoy to enter the besieged old city of Homs, where some six thousand people had been besieged by Syrian government forces for almost two years. During that time, the old city had been denied food, water, medical aid, and electricity, bombarded from the air, and subjected to relentless ground attacks by Hezbollah and Iranian Republican Guards. The rebel holdouts were now mainly hardened Islamists allied with al-Nusra. Al-Nusra regularly used car bombings in regime-controlled areas of the city to relieve the pressure, but their targets and victims were mostly civilians.[56] The proposal was broached with Lavrov a week before the Montreux meeting, and the Russian—wanting to divert Geneva II away from political transition by focusing on humanitarian issues—had indicated his support. This, Brahimi, Kerry and others hoped, might be a first confidence-building measure, one that could build the trust needed to drive the peace process forward. For the Russians, though, humanitarian talks were an end in themselves.

The negotiations moved from Montreux to Geneva, where Brahimi engineered proximity talks between the Syrians, hoping he could find enough common ground to enable face-to-face talks the coming Friday. But while he claimed to detect some signs of willingness to discuss humanitarian access, local ceasefires, and prisoner exchanges, Friday arrived with no agreement on any of these issues. Aware the government was trying to divert attention away from the Geneva Communiqué, the opposition demanded the parties recommit to it as a precondition for face-to-face talks. Al-Moualem, unsurprisingly, rejected the demand. He would return to Damascus if no progress was made on confidence building, he warned.[57] Brahimi did his best to paper over the cracks, telling the opposition the government did "accept" the basic formula of the communiqué though its interpretation was different from the opposition's. That wasn't true, and both Brahimi and Jarba knew it. Damascus had never signaled acceptance of the communiqué and was instead advancing an alternative in the form of presidential elections. The Russians meanwhile counseled the government side to not reject the communiqué outright, and, concerned that they not to be held responsible for the talks' failure, the opposition also accepted the fudge that no one believed.

The two sides at last agreed to hold face-to-face talks while more work was done on the plan to deliver relief to the old city of Homs.[58] That involved an ICRC convoy taking essential supplies into the besieged old city and evacuating civilians. With the convoy assembled and ready to move, talks resumed the following Tuesday but broke down: the government argued there were no civilians left in the old city, only terrorists, and proposed a ceasefire in Aleppo instead. That was dismissed by the opposition in part because they thought Homs had greater symbolic value (as the first city shelled by government forces), but also for the more practical reason that it was the Islamic Front, not the SOC, that controlled things in Aleppo. Under pressure from the Russians, the government side changed tack and accepted the evacuation of Homs in principle but argued that only certain categories of civilians be allowed to leave. Men and boys would have to be registered and vetted by the Mukhabarat before being permitted to leave. Food and medicine could not be delivered into Homs, though, since it might fall into the hands of extremists. This was a demand Brahimi and his team thought worth discussing, despite the obvious parallels with the Srebrenica genocide of 1995 where women and girls had been allowed to leave a besieged enclave, while thousands of men and older boys were trapped and executed. Brahimi brushed off suggestions they were analogous, but an ICRC official went public, advising that the plan likely violated International Humanitarian Law.[59] The opposition agreed, adding it had no faith in government assurances, given its record of atrocity crimes. Talks on other confidence-building measures fared little better. A prisoner exchange was scuppered by the government side denying it held tens of thousands of prisoners and claiming that captured government troops were mainly held by terrorists, not formally represented at the talks. The discussion touched only briefly on the Geneva Communiqué, running immediately into the roadblock that the government did not accept even its most basic tenets. The talks broke up, Brahimi reporting "no progress to speak of."[60] He hoped they would reconvene in a couple of weeks, but Al-Moualem would not commit to that.

Back in Syria, the head of the UN's humanitarian mission in Syria, the Sudanese veteran Yacoub El Hillo, took over negotiations on the Homs deal. The government stuck to its offer that some civilians could be evacuated, but others must be inspected by the Mukhabarat. The rebels inside Homs demurred, the most extreme among them preferring to make a last stand. But El Hillo persisted, and a compromise emerged: a three-day "humanitarian pause" in the fighting to allow the delivery of food and evacuation of wounded civilians. A UN and Syrian Red Crescent convoy was allowed to enter Homs, and eighty-six civilians, women with young infants and elderly men, were evacuated in buses escorted by UN vehicles. But the following day a second Red Crescent and UN convoy came under mortar and sniper attack orchestrated by proregime militia and the Homs Mukhabarat.[61] Eleven Syrians, mostly civilians, were killed.[62] Meanwhile, the ICRC and the United Nations reported no easing of restrictions on humanitarian access elsewhere in the country.[63]

The Homs evacuation resumed a few days later, as more people volunteered to leave. The government insisted that men and older boys be assessed by the Mukhabarat first. Made desperate by their squalid conditions and perhaps expecting UN protection, many agreed. As the men stepped off the UN-escorted buses, they were spat on, hit with rifle butts, and verbally abused by government soldiers before a UN official's protests made them stop. Soldiers tried to abduct about a dozen, but another UN official stopped them. But the courage of a couple of UN officials could not paper over the fundamental problem with the deal or compensate for their boss's complicity. The men and boys were taken to a school and forced to participate in a "release ceremony" hosted by the regime's Homs governor and the UN's Yacoub El Hillo. Mukhabarat chiefs cut intimidating figures in the front row as El Hillo launched into a speech praising cooperation between the United Nations and the Syrian government and congratulating the men on being given a new chance by Assad's government. The governor told them they had been caught up in foreign conspiracies. The men the United Nations handed over to the Syrian government began disappearing soon afterward. Some were taken by the Mukhabarat, others were forcibly drafted into the army, and others simply disappeared. The UN's office in Syria denied it had any responsibility for the men's protection once they had been released and did nothing to follow up with the released men or to even check their whereabouts. Homs had been a "successful experiment" that should be replicated elsewhere, El Hillo explained. On the wall behind where he sat was a framed photo of the UN's man handing his credentials to Walid al-Moualem, and beneath that, a portrait of Bashar al-Assad.[64] El Hillo did get his way. Homs became a model for future government operations as, in city after city, government forces encircled and besieged opposition-held areas, bombarded and starved them into submission, and then negotiated the evacuation of whoever was left alive. In all this, the UN team at the Four Seasons Hotel in Damascus, a hotel partly owned by the Assad family, helped, making their organization complicit in a campaign of atrocity crimes. They delivered aid to government areas but not besieged areas, deposited millions of dollars directly into government and Assad-family bank accounts, and facilitated the final evacuations, which completed the forced displacement of civilians opposed to Assad.

The negotiating teams returned to Geneva on February 10. Once more, the government attended only because Russia urged it to. Once more the talks failed from the start. A face-to-face meeting broke down inside thirty minutes, as the government side insisted the negotiations focus on terrorism and bluntly refused to discuss violence reduction or political transition. Brahimi tried meeting it halfway, proposing a new two-day agenda giving equal time to terrorism and the communiqué. The government side said no. Its stubborn refusal, Brahimi later explained, "raises the suspicion of the opposition that, in fact, the government doesn't want to discuss the [transitional governing body] at all."[65] Geneva II had run its course, having achieved nothing. Brahimi later described the talks as an "exercise in futility."[66] "It was a mistake to go to Geneva II," said the envoy who had worked so hard to get there. "Everyone was under pressure to just 'do something,' but we went to Geneva with very little conviction that it would lead anywhere. The government was clear [as] daylight . . . that they were only there because of the Russians and did nothing but parrot the claim that the opposition were terrorists. The opposition . . . didn't represent anybody; for them, getting rid of al-Assad would resolve all issues."[67] Ever determined to be even-handed, Brahimi's criticism of the SOC seems harsh. Jarba and his team were never given an opportunity to represent Syrians, nor did they demand anything beyond what they thought had already been agreed—implementation of Annan's six-point plan and the Geneva Communiqué. Later, reflecting on his experience, Brahimi observed that except for a brief period of doubt in 2012, "it seems to me that Assad has never doubted for a single day that he would win through, and has never for a single day thought about concessions."[68]

As he left, Brahimi apologized for the failure of Geneva II.[69] It was time, he thought, much as Annan had two years before, to confront the fact that only real pressure would bring the parties to implement the Geneva Communiqué. Subsequent meetings with Russia's deputy foreign minister Gennady Gatilov and U.S. under-secretary of state Wendy Sherman yielded no new commitments. Brahimi stressed it was imperative that Assad not set a date for the 2014 elections as this would effectively kill off the Geneva process. But the diplomats washed their hands of it, both telling Brahimi that they had done all they could to encourage their side to negotiate.[70] Kerry and Lavrov, their personal rapport so central to the whole process, traded public barbs: Lavrov insisted America's obsession with regime change caused the talks to fail; Kerry claimed Moscow had broken its commitment to the communiqué. Brahimi traveled to Tehran to see whether Iran could revive the dying peace process. But instead, Javad Zarif and National Security Council Secretary Ali Shemkhani outlined their own four-point alternative to Geneva focused on countering terrorism, ending foreign interference, presidential elections, and an Assad-led government of national unity.[71] France tried desperately to keep the process alive by tabling a draft Security Council statement of support for Brahimi and Geneva, which also demanded that presidential elections be postponed until after a transitional government was established. The Russians rejected it, and despite apparently securing the agreement of the other fourteen members, the French quietly dropped the proposal.

Geneva II was always going to fail, because all the obstacles that had foiled Kofi Annan were still there. Damascus rejected the Geneva Communiqué outright and saw no reason to change its mind. This left the opposition little to negotiate over. For good reason, the SOC had no faith the government would abide by local ceasefires or humanitarian pauses, let alone that these could serve as stepping-stones to meaningful negotiations on political transition. But it was not just that neither side felt much need to compromise: Brahimi had no meaningful compromises to offer. Years later the envoy blamed the West and the opposition for the impasse, claiming it was their refusal to accept that Assad remain in power that had caused him to fail. He claimed the Russians had always had a more realistic view of the situation and that the West should have paid them more attention.[72] The UN's former envoy seemed to be echoing the views of its station-chief in Damascus—the world should learn to live with Assad no matter what he did to the Syrian people. But that is not what Brahimi had said at the time. More than once, Brahimi himself had said Assad would have to step down. More than once, he had complained that it was the government that refused to negotiate or compromise. For all its well-known problems, he had said, the opposition had at least always been prepared to talk.

The portents for peace after Geneva II looked worse than before for two main reasons. First, under the weight of war, both sides were fragmenting. As a result, even had they wanted to compromise, their capacity to do so was shrinking. The opposition's difficulties were well known. The SOC had little presence in Syria and limited influence over the armed groups. What is more, the FSA was in terminal decline in the face of the growing influence of the Islamic Front, al-Nusra, and ISIS. But fragmentation affected the government, too. The Syrian Army was battered and in many parts of the country defeated, propped up by air power, artillery, and foreign allies. Its numbers seriously depleted, the army ceded control of territory to Iranian republic guards, Hezbollah, Iraqi Shi'ite militia, the NDF, *shabiha* gangs, and a growing number of foreign mercenaries.[73] Second, international political positions remained basically unchanged since Geneva I. For all their rhetoric, Lavrov and Kerry were no closer to agreeing on what the communiqué meant, and any momentum created by the chemical weapons deal had long-since stalled. Within a week of Geneva II's collapse, events in Ukraine drove Western-Russian relations toward a new Cold War.

NEW PRIORITIES, NEW STRATEGIES

In late February Viktor Yanukovych, Ukraine's Russian-backed president, was driven out of power by a popular uprising led by pro-European protestors eager that Ukraine conclude a partnership agreement with the European Union. Outraged by what he saw as a Western-orchestrated attack on the Russian near-abroad, Putin sent unmarked Russian forces into Crimea. A few days later, Russia formally annexed Crimea. Then it launched a military campaign supporting Russian separatists in the Donbas region in Ukraine's East. Europe and the United States responded with condemnation and sanctions.

Brahimi limped on for a while, looking for new leverage or angles, but resigned in early May. In a final private briefing to the UN Security Council, the envoy explained that the heart of the problem was Assad's unwillingness to accept the Geneva Communiqué. Plans for a presidential election later in the year were incompatible with Geneva, yet the government had formally announced its intention to hold the election, and Assad lost no time announcing his candidacy.[74] Brahimi blamed the Security Council, too, and especially the West, for its unwillingness to either compel the government or force a compromise with Assad.

On balance, the momentum of battle seemed to be with the opposition as winter turned to spring in 2014, though they were no closer to a decisive breakthrough. Not only were the major Islamists, united through the Islamic Front, now cooperating at the operational level with the FSA, but overall leadership of the armed opposition was tilting away from the extreme radicals and back toward more moderate factors, thanks to the better funneling of U.S., Saudi, and Qatari support. This was especially true in the South around Daraa and northern Idlib, where the MOCs had most influence. Politically, though, the collapse of Geneva was a success for Damascus and a bitter blow for the opposition. The Geneva Communiqué—and with it the idea of a negotiated political transition—was now effectively dead. To underscore that very point, in mid-March Iran convened its own conference on elections, attended by parliamentarians from Russia, Algeria, Iraq, Cuba, Syria, Lebanon, and Venezuela, which conveyed support for Assad's plans to hold elections later that year.

Though it was obvious the U.S. strategy of coercing Damascus to a negotiated political transition was failing, there was no serious discussion of reevaluating that strategy. Instead, the United States made barely perceptible adjustments. Syria's ambassador to the United Nations, Bashar Jaafari, was added to the list of officials subjected to travel restrictions, and Syria was instructed to close its embassy and consulate offices in the United States. Meanwhile, the United States rewarded the SOC for participating in Geneva II by restoring the delivery of nonlethal aid into the North and easing restrictions on the flow of arms through the MOCs. Obama agreed to go one step further in March by permitting the supply of weapons and ammunition to carefully vetted moderates (around fifty armed groups, mostly asso-ciated with the FSA and an emerging southern network backed by Jor-dan) on a limited basis. There were signs of the CIA's support pro-gram bearing fruit. Vetted Northern Brigade (formerly Liwa Fursan al-Haqq) members and the recently formed Harakat Hazzm—a poster child of the new U.S.-Saudi initiative to strengthen the moderate opposition formed by the amalgamation of a dozen smaller groups—employed U.S. BGM-71 TOW anti-tank guided missile systems to good effect around Idlib.[75] Two decades old, these were no better than the Russian- and French-made variants already in opposition hands, but their arrival in greater numbers stiffened opposition capa-bilities and inflicted significant damage on government armor.[76] The weapons were not provided directly by the United States but were likely sourced via Saudi Arabia's extensive stockpile with the Penta-gon's approval, all coordinated by the MOC in Turkey. This was an extension of existing strategy, however, and though the president him-self doubted that U.S. strategy could achieve its stated goals, there was no rethinking of either the goals or the strategy. Instead, the administration became cynical about its own strategy, which, always limited, became half-hearted and badly managed, too.

At the UN Security Council, Australia, Luxembourg, and Jordan argued that the collapse of the Geneva process underscored the need for more humanitarian action, especially an end to sieges, unre-stricted humanitarian access, and the authorization of cross-border deliveries of aid into opposition territory. Russia and China objected: the Russians argued that the council should focus on counterterror-ism; the Chinese, that the peace process should take precedence. But in truth neither seriously opposed the humanitarian track. The Krem-lin was quite comfortable allowing the Security Council to focus on local ceasefires and humanitarian pauses and access, especially if that meant redirecting attention away from political transition.[77] Yet the Russians were in no hurry to agree to a resolution and wanted to see what concessions they could extract in return. Thus Churkin's team raised five concerns with the nonpermanent trio. First, there should be no reference to chapter 7 of the UN Charter or any threat of sanc-tions should the government not comply. Second, the resolution must not single out the government for criticism. Third, there must be no reference to the International Criminal Court (ICC). Fourth, the council must not demand unhindered humanitarian access across Syria's international borders. Fifth, the humanitarian issues must be decoupled from the political issues. Specifically, humanitarian resolutions must not voice support for the Geneva Communiqué—an obvious gambit to undermine the text. Excited they might get a resolution, the three nonpermanent members offered compromises on each of these points: references to chapter 7, the ICC, and the cross-border deliveries were dropped entirely, and criticism of the government became criticism of all parties. At the insistence of the United States, the UK, and France, reference to the Geneva Communiqué was retained, but the reference to political transition was worded so vaguely that Moscow could interpret it as being consistent with its own view on the communiqué. That was enough to satisfy the Kremlin, and Security Council Resolution 2139 was passed unanimously on February 22, 2014. It changed nothing. When France proposed a new initiative, one that might have an effect, Russia and China brought out their vetoes once again to protect Assad and his henchmen.

Francois Hollande's French government was among those most disappointed by Obama's decision not to use force in 2013. Hollande, his activist foreign minister Laurent Fabius, and Eric Chevalier, the former ambassador to Damascus, still believed Obama had made the wrong call. One way of deterring atrocity crimes and ratcheting up pressure on Assad would be to refer Syria to the ICC. Under the court's statute, the Security Council could refer any situation to it for investigation and prosecution, as it had Libya in 2011 (Resolution 1970). The French had delayed pushing the idea to allow the Geneva process to run its course. Now that it had, they were determined to pursue it. Fabius knew that to have any hope of success, the referral would need the support of all the council's nonpermanent members as well as the United States. That would be difficult enough. But if thirteen of the council's fifteen members could be persuaded, then China might also be persuaded to allow a referral, as it had on Libya. In that event, an isolated Moscow might buckle. Fabius knew it would be a long shot, but there was at least a potential path.

The groundwork was laid carefully. France invited UN high commissioner for human rights, Navi Pillay, to brief the council on the human rights situation in Syria. They knew what she would say since

February 12, 2014, the UN's Commission of Inquiry had reported that attacks on civilians, including murder, rape, torture, enforced disappearances, and the denial of food and supplies to civilians, continued with "absolute impunity," and the commissioner's own office had reported on grave violations in besieged areas.[78] Russian diplomats also knew what Pillay would say and tried to block her briefing.

The following month, Chevallier attended a public meeting in Paris hosted by Amnesty International. The meeting concerned a file smuggled out of Syria by a defector code-named "Caesar," a Syrian army photographer who had been given the gruesome task of photographing some of the tens of thousands of detainees tortured to death in prisons like Hospital 601. Caesar courageously smuggled the photos and himself out of Syria. Chevallier had first heard about Caesar when Qatar's foreign minister, Khaled bin Mohammed al-Attiyah, had briefed the "London 11" that January, projecting photos from Caesar's files that showed dozens of tortured, mutilated, and emaciated corpses, some of the victims with their eyes gouged out. The Caesar files contained more than fifty-five thousand such photographs documenting the killing of more than eleven thousand separate detainees. The Caesar files were a smoking gun, clear evidence of widespread and systematic crimes against humanity by the Assad regime. There was no better evidence with which to persuade the council to act.[79] It was no coincidence, therefore, that Chevallier was at the Amnesty meeting that day. He wanted to meet Caesar's group and figure out ways of verifying the files. Afterward, he arranged to travel to Istanbul to meet Caesar himself. Then, with Qatar, he established a team led by Sir Desmond de Silva, former chief prosecutor of the Special Court for Sierra Leone, to study the files and judge their authenticity.[80] De Silva's report, which indeed confirmed that the photos portrayed exactly what they claimed to portray, was presented to an informal "Arria formula" Security Council meeting.[81] The Americans were persuaded, as were the council's wavering nonpermanent members: Argentina, Chad, Jordan, and Rwanda. Support mounted outside the council, too. A year earlier, fifty-six countries had signed a letter calling on the Security Council to refer Syria to the ICC.[82] Now, France recruited sixty-four states to cosponsor its draft resolution. Everything hinged on Moscow and Beijing.

French diplomats circulated their draft resolution in early May. It avoided assigning responsibility and simply called for the ICC to investigate all alleged violations of the Rome Statute, including those perpetrated by the opposition. Ominously, Russian diplomats refused even to engage in serious discussion, prompting others to question whether the draft resolution should be tabled, given that a Russian veto seemed inevitable and the whole thing might complicate negotiations with Assad. The vote came on May 22. Thirteen of the council's fifteen members—including Argentina, Chad, Jordan, Nigeria, and Rwanda—voted to refer the situation in Syria to the ICC. Russia and China cast their vetoes.[83] The Security Council decided there would be no justice for the thousands tortured to death in Assad's prisons, the thousands gassed to death in their basements, or the thousands blown and ripped to pieces by barrel bombs. A few days later, six of the UN Human Rights Council's special rapporteurs warned that the vetoes reinforced Syria's climate of impunity and encouraged more atrocity crimes.[84] The high commissioner for human rights, Navi Pillay, agreed. Tragically for Syria, they were right.

Syrian government forces tightened the screw on the old city of Homs. What was left of it endured intense bombardment until the defenders at last gave up. The UN's ever-compliant Yacoub El Hillo was invited back to supervise an evacuation deal hashed out by Iran, Qatar, and Turkey. It was agreed fighters could be transferred to rebel-held territory further north, in return for which the opposition agreed to release an Iranian woman and seventy Alawite and Shi'ite civilians they held captive.[85] It was a major victory for Assad. Though all he inherited was the devastated shell of a city, Homs had once been a symbolic center for the opposition. Now it was back in government hands. But it was much more than just a symbolic victory. It provided the government a strategic template that it would use again and again in the coming years:

- Step 1: government forces surround and besiege opposition towns and villages, prevent the delivery of humanitarian aid, and indiscriminately bombard areas with impunity—and sometimes gas.
- Step 2: depleted in number, living in utter squalor, malnourished, terrified, and completely demoralized, opposition fighters and civilians either surrender or negotiate their evacuation.

- Step 3: the government allows the United Nations or some other third parties to negotiate a "local ceasefire." "Reconciled" civilians are turned over to the government for assessment, relocation, sometimes imprisonment or forced recruitment; unreconciled civilians and fighters are dispatched with their side arms only to some other rebel-held territory, usually Idlib.

- Behind government lines: foreign aid flows freely thanks to the United Nations and others, mitigating the effects of Western and Arab sanctions and the collapsing economy. Foreign aid also ensures government areas never want for food, medicine, shelter, or any of the other basic supplies opposition areas are being deliberately starved of. This helps the regime sustain and legitimize itself while corroding opposition-held areas.

Thus the manipulation of humanitarian aid became a core plank of the government's siege-and-starvation strategy, the UN's humanitarian and development agencies willing accomplices to atrocity crimes recorded and denounced by the UN's human rights rapporteur and commissioners. This was the course allowed to be set by the failure of Geneva II and the blocking of international criminal justice. It created fertile ground for the rise of Islamist extremism.

7

RISE OF THE CALIPHATE

THE UNITED STATES intervened militarily in Syria in the early fall of 2014, but against the Islamic State (ISIS), not Assad. The rise of ISIS was a disaster for Syria's civilians and opposition and a gift for Assad. Syria's president had always portrayed the opposition as jihadist terrorists and had tried to make them so by releasing imprisoned jihadists onto the streets. The rise of ISIS gave him all the evidence he needed. It supercharged Western fears of Islamist terrorism, justified Russian military intervention, and realigned regional politics. For instance, where Egypt once backed the Muslim Brotherhood, now the sympathies of Abdel Fatteh el-Sisi's military regime, itself backed by Saudi Arabia, lay squarely with Damascus. Inside Syria, ISIS expended far more energy on the opposition than on the government, affording Assad and his allies an opportunity to strengthen their hand in Homs and Damascus.[1] Yet for all their preoccupation with jihadism, Western governments did not see ISIS coming. The CIA had warned of rising Islamism in Syria in mid-2012; Hillary Clinton and David Petraeus had based their case for arming the moderate opposition on the argument it would prevent an opposition slide towards extremism.[2] But Barack Obama had thought a limited footprint the best way of curbing the Islamist threat to the United States. In January 2014 he belittled the ISIS threat, comparing it to a junior varsity football team, a local challenge and nothing more.[3] What the president apparently failed to understand was that ISIS in Syria was a reincarnation of a group that had already wreaked havoc on the United States and its allies: Al-Qaeda in Iraq.

ISIS can be traced to Jordan in the 1990s and Abu Musab al-Zarqawi. After a turbulent youth, Zarqawi had embraced Islamism and joined the mujahedeen battling the Soviets in Afghanistan in 1989. He had a stint in Jordanian prisons before returning to Afghanistan in the late 1990s, where he met al-Qaeda leader Osama bin Laden. Theirs was an uneasy alliance. Zarqawi refused to pledge allegiance to al-Qaeda, and bin Laden objected to the Jordanian firebrand's extreme sectarianism. But he thought Zarqawi could be useful and awarded him control of a training camp. Zarqawi used the opportunity to establish Jama'at al-Tawhid wa'l Jihad, a group composed mainly of militant Jordanians and Palestinians. When the United States invaded Afghanistan after 9/11, Zarqawi was wounded and fled first to Iran and then to Kurdish northern Iraq, where he joined Ansar al-Islam, a Salafist militia led by former al-Qaeda members. It was Zarqawi's presence in Iraq that the United States pointed to when it claimed Saddam Hussein harbored al-Qaeda associates. But Zarqawi was no ally of Saddam's. Nor was he an al-Qaeda member.[4] The U.S.-led invasion of Iraq in 2003 catapulted Zarqawi to prominence by opening a new front in the war between the West and radical Islamism.[5] Zarqawi's group—which now included foreign fighters and former Ba'athists—joined the anti-U.S. insurgency hoping to drive out the invaders and incite a sectarian war to reawaken the Sunni minority.[6] As he saw it, Iraq's Sunnis faced the terrible prospect of democratic government inevitably dominated by Shi'ites, and he was determined not to let the United States hand Iraq over to Iran. On August 7, 2003, Zarqawi's group bombed the Jordanian Embassy in Baghdad, killing seventeen. On August 19 a massive truck bomb destroyed the headquarters of the newly installed UN Assistance Mission in Iraq (UNAMI) at the Canal Hotel, killing more than twenty. Ten days later they detonated a suicide bomb outside the Shia Imam Ali Mosque, killing at least ninety-five. In May 2004 they beheaded the American Nicholas Berg.[7] In October that year, Zarqawi finally pledged allegiance to bin Laden and rebranded his militia Al-Qaeda in Iraq (AQI). By 2006, AQI exerted control over much of Sunni-dominated western Iraq and had begun imposing its extreme interpretation of Sharia law, refashioning itself as the Islamic State of Iraq (ISI). That put Zarqawi squarely in American crosshairs, and on June 7, 2006, he was killed by U.S. special forces.

ISI's growing dominance provoked a backlash. Iraq's fiercely proud Sunni tribes resented the outsider, Zarqawi, and bridled at ISI's extremism. Tribal leaders joined forces in September 2006 to expel ISI from Anbar province. This was the beginning of the Sunni "Awakening," which the United States was quick to take advantage of as part of its "surge" strategy. Washington formed alliances with the Awakening councils, providing arms, money, and military help to the tribal militia, which by 2007 numbered some eighty thousand.[8] Under concerted pressure, ISI lost its grip across much of Anbar but retained a foothold further north, especially in Mosul, Iraq's second city, where it established a clandestine network. It reverted to terrorism, hoping to spark a sectarian war it could feed from. On August 14, 2007, it bombed the Yazidi towns of Til Ezer and Siba Sheikh Khidir, killing 796 Yazidis and wounded more than 1,500: a warning of what was coming.[9]

The Awakening dealt a serious blow to ISI, and by mid-2009 it had been reduced to a small underground network once again, incapable of holding territory, let alone governing. Approximately three-quarters of its senior leaders had been killed or captured.[10] But the incoming Obama administration was less interested in exploiting this advantage than in pulling up the drawbridge on U.S. involvement in Iraq, and so the United States withdrew support from its Sunni allies and stood aside when Iraq's sectarian Shi'ite president, Nouri al-Maliki, used underhanded tactics to cling to power.[11] The gains made by the Awakening were whittled away. Increasingly beholden to Shi'ite strongmen and Iran, Maliki's government became more sectarian, and discrimination against Sunnis became widespread and systematic. ISI offered disaffected Sunnis money, arms, encouragement, and an ideology. Many of its imprisoned leaders were released as the Americans withdrew from Iraq and people lost interest. Among them was Abu Bakr al-Baghdadi, an Islamic scholar with extreme Salafist views. He had founded a militia in late 2003 but was captured in Fallujah and held alongside hardened jihadists at the U.S.-run Camp Bucca. Al-Baghdadi used his prison time productively, inserting himself into jihadist circles and spreading radical ideas about a new Sunni caliphate. After his release from prison, he joined ISI and climbed to become its leader. Under his leadership, in 2012 and 2013 ISI orchestrated a series of prison breaks that brought hundreds of experienced jihadists into its ranks.[12] His political agenda extended well beyond Iraq, and al-Baghdadi established an ISI franchise in Syria that we have already met: Jabhat al-Nusra. But when he tried reintegrating al-Nusra back into ISI in April 2013, al-Nusra's leadership resisted, preferring instead to keep their focus squarely on ousting Assad. That marked the birth of ISIS—the Islamic State of Iraq and Syria, sometimes also referred to as ISIL (Islamic State of Iraq and the Levant) or simply IS (Islamic State)—and its struggle for a region-wide caliphate. While Syria burned, ISIS focused its efforts on Iraq, where it waged a campaign of murder and intimidation. By the end of 2013, ISIS had amassed an underground network of followers across western Iraq, especially in Mosul, Fallujah, and Tikrit.[13]

ISIS ranks swelled with foreign fighters. Many were encouraged to take up arms by the violent overthrow of Mohammed Morsi's Muslim Brotherhood government in Egypt. The Brotherhood had stood apart from other branches of Sunni conservatism by insisting that Islamic government could be built through the ballot box. Morsi's rise had seemed to vindicate that claim, but his violent removal dashed those hopes. Angry Islamists across the Middle East and Europe looked for new leadership. They found it in al-Baghdadi.[14] Some of ISIS's foreign fighters came from the Russian Caucasus, and there are even reports Russian intelligence may have helped them get to the Middle East, intent they should never return to Russia.[15] Whatever the case, by the end of 2013, with its underground network in Iraqi cities and backbone of foreign fighters, ISIS was ready to strike. But where? Between its creation in mid-2013 and the June 2014 offensive in Iraq, ISIS had not fared particularly well in Syria. Lacking popular support, relatively small in size, and composed primarily of foreign fighters, it had been subjected to a withering offensive by the FSA, Islamic Front, and al-Nusra in the first weeks of 2014, which had succeeded in pushing the group out of population centers (see chapter 6). It was failure in Syria that prompted ISIS to go on the offensive in Iraq.

THE STORM BREAKS

June 3, 2014, was a portentous day. In Syria, Assad romped to victory in his sham presidential election designed to undercut the Geneva Communiqué. The voting was conducted only in government-held areas and was obviously rigged. Assad secured 88.7 percent of the vote and another seven years in power. But as the votes were being tallied in Damascus, neighboring Iraq was being plunged into crisis. ISIS fighters in utility trucks and stolen Iraqi Army Humvees stormed into the city of Samarra, capturing most of the city before being repulsed by security forces. They attacked Mosul, Iraq's second city, the following day. They were initially repulsed there, too, but launched a new attack on June 9. With a force of just thirteen hundred, they pushed around thirty thousand Iraqi troops into retreat and took the whole city in a single day, and with it a huge bounty of U.S.-made military vehicles, weapons, and ammunition. When they overran the city's Badush prison, the extremists separated the Sunni and Shi'ite prisoners, forced at least 670 Shi'ites to kneel beside a ravine, and shot them.[16] Other massacres followed. ISIS encircled Tikrit, causing mass panic as soldiers and police fled, throwing off their uniforms. Hundreds were captured, and according to Human Rights Watch, 770 executed. ISIS itself claimed to have killed 1,700.[17] At Camp Speicher, 1,500 Shi'ite air cadets were captured and executed.[18] Tel Afar fell on June 15, and 170 captured Iraqi soldiers were killed. Two weeks later, ISIS shocked global Islamism by declaring a caliphate under the leadership of Abu Bakr al-Baghdadi.[19] Iraq splintered in less than a week and was in danger of collapsing entirely. Baghdad found itself dependent on two groups whose principal loyalties lay elsewhere. In the North, Kurdish Peshmerga moved quickly to secure territory, including Kirkuk, and block the extremists.[20] From Karbala in the South, Shi'ite militia were bused northward, and hundreds of Shi'ites in eastern Baghdad signed up to reinforce the capital's defense.

Events in Iraq had an immediate impact on Syria. There, an immediately revitalized ISIS had three main priorities: secure its "capital" in Raqqa (from which it had been recently ousted by FSA and Islamic Front elements), secure an access route for foreign fighters by establishing itself along the Syria-Turkey border (which brought it into conflict with the Kurds), and control the Euphrates corridor into Iraq (which required a new push into Deir ez-Zor province in Syria's East).[21] ISIS poured recently captured arms into Deir ez-Zor as forces from Raqqa advanced south to take the governate and connect with ISIS forces running amok across the border in Iraq's Anbar province.[22] They routed al-Nusra and other opposition groups and seized almost the whole governate—and with it more than half of Syria's oil production capacity—in just ten days.[23] Their military and financial prowess encouraged dozens of eastern Syria's tribes and factions to join up, and ISIS reportedly paid as much as $2 million to secure tribal loyalty. The comparatively generous salaries it paid its fighters lured them away from other groups.[24] Those who didn't join up suffered a terrible fate. The al-Shaitat tribe resisted, but when they were defeated, ISIS shot, beheaded, and crucified at least seven hundred of their men. (Evidence from mass graves suggests closer to nine hundred.)[25]

Having defeated ISIS once, the Syrian opposition launched a new offensive against them in Aleppo. But ISIS now had much better armaments, more fighters, and much more money—the latter in part thanks to Damascus, which bought its oil and gas from the extremists.[26] The beleaguered FSA and its allies found themselves targeted by both the regime and ISIS, while Damascus presented itself as a victim of terrorism. ISIS turned its guns seriously on the Assad regime only in July, first taking the al-Shaer gas field in Homs governate (July 16), executing more than two hundred prisoners and then attacking regime units in the governates of Hasakeh, Aleppo, Deir ez-Zor, and Raqqa. By July 25 the main military bases in Raqqa and Hasakeh were in ISIS hands.[27] Yet despite all this, Syria's air force refrained from striking the organization's headquarters in Raqqa, causing consternation for some of the regime's supporters.[28] ISIS also took its campaign into Europe, inspiring Islamist terrorism there. On May 24 Mehdi Nemmouche, a French and Algerian citizen, killed four people at the Jewish Museum in central Brussels. It later emerged he had traveled to Syria in 2012 and spent a year there training and fighting with the extremists.[29] Terrified Europeans saw Syria as the source of this Islamist threat and concluded that their governments should prioritize countering this, not ousting Assad.

Under stress at home and abroad, divisions within Syria's opposition became more pronounced. An increasingly anxious al-Nusra tried to stem the defection of its fighters to ISIS by imposing stricter Sharia law in the parts of Idlib it controlled and conducting "anticorruption" campaigns against FSA-aligned people in Aleppo and Deraa.[30] This put them on a collision course with moderates. In response to the new challenge, in early August a group of Islamic preachers and Muslim Brotherhood members in Idlib launched the "Watasimo" (hold fast) initiative, an attempt to unify opposition forces in the North, under a Revolutionary Command Council (RCC) of twenty-six representatives who would coordinate Syrian opposition forces. Heavily backed by Turkey and Qatar, on whom many of the groups were dependent, the initiative quickly gathered momentum.[31]

INHERENT RESOLVE

Mosul's fall stunned political leaders in the West. Obama was incensed that the expensively constructed Iraqi Army had melted away so easily and irritated he had not been forewarned about ISIS. He was also frustrated at being backed into a corner he didn't want the be in—forced to choose between sending U.S. forces back into Iraq and possibly watching the state, for which so much American blood had been spilt, collapse. Beyond that, the rise of ISIS reinforced the growing sense that it was Sunni jihadism, not Assad or Iran, that posed the gravest danger to regional security and U.S. interests.[32] In the longer term, it gave the West common cause with Assad and moved opinion closer to Russia's point of view.[33] But at that moment there was an immediate problem to address—that of defending Iraq.

Maliki pleaded for immediate U.S. assistance to shore up his government, but Obama was hesitant. On the one hand, the Americans "needed a policy that would ensure that they [ISIS] never achieved the full-fledged caliphate they sought," recalled John Kerry.[34] But on the other, Maliki was part of the problem: in the words of Susan Rice, he was a "venal Shia sectarian whom we did not trust to govern in the interests of all Iraqis."[35] Without fundamental political reform, military aid would do little more than paper over the cracks. To address the immediate security concerns of Americans in Iraq, the president authorized a small deployment of 275 ground troops: around 170 to secure and support the U.S. Embassy in Baghdad, and the rest deployed in Qatar, ready for insertion into Iraq at short notice if needed.[36] Over the next month, a small number of U.S. special forces provided support to the Kurdish peshmerga in northern Iraq, but it wasn't enough to stem the tide.

It was not only Washington that was stunned by the collapse of Mosul and seemingly relentless march of ISIS: Tehran was, too. The Islamic Republic had also underestimated ISIS, but that changed as Humvees and technicals bearing the extremists' black flags hurtled across the Iraqi desert. Iran drew its own "red line," announcing that any attempt by ISIS to seize the holy Shi'ite cities of Karbala and Najaf would provoke direct intervention. It also summoned Shi'ite militia to counter the threat and responded positively and quickly to Baghdad's request for Russian ammunition to replenish its depleted stocks.[37] Russia, too, offered help, supplying Baghdad with Su-25 aircraft and military advisers.[38]

In early August 2014 ISIS seized the Yazidi-majority town of Sinjar and unleashed genocide. Yazidi men and older boys were rounded up and executed, while thousands of Yazidi women and girls were kidnapped into sexual slavery.[39] Women deemed too old or ugly for sex were killed and buried in mass graves. The battered and traumatized survivors fled to the barren Mount Sinjar. There they would be safe for a time from ISIS, but since there was no food, little water, and scarce shelter, they could not survive there long.[40] Those who tried to flee the mountain were captured by ISIS, and many were killed. None of this should have come as a surprise. The Yazidis had cooperated with U.S. occupation forces in Iraq and been targeted by ISIS before. The U.S. leadership met in the White House Situation Room to consider its options. Kerry recalled the "unspoken but palpable" reality that a president elected to end a war in Iraq was now deciding whether to join a new war to protect the Yazidis from genocide and defeat ISIS.[41] The pressure to act was immense. Kerry, Ben Rhodes, and Samantha Power pressed Obama to order air strikes and drop supplies to the Yazidis. The president agreed the United States should use its capabilities "carefully and responsibly" to prevent massacres where it could but doubted that was possible in Syria and was reluctant to give military support to al-Malaki.[42] It was not just the Yazidis who were imperiled, though, since ISIS threatened Iraq itself and was already championing terrorism in the West. This was a national security issue, not an exclusively humanitarian one. That sentiment was reflected in American public attitudes. More than two-thirds of Americans polled signaled support for military action against ISIS, though most were uncertain about the objectives, and only around half supported the use of ground forces.[43] Public support for war with ISIS was sustained over time, reflecting the fact that most Americans saw ISIS as a threat to them.[44]

To confront ISIS meant going to war. Obama recognized that but wanted military action to be part of a broader political strategy, not an end in itself. The United States would use force, he decided, so long as three conditions were met: progress toward better governance in Iraq (the replacement of Maliki with a less divisive figure), a coalition of allies committed to the campaign, and a viable long-term political strategy.[45] But what about congressional support? Little more than a year after he'd made a principled defense of congressional authorization for the use of force, the president now decided the general authority granted after 9/11 to combat al-Qaeda gave him authority to undertake an open-ended mission against ISIS.[46] It is difficult to think of a clearer example of how priorities—in this case the priority afforded the war against ISIS by its association with national security as compared to the lesser priority afforded the protection of Syrians, seen as a humanitarian issue—shape the realm of the politically possible. The State Department drew up a plan that situated air strikes within a broader strategy to counter ISIS, which included going after the group's finances, stopping the flow of money, oil, and foreign fighters to it, challenging its propaganda, and building a broad anti-ISIS coalition, while using air power and local allies to degrade the group's military capacity.[47]

Kerry assumed it would be difficult to build the sort of international coalition Obama wanted, anticipating that Sunni leaders in Saudi Arabia, the Gulf, and Turkey might be wary about aligning themselves on the wrong side of the sectarian divide. Some had earlier raised the possibility of moving against ISIS and other extremists only after Assad was deposed.[48] What is more, King Abdullah bin Abdulaziz of Saudi Arabia was still angry about the Iran nuclear deal and the U.S. decision to step back from its red line on chemical weapons. But it transpired that Kerry was pushing at an open door. Whatever their reservations, Sunni governments themselves feared ISIS and knew it was imperative that they be seen to be countering it.[49] King Abdullah convened a regional meeting in Jeddah to marshal support for the campaign against ISIS that comprised ministers from Egypt, Jordan, Lebanon, Kuwait, Bahrain, Oman, Qatar, Saudi Arabia, Iraq, the UAE, and Turkey, all of whom were only too keen to enlist America's help.[50] Meanwhile, the Saudis, Qataris, and Turks agreed that Syria's new realities required that they set aside their differences and work together to corral the opposition into a more effective political and military force. Support from other Western governments was also not difficult to find: France, Germany, Canada, the Netherlands, and Australia quickly lined up to join the emerging coalition. On September 26 the British House of Commons voted 524–43 to permit British air strikes against ISIS in Iraq.[51] Clearly, the sense that ISIS threatened *British* security (rather than merely that of Syrians) easily overwhelmed any doubts Parliament may have had about open-ended military interventions. Indeed, despite energetic campaigning by leftists like Jeremy Corbyn and the "Stop the War" coalition, who even opposed military action to protect Yazidis from genocidal massacre, around 60 percent of British people polled supported military action against ISIS, even if it meant acting in Syria as well as Iraq— another stark contrast with public attitudes when it was only Syrians under threat.[52] By early 2015 more than sixty governments were part of the coalition, and by 2016 Australia, Canada, France, and the Netherlands had all extended military operations into Syria.

Satisfied he had sufficient political support but still uneasy about propping up Maliki and uncertain about his long-term strategy, on

August 7, 2014, Obama authorized a characteristically limited air campaign against ISIS in Iraq (ISIS operations in Syria would continue unmolested for another month). Initial planning tasked the U.S. military with protecting American installations and personnel embedded with the Kurdish peshmerga and targeting ISIS forces attacking Yazidis on Mount Sinjar. Transport aircraft would deliver much-needed food, water, shelter, and medical supplies to the imperiled people trapped on the mountain. This was not, the president explained, the start of a major new military engagement in the Middle East, but a modest and limited response to a grave threat.[53] In truth, the administration was unsure about what it was getting into, how it would prevail, how long and big the commitment would be, and what victory would look like. In other words, it had no clearer idea about where this intervention would lead than it had had about where a military response to chemical weapons use in Syria would take it, but because it believed its own security was at stake, it decided to take the plunge anyway. The one thing the president was clear on was that there would be no major deployment of American ground forces. Iraqi and Kurdish forces must take the lead in ground combat.

Operation "Inherent Resolve" as it became known, slowed ISIS advances in northern Iraq and, combined with peshmerga efforts on the ground, relieved the immediate pressure on Yazidi survivors, who were able to flee ISIS and reach the relative safety of Kurdish Iraq. ISIS retaliated by beheading kidnapped American journalist James Foley—subject of a failed rescue operation by U.S. special forces in early July.[54] By publicizing their brutality so openly, ISIS hoped to draw in followers and terrify their opponents. In the first aim, ISIS initially succeeded, and foreign jihadists joined in huge numbers, estimates suggesting that as many of two-thirds of ISIS fighters in Syria were foreign, most coming from Saudi Arabia, Libya, and Tunisia, bolstered by a hardened elite from Chechnya and Dagestan.[55] With respect to the second goal, the murder of James Foley and other brutal atrocities were counterproductive and produced a collective determination to defeat the extremists that proved to be their undoing. Seeking to exploit the opportunity to reorient international policy toward Syria this presented, in late June Russia proposed that the Security Council adopt measures to prevent ISIS and al-Nusra from raising revenue by selling oil abroad, a move broadly welcomed by the West. In August Russia and China embraced a British-drafted resolution that targeted the extremists' finances, moved to prevent the inflow of foreign fighters, and imposed sanctions on six leaders, including Abu Bakr al-Baghdadi (Resolution 2170, August 15, 2014). The following month Obama chaired a high-level meeting of the Security Council that adopted another resolution with ISIS and the other extremists in its crosshairs (Resolution 2178, September 24). Resolution 2178 called on all states to prevent the flow of foreign fighters to terrorist organizations, ISIS, al-Qaeda, and al-Nusra especially.

This activism slowed ISIS's advance in Iraq but did not altogether stop it because the group's nerve center was not in Iraq but in Syria and the caliphate's "capital," Raqqa. When ISIS forces were attacked in Iraq, they could slip to safety across the border in Syria, where Operation Inherent Resolve made little difference. ISIS adapted by hunkering down in Iraq and using its vast stockpile of stolen vehicles, arms, and ammunition to go on the offensive in Syria. It captured the Tabqa air base—the last government-held position in Raqqa governate—from the Syrian Army and launched a devastating raid on the al-Sha'er gas fields close to historic Palmyra. All the while the litany of ISIS massacres grew. Approximately four hundred soldiers taken captive during the advance on Sha'er were executed, causing panic among Syria's Alawites and an outpouring of complaints about the government's failure to protect them.[56] Iran, Hezbollah, and Shi'ite militias responded by taking more prominent roles, not just in the campaign against ISIS but in the government's war effort overall.

The spiraling chaos threatened to push the war westward into Lebanon and the Golan Heights. On August 28 al-Nusra and Ahrar al-Sham attacked Syrian Army positions in Quneitra, along the border of the UN-policed Golan Heights. This was not the first time they had entered the zone but was the most aggressive incursion yet. After heavy fighting, al-Nusra captured several border posts as well as forty-five Fijians serving as UN peacekeepers. They also surrounded two other UN observation positions held by seventy-two Filipino peacekeepers and offered safe passage in return for their weapons. The Filipinos refused. After two days of tense standoff, al-Nusra fighters attacked one of the Filipino positions and met fierce resistance. During a seven-hour firefight, in which three al-Nusra fighters were killed, the Filipinos fought off their assailants. Meanwhile, with the militants focused on one of the observation posts, Irish peacekeepers helped peacekeepers at the other post escape. Unable to take the post by force, al-Nusra imposed a blockade on the remaining Filipino position, manning the siege with an estimated two hundred fighters and twenty vehicles. The UN's force commander, India's General Iqbal Singha, ordered the peacekeepers to surrender, but the Filipino chief of staff refused. On the night of August 30, the besieged Filipinos escaped across the lines to safety. Singha later accused them of "cowardice" for refusing to surrender, but the Filipinos had acted with bravery and dealt a blow to the extremists by refusing to buckle. Singha himself was at fault for having taken too long to reposition his troops when the threat first emerged. During the crisis itself, he evinced little idea about how to respond beyond capitulation, leaving his troops to figure it out for themselves. The Fijians who surrendered spent two weeks detained by al-Nusra before their release was negotiated by Qatar. The Filipino government withdrew its peacekeepers from the UN Disengagement Observer Force (UNDOF), citing a loss of confidence in the mission's leadership. General Singha was relieved of his duties the following year.[57] Subsequent offensives left the opposition with around 70 percent of Quneitra governate bordering Golan by mid-September.[58]

Despite its slowing advance in Iraq, ISIS remained on the front foot into September, helped by sanctuary and resupply from Syria. On September 2 the extremists released footage of the beheading of another American hostage, Steven Sotloff. Panicked Americans demanded a military response. But though Obama realized he would have to escalate military operations, he remained painfully aware of the traps. "I can see how the Iraq War happened," he told Ben Rhodes, "people are so scared . . . it'd be easy for me as president to get on that wave and do whatever I want."[59] Obama feared that was a path back toward endless war. So while he accepted the need to expand anti-ISIS operations, he required that strict limits be imposed, much to the chagrin of the Pentagon. In particular, he insisted the United States would not assume primary responsibility for defeating ISIS in Iraq: that was Baghdad's job. It would deploy advisers to help the Kurdish peshmerga, but only in small numbers; air strikes would be expanded to include ground support to allies, but only in a limited fashion. One of the principal political obstacles to doing more was removed in early September with Maliki's resignation. Under intense pressure from Washington to step aside, Maliki was then abandoned by Tehran too, which proved decisive. He was replaced by the less obviously sectarian Haider al-Abadi.

Iran's role in the removal of Maliki underscored just how dependent U.S. strategy had become on the Islamic Republic. Iran was crucial to the defense of Baghdad, and its Quds force and proxy Iraqi Shi'ite militia were pivotal to the ground campaign against ISIS in areas not abutting Kurdish lands. Shi'ite militias deployed alongside regular Iraqi Army units in increasing numbers. This uneasy dependence impacted the administration's thinking on Syria since it worried any future confrontation with Assad (for example, over chemical weapons usage) might expose the approximately three thousand American troops inside Iraq to attack by Iranian proxies or their abandonment and exposure to ISIS.[60] More likely, though, was the possibility that Iran might simply hold back support for anti-ISIS operations in Sunni majority areas where it had fewer direct interests, leaving the United States to shoulder the responsibility. In the immediate term, however, containing ISIS displaced the administration's other regional concerns, including Assad, and on this the United States saw Iran as a key partner. On Syria, U.S. leaders came to see the relationship between ISIS and Assad in increasingly zero-sum terms whereby weakening the latter would only help the former. Since defeating ISIS was the priority, there was less incentive to coerce Assad. That raised questions about whether the United States should continue providing arms and nonlethal support to Syria's opposition since this could help the extremists. U.S. TOWs (tube-launched, optically tracked, wireless-guided weapons) were in circulation by the fall of 2014, exacting significant casualties on government armor, and it was not long before both al-Nusra and ISIS were filmed using the sophisticated U.S. weapons, having captured them from their initial recipients.[61] Some suggested the United States should rethink its approach to arming Syria's opposition.

As summer waned, it was evident that since ISIS could not be defeated in Iraq alone, it would have to be challenged in Syria, too. But the situation there was more fraught. Iran acquiesced to U.S. intervention in Iraq but would be much less welcoming in Syria. And while U.S. and coalition aircraft enjoyed freedom of the skies above Iraq, they would not enjoy the same over Syria. Not only did the Syrian government have Russian-made air defense systems capable of threatening U.S. aircraft, Iran deployed portable anti-aircraft weapons there, too. Confrontation over Syria might derail the relationship with Iran, imperiling cooperation in Iraq and the nuclear deal. But against all that, the Pentagon's advice was clear: that ISIS could not be defeated comprehensively unless Inherent Resolve was extended into Syria. Characteristically, the president was unhappy at being asked to escalate the war while there was still no comprehensive strategy for defeating ISIS. Only when that was done did he accept the case for expanding military operations, and on September 10 Obama publicly announced a strategy to "degrade and ultimately destroy" ISIS.

There was nothing especially novel about the plan, but its articulation underscored just how far American priorities in Syria had shifted from coercing Assad to defeating ISIS. The first strand of the strategy involved a concerted air campaign targeting ISIS members "wherever they are," including in Syria. The target set would be expanded to the organization's leadership, operational capacity, and logistics. Securing airspace over Syria meant cooperating with the government in Damascus. The Pentagon initially claimed there would be no cooperation beyond a message from Samantha Power to her Syrian counterpart at the UN providing forewarning of U.S. plans and likely target areas.[62] But in practice, the U.S. Air Force informed Damascus of its operations and deconflicted them with other military flights, agreeing to share the skies with the Syrian Air Force as it pummeled civilian areas. The second strand involved increased support for local allies. The United States would "lead from behind" by backing allies on the ground rather than committing its own troops. The seeds had been sown shortly after the fall of Ramadi when U.S. special forces embedded themselves within peshmerga units to coordinate close air support for Kurdish ground operations. The president still doubted Syria's armed opposition but recognized an effective ground presence was necessary to defeat ISIS. One option, deferring to Assad, was unacceptable. The other was to identify and support armed groups judged reliably willing to counter ISIS. This involved expanding and repurposing the assistance program to Syria's opposition. Back in June the White House had asked Congress for $500 million to support a train-and-equip program to help select Syrian opposition groups combat ISIS. Now, Obama announced the United States would increase that support in both Iraq and Syria. In Iraq, the principal beneficiaries would be the Iraqi government—supported by a new team of 475 Americans—and the Kurdish peshmerga. In Syria, the United States would help construct a force of five thousand carefully vetted opposition fighters to battle ISIS. Where U.S. military assistance to Syria's opposition had once focused on increasing pressure on Assad, it would now be focused on countering ISIS. The strategy's third element involved combating ISIS's global propaganda.[63]

While those around the SOC welcomed American support—they had, after all, been battling ISIS for much of the past year—many opposition figures worried about the implications. Syria's Muslim Brotherhood voiced opposition to any foreign intervention not targeting the government.[64] Iranian and Russian attitudes were mixed. On the one hand, they welcomed the obvious drift in Western priorities toward closer alignment with their own. On the other, they publicly opposed extension of U.S. coalition activities into Syria and worried that having crossed the threshold on using military force, the United States and allies might later broaden their campaign to include Assad in their crosshairs, too. The Syrian government shared that fear and warned any use of force without its consent would be regarded as an act of aggression, but its overriding concern to avoid conflict with the Americans meant that in practice it did little to hinder U.S. operations.[65] At the time, Assad and his allies did not know for sure that there was no likelihood of the United States expanding its campaign in the way they feared. If anything, it was the very idea of a political transition in Syria that was being questioned in the White House. At the November 2014 G20 meeting in Brisbane, Australia, Obama spoke of the need for a "political solution eventually within Syria that is inclusive of all the groups who live there"—including those still loyal to Assad. Asked whether the leaders were discussing ways of removing Assad through political transition, Obama replied "no."[66] A few weeks earlier, Lakhdar Brahimi had explained to an audience in London that Syria's president was being far from delusional in continuing "to bet on the military solution" and for thinking he could ultimately "win and recover rule over all of Syria."[67]

But it was not the subtleties of American policy at the forefront of Vladimir Putin's mind as he returned home from Brisbane. The G20 was overshadowed by war in Ukraine and the downing of Malaysian airliner MH17 by Russian-backed separatists using sophisticated weaponry given to them by Russia. Western leaders, including the Australian host Tony Abbott, whose country had lost twenty-seven citizens when MH17 was destroyed, were determined to make a point. Hectored by the Australian press to explain how he would address the visiting Russian president, the combative Abbott promised to "shirt-front" Putin—a colloquialism for hitting someone in the chest drawn from Australian rules football. Putin came armed: accompanying his aircraft, four naval vessels, including a destroyer and a guided-missile cruiser, approached the Australian coast unannounced, prompting the Australians to dispatch two frigates and an aerial surveillance aircraft to keep tabs on them. There was no "shirt-fronting," but there was plenty of humiliation for Putin. There was no question that Barack Obama was the star of the show in Brisbane as thousands lined the street to catch a glimpse of the president. By contrast, half of the Australians polled believed Putin should not have even been invited. When it came to the group photo, Putin was placed not in his customary position in the center with Obama and Chinese leader Xi Jinping but on the edge next to South Africa's Jacob Zuma. At the leaders' lunch, Putin was shown to a table accompanied only by Brazil's Dilma Rousseff. When he reached to greet Canada's Stephen Harper with a handshake, the Canadian responded, "I guess I'll shake your hand but I have only one thing to say to you: you need to get out of Ukraine."[68] Unaccustomed to this sort of treatment, Putin left the G20 early, resolved to not accept any future invitations to visit the West until he—and Russia—could be sure of receiving the deference and respect they believe they deserved. It took the Russian president less than a year to reassert his country's status as a great power that others should pay attention to, an achievement that owed much to Russia's policy on Syria.

THE BATTLE FOR KOBANE

On September 16, 2014, ISIS launched a major offensive against Syria's Kurdish heartland, aiming for the strategic town of Kobane, abutting the Turkish border. The Kurdish peshmerga had already established themselves as the extremists' principal enemies in Iraq. In Syria, Kurdish Rojava posed an ideological as well as strategic threat to the extremists. Its secular administration was an abomination, good only for extermination, but Rojava also stood in the way of ISIS securing contiguous territory stretching from Raqqa through Deir ez-Zor to Mosul and the lucrative oil and gas fields there. It also commanded access to Turkey. An unusually large ISIS force, including tanks, armored vehicles, and artillery, caught the YPG by surprise and captured fifty villages and towns as it moved close to Kobane's outskirts.[69] With ISIS forces poised to strike Kobane, spokesman Abu Muhammed al-Adnani issued a chilling call for jihadists everywhere to launch lone-wolf attacks to kill disbelieving Americans, Europeans, Australians, and Canadians in "any manner or way." "If you are not able to find an IED or a bullet, then . . . smash his head with a rock, or slaughter him with a knife, or run him over with your car, or throw him down from a high place, or choke him, or poison him."[70]

Al-Adnani's blood-curdling call to arms certainly provoked a wave of ISIS-inspired terrorism and reinforced the deep sense of panic in the West. But it also galvanized support for beleaguered Kobane, now a heroic symbol of resistance to ISIS. The commander of U.S. CENTCOM forces, General Lloyd Austin, advised Obama that Kobane would fall unless the YPG received urgent U.S. aid. He also counseled that the YPG was the best possible local ally the United States could find to lead the ground war against ISIS in Syria since it was battle-hardened, committed, and reliably secular. The United States should set aside concerns about its ties to the PKK and support the YPG, he argued, starting with the defense of Kobane.[71] The president broadly agreed but was more cautious than Austin about allying so fulsomely with the YPG. On September 22 the United States launched its first round of strikes in Syria, targeting ISIS positions in Raqqa, Deir ez-Zor, and Hasakah. Aircraft from Bahrain, Saudi Arabia, Jordan, Qatar, and the UAE also participated in the first wave. Drones, missiles, and aircraft also targeted Raqqa and al-Nusra elements in Aleppo and Idlib that U.S. intelligence alleged were part of the "Kharosan group," a high-level al-Qaeda cell planning terrorist operations against the West.[72]

Some analysts reckoned the attack on the Kharosan group was more about stiffening moderate forces around Aleppo than anything else. Whatever the intent, it set the tone for the rest of the campaign. Whether on the ground or in the UN Security Council, the West insisted on treating ISIS and al-Qaeda-affiliated al-Nusra as part of a common problem—a position that accorded well with Russia's view. As Moscow saw it, linking ISIS to al-Nusra was a way of discrediting much of Syria's armed opposition since even moderates such as the FSA and more moderate Islamists like the Islamic Front sometimes fought alongside al-Nusra.

The extension of Operation Inherent Resolve into Syria didn't immediately halt ISIS in its tracks, and its fighters pressed on toward Kobane. In early October U.S. State Department officials traveled to Kobane and other places to test Kurdish reliability and to assess whether a deeper alliance might be possible. They found Kobane ablaze amid its third week of battle, the Kurds anxious for reinforcements from Turkey and Iraq, and their brethren watching helplessly from across the border in Suruc, desperate to help but blocked from doing so by Turkish soldiers and armed police. For ten crucial days the Turkish government refused to allow Kurdish fighters to cross the border, and there were armed clashes when some tried to evade the border guards. The optics for Turkey were terrible—Ankara seemed more concerned about Kurdish malfeasance than about the jihadist extremists threatening to tear up the region. Palpable Kurdish—and American—frustrations weren't helped by images of Turkish tanks and armor lined up on the Turkish side of the border, doing nothing to help despite being literally within sight of battered Kobane, a town defended by at most eighteen hundred YPG fighters and under heavy attack from ISIS. Kurds in Turkey seethed and, egged on by the PKK's leader, Abdullah Ocalan, who warned the peace process would be dead if Kobane fell, erupted into three nights of violent protest on October 7. Thirty-one people were killed before an order of sorts was reimposed, but the damage to Turkey's peace process and its fragile ceasefire was done.[73] Both collapsed irredeemably under the weight of the crisis in Kobane. As if to signal that, on October 14 —Kobane's most perilous hour—Turkish jets bombed PKK positions in south-eastern Turkey, close to the Iraqi border.[74]

Ankara's position was more complex and difficult than it may have appeared. More complex because Turkey was doing more than most to help Kobane's Kurds, though Erdogan tended not to advertise his good deeds for fear of antagonizing Turkish nationalists. Turkish authorities housed some 200,000 refugees from Kobane in a newly built, high-spec refugee camp. They also sent ambulances across the border to ferry injured fighters to hospitals in Turkey and return the bodies of the dead to their families. Certainly, the Turkish authorities had initially turned a blind eye to the transit of jihadists and the flourishing black-market trade in Antakya and elsewhere, and had per-haps gambled this would help bring down Assad. But Ankara had already begun to rethink that assumption before the fall of 2014 and to crack down on the smuggling of people, weapons, and goods. It was not immune to the global panic ISIS provoked but feared terrorist blowback should it crack down too fiercely.[75] Its position was more dif-ficult than appeared because Syria's YPG was, after all, a PKK off-shoot and an autonomous Kurdish region in northern Syria did pose a potential threat. In Iraq, the Kurds had already profited from the col-lapse of national authority caused by ISIS by taking control of Kirkuk. Though Iraq's Kurdish leader, Masoud Barzani, was on good terms with Ankara, he had promptly announced a referendum on an inde-pendent Kurdistan, causing shock and anger in Turkey.[76] Meanwhile the defense of Kobane brought the United States into a close relation-ship with the YPG. Thus Kobane exposed acute difficulties for Turkey and deep contradictions in its policies. It also put Ankara on a colli-sion course with its Western allies and regional neighbors.

ISIS fighters entered Kobane's outskirts on October 1 and by Octo-ber 5 were engaged in house-to-house fighting inside the town. To warn outsiders not to interfere, they released another grizzly video, this time showing the beheading of British hostage Alan Henning—a reprisal, ISIS said, for the UK's decision to join the military coalition ranged against it. On October 6 ISIS raised its now notorious black flags on the strategic Mishtenur Hill overlooking the town. More and more fighters pushed into the town and over four days of brutal close-quarter fighting seized a significant proportion, including the town center and YPG headquarters. The UN warned of a humanitarian catastrophe and called on Turkey to allow Kurdish volunteers and military equipment into the enclave. Only around seven hundred civilians were left in the town, twelve thousand in the whole enclave. It was feared they would all be massacred.[77]

In Washington, State Department officials recently returned from the front reported that the YPG would be reliable partners, able and willing to take the fight to ISIS. But their capacity to fight hinged on the successful defense of Kobane. Pleased to finally have a reliable partner, Obama ordered that the United States step up support for the town's defense. The United States air-dropped weapons and medical supplies to YPG units inside the enclave on October 19.[78] Agreement was also reached to allow YPG fighters to pass on the coordinates of ISIS positions to the United States to guide its air and missile strikes. This had the almost immediate effect of increasing the number and lethality of strikes against active ISIS positions around Kobane, causing the advance to falter while seriously denting the extremists' supply lines. Obama applied diplomatic pressure too, calling Erdogan to explain that the United States intended to align itself with the YPG in Syria, urge the Turkish leader to rethink his own position, and request the use of Incirlik airbase. Outraged and fearful, Erdogan pushed back. Since Turkey believed there was no meaningful difference between the PKK and the YPG, the United States was effectively supporting terrorists, he exclaimed.[79] The obstinacy of a wounded Erdogan risked not only his alliance with the United States but his global standing, too, his reputation now in free fall owing to more ISIS lone-wolf attacks, this time in Canada on October 20 and 22, which he seemed unwilling to counter. But beneath the angst about Kurdish revivalism, the reality was that ISIS threatened Turkey, too.

Under intense international pressure, Erdogan permitted some relief. Border guards allowed Syrian FSA fighters to cross from Turkey into the Kobane enclave and convoys of Barzani's Iraqi peshmerga to transit through its territory and into Syria. As for Incirlik, Erdogan was not yet ready to sacrifice that piece of leverage: the United States would have to clarify its plans before permission was given. Around fifty FSA fighters entered the town on October 29, and twenty vehicles with approximately 150 Iraqi peshmerga arrived two days later.[80] Although only a small injection, the reinforcements stiffened the beleaguered defenders' resolve while intensive U.S.-led air and missile strikes inflicted a punishing toll on the extremists, whose casualties soared. Its supply routes subjected to constant aerial harassment, ISIS found it difficult to sustain fighters inside the town. The bitter street-by-street, often hand-to-hand fighting dragged on right through November and into December, but the tide had turned. ISIS may have lost the momentum it had enjoyed in October, but it put up dogged resistance, using suicide car bombings and booby traps to hang on to parts of the town for as long as possible and inflict serious casualties on the advancing YPG. But the YPG kept inching forward, able to call in U.S. firepower to blast out entrenched pockets of resistance. ISIS losses soared again in December as the United States intensified strikes still more. Of the 152 strike packages launched against ISIS across Syria in December, 127 focused on Kobane.[81] The YPG retook Mishtenur Hill on January 19, signaling that the immediate danger had passed. ISIS fell into retreat, but fighting continued for another two months before the extremists were ejected from the enclave altogether.

U.S. airpower had proven decisive. It had taken more than seven hundred sorties, around three-quarters of the total U.S. air effort over Syria, and had exacted an enormous toll on ISIS. Some estimates suggest the extremists lost sixteen hundred fighters in the battle for Kobane.[82] The campaign had also revealed a Syrian opposition partner the United States believed it could rely on: the YPG. They had proven themselves committed and capable fighters, able to take and govern territory, and fiercely anti-Islamist. In Washington, analysts wondered whether the YPG might provide the vanguard for a new Syria-wide strategy. But the U.S. strategy of targeting ISIS and other extremists like al-Nusra and not Assad's government had also created friction in its relationship with the non-Kurdish Syrian opposition. For all its brutality, even at the peak of its powers, ISIS never came close to matching Damascus in the killing of Syrian civilians. In the six months after Baghdadi proclaimed his caliphate, ISIS never accounted for more than 20 percent of Syria's civilian casualties.[83] Detailed studies from the month of December 2014, for example, show that ISIS and other jihadist groups accounted for 18 percent of civilian deaths, while the government and its allies accounted for 76 percent.[84] John Kerry recalls hoping that a combination of Syrian opposition progress on the ground and the U.S. campaign against ISIS "might finally force the regime back to the bargaining table."[85] But that was wishful thinking since the U.S.-led campaign against ISIS emboldened Assad and his allies, especially as it became clear the United States had no intention of extending its campaign to include the government. In practice, U.S. forces went out of their way to avoid confronting government forces whose artillery and barrel bombs rained down on civilians in plain sight of U.S. aircraft sometimes operating only a few kilometers away.

U.S. targeting of al-Nusra proved particularly controversial in opposition circles because of that group's strong reputation for battling the government. Even those who rejected al-Nusra's Islamist ideology acknowledged that it was at least a committed and determined opponent to Assad. This boded ill for the FSA's popular legitimacy, since it was tied in the popular imagination to the United States.[86] The Islamic Front's denunciation of U.S. strikes on al-Nusra was predictable, but even U.S.-aligned groups, such as Harakat Hazzm and the FSA, voiced displeasure. The SMC warned the U.S. strategy would only "benefit the regime."[87] Just how was being made plain in Aleppo. With the world's eyes fixed on Kobane in October, government forces backed by Hezbollah unleashed a major offensive in northeastern Aleppo. Government artillery and barrel bombs mercilessly battered opposition-held parts of the city. At the same time that U.S. aircraft struck al-Nusra positions there, the group was targeted by U.S. air strikes in Idlib and Aleppo on November 5, 13, and 19 as the government offensive continued.[88] To opposition fighters and civilians cowering in their Aleppo basements, the U.S. strikes were a bitter pill: Western bombs were falling on besieged areas, not on their tormentors. Indeed, U.S. airstrikes in Aleppo that November helped the government, not the opposition, a sign of changing Western priorities.

8

BETWEEN BARREL BOMBS
AND BEHEADINGS

IN JUNE 2014 Paulo Pinheiro, chair of the UN Human Rights Council's Commission of Inquiry on Syria, reported a sharp escalation of violence, much of it unrelated to ISIS. Nevertheless, this prompted only thirty-three of the UN Human Rights Council's forty-seven members to vote to condemn the continuing attacks on civilians.[1] The UN's secretary-general, Ban Ki-moon, was growing worried about the effect ISIS was having on international attitudes as governments came to see Syria as more of a counterterrorism problem than human rights one. Ban knew that this perception risked further downgrading the importance governments attached to protecting civilians and played into the dangerously flawed assumption that the extremist problem could be resolved independently of Syria's political problem. With few levers of influence, the secretary-general used his bully pulpit to remind governments that ISIS was only one part of Syria's tragedy, one of several urgent priorities, the others being to end government violence, resume negotiations about implementation of the Geneva Communiqué, ensure accountability for atrocity crimes, and complete the destruction of chemical weapons.[2] His audience clapped politely, but few governments heeded his message.

NEW APPROACHES, SAME RESULTS

The UN's third envoy for Syria was Staffan de Mistura. In a break from past practice, he did not simultaneously represent the Arab League. De Mistura was an interesting choice. An Italian aristocrat who also held Swedish citizenship, he had joined the humanitarian sector in the 1970s. He had served with the World Food Program and UNICEF before rising through the ranks of the UN bureaucracy to become the organization's top political officer in Iraq and Afghanistan and one of Italy's deputy foreign ministers—a position he held for a month in 2013. He came to the job with no firsthand experience of leading high-level mediation in an active war zone and a decidedly mixed track record of sometimes overlooking gratuitous violence to keep from causing offense.[3] Convinced his predecessors had taken the wrong path by becoming too confrontational with Assad, he stressed the importance of cultivating better ties with Damascus and Moscow.[4] He was eager to strike a new public tone, too, evincing a relentless optimism about the power of diplomacy to solve Syria's problems that contrasted sharply with Brahimi's practiced gloominess. Exuding confidence in his powers of persuasion, de Mistura resurrected and for five years curated what could only be described as a zombie peace process, one alive only in the minds of its participants, while blithely ignoring how the process itself served Assad's goals.

Like his predecessors, the new envoy began by touring the region, visiting Damascus, Ankara, Cairo, Doha, Riyadh, and later Moscow, Amman, and Tehran to sound out opinions on the Geneva process. He found predictable deadlock on the transitional government and Assad's future role, but his curiosity was piqued by what he heard in Tehran and Moscow. De Mistura received a warm welcome in Tehran, where he was briefed on Iran's four-point plan presented to Brahimi a few months before. But where Brahimi had politely dismissed the plan, seeing it as little more than a ploy to keep Assad in power, de Mistura thought it the potential silver bullet he was looking for, an opportunity to find the middle ground that had eluded his predecessors. He discovered more reason for optimism in Moscow, where he described Sergei Lavrov as a "dear friend" and heard Russian support for local ceasefires and humanitarian access to besieged areas, a seemingly useful starting place for his peace efforts. De Mistura mused that Annan and Brahimi had failed because of their "top-down" approach to peace. Surely a "bottom-up" strategy based on local ceasefires was better? That meant setting aside awkward questions about accountability for atrocities and Syria's future government, but, as he explained to opposition activist Mazen Darwish, "there won't be peace if you want to put the justice and accountability file on the table. You must choose: accountability or peace."[5] The new envoy set out his thinking—which he dubbed an "action plan," not a "peace plan"—at a closed briefing with the Security Council in late October. It involved "seeing if we can implement some freeze zone or incremental freeze-zone in order to make sure that in those areas we will be able to build first some political process at a local level and then eventually at the national level." That, he reckoned, would create "drops of hope"—and "many drops produce a lake and a lake can produce a sea." He proposed his new approach be tried in Aleppo.[6]

The end of the siege of Homs had, of course, already revealed the pitfalls of a localized approach. No wonder Lavrov had spoken so warmly of it, as he had for months. The approach aided and encouraged Assad's siege tactics by awarding the government immense leverage through its capacity to control ceasefires and humanitarian access. Government tactics were dictated by its chronic manpower shortage. Even with help from Hezbollah, Iraqi Shi'ite, Iranian, and other irregular forces, the Syrian government was unable to sustain operations across its extensive front lines thanks to a steady stream of defections and combat casualties that depleted its numbers. By now, defections numbered approximately 100,000, which, combined with casualties (which disproportionately affected its elite, Alawite-led, fighting units) and widespread draft dodging, meant that the Syrian Army's overall size was half what it had been in 2011.[7] To cope with the shortfall, the government looked to isolate opposition enclaves and thereby concentrate its forces to defeat them one by one. The government could bring overwhelming firepower to bear on one or two places at a time, just not everywhere along the front simultaneously. For that, it needed relative quiet in some areas so that the concentration of forces in one place didn't provoke an opposition counteroffensive elsewhere. Local ceasefires were not just helpful, therefore, they were essential to the government's siege-and-starvation strategy. That is why de Mistura found Damascus so receptive. Indeed, by the time the UN envoy got to work negotiating his own deals, at least thirty locally negotiated ceasefires were already in place. Fragmented opposition groups were often only too happy to negotiate individual deals that gave them respite even if that came at the expense of the opposition's overall strategic position. As former U.S. ambassador to Damascus Robert Ford astutely observed, "These 'cease-fires' have several common characteristics: They all followed lengthy sieges where manpower-short regime forces, unable to take the districts in full-scale assaults, besieged them instead and compelled the defenders to accept cease-fires in return for food. And in nearly all the instances, the regime subsequently blocked food supplies again, trying to extract more concessions from the opposition. Sporadic fighting has broken out again in most of them."[8] That should have been apparent to the UN, too.

Local ceasefires rarely held for long. They were helpful tactical and occasionally operational pauses, nothing more. The ceasefire in Barzeh, a Damascus suburb, is a good example. The truce there was one of the more durable. Agreed to in January 2014, it still held at the end of the year. But there was a reason for that. Opposition forces there controlled the road to a military hospital the Syrian Army desperately needed. The suburb also provided a route between Damascus and Latakia. When a government offensive failed to retake the road, a ceasefire was agreed on that permitted the government to use it. Why did the opposition agree to that? The answer lies inside Barzeh. The uprising there had been led by moderate FSA-aligned groups, but in 2013 al-Nusra and other extremists had become increasingly influential. Truce with the government allowed the moderates to focus their efforts on ejecting the extremists, which they did.[9]

The "local ceasefires" approach thus allowed the government to negotiate limited deals, which then freed it up to concentrate its military efforts in one or two theaters. By its very architecture, this method weakened the opposition's hand. Local deals engaged opposition armed groups individually rather than collectively, diminishing their position relative to the government and exacerbating tensions by encouraging groups to cut deals to suit themselves, even at the expense of other opposition members. The opposition had repeatedly demanded it be treated as a single negotiating bloc, while Assad had repeatedly pushed in the other direction. Annan and Brahimi had tried as much as possible to accommodate the opposition, but under the guise of the "local turn," de Mistura reshaped the political landscape to suit Assad much better. Moreover, the new plan undermined the Geneva Communiqué by taking political transition off the agenda. Brahimi well understood the flaws in de Mistura's thinking. Always pessimistic about the prospects for peace, he had contemplated something like the new envoy's approach, largely because Moscow had seemed so enthusiastic about it.[10] But, as he explained to an audience in London, he had rejected it since it offered little prospect of a just or sustainable peace.[11]

Meanwhile, the UN's top humanitarian, Valerie Amos, reported no progress was being made on the Security Council's demands on cross-border humanitarian access, access to besieged areas, and the protection of medical workers.[12] If anything, the regime was making it more difficult to get aid to where it was needed most. Amos pointed to evidence the regime was using aid distribution as a weapon of war: siege and starvation was now a commonly used tactic employed against opposition-held enclaves, while aid flowed freely in government-held areas, where the government oversaw its distribution. Foreign aid thus helped shore up government-held areas and lend credence to the government's claim that life was better there. Outside Syria, the displacement of now more than three million refugees to Jordan, Lebanon, and Turkey contributed to growing concerns about regional stability. Citing security and economic worries, all three restricted the inflow of refugees, the latter in tandem with measures to slow the flow of fighters and contraband across the border too.

The Security Council delegated leadership on Syria's humanitarian issues to three of its nonpermanent members: Australia, Luxembourg, and Jordan. They proposed that one way of breaking the logjam over humanitarian access to besieged areas would be a chapter 7 resolution authorizing the cross-border delivery of aid without the government's consent, if necessary. That would allow UN aid to reach opposition-held areas abutting international boundaries, though it would do little to help those in isolated enclaves such as eastern

Ghouta. The council would threaten sanctions should the government not comply. It had never done anything like this before—permitting humanitarian agencies to cross international borders without the government's consent challenged the sovereign's legal jurisdiction—but Australian diplomats engaged in the negotiations recalled that although the Russians were tough negotiators, they expressed a degree of openness from the start.[13] Chapter 7 and the threat of sanctions remained red lines for the Kremlin, and both were quickly dropped. So, too, was language laying responsibility for the humanitarian crisis at the government's feet. Other sticking points involved Russia's insistence that the enterprise be overseen by a UN monitoring mechanism and that aid be imported only through four designated border crossings, and a government demand that it be allowed to inspect the aid before it was delivered—at move that would at one swoop undermine the whole arrangement by giving Damascus a physical presence at the border and a veto over what came in.[14]

It is not difficult to see why the Kremlin was open to this idea. It would be difficult to justify blocking a purely humanitarian resolution without sacrificing international legitimacy. Dozens of states had already called for a moratorium on the use of the veto in mass atrocity situations, and momentum was growing. Indeed, by 2016 more than a hundred states had signed up to the idea. At the same time, Moscow saw little harm in the draft resolution and some ways in which it might help Assad. The Kremlin had always been always somewhat bemused by the self-restraint shown by humanitarian agencies in not delivering aid across the borders Damascus no longer controlled. Since there was little that Damascus or Moscow physically could do to stop aid entering by these routes, it made sense to try to restrict it by whatever means possible, including this. What is more, the Kremlin sensed an opportunity to capitalize on the swing of international priorities toward humanitarian issues and to build momentum behind local ceasefires, thereby reinforcing the Homs model and sidelining the Geneva Communiqué.

Negotiations about the resolution almost collapsed more than once. Though willing to compromise with Russia, Australia and its partners balked at the Syrian government's demand that it be allowed to inspect the aid. That was a problem, since Moscow insisted it would not agree to anything Damascus could not live with. The three humanitarian leads proposed that, instead of the government, the UN be required to inspect each aid convoy as it crossed into Syria through four designated entry points (Bab al-Salam in Idlib governate and Bab al-Hawa in Aleppo, both bordering Turkey, the Al Yarubiyah border crossing into Iraq in largely Kurdish-controlled northeastern Al-Hasakeh governate, and the Al-Ramtha crossing into Jordan in Daraa) and to notify the authorities of their contents. The Russians were not entirely satisfied but conceded the point and insisted instead that authorization be limited to a fixed period of 180 days, which could be extended only by a new resolution. Indeed, it was extended at the end of the year (Resolution 2191, December 17, 2014). The compromises helped secure a resolution—Resolution 2165, adopted unanimously on July 24—but also gave Damascus ample scope to continue manipulating the flow and distribution of aid and Russia a significant source of leverage over the council each time the mandate was due for renewal.[15]

The new resolution facilitated the delivery of aid into previously hard-to-reach areas. The first convoy crossed into Syria from Turkey at the Bab al-Salam crossing just ten days later, carrying food, shelter, water purification equipment, and sanitation to beleaguered civilians in rural Idlib.[16] At the end of August 2014, the UN reported improved access to Aleppo, Daraa, and even rural Damascus. Indeed, over the coming year more than sixty convoys reached besieged populations. But it was hardly the humanitarian game-changer its proponents had hoped for, and that Syria's civilians needed, and had little discernible impact on the government's siege-and-starvation strategy. Though it lost countrywide distribution rights, the government retained its ability to restrict humanitarian movement and quickly centralized decision making on access to ensure local decisions matched national strategy. Where local governors had once had discretion to approve humanitarian movements, a new edict required that every humanitarian convoy passing through government territory obtain approval from Damascus. This slowed things immensely—the national authorities, for example, insisted on comprehensive background checks for every UN and ICRC official allowed access—and reinforced the central authorities' control over who received aid, who delivered aid, and when aid would arrive. Meanwhile, progress on other humanitarian issues remained elusive. At the end of August, the UN reported that medical workers, medical facilities, and civilians were still being targeted despite Resolution 2165's insistence they not be.[17]

BOMBARDMENT, SIEGE, AND STARVATION

With the world's attention fixed squarely on ISIS, the Syrian government had seized an opportunity to tighten its stranglehold on besieged areas, especially eastern Aleppo and the suburbs of Damascus. Through September 2014 there was a significant escalation of indiscriminate aerial and artillery bombardment on these sites, and chemical weapons were also employed with greater frequency. The first had come earlier in the year, in April, when chlorine bombs were dropped on the opposition-held village of Kafr Zita, north of Hama. The regime blamed al-Nusra, but evidence pointed squarely at the government.[18] By September it was evident that chlorine was being used with growing regularity. The Organization for the Prohibition of Chemical Weapons found "compelling confirmation that a toxic chemical was used as a weapon, systematically and repeatedly, in the villages of Talmanes, Al Tamanah, and Kafr Zeta in northern Syria."[19] With no mandate to identify perpetrators explicitly, the OPCW pointed the finger squarely at the regime when it reported that the bombs were delivered from helicopters, since only one side had those. Reported chemical weapons use coincided with increasingly negative assessments of the government's compliance with its undertaking to hand over its chemical arsenal.[20] Clearly, Damascus was protecting and using its chemical weapons capabilities.

By October Aleppo had become the epicenter of a fierce government offensive, focused on the strategically important Hanadarat area to the north. De Mistura decided this was where he should focus his energies by testing the local ceasefires strategy. He floated the idea of a limited plan to "de-escalate" or "freeze" the conflict: a temporary ceasefire followed by the delivery of humanitarian aid into besieged parts of Aleppo and a safe route for civilians to flee. Assad responded positively, telling de Mistura the plan was "worth studying" but would need revising to allow the authorities to restore order in conflict affected zones, a position driven entirely by political and military concerns, not humanitarian.[21] Critics feared de Mistura's plan for Aleppo amounted to an opposition surrender. Opposition commanders and astute observers were also aware that in the absence of a national ceasefire, government forces stood down by a local ceasefire in Aleppo would simply be redeployed elsewhere. The Syrian government, meanwhile, was not yet ready to draw a temporary line under its Aleppo offensive, which had made steady progress toward the government's goal of encircling the opposition-held eastern part of the city. A ceasefire now, while the opposition still held a land bridge out of east Aleppo, would stem the government's momentum and give its opponents time to regroup. Far from "de-escalating," therefore, government forces stepped up their offensive, launching Operation Rainbow in early December, in which combined government and Hezbollah forces tried to set the siege. Despite early gains, the offensive ground to a halt in the new year and was called off in March 2015 with the government having fallen short. All the while, de Mistura shuttled around the world trying to secure a ceasefire, yet it was not until December, nearly three months after he had first mooted the idea to Assad and with the battle for the northern approaches to Aleppo raging, that he finally sat down with Aleppo's opposition leaders.[22] He found them uncertain and distrustful. Some saw merit in what the envoy had to say, but only if the ceasefire happened quickly, with the eastern city still connected to the opposition heartland. In that situation, a freeze could help them stabilize their position and bring respite for the winter. Most, however, were skeptical about de Mistura's ability to persuade Assad to honor a ceasefire.[23] It was also imperative, they argued, that the "freeze" not become a siege, something that could be guaranteed only if the freeze zone extended all the way to the Turkish border and was overseen by UN monitors. The UN would also have to recognize and support public administration within the zone. The SNC's delegates pressed de Mistura to attach a national approach to peace, including "safe zones" along the borders with Turkey, Lebanon, and Jordan, to his local ceasefires plan.

Ramzy Ezzeldin, a former career Egyptian diplomat now serving as de Mistura's deputy, traveled to Damascus to hash out the local ceasefire for Aleppo. He found a government willing to talk but in no rush to conclude a deal. With their forces still pounding the city and determined to set the siege, officials in Damascus dragged their heels. The question of employing UN ceasefire observers proved especially thorny. The opposition insisted on it; Damascus opposed it: the UN team had neither will nor mandate to put its own people into besieged eastern Aleppo, lest they be harmed, trapped, or used as bargaining chips. Ezzeldin suggested that small numbers of UN monitors operating only at agreed crossing points might monitor the ceasefire; none would go into besieged east Aleppo itself. Wanting to prolong the talks, not collapse them, government negotiators talked at length about essentially irresolvable issues, such as the restoration of order inside the city and disarming of armed groups. They also wanted to ensure, as far as possible, that the "freeze" *did* amount to a stranglehold—the very thing the opposition feared most. So, whereas the opposition urged an expansive zone of peace, reaching all the way to Turkey, the government insisted the freeze be limited to Aleppo city itself, leaving it a free hand to set a siege beyond the city limits.

The war rumbled on. As 2014 ended and the situation in Kobane eased, the U.S. coalition again targeted al-Nusra as its fighters advanced close to the Baba al-Hawa border crossing. It also struck an Ahrar al-Sham compound close to the crossing.[24] In late December 2014 a Jordanian fighter jet crashed near Raqqa and its pilot, Muath al-Kasasbeh, was captured by ISIS. The extremists pretended to negotiate his release, but Kasasbeh was already dead, burned alive. A public outpouring of horror pushed Jordan to intensify its air campaign against ISIS. Yet the basic fact remained that the Assad government was killing far more Syrians than ISIS was.[25]

GOVERNMENT AT THE BRINK

On January 7, 2015, Said and Cherif Kaouchi walked into the headquarters of a satirical magazine in Paris, *Charlie Hebdo*, and opened fire, killing twelve people. The next day, a police officer was gunned down in the city's Montrogue district. The day after that, the man responsible for that murder, Amedy Coulibaly, killed four people at a kosher supermarket before he himself was killed. The Kaouchi brothers had pledged allegiance to al-Qaeda in Yemen; Coulibaly to ISIS. Tens of thousands of people gathered in cities throughout France to mourn the victims and condemn the terrorists. None of these terrorists were Syrian. None had even visited Syria. But that didn't matter. Nor did it matter that Europeans traveling to Syria under the banner of ISIS killed far more people than Syrians traveling under the same banner in the opposite direction. In the minds of Western leaders and publics, ISIS was a major threat, one rooted in Syria. There, the new year had opened with a new grim statistic—that the war had claimed at least 210,000 lives and maybe closer to 300,000.[26]

Meanwhile, the battle for Aleppo continued unabated. Away from where its forces were concentrated, the government's military position looked more precarious. ISIS had brought the regime some respite, first by distracting the opposition and then by bringing the United States and its allies into a campaign against it. Despite that, the government's chronic military manpower shortage was becoming acute. Gaps were plugged to some extent by the progovernment NDF, Hezbollah, Iraqi Shi'ite militias, and new waves of Shi'ites from Afghanistan, Pakistan, and Yemen—some of them children—but the regime struggled to conduct simultaneous operations in different theaters, a problem being exposed in Aleppo.[27]

Elsewhere, Damascus was losing control of its own forces altogether. For instance, Hezbollah and Iran conducted operations in Quneitra, close to the prized Golan Heights, independently of the government, even assuming command over regime and NDF forces. This drew a military response from Israel, whose helicopters killed several Iranian-linked fighters, including reportedly an Iranian general and several Hezbollah commanders.[28] Rockets were launched from a Syrian government position into the Golan Heights in retaliation, drawing further Israeli responses and returned fire. To the north of Aleppo, a government offensive on the outposts of Nubl and al-Zahra was led by a frontline force mainly composed of foreign fighters. They made early gains against ill-prepared defenders but were forced back to starting positions by a rapidly cobbled together opposition alliance, which included al-Nusra.[29]

In both northern and southern theaters, therefore, government forces exhibited clear signs of overstretch. Overstretch had two effects on the government. First, it made Damascus still more dependent on its foreign allies, chiefly Iran. Always reliant to some extent on Tehran, the Syrian Army was ceding it command. This caused some disquiet, but Iran continued to prove itself a loyal ally. In March 2015 it supplied Damascus with ten overhauled Su-22 fighter bombers, which were put into immediate use above Homs.[30] Second, overstretch forced the government to become more reliant on its siege-and-starvation strategy. Through the winter of 2014–2015, it was not just eastern Aleppo but also Daraa, eastern Ghouta, and parts of Homs governate that were subjected to this strategy and its relentless indiscriminate bombardment. The increased pressure inhibited opposition offensives, worsened living conditions, and heightened tensions between opposition factions, but it also exemplified the government's own weaknesses, especially its chronic shortage of soldiers which made it reliant on Syrian irregulars, foreign militia, and the ability of its air and artillery power to wreak carnage on areas its ground forces could not take and hold.[31] By early 2015 the besieging of rebel-held territories, denial of aid into those territories, and persistent bombardment of critical infrastructure such as hospitals and medical centers, bakeries, markets, housing blocks, transport links, and aid distribution points had become the regime's principal military strategy. These bombardments made increasing use of barrel bombs and chlorine.

The government's problems were amplified when the opposition's foreign backers changed their approach, too. Mindful of ISIS and worried about the Kurdish People's Defense Units' (YPG) deepening cooperation with the United States, Ankara desperately wanted the opposition in the North to do more to confront Assad and hold back ISIS. To achieve that, it increased the supply of arms to groups like Ahrar al-Sham and Faylaq al-Sham, which received rockets, mortars, tank shells, assault rifles, and ammunition.[32] But since there were limits to what could be achieved while the opposition was so bitterly divided, Turkey also invested in a new political initiative. Through the summer and fall of 2014, Turkish officials had quietly encouraged factions to join the "Watasimo" initiative launched earlier in the year, a new coordinating framework that would improve opposition unity and allow Turkey, Qatar, Saudi Arabia, and others to increase their assistance and make their fighting forces more effective. The message was well received. By the winter, the FSA-aligned groups that had signed up at the start were joined by the Muslim Brotherhood and Islamic Front–aligned groups, including the powerful Ahrar al-Sham. Leaders representing some seventy-two factions gathered in the Turkish city of Gaziantep in late November and, prodded, cajoled, and in some cases bribed by Turkish officials, agreed to establish a Revolutionary Command Council (RCC) to coordinate military and political operations and even establish joint military units.

The RCC quickly bore fruit. Still battling the government offensive and ISIS, Aleppo-based RCC factions, including the Tawheed Brigades, Ahrar al-Sham, and the mujahedeen army, established a unified command and built a thousand-strong joint force.[33] Encouraged, Turkish intelligence urged Ahrar al-Sham to reach out to other opposition groups and establish a common command structure for neighboring Idlib. In this new spirit of cooperation, Qatar and Saudi Arabia joined forces to support the initiative. Dozens of groups, including al-Nusra, which together with Ahrar al-Sham provided most of the fighters, joined the new Idlib coalition, known as Jaysh al-Fatah. Some U.S.-backed groups, like Liwa Fursan al-Haqq, remained formally aloof to protect their patronage but in practice coordinated operations with the new formation.[34] The three foreign sponsors promised material support, later reports suggesting almost half of Jaysh al-Fatah's material needs were met by Saudi Arabia and Qatar.[35] Division was never far from the surface of opposition politics, however. Toward the end of 2014, for example, the CIA stopped supplying Harakat Hazzm with funds and weapons, having noticed that several Hazzm fighters had defected—with their American money and weapons—to al-Nusra. Desperate to get back into the Pentagon's good books, in February Hazzm fighters in Aleppo governate arrested and executed several al-Nusra fighters. The response was predictably sharp. Al-Nusra attacked several Harakat Hazzm bases, eventually driving its leadership out of Syria entirely.[36] Yet, these conflicts aside, encouraged by Turkey, the opposition in the North showed clear signs it was finding ways of cooperating more effectively. The effects would not be slow to show themselves.

Two other aspects of Turkey's new thinking post-Kobane are also worth mentioning here. Aware it was losing the battle with the Kurds for American hearts and minds, Erdogan tried to curry American favor by agreeing to support the CIA's train-and-equip program and provide Turkish trainers, facilities, and materiel.[37] At the same time, he dusted off plans for "safe zones" in northern Syria and offered the United States permission to use the Incirlik air base in return for U.S. support for the safe zone. To Ankara it was a win-win: a way of addressing the refugee crisis while pushing out ISIS and creating a buffer zone between itself and Rojava. To the United States, though, it seemed like a fool's errand. The White House declined, concerned the project was unfeasible, was opposed by the Kurds, and involved collaboration with unsavory Islamists among Turkey's northern allies.

It was not just in the North that the opposition was forging new coalitions. Things looked even more promising in the South. In early 2014 the U.S.-run Military Operations Center (MOC) in Amman had summoned more than fifty southern-based secular and moderate factions to a council of war. Promised financial, material, and technical support, they had agreed to form the Southern Front to challenge both Assad and ISIS/al-Nusra. The new front had a lot going for it. Its secular leadership pledged to uphold the laws of war and protect minorities and generally avoided ideological posturing, presenting itself instead as a military coalition dedicated to overthrowing Assad.[38] By the winter of 2014–2015, it comprised around thirty-five thousand fighters based largely in Daraa and southern Damascus and boasted sufficient military muscle to take and hold territory. Assistance was channeled through the Amman MOC, Jordan's King Abdullah revealing the Southern Front received help from British special forces.[39] By February 2015 Western and Jordanian tutelage had helped it establish a command center capable of orchestrating combined operations. It began work on a plan to take Daraa.

Far removed from all this, the UN's de Mistura spent his winter pursuing the elusive "conflict freeze" or "de-escalation" for Aleppo. He made further adjustments as he went. To address the opposition's fear the freeze was effectively a surrender, he jotted an amendment allowing them to retain weapons. To address the problem of government

forces simply redeploying to other theaters, he proposed they be prohibited from moving out of their zone—though quite how that would
be achieved in practice was unclear to everyone, including the envoy
himself. There would be a mechanism for the parties to raise and
resolve disputes. The United States, Russia, and Iran were all broadly
supportive, but winning over Syrians was another matter entirely. The
government was uninterested so long as the siege in Aleppo remained
incomplete, and when de Mistura visited Damascus on February 11,
he found the government's position unchanged from two months earlier. Assad did, though, promise to consider a six-week bombing
pause should the opposition agree to a ceasefire. This was an obvious
trap—the ceasefire would be used to consolidate the government's
military position and prepare a renewed offensive—but de Mistura
judged it a price worth paying to move closer to his deal and so agreed,
announcing in public that he saw Syria's president as "part of the solution." His spokesperson, Juliette Touma, was quick to clarify that he
was referring only to "short-term efforts to de-escalate violence" rather
than to the Geneva peace process that envisaged a transitional, not
Assad-led, government. She later issued an email clarifying that the
envoy still supported the Geneva Communiqué.[40] But the damage had
been done. That the United Nations felt the need to clarify that its
envoy supported its own plan confirmed rather than allayed opposition doubts. The timing of this gaffe could barely have been worse.
De Mistura's visit to Damascus came at the end of a week of intense
and indiscriminate bombardment in eastern Ghouta, which had
reportedly killed at least 350 people, including 120 children. The killings had occurred less than twenty kilometers from where de Mistura
sat, yet the envoy failed to even mention let alone condemn them.
Press photos of the envoy bowing before Assad only reinforced the
sense he was seriously out of touch with Syrian realities. The SNC and
SOC condemned the envoy and refused to meet him, and the new
opposition formation in Aleppo rejected the freeze plan entirely.[41]
At the UN, officials questioned de Mistura's myopic focus on conflict
freezes and his downplaying of the Geneva Communiqué.

ISIS, too, was on the move that winter, cutting unpredictably across
Syria and establishing a patchwork network of pockets of influence
and terror. After defeat in Kobane, the extremists faced a sustained

YPG offensive supported by U.S. airpower. While fighting this holding battle, they picked up isolated pockets of territory along the northern Syria border and launched their own offensive southward. One
line of advance headed toward villages populated by members of the
Christian Ismaili sect, prompting fears of another Yazidi-style genocide. One Western diplomat told American analyst Charles Lister that
a concerted ISIS attack on the Ismailis might have triggered a new
front in the West's military action against ISIS.[42] Neither of those
things materialized, but the ISIS threat remained real.

As winter turned to spring in 2015, the opposition, strengthened by
new alliances, command and control arrangements, and weapons,
went on the offensive. So successful was it that by August the government was in serious trouble. The turnaround began in February when
the government's Aleppo offensive was fought to a complete standstill,
its objective unachieved. The following month Jaysh al-Fatah, Ahrar
al-Sham, and al-Nusra led the largest and best coordinated rebel offensive yet, which overran Idlib city in just four days. An artillery bombardment facilitated by the Turkish materiel mentioned earlier was
accompanied by a wave of suicide attacks that quickly overwhelmed
government positions. A lightning-quick advance by opposition standards routed governments forces. To take another provincial capital
was a major achievement; to do it in four days was astonishing. The
rebels displayed a degree of operational planning and coordination not
seen before.[43] Celebrations were short-lived, however, as the regime
responded with a devastating indiscriminate air and artillery campaign that destroyed much of Idlib's old city.[44] But despite the withering firestorm, opposition forces continued their advance and took
the de facto capital of the Idlib governate, Jisr al-Shughur, too.[45] Al-
Nusra moved into Al-Mastumah the following month, leaving proregime forces clinging to just a few positions across the whole of Idlib
governate.[46] Meanwhile, the Southern Front, preparing an offensive on
Daraa, advanced into the strategic Nasib border crossing with Jordan—
Assad's last border crossing in the South—and the town of Busra al-
Sham on March 25. The loss of the Nasib crossing seemed especially
portentous. Jordan had until then kept a tight hold on its border crossings. Only with Amman's permission would the Southern Front have
dared attack the crossing. A further offensive in the North was delayed

to allow opposition forces to regroup, but it cost them momentum and the opportunity to exploit the panic engulfing Damascus.[47]

That sense of panic was fueled by chaos in the capital itself, where the struggle for control in Yarmouk had descended into a three-way battle between the government, opposition, and ISIS. On April 1 ISIS stormed the besieged Yarmouk Palestinian refugee camp, a dense two-square-kilometer neighborhood about six kilometers south of the al-Hamidiyah Souq. By then, Yarmouk housed around 18,000 refugees (from a prewar population of around 120,000). The extremists took control after two days of intense fighting with both pro-FSA and progovernment militias. Unusually, al-Nusra, which also had an armed presence in the camp, refused to get involved, effectively aligning itself with ISIS. Control established, ISIS executed captured enemy fighters and several civilians. The proximity of ISIS to the Syrian capital threw not just the Syrian government into a panic. The UN Security Council quickly agreed on a press statement condemning the ISIS incursion in Yarmouk, though not the government's siege that had precipitated it.[48] Ramzy Ezzeldin hastened to Damascus to propose a conflict freeze that would permit the government to concentrate on combating ISIS. Some of the Palestinians agreed; others did not. Hamas—whose allies in Yarmouk had already fought ISIS—complained the proposed deal gave the Syrian government a pretext for overrunning the camp.[49] The PLO broadly agreed with Hamas.

Meanwhile, ISIS attacked Deir ez-Zor city, claiming several suburbs, before advancing on the ancient city of Palmyra, a UNESCO World Heritage site, and taking it on 20 May. The fall of Palmyra, which coincided with the fall of Ramadi in western Iraq to the extremists, offered vivid evidence that, despite its setbacks, ISIS was not defeated.[50] In Syria, the extremists were positioning themselves east of Damascus, from where they might take advantage of any sudden regime collapse. The strategy was perhaps also focused on winning back floundering Sunni support through dramatic deeds, and they had not forgotten Kobane. On June 25 approximately thirty jihadists disguised in civilian clothes smuggled themselves into Kobane and began a killing spree, killing more than 220 civilians before being killed themselves.[51] In truth, though Palmyra and Kobane gave the impression ISIS was still a force in Syria, its strategic position was deteriorating as it consistently lost ground where it mattered most. For example, a rare joint FSA-YPG offensive, backed by U.S. airpower, drove ISIS out of Tel Abyad, close to Turkey's border, and severed a supply line into Raqqa.

With the government assailed on three fronts and incapable of imposing its will on any, it was clear the military balance was tilting away from Assad, perhaps decisively so. Overstretched and dependent on foreign help, government forces fragmented into a loose-knit coalition of regular troops (and air force), foreign fighters commanded by Iranians, Hezbollah, and Iraqi Shi'ites, the NDF, and local militias led by gangsters and the *shabiha*.[52] Repeated offensives had failed to close the Aleppo siege, Idlib city and much of the governate was lost, the government had sustained reverses in the South, and there was panic and violence near the center of Damascus. In both North and South, the opposition demonstrated newfound unity and a capacity to conduct complex coordinated operations. Forced to set their animosities aside, Turkey, Qatar, and Saudi Arabia were for the first time pulling in a similar direction: Turkey especially assumed a leadership role in the North, Qatar and Saudi Arabia instructed their proxies to work together, and in the South the United States and Jordan stood behind the Southern Front.[53] All this boded ill for Assad, and there were signs the government understood its peril.[54]

The regime's tactics became progressively more desperate. It used chlorine gas with increasing frequency. In February the OPCW reported with "a high degree of confidence" that chlorine gas had been used.[55] More reports emerged in the weeks that followed.[56] These were flagrant violations of the UN Security Council's demand that Syria disarm its chemical weapons. The United States, the United Kingdom, and France, backed by several nonpermanent Security Council members, including Chile, New Zealand, Malaysia, and Nigeria, insisted the council condemn the use of chemical weapons and demand that those responsible be held accountable. This put Russia in a difficult position. On the one hand, Moscow opposed punitive action against Assad. On the other, it was annoyed Damascus had breached its commitments and concerned that chemical weapons use might provide the West a pretext for armed intervention. It hoped a rap on the knuckles from the Security Council might push Assad back into line but was determined it must not become something more. Russia therefore argued a nonbinding presidential statement would be better than a resolution; Western diplomats responded that only a chapter 7 resolution would do the job. Russia relented but demanded the resolution not specifically name the government; the United States, the UK, and France argued that it must. They wanted the council to threaten sanctions; Russia insisted that it not. Both sides, though, wanted the council to issue a demarche and so instructed their diplomats to find a compromise, which they did. Resolution 2209 was adopted on March 6 with all but Venezuela, which abstained, voting in favor. The resolution condemned the use of chemical weapons but at Russia's request did not attribute responsibility to the government. Most significantly, and disturbingly for Damascus, while Russia won the argument over whether this resolution would be under chapter 7, it agreed the text should warn of future chapter 7 sanctions should Damascus not comply. This was something the Kremlin had adamantly opposed since 2011, claiming any reference to chapter 7 created a slippery slope to military intervention, but though Russia's ambassador, Vitaly Churkin dampened expectations about what would follow, Russia's affirmative vote sent a sharp message about chemical weapons use to Damascus.[57] This was the first time the Security Council had threatened Syria with sanctions. Syria responded as it had before to Russian threats, by forcing the Kremlin to choose between supporting the government or risking its defeat. Just two weeks later, chlorine was again used, this time in Idlib, killing six people. Backed into a corner, Russia tried hedging. It looked to defuse pressure by insisting there was insufficient evidence to prove the government responsible. But embarrassed by its apparent failure to influence the Syrian government, the Kremlin also agreed in early August to allow the establishment of a UN-OPCW Joint Investigative Mechanism (JIM) to investigate the use of chemical weapons in Syria and determine responsibility (Security Council Resolution 2235, August 7, 2015).[58] But just as it seemed that the military and political net was tightening around Assad, events outside Syria—specifically, civil war in Yemen, ISIS-inspired changes to Western policy, and the UN peace process—loosened it.

The outbreak of an internationalized civil war in Yemen complicated things immensely. Iranian-backed Houthis took the offensive
trying to topple the government but were met by Saudi Arabia, which
led a Gulf coalition to intervene in support of the government on
March 26. The intervention was the first major foreign policy initiative of the kingdom's new king, Salman bin Abdulaziz Al Saud, who
had succeeded King Abdullah on his death in late January, raising
hopes in some quarters that the new leadership in Riyadh intended
to counter Iran more assertively, a policy that might see it more actively
involved in Syria. Indeed, Saudi diplomats explored whether more
concerted action over Syria might be taken with Qatar and Turkey, an
initiative warmly welcomed by Erdogan.[59] Another immediate effect
of events in Yemen was rapprochement between Saudi Arabia and
Qatar on Syria, a shaky and short-lived partnership of mutual convenience. This broke down as the Saudi-led intervention dragged on
inconclusively and Riyadh and Qatar found themselves backing different armed factions—much as they had in Syria. Meanwhile, ISIS
attacked the anti-Houthi coalition (the Houthis follow the Zaidi
branch of Shi'ism, heavily influenced by Iran's official doctrine), presumably because the coalition's chief architect, Saudi Arabia, was wag-
ing war against it in Syria. But by putting itself on the side of the
Houthis, ISIS undermined its self-image as the guardian of true Sunn-
ism everywhere, disillusioning many devout Sunnis.[60] Moreover, by
targeting the Saudi coalition, ISIS elevated itself above Assad in
Riyadh's list of foreign priorities. So as its military commitment in
Yemen grew, Saudi Arabia's commitment to defeating Assad shrank
correspondingly.[61]

Western priorities continued to slide toward accommodation with
Assad, taking the pressure *off* his government. As Syrian helicopters
resumed barrel and chlorine bombing in Idlib, John Kerry gave signs
the United States was prepared to walk away from the Geneva Communiqué.[62] This reflected growing American unease about the risk of
jihadism filling the vacuum should Assad fall and the administration's changing view about the relative importance of countering
Islamist extremism and Assad. Indeed, CIA director John Brennan
publicly questioned whether Assad's fall was desirable.[63] Washington
insiders had been saying this for some time, of course, but now that

it was being publicly stated, it drew criticism not only from the opposition but also American allies like France and Turkey, who insisted Assad remained part of the problem, not the solution, but the slide was unmistakable.[64]

De Mistura, meanwhile, came up with the idea of bringing delegations to Geneva for working-level negotiations to establish a framework for dialogue on practical issues such as his "conflict freezes" plan. Damascus readily agreed, but the opposition was skeptical since there was nothing new on the table. It took significant American and Turkish pressure to persuade the SOC's new leader, Khaled Khoja—a Syrian Turkmen politician with Turkish parents and citizenship—to send a delegation. The RCC, however, rejected the talks, arguing de Mistura's approach undermined opposition unity (by insisting that each group negotiate separately), supported the government's (by allowing it and its allies to present a common position), and legitimized Iranian interference.[65] This left Khoja little choice but to follow suit. Low-level talks limped on, and the parties established working groups to explore political and constitutional issues, military and security issues, public institutions, and reconstruction and development in more detail, but this had zero impact inside Syria.

As if to underscore the point, on May 30 barrel bombs were dropped from a helicopter onto a market in eastern Aleppo, killing at least seventy people.[66] The Security Council agreed on a press statement expressing "deep concern" about "violence directed against civilians," including the use of barrel bombs in Aleppo, though it omitted to assign responsibility. Indeed, the only actors named explicitly were ISIS and al-Nusra, condemned for their continuing terrorism attacks though neither was responsible for the bombing in Aleppo.[67] The UN's wider membership was far from satisfied by the feeble response. Seventy-one states signed a letter to the Security Council expressing outrage at the indiscriminate use of barrel bombs and demanding that the council take concrete steps to protect civilians.[68] But the council did nothing. De Mistura reportedly raised the issue of barrel bombs at a Damascus meeting with Assad on June 15–17, but his concerns were batted away. The Syrian government may have dropped as many as seventy thousand barrel bombs by the end of 2017.[69]

It was the opposition that held the initiative on the battlefield, though, and in late June it launched its "Southern Storm" offensive on Daraa. A combined assault involving four simultaneous thrusts toward Daraa by Southern Front, al-Nusra, and Ahrar al-Sham forces, the operation aimed to take Daraa city and force the government to withdraw toward Damascus. Had it succeeded, Southern Storm might have dealt the regime a near-mortal blow. But it failed. Where the Idlib offensive had taken government forces preoccupied with Aleppo by surprise, Southern Storm was telegraphed long in advance and thus confronted well-prepared defensive lines. Government forces would always have an advantage in airpower and artillery, but the failure to take al-Thaala air base prior to the main offensive proved crucial since the government's ability to rain down munitions remained intact. Regime airpower and artillery pulverized the advancing opposition forces to a halt. Some territory was taken to the north, where the government held only a relatively small corridor astride the main highway to Damascus, but nowhere near enough to force a breakthrough. Two of the four lines of advance made almost no progress at all as government forces degraded their opponents in detail. To make things worse, Islamist gunmen attacked the Southern Front's central command post, forcing its evacuation at a critical moment. As the plan unraveled, the lack of cohesion among the different factions started to hobble operations. Southern Storm ground to a complete halt after just two weeks, opposition units forced back to starting positions having sustained significant casualties.[70] A second attempt weeks later was aborted when it yielded equally poor results.

Failure in the South resurfaced old doubts about opposition unity and capability. Its principal cause was the opposition's own shortcomings, especially its lack of coordination. True, Daraa was a bigger ask than Idlib: its proximity to Damascus made it more critical to the government and easier to both reinforce and bring aerial firepower to bear upon. What is more, the government *expected* an offensive in Daraa. Some complained the Southern Front's main foreign backers—the United States, Jordan, and to some extent Israel—were less committed than Jaysh al-Fatah's backers had been and more hesitant about delivering a decisive blow against Assad. Indeed, neither Jordan nor the United States wanted the Southern Front to push the government out of Daraa entirely nor to advance on Damascus itself should they succeed in the South. The United States and Jordan were focused more on ISIS than Assad; Israel, on Iran and Hezbollah.[71] While this didn't cause the debacle in the South, it does point to a crippling disunity of purpose and to the fact that the patronage relationships between Syria's new opposition coalitions and their foreign backers, so carefully constructed over the winter, were already fraying. One of the principal lines of tension was between the United States and Syrian groups aligned with Islamists. Officially, the United States demanded the groups it back not cooperate with Islamists, but this was impossible in practice since by now Islamists were among the most numerous and effective of the opposition's armed groups. Tension and conflict were inevitable. In August, U.S. missiles struck a depot belonging to Jaysh al-Sunna in Idlib, a group that had originally been one of the FSA's Farouq Brigades that had fled north after the opposition's defeat in Homs in 2013.[72]

The U.S. train-and-equip program meanwhile descended into farce. It had aimed to train small groups of carefully vetted Syrians who could then be inserted into larger vetted factions to help combat ISIS by conveying information to U.S. forces. The model was flawed from inception, however, since it depended on heavy investment in a tiny military capability incapable of defending itself. The program's initial focus was the northern Aleppo theater, where, in the summer of 2015, the first team of fifty-four fighters, with trucks and U.S. weaponry that included mortars and machine guns, crossed into Syria to great fanfare. They didn't get far before being challenged at an al-Nusra checkpoint and warned to keep out of its territory. This they did, but when U.S. missiles hit al-Nusra positions, the extremists kidnapped ten of the American-trained fighters, including their commander, and attacked a newly built FSA-affiliated base. Thus it took just a day for al-Nusra to dismantle and destroy the first batch of U.S.-trained soldiers. In mid-September General Lloyd Austin, chief of the U.S. Central Command, revealed that only "four or five" fighters from the expensive program remained in the field.[73] When the next group of seventy-one fighters arrived, their commander was so determined to avoid a repeat he promptly handed half his trucks and a quarter of his ammunition to al-Nusra in return for safe passage through Aleppo. The U.S. press immediately reported that American arms had fallen into Al-Qaeda-linked hands. The program was shut down in ignominy in October 2015, having cost $384 million and achieved nothing besides making the United States appear incompetent. Slow and poorly organized, the train-and-equip program was always detached from the aims and objectives of the people it tried recruiting. Except for the Kurds, most who joined the armed opposition did so to fight Assad. Yet the United States wanted them to fight ISIS, not Assad, and thus patron and client had different goals and different motivations.[74] The underlying problem was in Washington, where the administration's strategy had long rested on the obviously false assumption that Assad could be coerced by a combination of military pressure from the opposition, economic sanctions, and multilateral measures into negotiating a political transition. Now, even that had been subordinated to the goal of defeating ISIS—a project in which Assad was a vital partner. Driven by false assumptions and contradictory objectives, U.S. policy became a confused jumble.[75]

Thus, although the Syrian government was under immense strain in the spring and summer of 2015, it was not defeated. It had lost Idlib, lost ground in Daraa and Quneitra, and failed to besiege Aleppo, and its route between Damascus and Homs was threatened by a Jaysh al-Islam offensive out of eastern Ghouta. But it had weathered the storm and held its own in Daraa, albeit at the cost of increasing dependence on Iran and Hezbollah.[76] Southern Storm persuaded everyone that neither side was close to victory. The government pressed on with more indiscriminate bombing. On August 16, for example, the Syrian Air Force fired four missiles at Douma's main market, killing at least 96 people and wounding 530. Approximately four surface-to-surface missiles then crashed into the site as people rushed to help survivors.[77] Another 55 people were killed in the same place the following week.[78] Munitions fell indiscriminately on Idlib and east Aleppo, too. Médecins san Frontières reported that nine hospitals were targeted in Idlib alone in the three days after August 7, killing dozens of patients and medical workers.[79]

"SAFE ZONES"

On July 20 an ISIS suicide bomber killed thirty-three leftist Turkish activists as they demonstrated in support of Kobane. A few days later ISIS attacked the Turkish border post at Elbeyli, killing a soldier and wounding two others. The PKK blamed Ankara, accusing the authorities there of colluding with ISIS. It killed two policemen as retribution, a further sign their ceasefire was over. Across the country, Turks took to the streets in force, demanding the government respond to the twin threats of ISIS and the PKK. Erdogan positioned himself at the head of that movement, and Turkish F-16s conducted strikes on ISIS in northern Syria and PKK positions in northern Iraq over the course of the next forty-eight hours, the latter signaling the full collapse of the ceasefire.[80] The strikes reportedly killed thirty-five ISIS militants and more than a hundred PKK fighters. At home, Erdogan ordered a major crackdown on both organizations, and six hundred suspected ISIS and PKK members were arrested, prompting violent protests by Kurds.

Erdogan had already called Barack Obama to inform the U.S. president of his intent to intervene against ISIS and to grant the United States its long sought-after permission to use the Incirlik air base. In return, he asked for Obama's support in establishing a "safe zone" in northern Syria. The White House remained wary, worried about its impact on the Kurds and suspicious that a "safe zone" was just a no-fly zone by another name. But since it also wanted to reward Erdogan for his new anti-ISIS zeal and to restore its battered relationship with Ankara, the administration signaled it might be willing to consider to a more modest arrangement. The Pentagon dusted off an old plan it had drawn up for an "ISIS-free" zone in northern Aleppo governate—a strategically important part of the Syria-Turkey border that ISIS still operated within. The plan envisaged the United States and Turkey conducting joint air operations to establish an "ISIS-free" zone—the United States refused to call it a "no-fly" or "safe" zone, though Turkey used the latter label—along a strip of land running ninety-two kilometers along Syria's northern border between Jarabulus and Marea, reaching some forty kilometers in depth to the outskirts of

Aleppo and Dabiq—a small town ideologically important to ISIS since it featured in prophecies about the defeat of the Roman West. Neither ISIS nor the YPG would be permitted to operate in the zone. Moderate opposition groups would lead ground operations against ISIS, take control of vacated territory, and maintain order—in essence the disastrous U.S. train-and-equip program replaced by Turkish proxies. The YPG would not be targeted directly, but the United States would use its influence to persuade it to withdraw. Neither side got everything it wanted, but both were satisfied. While the arrangement was far from being the "safe zone" Ankara had in mind, it was a start, and Turkey's Foreign Ministry assumed the zone would widen and arrangements deepen over time.[81] The American view was different. They saw the bargain as a limited deal to clear out ISIS, nothing more. Air operations began on August 23 and enjoyed the almost unanimous support of Aleppo's opposition factions. Damascus recoiled in horror, fearing that whatever their stated objective, both Turkey and the United States had something more comprehensive in mind. Indeed, even the limited plan placed Turkish forces close to land the government needed to besiege Aleppo, jeopardizing that whole front. The Kurds, too, opposed the plan, though public criticism from the YPG leadership was constrained by its need to protect good relations with the United States. An ISIS backlash was inevitable. On October 10 ISIS suicide bombers killed more than a hundred people and injured five hundred more in Istanbul.

Turkey became more active on other fronts, too. Between July and September 2015 it facilitated negotiations between Ahrar al-Sham and Iran about the besieged towns of Zabadani (near Damascus, held by Ahrar al-Sham, al-Nusra, and others) and al-Fuah and Kafraya (both near Idlib and held by proregime militia). Several ceasefires were agreed through August, but all collapsed quickly. The United Nations then joined Turkey, and an agreement was reached in late September between Iran and Hezbollah, on one side, and Ahrar al-Sham and Jaysh al-Fatah, on the other. The result was a relatively stable six-month ceasefire that allowed for the evacuation of ten thousand civilians in return for the evacuation of fighters with their weapons from Zabadani. The first of its kind, to UN officials the agreement demonstrated that local ceasefires were possible. The Turks and Iranians, though, were more pragmatic—the deals were essentially mutually beneficial swaps of land and personnel. Crucially, Damascus was not a party to the talks or the final agreement, showing just how weak the central government had become.[82] While the parties fought and haggled, a combination of the war's immense human suffering and immensely cynical politics triggered a refugee crisis in the summer and fall of 2015.

9

EXODUS

ON THE morning of September 2, 2015, the tiny body of two-year-old Alan Kurdi washed up on a Turkish beach near the resort town of Bodrum. The bodies of his four-year-old brother, Ghalib, and an unrelated eleven-year-old boy lay farther along the beach. Alan's mother also lay dead. Bodrum-based photojournalist Nilufer Demir went to the beach that morning after receiving reports of bodies washing ashore overnight. She froze when she saw tiny Alan, the waves gently lapping against his lifeless face. "There was nothing to do except take the photograph," she remembered. "This is the only way I can express the scream of his silent body."[1] Demir took several photos of Alan. One tweeted with the hashtag, in Turkish, "humanity washed ashore" quickly became the iconic image of the suffering of Syria's refugees.

As their surnames suggest, the Kurdis are a Kurdish family who before the war had enjoyed a comfortable life in a Damascene suburb. Born in Kobane, Alan's grandfather moved to Damascus after his military service and set himself up as a barber, spending summers back in Kobane helping the extended family harvest olives. Abdullah, Alan's father, was one of six children. As an adult, Abdullah stayed in Damascus and worked in his father's barbershop. He married a cousin from Kobane, Rehenna, and started a family. They could not have picked a worse time. It was 2011, and all around them violence, lawlessness, and unease were growing as Syria's Arab Spring protests and the government's violent response escalated. They decided that Rehenna should return to the comparative safety of Kobane to give birth to their first son, Ghalib. Abdullah spent his time shuttling between there and work in Damascus. But that became more dangerous as increasingly nervous security forces picked people off the streets, especially Kurds, seemingly at random, some of them never to return. There were also kidnappings. Abdullah closed the barbershop and joined his family in Kobane. They struggled financially, but they were safe there.

When Alan was barely a year old, everything changed when ISIS shattered the safety of Kobane. The Islamists bombed, murdered, raped, and enslaved their way to the very doorstep of the Kurdi family's home. Their prized olive trees were put to the torch, their houses destroyed, and eighteen members of their extended family killed. Rehenna and the boys crossed into Turkey and, with Abdullah, went to Istanbul. Once more they were safe, but housing was unaffordable, living conditions declined, and the children were frequently unwell. Other members of the family struggled, too. Abdullah's older brother Mohammed, his wife, and three children were also in Turkey, having made the same journey, and were in a similar situation. Abdullah's sister Fatima (Tima) had immigrated to Canada in 1992, and she decided she would try to get them out, starting with Mohammed's children. She filed papers to sponsor their migration to Canada, while in Turkey Mohammed filed a corresponding application with the embassy. Their application was rejected on the grounds that the paperwork was incomplete. Their savings dwindled. With no hope of returning to Kobane or Damascus and official channels seemingly blocked, Abdullah and Rehenna took the fateful decision to make a desperate bid to reach Europe by boat and from there join Tima in Canada. Tima wired them five thousand dollars, enough to pay people smugglers for two trips across the water from Turkey to a Greek island. Abdullah, Rehenna, and the two boys traveled down to the coast.

The Greek island of Kos lies just 24 kilometers west of the beaches of Bodrum. Ferries take an hour and a half to make the crossing, but the people smuggled left from a remote beach on a peninsula, even closer to Kos. Two attempts were aborted, but on the night of September 1 Rehenna, Abdullah, Ghalib, and Alan were taken to the launch beach by smugglers and put aboard a sixteen-foot dinghy with seven others. They were each given a life jacket. Only when they needed them most did they discover the devastating truth: the jackets were fake and didn't float. "We are leaving right now," Abdullah texted his sister in Canada. Barely five hundred meters off the coast, the boat started taking in water, then began deflating, plunging its victims into the water. In the chaos and darkness, Abdullah tried to hold on to his sons. Ghalib was already dead. Alan slipped from his arms into the tumult, too.[2] Tima never received the second text she was anxiously awaiting, the one telling her they had arrived in Greece. Abdullah was the only survivor.

Alan Kurdi was one of millions of Syrians forced to flee the bloody war in their homeland. That summer, the number of refugees and asylum seekers arriving by boat in Greece and Italy increased dramatically. Europe "watched in alarm" as "hundreds of thousands of people crossed seas, walked great distances, climbed barbed wire fences, forged rivers, endured indignity and ill-treatment, battled the elements, experienced lack of food, water, and shelter, and risked their lives" to gain asylum in the European Union.[3] Between March and October around one million people arrived, approximately half of them from Syria, landing on the small islands of Lesbos and Kos.[4] Just like Alan, many never made it. According to one estimate, there was on average one death at sea in the Aegean for every four hundred arrivals.[5] This means almost a thousand Syrians may have died at sea that summer. Their stories will most likely never be known. The crisis was neither unprecedented (more than 1.3 million refugees had fled Yugoslavia's bloody wars in the 1990s), unexpected (the number of refugees traveling to Europe had been increasing since 2011), or unusually large (Turkey housed more than two million Syrian refugees, Lebanon more than a million, Jordan more than 600,000, and even Iraq hosted around 200,000), yet it unleashed a political crisis in Europe that exposed deep fissures within the EU, subjected Syrians to yet more harm, and further eroded European sympathy for Syria's plight.[6]

There were four main reasons for the rapid increase in the number Syrians choosing the perilous crossing over the Aegean that summer. First, the pace of displacement inside Syria had increased sharply because of Assad's war on the cities, intense fighting in Idlib and Aleppo, and ISIS.[7] Around a quarter of all the Syrians who left the country in 2015 and headed for Europe did so because they either feared ISIS or had been in communities attacked by ISIS.[8] An equally significant proportion had fled the devastation in Homs, Damascus, and Aleppo. Second, attitudes and policies in Turkey had changed, making it less hospitable than it had once been. The sheer scale of the refugee crisis in Turkey placed Ankara's relatively generous policies under pressure. By 2015 Turkey had spent $6.5 billion supporting Syrian refugees. That was barely sustainable in economic boom times, but economic growth was slowing, and as a result Turkish public attitudes toward the refugees shifted. Many opposed further expenditures. Sixty percent of Turks surveyed believed Syrian refugees were responsible for rising crime.[9] Ankara had first banked on a Syrian opposition victory, then on its "safe zone" idea, but neither had come to fruition. Turkey called on other governments to help, but despite all its pretensions to humanitarianism, the West's response was pathetic. The EU accommodated some 81,000 refugees; Sweden, whose government likes to lecture the world on humanitarianism, agreed to accept just 1,200. Fewer than 10,000 were accepted by the United States, 1,300 by Canada, and 300 by Australia.[10] All in all, less than 3 percent of Syria's refugees were resettled outside the immediate region. In March 2015 Turkey closed its border to all except those with medical grounds for travel to reduce the transit of ISIS jihadists in one direction and refugees in the other. This attracted stinging international criticism—despite the fact the West frequently demanded Turkey do more to control its border—and had only a limited effect, since Syrians used smugglers and familial networks to get them over the long border.[11] Then, in the spring, Ankara put pressure on the West to do more by restricting the ability of Syrian refugees to work and earn money in Turkey while simultaneously relaxing the obstacles preventing refugees crossing into Europe. With customs officials told to turn a blind eye to their outward migration, Syrians took advantage of the opportunity this created, just as Ankara knew they would. Third, the living conditions endured by Syrian refugees were worsening, creating a powerful incentive to leave. In addition to the tough situation in Turkey already discussed, the UNHCR estimated that 70 percent of Syrians in Lebanon and 85 percent of those in Jordan were living below the poverty line.[12] The UN's Regional Refugee and Resilience Plan, developed to support Syria's refugees, secured only 40 percent of its required funding. In Lebanon, kidnappings and disappearances were increasingly common. Refugees pointed to the long arm of the Syrian Mukhabarat, which had an extensive network in the country thanks to the long years of Syrian occupation, and its ally Hezbollah. The change of government in Egypt made life difficult for the much smaller community of refugees there. Where they had been welcomed and protected by Mohamed Morsi, Syrian refugees—most of whom had intended to see out the war in Egypt—found themselves vilified, harassed, and sometimes forcibly returned by Sisi's government. In 2014 and 2015 Algeria, Morocco, Egypt, Tunisia, Jordan, and Lebanon all imposed harsher visa restrictions on Syrians.[13] Fourth, though Assad had not consciously engineered the summer crisis, forced displacement was a critical component of his overall strategy. Damascus wanted to clear cities, towns, and villages of people sympathetic to the opposition. Internal displacement heaped pressure on the opposition, which strained to cope with massive influxes of civilians. Forcing large numbers of Syrians out of the country altogether helped put pressure on neighboring governments like Turkey and Jordan that were hostile to the Syrian government.[14]

The crisis was compounded by serious flaws in the EU's migration regulations and the fact that both Greece and Italy had relatively weak systems for managing and protecting asylum-seekers.[15] Under the EU's "Dublin system," agreed in 2013, asylum-seekers entering the EU were required to lodge their claim at their port of entry. Once claims were accepted, they could be resettled elsewhere in the EU according to a system designed to distribute refugees evenly across the union. Quickly overwhelmed by sheer weight of numbers in the summer of 2015, the Greek and Italian systems collapsed, the authorities there allowing asylum-seekers to continue their journeys into second, third, and fourth countries.[16] Most Syrians who survived the perilous crossing to Greece traveled north by whatever means possible—often on foot—hoping to reach Germany and Scandinavia. This triggered an antimigrant backlash, sometimes violent, in some transit countries. Hungary's far-right president, Viktor Orban, closed his country's southern borders and erected barbed-wire fences to keep refugees out.

One leader bucked the trend. German chancellor Angela Merkel was Europe's longest-serving premier, elected in 2005. She had always been resolute in her condemnation of Assad and concern for Syria's civilians but less bullish about military intervention than British and French leaders. As Europe's migration system teetered on the brink of collapse, Merkel took the bold decision to suspend the Dublin regulations and declare that Germany would accept, process, and resettle any Syrian refugees who arrived there. She argued that Germany had a "duty" to assist and called on the UK and France to follow suit. Germany's far right was horrified, but the number of protesting neofascists was dwarfed by the number of Germans who turned out to help the refugees. Thousands volunteered to staff temporary reception centers and train stations to welcome refugees with food, essential clothes, and help finding accommodation.[17] Local mayors and town councils were tasked with identifying spare accommodation and preparing to house refugees. Dozens of communities embraced the challenge. Signs, posters, and graffiti reading "refugees welcome" sprang up across the country. There were innumerable challenges, but along with Syria's own White Helmets volunteers, who courageously volunteered to pull people from destroyed buildings, this was one of the few times in Syria's war that humanitarian compassion overrode all else.[18]

Merkel had hoped her stand would prompt other Europeans to follow suit. The German government's display of humanity was rightfully praised by humanitarians and made good strategic sense too.[19] Indeed, thousands of Europeans rallied to offer aid and assistance. Volunteers, charity workers, humanitarians, and "ordinary people" provided food, water, shelter, and comfort to Syrian refugees. Some met them on the beaches of Kos and Lesbos; others set up support stations along their road north. Charities in Europe teamed up with Syrian charities to provide material aid, medical support, including mental health support, and educational assistance.[20] Several cities, including Amsterdam, Barcelona, Dusseldorf, and Lund, declared themselves cities of "sanctuary," "welcome," and "human rights" and opened their doors and labor markets to refugees.[21] But no other government followed Germany's lead. In fact, EU governments complained bitterly about German unilateralism and either kept their border shut or else hurried refugees through to Germany. As a result, the number of people arriving into Germany increased dramatically. In September 169,000 refugees registered in Bavaria alone.[22] By the end of the year, Germany had taken in more than 800,000 Syrian refugees. The sheer weight of numbers, though, and the fact that no other government offered to help, forced Berlin to change course and introduce border checks, though Syrians seeking sanctuary were still allowed in. By contrast, other countries, including Austria, France, Denmark, and Sweden, imposed tighter restrictions to prevent them from becoming a magnet as well. Meanwhile, Hungary's fence redirected refugees through Croatia and Slovenia, until that route, too, was blocked in October 2015. Europe's closed borders left some sixty thousand people stranded in Greece.[23]

EU governments rapidly negotiated a "temporary emergency relocation scheme" to rehouse some these refugees and tried to find ways of preventing people from making the journey. In March 2016 the EU made a deal with Turkey in which Syrian refugees who made it to Greece would be returned to Turkey, and for every refugee returned, the EU would resettle one other Syrian refugee—a scheme designed to deter dangerous crossings but without addressing any of the underlying causes or protection needs. In addition, Turkey agreed to prevent Syrians crossing into Greece by land or sea, in return for which the EU agreed to liberalize visa restrictions on Turkish citizens, grant three billion euros of aid to Turkey, spend another three billion euros on projects to assist Syrian refugees in Turkey, and revive talks about Turkey's EU membership. The negotiations revealed not only the limits of Europe's much professed humanitarianism but also Ankara's willingness to cynically manipulate Syrian suffering to serve its own interests. The deal they reached also raised awkward questions about the systematic violation of human rights by both sides.[24] But it did significantly reduce the number of Syrians arriving in Greece—98 percent by some estimates—and deaths at sea, so the arrangement was widely touted as a success.[25]

In the United States, the crisis reignited debates about Turkey's proposal to establish "safe zones" in Syria's North that would, among other things, allow some refugees to safely return to their country. Proponents, like Hillary Clinton and Senator John McCain, argued it offered a way of extending the protection of civilians into Syria, easing the refugee crisis, and increasing pressure on Assad without requiring military engagement on the ground. They pointed to the relative success of the safe haven imposed on northern Iraq to protect the Kurds in 1991 and the more recent operation to save the Yazidis on Mount Sinjar as evidence the concept could work. Neither the Pentagon, State Department, nor White House agreed. They countered that the concentration of civilians into safe areas would make the zone a prime target for the regime and ISIS, meaning that significant military effort would be needed to protect them—protection that could not be done from the air alone. Kerry estimated that between fifteen thousand and thirty thousand troops would be needed.[26] Moreover, the zone would need protecting from artillery and other long-range weapons, creating potential for mission creep. Kerry thought the idea was a diplomatic nonstarter, too. Russia and China would oppose it as a violation of Syrian sovereignty, denying the effort the legitimacy of a UN mandate. European allies would complain about the legal issues and probably not contribute to the military effort, and so it would fall to the United States to shoulder the burden of responsibility. And even were that all to be done, safe zones would never be anything more than a temporary stopgap.[27]

The refugee crisis not only exposed the EU's frailties, as mentioned earlier, it also had the perverse effect of diminishing whatever sympathy Europeans had for Syria's tormented civilians and arousing even greater panic about ISIS terrorism. Psychologists and peace activists alike promote "empathy" as the route to greater compassion. But in the summer of 2015, the experience of coming face-to-face with the battered and traumatized survivors of Syria's civil war *increased* the hostility many Europeans felt toward them. It was common to hear political and military leaders claim ISIS terrorists were concealed among Syria's refugees. General Philip Breedlove, commander of U.S. forces in Europe, warned that among the refugees, ISIS "is spreading like a cancer, taking advantage of paths of least resistance, threatening European nations and our own with terrorist attacks."[28] In fact, of the thirty-five major terrorist attacks in Europe, the United States, Turkey, and Russia claimed by ISIS between 2013 and 2018, only one—a bombing in the German town of Ansbach in 2016 that killed only the bomber himself—was perpetrated by a Syrian. The ISIS terrorists who targeted Europeans during this period came from nearly twenty different countries. They were French, Belgian, American, British, Moroccan, Algerian, and Tunisian. Meanwhile, thousands of European and North American extremists traveled to Syria to commit grievous atrocities there. Yet trapped by paroxysms of fear, many felt threatened by Syria's refugees, fears stoked not just by populist right-wing and neofascist parties.

Western attitudes toward Syrian refugees hardened further at the end of 2015, thanks to a string of terrorist incidents connected with ISIS and a spate of sex attacks across Germany on New Year's Eve. Yet although Syrians got the blame, the New Year's Eve attacks were mainly perpetrated by North Africans and a few Iraqis, not Syrians. Irrespective of the truth, Syrian refugees were tarred with the same brush: feared because they might harbor ISIS terrorists among them; loathed because Westerners believed they created chaos and crime.[29] Polls show that by early 2016, 52 percent of Americans, and 84 percent of Republicans, opposed taking in any Syrian refugees whatsoever.[30] A dozen republican governors declared that Syrian refugees would never be welcome in their states.[31] Similar views were aired in Europe. Around half of surveyed Germans, Italians, and Greeks said they believed immigrants were responsible for increased crime.[32] Not surprisingly, attitudes toward Angela Merkel's compassion hardened, too. Within a year of Merkel's humanitarian policy, many German voters and politicians alike seemed to agree that opening the doors had been a mistake.[33] American presidential candidate Donald Trump called the policy "a catastrophic mistake." Nigel Farage, leader of the right-wing UK Independence Party, called it "the worst decision a European leader has made in modern times," adding, "she's finished."[34] Some experts agreed. Merkel's failure to stop the "flotilla of migrants" into Europe would propel Germany's far-right parties into the ascendancy, claimed historian Niall Ferguson.[35]

But that is not how things turned out. Merkel's stance certainly cost her politically and the far-right did gain ground, but not to the extent Ferguson predicted. Germany's chancellor won a historic fourth term in office in 2017, and in 2019 polls showed that more than two-thirds of Germans wanted her to govern through to her retirement in 2021.[36] When Merkel did step down, her Christian Democrats lost not to the German far right but to the center-left Social Democrats. True, the program was expensive, costing more than twenty billion euros each year, or 6 percent of the entire federal budget. But the "swarm" of migrants predicted by British prime minister David Cameron failed to materialize. After peaks in 2015–2016, the number of Syrians trying to reach Germany declined significantly, with only around twenty thousand in 2019–2020. Moreover, Syrian refugees have largely settled successfully. Every refugee's journey is different, and many families experienced significant problems adjusting to new laws and customs. Some took better to the new language, and new rights, than others.[37] Yet of the approximately 700,000 Syrians who reside in Germany at the time of writing, more than half have jobs and pay taxes, more than 10,000 have sufficiently good language skills to be enrolled in university, and more than 80 percent of child and youth refugees report a strong sense of identification with Germany.[38] During that time, for all the challenges, Germany's economy has been western Europe's strongest performer, unemployment has declined, and the federal budget has chalked up consistent surpluses.[39]

Angela Merkel's decision to open her country's arms to refugees in the summer of 2015 was courageous. It stands out as a compelling, singularly humanitarian action and as a damning condemnation of other European and American leaders and societies, for they oversaw policies designed primarily to suit themselves and not the thousands of families in desperate need of protection that summer. Meanwhile, gripped by their own sense of crisis provoked by Syria's dispossessed victims of war, Western governments seemingly missed the fact that a significant change of strategy was being developed in Moscow.

10

RUSSIAN INTERVENTION

VLADIMIR PUTIN ended his self-imposed moratorium on traveling to the West by arriving in New York to deliver Russia's statement to the opening of the new UN General Assembly session
in September 2015. His remarks signaled a dramatic shift in Russia's
policy toward Syria. Insisting it would be "an enormous mistake to
refuse to cooperate with the Syrian government and its armed forces,
who are valiantly fighting terrorism," the Russian president called for
a broad-based international coalition to support Assad.[1] Caught off
guard, White House speechwriters quickly revised Obama's own
address, which rejected Putin's scheme and ruled out cooperation
with "tyrants like Bashar al-Assad" who drop "barrel bombs to massacre innocent children."[2] Back in Moscow, Putin asked the Federation Council, Russia's upper house, to approve military intervention
to counter terrorism in Syria, reassuring them Russia's involvement
would be limited to airstrikes. The council dutifully assented—
unanimously. Barely seventy-two hours after Putin's General Assembly address, in the early hours of September 30, a Russian general
walked into the U.S. Embassy in Baghdad to announce that air strikes
would begin in Syria within the hour and that the U.S. coalition should
vacate the skies.[3] An hour later, Russian bombs struck opposition targets in Hama and Homs.

Back in New York, the General Assembly's festivities were continuing. Hurrying between meetings, John Kerry bumped into his Russian counterpart, Sergei Lavrov, in a hallway. "Sergei—you guys are now bombing in Syria and moving troops? What's up?" he inquired. Lavrov expressed disbelief and hurried off, leaving Kerry unsure whether the Russian was bluffing to avoid a direct confrontation or the Russians were so confused they had not received instructions from Moscow and did not know what to do. Perhaps Lavrov had been blindsided too, Kerry speculated.[4] In fact, Kerry's speculation speaks volumes about just how out of touch America's senior leadership had become with the situation in Syria. There had been a hive of diplomatic and military activity in the weeks and months before Russia's military intervention, much of it involving Lavrov himself. The intervention was not a knee-jerk reaction concocted by Putin en route to New York. It was a carefully calibrated move to protect an imperiled Assad by changing facts on the ground inside Syria. Lavrov had been involved in the preparation every step of the way and was well aware of what his government's next steps would be.

The Kremlin had been considering military intervention for months, troubled by assessments that Assad's government was on the brink of collapse. Assad had repudiated Obama months earlier when the American president had commented that Iran and Russia saw a bleak future for the regime, but the U.S. president was right. Despite Iranian help, Syria's military was stretched thin, its acute personnel shortage worsening with time. The opposition, meanwhile, was becoming more capable with the emergence of the Southern Front in the South and Jaysh al-Fatah and its alliance in the North, two colossal blocs of opposition groups exhibiting a previously unseen capacity to cooperate in large and complex operations. The northern alliance had scored a dramatic victory in Idlib, and though the Southern Front had failed to repeat the feat in Daraa, the Kremlin judged that the long-term trends were tilted in the opposition's favor. Damascus was at its most vulnerable point in years, and the Kremlin knew it. Watching the situation with increasing alarm, Russian analysts concluded that Assad's defeat was becoming "inevitable" unless something was done to alter the balance of forces.[5] Defeat and state collapse would be catastrophic, since the vacuum left behind would be filled by jihadists. Indeed, the Kremlin believed 1,700 Russians had already joined the extremists in Syria.[6] That this posed a national security threat was made plain when the "Caucasus Emirate," the largest jihadist insurgency in Russia, pledged allegiance to ISIS, which then claimed responsibility for two terrorist attacks in Dagestan.[7] To the Kremlin, therefore, the Assad regime was an essential pillar of its war to protect itself from Islamist extremism. Moreover, with the West in diplomatic as well as military retreat, Putin sensed an opportunity to plug the leadership hole it had left behind by seizing the initiative, making Russia the indispensable power in Syria. As John Kerry later observed, "The Russians had upped the ante to a degree that they knew we would not match."[8]

Military intervention would achieve goals beyond Syria, too, by conveying Russian hard power and influence into the Middle East. That would strengthen Russia's global position as a serious military and political power and signal to its allies that, in sharp contrast to the United States, Russia was a reliable partner. Thus intervention in Syria might help Russia recover from the diplomatic isolation imposed by the West after the Russian invasions of Ukraine.[9] Tellingly, while the Kremlin publicly maintained the intervention would be limited and focused on countering terrorism, Russians in defense circles spoke of establishing "permanent" bases in Syria, indicating that while the immediate objectives might be limited, longer-term objectives lay behind them.[10] All this made good domestic political sense, too. Chastened by protests when he had returned to the presidency, Putin discovered that the more he stood up to the West, the more popular he became at home. The Russian Orthodox Church blessed his war against ISIS as a "holy war."[11]

Though it caught the Americans by surprise, the road to intervention can be traced back to a flurry of diplomatic activity between Damascus, Tehran, and Moscow beginning in June 2015, when Assad begged for more help and his allies deliberated on what to do. Russia and Iran shared an interest in protecting Assad, but their interests and objectives diverged in important respects, and they competed for influence over Damascus. Iran saw Syria's war as a part of its regional struggles, specifically its contest for influence with Saudi Arabia and its war on Israel. It wanted to keep the Alawites in power to keep the

Sunnis out and, in the process, to establish itself closer to the contested Golan Heights occupied by Israel. Moscow was not just uninterested in all that; it was concerned about it. Putin valued good relations with Israel, as well as with Saudi Arabia and Egypt. Russia wanted order and stability in the region, not Iranian hegemony. That Assad was an Alawite ruling a Sunni majority mattered little; that he held the state together mattered a great deal. Moscow had a strategic interest, therefore, in limiting Iran's military presence in Syria. Damascus itself was also less invested than Iran in regional sectarian struggles. Even before the war, it had been more concerned with its own survival than with ideological competition.

With the regime under serious military pressure in the summer of 2015, Iran's supreme leader Ali Khamenei had dispatched a senior envoy to appeal for Russian help. Putin had agreed, reportedly telling the envoy, "Okay, we will intervene. Send Qassem Soleimani." Khamenei duly dispatched the commander of Iran's Quds forces in Syria to Moscow that July, for the first of a series of secret trips, which, incidentally, violated a UN travel ban imposed in 2007 by Security Council Resolution 1747 (March 24). Soleimani found the Kremlin in a state of despondency, burdened by international isolation and economic sanctions and fearful Assad's days were numbered. The Russians were right to worry, Soleimani explained, since the dangers were quite real. Iran was doing all it could, but it too was buckling under the strain. The Syrian regime, meanwhile, was losing its grip on power altogether. He unfurled a large map on which was drawn a plan to reverse the military situation by taking the initiative in Aleppo, Hama, Daraa, Latakia, and Palmyra.[12] Battlefield losses would force the opposition to concede and negotiate a political settlement more conducive to the government's— and hence Russian and Iranian—interests. Soleimani claimed Assad was prepared to share power in a transitional government with opposition leaders not tainted by terrorism and to permit internationally monitored elections, on the condition that he or his nominee could stand. But to turn the tide, they needed Russia's military help.

Encouraged by Soleimani's plan, the Russians prepared the military and political paths. Lavrov met Kerry and Saudi foreign minister Adel al-Jubeir in Doha to press them to focus more on countering ISIS and less on removing Assad. Kerry expressed openness, unwittingly confirming the Kremlin's expectation that the United States could be persuaded to compromise on Assad's participation in a transitional government. Lavrov invited the SOC's Khaled Khoja to Moscow for talks on August 14 to test the opposition's willingness to do the same but found Khoja more implacable than Kerry and al-Jubeir. This helped convince the Russians that military facts on the ground would need to be changed to make the opposition more pliable. On August 26 Syria signed over control of Khmeimim air base, near Latakia, to Russia. Satellite footage showed significant work to improve the runway and facilities there. Within a month, they showed evidence Russian aircraft and troops were on the ground, too. Russian reports estimate that some two thousand troops, including elite marines, were deployed to the airbase with initially twenty-four aircraft, supported by tanks, helicopters, and anti-aircraft weapons. A further seventeen hundred troops were deployed at the naval base in Tartus, which the Russians were also busy upgrading.[13] Around fifteen warships, mainly from Russia's Black Sea fleet, took up position off the Syrian coast, and warships in the Caspian Sea also set their sights on Syria.[14] The buildup was careful and deliberate, but it was not shrouded in secrecy.[15] Despite that, neither the flurry of diplomatic activity nor the military buildup attracted much Western attention. In mid-September U.S. intelligence warned the Russian military buildup was significant, but the White House was dismissive.[16] Nor did anyone much notice that on September 21–22 the UN's Staffan de Mistura met with the four mediators who would lead his working groups, or his bizarre claim that the groups would "set the stage" to end the war. That oversight, however, was much less consequential.[17]

RUSSIA AT WAR

As the first Russian bombs and missiles rained down, the Kremlin insisted its intervention was limited to countering ISIS and other Islamist terrorist groups. Putin reassured Russians that "we certainly are not going to plunge head-on into this conflict." The mission, he explained, would be limited to "supporting the Syrian army purely in its legitimate fight with terrorist groups," and the commitment limited to "air support without any participation in the ground operations."[18] The war aims and strategic commitment were indeed limited, but not in the way the leadership claimed. The primary goal was to prevent the Syrian regime from collapsing, not to single-handedly defeat ISIS or lead Damascus to outright victory. Putin wanted influence without assuming responsibility for Syria's long-term future. And he wanted to minimize Russian losses. The Kremlin feared a quagmire just as much as the Pentagon did and wanted to avoid an open-ended commitment that might drag it into a protracted and bloody insurgency. This was no idle fear. Going to war in Syria made Russians a target, a point underscored when, on November 17, ISIS affiliates bombed a Russian passenger plane leaving Cairo, killing 224 people, mostly Russians. The secondary goal was regional stability and a peace that protected Russian interests. Moscow was convinced that whatever the outcome on the battlefield, Syria's long-term stability depended on achieving a political settlement with sections of the opposition, and it expected Assad to play his part.[19]

Military intervention in Syria was Russia's largest campaign outside the former Soviet space since the Soviet Union's disastrous war in Afghanistan.[20] Russia's initial military commitment was relatively small, intended for "reasonable sufficiency"—enough to tilt the balance and exert influence, but not enough to drag Russia into the civil war or ensure decisive victory.[21] It comprised thirty-three aircraft (twelve Su-24M bombers, twelve Su-25SM ground attack aircraft, four Su-34 bombers, four Su-30SM fighters, and one IL-20M1 reconnaissance aircraft) and seventeen helicopters (twelve Mi-24P combat helicopters and five Mi-8AMTSh transport helicopters), in addition to the naval armada. The number of aircraft based in Syria had grown to forty-four by February 2016, augmented by the use of Cold War era long-range Tu-160 and Tu-95MS bombers operating from bases in the Caucasus.[22] Russia provided support to ground operations, including by providing arms to Hezbollah, but did not—yet—want to directly engage on the ground.[23] The Russian Navy also got in on the intervention, firing long-range missiles from the Caspian Sea onto targets in Raqqa and Idlib.

Despite trumpeting intervention as a war on ISIS and terrorism, Russian forces chiefly targeted factions once aligned with the FSA, and especially those receiving support from the United States. In the first few hours, Russian aircraft attacked al-Lataminah in northern Hama three times, targeting Tajammu al-Aaza, an FSA-aligned group with moderate secular views supplied with TOW missiles by the United States. The group had been in place in northern Hama for four years, in an area far removed from ISIS or al-Nusra. This was perfectly consistent with Russia's objective of protecting Assad but entirely contrary to its stated goals.[24] By targeting this group, the Russians implicitly confirmed it saw the use of TOWs by opposition factions a particular threat to Assad.

The pattern continued. On October 7 Russian aircraft attacked a storehouse containing ammunition, artillery, armored personnel carriers, and tanks belonging to Liwa Suquor al-Jabal, another U.S.-backed group, led by defectors from the Syrian Army. On the same day, Syrian government forces backed by Iranian, Hezbollah, and Iraqi Shi'ite forces launched offensives against non-ISIS opposition groups in northern Hama and Aleppo. The following week, government forces went on the offensive in Homs, Idlib, Daraa, and the surrounds of Damascus, Russian aircraft providing close air support. The UN reported that the increased violence in the first two weeks of October displaced more than 120,000 civilians. The White Helmets, a volunteer civil defense group that courageously battled to pull victims out of ruined buildings, reported more than 400 civilian deaths in the same period, over half attributed to Russian airstrikes. The Syrian Network for Human Rights counted 1,438 barrel bombs dropped in October alone. Russian diplomats claimed they urged the Syrians to stop using barrel bombs. If they did, it had little effect.[25] The UN's Commission of Inquiry reported an "overwhelming yet consistent" intensification of violence with "devastating consequences for civilians."[26]

Sensing an opportunity to join the attack on the mainstream opposition, ISIS sent a car bomb against an FSA-aligned group in eastern Aleppo. Yet despite their all too obvious presence around Aleppo, Russian aircraft largely avoided targeting the extremists. In this first phase, only a tiny fraction of Russian airstrikes—less than 10 percent of the total—were directed at ISIS or al-Qaeda-affiliated targets. By the end of its first month, the United States claimed that still only

20 percent of Russian attacks were targeting the extremists. The investigative website *Bellingcat*, which specializes in the use of open-source data and analysis, estimated that only 7.5 percent of Russian airstrikes targeted areas controlled by ISIS. Russia was seemingly quite happy at this stage to allow ISIS to continue targeting opposition forces, its own forces targeting ISIS only when it posed a direct threat to government positions such as in northern Damascus and Aleppo—where a twelve-month ISIS siege of the Kuweires air base was ended by Russian airpower and Iranian and Iranian-backed ground forces. When Russian aircraft attacked areas where ISIS did have a presence, they often unloaded more munitions on civilians than on the extremists. In November 2015, for example, Russia reportedly conducted fifty-five strikes on Deir ez-Zor, mainly hitting civilians, seventy-one of whom were killed in a single strike.[27] Indeed, evidence soon emerged that Russia routinely used indiscriminate force that resulted in civilian deaths.[28] Yet its target set changed only slightly. Moscow sometimes went to absurd lengths to justify itself, in one instance inventing a fictitious Islamist group called "Sham Taliban"—or Syrian Taliban.[29] In the immediate term, all this helped ISIS by weakening its principal foe (the mainstream opposition) and forcing moderates—facing a war on two fronts against Assad/Russia and ISIS—to align more closely with jihadists.[30]

Over time, Russian intervention gradually turned the tide of Syria's war. In targeted locations in east Aleppo and to the south of the city, the opposition lost ground. They were also pushed back into the north Latakia hills, and by January 2016 the last remaining rebel strongholds in Latakia were cleared out. Regime forces pushed toward the outskirts of the city of Jisr al-Shughur and seized the town of Jabal al-Akrad, held by the rebels since 2012. Attempts to clear the north of the Hama governate were less successful, though. Former FSA units from Hama, equipped with TOWs and reinforced by jihadists from the North, pushed regime forces back. The regime fared better in the South, where with Russian help it solidified its grip on the Daraa-Damascus highway.[31] On Christmas Day a Syrian government air strike in Ghouta killed Jaysh al-Islam's commander, Zahran Alloush, a key Saudi ally.[32] Considered a highly sectarian Salafist extremist, Alloush had also been stridently anti-ISIS. Jaysh al-Islam had battled

ISIS from the start and was largely responsible for keeping the extremists out of Ghouta. Alloush was reportedly killed as he prepared to send representatives to talks in Switzerland orchestrated by the U.S. State Department.[33]

SCRAMBLING TO RESPOND

Russian intervention crippled the U.S. strategy of coercing Assad into accepting a transitional government by robbing the United States of any lingering leverage.[34] The Obama administration therefore entered its final months in office bereft of either objectives or strategy and its positions became more reactive and inconsistent. Over the course of several meetings, the White House narrowed U.S. objectives in Syria to: (1) prosecuting the war on ISIS by continuing air strikes and adding military aid to a new Kurdish-led entity (though without a clear idea of what would come afterward), and (2) alleviating the humanitarian aspects of the crisis. "For some of my colleagues in Washington," Kerry recalled, "this was enough"—the United States had reached the limit of what it could, and would, do for Syria.[35] Kerry himself, though, still believed that with hard work and patience he might still negotiate a political settlement.

In relation to the first goal, by the autumn of 2015, the ground campaign against ISIS in Syria had slowed significantly. Having largely displaced the extremists from Kurdish lands, albeit at great cost, the YPG was reluctant to expand operations beyond Kurdish territory toward the extremists' headquarters at Raqqa. Kurdish fighters would not be warmly welcomed by the majority Sunni population there, and, looking ahead, moving forces south would weaken the protection of its northern approaches from Turkey. What is more, the Kurdish goal of creating a unified and conterminous state, which they called Rojava, was not yet complete as there was still the unfinished business of connecting Kurdish Kobane with the northwestern Kurdish enclave in Afrin, separated still by territory held by Sunni groups and ISIS. This contested land included the precious land bridge between Sunni opposition-held east Aleppo and Turkey. The Pentagon's ground campaign against ISIS hinged on the Kurds moving southward but could be sustained only if it recruited Sunnis to take up the fight, too. The solution was to embed the YPG in a broader U.S.-backed force comprising both groups.

American agents offered the Kurds military equipment and hard cash in return for the YPG agreeing to join a new political front and committing to a Raqqa offensive. This, they explained, would distance the Kurds from the PKK and make it politically easy for the United States to funnel arms and protect them from Turkey. A new entity like this would also help the United States transition away from supporting a broad range of opposition coalitions, toward a more exclusive arrangement focused more directly on combating ISIS—though it might also have the secondary effect of increasing military pressure on Assad in the North, too. The Kurds were enthusiastic since here was an opportunity to deepen their alliance with the United States and thereby secure much-needed military hardware, political legitimacy, and influence. The new initiative would also divest the YPG, and its ostensible political master the Democratic Union Party (PYD), of its exclusively Kurdish outlook and afford it a more representative mantle, underscoring its demand to be included in the peace talks. So, with American help, the PYD and YPG worked with Sunnis to establish the Syrian Democratic Forces (SDF) that October. With the Kurdish YPG force at its core, the new force also contained Sunni militia (including vetted U.S.-backed units), multiethnic and secular leftist armed groups with Christians, Armenians, and Turkmens in their ranks, and Arab tribal groups. All were promised access to the organizational, logistical, tactical, and political goods and U.S. support that only membership could provide.[36] The United States intended to use the SDF to train and support new moderate Sunni and minority militia that would in turn be employed in ground campaigns against ISIS, especially the offensive on Raqqa. A parallel political entity—the Council of Democratic Syria—was established that December, comprising PYD and other Kurdish representatives (making up less than half of the whole), secular and left-wing Sunnis, former regime figures, and representatives from other minority groups gathered into multiethnic parties.[37] In October 2015 the United States dropped fifty tons of ammunition to the newly formed group and the following month deployed special forces around Kobane to support the Kurds.[38]

Meanwhile, it introduced tougher vetting checks, flying some rebel fighters to Qatar for interrogation on their religious beliefs.[39]

The alliance with the SDF was always a short-term marriage of convenience, driven initially by the imperative to liberate Raqqa from ISIS. It is not clear that anyone in the Obama administration thought much about what would happen after Raqqa's liberation or what sort of political entity would emerge from the SDF. Immediately, creation of the SDF sharpened tensions with Turkish-backed opposition coalitions like Jaysh al-Islam and Ahrar al-Sham, tensions arising not just from traditional antagonisms but also from their different interests and priorities—the SDF were squarely *not* concerned about toppling Assad. Clashes between the two were inevitable and could only help Assad. In the South, too, there was evidence the United States was narrowing its aspirations to fit the new realities post-Russian intervention. In Amman, the MOC urged the Southern Front to abandon its goal of taking Daraa and instead focus on countering ISIS, al-Nusra (its ally in the Daraa offensive), and other Islamist groups.[40] "Those that join our program are forbidden from fighting the regime," an American general reportedly told one applicant.[41]

At least one member of the administration was deeply uncomfortable with this narrowing of goals. Described by his colleague, Susan Rice, as "dogged, relentless, and always willing to mount the hill ahead," John Kerry beseeched the president to create some leverage to support U.S. diplomacy, perhaps by deploying troops to support the SDF, conducting concerted air and missile strikes against the regime or a targeted strike against an individual target, or crafting a no-fly or "safety" zone, as Turkey requested. Without leverage, he argued, the United States had no capacity to influence things. In this, he was supported by Samantha Power, who continued to urge more forceful intervention and CIA director John Brennan. Susan Rice and the Pentagon, however, were opposed.[42] In one testy exchange, Kerry challenged General Lloyd Austin, CENTCOMM commander, directly—"Do realistic military options exist that could end this war in six to nine months?" "Of course there are options," Austin replied, but the president is opposed to all of them. Austin was right. Obama refused to even consider using force to create political leverage since none of the old problems had disappeared and additional ones had arisen.[43] Most obviously, since Russia now controlled much of the airspace over Syria, any U.S. action risked direct confrontation with a great power. Equally problematic, though, were the growing ties between the mainstream opposition and Islamists, in particular the intermingling of al-Nusra and other opposition groups on the ground. On reflection, Obama was comfortable with America's narrower objectives of defeating ISIS and alleviating humanitarian suffering where possible. But he was also happy to let Kerry chance his arm at diplomacy, though without the leverage the secretary of state felt he so sorely needed.

Without leverage, any diplomatic initiative would be dependent on Russia for its success.[44] Kerry cast around for ideas. One was that Assad might be persuaded to rein in indiscriminate attacks on civilians and grant humanitarian access to besieged areas in return for the United States withdrawing its objection to his participation in the transitional government. Privately, the administration and some of its allies, including the UK and France, had for a while accepted that Assad might play a role in transitional government, and some were beginning to express this view publicly. But Obama's team was skeptical, arguing—with good reason—that having seized the military initiative thanks to Russian airpower, there was little reason why Damascus would agree to ceasefires, let alone negotiations based on a decrepit formula it had never accepted. Earlier in the year Steven Simon, a former director on the National Security Council, had traveled to Damascus to gauge Assad's interest in local ceasefires and humanitarian action but had gotten nowhere.[45] They doubted the Russians would buy it either, though Kerry believed Russia was sensitive to the danger of being dragged into a protracted war and would therefore be grateful for a political way out.[46] Doubtful, but with few options and little at stake, Obama sanctioned a private approach. Kerry used intermediaries to convey a message to Syria's president indicating that the United States no longer sought his removal from power and would make a public commitment to that effect if Syrian forces stopped dropping barrel bombs on civilians. But America's confused diplomacy had little credibility, and, as predicted, Assad saw no need to compromise. He replied that government forces would relent only when the United States stopped "backing the rebels."[47]

Obama was not alone among Western leaders in now seeing Assad as the lesser evil. Attacked at home by ISIS, other Western governments were drawing the same conclusion. A horrific wave of ISIS terror attacks in Paris, which killed more than 130 and injured more than 400 on November 15, solidified that view. In the weeks that followed, panic and fear spread through Europe, pushing more to the conclusion that it was ISIS, not Assad, that posed the biggest threat. To nervous Europeans, it was a short line from ISIS to al-Qaeda to the Syrian opposition. As if to underscore the point, ISIS released a video in January 2016 claiming the Paris attacks had been planned in Raqqa.[48] And all the while, ISIS seemed indestructible. Smashed in one place, it simply reemerged somewhere else, the extremists enjoying the limelight and proudly exhibiting their brutality.[49]

Putin was quick to exploit European fears by drawing a direct link between support for Syria's opposition and terrorism at home. Although none of the perpetrators of the Paris atrocity were Syrian—all hailing from Belgium and France—his arguments hit home. The French government, once a staunch champion of regime change, began altering its course. Within days of the Paris attack, Foreign Minister Laurent Fabius—the man who had pushed so passionately for Syria to be referred to the International Criminal Court—now proposed that France cooperate with Assad to combat ISIS.[50] President Hollande visited Washington and Moscow in quick succession to make the case for a united coalition against ISIS—much like the sort of thing Putin had proposed the previous fall. Obama balked, but in Moscow, the French president was in more receptive company as Putin agreed to cooperate.[51] All this put Turkey in a yet more uncomfortable position. It too was rattled by Russian intervention and the seeming intractability of ISIS. Despite pronounced differences over Syria, Erdogan had nurtured good relations with Putin and was offended he had not been consulted in advance of the military intervention. Russian airpower helped Damascus reverse some of the hard-won gains made by Turkish-backed groups over the past year and jeopardized Ankara's hopes of establishing a "safe zone." Things escalated on November 24 when a Turkish F-16 shot down a Russian Su-24 Ankara claimed had strayed into Turkish airspace. The pilots ejected, but one was caught and shot by Syrian rebels. The other was rescued, but not before the Russian team sent to do it came under fire, killing a marine. The Kremlin reacted angrily, imposing economic sanctions, blocking Russian package tours to Turkey, permitting the PYD to open an office in Moscow, and offering military aid to the YPG around Afrin. There was more behind the decision to support the Kurds than the impulse to annoy Ankara, though. Moscow harbored hopes they could be weaned off their alliance with the United States and persuaded to agree to a separate peace with Damascus.[52]

IF NOT GENEVA, THEN VIENNA?

Given a green light to explore diplomatic options, Kerry pressed Lavrov for talks and found he was pushing at an open door. For four main reasons, the Kremlin was eager for a political process and wanted to draw the Americans in. First, it was convinced a political deal favorable to Assad but encompassing at least some opposition elements was necessary for Syria's future stability. Second, since it did not want to assume full responsibility for Syria's future, Russia wanted to bind the United States into a political process on Russian terms. Third, Russia's limited-war strategy hinged on the opposition's foreign backers not counterescalating. The effectiveness of Russian airpower could be neutered and potential costs increased if Saudi Arabia, Turkey, Qatar, or the United States supplied sophisticated anti-aircraft weapons or armed drones to the opposition. Reviving the political process might forestall such counterescalation.[53] With hindsight we know there was little serious prospect of the kind of counterescalation the Kremlin feared. Washington was as keen as Moscow to ensure anti-aircraft weapons not find their way into jihadist hands and made sure its allies felt that way too. The Saudis, Qataris, and UAE meanwhile were increasingly preoccupied with the escalating civil war in Yemen, which was not at all going to plan. Fourth, Putin's vision of a new global order managed by the great powers, including Russia, required the legitimacy only American assent could provide.[54]

As if to signal Russia's indispensability, Assad was summoned to Moscow on October 20 to pay his respects to Putin. Assad thanked Putin for his help, and the Russian president advised that his ally consider a long-term political solution based on a process including "all political forces."[55] To the West, Russia signaled a willingness to consider compromises such as power sharing and elections but insisted any deal be approved by Damascus and include only groups unconnected to terrorism. It also insisted that counterterrorism be prioritized and, to reinforce the point, tabled a draft resolution in the Security Council in early October calling for the coordination of anti-ISIS operations with the Syrian government. U.S. diplomats objected and the draft went nowhere, but the gambit showed the direction Russian diplomacy was heading.

On October 23, Kerry, Lavrov, Turkey's interim foreign minister Feridun Sinirlioglu, and Adel al-Jubeir, Saudi Arabia's foreign minister, assembled in Vienna to examine whether a new political process might be possible. Lavrov demanded better terms than those offered at Geneva II, in particular the inclusion of Iran. Kerry—who had always thought Iran should have been represented—readily agreed, and an invitation was dispatched.[56] The Americans proposed the negotiations be steered by a new grouping of committed states including Iran and led by the United States and Russia. Quite at home with great power brinkmanship, Lavrov agreed. After all, a partnership with the United States that bypassed the region, the UN, and preferably Geneva, too, was precisely what the Russians were after. The question of Assad's future role remained vexed, however. Lavrov insisted Assad be allowed to participate in any transitional government. Kerry was cautiously open to the idea, but al-Jubeir rejected it out of hand.[57] Publicly, Kerry avoided the issue, hoping an artful compromise would arise, while U.S. diplomats privately suggested that the inclusion of Iran indicated American flexibility on Assad's future. Options included granting Assad a temporary role in the transitional government or reviving the ill-fated "Yemen model" touted in 2012.[58] While it is unclear whether the Americans had yet raised this with Saudi Arabia, officials indicated that as many as nine key governments, including Iran, Turkey, the UK, and the United States, expressed a willingness to consider allowing Assad to remain at the head of a transitional government for a fixed period.[59] There was no agreement, though, on whether he should be permitted to stand for election after that period.

The talks proper opened in Vienna a week later, on October 30. Foreign ministers and diplomats from the United States, Russia, Turkey, and Saudi Arabia were joined by the UK, Egypt, UAE, Qatar, Jordan, France, China, Germany, Italy, the EU, and de Mistura's UN team. They began by negotiating a joint statement of principles that was significant in several respects but most notably because it didn't explicitly reaffirm the Geneva Communiqué of 2012. While calling for "a political process leading to credible, inclusive, non-sectarian governance, followed by a new constitution and elections," there was no mention of a transitional government formed by "mutual consent." Nor was it even implied that Syria's president would step aside during the process. It was agreed that elections would be supervised by the UN, but the framework offered no reason why Assad might not stand. In contrast to its silence on Assad, the declaration was adamant that ISIS and other terrorists designated by the UN Security Council or as agreed by the participants "must be defeated." It also stated that Syrian institutions—presumably including the army and Mukhabarat—would remain "intact" through the transition. Finally, the statement called for steps toward a nationwide cessation of hostilities. Indeed, it said this was the main priority.[60]

Joined by delegates from the Arab League, the diplomats returned to Vienna two weeks later. They established themselves as the International Support Group for Syria (ISSG) and fleshed out their accord in more detail. It was clear that the refugee crisis that summer and fall's ISIS atrocities in Europe had fundamentally changed international attitudes. There was a sense of desperation in the air and a collapse of willingness to confront Assad. The goal of a national ceasefire was agreed, but at Russia's insistence it was also agreed the ceasefire would not apply to offensive operations against ISIS, al-Nusra, and other terrorist organizations as agreed by the ISSG. No one seriously objected, and the terrorist exception was grafted onto every subsequent ceasefire deal, even though it awarded Assad and his allies—who, recall, insisted *all* their main opponents were either terrorists or allied with terrorists—an obvious carte blanche to ignore ceasefires from then on. Nor would any ceasefire apply to the U.S.-led coalition or to Russia—which still claimed it was targeting only jihadists. It was an obvious hole in the arrangement that Damascus, Tehran, and Moscow exploited to the full and which little effort was made to reverse even when the consequences were clear. They also agreed in principle to reestablish a UN monitoring mission, but everyone except the United States was cool on the idea, and few thought it had much of a chance. At U.S. and European insistence, the new declaration reaffirmed the Geneva Communiqué (missing two weeks earlier) and set out an ambitious (some might say wholly unfeasible) timetable for elections inside eighteen months.[61] The UN's Staffan de Mistura was asked to convene talks between Syria's parties and to determine who should represent the opposition by January 1, 2016.

It was apparent from the start that de Mistura would be unable to marshal the opposition into a negotiating team, so the United States stepped in to help. It was no easy task. Besides differences between the groups themselves, Turkey insisted the SNC take the lead, Egypt insisted the Muslim Brotherhood be sidelined, and Russia demanded the so-called loyal opposition be included. The United States passed the buck to Saudi Arabia, which summoned the parties to Riyadh. Beginning on December 10, the talks brought together the SOC, including the Muslim Brotherhood, opposition figures from the National Coordination Body for Democratic Change (NCB), part of Assad's so-called loyal opposition who had already negotiated with Moscow (and were thus included to keep Russia onboard), the Kurdish National Council, independent opposition figures, and armed groups including Jaysh al-Islam and Ahrar al-Sham. As before, al-Nusra and the PYD were excluded—the former at the West's insistence, the latter at Turkey's. The Saudis, Turks, and Americans succeeded in strong-arming the factions into a single negotiating team—the Higher Negotiations Committee (HNC). Ahrar al-Shar at first objected to the NCB's inclusion but was persuaded to relent.[62] They drafted a joint statement setting out their common position, which contained little that was new. The crucial notes were that Assad must step down at the beginning of the political transition and the new state should be democratic.[63]

Kerry visited Moscow to underscore the new political alignment and hash out the terms of a new Security Council resolution, beginning a distinct slide away from the UN-convened framework towards a bilateral approach spearheaded by the United States and Russia. The two sides agreed on a process for negotiations, Putin welcoming the fact Washington's thinking now aligned with his own. Kerry reciprocated, underlining that the United States was not pursuing regime change in Syria and that Russian and American policies were "moving in the same direction."[64] The UN Security Council gave the new initiative its stamp of approval on December 18, passing Resolution 2254 at a ministerial-level session. Though Lavrov and Kerry had already agreed on the parameters, the negotiations still proved difficult, and the text was settled only a few hours beforehand. Though it involved compromises for both, the resolution signaled that the ground was shifting in Russia's favor. Besides endorsing the Vienna platform and elections within eighteen months, the resolution reaffirmed the Geneva Communiqué despite initial Russian objections, though without clarifying what was required with respect to Assad. American diplomats agreed to drop references to a "political transition"—the formula agreed on in Geneva—in favor of "political settlement," a phrase much more in keeping with Russian aspirations. But this was still a step too far for the British, French, and Gulf Arab states, so the final text included references to both "transition" (four times) and "settlement" (three times).[65] Ultimately, the Kremlin calculated it could live with the communiqué for the time being as the price for having the Security Council endorse a Vienna process more amenable to its interests and likely to supplant Geneva anyway.[66] Most of the key international players now accepted that Assad would be part of any transitional government and that it would be the government, not the state itself, subjected to reform. The council emphasized the need for an internationally monitored ceasefire but—as agreed to in Vienna—stressed this would not apply to groups designated terrorists by the council or ISSG. On that, Russia failed to have Ahrar al-Sham added to the list of proscribed terrorist groups excluded from the ceasefire, though that made little difference in practice since it insisted that all opposition groups were tainted by association with the proscribed groups. Russia had more success preventing the HNC from being recognized as the legitimate representative of Syria's opposition. The council invited the UN secretary-general to develop plans for a monitoring mission, but few expected that would see the light of day.

Just three days after the Security Council had set out new terms for peace in Syria more favorable to Damascus and Moscow, Russian aircraft bombed a marketplace and residential streets in Idlib, killing at least forty-three civilians.[67] It was not a one-off. In the course of 2015 there had been a staggering 112 attacks on medical facilities, 85 percent of them by government forces and their allies—the Russians.[68] In early January 2016 the UN's humanitarian chief, Stephen O'Brien, told the Security Council that nearly 400,000 people still lived under siege. The situation in Madaya, northwest of Damascus, was particularly dire. Besieged by government, Hezbollah, and Iraqi Shi'ite forces, and without power, water, or medical services, Madaya had received no assistance since October the previous year, and what it had received then had been insufficient to meet immediate needs. O'Brien said the UN had credible reports that people were starving and that those who tried to flee faced being shot or blown up by land mines. Undeterred by the criticism, Russian diplomats complained that humanitarian assistance was being used to help ISIS and warned they would block the continuation of cross-border aid unless their concerns were addressed. They relented in the face of strong pressure from UN officials, who argued that the cross-border deliveries had improved the humanitarian situation, but Resolution 2258 (December 22, 2015), which extended the operations until January 2017, also stressed that ISIS and other extremists were responsible for blocking humanitarian aid and called on states to stem the flow of foreign fighters into and out of Syria. Damascus, meanwhile, agreed to grant humanitarian access to Madaya in return for the opposition granting access to al-Fuah and Kafriya. The UN's Commission of Inquiry marked the new year by issuing a chilling report that documented the fate of detainees arbitrarily arrested by the government. Tens of thousands, the commission reported, had been subjected to torture and killed in government prisons.[69]

Once diplomats turned to the business of organizing the talks envisaged by Resolution 2254—named Geneva III—it was clear there was much they still disagreed about. They disagreed on the HNC's political status. They even disagreed about what a ceasefire ought to look like. De Mistura—backed by the Russians and to some extent the Americans—wanted an incremental approach based on local ceasefire arrangements and confidence building. Others, led by the French, expected a national ceasefire since local arrangements served the regime's siege-and-starvation tactics by allowing it to concentrate forces.[70] Consensus did start to emerge on ceasefire monitoring—not a monitoring mission but a "light footprint" proposed by de Mistura, something smaller and much less intrusive than UNSMIS, comprising a small, Damascus-based UN team to investigate alleged violations. The mission would grow over time if conditions allowed. But the secretary-general's office objected even to this, complaining the situation on the ground was too dangerous to permit even a modest deployment of deskbound monitors.

The Geneva III talks began on January 29, 2016, and fared no better than Geneva II. First, the HNC demanded that sieges be eased, humanitarian access granted, and Russian air strikes ended as preconditions. There was no chance any of these would be accepted, and it took U.S. and Saudi persuasion to get the opposition to the table. Then Russia challenged the HNC's legitimacy and objected to the inclusion of Jaysh al-Islam and Ahrar al-Sham, which it branded as terrorists. Russia also insisted that the Kurdish PYD and Council for Democratic Syria (CDS)—the new label attached to the SDF's civilian governing body—be allowed into the talks. Turkey objected strongly to the PYD and de Mistura agreed, but the UN envoy bought Jaysh al-Islam's participation by offering the CDS places as advisers and observers in return.[71] Squabbling over invitations pushed the talks back into February, and as the diplomats haggled, inside Syria government forces and their allies prepared a new offensive against Aleppo's northern approaches as some three thousand soldiers were redeployed from Damascus to Aleppo's front lines.

The parties eventually gathered on February 1. To avoid the opening ceremony acrimony that had soured earlier conferences, de Mistura orchestrated a muted opening of proximity talks about the ceasefire and transition process, charging his UN team with conveying messages between the parties. He envisaged that direct negotiations could begin after some trust and common ground was established first. This was not the first time this approach had been tried, and not the first time it had failed. This time, however, the talks never got going. Instead, delegates breakfasted to news of a combined Syrian

Army, Hezbollah, and NDF offensive on opposition positions north of Aleppo. Fearing a trap, HNC delegates vowed they would not negotiate while the regime prosecuted its war. De Mistura was left fruitlessly talking to the government delegation about lifting sieges and releasing political prisoners.

Naturally, the Syrians and Russians blamed the opposition for the failure.[72] So too did an irritated John Kerry. "Don't blame me," he told participants on the sidelines of a donor conference in London hours after the Geneva talks collapsed, "go and blame your opposition. . . . It was the opposition that didn't want to negotiate and didn't want a ceasefire, and they walked away." Pressed on why the United States had not done more, he retorted, "What do you want me to do? Go to war with Russia? Is that what you want?" The rebels' obstinacy would bring only more months of Russian bombing that would "decimate" them, Kerry exclaimed.[73] Blaming the opposition for the failure of peace talks when it was the government that had gone on the military offensive was a bizarre refrain, but it spoke volumes about Kerry's frustration and about his inability to influence events in and around Syria. As the secretary of state vented, around seventy thousand Syrians fled northward toward Turkey, seeking sanctuary from the government offensive. The Turkish Army lobbed shells in the opposite direction, aiming at the YPG.

11

MELTDOWN OF HUMANITY

ERGEI LAVROV and John Kerry were determined keep their peace process going: Lavrov because he had the Americans where he wanted them—working bilaterally on a deal that would allow Assad to remain in place; Kerry because he still aspired to do some good with the time he had left in office. The two kept in almost constant contact and on February 11, 2016, met in Munich with the other International Syria Support Group members to revive their stalled process. Kerry pressed Lavrov to support a cessation of hostilities, which the Russian readily did. They each agreed to exert influence over their Syrian allies to make it happen and that the ceasefire should be monitored and alleged infringements investigated, though precisely how remained unclear. They agreed humanitarian access should be granted to besieged areas, beginning with Madaya, Mouadhimiyeh, and Kafr Batna, and aid air dropped into Deir ez-Zor. They also agreed the cessation should not apply to ISIS and al-Nusra. Once the cessation of violence was established, the parties would return to Geneva to resume talks on the political settlement.[1] Lavrov and Kerry left Munich satisfied, seemingly set on a bilateral approach that cut the ISSG and UN from the picture. Syrians themselves were less satisfied. The opposition's Higher Negotiations Committee was wary, concerned the government would use this cessation as it had the last, to consolidate territorial gains and prepare its next offensive. Damascus was also unenthusiastic since it believed that, with Russian help, victory in Aleppo was within its grasp.

THE KERRY AND LAVROV CESSATION

Talks about talks dragged on while regime forces secured most of their objectives around Aleppo. The Syrian government relieved the sieges of loyalist Nubl and Al-Zahraa, linking up with the Syrian Democratic Force in Afrin to close the Sunni opposition's land route between Turkey and Aleppo. Meanwhile, to the north, the SDF exploited Sunni opposition vulnerability by forcibly taking the Menagh air base, held by FSA-aligned groups, after several days of fierce fighting during which it received help from around thirty Russian airstrikes.[2] The Russians, who favored rapprochement between Damascus and the Kurds, were only too happy to assist the SDF, sow discord, and weaken eastern Aleppo's defenders. These offensives cut the route from east Aleppo to Turkey to a single road.

Immediate objectives largely achieved, the government at last agreed to sit down and consider the Kerry-Lavrov plan. American and Russian diplomats had spent much of February 2016 hashing out the terms. They stipulated that the parties would limit the use of force to counterterrorism and self-defense, grant unfettered humanitarian access to besieged areas, and release detainees. Political talks would resume once basic stability was achieved. Differences remained on ceasefire monitoring. The Russians objected to an independent or UN mechanism, but for the time being the Americans were happy to concede the point to get the deal. The agreement was presented to the Security Council as a fait accompli on February 22 and adopted unanimously four days later (Resolution 2268, February 26, 2016). Damascus swiftly accepted the terms. The HNC remained suspicious, not least because the arrangement left ample scope for the government to continue using force against alleged terrorists, but reluctantly consented to give the initiative two weeks. The cessation finally came into effect on February 27.

Ceasefire monitoring was rudimentary at best. The parties were invited to submit alleged violations to the ISSG's "ceasefire task group," cochaired by the United States and Russia, either directly or through Staffan de Mistura's office. The ISSG would investigate and determine what, if anything, should be done. Both sides reported violations, but overall violence declined markedly. De Mistura reported that the Syrian Defense Ministry gave Russia an undertaking to cease aerial bombardment—though he had reported something similar the previous November, only for it to emerge that what he had taken as an undertaking not to bomb civilians was in fact a letter denying it ever had. Kerry claimed the cessation "hugely reduced" violence in Syria by 80–90 percent.[3] The UN reported significant improvements in humanitarian access. More than five hundred truckloads of aid were delivered to 240,000 people in several besieged towns, but access to others, including east Aleppo, was denied. The Syrian Observatory for Human Rights declared March 2016 Syria's most peaceful time since 2011. Some speculated about political settlement and an end to war.[4]

What was going on? The cessation was made possible by direct U.S. and Russian activism. Both invested heavily in and applied significant pressure on allies to secure compliance. But the heart of the matter lay not in international diplomacy but in the balance and disposition of forces on the ground. To the HNC, the hopes of early 2015 were long since gone. Assailed by the regime, Iran, Hezbollah, Shi'ite militia, ISIS, and now Russia and the SDF as well, its military position was under serious stress, not just in Aleppo but almost everywhere. Dependent on foreign help, its members had little option but to do as the United States and Saudi Arabia asked. Things were very different for Damascus. Assad and his allies were impatient to press their advantage, but battlefield gains had been slow and costly. Though hard-pressed, the opposition hadn't collapsed under the strain of Russian airpower as some thought it would, and government forces were exhausted and stretched thin. A strategic pause made sense not only because it pleased Russia but also because it gave the army time to regroup. The cessation's apparent success therefore owed little to the power of diplomacy and everything to the fact that it suited the parties to take a momentary pause. Damascus certainly had no intention of letting it become permanent.

With the ceasefire in place, the government and HNC reconvened in Geneva on March 14, 2016, for proximity talks, a low-key affair focused on abstract issues like constitutional reform. Moscow suggested Syria be a federal state like Russia, with autonomy granted to the Kurds. It had long thought the government should negotiate a deal with the Kurds that granted them autonomy and offered a path to reintegrating the more than one-fifth of Syria's territory controlled by the SDF, without having to fight for it. The PYD, not represented in Geneva, was enthusiastic, declaring their intention to establish federal-like authorities immediately. But Damascus was horrified and rejected federalism outright. On this, the HNC agreed with the government. The recent offensive near Aleppo had irreparably damaged its ties with the Kurds.

Perhaps unnerved by the government's display of independence, Putin shocked everyone with what appeared a stunning change in policy. Declaring that Russia had achieved its military objectives, he announced it would withdraw the main part of its force from Syria. This was clearly intended as a message to Assad: that in return for Russian military support, he was expected to accept Russian political leadership and the deal Russia wanted. Russia's exit strategy pivoted on securing an international agreement on favorable terms, and for that Putin needed Assad's acquiescence. There were other considerations, too: convincing the United States and HNC that Russia was serious about the peace process; containing the influence of Iran and Hezbollah, which had grown relative to Russian influence as the immediate threat to the regime had declined; limiting the political damage being done by the intervention to Russia's relationships with Turkey, Saudi Arabia, and Israel; concerns about the mounting chorus of international criticism; and a genuine sense that the intervention *had* achieved its initial objectives.[5] On the latter point, some suggest that it was precisely the fact the intervention had *not* had the immediate and decisive effect the Kremlin had expected that forced Putin's hand, an effort to prevent Russia being dragged further into Syria's quagmire. According to this view, it was not the Geneva talks but impending legislative elections in Russia that dictated the announcement's timing. All these factors probably played some role, but if Putin was hoping to cow Assad, he was to be disappointed, as Syria's president responded with an acerbic public comment that Iran had always been his regime's "chief supporter."[6] Putin had succeeded, however, in wrong-footing the West once again.

Despite Russian efforts to jolt negotiations in Geneva toward a resolution, talks broke down over the timing of presidential elections, who would be permitted to stand, and Assad's fate in the interim. Another jolt brought the Russians and Americans closer on these questions. On March 22, ISIS conducted a wave of bombings in Brussels, which killed thirty-two. A few days earlier, U.S. special forces operating in Kurdish territory close to the Syria-Iraq border had killed the group's deputy leader in Syria, Abu Ali al-Anbari.[7] ISIS loomed large, therefore, when Kerry visited Lavrov in Moscow to gauge whether Putin's withdrawal announcement signaled any waning support for Assad.[8] He found it hadn't, but the two sides decided nonetheless that this shouldn't stop them proceeding on other issues. Beneath the surface there was an emerging if still tacit understanding that the Americans were coming over to Russia's view of things—that Assad would stay in government for the transition, with the issue settled long-term by presidential elections.

By now, though, the ceasefire in Syria was falling apart. The collapse was orchestrated by the government, which continually probed the arrangement by exploiting the deal's loopholes to justify continued air and artillery attacks, by claiming to be targeting terrorists, as permitted. Each government violation drew an armed reaction from the other side, and the government gradually increased the pressure so that by late March, violence was back at pre-ceasefire levels. Humanitarian access dried up, too, with six of the eighteen besieged areas having not received any aid at all. Daraya and Douma in the embattled eastern Ghouta region remained firmly out-of-bounds to humanitarian aid, efforts to bring relief to trapped civilians blocked by their besiegers. It was not hard, therefore, to predict where the government's next offensive would land. Chastened by Putin's strong-arm tactics, Assad was repeating a trick he had used to good effect before: calling the Kremlin's bluff. Worried now that Putin might agree with the Americans to ease him out of power at the end of the transition, something he was no more willing to consider now than he had been five years before, Assad wanted to force Moscow to make a choice between him and the risk of state collapse. In truth this was not the high-stakes game of chicken it had once been for Assad. His military position—though not great—was better than it had been for a while, and his other ally, Iran, was bridling at being frozen out by Kerry and Lavrov. Assad's gamble worked. As he had done before, when pushed into a corner by Assad, Putin backed off.

Observers on the Bosporus looking for signs of Russian withdrawal reported, instead, that more military equipment was moving from Russia to Syria than in the other direction.[9] In the last week of March, Russian ground forces and attack helicopters became heavily engaged in a successful lightning offensive to retake Palmyra from ISIS. They celebrated by flying the Mariinsky Symphony Orchestra from St. Petersburg to play among the city's UNESCO-listed ruins—indeed, at the very spot where ISIS child soldiers had massacred two dozen captured government troops.[10] The celebration was short-lived, since ISIS retook the site that December, but, seriously depleted, their position was untenable. With Russian and U.S. help, Palmyra was finally liberated the following January. All that was in the future. For now, what mattered was that Russian withdrawal was a mirage.

In Geneva, the government side brought the talks close to collapse by refusing to even discuss Assad's future—a position that undermined any talk of future constitutions. De Mistura tabled a paper identifying "Points of Commonality" between the two sides, a feat achieved by restating banal points about the need for a new constitution and elections, Syria's "nonsectarian" future, the granting of equal rights to women, renunciation of terrorism and revenge, and return of refugees and the displaced, but omitting awkward details about transitional government or implementation.[11] Yet even this tepid document drew a sharp response from Damascus, which issued a written rebuttal and bewildering list of amendments. Then, disregarding the Geneva talks entirely, the government announced its own plans for a new constitution and legislative elections. Not far from where the two delegations were housed, the UN's Human Rights Council adopted yet another resolution that condemned Syria's many violations of human rights, urged a rethink on the decision not to refer the situation to the ICC, and demanded humanitarian access to besieged communities. But almost as many states didn't support these anodyne claims as supported them, with twenty-seven voting in favor and twenty either abstaining or opposing it—a clear sign of waning international concern that Damascus surely noted.[12] The Security Council itself was tested on March 31, when government aircraft bombed a school and hospital and Deir al-Asafir, south of Damascus, killing more than thirty civilians. Outraged Western governments demanded the council respond to this blatant ceasefire violation. American diplomats drafted a Security Council press statement condemning the attack, hardly a stinging riposte.[13] Yet even that was more than the council could stomach, as the Russians rejected the statement, insisting the ISSG procedures be followed first. The ceasefire was finished.

It did not take long to see how the Syrian Army had used its strategic pause. Government forces launched a concerted offensive against opposition pockets close to Damascus, especially in eastern Ghouta. Supported by Russian airpower and Hezbollah fighters, and helped by internecine conflict among Jaysh al-Islam, al-Nusra, and FSA-aligned Faylaq al-Rahman, they quickly captured around one-third of opposition-held territory in eastern Ghouta.[14] A shrunken eastern Ghouta could now be subjected to the full weight of the regime's siege-and-starvation tactics. Further north, more civilians were killed on April 20 by government bombardment of two of Idlib's markets.[15] More than sixty died the same way in Aleppo when a hospital and other civilian buildings were bombed.[16] Indiscriminate barrel bombs were used in both attacks. The HNC stormed out of the Geneva talks in protest, and opposition armed groups announced they would no longer honor the ceasefire. Adding to the growing sense of chaos, a wave of ISIS suicide bombs in Jableh and Tartus killed more than 150. In Jableh, the extremists sent a suicide bomber into the hospital treating victims of the first attack, killing doctors, patients, and visitors alike.

Lavrov proposed that he and Kerry adopt a new approach. Instead of a nationwide cessation, they should sponsor a "regime of calm," basically a temporary and localized (forty-eight- or seventy-two-hour) truce.[17] It was something the Russians had been pressing for a while and that the Americans were becoming increasingly comfortable with as their priorities shifted. Kerry agreed to cosponsor a two-day "regime of calm" for Aleppo in the first week of May. Another to the north of Latakia was unilaterally declared by the government. On May 24 two more "regimes of calm" were declared for Deraya and eastern Ghouta—the latter coming only after the government's offensive reached its culmination. All four truces came and went, but violence continued. Grasping at whatever straws they could find, de Mistura and Kerry pressed Lavrov to extend Aleppo's "regime of calm" and Lavrov agreed, suggesting an extension could be negotiated within hours while in practice Russian air operations over Aleppo, supported by Russian artillery, escalated. Kerry claimed U.S. patience was wearing thin: "either something happens in the next few months, or they are asking for a very different track," he warned.[18] He was bluffing, of course. There was no "different track," and everyone knew it.

The smaller opposition pockets in western Ghouta, to the south and west of Damascus, now suffered the same fate as their counterparts in eastern Ghouta. Subjected to months of besiegement and facing severe malnutrition, besieged Daraya and Mu'adhamiyat al-Sham relented in August and September 2016, respectively. The assault on Daraya recommenced in April and escalated dramatically in June. The UN's pleas for access were rebuffed by Damascus, and neither could Moscow be persuaded to exert influence over its ally, Russian diplomats arguing that since Daraya was controlled by al-Nusra and ISIS, it was a legitimate target under the terms of Resolution 2254. This was patently untrue since Daraya was defended by the FSA-aligned Martyrs of Islam, had no discernible al-Nusra presence, and had never been occupied by ISIS. But it didn't matter. De Mistura eventually succeeded in persuading the government to allow a humanitarian assessment team to enter the enclave. What they found was shocking: a civilian population in desperate need of medical supplies and food. Yet still the government refused to allow aid convoys to cross the lines. A few weeks later, no doubt helped by a nudge from Moscow, the ICRC, UN, and Red Crescent persuaded the government to allow five trucks of food and vaccines into Daraya. But after trundling its way between checkpoints and potholes, the convoy was stopped by Syrian Fourth Armored Division troops, commanded by Bashar's younger brother, Maher al-Assad. The soldiers seized nutritional and medical items, claiming the government's permit only extended to vaccines, baby formula, and school supplies.[19] As the forlorn convoy turned back, government forces shelled where civilians had gathered to receive aid, killing several. This blatant denial of aid prompted calls for assistance to be dropped by air, as it had already done to areas besieged by ISIS in Deir ez-Zor.[20] Perhaps fearing this might cause it to lose control over the inflow of aid, the government relented and allowed some supplies into Daraya. A convoy carrying vaccines and other medical items made it through the lines on June 5, 2016, and a few days later the World Food Program and Red Crescent brought in food—the first time since 2012. Once more, though, government forces rained barrel bombs down on the area.[21] About twelve barrel bombs hit the enclave in the week following the aid delivery. On August 19 a barrel bomb was thrown at Daraya's last functioning hospital, which was then repeatedly hit with incendiaries.[22] Its hospital ablaze, meager supplies all but gone, and fighters bereft of ammunition, Daraya's resolve crumbled, and it accepted the government's offer of surrender, removal, and "reconciliation." Under the deal, rebel fighters were bused to Idlib and civilians given the option of either joining them or submitting themselves to the government for "reconciliation" and rehousing elsewhere.

The surrender arrangements at Daraya represented a refining of the Homs deal to make it more acceptable to the rebels and UN. Though the UN was not involved this time, this deal became a model for the government's future strategy implemented with UN help: siege, starvation, and bombardment, followed by a tightening of the noose until resolve collapses, and the government's "reconciliation" terms are accepted. The UN frequently assisted in that final stage, officials rationalizing their complicity by claiming it was the only way of protecting civilians. What they apparently failed to understand was that each deal only encouraged the government to continue the siege-and-starvation tactic elsewhere. What was done in Daraya and then Mu'adhamiyat al-Sham became government strategy across the country—aided and abetted by the United Nations.

ALEPPO: SETTING THE SIEGE

Aleppo was next on the government's to-do list. Though the government had failed to close the siege entirely, the winter offensive in 2015–2016 had strengthened its position, creating new tactical opportunities. There was a degree of urgency, too, since November would bring presidential elections to the United States and a new administration likely led by Hillary Clinton, who was expected to adopt a more forceful approach to Syria. With Clinton in the White House, a major offensive on east Aleppo might attract American intervention. Moscow was more cautious, worried an offensive might undermine partnership with the United States and distract attention away from ISIS. Yet as the U.S. position on the big issues showed little sign of changing through the spring, Russia's sense of caution ebbed. The main U.S. priority was ISIS, and its main strategy was using SDF ground forces to defeat the extremists. At the end of May it backed an SDF offensive with aircraft and special forces, some photographed wearing YPG insignia, to liberate Manbij in northeast Aleppo governate from ISIS.[23] When NDF militia clashed with Kurdish forces, U.S. diplomats cabled Damascus, warning them to stop immediately. U.S. fighter jets took to the skies to deter them.[24]

The deepening U.S.-SDF alliance sent a cold chill through Ankara. A month before the Manbij offensive, the United States had asked Turkey to join the campaign and encourage its Syrian protégés to do likewise. Erdogan hoped to counteract the U.S.-Kurd alliance by demonstrating Turkey's value to the anti-ISIS campaign, but the Manbij offensive posed a problem for him since the SDF could take advantage to grab more land west of the Euphrates. Turkey's president therefore attempted a difficult balancing act by expressing willingness to join the offensive without fully committing.[25] Erdogan urged Obama not to allow the SDF to take unilateral control of towns west of the Euphrates, especially Manbij and Jarabulus. He stressed his support for the planned offensive but proposed that non-Kurdish units be pulled out of the SDF's command structure and that coalition air strikes do more to support operations undertaken by others. Obama replied that he was unable to deliver the first request and reluctant to deliver the second because Turkey's Syrian proxies were—in the words of Brett

McGurk, who served both Obama and Trump as envoy to the anti-ISIS coalition—"riddled with extremists, many tied to Al Qaeda."[26] But the Americans were not entirely unsympathetic to Erdogan's position. They proposed that the SDF prioritize the recapture of Raqqa, east of the Euphrates and well away from Turkey and the Kurdish heartland, before turning to the more sensitive Manbij and Jarabulus. But the Kurds themselves refused, insisting the liberation of Kurdish-populated towns take priority. Since the U.S. campaign against ISIS in Syria depended on YPG ground forces, the Kurds were confident the Americans would back down. And they did.[27] A further 250 American special forces soldiers were deployed to support "Operation Martyr"—the SDF offensive on Manbij.[28]

Still, Ankara tried to delay the offensive and dilute U.S. dependence on the SDF, this time by proposing a plan to establish a new "Northern Army" (Jaysh al-Shamal) composed of around three thousand Sunni fighters aligned with the Saudi-backed Islamist Harakat Nour al-Din al-Zenki and other, similar groups.[29] This new force would lead an offensive against al-Nusra and ISIS in Idlib before spearheading the fight for Manbij and Jarabulus. The United States would supply the weapons, Qatar and Saudi Arabia the finances, and Turkey would facilitate its movement and provide artillery and air cover. Though Qatar and Saudi Arabia bought into the idea, the United States wavered, citing persistent concerns about the Islamist credentials of some of the groups it was being asked to support, and the SDF opposed it outright.

With the help of an American Armored Vehicle Launched Bridge (AVLB), SDF forces crossed the Euphrates from the east on June 1, beginning their offensive on Manbij. They made rapid progress, taking just a couple of days to secure a bridgehead on the western banks and then a little more than two weeks to encircle Manbij city itself. An ISIS counteroffensive in early July inflicted serious casualties and forced the United States to send in more special forces and materiel, but the fighting dragged on into August. With each day that passed, cooperation between the United States and the SDF deepened, putting the United States squarely on a collision course with its other ally, Turkey.[30]

The turmoil caused by the Manbij offensive created just the window of opportunity for a renewed push on Aleppo that Damascus had been looking for. Barrel bombing and indiscriminate artillery fire increased markedly in May and June. The opposition fired back indiscriminately, too.[31] Not only did Moscow not dissuade Damascus from its chosen course, by mid-May Russian aircraft were actively participating, clinging to the claim they were targeting only al-Nusra and ISIS. The escalating violence around Aleppo through May was tempered only somewhat by American efforts to negotiate new "regimes of calm." Russian diplomats went through the motions but clearly had little intention of reviving the idea. More determined than anyone else to keep what was left of the peace process alive, John Kerry met his Iranian counterpart, Mohammed Javad Zarif, on the fringes of the Oslo Forum in mid-June. The secretary of state had been handed an intelligence assessment suggesting the Iranians might compromise on Syria in return for an easing of international sanctions, but Kerry detected no such flexibility, and Hezbollah announced it was sending reinforcements to Aleppo.

In late June the Syrian government, backed by Russian airpower, directed an offensive at the Castello highway—the last route between eastern Aleppo and the outside world. The final push to encircle Aleppo was on.[32] Both sides understood the stakes. Victory for Assad would deliver a major blow to the opposition and allow the government to ratchet up the pressure on Deraa, Ghouta, and Idlib, creating a domino effect that could pave his way to victory. Should the offensive fail, things would look very different, however, and Moscow would have to choose between increasing its military commitment, coercing Assad into a workable compromise, or cutting him loose. It took four weeks of vicious fighting, but the government succeeded.[33] Partly equipped by Turkey and Qatar, the opposition responded with a counterattack in the South to open a new route to opposition-held territory east of Aleppo, which succeeded for a while, simultaneously breaking the siege again and besieging a pocket of government forces in west Aleppo. The government, reinforced with two thousand Iraqi Shi'ites, escalated air and artillery attacks, helped by Russia, which stepped up air strikes and called on the *Admiral Kuznetsov* aircraft carrier for additional sorties.[34] The counteroffensive was reversed and eastern Aleppo fully besieged. Some twenty-five hospitals and clinics had been destroyed there since January; more than two million people now lacked access to clean water.[35]

Now preparing for a final offensive on eastern Aleppo, Russian officials floated the idea of creating humanitarian corridors to allow civilians to leave. There was an obvious strategic logic here—encouraging civilians to leave weakened the enclave and gave the besiegers a freer hand to target those who remained. The UN's Stephen O'Brien swiftly agreed and appealed for a weekly humanitarian pause to allow aid in and civilians out.[36] De Mistura backed it too. Not surprisingly, since it was their idea, Russia and Syria declared the humanitarian corridor open, while the HNC condemned it as tantamount to forced displacement. Undeterred, de Mistura offered to coordinate UN actions with Russia to implement the plan to evacuate civilians and disarmed fighters.[37] On August 3 he delivered a UN position paper to Russia proposing that the UN's humanitarian agencies establish corridors to evacuate people from Aleppo but stressing that the organization would not agree to a repeat of the Homs deal of 2014. The Russians agreed to consider it.

EUPHRATES SHIELD

The government's Aleppo offensive in full swing, by early August 2016 ISIS-held Manbij was close to falling to the SDF and American forces. Successful as the offensive may have been, it had proven difficult to prize ISIS out of its defensive positions. The SDF claimed it lost 360 fighters, but other estimates suggest the figure was double that number.[38] This was Ankara's worst nightmare: the United States brushing off Turkish entreaties and helping the Kurds take Manbij. Jarabulus to the north, close to the Turkish border, would be next in line, spelling political disaster for Erdogan unless Turkey got there first by intervening itself or sending in proxies. Since it was having so little joy appealing to Washington, perhaps it was time for Ankara to swallow Turkish pride and look elsewhere for support: to Russia. Channels were opened, and in early July Erdogan apologized for the downing of the Russian fighter jet the year before.[39] Sensing an opportunity,

Moscow responded warmly, terminating the sanctions imposed in 2015. Emergent rapprochement was then supercharged by events in Turkey itself just weeks later. Turkey's crisis was over in less than twelve hours, but its effects were longer lasting. They realigned the geopolitics of Syria's civil war.

On the evening of July 15, military aircraft took to the skies above Ankara, and soldiers blocked bridges across the Bosporus in Istanbul. Around the country, soldiers and police tried seizing control of key buildings. Dozens of people were killed as renegade military leaders calling themselves the "Peace at Home Council" launched a coup against Erdogan's government. As Western governments struggled to comprehend what was happening and what they thought about it, Vladimir Putin left no doubt. Putin called Erdogan, who was holidaying in Marmaris, to offer whatever support he needed, including military. Some reports suggest it was Russian intelligence that informed Erdogan that military helicopters had been dispatched to Marmaris carrying soldiers ordered to kidnap or kill the president. Erdogan escaped the net and the tide quickly turned. Buoyed by news the president remained at large and roused by AKP loyalists, popular demonstrations in support of the president reclaimed the streets. Meanwhile, it became clear only a relatively small fraction of the army had in fact revolted. Fighting at key locations continued for hours, claiming some three hundred lives, but the situation was brought back under control. Only then, when it was clear Erdogan would prevail, did Western governments and the EU issue their criticisms of the attempted coup. Erdogan could hardly have failed to notice that, as he accused a network led by the U.S.-based activist Fethulleh Gulen of being behind the plot.

Much about the attempted coup remains shrouded in mystery, but what is clear is that Putin immediately used the opportunity to position himself with Erdogan as a reliable ally, counterpoised to unreliable Washington. A few weeks later, Turkey's pivot was signaled by Erdogan visiting Putin in St. Petersburg to patch up their relationship face-to-face and set in train a major realignment on Syria. Putin expressed sensitivity about Turkey's Kurdish problem, reminding Erdogan that Russia faced similar challenges of its own and reassuring him Russia would always take account of Turkish interests.

Erdogan suggested Turkey could back Russia's constitutional plans for Syria in return for the Kremlin consenting to a "safe zone" in the North. Putin proved far more receptive to the idea than Obama ever had. Frustrated its engagement with Kerry had not borne fruit, the Kremlin wondered whether Turkey might be a more pliable and influential partner to support its Syria strategy. The Moscow meeting left Putin with the impression it would, and the sentiment was reciprocated. While the West condemned Erdogan's postcoup crackdown and imposed political sanctions, Russia public expressed nothing but sympathy and solidarity. As Ankara saw it, Putin was now more dependable partner than villainous puppet master; Russia displacing the United States as the power most likely to help Turkey protect its core interests in Syria.[40]

The first test of this new rapprochement was not slow in coming: Manbij began to fall, and Kurdish eyes turned to Jarabulus. The Turks "need to prioritize, they can't fight everyone at the same time," a Western diplomat based in Ankara noted.[41] In order, those priorities were: (1) contain the YPG and PKK, (2) secure the return of some of the 3.6 million refugees to a safe zone inside Syria, (3) get the best political deal possible for its Syrian allies, and (4) eliminate ISIS. But what could Turkey do to stop the Kurds taking Manbij and Jarabulus? Military action seemed untenable since the YPG/SDF was being actively supported by U.S. airpower and special forces. As Erdogan's government weighed the options, another ISIS suicide bombing on August 21 killed more than fifty guests at a wedding in Gaziantep. Protestors demanded a military response, and the government saw an opportunity to achieve two goals with one blow: deploying under the guise of clearing out ISIS, Turkey could get its forces into Jarabulus and establish a "safe zone" before the Kurds could get there, denying the territory to both ISIS and the Kurds without risking contact with the Americans.

The United States had always been unenamored about safe zones in Syria, which was one of the reasons Turkey had not already acted to create them. But if Putin consented, the Americans would be unable to do much about it, their relationship with Turkey already quite sour. Turkish diplomats quietly presented the idea to the Russians, and though they couched it squarely in terms of countering ISIS, the Russians knew instantly that this was about so much more than that and understood they could extract serious concessions in return. What they asked for in return was that Turkey withdraw its support from the rebels defending eastern Aleppo. Turkey wielded significant influence over rebel armed groups in Aleppo—indeed, so great that some referred to Aleppo as a "Turkish card guarded by jihadists."[42] Should Turkey withdraw support from east Aleppo, the enclave would be doomed. In return for that, Erdogan could have his safe zone. For a Turkish leader who had styled himself the champion of Syria's Sunni opposition, this was a hard and agonizing bargain. It was personal, too; Assad had crowed Aleppo would be "Erdogan's graveyard."[43] But he no doubt rationalized that since eastern Aleppo would fall eventually anyway, it was better to do a deal and achieve a cherished goal than not do a deal and lose out on all fronts. Erdogan felt abandoned by the West and believed there was now no hope of defeating Assad thanks to Russia's intervention. Like everyone else, he had to narrow his objectives to protect Turkey's interests. That meant securing territory in northern Syria before the American-backed Kurds did. It was with a grim sense of inevitability, then, that Erdogan agreed to sacrifice (some might say betray) eastern Aleppo in return for a green light from Russia to establish a "safe zone."

Ankara promptly engineered the redeployment of thousands of opposition fighters from eastern Aleppo to positions further north, where they were put to work countering the SDF/YPG. This quiet with-drawal crippled east Aleppo's defenses. Indeed, whatever the enclave's long-term prospects, eastern Aleppo probably would not have fallen when it did without this withdrawal. Meanwhile, Turkish comman-dos, aircraft, and their Syrian opposition allies waded into Syria's civil war, launching Operation Euphrates Shield in late August to clear around five thousand square kilometers of territory between Afrin and Manbij, and as far south as al-Bab, of ISIS and deny it to the Kurds. Their initial target, unsurprisingly, was Jarabulus, their offen-sive helped by U.S. strikes against ISIS positions there.[44] Jarabulus and half a dozen villages fell within hours. Surprised not for the first time by events in Syria, the White House welcomed Turkey's intervention against ISIS, and Vice-President Joe Biden called on YPG elements in the SDF to withdraw east of the Euphrates.[45] The Kurds complied, stating that the territory around Manbij would be controlled by non-Kurdish SDF elements instead. Clashes between pro-Turkish and pro-SDF forces continued for weeks, but in some areas they joined forces to combat ISIS while U.S. officials worked frantically to arrange a ceasefire between its two allies, confirming on August 30 that the bulk of the YPG force had indeed retreated eastward in preparation for an offensive on Raqqa.[46] Russia's public response was cool but acquiescent.[47] After taking Jarabulus and the surrounding area, the Turkish offensive turned westward against ISIS in northern Aleppo, liberating Dabiq on October 16.

KERRY AND LAVROV: THE FINAL DEAL

Forlorn about events in Syria and his inability to influence them for the better, John Kerry still firmly believed a political deal could be negotiated.[48] In his eagerness, the secretary stumbled into another diplomatic scheme that ultimately revealed just how muddled—and Russia-dependent—U.S. policy had become. Kerry thought the cessation of hostilities had collapsed primarily because the government had never fully committed to it. He wanted it reinstated but judged this would work only if Syria's air force was grounded. Given that his president had no intention of ordering U.S. military force to apply pressure on Assad, Kerry supposed the key to achieving that lay with Putin. Back in June, as battle raged around Aleppo, U.S. diplomats had approached the Russians to gauge whether they might be prepared to persuade Assad to ground his air force and ascertain what they would want in return. The Russians detected an opportunity to achieve what they had wanted since the previous September: U.S. support for a Russian-led peace process. Knowing the United States would likely reject that outright, they instead proposed that, in return for grounding the Syrian Air Force, the U.S. military should cooperate directly with Moscow on counterterrorism. Kerry thought this a small price to pay and hastened to Moscow on July 14 to hash out a deal. Putin promised he would urge Assad to restrain his air force if in return the United States did more to combat al-Qaeda-aligned al-Nusra and ISIS. Should the deal succeed, Putin explained, it would lay the groundwork for a new nationwide ceasefire and political talks.

It was an obvious trap, and recently installed secretary of defense Ash Carter recognized the problem immediately. The Russian gambit was as much about Ukraine as Syria. Russia's annexation of Crimea in 2014 had been met with sanctions and diplomatic isolation, exemplified by Putin's humiliation at the Brisbane G20. Much had changed since 2014, but Moscow wanted to regain its seat at the top global diplomatic table, and military cooperation with the United States was a good way to get it. Carter realized this would send a terrible signal to U.S. allies everywhere, especially nervous allies in eastern Europe and the Baltic. He also understood that Moscow was unlikely to keep its side of the bargain: Putin was promising only to urge Assad, not compel him. The Kremlin would be left to pocket the political boon, without assuming any responsibility for what happened in Syria. The February cessation deal had demanded that neither side take territory, a provision Damascus and Moscow blithely ignored as they gobbled up land in Ghouta, Aleppo, and Idlib. What is more, there were gaping holes in the plan: it covered Syria's air force, not its ground operations, and said nothing about Russian air operations. All the while, the noose tightened around east Aleppo. Yet desperate as he was to achieve any progress at all, Kerry "couldn't . . . understand Ash's rigidity." The secretary of state firmly believed the deal was a viable way of de-escalating the war.[49] The UN's Staffan de Mistura also thought the proposed arrangement a good one.

Over Carter's objections, Obama agreed to consider a detailed proposal. What emerged was something much more comprehensive than the original idea: an immediate countrywide ceasefire during which Syria's air force would be grounded. Humanitarian convoys would be permitted to enter besieged communities, and if that held for forty-eight hours, the U.S. military would begin to share intelligence and coordinate counterterrorism operations with Russia through a Joint Implementation Cell. Once that was operational, negotiations could begin on ending the war. Carter wasn't convinced. He thought forty-eight hours an insufficient test of Moscow's sincerity, and the president agreed, demanding the period of calm be extended to seven days, which Kerry felt undercut the whole thing.[50]

The plan's fatal flaw was that it relied on Moscow's good faith. A deal seemed possible only because the timing happened to suit

Moscow. The siege of eastern Aleppo having just been set, a cease-fire suited the Russians and their Syrian allies. They could use it as they had the ceasefire in Homs to consolidate gains and dig in their new siege positions. Moreover, the presence of al-Nusra fighters inside Aleppo meant that artillery and airpower could still be used on the enclave irrespective of any ceasefire—since offensive operations against "extremists" were permitted and Russia considered all opposition forces in Aleppo to be either extremists or allies of extremists. Indeed, the United States would now cooperate in such operations. Russian diplomats explained that under the terms of the deal they expected the Americans to do the patently impractical job of separating out moderates from the extremists so the latter could be attacked.[51] What is more, with the clock ticking down on the Obama administration and the widely expected Clinton administration thought likely to adopt a more hawkish foreign policy, Putin was keen to do deals that might limit the new president.[52] The two presidents met for a ninety-minute conversation on the sidelines of the G20 summit in Hangzhou, China, on September 5 and agreed a deal should be done, though Obama warned he would walk away if there was no progress on humanitarian access to besieged areas or grounding Syria's air force. Carter remained skeptical.[53]

Obama also confided with Erdogan on the sidelines of the G20 and offered military cooperation against ISIS in return for Turkish restraint against the Kurds. Erdogan replied that Turkey's ability to counter ISIS was contingent on the YPG remaining east of the Euphrates and relinquishing control of areas to the west. Turkey's leader had a more productive meeting with Putin. The Russian president again reassured Erdogan that he understood Turkey's concerns about the Kurds, was unsurprised by Ankara's actions, and would not oppose them. He expressed appreciation for Turkish actions in Aleppo and requested Turkey refrain from targeting Syrian government forces. Erdogan agreed.[54]

Shortly afterward, Lavrov led a Russian delegation to Geneva on September 9 to finalize the agreement with Kerry. A deal was reached over several hours of tense negotiations, Kerry complaining that the White House's fussiness over language—inspired by Ash Carter—infuriated Lavrov. The Russians agreed humanitarian aid would be allowed into eastern Aleppo but presented a long list of opposition groups they deemed terrorists and therefore excluded from the cease-fire.[55] The two sides haggled over the list and pored over maps to determine zones of al-Nusra and ISIS control that would be targeted jointly by the United States and Russia. Naturally, Russia preferred a more expansive interpretation, the United States a more restrictive one, but a compromise was reached.[56] The new Kerry-Lavrov agreement came into effect at 7 p.m., local time, on September 12 and took hold on the Aleppo front. Violence eased, but there was no easing of humanitarian access. A humanitarian convoy—the first since July bound for east Aleppo—was held up to the north between Turkish and Syrian lines as officials haggled over what goods could be allowed in.

Then, in the space of a few hours, it all unraveled. On September 17, with the period of calm five days old, U.S., British, Danish, and Australian aircraft launched a wave of thirty-seven air strikes at ISIS forces besieging the government stronghold of Deir ez-Zor in the country's East but mistakenly hit Syrian government forces.[57] Alerted to this by a Russian military liaison officer, the coalition called off the attack, but not before as many as sixty government troops had been killed and thirty more injured. Kerry immediately called Lavrov to explain the mistake and offer regrets but found the Russian "furious," accusing the Americans of taking advantage of the calm to attack the Syrian Army. Russian and Syrian media were immediately filled with claims the strikes were deliberate and showed that the West's true sympathies lay with ISIS, ironic since the accident was caused by the fact coalition aircraft were essentially providing close air support for Syrian government forces actively engaging ISIS.[58]

Payback came swiftly, but against a much softer target than the U.S. military. Two days after the Deir ez-Zor incident, Syrian helicopters and possibly Russian jets bombed and strafed a UN and Syrian Red Crescent humanitarian convoy as it unloaded supplies at Urum al-Kubra. This was no mistake. The vehicles were clearly marked with Red Crescent and UN insignia, their coordinates had been shared with the Syrian authorities, and the convoy had been stationary for around five hours prior to the attack. This was a meticulously planned war crime that killed fourteen aid workers and destroyed eighteen vehicles.[59] The convoy had been on the road since close to 11 a.m., monitored for much of the day by a Russian drone. The Russians claim the drone was withdrawn at around 2 p.m., though witnesses report seeing it three hours later. The convoy reached its destination at 2 p.m., and at around 7.15 p.m. Syrian government helicopters appeared above the warehouse, dropping several barrel bombs. Fighter jets then launched rockets and strafed the area. The United States believes Russian Su-24 aircraft also participated at this stage. It detected two fighters departing Khmemim air base toward Aleppo earlier that afternoon and reported that these were the only fixed-wing aircraft operating in the area at that time. Russian bomb remnants were found among the debris. The attack lasted until nearly midnight.[60] It was, John Kerry explained, "the final shredding of the diplomatic process into which so many had put so much." In New York, the Security Council fell into bitter recriminations. Lavrov denied Russian or Syrian involvement; Kerry condemned Lavrov's dissembling.[61] The Kerry-Lavrov process was over. In truth, the partial ceasefire was probably never much more than a temporary respite on the road toward meltdown in east Aleppo.

FALL OF EAST ALEPPO

Government forces launched their final assault on east Aleppo within just a few days of the Deir ez-Zor incident, on September 21. The offensive involved massive and indiscriminate bombardment. Hospitals and medical centers were systematically targeted; cluster bombs and incendiary devices were dropped on civilian areas to maximize terror and suffering; government helicopters hurled barrel bombs and chlorine-gas bombs into the chaos, destruction, and turmoil below. The UN's Commission of Inquiry reported that "in eastern Aleppo, pro-Government forces pummeled vital civilian infrastructure, with disastrous consequences. Day after day, hospitals, markets, water stations, schools and residential buildings were razed to the ground. Fearing bombardments, civilians avoided hospitals, including pregnant women, who increasingly gave birth at home without medical assistance or opted for caesareans to avoid hours in labour in hospital."[62] "Let us be clear," Secretary-General Ban Ki-moon told the

Security Council, "they know they are committing war crimes."[63] Civilians in west Aleppo suffered, too, as opposition groups lobbed shells indiscriminately in their direction. Access to food, water, medical services, and fuel was cut.

The UN's response was confused and fragmented. Its high commissioner for human rights, the Jordanian Zeid Ra'ad Al Hussein, declared the attacks on Aleppo's civilians likely war crimes and crimes against humanity, yet the organization's humanitarian chief, Stephen O'Brien, and its special envoy, Staffan de Mistura, focused not on stopping the violations but on evacuating eastern Aleppo's population. The envoy made a dramatic gesture by telling the media that he would personally escort the nine hundred or so al-Nusra fighters out of Aleppo if it meant ending the bombardment.[64] Russia welcomed his intervention but was working on another string to push the remaining opposition fighters out of Aleppo. Turkey's Euphrates Shield had set al-Bab, some thirty kilometers south of the border, as its objective, well south of what Putin had anticipated and a potential problem since it placed Turkish-based forces perilously close to Aleppo. Now, the Russians offered Turkey access to al-Bab without having to fight their way past the Syrian government in return for help evacuating opposition fighters from eastern Aleppo.[65] Erdogan reluctantly agreed in principle but wavered, hoping some alternative might present itself.

The UN Security Council was, as usual, divided: France and Spain proposed a resolution demanding an immediate ceasefire; Russia preferred de Mistura's initiative and threatened to veto any draft resolution demanding an immediate halt to military operations. It wasn't just the Russians that were concerned with the text: Egypt was reluctant to support a resolution that might slow the squashing of jihadists, while China remained aloof. Still, the French and Spanish pressed on. They amended their text, adding in stronger references to combating terrorism, toning down references to ceasefire monitoring, and leaving out explicit references to Syrian government and Russian operations. France's new foreign minister Jean-Marc Ayrault hurried to Moscow to urge a compromise. Lavrov replied he would negotiate but offered no concessions. Still, with time running out in east Aleppo, France and Spain, joined by more than forty other cosponsors brought the resolution to a vote. Russia tabled an alternative text, resulting in one of the council's most acrimonious public debates since the Russians and Chinese had blocked Syria's referral to the ICC more than two years earlier. Eleven members supported the French/Spanish resolution, including Egypt and Malaysia. Russia cast its veto, but only Venezuela joined it in voting no. China and Angola abstained. Only these four states supported Russia's alternative text. Russia's veto aroused palpable anger, and its obvious isolation, made plain by China's abstention, may have stung Putin into suspending Russian airstrikes. But this anger was impotent, and so the pause lasted only a few days, Russian bombing continuing until mid-November, when the enclave's end was near.

The indefatigable John Kerry was not done quite yet. He still hoped negotiations could find a way to manage the situation and hastily convened a meeting with Lavrov, de Mistura, and the foreign ministers of Egypt, Jordan Iran, Iraq, Qatar Saudi Arabia, and Turkey at the Swiss resort town of Lausanne. In his haste to talk, however, Kerry had nothing new to put on the table, so the meeting achieved nothing.[66] De Mistura offered more thoughts on his plan to escort nine hundred al-Nusra fighters out of Aleppo. Lavrov welcomed it; some Western governments expressed doubts. Since French intelligence reported fewer than 200 al-Nusra fighters still in east Aleppo, diplomats questioned where de Mistura had got his figure of 900 from and pressed him on how they would be identified. The envoy replied that the number was fluid and that the UN would ascertain who were al-Nusra fighters.[67]

Meanwhile, the situation in Aleppo deteriorated. "The tactics are as obvious as they are intolerable—make life intolerable; make death likely; push people from starvation to despair to surrender; push people to leave," the UN's Stephen O'Brien reported. Since late September alone, four hundred people had been killed and over two thousand injured.[68] Meanwhile, UNICEF reported the deliberate and systematic targeting of schools.[69] Churkin responded with an astonishing broadside, taking exception at O'Brien's "supercilious smile." "If we needed to be preached to, we would go to church. If we wanted to hear poetry, we would go to a theatre." Churkin's view was "absurd and surreal fantasy theatre," Britain's ambassador retorted. Churkin knew that, of course. He could see what everyone else, including the Chinese, could

280 MELTDOWN OF HUMANITY

see about the indiscriminate destruction of east Aleppo, but he also knew that no one intended to do anything about it.

There were some who pressed for a meaningful response to the carnage. In the United States, Samantha Power and John Kerry urged for a military response in the form of air strikes against Syrian air bases, anti-aircraft capabilities, and munitions stores. Besides the unfolding humanitarian catastrophe, the United States risked losing influence with the moderate opposition, Arab and Turkish allies, and the Kurds if it stood aside as Aleppo fell, they argued. But they were a distinct minority. Russian presence in the air and the comingling of Russian personnel with Syrian government forces on the ground had greatly increased the risk of escalation. Moreover, always reluctant to use force in Syria, Obama was never likely to change course in the final days of his presidency. That decision was compounded by the shock result of the November 8 U.S. presidential election, with Hillary Clinton defeated by erratic Republican self-styled entrepreneur and television personality Donald Trump. What this meant for U.S. foreign policy was anyone's guess, but during the campaign Trump had repeatedly professed his admiration for Putin and desire to pull back from the Middle East. In the immediate term, though, it meant the Obama administration was a lame duck.

The final push began soon after, spurred on, perhaps, by an intent to deliver the new U.S. president a fait accompli. On November 15, with Russian strikes, including cruise missiles fired from the Mediterranean, the civilian death toll soared as indiscriminate bombing and artillery fire rained down with greater intensity. The UN reported that eastern Aleppo now had no functional hospitals. Close to 1,000 civilians had been killed during this final stage of the campaign, all except 150 at the hands of the government and its allies.[70] The defenders set hundreds of tires alight, hoping the smoke would prevent or misdirect the air attacks. All it did was choke themselves. With a "sinking sense of futility," John Kerry summoned another diplomatic gathering to Lausanne.[71] At the UN, O'Brien presented Damascus with a plan for a ceasefire, humanitarian evacuations, and the delivery of aid. The Syrian government rejected it. It still preferred de Mistura's idea—one modeled on Homs and Daraya. De Mistura met Syria's foreign minister Walid al-Moualem on November 21 but made no progress.

Moualem denied the government had bombed hospitals and said he couldn't accept the delivery of food, medical supplies, and doctors into the enclave. Assad's allies were being obdurate in the Security Council, too. New Zealand, joined this time by the other humanitarian leads Spain and Egypt, circulated another draft resolution calling for an immediate ten-day pause in the fighting. The talks ambled on, but Russia refused to budge from its view that nothing be allowed to hinder counterterrorism. For sure, nobody wanted the siege to end in a bloodbath of street-to-street fighting—even Russia was keen to avoid that—but Moscow was now committed to completing the takeover of east Aleppo and saw little reason to accept a ceasefire now. What it wanted was an evacuation. After a month of consultations and debate and having allowed a full week for the Security Council to view and discuss the final draft, New Zealand, Spain, and Egypt presented a draft resolution calling for an immediate seven-day pause. Eleven states supported it, including Egypt, Malaysia, Japan, and Senegal. Russia cast its veto, this time joined by China. Britain's Matthew Rycroft let fly a sharp criticism of China, which had feebly claimed there had not been enough time for consultation and deliberation—a patently ridiculous claim that couldn't cover the fact China was simply choosing Russia over its pretensions of humanitarian concern.[72]

East Aleppo fell the following week amid an orgy of violence. Progovernment militia executed civilians and surrendered fighters on the spot. Other civilians were forcibly recruited into militia.[73] In one incident, an Iraqi Shi'ite militia Harakat al-Nujaba killed eighty-two prisoners. Many more men and boys simply disappeared. A UN spokesperson aptly described the situation a "meltdown of humanity."[74] By the end of the second week of December, some 95 percent of the enclave was in government hands as thousands of people remained huddled in what was left. After wavering for so long in the hope of deliverance, Turkish diplomats scrambled to find a way Erdogan might keep his promise to Putin and facilitate the evacuation of eastern Aleppo. They proposed making Aleppo a "safe zone" free of all foreign fighters, by which they meant al-Nusra as well as the Hezbollah and Iraqi Shi'ite forces supporting Assad. Not surprisingly, the Kremlin rejected that idea.[75] The need to do better to keep Moscow happy was rammed home on November 27when Syrian government aircraft attacked and killed four Turkish soldiers north of al-Bab. So worried was he about the implications, Erdogan called Putin directly to seek assurance that the attack had not come from the Russians. Putin responded favorably but reminded Erdogan of his yet unfulfilled pledge.

Turkish officials mediated talks between Russian officials and two Turkish-backed factions still active in east Aleppo, Ahrar al-Sham and Jaysh al-Islam. Moscow agreed they would be admitted to future peace talks if they cooperated on Aleppo. Turkey then proposed a deal like that used in Homs and Daraya: a surrender in east Aleppo that would allow fighters and civilians to evacuate to Idlib. This was precisely what the Russians wanted. Neither the United States nor the United Nations was involved in the talks that gave rise to an agreement under which civilians and fighters would be evacuated to Idlib. It was accepted by Aleppo's rebels on December 13, and the evacuations began shortly afterward. But there were problems. Buses came under fire, some people were removed from buses and shot, and then the government suspended its cooperation, demanding the rebels give up the besieged villages of al-Fuah and Kafriya. Civilians waited in limbo. Turkish diplomats pressed their Russian counterparts to move things forward, which they did. Under pressure, the government relented, and the evacuations recommenced. Civilians and fighters carrying light arms were bused out of Aleppo and into Idlib, while, under the deal, Russian military police, composed largely of Sunni Chechens, moved into east Aleppo.[76] The new arrangements were endorsed by the Security Council, which unanimously passed Resolution 2328 on December 19.

Over the course of fifteen months, Russia had succeeded in reversing the Syrian government's fortunes in Syria and in reestablishing itself at the top table of international diplomacy. Russia's intervention in Syria was a masterstroke for the Kremlin and a disaster for the West and its allies, the Syrian opposition, and Syria's civilians. Military intervention achieved all the Kremlin's major objectives: it saved the Assad regime from collapse, made Moscow the indispensable partner in Syria, restored Russia's place in global politics, sidelined both the UN and the United States, and badly dented the West's liberal international order. But it was not all one-way. ISIS was still a problem, and government forces were exhausted and overstretched. The collapse of eastern Aleppo had been possible only with Turkey's acquiescence—and at the price of giving Turkey the foothold it wanted inside Syria itself. Moreover, Moscow's political strategy had not borne fruit. Russia's intervention had always aimed at reshaping the battlefield to create favorable conditions for a political settlement to stabilize the country. Moscow had searched for a political process to achieve this end and had hoped that the various rounds of negotiations with Kerry would deliver that. It hadn't, largely because both Assad and the United States proved unwilling to bend to Moscow's will. By the end of 2016, however, Russia had found a new international partner in Turkey. In return for concessions to Turkey's security interests, Russia could use Turkey to persuade enough of the Syrian opposition to accept a deal favorable to Assad. Turkey, of course, had already shifted its position on Syria profoundly. It no longer thought regime change possible and was starting to prioritize a narrower set of objectives centered on its own interests. Moreover, after the failed coup, Erdogan felt less beholden to the West and more able to pursue an independent foreign policy. As the United States and SDF became more closely aligned, Ankara feared its own vital interests were threatened and so abandoned east Aleppo to concentrate on beating the Kurds to territory vacated by ISIS.[77] Assad did not appreciate being compelled to deal with Turkey and the opposition, but Putin had left him with little choice. The Geneva framework agreed to in 2012 was now effectively dead. The new framework taking shape in the Kremlin would be a settlement that left an Assad-led government at the helm. Looking to the future, other besieged areas could expect the same fate as Homs, Daraya, and now eastern Aleppo—siege and starvation, indiscriminate bombing, executions, and finally surrender and deportation. They could also expect that for all the howls of condemnation, promises, commitments, demands, and anguish, the besieged would receive no help from the outside world.

12

RUSSIA'S ENDGAME

THE NEW YEAR brought change at the top of the United Nations and the United States. In New York, Ban Ki-moon was replaced by Antonio Guterres, the former socialist prime minister of Portugal, who had presented himself as a tough-minded advocate of human rights during his time as the UN's high commissioner for refugees. He would prove to be anything but when it came to Syria, overseeing a UN policy of acquiescence with Syrian government strategy. Meanwhile, in Washington, D.C., Barack Obama was succeeded by Donald Trump. As a candidate, Trump had repeatedly promised to withdraw U.S. forces from the Middle East. While this wasn't all that different from Obama's aspirations, there were sharp differences in the new president's character and his position on human rights and multilateralism. Trump argued that national interests, not human rights, should drive U.S. foreign policy, foreshadowing that the gap between U.S. goals and means in Syria might be closed by a narrowing of the former.[1] Whereas Obama's decision making had been cerebral and ordered—sometimes overly so—Trump's was erratic and chaotic. The new president was ignorant, impulsive, and uninterested in details and he had a short attention span and few ideas of what he wanted to achieve in the world, beyond asserting his own greatness.

Life in Syria, meanwhile, hewed to a familiarly brutal pattern. The UN's high commissioner for human rights described it as "the worst man-made disaster the world has seen since World War II."[2] That ugly assessment was matched by the UN Human Rights Council's Commission of Inquiry, which detailed a litany of atrocities: civilians tortured and killed; hospitals, schools, and markets systematically bombed; water stations destroyed; chlorine gas repeatedly used.[3] But the UN itself had become complicit in these atrocity crimes. In the name of humanitarianism, it funneled hundreds of millions of dollars' worth of goods and cash into regime-held areas and tens of millions of dollars directly into the hands of the Assad family and some of its closest allies.[4] UN documents show the organization paid the government $13 million for agriculture projects. It paid another $4 million to a state-owned fuel company sanctioned by the European Union that helped keep the government's planes in the air and tanks on the road. The World Health Organization gave $5 million to the state's blood-bank initiative despite concerns it was being used for military purposes. In 2016 alone, the UN spent $9.5 million on food and accommodation at the luxurious Four Seasons Hotel in Damascus, partly owned by the government. Two UN agencies awarded contracts worth at least $8.5 million (and possibly more than $13 million) to the Syria Trust for Development—an "NGO" in the loosest sense, headed by the president's wife, Asma al-Assad.[5] The UN contracted Syriatel—owned by Assad's rapacious cousin Rami Makhlouf—to provide its telecommunications, ensuring not only the regime could easily listen in to everything they said, but also that it profited directly from the UN. UNICEF awarded contracts worth hundreds of thousands of dollars to the al-Bustan Association—another of Makhlouf's organizations, which also ran three *shabiha* units. By the end of 2016, the UN had bestowed contracts to more than 250 companies directly connected to the Syrian government, with a total estimated worth more than $500 million.

It was not just that the UN helped bankroll the Syrian government. By pouring aid into government-held areas despite being unable to do the same in opposition held areas, the UN reinforced the imbalances between them and directly helped the regime's siege-and-starvation strategy—a strategy prefaced on atrocity crimes. According to figures provided by the World Food Program, awarded the Nobel Peace Prize in 2020, approximately 96 percent of UN food aid delivered from inside Syria was distributed in government-held territory and by government agencies and their preferred partners. Overall, in excess of 90 percent of the more than $900 million worth of aid delivered by the UN into Syria in 2015 passed through government hands.[6] Thus the UN's food aid delivered resources directly into the hands of the government, provided it a means of rewarding allies and enticing opponents, and allowed the regime to redirect its own resources to the military, satisfy basic needs, and display an image of comparative security.[7] Meanwhile, the denial of aid to besieged nongovernment areas crippled them. Prices skyrocketed, infrastructure collapsed, and poverty, malnutrition, and sheer desperation bred conflict and endemic violence. In December 2016, the month eastern Aleppo fell to the government, only six thousand people in besieged communities received any humanitarian aid at all—less than 1 percent of those living in besieged communities judged to need assistance.[8] In government areas, food prices were kept artificially low by foreign aid.

While humanitarians struggled to get basic life-sustaining supplies into besieged opposition-held areas, the UN's activities in government areas extended to reconstruction. There, the UN paid for rebuilding initiatives, education programs, and economic projects to support livelihoods. There was a clear pattern here: the Syrian government manipulated aid to fund its military, advance its interests, punish opponents, and starve out the opposition. This was well known, yet the UN proved a willing partner.[9] Humanitarian aid played a crucial role in sustaining refugees in Turkey, Jordan, Lebanon, and elsewhere, and European governments and the United States shared much of the financial cost. Sometimes, though, that aid was used to evade responsibility for resettling Syrian refugees in third countries, and sometimes, when delivered directly into Syria, it aided and abetted the government's atrocity crimes.

FALLOUT FROM ALEPPO

The fall of eastern Aleppo realigned the political currents around Syria's civil war. For one thing, it convinced Saudi Arabia and Qatar that regime change was impossible. The Saudis quickly adapted, withdrawing support from the armed opposition and looking to normalize relations with Damascus, effectively returning to their initial 2011 stance of prioritizing order over revolutionary change. This put Saudi Arabia on a collision course with Qatar, which still championed the Sunni revolutionism encapsulated by the Muslim Brotherhood. More obviously, at least initially, the frantic diplomacy at the end of Aleppo's siege created a new axis to guide Syria's peace process. Growing in confidence, the Kremlin still doubted Assad could win a military victory sufficiently decisive to achieve sustainable long-term peace. Wary of being drawn in more deeply, Russia thought a deal with some opposition elements would be necessary but expected that the shock of Aleppo would make them more pliable.[10] It thought a separate deal could be struck with the Kurds. This put it at odds with Damascus and Tehran, which believed Aleppo showed that outright victory was possible and no compromises were needed.

With hindsight, we can see the main elements of an emerging Russian endgame strategy developing after Aleppo, one that involved using locally negotiated arrangements and "de-escalation" zones to isolate opposition enclaves from one another and then pressuring each to accept a political settlement—"reconciliation"—favorable to the government. The isolation of each de-escalation zone would enable pressure to be brought on them one by one. It also created military options should coercion fail, by allowing the government to concentrate its forces in a single theater at a time, using siege, starvation, and bombardment until they all gave out. Tactics employed in Aleppo, Homs, and Deraya could be brought to bear on the remaining holdouts one at a time, while a political process focused on extending the government's authority and a new constitution that preserved the state—and Assad—intact but offered just enough power sharing to co-opt some opposition elements. The U.S. State Department detected this emerging strategy quite early, indeed before the collapse of eastern Aleppo. By mid-2017 it had drawn up in-house maps forecasting gradual regime gains in what became known as the de-escalation zones.[11] Other Western governments seemed aware of the emergent strategy, too.[12] Yet they and the UN did little to stop it, first as the zones were established and given the stamp of international approval, then as the Russians tried strong arming the opposition into accepting

Moscow's terms, and finally when, having failed at diplomacy, the government—backed by Russia and Iran—used military force to eliminate the enclaves one by one. Ultimately, of the outside powers professing sympathy for Syrians tormented by their government, only Turkey put up any meaningful resistance.

Turkey's Erdogan had little faith in the West. The West's inaction on Aleppo seemed to confirm its waning interest and influence, while its deepening alliance with the Kurds was a source of extreme concern. Ankara expected neither trend to change with the arrival of Trump, the new president having spoken warmly of the Kurdish contribution to the war on ISIS.[13] Erdogan felt betrayed by Westerners who had encouraged and then abandoned the uprising, leaving Turkey to bear the costs of supporting the armed resistance and caring for refugees. This sense of betrayal was compounded by Western toleration of the coup in Egypt in 2013 and its muted response to the attempted coup in Turkey in 2016. Since then, Ankara had pivoted toward Russia in the hope it might still influence events in Syria and protect vital interests along its southern border. This was a painful marriage of convenience, especially for a Turkish government previously so unequivocal in its support for the anti-Assadists. Even now, Ankara found it difficult to disavow regime change completely, eliciting occasional criticism from Moscow.[14]

Turkey also had its own military campaign to think about. Entering 2017, Operation Euphrates Shield had still not achieved its objective of reaching all the way south to al-Bab and clearing the YPG and ISIS. For that, Turkey needed Russia's help. Its advance had ground to a halt, stalled by withering ISIS resistance. Part of Turkey's problem was that the United States had suspended airstrikes against ISIS in the area the previous December, out of concern it might alienate the YPG, which it was hoping to use to spearhead an SDF offensive on Raqqa later in the year. Turkish ministers angrily threatened to close the Incirlik airbase to U.S. aircraft once again.[15] With the United States proving unhelpful, Ankara turned to Moscow and found it only too willing. Putin had already agreed that Turkey could extend its zone of control to al-Bab. Thus he saw no harm in cementing their new partnership and drawing Ankara still further away from the United States by offering help. The Russian Air Force, which less than three years earlier had been instructed to shoot down Turkish fighter jets should they stray into Syrian airspace, now conducted air strikes in support of Turkish-backed ground operations.[16] This helped get Turkey's offensive moving again, and even a friendly fire incident, in which Russian jets accidentally killed three Turkish soldiers, failed to knock them off their stride. By the end of February al-Bab was in the hands of Turkish-backed Sunnis and Euphrates Shield wound down.[17] It had achieved its objectives, albeit at a cost of almost 70 Turkish soldiers killed and 250 wounded. Its Syrian allies sustained some 600 wounded and dead. ISIS losses were far heavier, Turkey claiming to have killed 2,300. Turkey also claimed to have killed more than 300 "PKK-PYG" fighters.[18] Clashes between Kurdish and Turkish-backed fighters continued even after al-Bab's fall, and to defuse tensions, American and Russian officials tried to create buffers between Turkish-backed groups and the Kurds. In the area between Manbij and Afrin, local arrangements were established whereby the SDF transferred control over some villages and border posts to the Syrian government to protect them from the Turkish-backed militia. Elsewhere American and Russian soldiers moved into frontline SDF positions to provide a buffer between them and Turkish-backed forces. Beyond seriously complicating the situation in Syria's North, the culmination of the initial phases of Euphrates Shield signaled the rise to prominence of the new Turkish-Russian axis and waning American influence, which, besides reorienting the geopolitics surrounding Syria's war, foreshadowed serious troubles ahead for the Kurds.

ASTANA PROCESS

During the frantic negotiations at the end of Aleppo's siege, the Russian and Turkish governments agreed to establish a trilateral dialogue including Iran to negotiate future arrangements for Syria, effectively ditching the International Syria Support Group.[19] On December 20 the country's three foreign ministers agreed to a new process of negotiations between government and opposition, to be held in the Kazakh capital Astana. The talks would first focus on establishing ceasefires and "de-escalation zones" in critical areas before addressing the larger political questions. The summit would bring the armed groups themselves, except ISIS and al-Nusra—which in January 2017 renamed itself Hei'at Tahrir al-Sham (HTS)—into direct dialogue with the government, displacing the civilian intermediaries represented in Geneva. While the Russians dutifully acknowledged the importance of the UN's Geneva talks, which staggered on, Astana became their political vehicle for engineering an endgame. This reality was apparent to everyone except the UN's Staffan de Mistura, for whom the mission had become "the extension of the mission."[20] There were major differences between the new triumvirate powers, however, and it was Turkey that conceded most. Their agreement made no mention of political transition or constitutional reform. The Russians and Syrian government wanted eastern Ghouta—considered the regime's likely next target—exempted from de-escalation, Turkey insisted it be included. The demand by Turkish foreign minister Mevlut Cavusoglu that Hezbollah be treated identically to HTS received short shrift from Iran, though he succeeded in blocking the PYD from the process. Turkish media proclaimed the "collapse" of the government's Syria regime-change policy.[21] But foundations had been laid. Russia and Turkey agreed a national ceasefire to begin on January 1, 2017, and invited Damascus and select opposition armed groups to Astana to negotiate de-escalation.

On the eve of the talks, the Kremlin leaked a draft constitution it had prepared, the timing seemingly engineered to secure leverage over both Turkey and Assad. In some respects, the draft offered Turkey (and the opposition) some concessions. It promised democracy, human rights, and minority protection, including a fixed-term elected presidency (presidents permitted two seven-year terms), an elected People's Assembly to legislate, and a second, review, chamber known as the Assembly of Territories empowered to remove presidents, all overseen by a constitutional court.[22] Some saw evidence of flexibility on Assad's political future, though that might have been overly optimistic. More controversially, the text envisaged Syria as a federal state with an autonomous Kurdish region. The Kremlin had long thought that Damascus ought to do a deal PYD, but the provision was also a broadside at Turkey—a warning of what might happen should Ankara not exhibit flexibility of its own.

The talks got under way in the Kazakh capital on January 24 and began, as usual, with disagreement about the agenda and expected outcomes. Flush with confidence by its recent victory in Aleppo, the government saw the process as a means of consolidating territorial gains, extending local ceasefire initiatives to the remaining opposition-held pockets, and dividing the opposition. Conversely, with few cards to play, the opposition delegation, drawn mainly from Turkish-backed armed groups in the North and headed by Jaysh al-Islam's Moham-med Alloush, sought concessions on access to besieged areas and release of detainees, lambasted government atrocities, and demanded that Iran (and Hezbollah) be excluded from the process.[23] Reluctant to concede the political transition embedded in the UN's Geneva pro-cess, opposition figures also questioned the legitimacy of the Astana process itself, drawing fire from Turkish diplomats, who insisted this was the only viable process left open to them. Government delegates stuck to their usual playbook. Hoping to derail the talks by focusing on counterterrorism, they complained jihadists were embedded among the opposition fighters in Wadi Barada, a claim the opposition denied. Away from the Syrians, the three conveners tried to deepen their own consensus, but there were problems here, too. The Iranians accused Turkey of undermining the process by supplying weapons to the opposition; Turkish delegates countered that Hezbollah should be treated the same way as other foreign terrorists.[24] The Iranians and Russians disagreed with each other on Hezbollah. Where all three did agree was on the utility of the process itself as a vehicle for managing the end of Syria's war. Setting their differences aside, they established a trilateral commission to monitor the ceasefire and encourage vio-lence reduction and issued a general statement recapitulating general points agreed to earlier.[25]

Leaving Astana, some opposition delegates foreshadowed their own peace plan, but it was the government in the ascendancy, and it would be setting the terms.[26] That was underscored a few days later when the opposition's fragile hold on Wadi Barada collapsed and the beleaguered defenders agreed to a surrender and evacuation deal. On January 28 the government took control of Wadi Barada, and the enclave's fighters and civilians were evacuated to an increasingly over-crowded Idlib, already beset by large influxes of displaced, desperate, and traumatized civilians and a combustible mix of hardened fighters from around Syria.

The triumvirate members, joined this time by the United States, Jordan, and the UN, returned to Astana on February 6 to establish a ceasefire-monitoring mission. Initial plans to reconvene the Syrians were quashed when Alloush refused to attend, citing ongoing ceasefire violations by the government. Even without the Syrians, though, agreement was difficult. The Russians suggested strengthening the process by bringing in the United States—a move that might also secure UN backing for Astana—but the Iranians (and presumably Damascus) were implacably opposed since that would seriously dilute Tehran's influence.[27] The Americans weren't enthusiastic either. That proposal dropped, the triumvirate agreed to a trilateral mechanism— the Joint Operational Group (JOG)— comprising experts from each guarantor nation to observe the ceasefire and investigate alleged violations. They also agreed to trial confidence-building measures such as prisoner transfers. They returned to Astana ten days later, accompanied by small government and opposition delegations, but once again, talks among the Syrians yielded no agreement.[28] The Astana process was becoming bogged down.

Things were no better in Geneva, where the UN process limped on, zombie-like. Geneva still mattered to the United States, Europe, and the UN since it was now their only point of political influence, but even they no longer pressed for a transitional government. Instead, they hoped to persuade Assad to accept terms that at least some in the opposition might also accept.[29] Their one remaining bargaining chip was financial support for reconstruction. If Russia wanted Western money to help rebuild Syria, diplomats in Geneva insisted, it would need to offer an acceptable political deal. But their position was weak. The Trump administration's ambivalence was palpable, and with Assad firmly in the ascendancy on the battlefield, Russia's always limited ability to persuade Damascus to share power was much diminished.

There was therefore much déjà vu about the new round of meetings in Geneva, referred to as Geneva IV. Squabbling over the attendance list and agenda delayed proceedings. De Mistura strong-armed the HNC by threatening to nominate opposition delegates himself if they did not, further souring that relationship. Sergei Lavrov proposed that the PYD be represented, a move opposed by Turkey and Syria's Sunni opposition groups.[30] Nonetheless, the Russians forced a compromise to include, not the PYD, but the Kurdish National Council (KNC), a political body with limited influence. Another problem was the inclusion of the "loyal opposition" Cairo and Moscow groups: the former including representatives of Syria's Christian and other minorities; the latter, opposition activists who remained loyal to the state. The HNC objected strongly to their inclusion, arguing that these were government proxies, but Moscow insisted and De Mistura agreed, forcing the HNC—desperate to keep Geneva alive—to relent.[31] Getting down to business, the parties sat in the same room but did not address one another directly. Nor did they make headway. By far the most energetic of the delegations were the Russians, shuttling constantly between them. The Syrians may not have been talking to each other, but they were all talking to Russians.[32] Russia's frenetic activity showed who was now leading Syria's peace process, but also the importance the Kremlin still attached to a political settlement, necessary, it thought, for sustainable peace, and just how difficult it was finding the task. The Syrians were pushed to agree to a Geneva V meeting and some generic agenda items—mostly things on the agenda since Geneva I. These would be placed into four "baskets," on governance, the constitution, elections, and counterterrorism, to be negotiated separately by teams of experts. The Security Council welcomed agreement on de Mistura's baskets, but the discussions did not get very far.[33]

Things were little better when the Astana triumvirate reconvened in mid-March. The opposition simply refused to turn up, citing government ceasefire violations. Russian and Turkish officials used the opportunity to work through the details of the de-escalation zones plan, bringing it close to a point where it could be presented as a fait accompli to the absent Syrians. In Geneva, another round of talks on de Mistura's four baskets in the last week of March proved as fruitless as previous rounds, while in Syria Tahrir al-Sham, backed by FSA units, launched the first opposition offensive in over a year around Hama, drawing a counteroffensive that retook all the lost land over the course of three weeks and an escalation of bombing on opposition enclaves near Damascus.[34] The opposition had nonetheless demonstrated it still had capacity to fight, reaffirming the Kremlin's belief that a political settlement had to be part of its endgame.

THE APPRENTICE GOES TO WAR

Not until August 2018 did the new U.S. president appoint an envoy for Syria, seasoned ambassador James Jeffrey. Discerning his Syria policy was a difficult business. The one thing that was well telegraphed was Donald Trump's eagerness to withdraw U.S. forces from the Middle East. Beyond that, four priorities were detectable, discussed here in roughly descending order. The first priority was to ensure the lasting defeat of ISIS. President Trump was determined to finish what Barack Obama had left undone, and quickly so he could also complete an American withdrawal. To speed things up, the administration expanded the scale and tempo of U.S. operations in Syria and extended partnership with the Kurds. In 2017 the United States conducted 49 percent more strikes than the previous year, and civilian casualties rose by 215 percent to a reported figure between 3,900 and 6,100.[35] The United States also deployed more special forces and military "advisers" to operate alongside the Kurds in preparation for an offensive on Raqqa— the planning for that undertaken by the Obama administration but accelerated under Trump. By the end of 2016 there were at least three hundred U.S. Special Operations Forces inside Syria and two hundred others on close standby in the region.[36] Trump authorized the deployment of a further 400 Marines to provide artillery and other support for the SDF's Raqqa offensive and the shipment of arms to the SDF/YPG.[37] Turkey responded angrily, bombing the YPG's headquarters near al-Malikiyah and YPG positions in al-Hasakeh.[38] In that context, the strategy of increasing military support to the Kurds to engineer a rapid victory over ISIS created a serious long term dilemma for the United States: how to withdraw while simultaneously protecting the Kurds from Turkish military retribution and ensuring ISIS stayed beaten.

The second U.S. priority was to contain Iranian influence. One of Trump's short-lived national security advisers, John Bolton, captured the essence of the administration's attitude well when he wrote: "From our perspective, Syria was a strategic sideshow . . . who ruled there should not distract us from Iran, the real threat."[39] On this, Trump's position aligned with Israel's, whose prime minister, Benjamin Netanyahu, repeatedly pressed Putin to ensure that there would be no permanent Iranian bases in Syria. Indeed, Putin was concerned about growing Iranian influence, but Russia's ability to counter Iran was constrained by Assad's dependence on the Islamic Republic.[40]

The third priority, very much subordinate to the first two, was to change the Syrian government's behavior without pursuing regime change.[41] This objective carried a renewed focus on deterring the use of chemical weapons, a matter of personal reputation for Trump, who had been sharply critical of his predecessor's handling of the issue, which he had described as a "national humiliation."[42] Paradoxically, Trump wanted to differentiate himself from his predecessor by adopting a tougher stance on chemical weapons while simultaneously softening the stance on almost everything else. As if to signal that shift, in the administration's second week, the Treasury Department imposed unilateral sanctions against eighteen Syrians associated with its chemical weapons program.[43]

Finally, the administration wanted to stem the flow of refugees and ensure their return. This objective was related to candidate Trump's trenchant criticisms of his predecessor and European allies. As a candidate he had favored establishing "safe zones" in Syria—at one point suggesting he would "take a big swatch of land" for "the right price" and build a "big beautiful safe zone" to make Syrian refugees "happier"—and a unilateral ban on Syrian refugees entering the United States.[44] Quite how he would square this policy with his surge of military support for the Kurds was anyone's guess.

Having imposed unilateral sanctions on Syrian officials in week two of his administration, in week three Trump promised the United States would "absolutely do safe zones in Syria." This firmly stated commitment triggered a presidential order requesting that the Departments of State and Defense prepare plans "to provide safe areas in Syria and in the surrounding region in which Syrian nationals displaced from their homeland can await firm settlement, such as repatriation or potential third-country resettlement." Whether this would entail a no-fly zone or putting U.S. troops on the ground was left unclear, as was the question of just where those "safe zones" would be.[45] U.S. officials urged Gulf allies and Turkey to not just support the plan but pay for it. The Saudis expressed interest but warned the United States would have to lead militarily and financially. Having already established one "safe zone," Ankara was more skeptical about what Washington had in mind and made its support contingent on any such zone being free not just of ISIS but of the Syrian government and YPG/SDF, too. Closer to home, the Pentagon was openly hostile to U.S. involvement in any such enterprise. Defense chiefs advised it would involve exorbitant costs—between fifteen thousand and thirty thousand ground troops at a cost of more than $1 billion. That alone was enough to make the president think again.

Russia pushed back, too. Sensing a lack of seriousness on the part of the White House, the Kremlin simply co-opted Trump's safe zones idea into its "de-escalation zones" plan. Indeed, there were signs as early as March 2017 that the U.S. administration was redefining what it meant by "safe zones" to better reflect the Russian model.[46] Meanwhile, the contradictions in its overall approach were being made apparent: the United States needed the Kurds to counter ISIS but Turkey for its safe zones, a problem underscored on the ground, where U.S. soldiers and officials (aided by British and French special forces) were preoccupied preventing open conflict between the YPG/SDF and Turkish-backed forces around Manbij.[47] The Russians tried to capitalize on the confusion with a concerted diplomatic campaign to undermine the OPCW's Joint Investigation Mechanism. In February the UK and France tabled a draft Security Council resolution imposing travel bans and asset freezes on individuals associated with chemical weapons use verified by the JIM and an embargo on the importing of arms, chlorine, and other items used to make chemical weapons. Russian diplomats characterized the draft a "provocation" and, after weeks of fruitless talks, cast their veto (joined by China, and Bolivia, which also voted against), describing the JIM's reporting as "unconvincing."[48]

It was on precisely the issue of chemical weapons that things came to a head. In the last week of March Secretary of State Rex Tillerson bluntly explained to his Turkish counterpart that the United States was unconcerned about whether Assad stayed in power, a view consistent with the four priorities mentioned earlier and confirmed over the coming days by U.S. ambassador to the UN Nikki Haley and the White House itself.[49] Countering ISIS and Iran were the priorities; Syria's government was for Syrians to determine. The green light to Assad could not have been clearer, and it took less than a week for the regime to test it. At around dawn on April 4, the early morning peace in Khan Shaykhun, a town at the southern end of the Idlib enclave, was shattered by a rocket attack and air strike. A Syrian Air Force Su-22 dropped a mainly conventional payload of bombs, but among them was a bomb laced with sarin. People soon started presenting at the town's underground hospital with symptoms consistent with Sarin poisoning, including convulsions and foaming at the mouth, while jets fired rockets at the hospital, plunging it into darkness and forcing a hasty move to Bab al-Hawa and another makeshift hospital housed on the Turkish border. In all, ninety-two people were killed, including thirty-three children. More than six hundred were injured.[50] The OPCW-JIM reported it was "confident that the Syrian Arab Republic is responsible for the release of sarin at Khan Shaykuhn."[51]

At the time, Trump was at his Mar-a-Lago resort in Florida hosting a meeting with Chinese premier Xi Jinping. By all accounts, a moved and outraged president immediately tasked the Pentagon with preparing a military response and tweeted: "These heinous actions by the Bashar al-Assad regime are a consequence of the past administration's weakness and irresolution. . . . President Obama said in 2012 he would establish a 'red line' against the use of chemical weapons and then did nothing."[52] Assad was an "animal" and there would be a "big price," he warned. European allies joined the chorus of condemnation, but none countenanced a military response. The problem for Trump's national security team was how to satisfy the president's demand for action without completely trashing the administration's view that Assad might stay in power. The National Security Council reviewed different military packages, and Trump requested more detailed plans for two: a comprehensive package that would ground Syria's air force and a more limited missile attack against the Shayrat air base used to launch the Khan Shaykhun strikes. A third option—destroying the regime's sarin storage facilities at the airport—was discounted because it risked releasing a large amount of gas into the atmosphere. Along with the Pentagon team, National Security Adviser H. R.

McMaster, a retired general with operational experience in Afghanistan and Iraq and one of the more highly regarded officials in the administration, urged the president to take the more limited option and thereby demonstrate resolve without risking civilian casualties, dragging the United States toward a protracted campaign, or shifting his Syria policy.[53] Others in the administration leaned towards the more robust option, among them Tillerson who seemed to hedge his bets at different points.[54]

In the end, Trump authorized the more limited option and called allies that evening to inform them and stress that this would be a unilateral action. In the early hours of April 7, USS *Ross* and USS *Porter* fired fifty-nine Tomahawk missiles, damaging buildings at the Shayrat base and damaging or destroying ten to twenty aircraft. Between four and nine people were killed. McMaster admitted the strikes had not significantly degraded Syria's military capacity—indeed, the very next morning, Syrian jets were again flying from the air base to attack targets in Idlib.[55] Standing beside him, however, Tillerson insisted they *had* conveyed a tough message.[56] The strikes achieved some measure of retribution and exposed Russian vulnerability, for it had been able to do nothing to prevent the United States hitting government installations in its heartland at will. But beyond that, the message—if there was one—was hard to discern. The strikes certainly garnered positive reactions at home, and trading insults with the Kremlin helped the president bat away accusations of Russian help in his election. Allies supported the action, too, and international criticism was muted. In the UN Security Council, Russia condemned the strikes as a "flagrant violation of international law" but was joined only by Bolivia and Syria, and pointedly not by China.[57] Russia delivered sophisticated Pantsir anti-aircraft systems to Syria and took what was left of Syria's air force under its protection at Khmeimim, measures designed to neuter future U.S. strikes. It also briefly withdrew from an aerial deconfliction agreement with the United States, though the practice continued informally.[58]

Without direction from the president, still ensconced at his resort, administration figures began making their own policy. On April 6 Tillerson disavowed his March 30 self and claimed Assad's future was "uncertain." McMaster didn't follow suit, instead emphasizing the limited nature of U.S. strikes and warning Assad to refrain from further chemical attacks. Three days later, Secretary of Defense James Mattis weighed in, echoing McMaster's position. This seemingly encouraged Tillerson to change his mind, for he then told journalists that defeating ISIS was the priority and that the United States would pursue a political settlement through the Geneva and Astana processes. Negotiations would determine "Assad's fate," while regime change would be disastrous, Tillerson intimated. Then, Nikki Haley reversed *her* March 30 position, commenting that "regime change is . . . going to happen," while McMaster threw shade on his own position by observing that "it's very difficult to understand how a political solution could result from the continuation of the Assad regime."[59] Assad would have to go, but as part of a political transition, they appeared to be saying: a position more Obama 2013 than Trump March 30, 2017, or Trump April 7, 2017. Haley and McMaster pressed the president for a tougher stance on Assad and urged him to threaten further retaliation should sarin or barrel bombs be used on civilians again. Secretary of Defense Mattis lobbied against them.[60]

Amid the chaos, Tillerson spoke on the phone with his Russian counterpart, Sergei Lavrov, to finalize plans for his impending trip to Moscow and a traditional courtesy visit with the Russian president. Lavrov had cultivated a close working relationship with Tillerson's predecessor, John Kerry, and wanted similar ties with the new incumbent. On Syria, Lavrov complained U.S. strikes violated international law and helped ISIS, but what he really wanted to know was what all this meant for U.S. thinking on Assad's future. Like everyone else, Lavrov was confused. In a rare moment of clarity, Tillerson reassured him their top priority was defeating ISIS and that the United States favored a political solution to Syria's crisis.[61] But somewhere over the Atlantic, the secretary changed his mind again and, in Italy to chair a G7 meeting en route to Moscow, lambasted the Russians, blamed them for the Khan Shaykhun attack, and demanded the Kremlin change course, warning that it could not hope to normalize relations, ease sanctions, make progress on Ukraine, or cooperate with the United States on Syria unless it did. The problem in all this was not that senior members of the administration had different positions. That was true of the Obama administration, too. The problem was that the White House was completely dysfunctional. Since the president offered no guidance or leadership, no one seemed to know what their policy was. After his combative show at the G7, Tillerson flew into a Moscow storm, his position built on sand.

Tillerson's Moscow visit was the first face-to-face meeting between a senior Trump official and the Russian leadership. In some ways Tillerson seemed the ideal man to repair the U.S. relationship with Russia. He and Putin had a personal connection established when the secretary was CEO of ExxonMobil and had signed a massive deal with the Russian state-controlled oil company, Rosneft. They had gotten on well back then, but that counted for little now since Putin was bitterly aggrieved by the vitriol Trump and Tillerson had directed his way and confused about American intentions. To make a point, the secretary and his team were advised when they arrived that it would be unlikely the president would meet them. They should first meet Lavrov, and if that went well they might be granted an audience with Putin.

The meeting with Lavrov proved difficult. The Russian spoke at great length about the follies of American regime-change policies, upbraided Tillerson for the missile strikes, and insisted there was no evidence the government was responsible for Khan Shaykhun. Lavrov asked whether Trump really thought Assad an "animal." That was a characterization "brought upon himself," Tillerson countered, stressing the evidence against the Syrian president was compelling. Afterward, Putin kept the Americans dangling until the last possible moment before, at 5 p.m., sending word that he would meet them at the Kremlin but that there would be no press comments afterward. The meeting, which lasted nearly an hour, was tense and awkward. Putin tersely listed his grievances at length and repeated his argument that U.S. strikes only helped ISIS. Tillerson asked Putin to use his influence to restrain Assad and secure a political settlement.[62] They did, however, find something to agree on. Putin talked about the Astana process and the planned "de-escalation zones"; Tillerson responded that Trump's thinking was moving in a similar direction—perhaps recalling the U.S. president's safe zone idea. They agreed this might be an area for future cooperation, though in public the mutual recriminations continued.

With hindsight, the U.S. strikes were a key inflection point for the new Trump administration. At stake was the question of whether to pursue a more expansive policy of using limited force to restrain Assad and impose "safe zones." But the episode revealed not just a divided administration but a deeply chaotic one. After much back and forth, Tillerson, Haley, and to some extent McMaster seemed to favor a more expansive approach, while Mattis and the Pentagon were doggedly committed to the more limited path. The missing element was the president. It was not that he had nothing to say—he said and tweeted plenty—but that there was no coherence to his stream of words. Herein lay the source of the chaos. Trump gave little guidance and took no steps to see that a coherent policy was even developed, let alone acted on. For a moment, U.S. missile strikes had given Russia cause for concern, but as chaos engulfed the White House, the political initiative quickly swung back in Moscow's direction.

DE-ESCALATION

In early May, Syria's parties were back in Astana to consider the deal Russia and Turkey were hashing out on de-escalation zones. Three zones were essentially agreed on in advance: Idlib, Rastan/Talbiseh (northern Homs governate and southern Hama), and a southern zone comprising parts of Deraa and Qunaitra governates. A fourth, eastern Ghouta, outside Damascus, was still not agreed. Turkey pressed hard for its inclusion and threatened to walk out if it were not. The Syrian government obstinately refused—eastern Ghouta was the rebel enclave it wanted to clear next.[63] The Russians had initially backed Damascus on this, but the U.S. missile strikes, Washington's rhetoric about safe zones, Tillerson's message to Putin, and the opposition offensive in Hama had underscored the regime's precarity as well as uncertainty about U.S. intent and prompted a rethink. A deal was important since it would keep Turkey inside the Russian-led process and undercut American pretensions to political leadership or reversion to the UN. So, after resisting the proposition for months, the Russians relented and agreed that eastern Ghouta be added to the list of de-escalation zones—albeit a smaller zone than it would have been a

few months earlier, for regime forces had battered Qaboun and Barzeh since late February until the remaining HTS- and FSA-aligned
fighters and residents had agreed to evacuate to Idlib.[64]

Under the de-escalation plan, ceasefires would be established in
each of the zones for a period of six months, after which the three
guarantors—Iran, Turkey, and Russia—would decide whether to
extend them. During this period, the government would cease military overflights, grant humanitarian access, allow people displaced
from the enclaves to return, and work to restore damaged infrastructure, such as water supplies and electricity, would begin. The three
guarantors would establish checkpoints to ensure the unhindered
movement of civilians and humanitarians in and out of the zones.[65]
As with the UN's ceasefires, however, the cessation would not apply
to ISIS or HTS, effectively permitting government and Russian forces
to continue using force.

Four major obstacles remained, however: First, there were practical questions about how the zones would be demarcated, the ceasefires monitored, and transgressions punished. There was little point
having a ceasefire, Turkey argued, if there were no viable mechanisms
for its enforcement. Russia and Iran accepted the need for monitoring and reporting but nothing more. In the end, the memorandum
signed in Astana committed the guarantors to "tak[ing] all necessary measures to ensure the fulfillment by the conflicting parties of
the ceasefire regime," but each had their own idea about what that
meant.[66] Second, not all Syria's parties accepted the plan. Some opposition groups opposed what they saw as the extension of the "local
ceasefires" model that had accompanied the regime's siege-and-
starvation strategy. None of the largest armed opposition groups—
HTS, ISIS, and PYD—was party to the deal. The PYD complained it
would lead to the sectarian division of Syria and might threaten
Kurdish autonomy.[67] Third, the deal applied the same basic template
to four very different zones comprising different sets of actors.[68]
Fourth, the United States—largely quiescent thus far—expressed
strong opposition to Iran's role as guarantor and particular concern
about the southern zone abutting the sensitive Golan Heights. Under
no circumstances, it insisted, would Iran be allowed a presence in

Syria's far south. As if to underscore that point, on May 18 U.S. aircraft struck a convoy of Iranian-backed Iraqi Shi'ite militia near al-Tanf. The United States had established a base in Syria's southeastern desert close to the Iraq border to train Syrian militia combatting ISIS and had thrown up a fifty-five kilometer exclusion zone around the base. This was prized real estate close to a route the Iranians hoped to open connecting Iraq, Damascus, and Lebanon, the denial of which was now a U.S. priority. It was also ground hotly contested by the government and opposition. The United States claimed it had acted in self-defense as the convoy moved toward the base. Although Mattis insisted it was a minor incident, others judged it a sign of Washington's more muscular anti-Iranian posture.[69]

By far the largest and most complex of the four zones was Idlib, its population inflated to more than one million by the influx of hundreds of thousands of people forcibly displaced from eastern Aleppo and elsewhere, and its political situation complicated by the simultaneous influx of HTS, Jaysh al-Islam, and other veteran fighters. Idlib was by far the most important zone to Turkey. It had even mooted the idea of deploying its own monitors into the zone to supervise the ceasefire, a suggestion the Russians reacted to cautiously but without rejecting it outright. Idlib gave Erdogan his principal bargaining chip. For as long as it stood, the Syrian government and its allies would need Turkish cooperation. It also presented Ankara an opportunity to establish an extended safety zone that might also come to include Manbij and Jarabulus, into which some of the three million or so Syrian refugees in Turkey might be returned, creating a permanent buffer between Turkey and Syria's Kurds. At the same time, Ankara feared the regime would try to force as many civilians and fighters from other parts of Syria as it could into Idlib in the hope it would collapse into disarray and conflict or create a pretext for government intervention.[70] The signs were already ominous as fractious armed groups jostled for position. In January 2018 HTS attacked the Ahrar al-Sham headquarters in Idlib city, and in the days that followed, five armed factions defected from Ahrar al-Sham to HTS while several Jaysh al-Islam factions from Aleppo moved in the opposite direction, into an alliance with Ahrar al-Sham. The extremists were better equipped, disciplined, and motivated fighters, however, and in July 2018 HTS stormed opposition headquarters in Idlib city and seized control.

The second zone was also the smallest and straddled northern Homs and southern Hama governates. With around 180,000 civilians, it was the center of Islamist armed groups, including some backed by the Muslim Brotherhood and Qatar, as well as the Salafist Ahrar al-Sham, which was leaking fighters to HTS. The third zone was eastern Ghouta. In its newly shrunken form, this enclave spanned around 100 square kilometers of mostly dense urban sprawl, which housed around 400,000 civilians and 10,000–20,000 fighters (probably closer to the lower end). The largest armed group there was probably Jaysh al-Islam, which made up roughly half of the fighters, followed by the formerly FSA-aligned Faylaq al-Rahman. Ahrar al-Sham and Tahrir al-Sham also had a presence amid the ruined tenement blocks. ISIS had tried getting a foothold there but had been driven out after just six months; HTS never had an armed presence in eastern Ghouta.

The fourth de-escalation zone was in the South, bordering Jordan. Most of the territory here was held by the various organizations of the Southern Front, backed by the United States, Jordan, and Saudi Arabia. A small ISIS affiliate held pockets close to the Golan Heights. Periodically, the IDF conducted strikes against Hezbollah and Iranian units it thought were operating too close to the border or transporting weapons to Hezbollah units in southern Lebanon. In March 2017, for example, Israeli jets attacked a convoy carrying military supplies to Hezbollah. The Syrians responded with S-200 surface-to-air missiles but failed to hit any of the aircraft. One Syrian missile was shot down by Israel's countermissile defenses.[71] Six months later, Israeli jets overflew Lebanon to strike facilities west of Hama being used by Iran to build missiles and the government to revive its chemical weapons stockpile.[72] Russia usually acquiesced in Israeli strikes since it too worried about Hezbollah and was locked in a struggle with Iran for influence over Assad. Moreover, the Kremlin feared that excessive Iranian activism might attract not just Israeli but also American counter measures. But the Kremlin had to balance these concerns against the fact its own Syria strategy depended on Iran and Hezbollah to provide the ground forces it would not, so, typically, Russia did little to directly counteract them but acquiesced when Israel did.

The sheer diversity of conditions and groups in the proposed zones made it difficult to achieve a common plan through the triumvirate. Turkey lacked the interest and influence necessary to deliver the Southern Front. Iranian posturing also posed a real problem there. On June 6 U.S. aircraft again attacked Iranian-backed militia operating uncomfortably close to its al-Tanf base.[73] Meanwhile, though Iran wielded little direct influence in the North, its intransigence made it difficult for the Kremlin to broker deals with Turkey. To accommodate these problems, the Russians began operating independently of the triumvirate, moving unilaterally to negotiate separate deals for each of the zones. For them, this hub-and-spokes approach had the added advantage of confirming Russian primacy. The United States seemed to accept this new political reality, but its position remained difficult to discern. In July Tillerson said Russia was responsible for Syria's political future, but just three months he added that the United States expected that Assad would not be part of it.[74]

In the South, the Russians needed the Americans and Jordanians to exercise influence over the Southern Front, which had refused to participate in the Astana talks, preferring to deal directly with its backers and Russia. To facilitate that, Jordan convened a meeting between the Russians and the two Americans nominally responsible for Syria policy: Brett McGurk—an Obama appointee still responsible for diplomatic coordination of the anti-ISIS coalition—and Michael Ratney—Obama's special envoy, who, though now outside government, still operated informally. The Russians offered de-escalation in return for the Americans agreeing to restrain the Southern Front and stop arming them. McGurk and Ratney were receptive. De-escalation offered a pathway for reducing violence, blocking Iran, restraining Damascus, and establishing conditions for a political deal. They also calculated that dealing with the Russians might fortify the anti-ISIS coalition and create friction between Moscow and Tehran.[75] But their enthusiasm was somewhat tempered by doubts about Syrian government and Iranian compliance and the Kremlin's will and ability to curb them. Israel, too, was a problem. A senior Israeli told the American envoys his country opposed Russian involvement in policing the southern de-escalation zone since it could not be relied on to prevent Iranian infiltration of the zone. It would be better, the Israelis argued, if the United States assumed responsibility.[76] Back in Washington, D.C., the two envoys cautiously advised accepting Russia's offer, but only if there were clear mechanisms for verification and enforcement. Trump, though, was not much interested in technicalities. Convinced of his own deal-making skills, he saw an opportunity to build his "safe zone" while drawing down American forces and endorsed the Kremlin's proposal.

Not that Syria was at the top of even America's regional priorities at the time. Eager to ingratiate themselves to the new U.S. administration, likely to be much friendlier than the last, the Saudis had put on a show to flatter and impress the president during his visit to Riyadh that May. It worked. Trump spoke gushingly of his admiration and support for the Saudi ruling family. Emboldened, the Saudis moved against their troublesome Sunni rival, Qatar, which it suspected (not unreasonably) of fueling disquiet and revolution across the Sunni world through the Muslim Brotherhood, among others. In a coordinated move, Saudi Arabia, the UAE, Yemen, and Egypt imposed stringent sanctions on the emirate, claiming it was supporting terrorism and helping Iran by using Al Jazeera to undermine Sunni governments. Rumors of an impending invasion spread, and, enamored by Saudi hospitality, Trump gave Riyadh vocal support, pouring fuel onto the fire. Tillerson—who described his president as a "fucking moron"—and Mattis disagreed sharply with Trump and urged Riyadh not to use force, warning it would complicate Saudi Arabia's relationship with the United States. This intervention may have helped prevent another Middle Eastern war, but it also caused a rift with their president.[77]

It was against this backdrop that in early June 2017, Trump met McMaster and CIA director Mike Pompeo to discuss Russia's terms, specifically the Kremlin's demand that the United States end train-and-equip. Pompeo advised that the $1 billion Obama-era program had failed: only a tiny number of moderate fighters had been trained, and since most of their armed groups had been defeated by either Assad (especially during the fall of Aleppo) or the Islamists, the program was effectively obsolete. To make matters worse, American

weapons had leaked out to ISIS and other extremists, some were stolen by Jordanians at one of the program's two training bases and sold
on the black market, and in November 2016 a Jordanian soldier had
shot and killed three American soldiers.[78] Its effects were so limited,
the program gave the United States no meaningful leverage, Pompeo
warned. The president should cash it in and do the southern de-
escalation deal.[79] This was exactly what Trump wanted to hear. He
decided to terminate the program—groups would receive assistance
until the end of the year but none thereafter—and close the military
operations centers in Turkey and Jordan, giving Putin everything he
had asked for.[80]

American, Jordanian, and Russian officials met again in Jordan and
agreed on the details, beginning with a confidence-building forty-
eight-hour ceasefire around Daraa. It was one of the issues on the
agenda for the first meeting between the two presidents held on
the sidelines of the G20 summit in Hamburg on July 7. Originally
scheduled for forty-five minutes, the two presidents spoke for more
than two hours, with just Lavrov, Tillerson, and their translators in
attendance. We don't know much about what was said (presumably
because the meeting coincided with a scandal in the United States
about Russian interference to support Trump's election), but Tillerson and Lavrov later commented the talks were friendly and constructive. Syria was discussed, and the presidents agreed on the
broad outline of the deal being negotiated.[81] The Israelis were not
pleased. Prime Minister Benjamin Netanyahu, a political ally of
Trump's, publicly criticized the impending deal, complaining it did
not do enough to counter Iran.[82] To address Israeli concerns, the
United States insisted that a buffer be established along the de-
escalation zone's border, into which Iranian and Iranian-backed
fighters would not be permitted. The Americans wanted it to be five
kilometers deep between the front lines and ten kilometers deep
from the Jordanian border, expanded over time to twenty kilometers. The Russians went along with that, but agreement on expan-
sion was never finalized, nor was this part of the deal ever implemented.[83] The Russians persuaded Damascus and Tehran to accept
the arrangement, and within forty-eight hours of the Trump-Putin
meeting, the ceasefire came into effect. Violence receded, and the

skies were reported free of fighter jets for the first time in weeks.[84] Russian military police units moved into a checkpoint and observation posts around the zone's perimeter, while efforts to institutionalize the arrangement progressed apace. On August 23 the United States and Jordan established a joint monitoring center in Amman with Russia to monitor the ceasefire.[85] On November 8 the three concluded a memorandum of principles formalizing the arrangements, later endorsed publicly by Trump and Putin.[86] U.S. officials warned of a "strong response" should there be any sustained violations.[87]

The week following the U.S.-Russian deal in July, a further round of discussion in Astana focused, without success, on delineation problems in the three other zones. Now convinced of the merits of the hub-and-spoke model, the Kremlin sidestepped the triumvirate and negotiated separate arrangements for each. Turkey had demanded eastern Ghouta's inclusion, but Ankara lacked the clout needed to negotiate on behalf of the rebels there. So the Kremlin turned to Cairo for help, and the Egyptian government mediated direct talks between Russian defense officials and opposition armed groups, which delivered a second de-escalation agreement on July 23. As in the South, the parties agreed to a ceasefire, humanitarian and other forms of access, and a modest Russian military police presence along the boundary to observe compliance.[88] But monitoring and enforcement arrangements were even more opaque than in the South. In August Russia turned again to Egypt to help it negotiate a similar deal for the Rastan/Talbiseh zone.[89] Not until the triumvirate reconvened in Astana in September was a deal done for Idlib. The stumbling block here was Turkey's insistence on a monitoring mechanism far more definitive than that agreed on in the South, and Russian and Iranian opposition to that. Turkey eventually got its way, however, and the three guarantors agreed to deploy their own forces at certain locations to monitor compliance. Turkey deployed into the zone's northwest and established observation posts, Syrian and Iranian forces deployed to the southeast, and Russian soldiers and military police deployed in between.[90] Agreed for a renewable period of six months, the deal permitted Russia to continue overflights of Idlib but not to bomb it. The Syrian Air Force would not be allowed over the zone at all. Humanitarian access should be unhindered. Key questions remained unresolved, however. Not least, the presence of relatively large numbers of HTS fighters posed questions about how military operations against extremists, excluded from the ceasefire, were to be conducted and monitored. How would inevitable disputes concerning identification of fighters be resolved? Aware of these problems, Russia presumably wanted to retain a loophole for itself should it judge the use of force necessary, while Turkey was content to let the issue slide for now in return for a period of calm it could use to fortify its position in Idlib and address outstanding Kurdish questions.

ISIS OVERCOME

The de-escalation agreements brought temporary respite to the four zones. Unsure of how the guarantors might respond to ceasefire violations, the Syrian government turned its attention eastward to the war against ISIS, determined not to allow the SDF to scoop up territory from the collapsing extremists. In particular, Damascus wanted to ensure the SDF not move south of the Euphrates, and to do that it needed to retake the territory first. Government forces struck out east from Aleppo toward the Euphrates south of al-Bab, forcing the jihadists into retreat. Earlier, they had retaken Palmyra with the help of both the Russians and Americans. In Iraq, meanwhile, the final assault on ISIS-held Mosul got into full swing in February, backed by U.S. airpower, Shi'ite militia, and Kurdish forces. ISIS held on tenaciously, but Mosul was retaken in late July. Iraq's Kurdish KRG emerged from the war in a much stronger position—a potential model for the YPG/SDF—but victory came at an immense cost.[91]

The SDF's long-anticipated offensive against the ISIS capital, Raqqa, began in early June. Around thirty thousand fighters, half the SDF's total strength, were committed, and the offensive was supported by U.S. airpower and ground forces. Numbering around a thousand in the Raqqa theater (U.S. forces inside Syria totaled around two thousand, half supporting the SDF and half located in the Southeast mainly, at al-Tanf), U.S. Special Operations Forces and Marines were actively involved. Marines fired more than forty thousand shells during the Raqqa offensive—more than the total number of shells fired during the 2003 invasion of Iraq, and nearly two-thirds the number fired during Desert Storm, the battle to retake Kuwait in 1991.[92] For the YPG, alliance with the United States was becoming a mixed blessing. On the one hand, American airpower and political support were invaluable help in defeating ISIS, deterring Damascus and Turkey, and consolidating control in Rojava. On the other, U.S. pressure was pushing it to overextend into areas, such as Raqqa and eastern Deir ez-Zor, well beyond Kurdish homelands. These offensives inflicted enormous losses. The SDF lost between seven hundred and a thousand fighters in the final stages of the Raqqa offensive alone. It later estimated total losses at the hands of ISIS at eleven thousand.[93]

The Raqqa offensive began on June 6, 2017. Nobody expected a quick victory since the vicious fighting in Mosul showed that hard-core ISIS fighters would fight to the last to inflict as much harm as possible. As with Mosul, Raqqa had to be cleared street-by-street. To minimize casualties, the SDF depended heavily on U.S. air and artillery support, causing significant civilian casualties, likely numbering more than 1,500. The offensive's first two weeks displaced 160,000 more. ISIS used civilians as human shields, forced them to become suicide bombers, and situated fighters in civilian buildings, knowing that would draw coalition fire. They used IEDs, booby traps, suicide bombers, and suicide car bombs to inflict as many casualties as possible. There were complications in Syria's increasingly crowded skies, too. On June 18 a U.S. Navy F/A-18 shot down a Syrian government Su-22 it had been tracking at close range after the jet dropped ordnance on SDF forces in Ja'Din, south of Raqqa. The whole incident was observed by a Russian fighter jet flying above the American and Syrian aircraft. Still, the SDF made steady progress and by early August had control of more than half the city. The end involved brutal house-to-house combat as extremists, including many foreign fighters, fought doggedly from heavily fortified positions. But ISIS was bottled up, and those who didn't want martyring in Raqqa agreed to evacuate. Under a ceasefire agreement, four thousand fighters and their families were evacuated with some of their weapons to Abu Kamal, in Deir ez-Zor governate.[94] It was a Faustian bargain, but the SDF and their American allies judged the jihadists could inflict more harm fighting from well-prepared positions in densely populated Raqqa than they could in the eastern desert, though some would no doubt slip the net. Indeed, within a fortnight of their arrival in Abu Kamal, ISIS positions there were attacked by the Syrian government and its allies, and after little more than a month, the town was retaken. In Raqqa, meanwhile, the last pockets of resistance were mopped up in mid-October, and the town declared free of ISIS. The devastation was massive. The United Nations deemed more than 80 percent of the city uninhabitable, with 70–80 percent of its buildings damaged or destroyed.[95] Reconstruction posed an enormous challenge, complicated by the thousands of mines and booby traps left behind by ISIS. The city had yet more grisly secrets to reveal: mass graves unearthed the victims of ISIS's brutal rule. More than three thousand bodies were pulled from graves in the suburb of al-Fukheikha, where ISIS had established a "Vanguard Camp" to train children in the arts of killing.[96]

In the East, the government retook Deir ez-Zor city in September, while the SDF captured more territory east of the Euphrates, including the al-Omar oil fields, Syria's largest. Occasionally, U.S. forces cooperated with Syrian government forces battling ISIS. They also established a joint base with the SDF and concluded a deconfliction line along the Euphrates with Russia and the Syrian government: the SDF held the east bank, the government the west. By the end of 2017, ISIS had lost 95 percent of its territory in Syria and Iraq.[97]

MANAGING DE-ESCALATION

Though the world's attention was fixed on the territorial collapse of ISIS in the second half of 2017, difficult questions about the de-escalation zones remained unanswered. In eastern Ghouta and Homs/Talbiseh, government forces repeatedly violated the ceasefire, signaling that Damascus was not ready to forgo a military solution, despite the Kremlin urging Damascus to accept de-escalation. The Kurds were another complication: well armed, entrenched, battle hardened, and backed by the United States. Putin's priorities now were to (1) maintain and stabilize the ceasefire agreements, (2) support a negotiated extension of government authority through "reconciliation" arrangements with the zones, (3) wind back areas of UN oversight such as cross-border deliveries and the OPCW JIM and transfer more authority to Damascus, and (4) translate this into a general political settlement that the "legitimate" opposition could buy into.[98]

Russia manipulated humanitarian aid to promote goals two and three. The Kremlin understood that control of aid was one way the government could procure the grudging acquiescence of desperate civilians in the de-escalation zones while also reestablishing its authority and legitimacy in areas it already controlled. With one hand, it promoted opening access in cooperation with Damascus, and with the other, it moved against the UN's cross-border deliveries, both designed to promote government control of aid. Making a show of Russian magnanimity, in early August Defense Minister Sergei Shoigu wrote to de Mistura promising Russian military police would ensure the safe passage of UN humanitarian convoys into the de-escalation zones—coordinating with the Syrian government.[99] De Mistura replied that the UN and Red Cross could not agree to this without impairing their impartiality, but that they would appreciate Russian assistance in securing safe passage. A few days later, Russian military police stationed themselves along the planned route of an aid convoy of fifty trucks, which both delivered some aid and visibly demonstrated Russia's control of the aid.[100] The following month, Russia asked the UN to intensify aid deliveries into the eastern Ghouta and Rastan/Talbiseh zones.[101] In late September, meanwhile, Russia's new ambassador to the UN, Vassily Nebenzia, launched a broadside against the cross-border delivery of aid without government consent, which, he claimed, was being diverted to opposition armed groups. Russia would not grant a simple extension of the Security Council's authorization of cross-border aid, he warned, though in truth there was little Russia could do to stop the practice since Turkey, Jordan, and the opposition controlled the most relevant borders, not Syria or Russia. Its point made, Russia relented at the eleventh hour, as the humanitarian mandate expired, but only after extracting a price—a commitment to review cross-border deliveries. Russia moved against the OPCW's JIM, too, voting in October and November to block the extension of its mandate for another year.[102] Russia's biggest headache was Assad himself. Having vowed to "liberate every inch," Syria's president saw little reason to de-escalate now that he was in the ascendancy—a view shared by Tehran. Though he paid lip-service to the Russians, government forces prodded relentlessly at the de-escalation zones, especially the weakest—eastern Ghouta and Rastan/Talbiseh—where aerial and artillery bombardment persisted. Aware this ceaseless prodding could topple the edifice of de-escalation, Putin ended 2017 by outlining plans for the next stage of the Russian endgame: a new Russian-led political process spearheaded by a grand summit at his favorite resort, Sochi.

13

DE-ESCALATION DOMINOES

THE "CONGRESS OF SYRIAN NATIONAL DIALOGUE" was the center-piece of Vladimir Putin's strategy for Syria: 1,500 Syrian delegates summoned to Sochi to deliver a death blow to the UN's Geneva process and establish terms for a new peace drawn up by Russia. Putin intended to cajole delegates to endorse a largely preselected committee that would be charged with drafting a new constitution. This document would preserve the Syrian state intact and extend its territorial writ to the whole country—allowing for some Kurdish autonomy, modest power sharing, and future presidential and parliamentary elections in which Assad would be permitted to stand. Assad would remain in power throughout the transition, during which the de-escalation zones would be reintegrated into the Syrian state. But Syrians did not widely share Putin's vision. The Higher Negotiations Committee rejected Sochi on principle, insisting on the primacy of the UN's Geneva process. Assad, too, was unenthusiastic, for the military solution now seemingly in reach dispensed with the need for compromise. And Turkey balked, fearing Kurdish autonomy in Syria would empower the PKK.

With so much ambivalence, Putin was forced to invest his own time and energy in drumming up support. Above all, he needed Assad. The Syrian leader was summoned to an audience at the Russian president's Borochov Ruchey summer residence in Sochi in November 2017. What Putin said to Assad is not publicly available, but immediately afterward the Russian president explained that with ISIS largely defeated, it was time to wind down military operations and focus on politics. His political survival dependent on Russian military help, Assad acquiesced. Putin telephoned Trump the following day, intent on getting the Americans onboard, too. Over more than an hour, Putin reassured Trump that his Sochi plans complemented the UN's process and advised that Assad had agreed to constitutional reform and elections.[1] Trump was uninterested in the transition and pressed his counterpart on stabilization, counterterrorism, and refugee return instead—precisely what Putin wanted to hear.[2] Next, the Russian leader called Saudi Arabia's King Salman, Egypt's Fattah al-Sisi, and Israeli's Benjamin Netanyahu, finding no obstacles there either. Netanyahu complained about Iran's growing foothold in Syria and warned Israel might be forced to counter it. Putin offered understanding and reassurance.[3] Only two key foreign actors remained. Recep Tayyip Erdogan and Hassan Rouhani arrived in Sochi for direct talks in the last week of November. Rouhani readily agreed to Putin's plan, but Erdogan doubted Assad's commitment. His real concern, though, was not Damascus, but the Kurds. Worried the YPG might take advantage of the peace process to extend its territory, Erdogan argued it should be excluded from the Sochi talks and Turkey permitted to establish a buffer zone around Afrin. The Turkish leader drove a hard bargain, but his was a transactional approach that Putin understood and appreciated. Since Russia needed Turkey to deliver the Sunni opposition, he agreed to Erdogan's terms: Russia would acquiesce should Turkey launch an incursion toward Afrin, in return for which Turkey would throw its weight behind the Sochi plan. Western and Gulf governments joined Turkey in urging the opposition to accept the new strategic reality and deal with the Russians. Their pressure prompted a raft of resignations by HNC figures disgruntled at being instructed to compromise with Assad and consent to him remaining in government for a time.[4] Others lamented that the West and the UN's Staffan de Mistura seemed content to let Putin bypass the Geneva process. The UN envoy called on the opposition to drop its preconditions and negotiate at Sochi, undercutting his own UN process.[5] This he did, even though UN documents leaked to the press suggested the Russians satisfied few of the conditions set by his boss, Secretary-General Antonio Guterres, for a viable and just peace.[6]

Putin thus succeeded in getting his 1,500 Syrians to Sochi. But that proved to be his principal success. For a start, while the Russians certainly had numbers in Sochi, they did not have the *right* numbers. The HNC refused to attend despite Turkey's urging, while the opposition groups holding most territory—the YPG and jihadist HTS (the former al-Nusra)—were not invited. Most of those who did attend were either outright loyalists or members of the so-called loyal opposition—neither capable of negotiating on behalf of the armed opposition. The few genuine opposition delegates who attended complained that the airport and conference rooms were festooned with Syrian flags and heckled Sergei Lavrov's opening address—hardly the deference the Russians expected. Then they refused to negotiate until government forces complied with the ceasefire in Idlib.[7] In the end, enough delegates were cajoled into agreeing to form a constitutional committee, but there was no agreement on its size, composition, or mandate. Only de Mistura seemed to think that this was progress.

The Kremlin's assessment was quite different. In its view, political investment in the Sochi conference had achieved virtually nothing. They were no closer to the political process they required in order to manage the war's endgame and postwar reconstruction. A new strategy was needed, and one was crafted over the winter of 2017–2018 that involved using military force to compel the opposition—and Turkey—to accept Putin's terms. Putin's interest in the political track diminished markedly, and without Russia, it took the UN another two years just to establish the constitutional committee. By then almost no one outside the UN and the committee itself even noticed. In the weeks and months following Sochi, Russia expanded its military operations in Syria, and over the next seven months, Syrian government forces, backed by Russian air power, ground forces, and mercenaries, overran three of the four de-escalation zones. The Kremlin's "Plan A," using limited force to coerce a favorable negotiated peace, failed spectacularly at Sochi. "Plan B" involved using military force to compel a solution, and that is what they ended up doing.

U.S. DILEMMAS, TURKISH INTERVENTIONS

Early 2018 saw a period of introspection about Syria policy in Washington, D.C., too. With ISIS largely defeated—though still active in pockets in Syria's East and as a terrorist threat across the country, its fighters also infiltrated as far as the African Sahel and Horn of Africa—the Trump administration contemplated what to do with the two to three thousand American soldiers that remained inside Syria. Most had been deployed to support the Syrian Democratic Force's Raqqa offensive but were now policing the deconfliction zone along the Euphrates, deterring violence between Kurdish, Turkish, Sunni, and regime forces around Manbij, and stabilizing the eastern portion of the volatile Turkish-SDF/YPG border. Proponents of keeping the force in place, which included the Pentagon and State Department, argued it was also maintaining military pressure on ISIS and deterring Iran, which now controlled between 120,000 and 150,000 fighters in Syria—a force several times larger than the Syrian Army itself, which by now fielded only some 20,000–30,000 regulars and a total force of little more than 100,000. Iran had acquired military bases in Syria and operated dozens of bomb- and missile-building facilities pointedly directed at its true, and oft-stated, goal: the destruction of Israel. In March 2017 Harakat Hezbollah al-Nujaba, among the largest of the Iranian-backed Iraqi Shi'ite armed groups in Syria, had publicly vowed to liberate the Golan Heights and created a brigade specifically for that task.[8] Others, though, including the American president, wanted to withdraw U.S. forces as quickly as possible. America's last ambassador to Damascus, Robert Ford, wrote that the "United States' first priority should be avoiding further mission creep and, above all, taking care not to get ensnared in any costly new military campaigns."[9]

The very real risks of mission creep were forcefully demonstrated late on February 7, 2018, when an armed group comprising Syrian government forces, Iranian-trained Afghan militia, and Russian mercenaries belonging to the Wagner Group approached an SDF headquarters housing U.S. Special Operations Forces in Khasham, on the Euphrates, the boundary between government-held and SDF-held territory in the Deir ez-Zor governate. Simultaneously, a second group of government soldiers crossed the Euphrates to the south, seemingly intent on attacking the base. Around twenty to thirty shells landed, forcing U.S. personnel to take cover and request air support. As it had been when the al-Tanf base was threatened, U.S. air support was overwhelming. F-16 fighters, AC-130 gunships, Apache helicopters, and drones engaged the various armed formations over the course of four hours, inflicting significant casualties and forcing them into retreat. Casualty reports vary considerably, but most put government-side losses at between eighty and one hundred fighters killed, twenty to thirty of them Russian mercenaries—though some reports suggest that most of these were killed not by direct U.S. fire but by an exploding weapons dump.[10] The Pentagon had taken care to communicate with Russian headquarters during the operation, and beneath the angry rhetoric that followed the incident, both the United States and Russia were careful to avoid escalation. For Damascus and its allies, the incident was a sharp reminder of their vulnerability; for Washington, a warning that for as long as its forces remained inside Syria, it might be dragged into fighting on behalf of the SDF. To avoid this trap, the State Department and Pentagon looked for a way of shoring up the SDF to cover an orderly U.S. withdrawal. The key, they thought, was to help the SDF assert its authority through a process of "stabilization." If the SDF could be supported to develop state-like capacities through the rebuilding of infrastructure, institutions, and security forces, it could protect itself against Turkey (aided by U.S. diplomacy), deny territory to Iran and ISIS, maintain pressure on Assad, and force Damascus to grant it autonomy. What is more, if stabilization worked in SDF-held territories, the model could then be rolled out in the southern zone, too.[11] Yet, however sound it may have been in theory—and it was sound, if perhaps overly optimistic—the proposed strategy was clumsily unveiled, publicly mauled, and then abandoned.

The first initiative mooted in the stabilization plan was a proposal to create "Border Security Forces" in the Northeast and in the southern de-escalation zone. In the Northeast, the plan involved helping the SDF form a thirty-thousand-strong force capable of holding the territory it had prized from the regime, ISIS, and al-Qaeda, denying access to Iran, and (presumably) deterring Turkey as the United States gradually withdrew. The new force would be trained, partially equipped, and salaried by the U.S.-led anti-ISIS coalition and would deploy along parts of Syria's northern border with Turkey, eastern border with Iraq, and the Euphrates deconfliction zone. The SDF would be strongly encouraged to recruit more fighters from vetted Sunni Arabs to make it more broadly representative. Around half the new force would be filled with SDF veterans, with new recruits making up the other half. In the South, where the politics was arguably less complicated, the plan involved training and equipping existing vetted Southern Front fighters (previously managed through the military operations center in Jordan, closed in late 2017) and paying their salaries to form a border force capable of establishing a meaningful presence on the de-escalation zone's boundaries and maintaining order within.[12] It was generally understood that, unlike the SDF, the Southern Front was incapable of defending the zone from concerted attack.

The Americans apparently gave no thought to coercing or persuading Turkey to accept the plan, and its response was predictably fierce. Upon the first intake of SDF trainees, Ankara summoned the American ambassador for a brusque dressing-down while Erdogan accused the United States of building a "terror army" and vowed "our mission is to strangle it before it's even born," hinting that plans for an incursion into Afrin—greenlighted by Putin, recall—were well advanced.[13] The Kremlin, evidently not consulted by the United States, also expressed opposition, complaining the plan risked partitioning Syria. Strangely, the Pentagon appeared surprised by the vehemence of Turkey's response and, fearing Erdogan would indeed intervene, backtracked. The best alternative to a home-grown force, the Pentagon hastily concluded, was maintenance of the U.S. military presence.

Secretary of State Rex Tillerson attempted to cast this new, hastily drawn vision as a logical part of a new strategy in a speech at Stanford University on January 17, 2018. Tillerson argued that as Russia wound down its military role in Syria, the United States must act to protect its interests. He identified five core goals—none of them wholly original: (1) the lasting defeat of ISIS and al-Qaeda, (2) reduction of Iranian influence, (3) a political settlement for Syria, (4) the safe and voluntary return of refugees, and (5) elimination of the threat of weapons of mass destruction. Tillerson suggested that to achieve these goals, the United States should maintain a military presence in

Syria—something both Obama and Trump had balked at.[14] The secretary was short on detail as to *how* a small force mainly in the Northeast would achieve these effects, and the president's support was lukewarm at best. Trump had reluctantly signed off on Tillerson's plan but was far from committed to the approach.[15] Indeed, the secretary of state lasted a mere six weeks more in his position.

The previous week's U.S. policy—the Border Force—triggered a new round of conflict between Turkey and the YPG before the ink had even dried. Turkey had been preparing a military incursion into Afrin at least since Putin's green light the previous November. The Border Force proposal encouraged it to bring its plans forward. Turkish intelligence head Hakan Fidan and Chief of the General Staff Hulusi Akar visited Moscow in the second week of January 2018 to clear the way. The Russians were receptive; Putin had already agreed in principle, and although Turkey hadn't been all that helpful at Sochi, the Russians still saw it as crucial to their long-term plans in Syria. Moreover, the Kremlin wanted to dent Tillerson's plans and judged that careering the Kurds and Turks into each other was one way of upending America's new strategy, creating mischief between the United States and its allies, and illustrating to the Kurds that Washington was an unreliable partner. So the Russians agreed to withdraw air cover above Afrin as well as the small number of Russian ground personnel based there.[16]

The euphemistically titled Operation Olive Branch opened on January 19, 2018, with an artillery barrage and air strikes against YPG positions—Russia having ceded control of the skies. Erdogan claimed it was a justified act of self-defense.[17] Two days later, Turkish and allied Sunni Syrian units moved across the border, making only modest early gains amid intense fighting. Noting with alarm that Turkey had supplied its allies with shoulder-launched MANPADS anti-air missiles, Russia closed the skies for five days in early February. This allowed it time to counter by deploying its own sophisticated Pantsir anti-air systems and thus deter attacks on its own aircraft. Once they were deployed, Russia reopened the skies to Turkish aircraft—demonstrating not just its power to control but also its acquiescence in the Turkish offensive. By mid-February the Kurdish position in Afrin had become critical. Desperate Kurdish leaders appealed to

Damascus for help—a decision that many Kurds opposed and that left the PYD embarrassedly scrambling to claim there had been no *political* appeal to Assad.[18] Assad agreed, hoping to counter Turkey's growing influence and woo the Kurds back into the fold. He offered to send government forces into Afrin should the Kurds sign over authority. The PYD rejected the offer and instead proposed that the Syrian government deploy guards along the front line but leave administration of the territory to them. Damascus rejected this idea, yet, as Afrin's position worsened, the regime allowed Kurdish fighters in the East to cross government-held territory to reinforce the defenders in the West.[19]

Alarmed that Damascus might be contemplating intervening to help the Kurds, Erdogan appealed to Putin for help. He warned that Turkey would not be deterred by Syrian forces entering Afrin. Determined to avoid a clash, the Russian president agreed to do what he could but, as usual, wanted something in return: specifically, Erdogan's agreement that Turkey would not oppose government offensives against the de-escalation zones in eastern Ghouta and Rastan/Talbiseh. Erdogan readily agreed—the zones were vulnerable, Turkey had little influence and no capability to stop offensives there anyway, and it was highly unlikely that anyone else would intervene to save them either. The Turkish leader judged that since their fall was inevitable, it was better that Turkey extract a concession in return for acquiescence. Within hours, messages were sent from the Kremlin warning Damascus not to send the army into Afrin.[20] The Syrians grudgingly complied and instead dispatched a token force of several hundred pro-regime militia, drawn mainly from Iranian-backed Shi'ites who drove into Afrin in a triumphal convoy waving Syrian flags.[21] But this ragtag army was no match for the Turkish Army and its allies and was swept away without perceptibly delaying the advance. The YPG fought on doggedly, but after being surrounded on March 6, the city fell two weeks later. Most civilians and fighters fled before the advancing forces. Those who did not were forced out soon after, an almost complete exercise of ethnic cleansing that depopulated Afrin's Kurdish community. Between three hundred and five hundred civilians were killed, and upward of twenty-five thousand displaced by the fighting. Some Yazidi refugees from Iraq were threatened with forcible conversion by Islamist militia; their temples were destroyed. Turkish authorities began rehousing refugees from Turkey in dwellings abandoned by their Kurdish owners.[22]

Ankara learned some important lessons from this experience: First, its military was more than capable of forcing its way into Syria and taking territory. Afrin posed a greater challenge than Euphrates Shield had since the YPG was well dug into terrain comprising hills, heavily wooded areas, and dense urban zones, ideally suited for insurgent warfare, and could call on progovernment allies for help. Although Turkey sustained quite heavy losses (around fifty Turkish and allied troops), the operation was concluded quickly with its objectives met, and the YPG was dealt the blow of far heavier casualties.[23] Second, Turkey learned that military force could be used to strengthen its political position. Olive Branch dealt a blow to the YPG, countered Iranian influence, and created leverage with both Damascus and Moscow. Third, Turkey discovered that military action against the Kurds was immensely popular at home.[24] Fourth, they found that for all its apparent battlefield success, the Assad regime was militarily weak. Finally, Ankara began to see a way of stitching together a large contiguous "safety zone" into which refugees might be encouraged to return in larger numbers—easing domestic pressures and creating a permanent buffer between Turkey and the Kurds. Turkey already held territory to the east of Afrin taken during Euphrates Shield and exercised influence over the opposition-held Idlib pocket and the west Aleppo countryside to the southwest. Events in Afrin confirmed Russia's political and military primacy, but also that Russian interests were not identical to Assad's. Meanwhile, the PYD's appeal to Damascus for help portended a possible deal to reintegrate Kurdish-held territory into the Syrian state, something Moscow long believed possible and necessary, and which might also prove acceptable to Ankara as a long-term solution.[25] In the summer of 2018 PYD officials opened talks with the government about future governance in Kurdish-held areas and suggested they might be willing to step back from demands for federalism in return for decentralization.[26]

As war was waged for control of Afrin, foreign-policy making at the White House was thrown into chaos once again when Trump fired his secretary of state, Rex Tillerson. Beyond the fact Tillerson had called the president a "moron," it was his efforts to prevent Saudi Arabia invading Qatar during the 2017 crisis that proved the catalyst. Riyadh and its allies lobbied hard for Tillerson to go, and finally, in March the following year, Trump agreed, describing his secretary of state as "dumb as a rock."[27] Tillerson was replaced by Mike Pompeo, a former businessman, soldier, and Republican congressman, and a noted hawk on Iran, who had previously served as Trump's CIA director. Days later, National Security Adviser H. R. McMaster was also sacked, this time by presidential tweet after drawing the ire of conservatives for supporting the Iran nuclear deal, opposing confrontation with Iran, acknowledging Russian interference in the 2016 election, and expressing caution about talks with North Korea. McMaster was replaced by another Iran-hawk, John Bolton. The fate of Defense Secretary James Mattis was also called into doubt, and Mattis clashed repeatedly with Pompeo, Bolton, and Trump himself.

The appointment of two Iran-hawks to senior positions confirmed the administration's drift in priorities on Syria toward countering Iran—and that meant loosening ties with the Kurds. For all the president's professed admiration for them, countering Iran meant rebuilding ties with Turkey as a key regional counterweight to the Islamic Republic.[28] More immediately, the personnel change hinted that the president might get his way on withdrawing U.S. forces from Syria. In unscripted remarks on March 20, Trump indicated this was precisely his intention.[29] He also postponed a $200 million project to support the stabilization plan in SDF territory and the Southern Zone—in one swoop undercutting the stabilization program and throwing the administration's strategy for an orderly withdrawal into disarray.[30] That announcement caught both his own government and his allies by surprise. The president was urged to rethink at a "testy" meeting of the national security team on April 3.[31] Envoy to the anti-ISIS coalition Brett McGurk and commander of Central Command General Joseph Votel warned that since ISIS was not yet fully defeated, a hasty U.S. withdrawal could induce a resurgence. If the president wanted lasting victory, more must be done to stabilize the situation on the ground, Votel argued.[32] Trump reluctantly accepted the advice and instructed the Pentagon to withdraw U.S. forces from Syria within six months of having fully defeated ISIS.[33] Yet, he wondered aloud, why should the United States shoulder the burden alone? The Gulf Arab states and Europeans should contribute financially to stabilization. To that end, the suspended $200 million for stabilization should be released only if others made financial contributions.[34] The Arabs, meanwhile, should put together their own multinational force to take over from the United States. By August 2018 U.S. fundraising efforts had borne fruit, securing pledges of $300 million from coalition members to support reconstruction in areas liberated from ISIS, the donors hoping that if they shouldered some of the financial burden, the Americans might be persuaded to keep their troops in place.[35] Yet beyond its own coalition, the confused state of American policy between February and April 2018 conveyed one message very clearly: Washington had no appetite to resist the military conquest of the de-escalation zones. It was a message the Kremlin heard loud and clear above the sound of barrel bombs, artillery shells, and missiles crashing into eastern Ghouta.

FIRST DOMINO: EASTERN GHOUTA

In truth, de-escalation bypassed eastern Ghouta almost entirely. Artillery shells and barrel bombs had continued to smash into the besieged Damascus suburbs right through the second half of 2017, albeit arguably at a reduced rate. The bombardment gained renewed intensity, and chlorine gas, in early 2018.[36] After almost seven years under siege, conditions in eastern Ghouta were dire for the estimated 400,000 civilians there. Food, water, and electricity were all scarce. Hospitals, systematically targeted and dismantled, were starved of supplies and doctors.[37] Despite the de-escalation agreements, no humanitarian convoys made it across government lines in January. On that score, eastern Ghouta was not alone: none of Syria's besieged towns received aid that month.[38] The regime had been eager to take back rebel held areas close to the capital in 2017 but, under intense pressure from Moscow, had stayed its hand. Following the political failure in Sochi, the Kremlin gave it a green light, and the government began its offensive to retake eastern Ghouta just a few weeks later. It was an important test case for how the world would respond to an offensive on a de-escalation zone.

The immediate trigger was a small assault by Ahrar al-Sham and Tahrir al-Sham on an armored vehicle base in Harasta. The base was being used by the government to support artillery and rocket attacks against the enclave.[39] Fighting in Harasta continued sporadically until February, leaving the base in government hands while the rebels claimed the surrounding suburbs, but, most important, it gave Damascus and Moscow the pretext they wanted to launch a general offensive which began in early February. Intense artillery fire killed dozens of civilians. This initial bombardment was followed by a sustained artillery and air campaign.[40] Russian aircraft joined the fray, and the bombing continued without break for more than a week. Repeating tactics employed in Homs and eastern Aleppo, planes dropped leaflets urging fighters to surrender and warning civilians to leave or risk death.

UN officials predicted a bloodbath and called for an immediate cessation of violence. Several Security Council members shared these grim assessments, but without great power support there was little they could do. Repeating a cycle seen several times before, Kuwait and Sweden, the council's humanitarian leads, carefully drafted a resolution demanding an immediate ceasefire and unhindered humanitarian access. Russian diplomats objected, blaming the opposition for the violence and insisting it was pointless for the council to mandate a ceasefire it could not enforce. The council, they argued, should focus on locally organized ceasefires and ensure any ceasefire excluded "counterterrorism operations." The talks dragged on for more than two weeks, while Russian and Syrian ordnance fell on eastern Ghouta, killing "hundreds."[41] Eventually, so great was the disparity between what was being said in New York and what was happening in eastern Ghouta that even the Chinese abandoned the Russians and agreed to support the ceasefire. Isolated, Russia relented and allowed passage of Resolution 2401 (February 24, 2018), which demanded a countrywide ceasefire and unhindered humanitarian access. Sweden may have thought it a "resolute . . . attempt for the Council to take decisive . . . action," but that's not how Russia saw it.[42] There was nothing the council could do to enforce the ceasefire, since it did not invoke chapter 7.

Nor did the ceasefire include the terrorist organizations Damascus and Moscow claimed they were targeting, so neither felt any compunction to stop or even moderate their bombardment. Resolution 2401 had no effect whatsoever, the latest of a long line of dead letters from the Security Council. Government forces opened an evacuation route for five hours each day to allow those who wanted to heed their warnings to do so, but otherwise the bombardment continued unabated. With active clashes along the front lines, there was little hope of securing humanitarian access.[43]

Western governments flailed around with criticism. State Department officials described Russia's humanitarian plan "a joke" and accused Moscow—not unfairly—of "killing civilians."[44] But what exactly was the West going to do about it? Nothing, and everyone knew it. President Trump consulted with allies. Especially surreal was his conversation with Britain's prime minister, Theresa May. They agreed that the situation in eastern Ghouta was a humanitarian catastrophe, and that Assad and Putin were to blame. As for what should be done, they decided that *Russia* should persuade the Syrian government to desist. France's president Emmanuel Macron telephoned Iran's president Hassan Rouhani, telling him Iran bore responsibility because of its ties to Assad and urging him to persuade Assad to end the indiscriminate violence. Rouhani blamed the opposition but said he would do what he could.[45] He did nothing, and Macron did nothing

Eastern Ghouta's defensive lines began to break in the first week of March, splintering what was left of the enclave into a series of three tiny pockets, each controlled by a different armed group. Tens of thousands fled as the civilian death toll climbed above fifteen hundred.[46] The first of these pockets, Harasta, was controlled by Ahrar al-Sham. It capitulated around March 22. Approximately fifteen hundred fighters and forty-five hundred civilians were taken by bus to Idlib as part of the deal. A day or so later, another Islamist group, Faylaq al-Rahman, followed suit when its front lines collapsed at Hammuriyeh and Kafr Batna. They handed over control of a small pocket comprising the towns of Arbin, Zamalka, Ain Tarma, and Jobar in return for the transfer of around seven thousand fighters and their families to Idlib.[47] By the end of March, badly ravaged Douma, controlled by Jaysh al-Islam, was all that was left. Violence receded as the two sides haggled over a surrender agreement that could avert a bloody final showdown. But they couldn't agree on the evacuation of fighters, what weapons they would be allowed to take with them, and the transfer of prisoners. Things weren't helped by the fact that Jaysh al-Islam was itself divided about what to do. In early April the government looked to force the issue by intensifying bombardment.

Among the bombs dropped on Douma during this final assault on Saturday, April 7, were two carrying chemical weapons. At around 4 p.m. a chlorine bomb crashed into Saada bakery. Around three and a half hours later, a second chlorine bomb hit Martyr's Square. By 8 p.m. Douma's beleaguered medical staff were treating around five hundred people for respiratory problems, blueness of skin, oral foaming, and corneal burns—all symptoms of intense exposure to chlorine. In all, forty-three people were killed by exposure to a highly toxic chemical—later identified as chlorine by the OPCW.[48] If the attack was intended to break Douma's wilting morale, it succeeded. The following day, Jaysh al-Islam caved in and accepted the government's terms. Those fighters who wanted to were evacuated to Jarabulus and Idlib. In return, they agreed to free prisoners and leave their heavy weapons behind. Civilians who wanted to stay in Douma and reconcile with the regime would be allowed to do so. After vetting by the Mukhabarat (a process called "resolving their status"), they would be granted formal amnesty if found not to have been supporters of "terrorist organizations." Men of fighting age would be conscripted into the army, auxiliary forces, or police.[49] The government also agreed that Douma would be patrolled by Russian military police units—Muslim soldiers, many of them considered elite counterterrorism forces, recruited from Russia's northern Caucasus. This deal cushioned the blow for remaining civilians but also helped free up government forces for future offensives. The process was quickly managed, and by the following Thursday the government declared it had control of the whole zone. In total, twelve thousand to eighteen thousand people had been killed during the siege, mostly civilians. In the months that followed, the government prevented the UN's humanitarian agencies from getting regular access while it determined which of the survivors had been loyal, which had not been, and what to do with both.[50] As territory fell to the government, UN aid—like all foreign aid coming into government-held territory—was used to reward the faithful and the penitent. The government withheld it from those it judged more suspect, as a form of punishment.

Worried the United States might respond militarily to the chemical attack on Douma, government forces moved quickly to secure the area, while Russia orchestrated an at times macabre campaign of disinformation to cast doubt on what the basic facts showed. First the Kremlin denied there had been a chemical attack.[51] Then it claimed the White Helmets had staged the attack.[52] Then it blamed Britain, saying it had staged the attack to provoke U.S. intervention.[53] Then, in a grotesque homage to Stalin's 1930s show trials, it paraded eleven "witnesses" before the OPCW at The Hague, who claimed that there had been no chemical attack.[54] Damascus got into the act, organizing carefully staged trips for sympathetic journalists, such as Britain's Robert Fisk.[55] Yet, despite their best efforts to hide and destroy the evidence, the OPCW was still able to find clear proof of a chemical weapons attack.

The Russians were rightly worried, and their dissembling had little effect on Western leaders. Washington's assessment pointed "with a high degree of certainty" to Syrian government responsibility. Angry that U.S. deterrence had failed, Trump expressed outrage at what he condemned as a "sick" and "barbaric act." Theresa May and Emmanuel Macron both agreed there must be a rapid military response—May deciding that she and her government, not Parliament, would determine whether British forces would be involved.[56] As usual, Angela Merkel ruled out German involvement in any military action, making the case for diplomatic action instead. The diplomatic route was soon closed off, however. At the UN, the United States, Britain, and France proposed a Security Council resolution condemning the use of chemical weapons—though without specifically mentioning the Syrian government in a bid to win Russian acquiescence—and establishing a new UN mechanism to investigate allegations and identify the perpetrators. Negotiations were tense and frequently acrimonious but didn't make it past first base, the Russians clinging to their absurd denials of government responsibility and the United States responding that if the council was blocked, it would act unilaterally. When it came to a vote on April 10, Russia cast its veto, joined only by socialist

Bolivia.[57] Uneasy with the Kremlin's blatant complicity yet still unwilling to condemn the use of chemical weapons, China abstained.

Trump, though, wasn't much interested in diplomacy. He wanted a sharp military riposte and told his advisors to find options like ones he'd seen on Fox News, where a pundit had suggested that the United States destroy Syria's five main air bases and put Assad's air force out of action. Bolton agreed a strong response was needed to deter not just Assad but Iran, too. Mattis, though, thought differently.[58] The secretary of defense presented three sets of options, dubbed "heavy," "medium," and "light." The "heavy" option gave Trump what he said he wanted, a sustained campaign to degrade Syria's air capabilities; the "medium" package was a suite of strikes against air bases and other Syrian facilities associated with chemical weapons, larger in scale than the 2017 strikes and thus carrying a larger deterrence footprint but similar in focus and intent; the "light" option was a replay of 2017. Mattis argued that only the more limited option would prevent American forces becoming bogged down, jeopardizing the president's withdrawal plans.[59] To support his case, he presented Pentagon advice that the heavy and medium packages presented "high risk" since they might provoke counterescalation, leading to U.S. losses. The light package, meanwhile, would demonstrate presidential resolve, punish the Syrian government, convey U.S. military predominance, and thus restore deterrence—all without risking conflict with Russia. Trump, backed by Bolton and Vice President Mike Pence, still preferred the heavy option, but though this wasn't obvious from his public posturing, Mattis had planted seeds of doubt in the president's mind.[60] Worried about anything that might derail withdrawal, Trump tasked Bolton with sounding out regional allies on whether they might deploy their own forces to replace the Americans. The response was unenthusiastic. Mattis and the Pentagon, meanwhile, reverted to an old tactic and stalled. Knowing there was pressure from allies for a quick response and that this was the president's strong preference too, the Pentagon worked up detailed target sets only for the light option and advised that the other packages would take more time to develop. In effect, Mattis presented Trump with a choice between the light option and deferring the use of force altogether. Unsurprisingly, Trump took the only option he was given and authorized the light package.

Early on the morning of April 14 (Syria time), 105 missiles fired from U.S., British, and French submarines, ships, and aircraft hit three targets in Syria: the Barzah research center in Damascus, responsible for Syria's chemical weapons program, a military storage site at Him Shanshar west of Homs, which held chemical weapons precursors, and a bunker at the same site. The missiles hit their targets, while around forty Syrian missiles sent to intercept them missed theirs. But, as had happened a year before, the strikes were too limited to have much material effect on Syria's chemical weapons capabilities, and though it may be claimed they restored deterrence, this was only a temporary effect—Assad's forces began using chemical weapons again the following May.[61] Russia feigned outrage and summoned the Security Council to condemn the strikes. Though Russia won some support from the UN secretary-general, the move backfired politically, as only China and Bolivia shared the Kremlin's view.[62] Beneath the rhetoric and agonized debates about their legality, however, the limited strikes unintentionally signaled the West's disinclination to punish Damascus for its brutal routing of eastern Ghouta. The Assad government and the Kremlin read this as a green light to proceed with military offensives against the other de-escalation zones. The offensive on Rastan-Talbiseh began the very same week.

SECOND DOMINO: RASTAN AND TALBISEH

The de-escalation zone spanning northern Homs and southern Hama governates, including the towns of Rastan and Talbiseh, was the smallest and least defensible of the four. It was therefore the obvious choice of target following eastern Ghouta. On April 15 Syrian Army and NDF units, backed by Russian and Syrian air power, advanced into the zone, seizing Saleem and the surrounding area. Government forces made steady progress over the next few days, despite a counteroffensive, until April 20, when envoys for the embattled opposition fighters in Rastan approached Russian negotiators, offering a "reconciliation" deal like that brokered in Douma. Meeting at Dar al-Kabira in northern Homs, they agreed to a four-day ceasefire but not a reconciliation deal, as the government rejected opposition demands that fighters be allowed to withdraw with their heavy weapons, while, flush with confidence, the government saw little need to concede authority over the area to Russian military police.[63] To underscore the point, when the ceasefire expired, government forces unleashed a massive artillery and air barrage on Rastan and Talbiseh, forcing the opposition back to the negotiating table. Damascus offered an ultimatum: opposition fighters must agree to evacuate without heavy weapons to Idlib or Turkish northern Aleppo and transfer authority to the government. They were given forty-eight hours to decide and were told that if they didn't accept the terms, the enclave would be routed. With little room for maneuver, the opposition agreed. Most civilians opted to stay where they were and "reconcile" with the government. Around three thousand fighters—with their light weapons, families, and other civilians—were bused to the North.[64] By May 15 the government had reclaimed control of the whole pocket without attracting much international criticism. In an act of supreme otherworldliness, the UN's Staffan de Mistura briefed the Security Council by video link from Geneva and reassured it that Iran and Russia agreed that de-escalation was "indispensable"—as if two of the four zones had not just been crushed.[65]

THIRD DOMINO: SOUTHERN ZONE

The divided city of Daraa, birthplace of the revolution, held symbolic value for government and opposition alike. The southern de-escalation zone ought to have been far more difficult to overrun, since it was guaranteed by the United States and Jordan as well as Russia, defended by the Southern Front, and watched over by an Israel determined to prevent Iran establishing a foothold near the Golan Heights. With a population of around 750,000, the southern zone was also far more populous than the zones already eliminated. An attack here risked serious escalation. But in the event, Moscow skillfully prepared the way with Tel Aviv, the United States keeled over, and the whole business was wrapped up before UN officials broke for their summer holidays.

Israel and the United States presented serious complications to the ambitions of Damascus and Moscow. The threat of open war between

Israel and Iran was real. From the beginning of the Islamic Republic's involvement in Syria's war, Israel had anticipated that Tehran would use the crisis to strengthen its position and move fighters and arms closer to the Golan Heights.[66] These concerns escalated when Russian intervention tipped the balance in Assad's—and Iran's—favor. Periodically, the Israeli Defence Force (IDF) conducted air strikes against Iranian-related facilities in Syria, but Israel also supported half a dozen armed opposition groups in the South, providing salaries, civilian vehicles, light weapons, and cash.[67] In early 2017 the IDF acquired what it believed was credible evidence of an Iranian plan to establish itself in Syria long-term with a force of around 100,000 Shi'ite fighters modeled on Hezbollah, dedicated to war with Israel. By 2018 Israeli intelligence detected signs that the plan was being made a reality.[68] Hostilities almost boiled over in February that year when Israel shot down an Iranian drone overflying the Golan Heights and conducted a wave of strikes targeting Iranian facilities.[69] It reportedly took a "stern" telephone call from Putin to Netanyahu to prevent the Israelis escalating still further.[70]

Israel always worried Hezbollah would exploit the southern de-escalation zone and acquiesced only when Russia promised to keep the group well away from Golan. Yet Hezbollah never completely withdrew from the southern zone as required; indeed, Hezbollah itself denied it was under any obligation to withdraw.[71] As government operations wound down in Rastan, tensions in the South soared on the expectation it would be next. Hezbollah's leader, Hassan Nasrallah, seemingly confirmed Israeli fears. "The war in Syria with proxies is coming to an end," he told his followers on May 2, "the second war with the genuine enemies may soon begin." Tensions weren't helped either by Trump's May 8 decision to formally withdraw from the Iran nuclear deal. Within hours, Israeli intelligence detected unusual activities by Iranian-backed militia. The IDF placed soldiers in the Golan Heights on alert, moved antimissile batteries to forward positions, and called up reservists. Israeli aircraft launched missiles at Iran's el-Kiswah base to the south of Damascus.[72] Iranian-backed forces responded the following day by firing twenty rockets at Israeli forward positions on the Heights—apparently without first seeking the Syrian government's permission.[73] Some were intercepted; others fell short and landed in Syria. None hit their target, but the IDF responded anyway, conducting its most sustained set of attacks against Iranian and Hezbollah positions in Syria yet.[74]

Everyone knew what was coming. As early as March, opposition leaders had identified the imminent threat and developed plans for a preemptive offensive of their own to relieve the pressure. They anxiously pressed their U.S. contacts for more assistance, but to no avail. Meanwhile, probing maneuvers drew a series of government air strikes in late March and a warning from the Americans and Jordanians that they should avoid provocations.[75] With little prospect that a preemptive offensive would succeed without outside help, most opposition groups complied, though some small HTS-aligned groups still pressed the case for an offensive. On the other side, Russia was understandably wary, concerned a southern offensive might trigger forceful responses from Israel and the United States. Assad, too, supported a brief pause to allow his exhausted troops to regroup and reposition.

Russian defense officials prepared the way by sounding out the Israelis to see what could be done to prevent them intervening. The Israelis were initially bullish, warning they would use force should Iran or Hezbollah move too close to the Golan Heights. The Russians explained that Russian and Iranian were not identical and reassured Israel that it would be in its interests if they—not Iran—emerged as the preeminent hegemon in Syria. In return for Israeli quiescence, they promised to keep Iranian and Iranian-backed militia (including Hezbollah) out of the southern offensive and beyond fifteen kilometers from the Golan Heights. They also offered the IDF free reign to strike Iranian-linked targets whenever it chose. In the longer term, Russia would press for the withdrawal of all foreign forces from Syria, Hezbollah and Iranian included. Not everyone in Israeli defense circles thought this a good deal. Gadi Eizonkot, the IDF's chief of staff, and Netanyahu himself initially, thought it better to delay and prevent a southern offensive altogether. But Israel could not do that alone, and there seemed no chance the United States would act to protect the zone. Moreover, intelligence assessments indicated the Syrian Army was preparing an imminent offensive and might attempt to preempt any Israeli deal with Moscow. This would be the worst of all worlds, leaving Israel bereft of leverage and confronting Hezbollah on the

Golan Heights. Despite his misgivings, therefore, Netanyahu accepted Russia's terms, the deal finalized in a phone call between Russia's defense minister, Sergei Shoigu, and his Israeli counterpart, Avigdor Lieberman.[76] Tehran, too, grudgingly accepted Moscow's terms, and Iranian diplomats reassured the Jordanians they would play no part in the coming offensive. Clearly, Tehran felt it could not afford open confrontation with Moscow, but unlike the Russians, Iran was not looking for an exit strategy. It could afford to wait.

The Israel-Russia deal blindsided the United States. To the extent Washington had any idea at all about how the zone might be defended, it had banked heavily on uncertainty about Israeli intentions deterring a full-scale offensive.[77] Some Syrian opposition figures had also made this calculation.[78] The deal undercut all that. The administration's first reaction was to try substituting Israeli deterrence for American by issuing a blunt warning that the United States would "take firm and appropriate measures" should the Syrian government violate the zone agreement.[79] In fact, the White House never had the slightest intention of intervening—it seems that at no point was the question even discussed. Perhaps aware that deterrence lacked credibility, U.S. officials scrambled for a more realistic strategy and indicated to the Russians and Israelis that they would not block "reconciliation" agreements, hoping this might allow the government to retake the territory without the obvious destruction of a de-escalation compact guaranteed by the United States. The offer was well taken, since it accorded with the Kremlin's own strategy, and Russian and government officials set about offering deals to the opposition armed groups and municipal leaders inside the zone. But behind-the-scenes accommodation undermined U.S. deterrence by removing uncertainty about its likely reaction to an offensive.

The offensive began on June 18, and government forces made rapid gains. Backed by Syrian and Russian aircraft, they seized several towns and villages, displacing fifty thousand from Daraa in the first week alone. In New York the U.S. ambassador to the UN, Nikki Haley, condemned the offensive as an unambiguous violation of the de-escalation zone, raising fleeting hopes among the opposition that the United States would respond forcefully. That was never in the cards.[80] Judging that the Israel-Russia deal had probably done enough to contain Iran, the president abandoned the zone. U.S. officials handed opposition groups a terse note that explained: "You should not base your decisions on an assumption or expectation of military intervention from us." The United States promised to hold Russia responsible for violating the deal but would do nothing more to protect it.[81] Opposition forces launched counterattacks but failed to reverse the tide as, now confident neither the United States nor Israel would intervene, Russia stepped up its fire support. By July 5 approximately 60 percent of the pocket was in government hands and around 160,000 people displaced, many of them crossing into Jordan. Close to 400 barrel bombs, 250 rockets, and a similar number of artillery shells had fallen on the zone since the offensive began. As the front lines crumbled, the number of displaced grew rapidly, another 100,000 in just two days at the end of the first week of July. Civilian casualties mounted, and the area's four main hospitals came under sustained attack themselves.[82] The UN secretary-general timidly expressed "grave concern," but not even he seemed to think his words would make a difference.[83]

With two promontories reaching north divided by a regime-held strip along the Daraa-Damascus highway, the southern zone was always vulnerable to being split into isolated pockets. That became a reality in early July, despite fierce opposition resistance. Defeat seemingly now inevitable, dozens of towns rushed to spare themselves from the worst by making local reconciliation deals with the government.[84] Still nervous lest a prolonged offensive, chemical weapons attack, or Hezbollah outrage suddenly change U.S. or Israeli intentions, the Russians pursued these deals with vigor and engaged in intense negotiations with a twelve-member opposition team mediated by Jordan. Aware of the fate awaiting them, opposition negotiators sought assurances that Russian military police and local civilian authorities would assume authority over them, not Damascus. In return, they offered a phased evacuation of fighters with their weapons. This was a deal that Putin could accept, and he instructed Lavrov to invite his Jordanian counterpart, Foreign Minister Ayman Safadi, to Moscow to finalize arrangements.[85] There were some sticking points, however, especially disagreements over what weapons opposition fighters would be permitted to retain and who would control the international borders. Damascus saw little need to compromise since by July 7 its forces had advanced almost all the way to the Nasib crossing into Jordan. With no apparent alternative, rebels there accepted the government's terms.[86] Opposition forces held out for a few more days in Daraa, but intensified bombardment forced them to accept the reconciliation deal a week later.[87] A small pocket in the West held by ISIS and other jihadist groups was taken at the end of July.

The third de-escalation zone had fallen amid reports of widespread looting and summary executions, to which the Russian military police turned a blind eye.[88] Days later, Trump and Putin held a summit in the Finnish capital, Helsinki. According to John Bolton, Putin reassured Trump that Russia wanted the Iranians out of Syria but could not substitute Russian troops for Iranian. The Russian also pressed the U.S. president to abandon the al-Tanf base, warning forces there were surrounded by ISIS. Most significantly, though, Putin urged Trump to reengage with the peace process—a Russian objective dating back to the start of its military intervention in 2015. But Trump was interested only in ISIS and Iran, not the Syrian peace process.[89] In the press conference afterward, not only did the U.S. president not criticize Russia for violating the de-escalation agreement or flinch at Putin's claim to have been conducting counterterrorism in Syria's South, he lauded enhanced cooperation between their two militaries and claimed recent events helped Israel.[90] There was only one de-escalation zone left.

14

NORTHERN FIRES

B Y THE summer of 2018, three of the four "de-escalation zones" were overrun, and living conditions in the last one, Idlib, were dire. Around two-thirds of the beleaguered enclave was controlled by the HTS (former al-Nusra), a group excluded from the Astana process ceasefire. Brett McGurk, then the U.S. envoy to the coalition against the Islamic State, had spoken for many in 2017 when he described Idlib as "the largest al-Qaeda safe haven since 9/11."[1] HTS controlled the strategic Bab al-Hawa border crossing into Turkey and Idlib city itself and maintained a presence almost everywhere in the enclave. Though it had formally severed its al-Qaeda ties in 2016 to emphasize the primacy of Syria to its calling, the group's ideology remained staunchly Salafist jihadist. This positioned it as a direct rival to the conservative Islamist Ahrar al-Sham, which had always emphasized the Syrian nature of its struggle, as well as to the battered remnants of former Free Syrian Army–aligned groups. The HTS grew stronger through 2017, helped by the fact its main rivals did deals with Assad and Turkey.[2] It had loudly condemned Turkey's abandonment of eastern Aleppo when others had remained mute and stood alone among northern opposition groups in opposing Euphrates Shield and complaining that Turkey should be directing its efforts against Assad.[3] This dogged single-mindedness brought the HTS legitimacy even among those who rejected its ideology, while the influx of extremist fighters evacuated from elsewhere in the country strengthened its military capacity.

More than anything else, Turkey wanted stability in Idlib—a goal it shared with the United States.[4] Ankara feared Idlib's collapse would trigger a new refugee crisis and present the Kurds another opportunity for territorial growth. But stability meant somehow loosening the extremists' grip. Turkish strategy, evident as early as spring 2016, was to isolate the HTS politically, diminish its material resources, and challenge its legitimacy, while reinforcing its political rivals through military assistance and stabilization. A military offensive against the HTS and its allies was judged unfeasible because it would likely attract strong resistance, provoke a backlash inside Turkey, and—if the battle to retake Raqqa was anything to go by—cause immense civilian suffering. A subtler approach was needed, and for that Turkey needed time since in the immediate term the pocket's defense depended on the HTS.

The relationship among Turkey, its allies, and the HTS was understandably fraught. When the de-escalation zone was first agreed to in the fall of 2017, there were serious doubts as to whether the extremists would allow Turkish forces in to monitor the ceasefire since they well knew that Ankara wanted to displace them. For a few tense weeks in October, a military standoff pushed Ankara to the brink of armed intervention before the HTS relented and allowed it to establish three observation posts along the zone's northern border. HTS obstructions and ongoing fighting delayed further deployments on the eastern and southern borders. Taking the opportunity for mayhem this created, between October 2017 and February 2018 regime, Russian-, and Iranian-backed forces conducted a series of offensives against the HTS in the enclave's rural East, forcing the extremists to withdraw their objections to further Turkish deployments. By May 2018 the Idlib zone was effectively ringed by Turkish military observers peering across at Russian and Iranian posts established on the other side.[5] Only then could Turkey begin to seriously challenge the HTS's political supremacy in Idlib. In June 2018 Turkish intelligence cobbled together more than a dozen Sunni groups—many of them formerly FSA-aligned—into the National Liberation Front (NLF) by offering security guarantees and material assistance in return for decoupling from HTS and accepting Turkish oversight. The same model was employed in Afrin, where Turkish intelligence engineered a new "Syrian National Army" (SNA).

THE FIRST OFFENSIVE

Idlib's fate now hinged on Turkish resolve. The first test was not slow in coming since Damascus and Tehran were impatient to exploit the military momentum created by their victories in the other zones. Moscow, however, thought an all-out offensive "impractical" for the time being and urged Damascus to pursue more modest goals.[6] The Kremlin understood the wisdom of a quick and devastating offensive but was unsure about Turkish intentions. It wanted to avoid provoking Ankara into another military escalation. Moreover, Russian intelligence assessed that Idlib's opposition forces were much more capable than those in the other zones and likely to fight to the bitter end, given that this was the last remaining enclave. Even victory carried risks, since it could trigger a humanitarian catastrophe and mass displacement, leave Russia having to help occupy ground housing thousands of battle-hardened jihadists bent on revenge, and sour a hard-won relationship with Ankara that Russia thought was important to its regional interests more broadly. Then there was the relationship with Damascus itself to think about. With one eye on its struggle for influence with Iran, some in the Kremlin judged that keeping Idlib on the table gave Moscow precious leverage over Assad, which it would lose if the enclave was overrun. On balance, then, the Kremlin advised Damascus to conduct a limited offensive to improve its tactical position in the field and political position vis-à-vis Turkey, but that instead of overrunning the enclave, force should be used to extract a "reconciliation" style agreement.[7]

The Syrian Army and its allies massed within striking range of Idlib. Artillery and air strikes were stepped up in the last week of August, and Russia built up its naval presence off Syria's northern shore, adding ten ships and two submarines. Capable of firing missiles into Idlib, the naval buildup was also intended to deter Western intervention should the Syrian regime use chemical weapons once again.[8] On the political front, Moscow warned it intended to support an "antiterrorist operation" in Idlib to eliminate what Sergei Lavrov described as an "abscess" of terrorism.[9] That message was underscored by a surge of air strikes and artillery fire in the first week of September—dozens conducted by Russian aircraft. A major regime offensive seemed imminent.

UN officials floundered for a response to the seemingly inevitable. The secretary-general warned an offensive would trigger a massive humanitarian crisis. His genocide-prevention adviser, Adama Dieng, predicted "catastrophic" harm to civilians, and his special envoy, Staffan de Mistura, labored to prevent a "bloodbath" by figuring out ways of letting the government simply walk into Idlib.[10] To the Security Council, de Mistura proposed that opposition fighters withdraw from certain areas to help the creation of UN-monitored humanitarian corridors to allow civilians to escape, though precisely where close to three million displaced civilians were meant to escape to was unclear. He also proposed an immediate ceasefire and called for a deadline for the withdrawal of "militant" fighters from populated areas so that they could be targeted without risk to civilians. Control of these areas would be transferred to "local authorities" and "civilian police."[11] Russia's Vasily Nebenzia welcomed the UN's help but insisted there could be no ceasefire with terrorist organizations. Western diplomats complained bitterly but offered only new demands for a ceasefire backed by nothing more than well-intentioned argument.

There was more meaningful diplomacy between the three Astana guarantors, Russia, Turkey, and Iran. Turkey's foreign minister, Mevlut Cavusoglu, pleaded with Moscow for more time to separate out the extremists and moderates and establish a new civilian administration. A few days later the three leaders convened in Tehran. Erdogan urged Putin and Rouhani to agree to an immediate ceasefire, warning of a "bloodbath" and explaining that Turkey could not cope with another mass influx of refugees. A ceasefire would be "pointless," Putin replied, a means only of shielding terrorists.[12] Rouhani agreed with the Russian, insisting that armed groups be pushed out of Idlib and the government's authority restored. Erdogan left chastened and empty handed. Having already been forced into a humiliating back down on Aleppo, he had staked his personal credibility on promising to protect Idlib. Antipathy toward Syrian refugees had grown in Turkey, especially as the economy stagnated, and the collapse of Idlib would create a new and unwelcome refugee crisis. Moreover, whatever the public's complaints about refugees, support for Syria's opposition remained strong in Turkey, particularly among Erdogan's AKP supporters.[13] Erdogan could not simply sacrifice Idlib without paying a serious political price. Disappointment in Tehran forced him to confront the fact that diplomacy alone would likely prove insufficient. As he left, Erdogan delivered a telling parting shot. Should the world fail to protect Idlib, Turkey would "neither watch from the sidelines nor participate in such a game."[14] As if to underline the point, additional troops and heavy weapons were deployed to reinforce Turkish positions in Idlib.[15]

Erdogan's obstinacy and none-too-subtle threats persuaded Putin it was time to do a deal. The Russian president had always intended that any offensive be a limited one, and he was not prepared—yet—to risk escalation.[16] So a little more than a week after the Tehran meeting, Putin invited the triumvirate back to Sochi. This time, they agreed on a ceasefire for Idlib and a plan to establish a demilitarized zone within the territory of the former de-escalation zone between fifteen and twenty kilometers deep. HTS and other extremist groups should withdraw entirely from the demilitarized zone, though Turkish-aligned groups, such as the NLF, would be permitted to remain within it but would have to withdraw heavy weapons, including tanks, artillery pieces, and rocket launchers. Turkey would expand its network of observation posts inside the demilitarized zone, and Russia and Iran would do likewise on the government side. Turkish and Russian forces would then conduct joint patrols inside the demilitarized zone and monitor the area with drones. The deal also contained measures to encourage longer-term stabilization. Notably, the M4 and M5 highways connecting Idlib with the rest of Syria should be opened to encourage movement.[17] Turkey agreed to use its influence to dissolve Idlib's HTS-led administration and replace it with a new civilian authority.[18]

The Sochi deal appeared to be a diplomatic triumph for Erdogan, though it also satisfied Russian interests, not least by placing HTS drones and missiles out of range of Russia's Khmeimim base. What mattered most, of course, was that Putin had always intended that there be nothing more than a limited attack followed by a deal. A "disgruntled" Assad was forced to yield to Russian pressure.[19] But the new arrangements did not address the underlying problem or change the balance of forces, making it a case more of conflict delayed than resolved, the fate of three million civilians hinging on a game of military brinkmanship. There were dozens of minor ceasefire violations in the weeks that followed, including exchanges of fire between government forces and the HTS, but the deal held for the time being. Everyone knew it couldn't last.

At an Istanbul meeting of the triumvirate plus France (to represent the EU, who the triumvirate hoped could be persuaded to foot the reconstruction bill) that October, Russian delegates were at pains to insist that the ceasefire could not be permanent. Stabilization required the dismembering of HTS and conclusion of a "reconciliation" agreement with Damascus. Plainly, the Russians hoped to persuade Turkey, the West, and the UN to clear Idlib of its extremists and set up reconciliation and the transfer of authority to Damascus—much as they had in Aleppo and the other zones. Whether this had always been part of their plan for Idlib or was an ad hoc gambit is unclear, but it corresponds with Putin's initial intent. If a negotiated reconciliation were not achieved, the Russians warned, a military solution would be pursued. Much therefore hinged on Turkey's ability to push the HTS out of the demilitarized zone and change the zone's political leadership. It succeeded at neither.

During October opposition forces withdrew some—but not all—of their heavy weapons from the demilitarized zone. HTS and other jihadists remained firmly in place inside the zone, provoking frequent exchanges of small-arms fire. The continuing presence of HTS made it impossible to start joint Turkish-Russian patrols: opposition groups refused to consent to the joint patrols, and the two governments judged it too dangerous to proceed without it. Nor was there any movement on opening the highways, leaving the HTS in control of these key arteries. The duties it extracted on the flow of people and goods became a key source of income for the group. Turkey also failed to make headway in displacing the HTS's Salvation Front government. In fact, things got worse. In a botched attempt to change Idlib's government, Ankara broke off ties with the Salvation Front and elevated the NLF. Rather than cowing the extremists, this provoked a backlash, which came to a head in January 2019. The HTS violently attacked its local opponents and, after ten days of brutal fighting, forced the NLF (the second largest group in Idlib) to assign them authority over almost the whole enclave. Emboldened, the extremists tried to win a seat at the international table by offering the government a deal granting access to the highways. They were rebuffed. In fact, the putsch had only weakened Idlib's international position. Washington grew alarmed at the growing presence of extremists in Idlib, the CIA identifying another al-Qaeda-linked group, Hurras al Din, there. Idlib could expect little help from the West if Damascus moved against it. Through March and April Syrian Army units stationed along the front line exchanged small-arms fire with HTS fighters still occupying the DMZ. A new offensive was all but inevitable. The only questions were when it would come and how Turkey would respond. Erdogan had much to ponder. Just as Putin was plagued by uncertainty about Turkish intent, so Erdogan was unsure of Russia's. Stabilizing Idlib, preventing another refugee crisis, and, if possible, returning some refugees to Syria were certainly priorities, but the Kurdish question loomed larger still. The resolution of that issue hinged on the United States, which seemed itself not to know what its policy was.

President Trump tweeted on December 19, 2018, to publicize his long-promised decision to withdraw the two thousand or so U.S. troops from Syria following their "historic victories" over ISIS. But how could the United States withdraw and still hope to achieve its stated goals of completing the destruction ISIS and protecting the Kurds? One or the other would have to give unless conditions on the ground changed dramatically. Secretary of Defense James Mattis, backed strongly by the Pentagon—both always cautious about U.S. military involvement in Syria—and intelligence agencies, had pushed back hard against the president's withdrawal plan. Since ISIS had not been completely defeated, Mattis reasoned, withdrawal risked ISIS resurgence. Withdrawal would also expose the SDF—loyal allies—to a potentially catastrophic Turkish offensive. That would further exacerbate the ISIS threat, since war with Turkey would force the SDF to take its boot off the extremists' neck. What is more, the SDF guarded some eleven thousand former ISIS fighters in its prisons, which might become insecure in the event of conflict with Turkey.[20] U.S. withdrawal might also encourage Damascus—which had thus far stayed its hand in the Northeast—to move against the Kurds. Beyond all that, abandoning a loyal ally would send a terrible signal to U.S. allies worldwide and make it more difficult to recruit local partners in the future. But Mattis failed to persuade the president, who informed the Joint Chiefs of his decision at around the same time he tweeted it to the world.[21] The defense secretary resigned, and the president's special envoy on Syria, Brett McGurk, quickly followed suit.[22] The way seemed clear for Trump to get the withdrawal he wanted, but the Joint Chiefs and intelligence agencies had other ideas. The Pentagon slow-tracked planning for the withdrawal, counting on the president's short attention span to provide a stay of execution. The ploy worked, helped by a Christmas presidential visit to U.S. forces in the Middle East which so enamored the president he agreed to delay withdrawal still further and hold on to the Al-Tanf base in eastern Syria.[23] After several more weeks of confusion, U.S. policy settled on retaining around four hundred soldiers alongside the SDF in the North and maintaining the al-Tanf facility for the time being, with an understanding that the United States was working toward complete withdrawal once the ISIS threat was diminished.[24] Complete withdrawal, however, remained the president's primary objective.

If the Trump administration was struggling for clarity, the UN was struggling for relevance. The Security Council had long been deadlocked by Russian (and often Chinese) vetoes. By fall 2018 even the once proactive General Assembly and Human Rights Council had been reduced to issuing formulaic expressions of concern that were given little heed. In November only 106 of the UN's 193 member states bothered supporting a resolution condemning the "systematic, widespread and gross violations and abuses of international human rights law and violations of international humanitarian law." Some 58 states signaled their disinterest by abstaining.[25] Even de Mistura had run out of steam and wanted out, citing moral objections not hitherto seen to Assad's seemingly inevitable victory.[26] The cold reality was that the Astana process had reduced the UN's process to a sideshow. The envoy mainly spent tedious hours chairing pointless meetings about constitutional provisions no one paid any attention to. The UN's crisis diplomacy was reduced to an exercise in facilitating surrender. Throughout his time as special envoy, de Mistura had reported "important meetings" and "diplomatic progress" when everyone around him knew that what mattered was what happened on the battlefield. His final address to the Security Council spoke volumes of the UN's political irrelevance. De Mistura dwelt on the Sochi agreement he had played no part in negotiating before explaining why the long-promised constitutional committee had not yet materialized, pointing the blame at the shortfall in gender balance. Yet he ended with a flourish, claiming important progress *had* been made and that there were many vital meetings and much "absolutely urgent" work ahead.[27] And with that ethereal display, he was gone, the UN peace process he had been charged with overseeing long since zombified. De Mistura's replacement, Norwegian diplomat Geir O. Pedersen—veteran of the Norwegian team that oversaw the ill-fated Oslo Middle East peace process—promised to throw himself vigorously into renewed talks about the constitutional committee.[28] No one held their breath.

OFFENSIVE RENEWED: IDLIB DAWN

The calm was short-lived. In New York, Pedersen insisted "there is no military solution." In and around Idlib, however, Syrians spent the winter preparing for war. It duly returned in the spring of 2019 when, in the final days of April, Syrian and Russian aircraft and artillery opened a barrage into the demilitarized zone and wider enclave, apparently in retaliation for an HTS attack three days earlier that had left more than twenty Syrian soldiers dead. Their principal goals were to clear HTS from the demilitarized zone and secure positions behind some of Turkey's observation posts to facilitate their encirclement, should that become necessary, and to prevent Turkey establishing a hard border. Once again, civilian infrastructure was deliberately targeted, especially hospitals. The World Health Organization reported that eighteen hospitals were hit. Another report claimed that Russian jets hit four hospitals in a single day.[29] Among the civilian casualties were more than a dozen children, killed by barrel bombs that tore into schools, medical facilities, and homes.[30] After a week or so of bombing, which killed more than sixty civilians and forty fighters, on May 6, 2019, Syrian government forces advanced into the demilitarized zone in the south of the Idlib pocket (northern Hama governate), taking several villages from the HTS.[31] The offensive was spearheaded by the army's Tiger Force and 5th Corps, units built or reconstituted, trained, and equipped by Russia.[32] Iranian Quds forces also took part.[33] Opposition forces responded with a desperate mortar attack on the Khmeimim base, drawing an intense response from the Russian Air Force. Western governments condemned what they described as a flagrant violation of the ceasefire arrangement, but Moscow blamed the opposition, pointing to the failure of extremists to withdraw fully from the demilitarized zone and their frequent ceasefire violations. The UN was left to report the costs, express concern, and urge a return to ceasefire. What mattered was that Damascus faced much stiffer resistance than it had expected, made only modest gains at considerable expense, and discovered to its dismay that Turkey would not be so easily outmaneuvered.

Government forces continued to advance through early May, taking Kafr Nabudah in the far Southwest, but faced stiff resistance as NLF forces joined the fray. Meanwhile, Turkey orchestrated the deployment of SNA units—including Jaysh al-Islam, Ahrar al-Sham, and Hasakah Shield forces—to reinforce the defense.[34] In the first weeks of May, the SNA added around a thousand fighters equipped with T-72 tanks, TOW launchers, GRAD rocket launchers, antitank weapons, and other advanced equipment to the fight. Meanwhile, at least one Turkish military convoy of more than a dozen vehicles supplied NLF fighters with TOW launchers and other critical equipment—a move reportedly given a green light by Washington.[35] Alarmed at this turn of events, on May 18 Russian officials offered their Turkish counterparts a seventy-two-hour ceasefire, the pause intended to give the government a chance to consolidate its modest gains. Hoping its point had been made, Ankara agreed but had less success persuading its Syrian allies, who insisted that government forces retreat to their starting positions. The Russians rejected that but concluded a temporary truce arrangement with Ankara anyway. Fighting fell into a lull but never entirely stopped.

The lull was shattered on May 21, when—again accusing the rebels of violating the ceasefire first—the Syrian Army and NDF units resumed their offensive on Kabani in the west. Once more the attack stalled under fierce resistance, and the opposition counterattacked at Kafr Nabudah, retaking it on May 24. Panicking, government forces hurled chlorine gas at HTS fighters.[36] Things were not going as planned on other fronts, either. To the east, government forces attacked Turkey's southernmost observation post, near the town of Morek, expecting the Turks to abandon the position. But the Turks did not retreat as expected, and instead Ankara issued a warning that they would not withdraw and would return fire if necessary. Damascus and Moscow ducked for cover and claimed that jihadists were responsible for the attack.[37] With the offensive already stalling, Russian military advisors proposed a rethink. In the South, government forces withdrew to a perimeter around Kafr Nabudah and began an aerial and artillery bombardment to soften the town up for another offensive, which succeeded in taking the town on the final day of May. In the West, however, yet another offensive on Kabani was beaten back. Meanwhile, further Turkish convoys brought arms into Idlib. For a second time, Russian and Turkish officials sat down to hammer out a ceasefire, but this time Ankara's position was more uncompromising. Aware that government forces were taking heavy losses and struggling to advance and that the NLF would not accept anything less, Turkish officials now demanded that government forces return to their starting positions. The Russians refused, unwilling to sacrifice hard-won gains and aware that Damascus was unlikely to accept such an arrangement. Fighting escalated as the bargaining dragged on. At the start of June the Tiger Force consolidated its position around Kafr Nabudah, but the NLF and HTS mustered yet another counteroffensive, at one point threatening to isolate several government units. Only intense Russian air strikes allowed them to stabilize the situation.

Two things were becoming clear to the Kremlin: Damascus was incapable of imposing its will on Idlib without significant Russian military assistance, and any durable ceasefire would have to revive the original Idlib memorandum. Yet there could be little prospect of either a stable ceasefire or a longer-term political arrangement while the HTS retained its potency. Perhaps, though, Turkey could be persuaded to deal with the HTS in return for the restoration of the status quo. Sergei Lavrov proposed just such a deal to his Turkish counterpart—a cessation of violence in return for a Turkish commitment to clear the DMZ of fighters and separate HTS from the other armed groups, as agreed at Sochi. Ankara assented, and Moscow turned the screws on Damascus to get it to follow suit. Frustrated, the Syrian government announced a unilateral seventy-two-hour ceasefire on June 12, but the NLF and HTS both refused to accept the arrangement, forcing Ankara into an embarrassing diplomatic retreat.[38] As the seventy-two hours wound down, government forces eager for the ceasefire to collapse shelled another Turkish observation post, near Jabal al-Zawiya.[39] Turkey responded by repeating its warning and hurrying reinforcements to the two attacked posts.[40] Russian defense minister Sergei Shoigu tried to revive the deal by calling his Turkish counterpart, the recently installed former general Hulusi Akar, but no agreement was reached.

With the agreement in tatters, fighting continued through June and July without either side making much headway. Some governments tried, but failed, to persuade the UN Security Council to at least express mild concern about attacks on the civilian population.[41] In early July Hezbollah and other Iranian-backed Shi'ite militias deployed additional units to relieve the Tiger Force. Unleashed on the opposition to great fanfare, the Tiger Force had performed quite poorly—losing a string of key battles in Kafarnabouda, Tal Meleh, al-Jibain, and al-Hamamyat and more than once being forced into disorderly retreat. The tipping point seems to have been the killing of its leader, the "tiger" himself, Suhail al-Hassan—one of a new generation of Syrian Army officers beholden more to Russia than Iran and once touted as a potential future rival to Assad. His death threw the force's already shattered morale into free fall.[42] Hezbollah steadied the ship, but even its fighting capacity was not what it once was, and a financial crisis at home was jeopardizing Iran's ability to bankroll the war effort.

After a few weeks of pause, the offensive was renewed in late August, coinciding with a new round of talks in Astana (recently renamed Nur Sultan) between the triumvirate's foreign ministers, Damascus, and opposition figures. The government and Russians offered new terms: a cessation of force in return for full implementation of the Sochi agreement, meaning the withdrawal of all forces from the DMZ and opening of the M4 and M5 highways, within twenty-four hours. Damascus also demanded that the HTS withdraw its heavy weapons twenty kilometers behind the zone, while Iran's foreign minister insisted that the ceasefire not apply to the HTS at all. This was wholly unrealistic. There was no way Ankara could engineer all that within a day—it simply did not have that sort of influence over the HTS. An agreement of sorts was reached, but nobody seemed quite sure as to its contours. In their press statements afterward, the foreign ministers each offered a different view.[43]

Unsurprisingly, this latest deal never came into effect, as fighting in and around the DMZ continued. Damascus and Moscow agreed a further escalation was needed to dislodge the extremists and launched a new ground offensive, backed by more intense Russian air strikes, to envelop and take Khan Shaykhun in the enclave's South. Through the first half of August, government forces made steady progress along two fronts, though the fighting was intense and opposition losses were matched by equally heavy government losses. To the west, another assault on Kabani was repelled, the government side losing at least one aircraft shot down as well as several tanks and APCs destroyed by TOWs. The civilian toll was immense. Between May and August some 400,000 civilians were displaced as government forces deliberately shelled civilian infrastructure inside the DMZ to terrorize the population and force it to flee. Civilians displaced by the shelling found little safety elsewhere. On August 26 fighter jets—most likely Russian—targeted a displaced-persons camp, killing at least twenty civilians, including eight women and six children. The strike also damaged the camp's food store, medical center, and school. A string of attacks on medical facilities dating back to March "strongly suggested" to the UN's Commission of Inquiry that they were being targeted systematically.[44]

The turning point came on August 19. Opposition forces defending Khan Shaykhun were reinforced by men and materiel from the SNA, which fortified the defenders—another government tank was destroyed by TOW and a counteroffensive launched at Sukayk. To put

the loss of government armor into perspective, military experts estimated that at the start of the war in 2011, the Syrian Army had between
3,500 and 4,800 tanks—not all of them serviceable, but the sixth largest tank fleet in the world. In 2020 the investigative group Bellingcat
used publicly available visual data to confirm that at least 1,900 of
those tanks had been lost and estimated that the actual number of
losses was likely much higher since not all losses left a publicly available visual trace.[45] This steady stream of losses seriously weakened the
Syrian armor capabilities and explains why opposition defenses had
such an impact on Syrian government advances now. But despite this,
the opposition couldn't turn the course of battle, thanks in part to
Russian airpower and in part to deep animosity between the SNA and
HTS. As government forces reached the outskirts of Khan Shaykhun,
Turkey faced a dilemma: should it allow the town to fall or introduce
its own forces? Hulusi Akar, the defense minister running Turkey's
operations in Syria, settled on what he hoped would be an artful way
of deterring the government without direct confrontation. He dispatched a twenty-eight-vehicle military convoy carrying supplies,
tanks, APCs, and other equipment destined for its two observation
posts in the far south of the enclave. Ankara calculated that should
the convoy reach Khan Shaykhun before the town fell, Damascus and
Moscow would be forced to halt their offensive to avoid contact with
the Turkish Army.

Watching the approaching convoy with an increasing sense of
alarm, Syrian government commanders understood the stakes and
believed they extended well beyond Khan Shaykhun. If Turkey established itself inside Idlib, that would effectively mean the end of Assad's
"every inch" objective. They opted for a massive gamble. Government
aircraft launched two separate attacks on the convoy, killing at least
one Syrian fighter allied to the Turks and three civilians, as well as
injuring some Turkish soldiers. The attacks were plainly designed to
deter and delay the Turkish reinforcement rather than inflict serious
damage, bombs landing on the road ahead and to the side of the convoy rather than directly on it, so as not to inflict casualties and thus
provoke Turkish retaliation. Some suggest Russian aircraft carried out
the attack, but both Moscow and Ankara were careful to attribute

responsibility solely to Damascus. The convoy was brought to a halt, and, once made aware that Turkish reinforcements were not en route, opposition forces withdrew from Khan Shaykhun. Within a few days government forces had taken the town and encircled Turkey's Morek observation post, too—drawing another terse warning from Ankara.[46] A "humanitarian corridor" was opened to allow civilians to flee north, and, objective achieved, the government announced a unilateral cessation of hostilities, confirmed by Moscow a few days later.

The ceasefire wasn't a humanitarian gesture; it was agreed because the offensive had reached what strategists call its culminating point. The government had achieved some of its more immediate objectives, such as taking control of much of the southern portion of the DMZ and clearing HTS from the area. In also taking Khan Shaykhun, the government had strengthened control over the M4 highway linking Homs to Aleppo. But these relatively modest gains had come at significant cost: the government side sustained serious casualties, and yet resistance in Idlib had not collapsed. Moreover, the reinforcement of the NLF and infiltration of the SNA had weakened the HTS's grip on Idlib, and although Ankara had opted against direct retaliation for the attack on its convoy, it had also shown itself unlikely to simply abandon its posts and the zone, as the United States had done in the South. If anything, Turkey's military position in Idlib was stronger at the end of the offensive than it had been at the beginning. Whether this meant that Erdogan was now resolved to defend Idlib by force if necessary remained unclear, but that uncertainty troubled Damascus.

Turkey's president was indeed rethinking his Syria strategy. The offensive had demonstrated not just the limits of the Astana process—he knew those all along—but also his limited ability to deter Putin and Assad by words and displays of force alone. Ankara had to confront the difficult question of whether it was willing to defend Idlib with force, since the government side would surely press again. For now, Erdogan decided that Turkey should certainly prepare for a more resolute military commitment to the defense of the enclave. He hoped that visible military preparations would strengthen deterrence, but they would also offer more credible military options should that be needed in the future.

More immediately, both sides were grateful to negotiate a cease-fire. But whose ceasefire counted? In New York, the Security Council's humanitarian leads, Belgium, Germany, and Kuwait, had circulated a draft ceasefire resolution in late August. Egged on by the P3 (United States, UK, France), who wanted to undercut Astana and reassert the Security Council's primacy, they proposed a resolution calling for a ceasefire, demanding unimpeded humanitarian access, requiring that all parties comply with international humanitarian law, and calling for accountability if they did not. From the start, Russia insisted that any ceasefire include an exception for "antiterrorism" operations—a move used before to get around inconvenient ceasefires—and threatened to veto any reference to chapter 7. It also objected to a proposed monitoring mechanism and pledge the council would consider further action in the event of noncompliance. In its place, the Russians and Chinese offered their own draft, which emphasized the threat of terrorism in Idlib, endorsed offensive operations against terrorists, and stripped out monitoring mechanisms and promises of further action. The ensuing haggling was mere shadowboxing. The Russians wanted a ceasefire but on their own terms, and nothing that could be said or done in New York was going to change that. Any hopes Western governments may have had of using the ceasefire to reinsert the Security Council into Syria's peace process were dashed by Russia's opening response to their text.[47]

Not for the first—or last—time, the main diplomatic action proceeded with little regard for the Security Council. While bargaining in New York continued into a third week, Erdogan hosted the triumvirate's two other leaders in Ankara, where they agreed to restore Idlib's status as a de-escalation zone and take steps to prevent ceasefire violations. Turkey chanced its arm with the "safe zone" proposal, but Rouhani and Putin were unsurprisingly cool on that idea.[48] Two days later, the Security Council met to vote on the two proposed drafts. Predictably, Russia and China vetoed the humanitarian troika's draft. Equatorial Guinea abstained, and the other members voted in favor. The P3 then returned the favor, vetoing a Russian and Chinese draft—which secured only two votes, their own.[49] The triumvirate's primacy was sustained.

PEACE SPRING

The ceasefire may have represented a tactical victory for Ankara, but Erdogan's domestic position was at its most fragile since the attempted coup in 2016. Economic growth had declined steadily from a peak in 2013–2014, and unemployment had increased significantly. Many blamed the country's economic woes on the more than three million Syrian refugees.[50] Erdogan's handling of the Syrian crisis pleased no one: Kemalists and leftists bemoaned political instability; moderate Islamists who formed the core of the AKP's support bemoaned the president's failure to oust Assad. The AKP won parliamentary elections in 2018, but its vote fell nearly 7 percent. Erdogan won the presidential election but with only 52 percent of the vote, despite a climate of fear, intimidation, the suppression of opposition media and voices, and a divided opposition slate. Things got worse in 2019, when the AKP lost its outright national majority in local government and was defeated twice in the bitterly contested Istanbul mayoral race—a particularly bitter pill for Erdogan since that was where his political career had begun. To add insult to injury, Turkey's Kurdish parties performed well in all these elections, its leftist agenda attracting votes even from outside the Kurdish community. These domestic political anxieties help explain Erdogan's caution during the Idlib crisis in the first half of 2019. The last thing the Turkish president wanted was for the enclave to collapse, forcing another three million Syrians into Turkey, but neither did he want Turkish forces bogged down inside Syria, much less a direct confrontation with Russia—whose cooperation he would need if he was ever to get his proposed "safe zone" up and running.[51]

With the situation in Idlib stabilized for the time being, Ankara's attention turned back to this question of the safe zone. Always fraught, relations with the YPG/SDF soured yet more during hostilities in Idlib when an exchange of fire in Tall Rifat, around thirty kilometers east of Afrin, left two Turkish soldiers dead. The SNA responded on Turkey's behalf by attacking YPG positions, killing more than twenty Kurdish fighters, in response to which the YPG heavily shelled SNA positions. That escalation prompted fears Turkey might launch a general offensive against the SDF, but with American forces still embedded with SDF units and with the situation in Idlib so fragile, Ankara wanted to avoid an unplanned escalation with the Kurds. Moscow, too, wanted to dampen tensions lest an escalation further complicate its Idlib offensive. So within hours of the Tall Rifat incident, Turkish and Russian officials hammered out a deal to restore the ceasefire and establish a new buffer zone.[52] The immediate crisis resolved, it showed just how combustible the situation between Turkey and the SDF was becoming. It also alerted the Pentagon to the fact than a potential future offensive to clear out the Kurds from northern Syria was still very much part of Ankara's thinking.

For the United States, a solution was needed to the pressing dilemma of how to withdraw its forces without inviting Turkish retribution against the Kurds or lessening military pressure on ISIS. Few thought Trump's flamboyant threat to "devastate" Turkey's economy should it move against the Kurds credible.[53] Since Trump's Christmas decision to postpone withdrawal, the Pentagon had been working on options.[54] Chair of the Joint Chiefs of Staff Joseph Dunford initially proposed that a NATO-led monitoring mission be deployed along Turkey's southern border with only minimal U.S. presence. The mission would be supported by U.S. intelligence, surveillance, and air cover and backed by a rapidly deployable stand-off capacity to respond to crises.[55] The whole thing could be funded by Saudi Arabia and the UAE, neither happy with Turkey's growing regional hegemony. But the idea gained little traction. The president's new envoy for Syria, Jim Jeffrey, proposed that Turkey be allowed to assume control of sensitive areas inside Syria and that the United States broker a zones of control deal between Ankara and the Kurds prior to withdrawing. The White House, it seemed, believed Turkish intervention imminent and wanted Americans out of the way before it came. Dunford disagreed. Backed by the Pentagon and Bolton, he preferred a more straightforward policy of keeping the Turks to their side of the border.[56]

There was little chance of persuading allies to commit forces to a monitoring mission, Dunford thought, unless the United States was prepared to keep boots on the ground. He proposed that "a couple of hundred" be kept inside the buffer zone. Trump reluctantly agreed, on the proviso the U.S. role would be minimal and short-lived. Erdo-gan, though, rejected this iteration too, insisting that Turkey be given exclusive control of the zone.[57] After more back and forth, a proposal emerged for a narrow buffer zone, around five kilometers deep, along the Syrian side of the Turkey-Syria border east of the Euphrates as far as the Tigris. The SDF would withdraw completely from the zone, which would be monitored by the United States and Turkey through joint ground and air patrols. This would provide Turkey the security guarantees it craved while also protecting the SDF from a Turkish offensive. It would also reduce the American footprint in Syria. Erdo-gan was receptive. Though far from perfect, since Turkey wanted exclusive control and thought the proposed strip too shallow, he thought it better than Washington's previous proposals. After all, the deal got Turkish forces into the zone and opened a pathway for get-ting the Americans out, even if in the first instance the buffer would be less deep and comprehensive than he had hoped for. In the first week of August 2019, three U.S. defense officials visited Ankara to final-ize the deal, knowing they would have to deliver a fait accompli to get their own president to buy in. They made a series of concessions to achieve that. They offered Turkey a wider buffer between ten and fif-teen kilometers deep in different places. They also agreed that not only would the SDF withdraw fighters and heavy weapons from the zone, they would also turn over control of the border crossings and dismantle fortifications. In return, it was agreed that the arrangement would not apply to Manbij and that while Turkish drones, helicopters, and reconnaissance aircraft would be permitted to overfly the area, fighter jets would not.[58] To the U.S. officials, the deal seemed to address the core dilemma of how to defend the SDF and its counter-ISIS activ-ities and deter Turkish intervention while simultaneously reducing America's military footprint.[59]

But as implementation began, on August 21, it became clear there were significant problems. Damascus, of course, condemned the agreement as a blatant violation of its sovereignty, though the Krem-lin was publicly ambivalent—suggesting some grudging acquiescence. Turkey and the SDF disagreed on where the demarcation line should be. Turkish officials claimed Trump had agreed to widen the buffer zone to thirty-two kilometers deep, well beyond the fifteen-kilometer depth agreed to in Ankara and still being proposed by U.S. defense officials.[60] Then there were differences over what, precisely, was meant to happen inside the zone. Ankara expected the SDF's full withdrawal, and Erdogan warned that Turkish forces would achieve exclusive control within weeks. The SDFs understanding was very different: that YPG elements would have to withdraw but control would remain with the SDF's military councils. The deal itself has never been published, so it is difficult to ascertain whose account is closer to the truth. On the boundary question, it seems likely that the Turkish government was pushing for concessions beyond what had been agreed and was banking on Trump's disinterest in details. On control, it seems likeliest that the hastily negotiated terms did not specify future arrangements. There is also every reason to think that knowing full well the U.S. president wanted complete withdrawal from Syria, Ankara was looking for ways to force America's hand. After all, a transfer of authority to Turkey gave Trump the exit he wanted. Whatever the truth, within days of agreeing to the deal Erdogan warned that Turkey intended to do the very thing it was supposed to prevent: attack the Kurds and establish Turkish control over the buffer zone.[61] Through the late summer of 2019, Turkey's dissatisfaction with the arrangements grew louder. Behind the scenes, Turkish officials sounded out American and Russian attitudes toward an offensive east of the Euphrates. Neither the White House nor Kremlin was enthusiastic, but neither stridently opposed the idea either.[62] Russia had long recognized Turkey's interests and knew it would have to compromise to satisfy those interests if it wanted Ankara's cooperation in Idlib. The problem was more acute for the United States: Trump wanted to withdraw from Syria and abandon the deal, but that would mean abandoning the SDF to its fate, something he could not do without contradicting his earlier gushing praise and pledges of support to the Kurds.

YPG units withdrew from the zone and the SDF dismantled fortified positions along the border, sometimes supervised by American soldiers. Joint U.S.-SDF ground patrols and U.S.-Turkish helicopter patrols began in the first week of September, and the following week the United States and Turkey conducted their first joint ground patrols. It was even reported in the United States that the administration was considering deploying additional troops to support the arrangement.[63] This was the last thing Ankara wanted. Foreign Minister Mevlut Cavusoglu issued a broadside, accusing the United States of "stalling" on its commitment to support a safe zone and warning that Turkey was prepared to act unilaterally.[64] In late September Erdogan took his case directly to the UN, making an impassioned plea for a "safety zone" 30 kilometers deep and stretching 480 kilometers east from Jarabulus, incorporating Kobane, Tal Abyad, and Qamishli, from which ISIS, the SDF, and Syrian government would be excluded. This, he promised, would facilitate the safe return of between one and two million refugees and was a task Turkey was already preparing for. It intended to act and would do so alone if necessary.[65] Turks broadly supported their president's plan—polls showed a slim majority now favored military intervention in Syria—but Erdogan's appeal did little to change international opinion, which remained almost uniformly hostile.[66]

Erdogan's speech had an audience of one, however: Donald Trump. Ankara was confident the U.S. president did not share the view of his defense officials and pushed repeatedly for the two presidents to have a direct conversation in the hope of drawing Trump out. In fact, Erdogan had wanted a one-on-one with Trump in New York on the sidelines of the UN General Assembly in September, but much to his chagrin, Trump's schedulers had kept the two apart—their paths crossing only at a well-attended formal reception. But now the other channels had failed and an invasion seemed imminent, Erdogan was granted an audience with Trump. They spoke by phone Sunday, October 6. It was a pivotal moment. Trump's brief was to reassure Ankara that the United States understood its security concerns, reinforce U.S. commitment to the buffer zone, and caution against military intervention. According to the White House, Trump opened on script, urging restraint and offering his Turkish counterpart the honor of a White House visit if he complied. Erdogan insisted Turkey must protect itself from terrorists and explained his plan for an intervention in northern Syria to establish a "safe zone." This would keep the area safe from ISIS, deny it to Assad, and resolve the standoff between Turkey and the SDF. Best of all, Erdogan explained, Turkish intervention would allow Trump to deliver on his promise of withdrawing U.S. ground forces. In fact, withdrawal could begin immediately. This must have sounded like music to Trump's ears. At last, here was somebody explaining how he could achieve what he wanted, not telling him why he mustn't. He took the bait and replied that a modest incursion to clear out a "safe zone" would be acceptable and that U.S. forces would withdraw out of the way. But he warned that a large intervention would prompt a complete U.S. withdrawal from Syria. Trump hung up the phone and ordered the immediate withdrawal of U.S. troops from the buffer zone.[67] As newly installed secretary of defense Mark Esper and the president's caretaker chief of staff Mick Mulvaney scrambled to make sense of what had just happened and communicate it to the Pentagon, Trump bragged on Twitter that he had just ended America's "endless wars." Around him, in the words of one administration official, "all hell broke loose."[68] Neither the White House, State Department, nor the Pentagon had anticipated the president's move. America's allies—including the British and French, whose special forces operated alongside U.S. forces keeping the peace in Manbij—were also caught by surprise.

All hell broke loose in northern Syria too. That evening the White House announced that Turkey would soon begin its intervention in Syria and that U.S. forces would withdraw out of the way. In the early hours of Monday morning, U.S. forces in Syria received an unexpected order to withdraw immediately from the buffer zone, and the SDF was advised about what was coming. London and Paris clambered to respond, putting in irate calls to their American counterparts while hurriedly figuring out what to do with their forces on the ground. The Turkish offensive—code-named Peace Spring—began less than forty-eight hours later with air strikes and artillery fire directed at YPG positions. In a letter to the United Nations, Turkey said it was acting under article 51 of the charter to defend itself from terrorism. YPG units returned fire, and the SDF declared its intent to resist Turkish incursions. It also threatened to suspend anti-ISIS operations as it defended itself against Turkey.[69]

In Washington, D.C., opinion on both sides of politics swung firmly against Turkey as commentators and politicians decried what they saw as America's "betrayal" of its Kurdish allies. One "senior administration official" described the move as "a betrayal of one of our best partners in the global war on terrorism." William Roebuck, the administration's most senior diplomat inside northern Syria, penned an angry memo to his bosses complaining that the administration "didn't try" hard enough to deter Turkey's offensive and that the resulting violence, which included "war crimes and ethnic cleansing" by Turkish-supported Islamist militias, "is to a significant degree of our making." In Congress, 129 Republicans crossed the floor to support a bipartisan resolution condemning the withdrawal of U.S. forces, the motion passing by a large majority of 354 to 60.[70] American allies voiced their concern—especially France, so often the target of ISIS terrorism. At stake, President Macron argued, was not just Middle Eastern security or the war on ISIS but the credibility of the Western alliance itself.[71]

Rattled by criticism, Trump backtracked quickly. The White House denied giving Erdogan a green light and explained the United States had never promised to defend the Kurds. The president himself fired off an extraordinary letter to Erdogan that not only reversed what he had told the Turkish president just a few days earlier but threatened sanctions if Turkey persisted with the course of action the American president had so recently okayed. "Don't be a tough guy. Don't be a fool!," he wrote. "You don't want to be responsible for slaughtering thousands of people. . . . I don't want to be responsible for destroying the Turkish economy." The SDF was prepared to negotiate a "good deal," Trump explained. "History will look upon you favorably if you get this done the right and humane way. It will look upon you forever as the devil if good things don't happen."[72] That the letter was meant more to assuage Trump's American critics than change policy on Syria was made plain by the fact that no sooner was it written, it was leaked to the press. Besides enraging the Turkish president, the letter had little impact. Erdogan threw it in the litter bin, Turkish sources claimed.[73] Threats and bluster ineffective, the United States and the EU imposed restrictions on trade and defense cooperation, and several European states—including Germany, France, the UK, and Sweden—imposed unilateral bans on the export of arms and defense-related equipment to Turkey. In response, Erdogan threatened to allow Syrian refugees to cross into Europe as they had in 2015 and announced that Turkey would purchase Russian S-400 anti-aircraft missiles instead of the American alternative.

The land offensive began on October 10, spearheaded by Turkish-backed SNA and allied groups, including Islamist Ahrar al-Sharqiya. Turkish-backed forces made significant gains, for example, reaching the M4 highway between Manbij and Qamishli, some 30 kilometers inside Syria, and taking towns such as Ras al-Ayn and Tall Abyad. Amid the chaos in Tall Abyad, nearly eight hundred ISIS prisoners broke free from a detention camp—a predictable, and predicted, consequence of the Turkish intervention. Trump quickly joined Turkey in blaming the SDF for the breach but was just as quickly corrected by his own officials who reported that the prisoners had been released by elements of the Turkish-backed SNA.[74] Equally predictably, the offensive triggered yet another round of mass civilian displacement—an estimated 100,000 civilians fled their homes in the first hours of the intervention—and a series of atrocity crimes.[75] Among the most shocking was the killing of Hevrin Khalaf, head of the moderate Future Syria Party, by Ahrar al-Sharqiya, an extremist group allied with Turkish-backed forces.[76]

Abandoned by the United States, the SDF turned to the one place it could for help: Moscow. The Kurds had always had an uneasy but complex relationship with Assad and Russia. The main Kurdish political parties wanted autonomy but not separation from Damascus and calculated an Assad government preferable to a Sunni Islamist government. At times, Kurdish armed forces had cooperated with the armed opposition—notably in the struggle against ISIS—but at other times they had come to blows, especially in Aleppo governate. Russia firmly believed that Assad could—and should—make a deal with the Kurds, something most Kurdish leaders were prepared to contemplate, though the Assadists were less keen. Although sometimes willing to turn a blind eye to Turkish incursions, Moscow had also at times helped the Kurds. When they appealed to Moscow for help, the Kremlin sniffed an opportunity.

Moscow proposed protecting the Kurds from Turkey by restoring the government's authority over the northern border. It suggested that the SDF should permit Syrian government and Russian forces to deploy along its borders and occupy the crossings. The Kurds could continue to administer Rojava, but Damascus would assume responsibility for the borders and defense. With few options available to it, the SDF agreed, and the Kremlin brokered a deal to allow Syrian government forces to move into Kobane and Manbij.[77] More than seven years after they had withdrawn, government forces supported by Russian troops returned to the sound of Kurdish applause. But Turkey and the SNA were not willing to give up Kobane and Manbij so readily and stepped up the tempo of their offensive in the hope of taking the towns before the Syrians and Russians could get there. Multiple sources report that withdrawing U.S. units blocked and delayed Syrian and Russian vehicles—though it is not clear whether this was a centrally orchestrated campaign to give the Turks and SNA more time or merely localized fits of pique by frustrated U.S. soldiers. Whatever, the result was an incredibly tense few hours in which no fewer than seven armies—Turkish, SNA, Ahrar al-Sharqiya, American, SDF, Syrian, and Russian—jostled for position in an area of a little more than sixty square kilometers. The potential for catastrophic miscalculation was immense. After mopping up villages around Manbij, the SNA began what it thought was its final offensive on the city on October 14, the same day as Syrian government troops reached the town.[78] The SNA offensive there quickly ground to a halt as government forces established themselves in Manbij. Attention turned northward to Kobane, where a similar story unfolded over the next couple of days. Withdrawing U.S. troops delayed a Syrian government convoy from moving into Kobane from Manbij, forcing it to turn around. Blocking the Syrian Army was one thing, but blocking the Russians another thing entirely. When Russia dispatched its own convoy toward Kobane, the Americans tactfully stepped aside. It was Russia, therefore, that won the race to Kobane, paving the way for the return of Syrian government forces the following day. Erdogan tried to put a positive spin on things, suggesting that the Syrian-Russian deployments achieved his goals anyway by denying control of the territory to Kurdish "terrorists." While that was certainly true, the reality was that Ankara's long desired "safe zone" was in tatters. The offensive had made nothing like the sorts of territorial gains Erdogan had hoped for—Kobane and Manbij were now under government/Russian control, Ras al-Ayn, right on the border like Kobane, remained in SDF hands—and the political and military obstacles were mounting by the hour.

In the wake of Trump's intemperate letter to Erdogan, Vice President Mike Pence rushed to Ankara to persuade the Turkish government to agree a ceasefire and limit the political fallout. He was not given a warm welcome, but as Peace Spring got caught in the bog, Ankara desperately wanted a diplomatic exit and Pence offered one. The vice president proposed that in return for an immediate cessation of hostilities, Turkey and the SNA would be permitted to create a "safe zone" on the land they already held—essentially a 120-kilometre-long front between Tall Abyad and Ras al-Ayn to a depth of between 30 and 40 kilometers. The SDF, which still held Ras al-Ayn itself while the SNA controlled the countryside around it, would withdraw as part of the deal. In return, the United States would not impose the withering sanctions Trump had threatened. It was far less than Erdogan had hoped for. He had envisaged a safe zone stretching 480 kilometers in length. Not only was he not going to get that, he was also not going to get another opportunity, because along the rest of the border, and along the line of demarcation, there would not be the SDF but instead the Syrian government and its Russian allies. Damascus would no doubt use its control of the border to prevent any large-scale return of refugees judged disloyal by the regime—denying Turkey one of its main objectives. But with few options left, Erdogan accepted the deal and agreed to a five-day ceasefire to permit the SDF to withdraw.[79] The United States used the opportunity to withdraw its forces, too. A convoy of American vehicles left the U.S.-run Metras air base near Sarrin (about thirty kilometers south of Kobane), heading southeast toward the Iraqi border to an ignominious chorus of boos and jeers from local Kurds. But even now there was still time for another impulsive change of direction. Rather than withdrawing U.S. forces entirely, Trump decided to leave around two to three hundred near the oilfields in the east of the Deir ez-Zor governate.[80] This seems to have been less about the oil and more about keeping tabs on the actor the administration was now most worried about overall: Iran. What likely stayed Trump's hand was the Pentagon's argument that complete U.S. withdrawal from the Syria-Iraq border area risked handing the territory to Iranian-backed militia, who might establish a land bridge of control reaching all the way to Iran itself. A few days after his agreement with Pence, Erdogan flew to Sochi to finalize arrangements with Putin. The Russian leader agreed to help supervise the withdrawal of YPG units, including from Manbij. Russia would also work with Damascus to establish observation posts along the new demarcation line and other portions of the Syria-Turkish border still controlled by SDF.[81] An uneasy peace, frequently punctuated, fell on northeastern Syria.

Outside Syria, analysts and media commentators depicted events as a victory for Turkey and the SNA and a devastating defeat for the SDF and YPG. The SDF were indeed the biggest losers. They had lost not just territory but also their principal ally, and with it hope of clinging onto Rojava in the longer term. The United States also lost out. It lost an ally, whatever limited leverage it had left to influence Syria's future, and the opportunity to inflict a decisive defeat on ISIS. Some in Turkey hailed Erdogan as a hero, with old supporters flocking back to the cause.[82] He now had his safe zone, albeit a truncated one that had come at the cost of alienating NATO and potentially reinvigorating ISIS. And, as in Idlib a few months earlier, Turkey had flinched when confronted with minimal military pressure from Syria and Russia, raising serious doubts as to whether it would defend Idlib if pushed.

The biggest winners were Damascus and Moscow. Without exerting much energy, they had secured control of most of Syria's northern border and reconfigured their relationship with the Kurds. Russian officials quickly got to work facilitating talks between Damascus and the Kurds on a new set of military and political arrangements. The balance of power between the two sides had changed significantly.[83] This made it much more likely that the Kurds could be persuaded to accept a political settlement with Damascus—a core Russian objective. But Damascus and Russia were not entirely of one mind on this question—the former still ruled out concessions such as formal autonomy that the latter was happy to embrace. The two allies also disagreed to some extent on the future of the SDF/YPG. Russia envisaged their integration into Syria's armed forces, but until that was possible, it was happy to let the SDF control the territory it held. Damascus was uneasy about integration and opposed to legitimizing SDF control. The changed balance of power reduced Assad's incentive to compromise, creating a potential source of tension with his

Russian patron.[84] Above all, Russia had once again proven itself the indispensable power, not just for the Syrian government but also for the opposition and other foreign powers, too. Russian soldiers replaced Americans on Syria's northern border.[85] Russia also took possession of two other former U.S. bases, at Manbij and Tabqa.[86] Once again, civilians suffered most. Far from stimulating the return of displaced Syrians, Erdogan's operation displaced 300,000 more. Civilians forced to flee into Syrian government territory risked arbitrary detention, violent retribution, and forced recruitment.[87] Those who remained were subjected to killings, sexual violence, and looting by Turkish-backed Islamist militia.

COMMITTEES, RESOLUTIONS, TALKING

As battles raged for control of the Idlib pocket and northeastern Syria, the UN's new special envoy, Geir Pedersen, spent long hours trying to breathe life into the Syrian Constitutional Committee, first mooted by the UN Security Council in 2015 (Resolution 2254) and then incorporated into the Astana process at Sochi in 2018. Intent on military victory and confident it could win, Damascus saw the committee as an irritant and felt little need to engage seriously. As for the opposition, except for the Kurds, there was now a profound gap between who the UN *wanted* to represent the opposition and who controlled the ground. The committee was to comprise 150 members organized into three blocs, each represented by 50 members: a government bloc, an opposition bloc referred to as the Syrian Negotiations Committee and a civil society bloc nominated by the UN. The committee's decisions would be made based on a 75 percent majority. The opposition bloc, though formally established under HNC auspices, comprised around twenty representatives from Turkish-aligned groups, including former FSA, seven from the loyalist Platform and National Coordination committees supported by Russia, five from the secularist "Cairo platform" backed by Egypt and largely cooperative with Assad, six from the National Coordination Committee of secular leftists, and around seven Kurds acting independently of the PYD or SDF. Unsurprisingly, the opposition bickered among itself and with others about the composition of its bloc—most Islamist groups boycotted the process entirely, but there remained the difficult question of Kurdish representation as well as the government's insistence that the so-called loyal opposition be included. In the end, neither the PYD, SDF, nor HTS was represented in the committee, and the triumvirate rejected the UN's selection of civil society representatives.[88]

That the process survived at all was largely down to Russian sponsorship. The Kremlin saw the constitutional committee as a potential way of legitimizing a postwar settlement, so through the summer and autumn of 2019 Russian diplomats encouraged the Syrian government to go along with the process while Pedersen cobbled together an opposition delegation. As if to underscore the point that, whatever the UN might think, this was very much a Russian-led exercise in peacemaking, when the talks resumed in Geneva in late October, the Syrian government delegation and parts of the opposition delegation arrived on planes laid on by Moscow.[89] Immediately, the 75 percent threshold on decision making proved a recipe for deadlock. The government suggested it might accept some minor constitutional revisions in return for opposition concessions, but that was all. The opposition insisted Syria's constitution of 1950, which curtailed the powers of the presidency, be used as the starting point. With Russian officials hovering in the background, the government delegation knew it could not just walk away. Staring military defeat in the face, the opposition delegation felt the same. Despite their differences, they agreed to leave forty-five delegates in Geneva to continue the discussions.

The delegations hunkered down in Geneva for a month, debating esoteric matters before hitting a roadblock over a code of conduct in late November. They agreed the word "Kurd" should not be included in the constitution, though. In November the opposition proposed a discussion on the constitution's preamble, prompting the government to table "national pillars of concern," which included ending foreign interference, combatting terrorism (by which the government meant all armed opposition), and terminating international sanctions. The opposition complained these were political positions, not constitutional points. Reminded by Russian officials that Moscow expected the dialogue to keep going, the government turned to a classic stalling tactic and argued that the full 150-strong committee be reconvened for a dialogue on basic principles for the constitution's preamble—a dialogue they knew would continue indefinitely without ever reaching the 75 percent consensus needed to approve any particular form of words. The opposition saw the trap immediately and rejected the proposal, and so the talks ground to a halt, having failed to even agree an agenda. Damascus blamed the opposition for rejecting an inclusive dialogue on basic principles.[90]

As usual, the real peacemaking, such as it was, was taking place away from the United Nations and was proceeding on two fronts: normalization of the government's relationships with its neighbors (except Turkey) and Russian-brokered negotiations between Damascus and the Kurds. By late 2019 the Assad government was well on the road toward reestablishing its international position. Recognizing Assad had all but prevailed, Syria's Gulf Arab neighbors began normalizing relations with the government, intent now on minimizing the political fallout caused by their earlier decisions to back the opposition. The UAE led the way on this in 2018 when the foreign ministers of Bahrain and Syria met on the sidelines of the UN General Assembly to discuss normalization, the UAE's foreign minister Anwar Gargash later confessing that suspending Syria's membership in the Arab League had been a mistake. Saudi Arabia and Jordan followed suit.[91] All three spoke openly about readmitting Syria into the Arab League.[92] In part, these moves were simple recognition of facts on the ground. Saudi Arabia, the UAE, and Jordan no longer had viable proxies inside Syria and so had to recalibrate their foreign policies to match the new reality. Their primary goal now was to ween Damascus away from Iran. To do that, they needed to create leverage by reestablishing bilateral relations and then using investment, financial incentives, and political inducements to encourage Syria back into Arabic political space. Moreover, Saudi Arabia hoped to further isolate Qatar and contain Turkey, not just in Syria but also in Libya. Normalizing relations with Damascus played into a broader struggle for influence in the eastern Mediterranean.[93] The well-being of Syrians was not a priority issue. In relation to the Kurds, Russian forces consolidated their positions in the Northeast in the final months of 2019, and Russian officials encouraged Kurdish factions to articulate a common position that might form the basis for bilateral negotiations with Damascus. Still resistant to formalizing Kurdish autonomy, Assad's government nonetheless expressed willingness to negotiate with the Kurds and made concerted efforts to persuade Arab members of the SDF to join the government's forces.

At the UN in New York, these developments emboldened Russian diplomats to push harder to wind back some of the measures imposed by the Security Council since the start of the war. They had already succeeded in terminating the council's investigatory mechanism on chemical weapons but had earlier backed down in the face of sharp international criticism when they had tried to limit the delivery of humanitarian aid without the government's consent. At the end of 2019 the UN's humanitarian mandate came up for renewal once again, and this time the Russians dug their heels in, prepared to use their veto. The authorization, first approved in Resolution 2165 (2014), allowed the UN to convey aid into Syria through four crossings—two from Turkey, one from Iraq, and one from Jordan—without the government's consent. The so-called humanitarian troika responsible for crafting the council's work on humanitarian issues—now Belgium, Germany, and Kuwait—called for the mandate's renewal in full, citing massive humanitarian need and the Syrian government's track record of manipulating aid.[94] The proposal also enjoyed the support of the P3 and all ten of the council's nonpermanent members, but the Russians and Chinese objected and cast their veto.[95] Council members played a game of diplomatic chicken over the Christmas period as the clock ticked down on the humanitarian mandate. The Russians prevailed. A new draft that bowed to Russia's core demands—a six-month authorization for the two border crossings into Turkey—was introduced, and though four of the council's five permanent members refused to support the revised text—the United States and UK because they objected to the concessions, Russia and China because they felt the language insufficiently deferential to Syrian sovereignty—eleven votes of the council's elected members and France carried the day.[96] But only just.

Assad was not having everything his own way, though. In December the U.S. Senate passed what became known as the "Caesar Act," after the brave Syrian photographer whose images had exposed the brutality and mass killing inside Assad's prisons. The bipartisan act imposed swingeing sanctions against not just Syrian officials linked to atrocity crimes but also their allies in Iran and Russia and individuals and corporations doing business with them, no matter where they were from. The act had begun life in 2016 but, after passing the committee stage, had been blocked by the Obama White House, anxious it would undermine the Kerry-Lavrov initiative and the Iran nuclear deal.[97] For all the expectation that Syria's war was essentially over and Assad's victory complete, at the end of 2019 the situation remained uncertain, not because of any concerted international action—which had all but withered away—but because of the uneven, unpredictable, ad hoc, and unilateral efforts of a couple of international actors and the growing exhaustion of the regime and its allies. For all its military success, Damascus had failed to defeat the opposition in Idlib. Now, the Caesar Act added to the government's multiplying economic woes and threatened its ability to fund an authoritarian peace.

15

"NO MILITARY SOLUTIONS"
AND OTHER ZOMBIES

FROM THE very beginning, Western leaders, officials, commentators, and humanitarians had insisted there was no military solution to Syria's crisis. This article of faith became a mantra, as if the more it was said, the more likely it was to become true. But Damascus never demurred from thinking there was *only* a military solution. Assad repeatedly stated his intent to reclaim "every inch" of Syria. Tehran too always believed there was a military solution and poured tens of thousands of fighters and billions of dollars into Syria to ensure there would be. The Kremlin thought a political settlement was required but that force was necessary to achieve the right sort of settlement. The brave Syrians who poured onto the streets in 2011 hoped a nonmilitary solution was possible; most were quickly disabused of that by Assad's snipers, tanks, barrel bombs, chemical weapons, and torture chambers. Many came to believe they would find no peace while Assad ruled Syria. For a while, governments in Turkey, Qatar, and Saudi Arabia thought regime change possible and tried, albeit half-heartedly, to engineer it. Yet while all around him pursued, prepared for, or pulled back from a military solution, the UN's Geir Pedersen believed that a "credible and inclusive United Nations facilitated political process" remained "the only path to end the conflict."[1] He could not have been more wrong. The West got things wrong, too. Its strategy always hinged on the flawed belief Assad could be coerced into sharing power. That was always a mirage.

Events in January 2020 hinted at the grave miscalculations underpinning UN and Western policy. On January 3 American drones killed Qassem Soleimani, the architect of so much of Syria's suffering, an act of retribution for an attack on the U.S. Embassy in Baghdad by Iranian-backed militias. Worse was to come for the regime. Soon afterwards, Russian and Syrian forces attempted once again to impose a military solution on Idlib. This time, Turkey countered with its own military and stopped the government in its tracks. Turkey had found a solution—albeit a partial and temporary one—to the immediate crisis bedeviling three million civilians in Idlib. It turned out to be a military one.

IDLIB: BATTLE RESUMED

From Assad's perspective, two pieces of unfinished business remained at the end of 2019: the Kurds and Idlib. On neither front did the United States now present a serious obstacle, but Syria's war planners were concerned about overextending their weakened and overstretched forces. The Kurds blocked the realization of Assad's ambition of reclaiming "every inch" of Syria. Despite Russian entreaties, the president still opposed a federal arrangement but believed some form of reconciliation possible. For now, the Kurds could wait. Although the SDF controlled significant territory and considerable economic assets—including 80 percent of Syria's productive oil fields and productive agricultural land—it posed no immediate threat.[2] The government could afford to play a long game of weakening the SDF by drawing in its Arab components and letting Russian diplomacy weaken its resolve. Idlib was a different matter entirely. Despite the headaches caused by Turkey's growing involvement, this could not wait. The longer the enclave held out, the more entrenched its defenders might become, and the more stable its manner of governing, a potential beacon for future resistance. Damascus worried that if it left Turkish-backed entities like the NLF and nearby SNA to fester, they might grow in strength and eventually even displace the extremist HTS and win international legitimacy. This was precisely what Turkey wanted to engineer, and though there were few signs it was succeeding, any moderation in Idlib's government would make it harder for Assad to retake "every inch" of Syria. That both Assad and Iran were worried by this prospect was evinced by their surprisingly cool response to the killing of ISIS leader Abu Bakr al-Baghdadi, holed up inside the Idlib enclave, by American Special Operations Forces on October 29, 2019. The Iranians claimed the killing was of little consequence; Assad suggested that al-Baghdadi might not be dead.[3]

Al-Baghdadi was located while hiding in a nondescript compound outside the town of Barisha, five kilometers south of Syria's border with Turkey. Supported by drones and fighter jets, U.S. Delta Force troops flying from Iraq in eight helicopters stormed the compound, forcing Baghdadi to flee into a tunnel. Cornered, the terror leader detonated his suicide vest, killing himself and two small children he had carried with him. Precisely how the United States tracked him down remains shrouded in doubt, but most accounts point to cooperation between the CIA and Kurdish and Iraqi intelligence.[4] The Turkish government was informed in advance and used its influence to prevent HTS and other fighters opening fire on U.S. forces during the operation. A week or so later, Turkish forces captured one of al-Baghdadi's wives during its own raid on an ISIS compound.[5] Baghdadi's death was certainly a coup for Donald Trump, but it was not a terminal blow to ISIS. Indeed, ISIS violence increased, thanks in large part to the lessening of Kurdish pressure as they redeployed to meet the threat coming from Turkey.[6] All this underscored just how internationally isolated Ankara's position in Idlib had become. Damascus and Moscow judged that so long as the pocket remained in largely HTS hands, they would enjoy a tacit green light from the United States and regional powers to move against it.[7] Who, after all, would mourn the defeat of al-Qaeda-connected terrorists? As they saw it, the Gulf states had already abandoned the zone. The UN and the West could be expected to loudly condemn any offensive while standing aside and accepting the result. They might even one day be persuaded to pay for Idlib's reconstruction. Since Idlib was not a Kurdish area, Turkey had few immediate national security interests at stake there. Since Erdogan was internationally isolated, it seemed reasonable to expect he would fold if put under enough military pressure. Damascus and Moscow thus believed they had a window of opportunity to resolve their Idlib problem.

After skirmishes through November, preparations for a new government offensive, likely orchestrated by Russian officers, got underway in December 2019. The initial targets were control of the M4 and M5 highways, the focus of a series of inconclusive offensives the year before. Bombing and shelling intensified markedly, causing more than 235,000 people to flee their homes, according to the UN.[8] Focused on the enclave's South, the bombing aimed to clear the area of civilians and took a colossal toll on civilian infrastructure, schools and medical facilities especially. By Christmas, Saraqib and Maaret al-Numan—the latter located astride the M4 motorway—were almost depopulated by the bombing.[9] From mid-December government and allied forces took up positions closer to opposition front lines at Maaret al-Numan, perhaps hoping to take the town's surrender without a fight. They also surrounded the Turkish observation post at Surman, intending to isolate and neutralize it. The SNA responded by redeploying hundreds of fighters from Afrin into Idlib, while the HTS and other militia launched counterattacks.

Knowing full well that these moves portended a fresh offensive, the UN's Antonio Guterres pleaded in vain for an end to the hostilities. Meanwhile, UN officials helped broker a six-hour bombing pause to facilitate the evacuation of civilians from the nearly two dozen villages and small hamlets that had fallen into government hands.[10] As before, though, the real diplomatic action was happening not at the UN but between the triumvirate, or Russia, Iran, and Turkey. Low-ranking officials from the three met in Nur-Sultan (as Astana had been renamed in 2019) on December 10, where the Russians and Iranians demanded territorial concessions and insisted Turkey recognize their right to attack the HTS and other jihadists throughout the zone. The Turks refused, and the three delegations parted empty-handed.[11] Amid escalating violence, two weeks later, Turkish officials rushed to Moscow to demand a ceasefire—a move backed by Trump, who, eager to repair his seriously damaged relationship with Ankara, warned Syria and Russia not to cause civilian casualties.[12] This direct appeal to the Kremlin seemed to give it pause for thought, and Russian diplomats agreed to urge a ceasefire.

It was another two weeks before that came into effect, in the early hours of January 12, 2020.[13]

The ceasefire was a dead letter within seventy-two hours. Citing HTS violations, the Syrian Army—backed by Hezbollah and intense Russian bombing—resumed the offensive on January 15, now attacking primarily from the East. Government forces made steady progress, which gradually turned into a rout as the front line collapsed in several places, largely because the HTS withdrew from the relatively flat ground under attack to more easily defensible positions in hillier areas to the rear. HTS commanders judged they could not defend the enclave without international aid and decided to protect their fighting capacity rather than risk its destruction.[14]

The fate of Idlib and its three million civilians rested in the balance. Since no one else was going to stop the offensive before the zone collapsed entirely, everything hinged on Ankara. Erdogan had staked his personal credibility on the Astana process. Its collapse in Idlib at the hands of Russian and Iranian duplicity would be a bitter personal humiliation. Moreover, Idlib's civilians could be expected to flee into Turkey should the zone collapse, massively increasing the number of Syrian refugees there at a time when Turkey's government was under intense pressure to reduce the number. Returning from a visit to Senegal, Erdogan expressed anger at the collapse of the ceasefire agreement and told journalists the Astana process was effectively dead.[15] But if the Astana process no longer defined Turkey's thinking on Idlib, what would replace it?

In fact, Ankara had been busy developing a new strategy for Idlib, a process that probably began after the May 2019 offensive and that had gathered pace in the second half of the year. The new strategy involved deploying additional forces into Idlib and exhibiting a greater willingness to use force in order to deter the Syrian government and Russia, create leverage, and establish a better bargaining position. If deterrence failed, Turkey's military posture would allow it to use graduated escalations of force to impose spiraling costs on Damascus and thereby create a stalemate. Turkish strategy hinged on an assumption that direct confrontation with Russia could be avoided if it targeted only Syrian government forces. That involved a dangerous game of highly militarized chicken, since Russian officers largely controlled the Syrian Army's active elite units, its land and air forces worked in close coordination with the Syrians, and Russian mercenaries, many employed by the Wagner Group, were embedded inside the Syrian Army. Still, in late 2019 and early 2020, Turkey significantly strengthened its military position in Idlib and established a new observation post near Saraqib.[16] One report suggests more than twelve hundred Turkish military vehicles entered the zone between February 2 and 8.[17] By mid-February Turkey had up to twenty thousand soldiers and two thousand armored vehicles inside the Idlib enclave—a dramatic escalation from the approximately one thousand troops deployed there at the start of the year.[18] As well as extending and reinforcing observation posts, these forces established defensive positions west of the M5 motorway to protect Idlib city. Turkey also increased its supply of arms, including antitank and air (MANPADS), and ammunition, to the NLF and SNA.

Turkey's response to the breakdown of the January ceasefire was consistent with this new strategy. It attempted first to deter escalation through presence. Ankara warned Damascus to back down and threatened to use force if it did not. Yet since both Assad and Putin still assumed it would be Erdogan backing down, neither thought the threat serious. As government forces crept along the M5 highway, they began probing Turkish resolve. On February 3 Syrian and Turkish forces exchanged fire at several places. According to some reports, eight Turkish and double that number of Syrian soldiers were killed in the exchanges.[19] Erdogan immediately tried to exploit any leverage this created to persuade Putin to call a ceasefire. Erdogan declared the attack on Turkish troops a "turning point" and demanded that Syrian government forces cease firing and withdraw behind Turkey's observation posts—that is, to the positions held before May 2019—by the end of February. If they did not, "Turkey will be obliged to take matters into its own hands. . . . Turkey's air and land forces will move freely in all operation areas and in Idlib and they will conduct operations if needed." "From now on," Erdogan warned, "we will not turn a blind eye."[20]

Was the threat real or mere bluster? On February 8 a Russian delegation charged with finding out arrived in Ankara. Three hours of talks didn't persuade it that the Turks were serious. Nor did it yield an agreement on what to do next. To Russian ears, Turkish demands seemed outlandish, their threats lacking credibility. For all their posturing, Turkish forces had merely returned fire when fired on. Their observation posts were being easily bypassed, and then surrounded, by advancing government forces. The Russians saw little reason to think that would change. Erdogan's rather extended deadline, the end of February, sounded more like an invitation than a warning—a threat issued by someone desperately hoping his bluff wouldn't be called. Proceeding at the pace established in the first week of February, government forces could expect to have inundated Turkish observation posts and advanced deep into the enclave by the end of the month, rendering Erdogan's threats irrelevant.

Meanwhile, the rout continued. The strategically important town of Saraqib fell as opposition coordination collapsed amid mutual recriminations. Assad's military solution seemed within his grasp.[21] A little more probing, he and his team assumed, and both Turkish resolve and the enclave itself would surely collapse. On February 10 government forces conducted a sustained mortar attack on a Turkish observation post at Taftanaz air base, killing five or six Turkish soldiers and destroying at least one tank and one armored personnel carrier (APC). Turkish forces responded with a sustained barrage of their own, which they claimed struck more than a hundred government positions, destroyed three tanks as well as other vehicles, and inflicted more than a hundred casualties.[22] Ankara clearly saw this as the very kind of step-up called for by its graduated strategy. Damascus and Moscow did not see it this way, though. For them, although Turkish actions were more intense than previously, it wasn't different in kind—still a punitive tactical response to a direct attack. By the end of the week, government forces were celebrating significant advances on the northeastern (Aleppo) front as Assad gave a rare television address promising outright victory.[23]

Erdogan summoned an emergency meeting of his senior security team on February 10. Deterrence and graduated response were plainly failing. Conscious that his own personal credibility was on the line, and fearing the pocket's collapse would push millions more refugees into Turkey, he made the case for a more dramatic escalation. His cabinet agreed.[24] Publicly, the president warned that Turkey's military preparations were almost complete and intervention "imminent." Still thinking that this was bluster, Lavrov warned Turkey not to act. Behind the scenes, Russian and Turkish officials were now in almost constant dialogue trying to manage the situation. The Kremlin tried to persuade Erdogan to accept the inevitable, while the Turks looked for a way to escalate their engagement without triggering Russian countermeasures.[25] Meanwhile, the Syrian government's offensive continued, and Turkish losses grew. The humanitarian situation—already dire—worsened, too. Government air and artillery attacks aimed at driving out the civilian population persisted right across the enclave.[26] For example, they bombed and shelled makeshift camps for displaced people in Dana, Sarmada, and Kafr Aruq. The UN reported that between February 13 and 16 some 160,000 civilians fled Atareb and Daret Azza districts, bringing the total number of recently displaced to a staggering 900,000.[27]

But there were signs the opposition was regaining its resolve. Certainly, its air defenses were improving—with Turkish help. By mid-February the regime had lost two helicopters to guided missiles fired from MANPADS provided by Turkey. On February 11 opposition MAN-PADS targeted but missed a Russian jet. They succeeded in destroying two Russian drones. Having already sustained relatively high losses (nineteen aircraft and helicopters by 2019) in its Syria campaign, Moscow was reluctant to take further risks with its aircraft. Russia thus reduced its sortie rate and confined aircraft to higher altitudes.[28] On the ground, Turkish artillery units and commandos supported rebel counteroffensives in Nayrab in the Idlib enclave's Southeast and Saraqib. This succeeded in briefly retaking Nayrab before Russian airstrikes tilted the balance back the other way. In the heat of the battle, Russian Defense Ministry officials contacted Turkish troops directly to urge them to cease firing, which they reportedly did. Although the opposition couldn't hold Nayrab, the counteroffensive stalled the government's advance, inflicted serious casualties, and raised opposition morale.[29] The counteroffensive in Saraqib helped raise opposition spirits but failed to take much ground.

For a second time, Erdogan tried to leverage the military situation directly with Putin on February 12, and the Kremlin agreed to receive a Turkish delegation. In what was clearly now a game of political brinkmanship backed by military force, the Turkish delegation, led by Deputy Foreign Minister Sedat Onal, arrived in Moscow on February 17 only to discover that Russia's position had become more inflexible. Still confident Erdogan would back down, Russia's presidential envoy for Syria, Sergey Vershinin, demanded a new arrangement more reflective of the situation on the ground: Saraqib and the highways should go to the government, and Turkey should withdraw its observation posts northward. To put Erdogan in his place and remind him who was boss, the Russians also insisted that negotiations wait until the next Astana triumvirate meeting, scheduled for Tehran on March 5. Erdogan might think Astana dead, the Russians were saying, but if he wanted a deal, he would have to pay it homage.[30] Erdogan bluntly rejected Russia's terms and turned to the Europeans for help. He called French president Emmanuel Macron and German chancellor Angela Merkel on February 20 to urge them to apply pressure on the Russians to stop the bloodshed. To circumvent the triumvirate, he proposed a rival European summit involving Russia, Turkey, France, and Germany that could be held in Istanbul also on March 5. The Europeans agreed, and both Merkel and Erdogan put in calls, but Putin rebuffed their entreaties.[31] Since the Russian president thought he held all the cards, Erdogan's feverish diplomacy only confirmed the Kremlin's view that Turkey was growing desperate and was close to folding.

Now it was Russia's turn to increase the military pressure. The Russian-built Tiger Force was redeployed from Idlib's eastern front to the more vulnerable southern front, where it took to the offensive against Turkish positions on February 23, backed by intense Russian and Syrian air strikes. Turkish casualties climbed. Two soldiers were killed in an exchange of fire with government forces at Nayrab, between five and ten more by air strikes and artillery. Syrian aircraft attacked Turkish positions at Taftanaz, and a Turkish surveillance drone was downed on February 25. The following day two more Turkish soldiers were killed. Kafr Nabul—an early site of anti-Assad activism, once labeled the "conscience of the revolution"—fell that day too, a significant symbolic victory for the government.[32] But far from backing down as the Kremlin expected, Turkey responded in kind by supporting a lightning counteroffensive on Saraqib. Backed by artillery and extensive Turkish drone strikes, opposition fighters overwhelmed government positions and retook the highly prized town in a matter of hours, cutting the M5 motorway once again and relieving pressure on four Turkish observation posts.[33] This turn of events caused shock and alarm in Moscow. Instead of buckling as expected, Turkish forces were not just responding in kind, they were taking the initiative. What is more, time and again they were proving more than a match for government forces. The counteroffensive at Saraqib was a serious escalation of Turkish force, well beyond tactical reprisals, and portended a creeping Turkish intervention that could seriously weaken the government's position. Still, though, Damascus and Moscow believed Turkish resolve was relatively weak and that Ankara could be compelled to accept their terms by a sharp escalation of casualties. It was a serious miscalculation.

The catalyst came in the late morning of February 27, when Turkish, SNA, or NLF MANPADS targeted Russian Su-34s as they conducted bombing runs over southern Idlib—site of the Tiger Force's most recent offensive. Russia claimed there were at least fifteen separate MANPADS attacks that morning and that its aircraft sustained damage.[34] They retaliated in force. Later that day at around 5 p.m., two Syrian Su-22 fighters and—according to initial witness and Turkish reports—two Russian Su-34 jets attacked a Turkish military convoy on the road between al-Bara and Baylun in the south of the Idlib pocket. First the Su-22s strafed the convoy, forcing it to stop. Turkish soldiers left their vehicles and took shelter in nearby buildings, which were then hit with large "bunker buster"-style bombs, most likely delivered by the Russian aircraft. These collapsed the buildings down on top of the Turkish soldiers, killing at least thirty-three—and maybe as many as fifty-five—and wounding many more.[35] Initial reports alleged that Russia refused Turkey permission to evacuate its injured troops by air, causing additional deaths.[36]

Turkey's international isolation was palpable. Its diplomats asked NATO for a show of support, but although the alliance's secretary-general Jens Stoltenberg promised cooperation in areas such as air defense, Greece used its veto in the North Atlantic Council to block a statement of support.[37] Turkey responded by once again manipulating refugees and European fears of them. It ordered its border guards to stand down and allow Syrian refugees to cross into Greece and Bulgaria, no doubt hoping this would put pressure on the Europeans and encourage them to back Ankara more fulsomely.[38] It didn't. Meanwhile, Erdogan appealed to the United States for help, but was rebuffed there, too. Secretary of Defense Mark Esper ruled out supporting Turkish countermeasures. Erdogan's next call was to Putin, angrily demanding an explanation for the convoy attack. Putin denied Russian involvement and claimed that once they had become aware of the incident, Russian officers had intervened with their Syrian counterparts to call off the attack.[39] Again, Putin warned Erdogan to accept Russia's terms, and again Erdogan refused. Shaken by the fact that, far from buckling, Erdogan now seemed set on escalation, Putin suggested they agree to not let their differences on Syria undermine their broader relationship. Erdogan agreed. Ankara publicly accepted that Russia had not been involved in the convoy attack and pinned the blame wholly on Damascus. Putin did not give the green light to Turkish intervention in Idlib, but he clearly understood it was going to happen and, whether or not this was actually expressed, at least tacitly agreed that so long as Russian forces were not targeted, Russia would not intervene directly. As if to set a prearranged timeframe for Turkish intervention, the two leaders agreed to set aside their rival summits and meet face-to-face on March 5. This set the tenor—and the timeframe—for the surprisingly extensive and effective Turkish offensive to come: Operation Spring Shield.

Starting on February 28, Turkish forces unleashed a barrage of artillery and drone strikes against more than two hundred Syrian government and Hezbollah targets, including Russian mercenaries and proxies, causing one hundred to three hundred casualties and destroying dozens of tanks, APCs, artillery pieces, trucks, and ammunition stores. Turkish missiles also hit chemical weapons research facilities and at least two government-held air bases in the Aleppo governate. MANPADS targeted Syrian and (according to Russian sources) Russian aircraft with greater ferocity. The UN was caught flat-footed again. Guterres spoke with Erdogan and Putin but could report only that the two leaders were "not ready" to agree to a ceasefire.[40] The secretary-general urged the Security Council to demand an immediate ceasefire, but despite winning the support of thirteen of the council's fifteen members, it saw Russia and China object, arguing this would hinder the government's "antiterrorism" operations. The timeframe for a ceasefire had in fact already been implicitly set bilaterally by Putin and Erdogan agreeing to meet on March 5. Until then, the battle would continue—a limited test of the two sides' relative strength. It was Turkey that came out on top.

In the skies, Turkey challenged Russian and Syrian government dominance and looked to impose a de facto no-fly zone over Idlib city. On March 1 Turkish F-16s shot down two Syrian Su-24s, missiles and artillery rendering the Nayrab air base inoperable. Drones destroyed Russian-made Pantsir S1 anti-aircraft systems. The apparent ease with which Turkish drones jammed and then neutralized Russia's most advanced systems was a particular embarrassment—and shock—to Moscow. Until then, only Israel had demonstrated a comparable drone capacity. Armed drones were also employed extensively against Syrian government, allied, and Hezbollah ground forces with devastating effect. By the time Erdogan boarded his Moscow-bound aircraft, Turkey was claiming to have inflicted more than three thousand casualties on the Syrian government and its allies, and to have destroyed or disabled 3 jets, 8 helicopters, 3 drones, 151 tanks, 47 howitzers, 52 launchers, and more than 140 other military vehicles.[41] While those figures are disputed, there is no doubt Turkey's intervention inflicted a heavy toll, stalled the government's offensive, and exposed its military fragility. Independent visual assessments suggest Turkey's grandiose-sounding estimates may not have been very far from the truth. By comparison, Turkish losses were light. In addition to those lost at Baylun, Turkey lost only a handful of soldiers and three drones, its approach calibrated to exact maximum damage with minimum risk using stand-off weapons supported by local proxies. Turkish drones proved highly effective at seeking out and targeting concentrations of Syrian ground forces, spotting targets for artillery fire, and neutralizing Syria's air defenses.[42]

Under withering fire, Syrian government forces became quickly dependent on Russian support. Since Turkish forces took great care to avoid Russian casualties, Russian military police were used to shore up the government's frontline by inhibiting Turkish attacks. Among other things, they followed up a Tiger Force counteroffensive into Saraqib and helped the government retake the battered town. Meanwhile, Russian Wagner Group mercenaries were rushed to the front in large numbers.[43] Iran also intervened to prop up government lines, among other things firing a barrage of missiles toward Turkey from positions inside Syria, all of which were intercepted. While this suc-ceeded in protecting the front line and with it Saraqib, there was no mistaking the seismic shift in Idlib's military balance. In deference to the Russians, Turkey made no attempt to recapture Saraqib or pre-vent Tiger Force commander Suhail al-Hassan doing a victory parade. Hours later, though, it sent a sharp reminder of its capacity to inflict pain, targeting a high-level Tiger Force meeting in northern Hama, wounding Hassan himself.[44]

By the time Erdogan landed in Moscow, on March 5, both sides were ready to make a deal. There was no disguising the fact that Assad's position in Idlib—and with-it Russia's—had been seriously weakened. The Kremlin now faced the unenviable choice it had tried to impose on Turkey. Continuing its air campaign over Idlib would mean replacing lost Syrian capabilities with additional Russian assets or transferring more assets to the Syrians. It would also mean accept-ing greater losses due to the threats posed by MANPADS and Turkey's very clear demonstration of superiority over the Pantsir system. Then there was the regime's chronic manpower shortage. Moscow and Teh-ran had helped paper over the cracks by importing thousands of for-eign fighters and mercenaries and fortifying regime forces with elite units like the Tiger Force, but it was clear the government side could not withstand the sort of losses inflicted by Turkey for long without serious repercussions. Moscow had already begun scrambling for a response. Worried Turkey might close the Bosporus to its military shipping, Russia hurried two frigates and amphibious assault ships, presumably carrying hundreds of Russian troops or mercenaries, into the eastern Mediterranean. But these were hasty, short-term fixes, not long-term solutions. Erdogan also wanted a deal. Turkey's interven-tion had always been about coercing Moscow and Damascus to end their offensive and deterring future offensives, and for that Ankara needed to translate military success into a sustainable political arrangement.

The two leaders quickly agreed a new ceasefire that offered both a little of what they wanted, but which overall represented a significant, though short-term, victory for Erdogan. Under the agreement, which was couched as an "additional protocol" to the Sochi Memorandum of Understanding of 2018, the two sides agreed a near-immediate ceasefire (commencing at midnight), a freeze of the front lines, and the establishment of a security corridor six kilometers to the north and south of the M4 motorway jointly patrolled and monitored by Russia and Turkey. The agreement also stipulated that the targeting of civilians was unjustifiable in any circumstance.[45] It gave Erdogan most of what he wanted. Although the ceasefire was likely temporary, it bought Turkey the time it wanted to shore up the military defense of Idlib and work on the enclave's treacherous internal politics. The deal would also make it easier for Turkey, which quickly reinforced its positions with an additional thousand vehicles and associated personnel, to justify future uses of force.[46]

But the agreement also left a lot of questions unanswered. First, implementation of the security corridor would be very difficult in practice. Turkey would be responsible for security north of the corridor, Russia for security to the south. The Russians were thus heading into territory housing a bitterly anti-Assad civilian population, Turkish proxy forces, and HTS-aligned jihadists—territory in which they might be vulnerable. But Turkey, too, faced a problem as the HTS retained a presence in force to the north of the highway and had always strongly objected to joint Turkish-Russian patrols along it. Second, Turkey's military intervention had limited but not entirely prevented a new refugee crisis. Erdogan's domestic problem thus remained, and the Idlib enclave was now more truncated that it had been at the start of the year. Third, the decision not to abandon observation posts and withdraw forces to defensible lines meant that some fourteen observation posts were now surrounded by Syrian and Russian forces, highly vulnerable, and critical points of leverage in Moscow's hands. Fourth, the thorny issue of counterterrorism remained unresolved. The agreement did not altogether prohibit counterterror operations, and although the HTS had been weakened, it retained a strong hold within the Idlib enclave.[47] So although the use of force and strengthened presence deterred further attacks on Idlib in the short term, the prospects remained high of a return to war in the future.

The settling of scores in Idlib will likely prove to be one of the catalysts for Syria's next civil war.

EPILOGUE

System Failure

ASSAD, OR WE BURN THE COUNTRY," government loyalists chanted in 2011. It had been a statement of intent. Nine years on, more than half a million Syrians were dead, more than six million had fled the country, and more than half of those who remained were either displaced, reliant on humanitarian aid, or both, and major cities, dozens of towns, and thousands of villages lay in ruins. And for all that, and all the ambivalence and complicity of foreign powers and international organizations, Bashar al-Assad had still not retaken every inch. As the dust settled on Idlib, the Syrian economy nosedived toward total collapse. Hyperinflation brought home a new reality to Assad's loyalist circle—that they had indeed burned the country, and that as a result the country could no longer sustain their lifestyles. As the war economy wound down, the Alawite elite confronted a future with limited income, destroyed infrastructure, and little hope of reconstruction. A new calamity, the COVID-19 pandemic, brought the global economy to a standstill and brought Iran, but also Russia, to its knees. The pipelines of men, materiel, and money that had sustained the regime through the long years of war began to dry up. At last realizing some of what they had wrought, members of the Alawite elite turned on itself. There were rumors of plots to remove Assad. Perhaps sensing this, the president reined in his cousin Rami Maklouf, who the authorities claimed owed more than $180 million in back taxes to the impoverished state, but that only compounded the feeling that Assad's was a regime confined to a state of near-permanent existential crisis. One theory suggests that Maklouf's fall from grace stemmed from a conflict with Assad's wife, Asma al-Assad, for control of the lucrative NGO sector.[1] Another holds that Russia demanded the oligarch's fall, concerned Maklouf was a divisive figure and economic competitor.[2] Whichever is true, both paint a picture of a brittle regime hollowed out from within. Amid the economic chaos, Ankara moved to insulate Idlib from Syrian hyper-inflation by introducing the Turkish lira as the currency of choice—further separating the enclave from the rest of Syria and enmeshing it into Turkey's economic as well as political orbit. The fact that the HTS agreed to the move pointed to Ankara's growing influence there.

In some of the territories nominally controlled by Damascus, the government ruled in name only. The security state on which Assad depended was no longer controlled exclusively by Syria's government or the Assad family, dependent as it now was on Russia and Iran. Russia all but controlled the remaining functional parts of Syria's armed forces; Iranian proxies in their tens of thousands established themselves across the country, causing resentment even among loyalist Syrians.[3] Government control also depended on a loose network of militias, each with its own loyalties and interests. And to compound things, already by 2020 the government's "reconciliation" policy was starting to fray. In devastated Daraa, where it all began in 2011, "reconciled" civilians were taking once more to the streets demanding reform and regime change. In regime-controlled Suwayda in June 2020, protestors chanted "We don't want to live, we want to die in dignity" and "He who starves the people is a traitor."[4]

It is not just that Assad's long-predicted victory remains incomplete. It is that by refusing to deal properly with a regime responsible for mass atrocities, international actors are storing up trouble for the future. The ghosts of Aleppo, Homs, Ghouta, Daraa, Hama, and the rest will haunt Syria's future until there is, at last, a reckoning. Yet the United Nations, an increasing number of governments, and even some human rights–focused NGOs believe an authoritarian peace is possible, that Assad victorious can be coaxed to reform, and his terrorized people persuaded to meekly accept their fate. They are wrong about that, because the one thing that all Syria's major political actors have learned is that there is always—sometimes only—a military solution. The war and with it the suffering of Syria's people will most likely continue—sometimes openly, sometimes by stealth—until there is a reckoning with Assad and his allies.

There were many points in the journey when world leaders could have taken different decisions from the ones they did. Different decisions could have saved lives or cost more lives. At the beginning, Assad could have chosen a path of conciliation. At the end, Erdogan could have chosen to let Idlib collapse. Different leaders in those situations—and the many other critical junctures in between—might have made different choices. Why, then, did things turn out this way? Why did the international legal obligations established after the Holocaust to protect civilians from exactly this type of violence, and the world's unanimous twenty-first-century promise that it had a responsibility to protect populations from atrocity crimes, amount to so little? The answer lies in Lakhdar Brahimi's comment in 2015 that "everybody had their agenda and the interests of the Syrian people came second, third, or not at all." It was not that Syrian lives mattered for nothing, but that again and again leaders decided that other things mattered more.

For Russia and Iran, protecting Assad was more important than protecting ordinary Syrians. For their ally, China, solidarity with political friends and an instinctive preference for brutal yet orderly authoritarianism were paramount. None of these powers gave the welfare of Syrians the slightest consideration. What concessions to humanity they made were wrung out of them either by intense diplomatic pressure, by lingering fears of Western military unilateralism, by calculations that it might serve their purposes in the long term, or simply because they judged they wouldn't make much difference anyway. The disarming of Syria's chemical weapons was agreed to only to forestall U.S. airstrikes. "Humanitarian" evacuation agreements were accepted because they facilitated surrenders and forced displacement. Yet of Assad's foreign allies, only Iran comes out of the war the stronger for it—its militias, weapons factories and stores, and networks now positioned across Syria and not far from the Golan Heights. Even this apparent success came at a colossal cost. Iran lost Soleimani, its Shi'ite militia and Hezbollah allies sustained heavy losses, and the Syrian meat grinder helped cripple Iran's economy. Spending $6 billion per year on Assad's defense, the Iranian economy spiraled downward in 2020, provoking fresh antigovernment protests. Russia has succeeded in reasserting its place on the global stage but finds itself politically isolated and backing a regime it knows cannot command the loyalty of most of its people, a collapsed state run like a loose network of mafia fiefdoms facing a huge reconstruction bill it will not be able foot alone. Looking back to its original goals, Moscow's policy failed completely in its first purpose: containing extreme violent Islamism. Its strategy of backing Assad helped embolden ISIS, which was suppressed only with significant American and Kurdish help. Even with ISIS seemingly defeated, it would be difficult to claim that Moscow faces less of a threat from jihadi terrorism in the 2020s than it did in 2011. Looking ahead, Moscow faces an unenviable choice between an open-ended commitment to protecting Assad and cutting the dictator loose, with all that that might mean.

From the Barack Obama administration, and U.S. allies in Europe, there was genuine humanitarian concern. Yet the shallowness of that concern was exposed time and again, for instance, by just how few states joined Angela Merkel in opening their borders and welcoming Syrian refugees in 2015. Humanitarian concern was always tempered by fears of international jihadist terrorism, political instability, and refugees, and the U.S. ambition to withdraw from the Middle East and avoid creeping military entanglements. The result was a dangerously contradictory strategy that involved vocal support for human rights and democracy without offering the support they needed to prevail. Concerns about getting drawn into new military commitments inhibited serious consideration of options such as safe zones, no-fly zones, or targeted strikes against the artillery and aircraft used to terrorize civilians—options that Turkey proved in 2020 could have been utilized to good effect all along. In 2011 the Obama administration hit on a strategy of trying to coerce Assad to share power by providing just enough support to keep the fight going but not enough to ensure an opposition victory. This approach rested on an assumption no less flawed than the belief that Assad's fall was inevitable: that Assad could be coerced into stepping down by a combination of diplomatic pressure, economic sanctions, and limited assistance to the opposition. It was a strategy that took no heed of the regime's nature or its oft-stated intent, a strategy that failed also to factor in the willingness of Tehran and Moscow to back Assad. It was thus a flawed strategy always doomed to fail. With the rise of ISIS from 2014, even this was pushed aside as new priorities surfaced. Combating the caliphate and managing the refugee crisis displaced all other concerns. For the chaotic Donald Trump administration, Syria—even with the ISIS problem—was never more than a "strategic sideshow," to use John Bolton's words.

The successors to the generation of leaders whose "war on terror" led the West into costly wars in Iraq, Afghanistan, the African Sahel, and elsewhere were determined to avoid the mistakes of the past. It is a tragic irony that in their determination to prevent resurgent jihadist terrorism, the West's approach to Syria's crisis contributed directly to the rise of first al-Nusra and then ISIS, and to the fragmenting and marginalization of Syria's peaceful protestors and mainstream opposition. The United States and its allies did eventually intervene militarily, but to counter ISIS, not protect Syrians. The U.S.-led coalition's intervention helped some Syrians—notably the Kurds—in the short term, but even that was tempered: it may have helped save Syria's Kurds from ISIS, but its haste to withdraw exposed those very same communities to Turkish encroachment. As a result, Kobane is now more or less in the hands of Damascus.

Regional powers, too, had their own priorities, and the protection of Syrian civilians was rarely near the top. Early on, regional priorities coalesced around the perceived need to protect authoritarian pseudo-stability. Once that temporary consensus collapsed, Syria's neighbors played out their geopolitical struggle through the lives of Syria's people. One of the greatest cruelties of all was that those states with vast resources and a proclaimed affinity with Syria's Sunnis—Saudi Arabia, Qatar, UAE, Turkey, and Jordan—privileged their own, narrow interests over the collective interests of the people they claimed they were helping. Thus, rather than helping build a united opposition, they fermented and rewarded factionalism. Rather than encouraging a Syrian-led Free Syrian Army, they tried to maximize their own influence by arming and funding a panoply of small and fractious armed groups. And rather than instilling in their clients the values of moderation and inclusiveness, they encouraged the lurch toward extremism. More concerned with their own interests than those of the Syrians they claimed to protect, regional powers created a competitive marketplace for arms, fighters, and funds that encouraged factionalism and rewarded extremism. Rather than help the opposition, these foreign patrons sowed the seeds of its destruction.

Everything else flowed from this core fact that the fate of Syria's people was no one's consistent priority. There were several critical junctures when things might have turned out differently had protection been prioritized. Yet at each turn there was always something else judged more important. The fate of UNSMIS and the Kofi Annan mission, effectively abandoned by a Security Council that had endorsed them, was one such instance. Obama's decision not to authorize air strikes in 2013 another. The decision not to refer the torture and killing of thousands trapped by Syria's detention system to the ICC another. Russia's decision to intervene to prop up Assad another. The West's decision to not back Sunni opposition groups battling ISIS another. Decisions to allow Assad to manipulate humanitarian aid to his advantage another. The series of decisions to allow the de-escalation zones to topple one-by-one yet another.

Once the fleeting belief that Assad's fall was inevitable evaporated, Western fears about regional instability and entanglement fed a deeply flawed assumption that drove a political strategy doomed from the outset to fail. That assumption, already mentioned, was the idea that Syria's president could be persuaded or coerced into negotiating a political settlement that would satisfy the opposition's core demands that the government share power and become democratic and that Assad himself step down. No paper agreement could end state terror while Assad held onto the levers of Syria's security apparatus. To think otherwise, that some sort of compromise was possible, was to misunderstand the personalized and patrimonial nature of Assad's regime and was willfully deaf to what Assad himself said repeatedly: that he would not be coerced; that he intended to reclaim "every inch" of Syria. Those who talked to him usually came to the same conclusion, though it took some longer than others to reach it. Kofi Annan reported that Assad had no interest in seriously negotiating. Lakhdar Brahimi quickly reached the same conclusion. For all his efforts to skirt around the problem, even Staffan de Mistura eventually reached the same conclusion. This assumption fed other, equally flawed beliefs—for example, that Russia might be persuaded to help engineer a just peace. No matter how often these flawed assumptions were exposed, governments persisted with a protection strategy dependent on the good graces of the very regime responsible for perpetrating most of the atrocities. We cannot be surprised that the strategy failed. The contending priorities of foreign powers compounded the disaster that befell Syria.

The story is also one of the UN's inexorable descent into political irrelevance and complicity with evil. Diplomats worked hard to find common ground, but almost from the outset the Security Council was blocked by Russian and Chinese vetoes. Together, these two states ensured the council became a sideshow. The same fate befell the UN's diplomatic efforts. From the first meetings in 2012, each round of the UN's peace process got farther and farther away from reality until it was supplanted altogether by Russian-style peacemaking. The UN persisted with a zombified peace process that existed only in the minds of those being paid to occupy hotels and conference halls keeping it going in Geneva. Under the guise of humanitarianism, the UN channeled millions of dollars straight into the hands of Assad's family and supporters and funded rebuilding activities in regime-governed areas. For years it continued to supply food and medical items to government held areas, while those same authorities indiscriminately bombarded and denied access to besieged areas, helping the government supply its friends and break the will of its opponents. When government forces began pushing besieged areas into submission, the UN facilitated their surrender, aided their displacement, and was more than once directly complicit in handing men and boys over to the security state from which many never reappeared. Some UN officials were undoubtedly well-intentioned as they engaged in a desperate search to do whatever they could to save lives in extremely difficult conditions. But too many UN officials, comfortably housed in the luxurious Four Seasons residences in downtown Damascus, were more than happy to cooperate with Assad and channel the UN's precious resources into state-run organizations, the UN's largesse going directly to Assad's own family.

As their peace efforts floundered, the UN's senior leadership also came to see Syria as a "sideshow"—even for atrocity prevention. In his report on "learning lessons" from atrocity prevention in 2019, Antonio Guterres concluded that "the best outcomes are achieved when atrocity prevention is made a priority." Yet the report contained no reflection on the UN's performance in Syria. Indeed, the word "Syria" did not appear in the report at all.[5] In sharp contrast to his predecessor Ban Ki-moon, who had repeatedly used his bully pulpit to decry the failure to prevent atrocities in Syria, for example, mentioning it no fewer than nineteen times in his final three annual reports on the "responsibility to protect," Guterres was reticent indeed, referring to Syria only once in his first three reports on the same subject. The UN's largest humanitarian donors—mainly in the West—were happy to use the organization as an alibi for their own relative disinterest. The Security Council blocked by Russian and Chinese vetoes and the ineffectual General Assembly and Human Rights Council served as convenient excuses for inaction. Diplomats busied themselves with meetings and dialogues about issues that mattered only to them and not at all to Syrians caught in the crosshairs. Only rarely did the question of circumventing these failing institutions arise, and when it did this was usually in the context of the West's actual priorities—countering Islamist terrorism and controlling chemical weapons.

The United Nations was not alone in its complicity. Syria's tragedy exposed a whole industry of peace activism and humanitarianism eager to prove its relevance and prepared to clutch at any straw. In their desperation, organizations displayed acute naiveté about the Syrian government, were easily manipulated by it, and expended resources on projects either wholly irrelevant, counterproductive, or complicit. Like the UN, this industry insisted on believing a consensus could be forged between Syria's parties and the great powers brought into alignment. As late as 2020, the Carter Center—an organization dedicated to promoting democracy and conflict resolution led by former U.S. president Jimmy Carter—cohosted a meeting with the pro-Assad British Syrian Society in London to discuss "restoring territorial sovereignty" and "how to secure the removal of armed forces operating in Syria without the Syrian government's consent."[6] The Carter program aimed to understand the "harm" caused by international isolation and promote "positive steps by the Syrian government." The Quincy Institute for Responsible Statecraft recommended that the

United States reestablish positive relations with Assad, form an international "contact group" to direct the flow of humanitarian aid into Syria by "mutual agreement" with his government, and turn to the World Bank and International Monetary Fund to provide "a massive infusion of technical assistance for capacity building" to help the Syrian state.[7] In other words, international actors should pay the Assadists to rebuild what they themselves had burnt down.

The tragedy of Syria holds an uncomfortable lesson for the peace and humanitarian industries: that some actors are unwilling to compromise and quite willing to use whatever violence they need in order to impose their will. Actors like Assad cannot be persuaded to reform or stand down by diplomacy or financial carrots. No amount of dialogue, abstract wrangling over constitutions, or workshopping will affect their base calculations. Motivated and determined leaders such as this can be pushed off their path only by the thing most liable to stop them getting what they want: military power. We can draw any number of conclusions about what this tells us about changing world politics and the relative merits of choices, policies, and strategies. I have offered some reflections on that throughout. Sometimes the wrong lessons have already been drawn. For example, the idea that the West and Gulf Arab states poured fuel on the fire of conflict in 2011–2012 and that they should have tried to de-escalate things by moderating support to the opposition has become canon. Events, though, have proven this lesson misguided. First, it wrongly assumes Assad could have been persuaded to reform. Second, it assumes, equally wrongly, that it was encouragement from outside, not their own experience inside Syria, that was the primary consideration pushing soldiers to defect and civilians to arm. This surely exaggerates the role of outsiders and diminishes the agency of Syrians. There is no evidence to suggest that dialing down rhetorical support for the opposition would have changed the opposition's demands. Indeed, the opposition was always ambivalent about Western intervention. It is probably true that Assad would have crushed his opponents more quickly had they not received external assistance, but that would still have involved mass killing—evidenced by the Caesar files—and would still likely have given rise to protracted armed conflict and jihadist terrorism.

A related but equally misplaced "lesson" is that a negotiated deal acceptable to both government and opposition was possible. In truth, this was never a promising avenue. The United States repeatedly told the opposition to compromise or be annihilated. Because the former would have required accepting that Assad remain president and in control of the security state, the opposition saw annihilation at the end of both paths and hoped that, by resisting, it might outlast the dictator. The problem lay not with the opposition but with Assad, who never contemplated a deal that might see him lose power. Moscow learned this early when it was unable to influence him out of this position. This presented it with a stark choice: back Assad or risk his fall. As early as 2012 the Kremlin chose to back Assad. From the moment Russia vetoed multilateral avenues of coercion, the idea of a negotiated settlement became a convenient fiction. From that point, the stage was set for a military solution, and only a military solution. This was something Moscow and Tehran understood long before their rivals in the West and Gulf did. Only when the de-escalation zones began to topple, one after the other, did the reality finally dawn on them. By then it was too late because Syria's suffering had become a geopolitical sideshow.

Ultimately, protecting Syria's civilians was never the top priority for any of these actors. When Syrian artist Aziz Asmar saw the shocking video of Minneapolis police officers choking an unarmed and handcuffed George Floyd to death on May 25, 2020, he saw strong parallels with the experience of his own people. From Binnish, inside the Idlib enclave, Asmar recalled how thousands of Syrian men, women, and children had lain in hospitals, on floors, and in rubble, complaining they couldn't breathe. In his final moments, George Floyd had pleaded for his life, just as so many Syrians had done. Asmar wanted to express his solidarity, and so on a wall of what was once a family's kitchen, he painted a mural depicting Floyd's face with the words, "I can't breathe."[8] Syria stands as a stark reminder of what happens when other things are taken to matter more than the protection of human life from atrocity crimes. The battered, displaced, and traumatized survivors live in hope that one day the world will recognize that their lives matter, too.

NOTES

PROLOGUE

1. Thorsten Gromes and Matthias Dembinski, "Practices and Outcomes of Humanitarian Military Intervention: A New Data Set," *International Interactions* 45, no. 6 (2019): 1032–48.

1. ARAB SPRING

1. Robin Yassin-Kassab and Leila Al-Shami, *Burning Country: Syrians in Revolution and War* (London: Pluto, 2016), 37.
2. Lina Khatib and Ellen Lust, eds., *Taking to the Streets: The Transformation of Arab Activism* (Baltimore: Johns Hopkins University Press, 2014), 161.
3. Sam Dagher, *Assad or We Burn the Country* (Boston: Little, Brown, 2019), 208.
4. Charles Glass, "Tell Me How This Ends: America's Muddled Involvement with Syria," *Harpers*, February 26, 2019.
5. Avi Asher-Schapiro, "The Young Men Who Started Syria's Revolution Talk About Daraa, Where It All Began," *Vice News*, March 15, 2016.
6. Dagher, *Assad or We Burn the Country*, 162–63.
7. Dagher, 178.
8. Philippe Droz-Vincent, "State of Barbary (Take Two): From the Arab Spring to the Return of Violence in Syria," *Middle East Journal* (2014): 34.
9. Michael Slackman, "Syrian Troops Open Fire on Protestors in Several Cities," *New York Times*, March 25, 2011.

10. David W. Lesch, *Syria: The Fall of the House of Assad*, updated ed. (New Haven, Conn.: Yale University Press, 2013), 70.

11. See Robert F. Worth, *A Rage for Order: The Middle East in Turmoil, from Tahrir Square to ISIS* (London: Picador, 2016), 66.

12. Bassam Barabandi and Tyler Jess Thompson, "Inside Assad's Playbook: Time and Terror," Atlantic Council, July 23, 2014.

13. Reinoud Leenders, "Repression Is Not a Stupid Thing," in *The Alawis of Syria: War, Faith and Politics in the Levant*, ed. Michael Kerr and Craig Larkin (London: Hurst, 2015), 145ff.

14. Michael Weiss and Hassan Hassan, *ISIS: Inside the Army of Terror* (New York: Regan Arts, 2015), 139.

15. Emile Hokayem, *Syria's Uprising and the Fracturing of the Levant* (London: Routledge, 2013), 150.

16. Christopher Phillips, *The Battle for Syria: International Rivalry in the New Middle East* (New Haven, Conn.: Yale University Press, 2016), 51.

17. Liz Sly, "Doomsday Scenario If Syria Falls," *Washington Post*, May 1, 2011.

18. Colin Dueck, *The Obama Doctrine: American Grand Strategy Today* (Oxford: Oxford University Press, 2015), 2, 34.

19. Transcript of Obama's speech against the Iraq War, Chicago, October 2, 2002.

20. Hillary Rodham Clinton, *Hard Choices* (New York: Simon and Schuster, 2014), 461.

21. "Acting Assistant Secretary Feltman Briefs on Meetings with Syrian Officials," U.S. Department of State, March 7, 2009.

22. William J. Burns, *The Back Channel: A Memoir of American Diplomacy and the Case for Its Renewal* (New York: Random House, 2019), 324.

23. Clinton, *Hard Choices*, 448.

24. Robert Gates, *Duty: Memoirs of a Secretary at War* (New York: Allen, 2014), 523.

25. "Senator John Kerry on U.S. Policy Toward the Middle East," Carnegie Endowment for International Peace, March 16, 2011.

26. *Face the Nation*, March 27, 2011.

27. Nicole Gaouette and Gopal Ratnam, "Clinton Says U.S. Won't Intervene in Syria, Sees Progress in Libya Fight," *Bloomberg*, March 28, 2011.

28. Phillips, *Battle for Syria*, 65.

29. Christopher S. Chivvis, *Toppling Qaddafi: Libya and the Limits of Liberal Intervention* (Cambridge: Cambridge University Press, 2014), 34.

30. Josh Rogin, "How Obama Turned on a Dime Toward War," *Foreign Policy*, March 18, 2011.

31. Jean Dufourcq and Olivier Kempf, "The Evolution of France's Policy in Syria," King Faisal Research Centre, March 2016, 3.

32. Dagher, *Assad or We Burn the Country*, 208.

33. Nikolaos Van Dam, *Destroying a Nation: The Civil War in Syria* (New York: Tauris, 2017), 77.

34. Richard Gowan, "How Not to Intervene in Syria," *Foreign Policy*, December 1, 2011.

35. Jubin N. Goodarzi, *Syria and Iran: Diplomatic Alliance and Power Politics in the Middle East* (London: Tauris, 2006), 271.

36. Payam Mohseni, "The Arab Awakening: Iran's Grand Narrative of the Arab Uprisings," Crown Center for Middle East Studies, Brandeis University, April 2013.

37. Lesch, *Syria*, 128.

38. Kristian Coates Ulrichsen, "Qatar and the Arab Spring: Policy Drivers and Regional Implications," Carnegie Endowment for International Peace, September 2014, 9.

39. Emile Hokayem, "The Gulf States and Syria," Peacebrief for the U.S. Institute of Peace, September 30, 2011, p. 3.

40. Hokayem, *Syria's Uprising*, 107.

41. Jim Muir, "Syria: Assad Regime Looks to Bolster Itself," BBC, March 29, 2011.

42. Marc Lynch, *The New Arab Wars: Uprising and Anarchy in the Middle East* (New York: Public Affairs, 2016), 109.

43. Yehuda U. Blanga, "Saudi Arabia's Motives in the Syrian Civil War," *Middle East Policy Council Journal* 24, no. 4 (2017).

44. Hokayem, *Syria's Uprising*, 111.

45. Hannah Lucinda Smith, *Erdogan Rising: The Battle for the Soul of Turkey* (London: Collins, 2019), 187.

46. Smith, 103.

47. Christopher Phillips, "Turkey's Global Strategy: Turkey and Syria," *IDEAS Reports*, London School of Economics, 2011.

48. Smith, *Erdogan Rising*, 57.

49. Delphine Strauss, "Erdogan Urges Assad to Hasten Reform," *Financial Times*, March 28, 2011.

50. Anthony Shadid, "Coalition of Factions from the Streets Fuels a New Opposition in Syria," *New York Times*, June 30, 2011.

51. Lesch, *Syria*, 97; UN document, S/PV.6524, April 27, 2011, 2.

52. Dagher, *Assad or We Burn the Country*, 219.

53. Yassin-Kassab and Al-Shami, *Burning Country*, 45.

54. Sonia Verma, "How a 13-Year-Old Became a Symbol of Syrian Revolution," *Globe and Mail*, June 1, 2011.

55. Dagher, *Assad or We Burn the Country*, 248.

56. Dagher, 209.

57. Hokayem, *Syria's Uprising*, 112.

58. Lesch, *Syria*, 142.

59. "Syria 'Drops Bid' to Join Human Rights Body," France 24, May 11, 2011.

60. Dagher, *Assad or We Burn the Country*, 209.

61. "A Statement by President Obama on Syria," White House, April 22, 2011.

62. S/PV.6524, April 27, 2011, 4.

63. S/PV.6524, April 27, 2011.

64. Lesch, *Syria*, 139.

65. Dmitri Trenin, *What Is Russia Up to in the Middle East?* (Cambridge: Polity, 2018), 41.

66. Tony Wood, *Russia Without Putin: Money, Power and the Myths of the New Cold War* (London: Verso, 2018), 98.

67. Samuel Charap, "Russia, Syria and the Doctrine of Intervention," *Survival* 55, no. 1 (2013): 35–41.

68. Roy Allison, *Russia, the West, and Military Intervention* (Oxford: Oxford University Press, 2013), 199.

69. Dmitri Trenin, "The Mythical Alliance: Russia's Syria Policy," *Carnegie Papers*, February 2013.

70. Allison, *Russia, the West, and Military Intervention*, 199.

71. "Libya Letter by Obama, Cameron, and Sarkozy: Full Text," BBC, April 15, 2011.

72. G8 Declaration, "Renewed Commitment for Freedom and Democracy," G8 Summit of Deauville, May 26–27, 2011, para. 64.

73. Roy Allison, "Russia and Syria: Explaining Alignment with a Regime in Crisis," *International Affairs* 89, no. 4 (2013): 797.

74. "Interview with Dmitry Medvedev," *Russia Today*, August 5, 2011.

75. Mikhail Zygar, *All the Kremlin's Men: Inside the Court of Vladimir Putin* (New York: Public Affairs, 2016), 331.

76. Phillips, *Battle for Syria*, 98.

77. Interview with European official.

78. S/PV.6531, May 10, 2011.

79. Nidaa Hassan, "Mass Grave Found Near Deraa, Residents Say," *Guardian*, May 18, 2011.

80. Interview with diplomats from Security Council members.

81. Yassin-Kassab and Al-Shami, *Burning Country*, 83.

82. Anthony Shadid, "Syrian Unrest Stirs New Fear of Deeper Sectarian Divide," *New York Times*, June 13, 2011.

83. "Syria Barring Humanitarian Mission to Deraa, UN Says," *Reuters*, May 9, 2011.

84. David E. Sanger, *Confront and Conceal: Obama's Secret Wars and Surprising Use of American Power* (New York: Penguin, 2013), 359.

85. Glass, "Tell Me How This Ends."

86. Rania Abouzeid, "U.S. Diplomat Causes Firestorm with Visit to Rebellious Syrian City," *Time*, July 8, 2011.

87. Lesch, *Syria*, 157–58.

88. Sanger, *Confront and Conceal*, 359.

89. "No Easy Answers for U.S. Involvement in Libya, Syria," *USA Today*, July 30, 2011.

90. Adrian Blomfield, "Syria: Bashar al-Assad's Tanks Renew Assault on Hama," *Telegraph*, August 1, 2011.

91. "No Easy Answers for U.S. Involvement in Libya, Syria."

92. "Syrian Army Kills at Least 95 in Hama: Activist," *AFP*, July 31, 2011.

93. "Syria: UN Chief Condemns Latest Bloody Violence Against Civilians," *UN News*, July 31, 2011.

94. "Alarmed at Syrian Bloodshed, UN Rights Chief Demands End to Brutality," *UN News*, August 2, 2011.

95. "France: Syria Will Answer for Protest Deaths," *AFP*, August 1, 2011.

96. Blomfield, "Syria: Bashar al-Assad's Tanks Renew Assault on Hama."

97. "Interview by Dimitry Medvedev," Russia Today, August 5, 2011.

98. Khaled Yacoub Oweis, "Syria Toll Rises, Russia Opens Way to UN Resolution," *Stuff* (New Zealand), August 2, 2011.

99. S/PV.6598, August 3, 2011. The Security Council presidential statement is SC/10352, August 3, 2011.

100. Bente Scheller, *The Wisdom of Syria's Waiting Game: Foreign Policy Under the Assads* (London: Hurst, 2013), 33.

101. Nada Bakri, "Turkish Leader and Other Envoys Press Syrian Leader," *New York Times*, April 9, 2011.

102. Hardeep Puri, *Perilous Interventions: The Security Council and the Politics of Chaos* (New York: Harper Collins, 2016), 125.

103. Adrian Blomfield, "Syria Unrest: Saudi Arabia Calls on 'Killing Machine' to Stop," *Telegraph*, August 8, 2011.

104. Nada Bakri, "3 Arab Countries Recall Ambassadors to Syria," *New York Times*, August 8, 2011.

105. "Qatari Ambassador Closes Embassy, Leaves Damascus," France 24, July 18, 2011.

106. "Turkey and Syria: One Problem with a Neighbour," *Economist*, August 20, 2011.

107. Nada Bakri, "Turkish Minister and Other Envoys Press Syrian Leader," *New York Times*, August 9, 2011.

108. Tulay Karadeniz, "Turkey Says Syria Tanks Leaving Hama City," *Reuters*, August 10, 2011.

109. "Recep Tayyip Erdogan Hails Success of Ankara Message to Syria," *Trend News Agency*, August 10, 2011.

110. Liz Sly, "Syria Gunboats Join Fresh Attacks Against Protestors," *Washington Post*, August 14, 2011.

111. "Middle East Allies Call for Syrian Government to Reform," CNN, August 29, 2011.

112. *Report of the United Nations High Commissioner for Human Rights on the Situation of Human Rights in the Syrian Arab Republic*, A/HRC/18/53, September 15, 2011.

113. "US, Saudi Arabia Demand End to Syria Violence," *AFP*, August 14, 2011.

114. *Syria: The Crisis and Its Implications*, Hearing Before the Committee on Foreign Relations, United States Senate, March 1, 2012, 6, 15.

115. Ben Rhodes, *World as It Is: A Memoir of the Obama White House* (New York: Random House, 2018), 157–58.

116. Dagher, *Assad or We Burn the Country*, 325.

117. "The Roads to Damascus: How the Elysee Manipulated Chemical Weapons Reports," *Al-Akbhar* (Lebanon), October 14, 2014.
118. Dagher, *Assad or We Burn the Country*, 324.
119. Athanasios Dimadis and Robert Ford, "What Went Wrong in Syria?," *Fair Observer*, December 21, 2017.
120. Phillips, *Battle for Syria*, 79.
121. Josh Rogin, "Why Has Obama Not Asked for Assad to Go Yet?," *Foreign Policy*, August 16, 2011.
122. Dimadis and Ford, "What Went Wrong in Syria?"
123. "President Obama: The Future of Syria Must Be Determined by Its People, but President Bashar al-Assad Is Standing in Their Way," White House, August 8, 2018.
124. Lesch, *Syria*, 145.
125. Nada Bakri, "Turkish Leader and Other Envoys Press Syrian Leader," *New York Times*, April 9, 2011.
126. Lyce Doucet, "Syria's Assad Should Step Aside, Says Jordan's Abdullah," BBC, November 15, 2011.
127. Phillips, *Battle for Syria*, 81.
128. "U.S. Policy in Syria Could No Longer Be Defended, Ex-ambassador Says," interview with Robert Ford, NPR Radio, June 4, 2014.
129. Chivvis, *Toppling Qaddafi*.
130. Lesch, *Syria*, 114.
131. Phillips, *Battle for Syria*, 88.
132. Khalid Ali, "Iran Calls on Syrian President to Consider Protestors' Demands," *Independent*, August 29, 2011.
133. Lesch, *Syria*, 182.
134. "Russia Opposes Calls for Syrian President to Resign," CNN, August 19, 2011.
135. *Report of the Human Rights Council on Its Seventeenth Special Session*, A/HRC/S-17/2, August 23, 2011.
136. Phillips, *Battle for Syria*, 68.
137. Author's interview with Security Council diplomats and observers.
138. S/2011/612, October 4, 2011.
139. S/PV.6627, October 4, 2011, 3–4.
140. Puri, *Perilous Interventions*, 22, 19.
141. S/PV.6627, October 4, 2011, 11.

2. REGIONAL SOLUTIONS?

1. Joseph Holliday, "Syria's Armed Opposition," *Institute for the Study of War*, Washington, D.C., March 2012, 13.
2. Martin Chulov, "Arab League Issues First Condemnation of Syria Violence," *Guardian*, June 14, 2011.

3. Lars Berger and Adrian Gallagher, "Shared Values or Shared Interests? Arab Publics and Intervention in Syria," *Politics* (2020): 1–17.

4. Ian Black, "Arab League Mission in Syria 'Has Only Just Started,'" *Guardian*, January 8, 2012.

5. "Arab States Seek to End Syria Crisis," Al Jazeera, August 28, 2011.

6. "Arab League Says Syria Reform Deal Agreed," Al Jazeera, September 11, 2011.

7. "Arab League Calls for Syria Dialogue Within 15 Days," BBC News, October 16, 2011.

8. "Syria Agrees to End Crackdown, Arab League Says," CNN, November 3, 2011.

9. "Syria Signs Deal to Allow Arab League Observers Into Country," *Guardian*, December 20, 2011.

10. Neil MacFarquhar, "Arab League Votes to Suspend Syria Over Crackdown," *New York Times*, November 12, 2011.

11. Paul Denahar, *The New Middle East: The World After the Arab Spring* (London: Bloomsbury, 2013), 237–388.

12. Kristian Coates Ulrichsen, *Qatar and the Arab Spring* (London: Hurst, 2014), 134–35.

13. MacFarquhar, "Arab League Votes to Suspend Syria Over Crackdown."

14. Bradley Hope, "Arab League Suspends Syria and Threatens Sanctions," *National*, November 13, 2011.

15. "Syria Unrest, Arab League Adopts Sanctions in Cairo," BBC, November 27, 2011.

16. Mujge Kucukelles, "Arab League's Syria Policy," *SETA Policy Brief*, no. 56 (April 2012): 8.

17. "Syria Soldiers Defecting in Increasing Numbers—UN," *Reuters*, November 10, 2011.

18. David W. Lesch, *Syria: The Fall of the House of Assad*, updated ed. (New Haven, Conn.: Yale University Press, 2013), 183.

19. Christopher Phillips, *The Battle for Syria: International Rivalry in the New Middle East* (New Haven, Conn.: Yale University Press, 2016), 94.

20. S/PV.6710, January 31, 2012.

21. Bashar al-Assad, "Interview with Barbara Walters," ABC, December 7, 2011.

22. Ian Black, "Arab League Mission in Syria 'Has Only Just Started,'" *Guardian*, January 8, 2012.

23. "US Skeptical of Syrian Agreement on Monitors; Opposition Criticizes 'New Tactic,'" *Al-Arabiya News*, December 20, 2011.

24. "Syria Signs Deal to Allow Arab League Observers Into Country," *Guardian*, December 20, 2011.

25. UN General Assembly Resolution 66/176, December 19, 2011.

26. "Sudanese General's Past Casts Shadow on Arab League Mission," France24, December 26, 2011.

27. Phillips, *Battle for Syria*, 90.

28. Ian Black, "Arab League Mission in Syria Has Only Just Started," *Guardian*, January 8, 2012.

29. *Report of the Head of the League of Arab States Observer Mission to Syria for the Period from 24 December 2011 to 18 January 2012,* January 27, 2011, paras. 45–56.
30. Phillips, *Battle for Syria,* 90.
31. Michael Peel, "Arab League Mission to Syria Branded a 'Farce,' " *Financial Times,* January 12, 2012.
32. "Arab League Suspends Syria Mission as Violence Rages," *Reuters,* January 28, 2012.
33. Dorothy Ohl, Holfer Albrecht, and Kevin Koehler, "For Money or Liberty? The Political Economy of Military Desertions and Rebel Recruitment in the Syrian Civil War," Carnegie Endowment for International Peace, *Regional Insight,* November 24, 2015.
34. "Syria Tanks and Troops Enter Protest Town, Zabadani," BBC, January 13, 2012.
35. Erika Solomon, "Zabadani, Former Syrian Resort, Now Rebel Stronghold," *Reuters,* January 17, 2012.
36. Sultan Barakat, "The Qatari Spring: Qatar's Emerging Role in Peacemaking," LSE Kuwait Program, Working paper no. 24, July 2012, 28.
37. "Arab League May Debate Syria Troops Call; UN Chief Tells Assad to 'Stop Killing,' " *Al Arabiya,* January 16, 2012.
38. *Report of the Head of the League of Arab States Observer Mission,* paras. 25–39.
39. "Gulf Arab States to Pull Observers from Syria," BBC, January 24, 2012.
40. Alistair Lyon, "Syria Denounces Arab League for Telling Assad to Quit," *Reuters,* January 23, 2012.
41. Ayman Samir and Erika Solomon, "Arab League Suspends Syria Mission as Violence Rages," *Reuters,* January 28, 2012.
42. Emile Hokayem, *Syria's Uprising and the Fracturing of the Levant* (London: Routledge, 2013), 160.
43. Hassan Hassan, "Syria: The View from the Gulf States," European Council on Foreign Relations, June 13, 2013.
44. Ian Black, "Syrian Acceptance of Arab League Ceasefire Plan Met with Scepticism," *Guardian,* November 3, 2011.
45. "Gunfire, Angry Crowds Greet Arab League Monitors in Syrian Protest Town Homs," *Reuters,* December 28, 2011.
46. "Syria Rejects Arab League Plan for Transition; Opposition Welcomes Initiative," *Al Arabiya,* January 23, 2012.
47. UN Security Council Resolution 2014, October 21, 2011.
48. Liz Sly, "Arab League Calls on Syria's Assad to Step Down," *New York Times,* January 22, 2012.
49. Lesch, *Syria,* 192–93.
50. S/PV.6710, January 31, 2012.
51. Hillary Rodham Clinton, *Hard Choices* (New York: Simon and Schuster, 2014), 450, 451.

52. Julian Borger and Bastien Inzaurralde, "West Ignored Russian Offer in 2012 to Have Syria's Assad Step Aside," *Guardian*, September 15, 2015.

53. Colum Lynch and Dan De Luce, "Did the West Really Miss a Chance to End the Syrian War?," *Foreign Policy*, September 15, 2015.

54. Ibrahim Freihat, "The Yemeni Model Probably Won't Fit Syria Now," Brookings Institution, August 21, 2012.

55. Clinton, *Hard Choices*, 451, 452.

56. Lesch, *Syria*, 193.

57. "US Says Assad's Fall Inevitable," Al-Jazeera, February 1, 2012.

58. S/PV.6710, January 31, 2012.

59. "UN Draft Resolution on Syria," *Guardian*, January 31, 2012.

60. S/2012/77, February 4, 2012.

61. S/PV.6711, February 4, 2012.

62. S/PV.6711, February 4, 2012.

63. Rosemary Foot, *China, the UN, and Human Protection: Beliefs, Power, Image* (Oxford: Oxford University Press, 2020), 163–89.

64. "More than 200 Killed in Homs Ahead of UN Resolution Vote," France 24, February 6, 2012.

65. Kim Sengupta, "Journalists Killed in Syria Rocket Strike 'Were Targeted,'" *Independent*, February 23, 2012.

66. Paul Wood, "Syria's Slide Towards Civil War," BBC, February 12, 2012.

67. Liz Sly, "Syria Activists: 64 Bodies Found Near Homs in One of the Worst Mass Killings," *Washington Post*, February 27, 2012.

68. Holliday, "Syria's Armed Opposition," 13.

69. "Syria Violence: Opposition Seeks Heavy Weapons and Support Abroad for Bosnia-Style War," *Reuters*, March 4, 2012.

70. Tom H. J. Hill, "Kofi Annan's Multilateral Strategy of Mediation and the Syrian Crisis: The Future of Peacemaking in a Multipolar World?," *International Negotiation* 20, no. 3 (2015): 449.

71. "France, Partners Considering Syria Crisis Group: Sarkozy," *Reuters*, February 4, 2012.

72. Aron Lund, "How Assad's Enemies Gave Up on Syria's Opposition," Century Foundation, October 17, 2017.

73. Aron Lund, "Stumbling Into Civil War: The Militarization of the Syrian Opposition in 2011," *AMEC Insights*, vol. 2 (2015): 2–24.

74. Elizabeth Dickinson, *Playing with Fire: Why Private Gulf Financing for Syria's Extremist Rebels Risks Igniting Sectarian Conflict at Home*, Brookings Institution, Analysis paper no. 16, December 2013.

75. Bernard Rougier, *The Sunni Tragedy in the Middle East: Northern Lebanon from al-Qaeda to ISIS* (Princeton, N.J.: Princeton University Press, 2015), 178.

76. "Syria's Secular and Islamist Rebels: Who Are the Saudis and Qataris Arming?," *Time*, September 18, 2012; Hokayem, *Syria's Uprising*, 87.

77. See Michael Weiss and Hassan Hassan, *ISIS: Inside the Army of Terror* (New York: Regan Arts, 2015), 140ff.
78. Charles R. Lister, *The Syrian Jihad: Al-Qaeda, the Islamic State, and the Evolution of an Insurgency* (Oxford: Oxford University Press, 2015), 65.
79. Lesch, *Syria*, 201.
80. Samer N. Abboud, *Syria* (Cambridge: Polity, 2015), 70–73.

3. LAST CHANCE FOR PEACE

1. Kofi Annan, *Interventions: A Life in War and Peace* (New York: Penguin, 2012), 369.
2. Tom H. J. Hill, "Kofi Annan's Multilateral Strategy of Mediation and the Syrian Crisis: The Future of Peacemaking in a Multipolar World?," *International Negotiation* 20 (2015): 456.
3. Michael Aaronson, "Has Kofi Annan Failed in Syria?," *E-International Relations*, May 30, 2012.
4. Emile Hokayem, *Syria's Uprising and the Fracturing of the Levant* (London: Routledge, 2013), 71–73.
5. Richard Gowan, "Kofi Annan, Syria and the Uses of Uncertainty in Mediation," *Stability* 2, no. 1 (2013): 3.
6. Hill, "Kofi Annan's Multilateral Strategy," 459.
7. Six-Point Proposal of the Joint Special Envoy of the United Nations and the League of Arab States, March 16, 2012 (as annexed to UN Security Council Resolution 2042, April 14, 2012).
8. Hill, "Kofi Annan's Multilateral Strategy," 460.
9. "Setback to Kofi Annan's Peace Mission to Syria After Meeting with President Assad," *Telegraph*, October 3, 2012.
10. SC/10564, March 1, 2012.
11. Raymond Hinnebusch and I. William Zartman, "UN Mediation in the Syrian Crisis: From Kofi Annan to Lakhdar Brahimi," *International Peace Institute*, March 2016, 6.
12. S/PRST/2012/6.
13. Jean-Marie Guehenno, *The Fog of Peace: A Memoir of International Peacekeeping in the 21st Century* (Washington, D.C.: Brookings Institution, 2015), 273.
14. Hill, "Kofi Annan's Multilateral Strategy," 453.
15. S/PV.6746, April 5, 2012.
16. Hillary Rodham Clinton, *Hard Choices* (New York: Simon and Schuster, 2014), 454.
17. Guehenno, *Fog of Peace*, 274.
18. James Traub, "Enough Talking Kofi," *Foreign Policy,* May 25, 2012.
19. Hill, "Kofi Annan's Multilateral Strategy," 461.
20. Hill, 463.
21. "Syria Ceasefire Violated, Says UN Chief," *Guardian*, May 2, 2012.

22. Christopher Phillips, *The Battle for Syria: International Rivalry in the New Middle East* (New Haven, Conn.: Yale University Press, 2016), 99.

23. *Report of the Secretary-General on the Implementation of Resolution 2043 (2012)*, S/2012/253, July 6, 2012, para. 12.

24. Transcript of press encounter with head of UNSMIS, Major General Robert Mood, Damascus, May 18, 2012.

25. Guehenno, *Fog of Peace*, 271.

26. *Report of the Independent International Commission of Inquiry on Syria*, UN Human Rights Council, A/HRC/21/50, August 15, paras. 41–50.

27. "Ban, Annan Condemn Syria Massacre," *AFP*, May 26, 2012.

28. "Syria Massacre: Rebels Share the Blame Says Russia's Lavrov," BBC, May 26, 2012.

29. SC/10658, May 27, 2012.

30. Michael McFaul, *From Cold War to Hot Peace: An American Ambassador in Putin's Russia* (New York: Penguin, 2019), 338.

31. McFaul, 258.

32. Hill, "Kofi Annan's Multilateral Strategy," 463.

33. Author's interview with Moscow-based analyst.

34. "UN Team 'Shot at' Near Qubair 'Massacre Site,'" BBC News, June 7, 2012.

35. *Report of the Secretary-General on the Implementation of Resolution 2043*, July 6, 2012.

36. Clinton, *Hard Choices*, 454; Arshad Mohammed, "Clinton Cool on Russian Call for Syria Meeting," *Reuters*, June 6, 2012.

37. Annan, *Interventions*, 369.

38. "UN Suspends Monitoring Activities in Syria Amid Escalating Violence," UN media release, June 16, 2012.

39. Paul Danahar, *The New Middle East: The World After the Arab Spring* (New York: Bloomsbury, 2013), 379.

40. "Opening Remarks to Press by Head of UN Supervision Mission in Syria," Major General Robert Mood, Damascus, July 19, 2020.

41. Lucky Gold, "Annan Peace Plan Clearly on Life Support, but Not Dead Yet," CNN, May 31, 2012.

42. *Report of an Independent Review on Sexual Exploitation and Abuse by International Peacekeeping Forces in the Central African Republic: "Taking Action on Sexual Exploitation and Abuse by Peacekeepers,"* A/71/99, June 23, 2016, 6.

43. Guehenno, *Fog of Peace*, 286.

44. Clinton, *Hard Choices*, 453.

45. Ian Black and Julian Borger, "Gulf States Warned Against Arming Syria's Rebels," *Guardian*, April 6, 2012.

46. Hill, "Kofi Annan's Multilateral Strategy," 451.

47. McFaul, *From Cold War to Hot Peace*, 335.

48. Charles Glass, "Tell Me How This Ends: America's Muddled Involvement with Syria," *Harpers*, February 26, 2019.

49. Clinton, *Hard Choices*, 455.

50. Clinton, 456–57.

51. Clinton, 457.

52. Colum Lynch and Dan De Luce, "Did the West Really Miss a Chance to End the Syrian War?," *Foreign Policy*, September 15, 2015.

53. Sam Dagher, *Assad or We Burn the Country* (Boston: Little, Brown, 2019), 300.

54. *Final Communique of the Action Group for Syria*, A/66/865-S/2012/522, July 6, 2012.

55. Nick Meo, "Geneva Meeting Agrees Transition Plan to Syria Unity Government," *Telegraph*, June 30, 2012.

56. Clinton, *Hard Choices*, 470.

57. Secretary Clinton press availability dollowing meeting of the Action Group on Syria, Geneva, June 30, 2012.

58. Meo, "Geneva Meeting Agrees Transition Plan."

59. Secretary Clinton press availability, June 30, 2012.

60. Kofi Annan, "My Departing Advice on How to Save Syria," *Financial Times*, August 3, 2012.

61. "Kofi Annan on Syria, Hard Choices for Peacekeeping," NPR, August 27, 2012.

62. Hill, "Kofi Annan's Multilateral Strategy," 463.

63. Hillary Clinton, statement to the Friends of Syria Ministerial Meeting, Paris, July 6, 2012.

64. Scott Stearns, "Clinton Says Assad's Days Are Numbered," Voice of America, July 8, 2012.

65. Karen DeYoung, "Syria Conference Fails to Specify Plan for Assad," *Washington Post*, June 30, 2012.

66. See Jeremy Shapiro, "The Qatar Problem," *Foreign Policy*, August 28, 2018.

67. Ian Black, "Emirati Nerves Rattled by Islamists Rise," *Guardian*, October 12, 2013.

68. "Department of Defense Information Report, Not Finally Evaluated Intelligence—Iraq, 3 July 2012," DoD release, April 10, 2015.

69. "Minutes of Assad-Annan New Truce Deal," *Arab Saga*, July 10, 2012.

70. Michael Hirsh, "The Syria Deal That Could Have Been," *Atlantic*, October 4, 2013.

71. "Syria Rebels Seize Key Iraq Border Crossings," Al Jazeera, July 21, 2012.

72. Neil MacFarquhar, "Details of a Battle Challenge Reports of a Syrian Massacre," *New York Times*, July 14, 2012.

73. Charles R. Lister, *Syrian Jihad: Al-Qaeda, the Islamic State, and the Evolution of an Insurgency* (Oxford: Oxford University Press, 2015), 78; Phillips, *Battle for Syria*, 128.

74. Harriet Allsop, *The Kurds of Syria: Political Parties and Identity in the Middle East* (London: Tauris, 2015), 204ff.

75. Roy Gutman, "How Assad Staged Al-Qaeda Bombings," *Daily Beast*, April 13, 2017.

76. Letter dated July 13, 2012, from the secretary-general to the president of the Security Council, annex, letter from Kofi Annan, S/2012/542, July 13, 2012.

77. Michael Hirsh, "The Syria Deal That Could Have Been," *Atlantic*, October 4, 2013.

78. Hill, "Kofi Annan's Multilateral Strategy."

79. S/PV.6810, July 19, 2012, 9.

80. S/PV.6810, 8–9.

81. Brookings Institution, *A Life in War and Peace: A Statesmen's Forum with Former UN Secretary-General Kofi Annan* (Washington, D.C., October 18, 2012), 20–21.

82. "Press Conference by Joint Special Envoy for Syria," August 2, 2012.

83. "Kofi Annan on Syria, Hard Choices of Peacekeeping," NPR, September 3, 2012.

84. McFaul, *From Cold War to Hot Peace*, 343.

85. Press conference by Joint Special Envoy for Syria, August 2, 2012.

86. A/RES/66/253 B, August 3, 2012.

87. J. Barnes-Dacey, "West Should Give Annan Plan Another Chance," CNN, July 31, 2012.

88. Rick Gladstone, "Annan Steps Down as Peace Envoy and Cites Barriers in Syria and the United Nations," *New York Times*, August 3, 2012.

89. A. D. Miller, "Will Annan Save Assad?," *New York Times*, March 29, 2012.

90. Gowan, "Kofi Annan."

91. Hinnebusch and Zartman, "UN Mediation," 10.

92. Kofi Annan, "My Departing Advice on How to Save Syria."

93. "Kofi Annan on Syria."

4. SYRIAN WINTER

1. *Periodic Update of the Independent International Commission of Inquiry on the Syrian Arab Republic*, December 20, 2012, para. 1.

2. William Harris, *Quicksilver War: Syria, Iraq and the Spiral of Conflict* (London: Hurst, 2018), 31.

3. Charles R. Lister, *Syrian Jihad: Al-Qaeda, the Islamic State, and the Evolution of an Insurgency* (Oxford: Oxford University Press, 2015), 86, 111.

4. Aron Lund, "Meeting Bashar al-Assad," *Hufvudstadsbladet*, November 20, 2016.

5. "Syrian Fighter Jets Bomb Palestinian Camp in Damascus—Activists," *Reuters*, December 16, 2012.

6. Jonathan Steele, "How Yarmouk Refugee Camp Became the Worst Place in Syria," *Guardian*, March 5, 2015.

7. Harris, *Quicksilver War*, 36.

8. See Martin Chulov, "War for Aleppo: Battle Rages in City That Will Determine Fate of Syria," *Guardian*, August 4, 2012.

9. Lister, *Syrian Jihad*, 86–87.

10. Paul Danahar, *The New Middle East: The World After the Arab Spring* (London: Bloomsbury, 2015), 396.

11. Lister, *Syrian Jihad*, 84.

12. Robin Yassin-Kassab and Leila Al-Shami, *Burning Country: Syrians in Revolution and War* (London: Pluto, 2016), 96.

13. "Terrorist Designation of the al-Nusrah Front as an Alias of al Qa'ida in Iraq," U.S. Department of State, December 11, 2012.

14. Michael Weiss and Hassan Hassan, *ISIS: Inside the Army of Terror* (New York: Regan Arts, 2015), 145.

15. Nickolaos Van Dam, *Destroying a Nation: The Civil War in Syria* (New York: Tauris, 2017), 98.

16. Danahar, *The New Middle East*, 391.

17. Roula Khalaf and Abigail Fielding-Smith, "How Qatar Seized Control of the Syrian Revolution," *Financial Times*, May 17, 2013.

18. Borzou Daragahi, "Libya Helps Bankroll Syria's Opposition," *Financial Times*, November 5, 2012.

19. Kristian Coates Ulrichsen, "Qatar and the Arab Spring: Policy Drivers and Regional Implications," Carnegie Endowment for International Peace, September 2014, 137.

20. Lister, *Syrian Jihad*, 106.

21. Daniel Byman, "Sectarianism Afflicts the New Middle East," *Survival* 56, no. 1 (2014): 79–100.

22. Rania Abouzeid, "Syria's Secular and Islamist Rebels: Who Are the Saudis and Qataris Arming?," *Time*, September 18, 2012.

23. Eric Schmitt, "C.I.A. Said to Aid in Steering Arms to Syrian Opposition," *New York Times*, June 21, 2012.

24. Samer N. Abboud, *Syria* (Cambridge: Polity, 2015), 133.

25. Nuh Yilmaz, "Syria: The View from Turkey," European Council on Foreign Relations, 19 June 2013.

26. "Widespread Middle East Fears That Syria Violence Will Spread," Pew Research Center, May 1, 2013, 3

27. Hannah Lucinda Smith, *Erdogan Rising: The Battle for the Soul of Turkey* (London: Collins, 2019), 185.

28. Abboud, *Syria*, 91.

29. Interview with Moaz al-Khatib, Al Jazeera, May 11, 2013.

30. Idea from Alex de Waal, *The Real Politics of the Horn of Africa: Money, War, and the Business of Power* (Cambridge: Polity, 2015).

31. Abboud, *Syria*, 91, xx.

32. Yassin-Kassab and Al-Shami, *Burning Country*, 86.

33. Khalaf and Fielding-Smith, "How Qatar Seized Control"; Emile Hokayem, *Syrian Uprising and the Fracturing of the Levant* (London: Routledge, 2013), 75.

34. Harriet Allsopp, *The Kurds of Syria* (London: Tauris, 2015), 201.

35. Allsopp, 218.

36. Allsopp, 198–207.

37. "Turkey Probes Possible Iran Link in Bombing Near Syria," *Haaretz*, August 23, 2012.

38. "Syrian Opposition Plans Fall Apart on Eve of Doha Conference," *Telegraph*, November 7, 2012.

39. Robert Ford, Twitter, December 10, 2018.

40. Christopher Phillips, *The Battle for Syria: International Rivalry in the New Middle East* (New Haven, Conn.: Yale University Press, 2016), 115.

41. Aron Lund, "How Assad's Enemies Gave Up on Syria's Opposition," *Century Foundation*, October 17, 2017.

42. "Syria: France Backs Anti-Assad Coalition," BBC News, November 13, 2012.

43. Daragahi, "Libya Helps Bankroll Syria's Opposition."

44. Josh Rogin, "Obama Administration Works to Establish New Syrian Opposition Council," *Foreign Policy*, October 30, 2012.

45. Regan Doherty and Amena Bakr, "Exclusive: Secret Turkish Nerve Center Leads Aid to Syria Rebels," Reuters, July 27, 2012.

46. Charles Glass, "Tell Me How This Ends: America's Muddled Involvement with Syria," *Harpers*, February 26, 2019.

47. Danahar, *The New Middle East*, 397.

48. Glass, "Tell Me How This Ends."

49. Michael Mazzetti, Robert F. Worth, and Michael R. Gordon, "Obama's Uncertain Path Amid Syria Bloodshed," *New York Times*, October 23, 2013, A2.

50. Josh Rogin, "Debate Over Syria Intervention Takes Shape," *Foreign Policy*, March 7, 2012.

51. "Syrian Military Says It Downed Turkish Fighter Jet," BBC News, 23 June 2012.

52. Hillary Rodham Clinton, *Hard Choices* (New York: Simon and Schuster, 2014), 463.

53. Sam Dagher, *Assad or We Burn the Country* (Boston: Little, Brown, 2019), 328.

54. Adam Entous, "Inside Obama's Syria Debate," *Wall Street Journal*, 30 March 2013.

55. Mona Yacoubian, "Critical Junctures in United States Policy Towards Syria: An Assessment of the Counterfactuals," U.S. Holocaust Memorial Museum, August 2017, 30.

56. Yacoubian, 30.

57. Nada Bakos, "Humility Now! The Miseducation of Jackson Diehl," *Foreign Policy*, April 2, 2013.

58. Nina Burleigh, "Obama vs. the Hawks," *Rolling Stone*, April 1, 2014.

59. Douglas Ernst, "Obama Staunchly Defends Syria Policy, Blasts Critics 'Magical Thinking,'" *Washington Times*, January 21, 2014.

60. Michael Mazzetti, Robert F. Worth, and Michael R. Gordon, "Obama's Uncertain Path Amid Syria Bloodshed," *New York Times*, October 23, 2013.

61. Ben Rhodes, *The World as It Is: A Memoir of the Obama White House* (New York: Random House, 2018), 197–98.

62. David Remnick, "Going the Distance: On and Off the Road with Barack Obama," *New Yorker*, January 27, 2014.

63. Lister, *Syrian Jihad*, 390.

64. Josh Rogin, "Exclusive: Obama Told Lawmakers Criticism of His Syria policy Is Horsesh*t," *Daily Beast*, August 11, 2014.

65. Thomas L. Friedman, "Obama on the World," *New York Times*, August 8, 2014.
66. Phillips, *Syria*, 145.
67. Larry Luxner, "Ford Doesn't Mince Words About US Failures in Syria," *Washington Diplomat*, October 1, 2014.
68. Yacoubian, "Critical Junctures," 31.
69. Doucet, "Brahimi Has 'No Illusions.'"
70. Kareem Fahim, "New International Envoy, Meeting with Syria's President, Says Crisis Is Worsening," *New York Times*, September 15, 2012.
71. Marwa Awad, "Egypt to Host Regional Meeting Over Syria Crisis," *Reuters*, September 10, 2012.
72. Tom Perry, "Morsi Cuts Egypt's Syria ties, Calls for a No-Fly Zone," *Reuters*, June 16, 2013.
73. Marwan Makdesi, "Assad Tells Syria Envoy Arms Flow to Rebels Must Stop," *Reuters*, October 21, 2012.
74. Danahar, *The New Middle East*, 397.
75. "UN's Syria Envoy Seeks China's 'Active Role,'" Al Jazeera, October 31, 2012.
76. "Speech and Answers of S. V. Lavrov, the Minister of Foreign Affairs of the Russian Federation, Cairo, November 4, 2012," Moscow, Foreign Ministry of Russia.
77. Raymond Hinnebusch and I. William Zartman, "UN Mediation in the Syrian Crisis: From Kofi Annan to Lakhdar Brahimi," International Peace Institute, March 2016, 14.
78. *Report of the Independent International Commission of Inquiry on the Syrian Arab Republic*, A/HRC/22/59, February 5, 2013, paras. 46–47, 121, and summary.
79. A/HRC/22/59 paras. 49, 71, 72, 127, and 129.
80. Erika Solomon and Peter Graff, "UN Envoy Says 40 Years of Assad Family Rule Is 'Too Long,'" *Reuters*, January 9, 2013.
81. Louisa Loveluck and Zakaria Zakaria, "The Hospitals Were Slaughterhouses: A Journey Into Syria's Secret Torture Wards," *Washington Post*, April 2, 2017.
82. Ian Black, "Bashar al-Assad Calls on Foreign Countries to End Support for Rebels," *Guardian*, January 6, 2013.
83. Tom Perry and Erika Solomon, "UN Envoy Says Assad Can't Be in Syrian Transition," *Reuters*, January 10, 2013.
84. Hokayem, *Syria's Uprising*, 77.
85. Dominic Evans, "Syria Accuses UN Envoy Brahimi of Interfering," *Reuters*, April 25, 2013.
86. "Opposition Leader Says Could Hold Talks Outside Syria," *Reuters*, January 31, 2013.
87. Interview with Moaz al-Khatib, Al Jazeera, May 11, 2013.
88. Phil Sands, "Syrian Opposition to Establish Moderate Form of Islamic Law," *National*, April 18, 2013.
89. Hokayem, *Syria's Uprising*, 77.
90. Interview with Moaz al-Khatib, Al Jazeera, May 11, 2013.
91. Ulrichsen, "Qatar and the Arab Spring," 141.

92. Glass, "Tell Me How This Ends."
93. Interview with Moaz al-Khatib, Al Jazeera, May 11, 2013.
94. Lister, *Syrian Jihad*, 120.
95. Danahar, *New Middle East*, 376.
96. Danahar, 377.
97. Marisa Sullivan, "Hezbollah in Syria," Institute for the Study of War, April 2014.
98. "Burgas Bomb: Bulgaria Names Anti-Israeli Bomber," BBC News, July 18, 2014. Also Trita Parsi, *Losing an Enemy: Obama, Iran, and the Triumph of Diplomacy* (New Haven, Conn.: Yale University Press, 2017), 128.
99. Weiss and Hassan, *ISIS*, 134.
100. Lister, *Syrian Jihad*, 128.
101. *Report of the Independent International Inquiry on the Syrian Arab Republic*, A/HRC/24/46, August 16, 2013, para. 10.
102. "Iran Spending $6 Bln Annually to Support Assad Regime: Report," Al Arabiya, June 10, 2015.
103. "March Was the Bloodiest Month in Syria: Rights Group," *Reuters*, April 1, 2013.
104. Guillaume Lavallee, "Syrian Rebels Seize 21 Filipino Peacekeepers," *AFP*, March 6, 2013.
105. Lister, *Syrian Jihad*, 114.
106. Jessica Stern and J. M. Berger, *ISIS: The State of Terror* (New York: Harper Collins, 2015), 42.
107. Weiss and Hassan, *ISIS*, 147ff.
108. Dominic Evans, "Syria Accuses UN Envoy Brahimi of Interfering," *Reuters*, April 25, 2013.
109. Danahar, *The New Middle East*, 405.
110. "G8 Leaders Close to an Agreement on Syria," BBC, June 18, 2013.
111. Final communiqué of the 2013 Lough Erne G8 Leaders Summit, Lough Erne, UK, June 18, 2013.

5. RED LINE

1. Remarks by the president to the White House Press Corps, August 20, 2012.
2. Helene Cooper, "Washington Begins to Plan for Collapse of Syrian Government," *New York Times*, July 18, 2012.
3. Andrea Shalal-Esa, "Sixth US Ship in the Eastern Mediterranean 'as Precaution,'" *Reuters*, August 31, 2018.
4. Ian Black, "Syria Insists Chemical Weapons Would Be Used Only Against Outsiders," *Guardian*, July 24, 2012.
5. Alister Bull and Jeff Mason, "Obama: Assad Will Be Held Accountable If Uses Chemical Weapons," *Reuters*, July 24, 2012.
6. "Allegations of Use of Chemical Weapons in Syria Since 2012," Foreign Ministry of France.

7. Alistair Dawber, "Chemical Weapons Were Used on Homs: Syria's Military Police Defector Tells of Nerve Gas Attack," *Independent*, December 26, 2012.

8. Robin Yassin-Kassab and Leila Al-Shami, *Burning Country: Syrians in Revolution and War* (London: Pluto, 2016), 104–5.

9. Simon Tisdall and Josie Le Blond, "Assad Did Not Order Chemical Weapons Attack, Says German Press," *Guardian*, September 9, 2013.

10. *United Nations Mission to Investigate Allegations of the Use of Chemical Weapons in the Syrian Arab Republic*, Final Report, December 12, 2013.

11. Interview with British Foreign Office official, November 2016; U.S. Department of Defense, transcript of media availability with Secretary Chuck Hagel, Abu Dhabi, April 25, 2013.

12. *United Nations Mission to Investigate Allegations of the Use of Chemical Weapons.*

13. Gwyn Winfield, "Interview with Ake Sellstrom," CBRNe World, January 30, 2014.

14. Susan Rice, *Tough Love: My Story of the Things Worth Fighting For* (New York: Simon and Schuster, 2019), 350.

15. Charles Glass, "Tell Me How This Ends: America's Muddled Involvement with Syria," *Harpers*, February 26, 2019.

16. Ewen MacAskill. "Obama and Romney Clash Over Foreign Policy in Final Presidential Debate," *Guardian*, October 23, 2012.

17. Hannah Lucinda Smith, *Erdogan Rising: The Battle for the Soul of Turkey* (London: Collins, 2019), 114.

18. Samantha Power, *The Education of an Idealist* (New York: HarperCollins, 2019), 363.

19. John Kerry, *Every Day Is Extra* (New York: Simon and Schuster, 2018), 526.

20. Mark Mazzetti, Adam Goldman, and Michael S. Schmidt, "Behind the Sudden Death of a $1 Billion Secret CIA War in Syria," *New York Times*, August 2, 2017.

21. Kerry, *Every Day Is Extra*, 528.

22. Mark Mazzetti, Michael R. Gordon, and Mark Landler, "US Is Said to Plan to Send Arms to Syrian Rebels," *New York Times*, June 13, 2013.

23. Power, *Education of an Idealist*, 364.

24. Mazzetti, Gordon, and Landler, "US Is Said to Plan to Send Arms to Syrian Rebels."

25. "Government Assessment of the Syrian Government's Use of Chemical Weapons on 21 August 2013," White House, August 30, 2013.

26. Power, *Education of an Idealist*, 365.

27. "Government Assessment of the Syrian Government's Use of Chemical Weapons."

28. Nina Burleigh, "Obama vs. the Hawks," *Rolling Stone*, April 1, 2014.

29. Burleigh, "Obama vs. the Hawks."

30. Power, *Education of an Idealist*, 365–66.

31. Kerry, *Every Day Is Extra*, 526–27.

32. Joint Intelligence Committee, "Syria: Reported Chemical Weapons Use," August 29, 2013.

33. Tim Ross and Ben Farmer, "Navy Ready to Launch First Strike on Syria," *Telegraph*, August 25, 2013.
34. Sam Dagher, *Assad or We Burn the Country* (Boston: Little, Brown, 2019), 381.
35. Kerry, *Every Day Is Extra*, 530.
36. Colum Lynch, "Saudis to Push General Assembly Vote on Syria Intervention," *Foreign Affairs*, September 6, 2013.
37. Cited in Thomas G. Weiss, David Forsythe, Roger A. Coate, and Kelly Kay Pease, *The United Nations in a Changing World*, 8th ed. (London: Routledge, 2018)
38. Kimberly Dozier and Matt Apuzzo, "AP Sources: Intelligence on Weapons No 'Slam Dunk,'" *Associated Press*, August 29, 2013.
39. Power, *Education of an Idealist*, 368–69.
40. Trita Parsi, *Losing an Enemy: Obama, Iran, and the Triumph of Diplomacy* (New Haven, Conn.: Yale University Press, 2017), 197–225.
41. Rice, *Tough Love*, 363, 364.
42. Burleigh, "Obama vs. the Hawks."
43. Power, *Education of an Idealist*, 373.
44. Adam Entous, Sam Dagher, and Siobhan Gorman, "US Allies Prepare to Act as Syria Intelligence Mounts," *Wall Street Journal*, August 28, 2013.
45. UN Mission to Investigate Allegations of the Use of Chemical Weapons in the Syrian Arab Republic, *Report on Allegations of the Use of Chemical Weapons in the Ghouta Area of Damascus on 21 August 2013*, September 13, 2013, paras. 27–28.
46. *Report of the Independent International Commission on Inquiry on the Syrian Arab Republic*, A/HRC/25/65, February 12, 2014, para. 128.
47. Power, *Education of an Idealist*, 373.
48. Rice, *Tough Love*, 363.
49. Glass, "Tell Me How This Ends."
50. Shaun Ley, "How Did the Government Allow a Defeat Over Syria to Happen?," BBC, November 10, 2014.
51. Oz Katerji, "If Jeremy Corbyn Opposes Intervention in Syria, He Should Have More to Say About Russia," *New Statesman*, April 20, 2018.
52. Government Motion, "Syria and the Use of Chemical Weapons," House of Commons, August 29, 2013.
53. Adam Withnall, "Government Sources Say Ed Miliband Is 'a Copper-Bottomed S***' Who 'Changed His Mind' on Syria," *Independent*, August 29, 2013.
54. "Chemical Weapons Used by Syrian Regime: UK Government Legal Position," Prime Minister's Office, 10 Downing Street, August 29, 2013.
55. Opposition manuscript amendment to motion no. 2, House of Commons, August 29, 2013.
56. James Forsyth, "Syria Vote? What Syria Vote? David Cameron's Strategy Is to Forget It Ever Happened," *Spectator*, September 7, 2013.
57. Kerry, *Every Day Is Extra*, 531.
58. Dagher, *Assad or We Burn the Country*, 382.
59. Burleigh, "Obama vs. the Hawks."

60. Rice, *Tough Love*, 363.
61. Burleigh, "Obama vs. the Hawks."
62. Kerry, *Every Day Is Extra*, 529.
63. Ramsey Cox, "Reid Files Resolution to Authorize Force Against Syria," *Hill*, September 6, 2013.
64. "Syria Joint Resolution Side-by-Side," Senate Foreign Relations Committee, September 3, 2013.
65. "The Hill's Syria Whip List: Obama Seeks to Turn Tide with House, Public," *Hill*, September 9, 2013, and Wilson Andrews, Aaron Blake, and Daria Cameron, "Where the Votes Stand on Syria," *Washington Post*, September 13, 2013.
66. "Will Congress Authorize a Strike on Syria?," *Huffington Post*, September 4, 2013.
67. "Public Opinion Runs Against Syrian Air Strikes," Pew Research Center, September 3, 2013.
68. Power, *Education of an Idealist*, 382.
69. Darlene Superville, "Americans Protest Military Action Against Syria," *Star*, September 7, 2013.
70. Allie Jones, "Obama Arrives at G20, Gives Putin 'Death Stare,'" *Atlantic*, September 5, 2013.
71. Dagher, *Assad or We Burn the Country*, 386–87.
72. Burleigh, "Obama vs. the Hawks."
73. Danahar, *The New Middle East*, 404; Hillary Rodham Clinton, *Hard Choices* (New York: Simon and Schuster, 2014), 467.
74. Security Council Resolution 2118, September 27, 2013.
75. S/PV.7038, September 27, 2013.
76. Derek Chollet, "Obama's Red Line Revisited," *Politico*, July 19, 2016.
77. David Remnick, "Going the Distance: On and Off the Road with Barack Obama," *New Yorker*, January 27, 2014.
78. Cited by Burleigh, "Obama vs. the Hawks."
79. Anthony Deutsch, "Special Report: How Syria Continued to Gas Its People as the World Looked on," *Reuters*, August 17, 2017.
80. OPCW, *Third Report of the OPCW Fact-Finding Mission in Syria*, December 18, 2014, para. 5.59.
81. Krishnadev Calamur, "Syria Is Now in Charge of the UN's Disarmament Efforts. Really," *Atlantic*, May 29, 2018.
82. Christopher Phillips, *The Battle for Syria: International Rivalry in the New Middle East* (New Haven, Conn.: Yale University Press, 2016), 171.
83. Charles R. Lister, *Syrian Jihad: Al-Qaeda, the Islamic State, and the Evolution of an Insurgency* (Oxford: Oxford University Press, 2015), 164.
84. Smith, *Erdogan Rising*, 111.
85. David Kenner, "Saudi Arabia's Shadow War," *Foreign Policy*, November 8, 2013.
86. Jamie Dettmer, "Syria's Saudi Jihadist Problem," *Daily Beast*, December 16, 2013.
87. Smith, *Erdogan Rising*, 105.

88. Ahmet S. Yayla and Colin P. Clarke, "Turkey's Double ISIS Standard," *Foreign Policy*, April 12, 2018.

89. Kerry, *Every Day Is Extra*, 541.

90. Jesse Byrnes, "Ex-Pentagon Chief Hagel: White House 'Tried to Destroy Me,'" *Hill*, December 18, 2015.

91. Dagher, *Assad or We Burn the Country*, 389.

6. DEATH AND DIPLOMACY

1. S/PV.7038, September 27, 2013, 3.

2. "London 11 Meeting on Syria," Foreign and Commonwealth Office press release, London, October 22, 2013.

3. Ian Black, "Syrian Rebels Urged to Take Part in Geneva II Peace Conference," *Guardian*, October 23. 2013.

4. Susan Rice, *Tough Love: My Story of the Things Worth Fighting For* (New York: Simon and Schuster, 2019), 368.

5. John Kerry, *Every Day Is Extra* (New York: Simon and Schuster, 2018), 542.

6. "Syria National Council Rejects Peace Talks," BBC, October 13, 2013.

7. "Lakhdar Brahimi Urges Syria's Warring Parties to Talk Without Preconditions," RFI, October 6, 2013.

8. Charles R. Lister, *Syrian Jihad: Al-Qaeda, the Islamic State, and the Evolution of an Insurgency* (Oxford: Oxford University Press, 2015), 173.

9. Cited by Lister, 173.

10. "Syria's Opposition Agrees to Geneva Peace Talks," *Telegraph*, November 11, 2013.

11. "UN Envoy to Syria: No Talks Without Opposition," *Times of Israel*, November 1, 2013.

12. Susanne Koelbl, "Syria Will Become Another Somalia: Interview with UN Peace Envoy Brahimi," *Der Spiegel International*, June 7, 2014.

13. Robert F. Worth, "Saudi Arabia Rejects UN Security Council Seat in Protest Move," *New York Times*, October 18, 2013.

14. S/PRST/2013/15.

15. *Assault on Medical Care in Syria*, report to the Human Rights Council, A/HRC/24/CRP.2, September 13, 2013.

16. "Syria Rebels Meet on Possible Peace Talks," Voice of America, November 9, 2013; "Boosted by Foreign Shi'ite Militia, Assad's Forces Advance on Aleppo," *Reuters*, November 13, 2013.

17. "Barrel Bombs Kill 517 in Aleppo Since 15 December," BBC News, December 29, 2013.

18. Asli S. Okyay, "Turkey's Post-2011 Approach to Its Syrian Border and Its Implications for Domestic Politics," *International Affairs* 93, no. 4 (2017): 829–46.

19. Human Rights Watch, *"You Can Still See Their Blood": Executions, Indiscriminate Shootings, and Hostage Taking by Opposition Forces in Latakia Countryside*, October 10, 2013.

20. Joshua Hersh, "The Lessons of Atmeh," *Virginia Quarterly Review*, Fall 2014.

21. T. Hamid al-Bayati, *A New Counterterrorism Strategy: Why the World Failed to Stop Al Qaeda and ISIS/ISIL and How to Defeat Terrorists* (Westport, Conn.: Praeger, 2017), 173.

22. Counter Extremism Project, *ISIS's Persecution of Religions*, New York, 2017, 10.

23. Loveday Morris, "Seven Syrian Islamist Groups Form New Islamic Front," *Washington Post*, November 22, 2013.

24. Ian Traynor, "Germany Fears Return of European Jihadists in Syria," *Guardian*, May 17, 2013.

25. EUROPOL, *EU Terrorism and Situation Trend Report*, 2013, 22.

26. Lorenzo Vidino, "European Foreign Fighters in Syria: Dynamics and Responses," *European View* 13 (2014): 217–24.

27. Nikolaos Van Dam, *Destroying a Nation: The Civil War in Syria* (New York: Tauris, 2017), 98–99.

28. Sam Dagher, *Assad or We Burn the Country* (Boston: Little, Brown, 2019), 391.

29. Mike Giglio, *Shatter the Nations: ISIS and the War for the Caliphate* (New York: Public Affairs, 2019), 36.

30. "US and UK Suspend Non-lethal Aid for Syria Rebels," BBC News, December 11, 2013.

31. "Gulf Ambassadors Pulled from Qatar Over 'Interference,'" BBC News, March 5, 2014.

32. Ruth Sherlock, "US Secretly Backs Rebels to Fight al-Qaeda in Syria," *Telegraph*, January 21, 2014.

33. "Syria: Soaring Number of Executions in Violation of International Law: Pillay," UN Office of the High Commissioner for Human Rights, January 16, 2014.

34. Michael Weiss and Hassan Hassan, *ISIS: Inside the Army of Terror* (New York: Regan Arts, 2015), 155.

35. Alexander Griffing, "How Assad Helped to Create ISIS to Win in Syria and Got Away with the Crime of the Century," *Haaretz*, October 7, 2018.

36. "Hundreds Killed as ISIL Insurgents Gain Ground in East Syria," *Reuters*, June 10, 2014.

37. Lister, *Syrian Jihad*, 206.

38. William Harris, *Quicksilver War: Syria, Iraq and the Spiral of Conflict* (London: Hurst, 2018), 49.

39. Lister, *Syrian Jihad*, 200.

40. "Turkey Downs Syria Military Jet in Airspace Violation," BBC, March 23, 2014.

41. Nick Cumming-Bruce, "UN Seeks Record Sum for Humanitarian Aid in 2014," *New York Times*, December 16, 2013.

42. "UN Implicates Bashar al-Assad in Syria War Crimes," *BBC*, December 2, 2013.

43. "Without a Trace: Enforced Disappearances in Syria," Thematic Report of the Independent International Commission of Inquiry on the Syrian Arab Republic, December 13, 2013.

44. Nick Cumming-Bruce, "UN Seeks Record Sum for Humanitarian Aid in 2014," *New York Times*, December 16, 2013.

45. Author's interviews.

46. Karen DeYoung, "Kerry Reassures Saudis, Says US Will Step Up Its Consultations with the Region," *Washington Post*, November 4, 2013.

47. Trita Parsi, *Losing an Enemy: Obama, Iran, and the Triumph of Diplomacy* (New Haven, Conn.: Yale University Press, 2017), 256; William J. Burns, *The Back Channel: A Memoir of American Diplomacy and the Case for Its Renewal* (New York: Random House, 2019), 295.

48. Matthew Weaver, "Syrian Civil War Peace Talks at Risk as Iran Accepts Invitation," *Guardian*, January 21, 2014.

49. Parsi, *Losing an Enemy*, 256.

50. Kim Sengupta, "Syria Peace Talks: Geneva II Is the Only Hope for Syria—and Iran Should Have Been Part of It," *Independent*, January 20, 2014.

51. "Iran Leader: Free Elections the Best Solution for Syria," Al Jazeera, January 23, 2014.

52. Cited by Ian Black, "Syria Peace Talks: War of Words Over Bashar al-Assad's Future," *Guardian*, January 23, 2014.

53. Kerry, *Every Day Is Extra*, 542.

54. Susanne Koelbl, "Syria Will Become Another Somalia: Interview with UN Peace Envoy Brahimi," *Der Spiegel International*, June 7, 2014.

55. Kim Sengupta, "Syria Peace Talks: John Kerry Leads Calls for Removal of President Bashar al-Assad," *Independent*, January 22, 2014.

56. Dagher, *Assad or We Burn the Country*, 399.

57. Ian Black, "Syria's Foreign Minister Threatens to Walk Out of Peace Talks," *Guardian*, January 24, 2014; Kim Sengupta, "Syria Geneva II Talks: The Long Road to Peace," *Independent*, January 25, 2014.

58. Anne Barnard, "Syria's Shaky Peace Talks Move Toward Solid Ground," *New York Times*, January 26, 2014.

59. James Bays, "Syria Peace Talks Struggle in Switzerland," Al Jazeera, January 29, 2014.

60. "UN Mediated Peace Talks Resume as Aid Lifeline to Homs Extended for Three Days," *UN News*, February 10, 2014.

61. Dagher, *Assad or We Burn the Country*, 399.

62. "UN Mediated Peace Talks Resume."

63. "Syria Peace Talks Break Up as UN Envoy Fails to End Deadlock," *Guardian*, February 16, 2014.

64. Dagher, *Assad or We Burn the Country*, 400.

65. Laura Smith-Spark and Michael Martinez, "Little Progress Made as Syria Peace Talks Close in Switzerland," CNN, February 17, 2014.

66. Christopher Phillips, *Battle for Syria: International Rivalry in the New Middle East* (New Haven, Conn.: Yale University Press, 2016), 190.

67. Raymond Hinnebusch and I. William Zartman, "UN Mediation in the Syrian Crisis: From Kofi Annan to Lakhdar Brahimi," International Peace Institute, March 2016," 17.

68. Ghassan Charbel, "Interview with Lakhdar Brahimi," *al-Hayat*, June 25, 2014.

69. "Syria Peace Talks Break Up."

70. George Baghdadi, "Syria Peace Talks in Geneva End in Failure," CBS News, February 14, 2014.

71. "Iran Daily, Mar 17: UN's Brahimi Holds Syria Talks in Tehran," *EA Worldview*, March 18, 2014.

72. Gwynne Dyer, "The Russians Were Right About Syria and Bashar al-Assad," *Sydney Morning Herald*, May 17, 2016.

73. Harris, *Quicksilver War*, 36.

74. Michael Pizzi, "Syria Announces June Election with Assad's Victory All but Certain," Al Jazeera, April 21, 2014.

75. Liz Sly, "Syrian Rebels Who Received First US Missiles of War See Shipment as 'an Important First Step,'" *Washington Post*, April 27, 2014.

76. Deborah Amos, "After a Long Wait, Syria Rebels Hope the Weapons Will Now Flow," *National Public Radio*, September 17, 2014.

77. S/PV.7116, February 22, 2014, 7.

78. *Report of the Independent International Commission of Inquiry on the Syrian Arab Republic*, A/HRC/25/15, February 12, 2014; Office of the UN High Commissioner for Human Rights, *Living Under Siege: The Syrian Arab Republic*, Geneva, February 2014.

79. Garance le Caisne, *Operation Caesar: At the Heart of the Syrian Death Machine* (London: Polity, 2018), 3.

80. *Report Into the Credibility of Certain Evidence with Regard to Torture and Execution of Persons Incarcerated by the Current Syrian Regime*, prepared for Carter-Ruck and Co. 2014.

81. Louis Charbonneau, "UN Security Council Members View Graphic Photos of Syria Dead," *Reuters*, April 16, 2014.

82. Letter dated January 14, 2013, from the chargé d'affaires a.i. of the Permanent Mission of Switzerland to the United Nations addressed to the secretary-general, A/67/694-S/2013/19, January 16, 2013.

83. S/PV.7180, May 22, 2014, 12–13.

84. "Syria: Door Remains Wide Open for Further Atrocities After Lack of Referral to the ICC, UN Experts Warn," Office of the High Commissioner on Human Rights, Geneva, May 30, 2014.

85. Dagher, *Assad or We Burn the Country*, 400.

7. RISE OF THE CALIPHATE

1. Sam Dagher, *Assad or We Burn the Country* (Boston: Little, Brown, 2019), 374.
2. Jessica Stern and J. M. Berger, *ISIS: The State of Terror* (London: Collins, 2015), 3–4.
3. David Remnick, "Going the Distance: On and Off the Road with Barack Obama," *New Yorker*, January 17, 2014.
4. Colin P. Clarke, *After the Caliphate* (Cambridge: Polity, 2019), 32ff.
5. Nada Bakos, "Humility Now! The Miseducation of Jackson Diehl," *Foreign Policy*, April 2, 2013.
6. Michael Weiss and Hassan Hassan, *ISIS: Inside the Army of Terror* (New York: Regan Arts, 2015), 31.
7. Weiss and Hassan, 28–33.
8. Peter R. Mansoor, *Surge: My Journey with General David Petraeus and the Remaking of the Iraq War* (New Haven, Conn.: Yale University Press, 2013), 120–47.
9. "Minority Targeted in Iraq Bombings," BBC, August 15, 2007.
10. Weiss and Hassan, *ISIS*, 78–81; Charles R. Lister, *Syrian Jihad: Al-Qaeda, the Islamic State, and the Evolution of an Insurgency* (Oxford: Oxford University Press, 2015), 269.
11. Emma Sky, *The Unravelling: High Hopes and Missed Opportunities in Iraq* (New York: Public Affairs, 2016), 334.
12. Jessica Stern and J. M. Berger, *ISIS: State of Terror* (New York: Harper Collins, 2015), 39.
13. Lister, *Syrian Jihad*, 271.
14. Marc Lynch, *The New Arab Wars: Uprising and Anarchy in the Middle East* (New York: Public Affairs, 2016), 162–63.
15. Maria Tsvetkova, "How Russia Allowed Homegrown Radicals to Go and Fight in Syria," *Reuters*, May 13, 2016.
16. "Iraq: ISIS Executed Hundreds of Prison Inmates," Human Rights Watch, Erbil, October 30, 2014.
17. Tim Arango, "Escaping Death in Northern Iraq," *New York Times*, September 3, 2014.
18. "Iraqi Court Sentences 24 to Death Over Speicher Massacre," *Middle East Monitor*, July 9, 2015.
19. Mark Tran and Matthew Weaver, "ISIS Announces Islamic Caliphate in Area Straddling Iraq and Syria," *Guardian*, June 30, 2014.
20. Fazel Hawramy and Peter Beaumont, "Iraqi Kurdish Forces Take Kirkuk as Isis Sets Its Sites on Baghdad," *Guardian*, June 12, 2014.
21. William Harris, *Quicksilver War: Syria, Iraq and the Spiral of Conflict* (London: Hurst, 2018), 50.
22. Lister, *Syrian Jihad*, 216.
23. "Islamic State Seizes Main Syrian Oil Fields," Al Jazeera, July 4, 2014.

24. Michelle Nichols, "UN Rights Inquiry Says More Syrians Joining Islamic State," July 26, 2014.

25. Liz Sly, "Syrian Tribal Revolt Against Islamic State Ignored, Fueling Resentment," *Washington Post*, October 20, 2014.

26. Weiss and Hassan, *ISIS*, 158.

27. Lister, *Syrian Jihad*, 245.

28. Anne Barnard, "Blamed for Rise of ISIS, Syrian Leader Is Pushed to Escalate Fight," *New York Times*, August 22, 2014.

29. "Brussels Jewish Museum Killings: Suspect 'Admitted Attack,' " BBC News, June 1, 2014.

30. Lister, *Syrian Jihad*, 244.

31. Aaron Lund, "The Revolutionary Command Council: Rebel Unity in Syria?," Carnegie Middle East Center, December 1, 2014.

32. Samantha Power, *Education of an Idealist* (New York: HarperCollins, 2019), 510.

33. Weiss and Hassan, *ISIS*, xv.

34. John Kerry, *Every Day Is Extra* (New York: Simon and Schuster, 2018), 543.

35. Susan Rice, *Tough Love: My Story of the Things Worth Fighting For* (New York: Simon and Schuster, 2019), 418.

36. Paul Lewis, Spencer Ackerman, and Saeed Kemali Dehghan, "Iraq Crisis: Barack Obama Sends in US Troops as ISIS Insurgency Worsens," *Guardian*, June 17, 2014.

37. Trita Parsi, *Losing an Enemy: Obama, Iran, and the Triumph of Diplomacy* (New Haven, Conn.: Yale University Press, 2017), 257.

38. Fred Weir, "Russia to the Rescue in Iraq? Moscow Delivers Jet Fighters to Baghdad," *Christian Science Monitor*, June 30, 2014.

39. Nadia Murad, *The Last Girl: My Story of Captivity and My Fight Against the Islamic State* (London: Little, Brown, 2018); Patrick Desbois, *The Terrorist Factory: ISIS, the Yazidi Genocide, and Exporting Terror* (New York: Simon and Schuster, 2018).

40. Loveday Morris, "Iraqi Yazidis Stranded on Isolated Mountaintop Begin to Die of Thirst," *Washington Post*, August 5, 2014.

41. Kerry, *Every Day Is Extra*, 545.

42. Power, *Education of an Idealist*, 511–12.

43. "Support for US Campaign Against ISIS: Doubts About Its Effectiveness, Objectives," Pew Research Center, October 22, 2014.

44. Shibley Talhami, "American Public Attitudes Towards Syria and ISIS," Brookings Institution, January 8, 2015.

45. Kerry, *Every Day Is Extra*, 545.

46. See Spencer Ackerman, "Obama's Legal Rationale for ISIS Strikes," *Guardian*, September 11, 2014.

47. Kerry, *Every Day Is Extra*, 546.

48. Kerry, 547.

49. Michael Crowley, "Kerry Enlists Saudi King in War of Ideas Against ISIS," *Time*, 15 September 2014.

50. "10 Arab States Agree to Join US Led Military Campaign Against Islamic State," *Jerusalem Post*, September 10, 2014.

51. Andrew Sparrow, "UK Parliament Approves Air Strikes Against ISIS in Iraq," September 17, 2014.

52. Joel Rogers de Waal, "Report on British Attitudes to Defence, Security, and the Armed Forces," *YouGov*, October 25, 2014.

53. Stern and Berger, *ISIS*, 48.

54. James Harkin, *Hunting Season: The Execution of James Foley, Islamic State, and the Real Story of a Kidnapping Campaign That Started a War* (New York: Little Brown, 2015).

55. Harris, *Quicksilver War*, 50.

56. Martin Chulov, "Islamic State Militants Seize Syrian Airbase," *Guardian*, August 25, 2014.

57. See "Syrian Rebels Surround Filipino UN Peacekeepers in Golan Heights," *Guardian*, August 29, 2014.

58. Lister, *Syrian Jihad*, 285.

59. Ben Rhodes, *The World as It Is: A Memoir of the Obama White House* (New York: Random House, 2018), 312.

60. Weiss and Hassan, *ISIS*, 245.

61. Lister, *Syrian Jihad*, 218.

62. Martin Chulov, Spencer Ackerman, and Paul Lewis, "US Confirms 14 Airstrikes Against ISIS in Syria," *Guardian*, September 23, 2014.

63. President Obama, "Statement by the President on ISIL," White House, September 10, 2014.

64. Lister, *Syrian Jihad*, 284.

65. "Syria Warns Against Foreign Intervention After Obama Speech," *Reuters*, September 11, 2014.

66. Cited in Paul Danahar, *The New Middle East: The World After the Arab Spring* (New York: Bloomsbury, 2013), 424.

67. Comments by Lakhdar Brahimi at a roundtable on "Syria's Conflict and the Impact on its Neighbours: The Long View," Chatham House, London, October 15, 2014.

68. Mikhail Zygar, *All the Kremlin's Men: Inside the Court of Vladimir Putin* (New York: Public Affairs, 2016), 332–33; "Stephen Harper at G20 Tells Vladimir Putin to 'Get Out of Ukraine,'" CBC News, November 16, 2014.

69. "Syrian Kurds Warn of Mounting Crisis as ISIS Advances, Take More Villages," CNN, September 19, 2014.

70. Yara Baymoumy, "Isis Urges More Attacks on Western 'Disbelievers,'" *Independent*, September 22, 2014.

71. Author's interviews with former U.S. officials, Washington D.C.

72. Lister, *Syrian Jihad*, 291.

73. Hannah Lucinda Smith, *Erdogan Rising: The Battle for the Soul of Turkey* (London: Collins, 2019), 184.

74. "Turkish Jets Bomb Kurdish PKK Rebels Near Iraq," BBC News, October 14, 2014.

75. Mike Giglio, *Shatter the Nations: ISIS and the War for the Caliphate* (New York: Public Affairs, 2019), 80.

76. Smith, *Erdogan Rising*, 188.

77. "Observer: Islamic State takes Kurdish headquarters in Kobani," DW News (via AFP), 10 October 2014.

78. Constance Letsch, "US Drops Weapons and Ammunition to Help Kurdish Fighters in Kobani," *Guardian*, October 20, 2014.

79. "President Erdogan Says PYD 'No Different than PKK' for Turkey," *Hurriyet*, October 19, 2014.

80. Humeyra Pamuk and Raheem Salman, "Kurdish Peshmerga Forces Enter Syria's Kobani After Further Airstrikes," *Reuters*, October 31, 2014.

81. Lister, *Syrian Jihad*, 313.

82. Weiss and Hassan, *ISIS*, 264.

83. A/HRC/27/60, September 16, 2014.

84. Syrian Network for Human Rights, "1851 People Were Killed in December; Death Toll for December 2014," January 2, 2015.

85. Kerry, *Every Day Is Extra*, 548.

86. Liz Sly, "US-Backed Syria Rebels Routed by Fighters Linked to al-Qaeda," *Washington Post*, November 2, 2014.

87. Tom Perry, "US-Led Airstrikes Pose Problem for Assad's Moderate Foes," *Reuters*, September 30, 2014.

88. Lister, *Syrian Jihad*, 305.

8. BETWEEN BARREL BOMBS AND BEHEADINGS

1. A/HRC/RES/26/23, June 27, 2014.

2. Ban Ki-moon, "Crisis in Syria: Civil War, Global Threat," address at the Asia Society, June 20, 2014.

3. "Afghanistan: Obama Condemns Killings of UN Staff," BBC News, April 3, 2011.

4. David Kenner, "Even a Diplomat's Diplomat Can't Solve Syria's Civil War," *Atlantic*, November 26, 2018.

5. Sam Dagher, *Assad or We Burn the Country* (Boston: Little, Brown, 2019), 456.

6. Staffan de Mistura, press briefing following UN Security Council closed consultations, New York, October 30, 2014.

7. Aram Nerguizian, "The Military Balance in a Shattered Levant," Center for Strategic and International Studies, Washington D.C., June 15, 2015, 19.

8. Robert Ford, "A 'Good Freeze' in Aleppo Is Not Enough," *Foreign Policy*, December 5, 2014.

9. Joshua Hersch, "Syrian Government Sees an Endgame: Block by Block," *Huffington Post*, February 27, 2014.

10. Patrick Wintour, "Ex-UN Envoy Says He Quit to Avoid Having to Shake Assad's Hand," *Guardian*, November 5, 2019.
11. Lakhdar Brahimi, remarks at Chatham House, London, October 14, 2014.
12. *Report of the Secretary-General on the Implementation of Security Council Resolution 2139*, S/2014/427, June 20, 2014.
13. Author's interviews.
14. S/2014/426, June 18, 2014.
15. Courtney Fung, *China and Intervention at the UN Security Council: Reconciling Status* (Oxford: Oxford University Press, 2019), 126.
16. Michelle Nicholls, "First UN Aid Convoy Enters Syria Without Government Consent," *Reuters*, July 25, 2014.
17. S/2014/611, August 21, 2014.
18. Nicholas Blanford, "Chlorine Attacks Sink Syria's Credibility on Chemical Weapons Deal," *Christian Science Monitor*, April 28, 2014.
19. OPCW, "Second Report of the OPCW Fact-Finding Mission in Syria: Key Findings," September 10, 2014, paras. 13, 14, 15, 29, and 30.
20. Press briefing by Sigrid Kaag, head of the OPCW-UN joint mission to Syria, New York, September 4, 2014.
21. "Syria's Assad: Aleppo Truce Plan 'Worth Studying,' " Voice of America, November 10, 2014.
22. Charles R. Lister, *Syrian Jihad: Al-Qaeda, the Islamic State, and the Evolution of an Insurgency* (Oxford: Oxford University Press, 2015), 317.
23. Dominique Soguel, "Can UN Envoy Sell Cease-fire to Syria Rebels? Not So Far," *Christian Science Monitor*, December 9, 2014.
24. "Syria's Ahrar al-Sham Says Coalition Strikes on It Killed Civilians," *Reuters*, November 7, 2014.
25. Michael Weiss and Hassan Hassan, *ISIS: Inside the Army of Terror* (New York: Regan Arts, 2015), 132.
26. "Syria Death Toll Now Exceeds 210,000, Rights Group Says," *Reuters*, February 7, 2015.
27. Heaven Crawley, Simon McMahon, Katherine Jones, Franck Duvall, and Nando Sigona, *Destination Europe: Understanding the Dynamics and Drivers of Mediterranean Migration in 2015*, final report of the Unravelling the Mediterranean Migration Crisis Project, November 2016, 38.
28. William Harris, *Quicksilver War: Syria, Iraq and the Spiral of Conflict* (London: Hurst, 2018), 76.
29. "The Opposition Takes Regime Fighters Hostage," Al Jazeera, February 19, 2015.
30. Lister, *Syrian Jihad*, 334.
31. Lister, 331.
32. Lister, 342.
33. Aron Lund, "The Revolutionary Command Council: Rebel Unity in Syria?," Carnegie Middle East Center, December 1, 2014.
34. Lister, *Syrian Jihad*, 342.

35. David Ignatius, "A New Cooperation on Syria," *Washington Post*, May 12, 2015.

36. "Syrian Rebel Group That Got US Aid Dissolves," *Washington Post*, March 1, 2015.

37. "US and Turkey to Train and Equip Syria's Rebels," Al Jazeera, February 20, 2015.

38. Haid Haid, "The Southern Front: Allies Without a Strategy," Heinrich Boll Stiftung (Beirut), August 21, 2015.

39. Tom Morgan, "Leaked Report: SAS on Ground in Libya for Months," *Telegraph*, March 25, 2016.

40. Anne Bernard, "UN Envoy Says Assad Is Crucial to Defusing Conflict in Syria," *New York Times*, February 13, 2015.

41. Rita Daou, "Syria Rebels Reject Envoy Plan to Freeze Aleppo Fighting," *AFP*, March 1, 2015.

42. Lister, *Syrian Jihad*, 336.

43. See Liz Sly, "Syrian Rebels Take Strategic Town of Idlib," *Washington Post*, March 28, 2015; Lister, *Syrian Jihad*, 342.

44. Lister, *Syrian Jihad*, 341.

45. Martin Chulov and Kareem Shaheen, "Syrian Rebels Hail Fall of Jisr al-Shughour as Sign of Growing Strength," *Guardian*, April 27, 2015.

46. "Syria Rebels Seize Key Regime Base," *Guardian*, May 20, 2015.

47. Harris, *Quicksilver War*, 71.

48. SC/11865-PAL/2187, April 20, 2015.

49. Anne Barnard, "Islamic State Seizes Palestinian Refugee Camp in Syria," *New York Times*, April 4, 2015.

50. Weiss and Hassan, *ISIS*, 250ff.

51. Kareem Shaheen, "Islamic State Attacks Kobani and Pro-regime Troops in Syria's North," *Guardian*, June 25, 2015.

52. Tobias Schneider, "The Decay of the Syrian Regime Is Much Worse Than You Think," *War on the Rocks*, August 31, 2016.

53. Lister, *Syrian Jihad*, 349.

54. Harris, *Quicksilver War*, 76.

55. *Note by the Director-General of the Organization for the Prohibition of Chemical Weapons Progress in the Elimination of the Syrian Chemical Weapons Programme*, S/2015/138, February 25, 2015.

56. "Syria War: 'Chlorine Attack' Video Moves Security Council to Tears," BBC, April 17, 2015.

57. S/PV.7401, March 6, 2015.

58. Kareem Shaheen, "Fresh Allegations of Chlorine Gas Attacks in Syria," *Guardian*, March 18, 2015.

59. Aaron Stein, "Turkey's Yemen Dilemma," *Foreign Affairs*, April 7, 2015. Also, Lister, *Syrian Jihad*, 344.

60. Weiss and Hassan, *ISIS*, 321.

61. Ginny Hill, *Yemen Endures: Civil War, Saudi Adventurism, and the Future of Arabia* (Oxford: Oxford University Press, 2017).

62. Aaron Lund, "What Did Kerry Really Say About Assad?," Carnegie Middle East Center, March 20, 2015.
63. Ian Black, "Bashar al-Assad Dismisses US Position on Negotiating End to Syria War," *Guardian*, March 17, 2015.
64. Ian Black, "Bashar al-Assad Dismisses US Position on Negotiating End to Syria War," *Guardian*, March 17, 2015.
65. RCC statement cited by Lister, *Syrian Jihad*, 350.
66. "Syria Crisis: Barrel Bomb Strikes Kill 72 in Aleppo Province," BBC, May 30, 2015.
67. Security Council Press Statement on Attacks Against Civilians in Syria, SC/11921, June 5, 2015.
68. S/2015/454, June 18, 2015.
69. Documented by Syrian Network for Human Rights, "The Syrian Government Has Dropped Nearly 70,000 Barrel Bombs on Syria: The Ruthless Bombing," December 25, 2017.
70. Aron Lund, "The Battle for Daraa," Carnegie Middle East Center, June 25, 2015.
71. Weiss and Hassan, *ISIS*, 275.
72. Michael Weiss, "Did the US Just Kill Five kids in Syria?," *Daily Beast*, August 12, 2015.
73. General Lloyd Austin's testimony to the U.S. Senate Committee on Armed Services, September 16, 2015, 35.
74. Weiss and Hassan, *ISIS*, 279, 277, 278.
75. Michael Weiss, "Syrian Defector from US Trained Force Found with US Hardware," *Daily Beast*, September 24, 2015.
76. Weiss and Hassan, *ISIS*, 133.
77. "An 'Official Massacre' of Civilians Alleged in Syria," CBS News, August 16, 2015.
78. "Syria's Attack on Douma a War Crime, UN Political Chief Says," *Associated Press*, August 19, 2015.
79. Martin Chulov, "UN Condemns Syria Market Attack as Witnesses Tell of 'Corpses Everywhere,'" *Guardian*, August 17, 2015.
80. Zia Weise and Chris Stevenson, "Turkish Airstrikes Against PKK in Iraq Throw Two-Year Ceasefire with Kurds Into Jeopardy," *Independent*, July 25, 2015.
81. Anne Bernard, Michael R. Gordon, and Eric Schmitt, "Turkey and US Plan to Create Syria Safe Zones, Free of IS," *New York Times*, July 27, 2015.
82. Lister, *Syrian Jihad*, 378.

9. EXODUS

1. Brandon Griggs, "Photographer Describes 'Scream' of Migrant Boy's 'Silent Body,'" CNN, September 3, 2015.
2. This account is based on Tima Kurdi, *The Boy on the Beach* (New York: Simon and Schuster, 2018); also Tristin Hopper, "The Sad Odyssey of Alan Kurdi and His Family: Their Search for New Life Ended in Death," *National Post* (Canada),

September 4, 2015; and Anne Barnard, "Five Years of Upheaval: The Story of Alan Kurdi's Family," *Irish Times*, October 13, 2020.

3. Dallal Stevens, "Asylum, Refugee Protection and the European Response to Syrian Migration," *Journal of Human Rights Practice* 9 (2017): 184.

4. UNHCR, "Europe: Syrian Asylum Applications," October 19, 2015.

5. Heaven Crawley, Simon McMahon, Katherine Jones, Franck Duvall, and Nando Sigona, *Destination Europe: Understanding the Dynamics and Drivers of Mediterranean Migration in 2015*, final report of the Unravelling the Mediterranean Migration Crisis Project, November 2016, 4.

6. Francois Heisbourg, "The Strategic Implications of the Syrian Refugee Crisis," *Survival* 57, no. 6 (2015): 7–20.

7. Heisbourg, 14.

8. Crawley et al., *Destination Europe*, 27.

9. Elizabeth Ferris and Kemal Kirisci, *The Consequences of Chaos: Syria's Humanitarian Crisis and the Failure to Protect* (Washington, D.C.: Brookings Institution, 2016), 40.

10. E.g., Anne Maree Belanger McMurdo, "Causes and Consequences of Canada's Resettlement of Syrian Refugees," *Forced Migration Review* 52 (May 2016): 82–84.

11. Crawley et al., *Destination Europe*, 24.

12. Harriet Grant, "UN Agencies Broke and Failing in Face of Ever-Growing Refugee Crisis," *Guardian*, September 6, 2015; Kelly M. Greenhill, "Open Arms Behind Barred Doors: Fear, Hypocrisy, and Schizophrenia in the European Migration Crisis," *European Law Journal* 22, no. 3 (2016): 329.

13. Crawley et al., *Destination Europe*, 23.

14. Daniel Byman and Sloane Speakman, "The Syrian Refugee Crisis: Bad and Worse Options," *Washington Quarterly*, 39, no. 2 (2016): 46.

15. Arnie Niemann and Natascha Zaun, "EU Refugee Policies and Politics in Times of Crisis: Theoretical and Empirical Perspectives," *Journal of Common Market Studies* 56, no. 1 (2018): 4.

16. A. J. Menendez, "The Refugee Crisis: Between Human Tragedy and Symptom of the Structural Crisis of European Integration," *European Law Journal* 22, no. 4 (2016): 397.

17. See E. Papataxiarchis, "Being 'There': At the Frontline of the 'European Refugee Crisis," *Anthropology Today* 32, no. 2 (2016): 5–9 and no. 3 (2016): 3–7.

18. Allan Hall and John Lichfield, "Germany Opens Its Gates: Berlin Says All Syrian Asylum-Seekers Are Welcome to Remain, as Britain Is Urged to Make 'a Similar Statement,'" *Independent*, August 24, 2015.

19. Byman and Speakman, "The Syrian Refugee Crisis," 45–60.

20. Alise Coen, "R2P, Global Governance and the Syrian Refugee Crisis", *International Journal of Human Rights* 9, no. 8 (2015): 1053.

21. Stevens, "Asylum," 8.

22. Heisbourg, "Strategic Implications," 8.

23. Niemann and Zaun, "EU Refugee Policies," 5.

24. "Turkey 'Illegally Returning' Syrian Refugees," BBC News, April 1, 2016.
25. Peter Slominski and Florian Trauner, "How Do Member States Return Unwanted Migrants? The Strategic (Non)use of 'Europe' During the Migration Crisis," *Journal of Common Market Studies* 56, no. 1 (2018): 101–18.
26. Justin Fishel, "Up to 30,000 Troops for Syria Safe Zones Kerry Says," ABC News, February 24, 2016.
27. Byman and Speakman, "Syrian Refugee Crisis," 53.
28. Lisa Ferdinando, "Breedlove: European Security Situation 'Serious, Complicated,'" U.S. Department of Defense press release, March 1, 2016.
29. Greenhill, "Open Arms," 323.
30. Elizabeth McElvein, "What Do Americans Really Think About Syrian Refugees?," Brookings Institution, March 4, 2016.
31. Gregory Korte, "Governors Have Little Power to Block Refugees," *USA Today*, November 16, 2015.
32. J. Poushter, "Refugees Stream Into Europe Where They Are Not Welcomed with Open Arms," *FactTank: News in Numbers*, April 24, 2015.
33. Greenhill, "Open Arms," 323.
34. Phillip Oltermann, "How Angela Merkel's Great Migrant Gamble Paid Off," *Guardian*, August 30, 2020.
35. Niall Ferguson, "The EU Melting Pot Is Melting Down," *Sunday Times*, June 17, 2018.
36. "Merkel's Staying Power: Two-thirds of Germans Want Chancellor to Serve Final Term," *Local* (Germany), March 12, 2019.
37. E.g., Aryn Baker, "Syrian Women Are Embracing Their New Lives in Syria, but at What Cost?," *Time*, January 3, 2019.
38. Oltermann, "How Angela Merkel's Great Migrant Gamble Paid Off."
39. Stefan Trines, "The State of Refugee Integration in Germany in 2019," *World Education News and Reviews*, August 8, 2019.

10. RUSSIAN INTERVENTION

1. "Read Putin's UN General Assembly Speech," *Washington Post*, September 28, 2015.
2. Remarks by President Obama to the United Nations General Assembly, September 28, 2015.
3. Shaun Walker, "Russian Parliament Grants Vladimir Putin Right to Deploy Military in Syria," *Guardian*, September 30, 2015.
4. John Kerry, *Every Day Is Extra* (New York: Simon and Schuster, 2018), 548–49.
5. Dmitri Trenin, *What Is Russia Up to in the Middle East?* (Cambridge: Polity, 2018), 57.
6. Michael Weiss and Hassan Hassan, *ISIS: Inside the Army of Terror* (New York: Regan Arts, 2015), 283.

7. Weiss and Hassan, 280.

8. Kerry, *Every Day Is Extra*, 549.

9. Emma Graham-Harrison and Alex Luhn, "Vladimir Putin Bids for Major World Role as His Forces Move Into Syria," *Guardian*, September 27, 2015.

10. Rod Thornton, "Countering Prompt Global Strike: The Russian Military Presence in Syria and the Eastern Mediterranean and Its Strategic Deterrence Role," *Journal of Slavic Military Studies* 32, no. 1 (2019): 1–24.

11. Gianluca Mezzofiore, "Russia in Syria: Air Strikes on Homs are 'Holy War' Against Terrorism Says Russian Orthodox Church," *International Business Times*, September 30, 2015.

12. Laila Bassam and Tom Perry, "How Iranian General Plotted Out Syrian Assault in Moscow," *Reuters*, October 7, 2015; and Sam Dagher, *Assad or We Burn the Country* (Boston: Little, Brown, 2019), 407.

13. Graham-Harrison and Luhn, "Vladimir Putin Bids for Major World Role."

14. Thornton, "Countering Prompt Global Strike."

15. William Harris, *Quicksilver War: Syria, Iraq and the Spiral of Conflict* (London: Hurst, 2018), 72.

16. Tom Perry, Laila Bassam, Jonathan Landay, and Maria Tvestkova, "The Road to Aleppo: How the West Misread Putin Over Syria," *Reuters*, February 26, 2016.

17. "UN Envoy Hopes Intra-Syrian Thematic Discussions Will 'Set the Stage' for End to Conflict," *UN News*, September 22, 2015.

18. Kathrine Hille, Geoff Dyer, Demetri Sevastopulo, and Erika Solomon, "Russian Air Strikes on Syrian Targets Raise 'Grave Concerns' in the US," *Financial Times*, September 20, 2015.

19. Roland Oliphant, Harriet Alexander, and David Blair, "Russian General Tells US Diplomats: We Launch Syria Air Strikes in One Hour, Stay Out of the Way," *Telegraph*, September 30, 2015.

20. Trenin, *What Is Russia Up to in the Middle East?*, 54.

21. Dmitry Adamsky, "Putin's Syrian Strategy: Russian Airstrikes and What Comes Next," *Foreign Affairs*, October 1, 2015.

22. Trenin, *What Is Russia Up to in the Middle East?*, 66.

23. Weiss and Hassan, *ISIS*, 358.

24. Cited by Weiss and Hassan, 286.

25. Author's interview with former official.

26. "Almost Five Years on, Syria Is a Country Destroyed with Civilians Paying the Biggest Price: UN Commission of Inquiry on Syria," *United Nations Human Rights Council News*, February 22, 2016.

27. Weiss and Hassan, *ISIS*, 286, 288, 289, 357.

28. Alec Luhn, "Russia's Campaign in Syria Leads to Arms Sales Windfall," *Guardian*, March 29, 2016.

29. Hugo Spaulding, "Five Huge Myths About Russia's Military Intervention in Syria," *Business Insider*, December 1, 2015.

30. Charles R. Lister, *Syrian Jihad: Al-Qaeda, the Islamic State, and the Evolution of an Insurgency* (Oxford: Oxford University Press, 2015), 369.

31. Genevieve Casagrande, Christopher Kozak, and Jennifer Cafarella, "Syria 90 Day Forecast: The Assad Regime and Allies in Northern Syria," Institute for the Study of War, February 24, 2016.

32. Christopher Phillips, *The Battle for Syria: International Rivalry in the New Middle East* (New Haven, Conn.: Yale University Press, 2016), 219.

33. Weiss and Hassan, *ISIS*, 357.

34. Kerry, *Every Day Is Extra*, 549.

35. Kerry, 551.

36. Aaron Lund, "Origins of the Syrian Democratic Forces: A Primer," *Syria Deeply*, January 22, 2016.

37. "Kurdish-Arab Coalition in Syria Forms Political Wing," Al Jazeera, December 11, 2015.

38. Peter Baker and Helene Cooper, "Obama Sends Special Operations Forces to Help Fight ISIS in Syria," *New York Times*, October 30, 2015.

39. Dagher, *Assad or We Burn the Country*, 409.

40. Weiss and Hassan, *ISIS*, 276.

41. Dagher, *Assad or We Burn the Country*, 409.

42. Susan Rice, *Tough Love: My Story of the Things Worth Fighting For* (New York: Simon and Schuster, 2019), 386, 369.

43. Kerry, *Every Day Is Extra*, 551.

44. Kerry, 549.

45. Nour Malas and Carol E. Lee, "US Pursued Secret Contacts with Assad Regime for Years," *Wall Street Journal*, December 23, 2015.

46. Kerry, *Every Day Is Extra*, 549.

47. Dania Akkad, "Kerry 'Blames Opposition' for Continued Syria Bombing," *Middle East Eye*, February 6, 2016.

48. Colin P. Clarke, *After the Caliphate: The Islamic State and the Future of the Diaspora* (Cambridge: Polity, 2019), 49.

49. Graeme Wood, *The Way of the Strangers: Encounters with the Islamic State* (London: Penguin, 2017).

50. Mark Tran, "Syrian Troops Could Be Used to Help Fight ISIS, France's Foreign Minister Says," *Guardian*, November 27, 2015.

51. Dagher, *Assad or We Burn the Country*, 426.

52. Phillips, *Battle for Syria*, 222.

53. Owen Matthews, "Putin's Bloody Logic in Syria," *Newsweek*, November 24, 2015.

54. Angela Stent, *Putin's World: Russia Against the West and with the Rest* (New York: Little, Brown, 2019).

55. "Syria Conflict: Assad in Surprise Visit to Moscow," BBC News, October 21, 2015.

56. Kerry, *Every Day Is Extra*, 550.

57. Arshad Mohammed and Francois Murphy, "Kerry Sees New Syria Talks Next Week, Does Not Rule Out Iran Role," *Reuters*, October 23, 2015.

58. Thomas Erdbrink, Sewell Chan, and David Sanger, "After a US Shift, Iran Has a Seat at Talks on War in Syria," *New York Times*, October 28, 2015.

59. Bradley Klapper and George Jahn, "Kerry in Vienna for Syria Talks Including Iran, Saudis," *Business Insider*, October 30, 2015; and author's interview with Western diplomat, April 14, 2017.

60. *Final Declaration on the Results of the Syria Talks in Vienna as Agreed by the Participants*, Vienna, October 30, 2015.

61. Statement of the International Syria Support Group, Vienna, November 14, 2015.

62. "Saudi Hails Syria Opposition 'Breakthrough,'" *Al Arabiya*, December 12, 2015.

63. "Syrian Opposition Find Common Ground at Riyadh Peace Talks," December 10, 2015.

64. Patrick Reevell, "US Not Seeking Regime Change in Syria, John Kerry Says After Meeting with Russian President," ABC News, December 15, 2015.

65. Author's interview with Security Council diplomats.

66. Harris, *Quicksilver War*, 80.

67. "Boy Rescued from Rubble After Airstrikes on Idlib, Syria," *Guardian*, December 21, 2015.

68. S/PV.7631, February 24, 2016.

69. UN Human Rights Council Independent Commission of Inquiry on Syria, *Out of Sight, Out of Mind: Deaths in Detention in the Syrian Arab Republic*, A/HRC/31/CRP.1, February 3, 2016.

70. Author's interview with French diplomats.

71. Aron Lund, "The Road to Geneva: The Who, When, and How of Syria's Peace Talks," Carnegie Endowment for International Peace, January 29, 2016.

72. "Syria Crisis Plan: Cessation of Hostilities, Airdrops, Peace Talks Laid Out in Munich," RT News, February 12, 2016.

73. Dania Akkad, "Kerry 'Blames Opposition' for Continued Syria Bombing," *Middle East Eye*, February 6, 2016.

11. MELTDOWN OF HUMANITY

1. Ian Black and Kareem Shaheen, "Partial Syria Ceasefire Agreed at Talks in Munich," *Guardian*, February 12, 2016.

2. Suleiman Al-Khalidi, "Kurdish Forces Said to Take Air Base Near Turkish Border," *Reuters*, February 11, 2016.

3. Colum Lynch, "Kerry Accuses Syria of Trying to Undercut Peace Talks," *Foreign Policy*, March 13, 2016.

4. Scott Lucas, Christalla Yakinthou, and Stefan Wolff, "Syria: Laying the Foundations for a Credible and Sustainable Transition," *RUSI Journal* 161, no. 3 (2016): 22–32.

5. Dmitry Adamsky, "Putin's Game in Syria: Why a Withdrawal Does Not Mean a Pullout," *Foreign Affairs*, April 3, 2016.

6. William Harris, *Quicksilver War: Syria, Iraq and the Spiral of Conflict* (London: Hurst, 2018), 85.

7. Damien Paletta, Adam Entous, and Ben Kesling, "Senior Islamic State Leader Killed," *Wall Street Journal*, March 25, 2016.

8. Shaun Walker, "US Secretary of State Arrives in Moscow for Syria Talks," *Guardian*, March 25, 2016.

9. Maria Tsvetkova, "Exclusive: Russia, Despite Drawing Down, Shipping More to Syria Than Removing," *Reuters*, March 30, 2016.

10. John Simpson, "Russia's Valery Gergiev Conducts Concert in Palmyra Ruins," BBC, May 5, 2016.

11. United Nations Office at Geneva, "UN Special Envoy's Paper on Points of Commonalities," March 24, 2016.

12. A/HRC/RES/31/17, March 23, 2016.

13. "Death Toll Rises to 33, Including Women and Children, as Regime Hits East of Damascus," *Daily Sabah*, April 1, 2016.

14. Harris, *Quicksilver War*, 86.

15. "Syria Conflict: Airstrikes on Idlib Markets 'Kill Dozens,'" *BBC News*, April 19, 2016.

16. Anne Barnard, "Divided Aleppo Plunges Back Into War as Syrian Hospital Is Hit," *New York Times*, April 28, 2016. Approximately twenty-seven people were killed at the hospital.

17. "Syria Civil War: Russia Calls for Regime of Calm," Al-Jazeera, May 24, 2016.

18. "US Asks Syria's Bashar al-Assad Regime to Stick to Transition Timeline," *Economic Times*, May 4, 2016.

19. "Red Cross Aid Convoy Denied Entry to Syrian City of Darayya," *Guardian*, May 13, 2016.

20. "Note to Correspondents: Statement of the International Syria Support Group," May 17, 2016.

21. "Besieged Town Gets First Food Aid Since 2012. Then Gets Bombed," *New York Times*, June 11, 2016.

22. Mike Thomson, *Syria's Secret Library: The True Story of How a Besieged Syrian Town Found Hope* (New York: Weidenfeld and Nicolson, 2019), 210.

23. Krishnadev Calamur, "Reversing Course on US Soldiers Wearing Kurdish Rebel Insignia," *Atlantic*, May 27, 2016.

24. Harris, *Quicksilver War*, 123.

25. Oren Dorell, "Turkey's President Erdogan Visits Washington Amidst Policy Rifts," *USA Today*, March 29, 2016.

26. Kathy Gilsinan, "Trump Is Killing a Fatally Flawed Syria Policy," *Atlantic*, October 8, 2019.

27. Manar Abdel Razzak, "Proposed 'Northern Army' in Syria Alienates Kurds," *Arab Weekly*, May 22, 2016.

28. "The New Coalition to Destroy the Islamic State," *Washington Post*, May 22, 2016.

29. Cedric Labrousse, "18 Syrian Revolutionary Factions Advancing Toward a One Army Project," *Arab Chronicle*, August 26, 2014.

30. Chris Kozak, "Aleppo Warning Update: April 7, 2016," Institute for the Study of War, April 7, 2016.

31. Kareem Shaheen, "Aleppo Hospital Hit as City Faces Humanitarian Catastrophe," *Guardian*, May 4, 2016.

32. Diana Darke, "Aleppo: Is Besieged Syrian City Facing Last Gasp," *BBC News*, July 22, 2016.

33. "Syrian Army Says Cut Off All Supply Routes Into East Aleppo," *Reuters*, July 27, 2017.

34. Dmitri Trenin, *What Is Russia Up to in the Middle East?* (Cambridge: Polity, 2018), 67.

35. A/HRC/33/55, August 16, 2016.

36. "Proposed Humanitarian Corridors in Aleppo Must Be Guaranteed by All Sides, Says UN Relief Chief," *UN News*, July 28, 2016.

37. Sarah El Deeb and Phillip Issa, "Russia, Syria Blockade Aleppo: Offer Corridors Out," Associated Press (Beirut), July 29, 2016.

38. Roy Gutman, "America's Favorite Syrian Militia Rules with an Iron Fist," *Nation*, February 13, 2017.

39. "Turkey 'Sorry for Downing Russian Jet,'" *BBC News*, June 27, 2016.

40. Emile Hokayem, "How Syria Defeated the Sunni Powers," *New York Times*, December 30, 2016.

41. Sam Heller, "Turkey's 'Turkey First' Syria Policy," *Century Foundation*, April 12, 2017.

42. Robert Worth, "Aleppo After the Fall," *New York Times Magazine*, May 24, 2017.

43. "Assad Vows to Fight On, Says Aleppo to Be Erdogan's Graveyard," *Reuters*, June 7, 2016.

44. "Turkish Tanks, Special Forces Launch First Major Into Syria to Battle IS," *Reuters*, August 24, 2016

45. "Remarks by Vice President Joe Biden and Turkish Prime Minister Binari Yildirim at a Press Availability," Cankaya Palace, Ankara, August 24, 2016.

46. "Turkey, Syrian Kurdish Ceasefire in Doubt Only Hours After US Confirmation," *Middle East Eye*, August 30, 2016.

47. Trenin, *What Is Russia Up to in the Middle East?*, 103.

48. William J. Burns, *The Back Channel: A Memoir of American Diplomacy and the Case for Its Renewal* (New York: Random House, 2019), 248.

49. John Kerry, *Every Day is Extra* (New York: Simon and Schuster, 2018), 552.

50. Kerry, 553.

51. Roberta Rampton, "Obama and Putin Tell Diplomats to Keep Working on Syria Argument," *Reuters*, September 5, 2016.

52. Patrick Wintour, "Ex-UN Envoy Says He Quit to Avoid Having to Shake Assad's Hand," *Guardian*, November 5, 2019.

53. "Remarks by Secretary Carter at the University of Oxford's Blavatnik School of Government, Oxford, England," U.S. Department of Defense transcript, September 7, 2016.

54. "Ankara Announced Putin's Support for the Operation in Syria," RBC Russia, September 6, 2016. Author's translation from the Russian.

55. Author's interview with official, November 18, 2019.

56. Julian Borger, "Russia and US Reach Tentative Agreement for Syria Ceasefire," *Guardian*, September 11, 2016.

57. Paul McLeary, "Russia Had to Call US Twice to Stop Syria Airstrikes," *Foreign Policy*, September 20, 2016.

58. Jared Malsin, "How a Mistaken US-Led Air Attack Could End the Syria Ceasefire," *Time*, September 18, 2016.

59. Nick Cummings-Bruce and Anne Barnard, "UN Investigators Say Syria Bombed Convoy and Did So Deliberately," *New York Times*, March 1, 2017.

60. Letter dated December 21, 2016, from Secretary-General Addressed to the President of the Security Council, S/2016/1093, December 21, 2016.

61. Kerry, *Every Day Is Extra*, 555.

62. *Report of the Independent International Commission of Inquiry on the Syrian Arab Republic*, A/HRC/34/64, February 2, 2017, para. 25.

63. Ban Ki-moon, "Briefing to the Security Council Debate on Protection of Civilians: Healthcare in Armed Conflict," September 28, 2016.

64. Raf Sanchez, "UN Diplomat Offers to Personally Escort 900 al-Qaeda Fighters Out of Aleppo in Hope of Ending Bombing," *Telegraph*, October 6, 2016.

65. Author's interview.

66. Lesley Wroughton and Alexander Winning, "Syria Talks in Lausanne End Without Breakthrough," *Reuters*, October 15, 2016.

67. Tom Miles, "Aleppo's Jabhat Fateh al-Sham Fighters Far Fewer Than UN Says: Sources," *Reuters*, October 14, 2016.

68. S/PV.7795, October 26, 2016.

69. Statement by UNICEF Executive Director Anthony Lake on Multiple Attacks on Schools in Syria, New York, October 27, 2016.

70. "Hundreds of Civilians, Rebels Evacuated from Aleppo," *AFP*, December 16, 2016.

71. Kerry, *Every Day Is Extra*, 555.

72. S/PV.7825, December 5, 2016.

73. *Report of the Independent International Commission of Inquiry on the Syrian Arab Republic*, A/HRC/34/64, paras. 25, 89–93.

74. Kareem Shaheen, "Aleppo: Russia-Turkey Ceasefire Deal Offers Hope of Survival for Residents," *Guardian*, December 14, 2016.

75. Harris, *Quicksilver War*, 155.

76. Trenin, *What Is Russia Up to in the Middle East?*, 67.

77. Emile Hokayem, "How Syria Defeated the Sunni Powers," *New York Times*, December 30, 2016.

12. RUSSIA'S ENDGAME

1. See David A. Graham, "What Is Trump's Syria Policy?," *Atlantic*, April 11, 2017.
2. "UN's High Commissioner for Human Rights Calls Syria 'a Torture Chamber,'" NPR, March 17, 2017.
3. *Report of the Independent International Commission of Inquiry on the Syrian Arab Republic*, A/HRC/34/64, February 2, 2017, and A/HRC/34/CRP.34/CRP.3, March 10, 2017.
4. Reinould Leenders and Kholoud Mansour, "Humanitarianism, State Sovereignty, and Authoritarian Regime Maintenance in the Syrian War," *Political Science Quarterly* 133, no. 2 (2018): 225–57.
5. Haid Haid, "Principled Aid in Syria: A Framework for International Agencies," research paper for Chatham House, Royal Institute of International Affairs, July 2019, 7.
6. Syria Campaign, *Taking Sides: The United Nations' Loss of Impartiality, Independence, and Neutrality in Syria*, June 2016.
7. Jose Ciro Martinez and Brent Eng, "The Unintended Consequences of Emergency Food Aid: Neutrality, Sovereignty, and Politics in the Syrian Civil War, 2012–2015," *International Affairs* 92, no. 1 (2016): 153–73.
8. Physicians for Human Rights, "Access Denied: UN Aid Deliveries to Syria's Besieged and Hard-to-Reach Areas," March 2017.
9. Human Rights Watch, "Rigging the System: Government Policies Co-opt Aid and Reconstruction Funding in Syria," June 28, 2019.
10. Patrick Wintour, "Russia in Power-Broking Role as Syria Peace Talks Begin in Astana," *Guardian*, January 23, 2017.
11. Charles Lister and William Wechsler, "Trump Has Big Plans for Syria. But He Has No Real Strategy," *Politico*, January 30, 2018.
12. John Irish, Stephanie Nebehay, and Tom Miles, "One Question at UN Peace Talks: What Does Russia Want?," *Reuters*, February 25, 2017.
13. "Transcript: Donald Trump on NATO, Turkey's Coup Attempt, and the World," *New York Times*, July 21, 2016.
14. William Harris, *Quicksilver War: Syria, Iraq and the Spiral of Conflict* (London: Hurst, 2018), 155–56.
15. "December 30: Turkey Claims Russian Air Support Against IS in Al-Bab," *Syriadirect.org*.
16. "Airstrikes by Russia Buttress Turkey in Battle v. ISIS," *New York Times*, January 9, 2017.
17. "Russian 'Friendly Fire' Kills Turkish Soldiers," BBC News, February 9, 2017.
18. Harris, *Quicksilver War*, 152.
19. Kathy Gilsinan, "What Are Turkey and Russia Doing in Syria?," *Atlantic*, December 19, 2016.
20. David Kenner, "Even a Diplomat's Diplomat Can't Solve Syria's Civil War," *Atlantic*, November 26, 2018.

21. Harris, *Quicksilver War*, 156.
22. "Power Split and Minority Rights Among Cornerstone of Russia-Proposed Syria Constitution," RT, January 27, 2017.
23. Dylan Collins and Zena Tahhan, "First Day of Astana Summit Ends Without Breakthrough," Al Jazeera, January 24, 2017.
24. Patrick Wintour, "Sponsors of Syria Talks in Astana Strike Deal to Protect Fragile Ceasefire," *Guardian*, January 24, 2017.
25. Joint Statement by Iran, Russia, Turkey on the International Meeting on Syria, Astana, January 23–24, 2017.
26. Wintour, "Sponsors of Syria Talks in Astana Strike Deal."
27. "Russia, Turkey, Iran Discuss Syria Ceasefire in Astana," Al Jazeera, February 6, 2017.
28. Daniel Schearf, "Astana Talks on Syria to Continue Despite Setbacks," Voice of America, February 18, 2017.
29. John Irish, Stephanie Nebehay, and Tom Miles, "One Question at UN Peace Talks: What Does Russia Want?," *Reuters*, February 25, 2017.
30. "Russia Pushes Hard to Include Syria's Kurds in Geneva Talks," *Rudaw*, February 10, 2017.
31. Dylan Collins and Zena Tahhan, "Syria Talks Hit Snag Before Opening Ceremony in Geneva," Al Jazeera, February 25, 2015.
32. Author's interview with Western diplomat, Geneva, March 14, 2018.
33. SC/12749, March 10, 2017.
34. "Fierce Fighting in Syria as Talks Restart in Geneva," Al Jazeera, March 24, 2017.
35. Alex Hopkins, "Airwars Annual Assessment 2017: Civilians Paid a Heavy Price for Major Coalition Gains," *Airwars*, January 2018.
36. "American Is Killed in First Casualty for US Forces in Syria Combat," *New York Times*, November 24, 2016.
37. Harris, *Quicksilver War*, 96.
38. "Turkey Bombs Kurdish Forces in Northeast Syria," Agence France Presse, April 25, 2017.
39. John Bolton, *The Room Where it Happened: A White House Memoir* (New York: Simon and Schuster, 2020), 46.
40. Dmitri Trenin, *What is Russia up to in the Middle East?* (Cambridge: Polity, 2018), 97.
41. Kathy Gilsinan, "Trump Is Killing a Fatally Flawed Syria Policy," *Atlantic*, October 8, 2019.
42. Michael Crowley, "Obama's Red Line Haunts Clinton, Trump," *Politico*, November 10, 2016.
43. "Treasury Sanctions Senior Officials in Connection with OPCW-UN Findings of Regime's Use of Chemical Weapons on Civilians," press release, U.S. Department of the Treasury, January 12, 2017.
44. Joe Macaron, "Trump's 'Real Estate' Approach to Safe Zones in Syria," Al Jazeera, January 31, 2017.

45. Justin Edwards Ainsley and Matt Spetalnick, "Trump Says He Will Order 'Safe Zones' for Syria," *Reuters*, January 26, 2017.

46. "Tillerson Addresses Coalition of 68 Nations to Defeat ISIS," U.S. Embassy in Bahrain, March 23, 2017.

47. "US Military Deploys Forces in Manbij in New Effort," *Reuters*, March 7, 2017.

48. S/PV.7893, February 28, 2017.

49. Michelle Nichols, "US Priority on Syria No Longer Focused on Getting Assad Out: Haley," *Reuters*, March 31, 2017.

50. Clarissa Ward, Waffa Munayyer, Salma Abdelaziz, and Fiona Sibbett, "Gasping for Life: Syria's Merciless War on Its Own Children," CNN, 2017.

51. Letter from the Secretary-General to the President of the Security Council, 2/2017/904, October 26, 2017, para. 45.

52. Domenico Montanaro, "After Syria Gas Attack World Waits to See What Kind of Leader Trump Will Be," NPR, April 5, 2017.

53. Mark Katkov, Jessica Taylor, and Tom Bowman, "Trump Orders Syria Airstrikes After Assad 'Choked Out the Lives' of Civilians," NPR, April 6, 2017.

54. Robert Jervis, "Rex Tillerson Might be the Weakest Secretary of State Ever," *Foreign Policy*, March 10, 2017.

55. Josie Ensor, "Syrian Warplanes Take Off Once Again from Air Base Bombed by US Tomahawks," *Telegraph*, April 8, 2017.

56. Jonathan Karl and Alexander Mallin, "Tillerson: Russia 'Complicit' or 'Incompetent' with Syria," ABC News, April 7, 2017.

57. S/PV.7919, April 7, 2017.

58. "Russia Notifies Intent to Suspend Communication Channel: Coalition Official," *Reuters*, April 7, 2017.

59. Jessica Schulberg, "Trump Administration Is Contradicting Itself on Regime Change in Syria," *Huffington Post*, April 10, 2017.

60. Spencer Ackerman, "What's Trump's Plan for Syria? Five Different Policies in Two Weeks," *Guardian*, April 11, 2017.

61. Max Greenwood, "Tillerson: Defeating ISIS 'First Priority' in Syria," *Hill*, April 8, 2017.

62. David Sanger, "Tillerson and Putin Find Very Little to Agree On," *New York Times*, April 13, 2017.

63. Tom Rollins, "The Unravelling of Syria's Eastern Ghouta," Al Jazeera, December 18, 2016.

64. See John Davison, "Last 1,000 Rebels Leave Damascus District Under Evacuation Deal," *Reuters*, May 16, 2017.

65. Memorandum on the Creation of De-escalation Areas in the Syrian Arab Republic, May 6, 2017. Also see "Russia, Iran, Turkey Set Up Syria De-escalation Zones for At Least Six Months: Memorandum," *Reuters*, May 6, 2017.

66. Memorandum on the Creation of De-escalation Areas, para. 5.

67. "Syrian Kurdish PYD Denounces Syria Deal for 'De-escalation' zones," *Reuters*, May 6, 2017.

68. See Emma Beals, "De-escalation and Astana," Atlantic Council, September 15, 2017.

69. Martin Chulov, "US Jets Attack Iran-Backed Militiamen in South-Eastern Syria," *Guardian*, May 19, 2017.

70. Harris, *Quicksilver War*, 98.

71. Steve Weizman, "Netanyahu: Syria Raids Targeted Advanced Hezbollah Arms," *Agence France Press*, March 17, 2017.

72. "Israeli Jets Hit Syria's Masyaf Chemical Sites—Reports," BBC News, September 7, 2017.

73. Christopher Woody, "The US-Led Coalition Destroyed More Pro-Assad Forces at a Growing Hotspot in the Syrian Desert," *Business Insider*, June 7, 2017.

74. Compare Colum Lynch and Robbie Gramer, "Tillerson Ready to Let Russia Decide Assad's Fate," *Foreign Policy*, July 3, 2017; and Max Greenwood, "Tillerson: 'Reign of the Assad Family Is Coming to an End' in Syria," *Hill*, October 26, 2017.

75. Harris Gardiner, "US, Russia and Jordan Reach Deal for Ceasefire in Part of Syria," *New York Times*, July 7, 2017.

76. Bethany Allen-Ebrahimian, "Russia and US Broker Another Ceasefire in Syria," *Foreign Policy*, July 7, 2017.

77. Jane Kinninmont, "The Gulf Divided: The Impact of the Qatar Crisis," research paper, Chatham House, London, May 2019.

78. Mark Mazzetti, Adam Goldman, and Michael S. Schmidt, "Behind the Sudden Death of a $1 Billion Secret CIA War in Syria," *New York Times*, August 2, 2017.

79. "Trump Ends CIA Support for Anti-Assad Rebels," Al Jazeera, July 20, 2017.

80. Greg Jaffe and Adam Entous, "Trump Ends Covert CIA Program to Arm Anti-Assad Rebels in Syria, a Move Sought by Moscow," *Washington Post*, July 20, 2017.

81. "G20: Trump and Putin Hold First Face to Face Talks," BBC, July 7, 2017.

82. "PM Opposes Syria Ceasefire, Says It Will Strengthen Iran," *Times of Israel*, July 16, 2017.

83. International Crisis Group, "Keeping the Calm in Southern Syria," *Middle East and North Africa Report*, no. 187, June 21, 2018.

84. Ellen Francis, "US-Russian Ceasefire Deal Holding in Southwestern Syria," *Reuters*, July 9, 2017.

85. "Monitoring Centre for Southern Syrian De-escalation Zone Starts Activities in Amman," *TASS*, August 23, 2017.

86. Joint statement by the president of the United States and the president of the Russian Federation, U.S. Department of State, November 11, 2017.

87. Emma Graham-Harrison, "Syria: Southern Towns Surrender to Assad Forces After Thousands Flee Homes," *Guardian*, July 1, 2018.

88. "Russia: New Ceasefire Deal Agreed in Syria's Ghouta," Al Jazeera, July 23, 2017.

89. "Russia Announces 'De-escalation Zone' North of Syria's City of Homs," *Reuters*, August 3, 2017.

90. "Final De-escalation Zones Agreed On in Astana," Al Jazeera, September 16, 2016.
91. Harris, *Quicksilver War*, 95.
92. Shawn Snow, "These Marines in Syria Fired More Artillery than Any Battalion Since Vietnam," *Marine Times*, February 6, 2018.
93. Ellen Ioanes, "11,000 Kurds Killed Fighting ISIS and Now the US Is Abandoning Them—Who Will Help America Next Time?," *Business Insider*, October 9, 2019.
94. "Raqqa's Dirty Secret," BBC, October 12, 2017.
95. "Syria Crisis: Northeast Syria Situation Report No. 16 (1–30 September 2017)," UN Office for the Coordination of Humanitarian Affairs, Geneva, September 30, 2017.
96. Hannah Lucinda Smith, "ISIS Families Are Buried in Shrouds, Infidels Piled Five High," *Times* (London), February 27, 2019.
97. "Timeline: The Rise, Spread, and Fall of the Islamic State," Wilson Center, October 28, 2019.
98. Dmitri Trenin, "Putin's Plan for Syria," *Foreign Affairs*, December 13, 2017.
99. Letter dated August 9 from Permanent Representative of the Russian Federation to the United Nations addressed to Secretary-General and the President of the Security Council, S/2017/693, August 10, 2017.
100. Transcript of stakeout by UN special envoy for Syria Staffan de Mistura and UN senior adviser Jan Egeland, *UN News*, August 17, 2017.
101. 'Russia's DM Urges UN to Step Up Humanitarian Assistance to Syria," KUNA (Kuwait), September 11, 2017.
102. S/PV.8073, October 24, 2017.

13. DE-ESCALATION DOMINOES

1. Katya Golubkova and Tom Perry, "Russia's Putin Hosts Assad in Fresh Drive for Syria Peace Deal," *Reuters*, November 21, 2017.
2. Anne Barnard, "Assad and Putin Meet, as Putin Pushes End to Civil War in Syria," *New York Times*, November 22, 2017.
3. Golubkova and Perry, "Russia's Putin Hosts Assad."
4. Barnard, "Assad and Putin Meet."
5. Patrick Wintour, "Putin Brings Iran and Turkey Together in Bold Syria Peace Plan," *Guardian*, November 23, 2017.
6. Patrick Wintour, "UN Envoy to Attend Syria Peace Talks Despite Boycott," *Guardian*, January 29, 2018.
7. Patrick Wintour, "Russia's Peace Conference Teeters on Farce," *Guardian*, January 31, 2018.
8. Ahmad Majidyar, "Iran-Backed Iraqi Militia Group Launches New Brigade to 'Liberate' Golan Heights," Middle East Institute, March 9, 2017.

9. Robert Ford, "Keeping Out of Syria: The Least Bad Option," *Foreign Affairs*, November 1, 2017.

10. Thomas Gibbons-Neff, "How a 4-Hour Battle Between Russian Mercenaries and U.S. Commandos Unfolded in Syria," *New York Times*, May 24, 2018.

11. Author's interview with former U.S. official, New York, September 21, 2018.

12. International Crisis Group, "Keeping the Calm in Southern Syria," report no. 187, June 21, 2018, nn. 41, 42.

13. Patrick Wintour, "Erdogan Accuses US of Planning to Form 'Terror Army' in Syria," *Guardian*, January 15, 2018.

14. "Secretary of State Rex Tillerson on the Way Forward for the United States Regarding Syria," U.S. Department of State, January 17, 2018.

15. Matthew Lee and Josh Lederman, "In Private, Trump Has Mused About Syrian Pullout for Weeks," *Associated Press*, March 30, 2018.

16. Noah Bonsey, "No Winners in Turkey's New Offensive Into Syria," International Crisis Group, January 26, 2018.

17. Identical letters dated January 20, 2018, from the chargé d'affaires a.i. of the Permanent Mission of Turkey to the United Nations addressed to the secretary-general and the president of the Security Council, S/2018/53, January 22, 2018.

18. "No Political Agreement Held with the Syrian Regime, Saleh Musallam Says," *Syria Call*, February 24, 2018.

19. International Crisis Group, "Prospects for a Deal to Stabilize Idlib," 2018.

20. Angus McDowell and Tuvan Gumrucku, "Turkey Warns Syrian Army Against Helping Kurdish YPG in Afrin," *Reuters*, February 19, 2018.

21. International Crisis Group, "Prospects for a Deal to Stabilize Idlib," 2018, n.73.

22. Patrick Cockburn, "Yazidis Who Suffered Under ISIS Face Forced Conversion to Islam Amid Fresh Persecution in Afrin," *Independent*, April 18, 2018.

23. Bonsey, "No Winners in Turkey's New Offensive into Syria."

24. "Nearly 90 Percent of Turkish Citizens Support Cross-border Military Operation in Syria: Survey," *Hürriyet Daily News*, February 19, 2018.

25. Aaron Stein, "Turkey's Afrin Offensive and America's Future in Syria," *Foreign Affairs*, January 23, 2018.

26. International Crisis Group, "Prospects for a Deal," n. 88.

27. Nahal Toosey and Quint Forgey, "Trump Trashes Tillerson for Saying Putin Outfoxed Him," *Politico*, May 23, 2019.

28. Charles Lister, "Pompeo's Appointment Could Mean a More Hawkish US Stance on Syria," March 13, 2018.

29. "Syria War: Trump Persuaded Not to Pull Out Immediately," *BBC*, April 4, 2018.

30. Felicia Schwartz, "Trump Freezes Funds for Syrian Recovery, Signaling Pullback," *Wall Street Journal*, March 30, 2018; Julie Hirschfeld Davis, "Trump Drops Push for Immediate Withdrawal of Troops from Syria," *New York Times*, April 4, 2018.

31. Lise Labott and Kevin Liptak, "Trump Gets Testy as National Security Team Warns of Risks of Syria Withdrawal," CNN, April 5, 2018.

32. "Syria War: Trump Persuaded Not to Pull Out Immediately," BBC News, April 4, 2018.

33. Karen DeYoung and Shane Harris, "Trump Instructs Military to Begin Planning for Withdrawal from Syria," *Washington Post*, April 4, 2018.

34. Michael Gordon, "U.S. Seeks Arab Force and Funding for Syria," *Wall Street Journal*, April 16, 2018.

35. David M. Satterfield and Brett McGurk, "Briefing on the Status of Syria Stabilization Assistance and Ongoing Efforts to Achieve an Enduring Defeat of ISIS," U.S. Department of State, August 17, 2018.

36. "Syria: UN Urges and End to Hostilities, Warns of Grave and Deepening Humanitarian Crisis," *UN News*, February 6, 2018.

37. Sharmila Devi, "Syria: Seven Years Into a Civil War," *Lancet* 391, no. 10115 (January 6, 2018).

38. Briefing by Mark Lowcock to the UN Security Council, February 28, 2018.

39. Suleiman al-Khailidi, "Russia, Syria Armies Step Up Attacks on Damascus Enclave Rebels," *Reuters*, November 16, 2017.

40. SG/SM/18890, February 10, 2018.

41. "Amid Outcry Over Ghouta, Russia Vows to Back Assad Against 'Terror Threat,'" RFE/RL, February 28, 2018.

42. S/PV.8188, February 24, 2018.

43. "Amid Outcry Over Ghouta."

44. Tom Perry and Stephanie Nebehay, "Assad Vows to Press Ghouta Assault, as Civilians Flee Government Advances," March 4, 2018.

45. Ken Bredemeier, "Trump, May Blame Syria, Russia for Eastern Ghouta Humanitarian Woes," Voice of America, March 4, 2018.

46. "Syrian Army Splinters Rebel Enclave in Ghouta Onslaught," *Reuters*, March 11, 2018.

47. "Syrian State Media Announces Agreement Reached to Evacuate a Second Area of E. Ghouta," France 24, March 23, 2018.

48. Interim Report of the OPCW Fact-Finding Mission in Syria Regarding the Alleged Use of Toxic Chemicals as a Weapon in Douma, Syrian Arab Republic, April 7, 2018.

49. Marika Sosnowski, "Reconciliation Agreements as Strangle Contracts: Ramifications for Property and Citizenship Rights in the Syrian Civil War," *Peacebuilding*, July 18, 2019.

50. *Implementation of Security Council Resolutions 2139 (2014), 2165 (2014), 2191 (2014), 2258 (2015), 2332 (2016), 2393 (2017) and 2401 (2018)*, Report of the Secretary-General, S/2018/619, June 20, 2018.

51. "Moscow Says Chemical Attack 'Fake News,' Warns Against Syria Intervention," *RT*, April 8, 2018.

52. "White Helmets Staged Chemical Weapons Attack on Civilians—Russian General Staff," *TASS*, April 12, 2018.

53. Ken Sengupta, "Russia Accuses Britain of Staging Suspected Syria Chemical Weapons Attack," *Independent*, April 13, 2018.

54. Patrick Wintour, " 'Obscene Masquarade': Russia Criticized Over Douma Chemical Attack Denial," April 27, 2018.

55. E.g., Robert Fisk, "The Search for Truth in the Rubble of Douma—and One Doctor's Doubts Over the Chemical Attack," *Independent*, April 17, 2018.

56. John Bolton, *The Room Where It Happened: A White House Memoir* (New York: Simon and Schuster, 2020), 45.

57. Draft resolution S/2018/32, April 10, 2018. For the meeting record, see S/PV.8228, April 10, 2018.

58. Bolton, *The Room Where It Happened*, 45.

59. Helene Cooper, Michael D. Shear, and Ben Hubbard, "Trump Orders Strikes on Syria Over Suspected Chemical Weapons Attacks," *New York Times*, April 13, 2018.

60. Bolton, *The Room Where It Happened*, 47.

61. Phil McCausland and Yuliya Talmazan, "Trump's US-Led Airstrikes on Syria Won't Stop Assad's Chemical Capabilities, Experts Say," NBC News, April 15, 2018.

62. S/PV.8233, April 14, 2018.

63. "4 Day Seasefire [*sic*] Agreement Between Homs and Hama Negotiating Commission with Russians," *Syria Call*, April 18, 2018.

64. "Syria War: Rebels Leave Last Major Besieged Enclave," BBC News, May 7, 2018; and "Syrian Rebels Surrender Last Rebel-Held Area Near Homs," Al Jazeera, May 4, 2018.

65. S/PV.8260, May 16, 2018.

66. Sune Engel Rasmussen and Felicia Schwartz, "Israel Broadens Fight Against Iran," *Wall Street Journal*, July 15, 2018.

67. Elizabeth Tsurkov, "Israel's Deepening Involvement with Syria's Rebels," *War on the Rocks*, February 14, 2018.

68. Seth G. Jones, "The Escalating Conflict with Hezbollah in Syria," *CSIS Briefs*, June 20, 2018.

69. Oliver Holmes, "Israel Launches 'Large Scale' Attack in Syria After Fighter Jet Crashes," *Guardian*, February 11, 2018.

70. Charles Lister, "The Israeli Airstrike on Syria Monday: A Message to Iran, Russia—and Trump: The Days of 'Rolling Back' Iran in Syria Are Gone," *Daily Beast*, April 9, 2018.

71. International Crisis Group, "Keeping the Calm in Southern Syria," *Middle East and North Africa Report*, no. 187, June 21, 2018, n.16.

72. Judah Ari Gross, "Alleged Israeli Strike Reported at Iran-Linked Military Site Near Damascus," *Times of Israel*, May 8, 2018.

73. "Iran Attacked Israel from Syria Without Notifying Damascus—Reports," *Times of Israel*, May 10, 2018.

74. See Raf Sanchez, "Israel Strikes Back Against Syrian Targets and Threatens 'Storm' on Iran After Golan Heights Attack," *Telegraph*, May 11, 2018.

75. Ofar Zeizberg, "Israel's Southern Syria Decision Time," International Crisis Group, July 4, 2018.

76. Josie Ensor and Raf Sanchez, "Russia and Israel 'Agree Deal' to Hold Back Iranian Militias So Assad Can Take Border Region," *Telegraph*, May 29, 2018.

77. "US Wary of Israel-Russia Deal to Remove Iranians from Southern Syria," *Times of Israel*, June 2, 2018.

78. International Crisis Group, "Southern Calm," n. 93.

79. "Assad Regime Intentions in the Southwest De-escalation Zone," U.S. Department of State, May 25, 2018.

80. Lara Seligman, "The Unintended Consequences of Trump's Decision to Withdraw from Syria," *Foreign Policy*, January 28, 2019.

81. "You're on Your Own, US Tells Syrian Rebels, as Assad Goes on Offensive," *Guardian*, June 24, 2018.

82. Kareem Shaheen, "Fear Grows for Safety of 270,000 Syrians Fleeing Fighting in Deraa," *Guardian*, July 4, 2018.

83. Statement attributable to spokesman of the secretary-general on Syria, United Nations, June 22, 2018.

84. Suha Ma'ayeh, "Jordan Mediating Russian and Rebel Talks for Southern Syria Handover," *National*, July 4, 2018.

85. Ma'ayeh, "Jordan Mediating Russian and Rebel Talks."

86. "Syria Rebels Say Close to Deal with Russia on South," France 24, July 6, 2018.

87. Kareem Shaheen, "UN Calls for Access to Syrians Stranded in Desert After Deraa's Fall," *Guardian*, July 14, 2018.

88. "Regime Looting Runs Rampant in Syria," *Ashaq al-Awsat*, July 22, 2018.

89. Bolton, *The Room Where It Happened*, 131.

90. Yury Barmin, "What Does the Helsinki Summit Mean for Syria?," Al Jazeera, July 17, 2018.

14. NORTHERN FIRES

1. "In a Syria Refuge, Extremists Exert Even Greater Control," *New York Times*, August 13, 2017.

2. Charles Lister, "Al-Qaeda Is Starting to Swallow the Syrian Opposition," March 15, 2017.

3. Charles Lister, "Al-Qaeda's Turning Against Its Syrian Affiliate," May 18, 2017.

4. Christopher Phillips, "Idlib's Fate Looks More Llikely to Be Settled in Moscow than in Ankara," *Middle East Eye*, August 31, 2018.

5. International Crisis Group, "The Best of Bad Options for Syria's Idlib," *Middle East Report*, no. 197, March 14, 2019, 3.

6. Bethan McKernan, "Idlib Is a Bargaining Chip: Civilians Brace as Assad Air Assault Escalates," *Guardian*, May 23, 2019.

7. See International Crisis Group, "Saving Idlib from Destruction," briefing no. 63, September 3, 2018.

8. Raf Sanchez, "Russia Amasses Warships Off Syria Ahead of Regime's Final Assault on Idlib," *Telegraph*, August 28, 2018.

9. See "Lavrov Says Terrorists' Use of Idlib for Attacks on Russian, Syrian Troops Unacceptable," *TASS*, August 31, 2018.

10. "UN Head Calls for Idlib to Be Spared 'Humanitarian Nightmare,'" *Guardian*, September 12, 2018, statement by Adama Dieng, special adviser on the prevention of genocide, on the situation in Idlib, Syrian Arab Republic, September 6, 2018; and "UN Says Russia and Turkey Hold Key to Averting Idlib Bloodbath," France 24, September 5, 2018.

11. S/PV.8345, September 7, 2018.

12. "Idlib: Turkey's Ceasefire Call Rejected by Russia, Iran," Al Jazeera, September 8, 2018.

13. International Crisis Group, "Turkey's Syrian Refugees: Defusing Metropolitan Tensions," report no. 248, January 29, 2018.

14. Denis Pinchuk, "Russia, Turkey, Iran, Fail to Agree on Ceasefire for Syria's Idlib," *Reuters*, September 7, 2018.

15. Leonid Issaev, "What Does Russia Want in Northwest Syria?," Al Jazeera, September 19, 2018.

16. Phillips, "Idib's Fate Looks More Likely to Be Settled in Moscow."

17. S/2018/852, September 18, 2018.

18. "Russia and Turkey to Create Syria Buffer," BBC News, September 17, 2018.

19. International Crisis Group, "The Least of Bad Options," 9.

20. Alex Ward, "Trump Just Reversed His Decision to Pull All US Troops Out of Syria," *Vox*, February 22, 2019.

21. Laurel Wamsley, "White House Orders Pentagon to Pull US Troops from Syria," NPR, December 18, 2018.

22. Letter from secretary of defense to the president, December 20, 2019.

23. John Bolton, *The Room Where It Happened: A White House Memoir* (New York: Simon and Schuster, 2020), 202.

24. Ward, "Trump Just Reversed His Decision."

25. A/C.3/73/L.50, November 16, 2018.

26. Patrick Wintour, "Ex-UN Envoy Says He Quit to Avoid Having to Shake Assad's Hand," *Guardian*, November 5, 2019.

27. S/PV.8406, November 19, 2018. Security Council briefing on the situation in Syria by Special Envoy Staffan de Mistura.

28. David Kenner, "Even a Diplomat's Diplomat Can't Solve Syria's Civil War," *Atlantic*, November 26, 2018.

29. Evan Hill and Christiaan Triebert, "12 Hours. 4 Syrian Hospitals Bombed. One Culprit: Russia," *New York Times*, October 13, 2019.

30. "Dozen Syrian Children Dead in Latest Ceasefire Breach," ITV News (UK), May 7, 2019.

31. "Intense Fighting in Northwest Syria as Army Tries to Advance," *Reuters*, May 7, 2019.

32. Reference the report on Russian reconstruction of Syrian Army.

33. Omer Ozkizilcik, "A Way Out for Russia and Turkey from Idlib's Spiral of Violence," Middle East Institute, July 1, 2019.

34. Ozkizilcik, "A Way Out for Russia and Turkey."

35. Suleiman al-Khailidi, "Turkey Sends Weapons to Syrian Rebels Facing Russian Backed Assault: Syrian Sources," *Reuters*, May 26, 2019.

36. "US Says There Are Signs Syria May Be Using Chemical Weapons, Warns of Quick Response," CNBC News/*Reuters*, September 21, 2019.

37. Orhan Coskun, "Turkey Says It Will Not Withdraw Posts in Syria After Government Attacks," *Reuters*, May 22, 2019.

38. "Turkey Says Ceasefire Not Yet Secured in Syria's Idlib," *TRT World*, June 13, 2019.

39. Daren Butler, "Turkish Outpost in Syria Shelled from Syrian Government Forces Area: Ministry," *Reuters*, June 16, 2019.

40. "Turkish Defence Minister Discusses Idlib with Russian Counterpart," *Ahval*, June 17, 2019.

41. Author's interviews with Security Council diplomats.

42. "Russia to Implement New Plan in Idlib Aimed at Influencing the Morale of the Revolutionaries," *Syria Call*, July 5, 2019.

43. "Parties to Syria Peace Talks in Kazakhstan Highlight Efforts to Prevent Civilian Casualties in Idlib," *Daily Sabah*, August 2, 2019.

44. *Report of the Independent International Commission of Inquiry on the Syrian Arab Republic*, A/HRC/43/57, January 28, 2020, paras. 24, 27, 30.

45. Jakub Janovsky, "Nine Years of War—Documenting the Syrian Arab Army's Armored Vehicles Losses," *Bellingcat*, March 30, 2020 (initially published March 27, 2018, updated in 2020).

46. Ellen Francis, "Syrian Army Takes Towns in Northwest That Rebels Held for Years," *Reuters*, August 23, 2019,

47. Author's interviews, February 20–21, 2020.

48. "Turkey, Russia, Iran Vow to Ease Tensions in Syria's Idlib," *RFE/RL*, September 17, 2019.

49. S/PV.8623, September 19, 2019.

50. Anna Getmansky, Toiga Sinmazdemir, and Thomas Zietzoff, "Most Turks Support the Syrian Invasion, Here's Why," *Washington Post*, October 25, 2019.

51. Christopher Phillips, "Idlib Offensive: Turkey's Tradeoffs with Russia Put It on the Losing Side," *Middle East Eye*, February 19, 2020.

52. "Turkey-Backed Syrian Rebels Launch Attack Into Kurdish Held Area," *Reuters*, August 5, 2019.

53. "Turkey, US Work to Create Buffer Zone in Northern Syria," *Deutsche Welle*, August 13, 2019.

54. Audrey Wilson, "US and Turkey Spar Over Syria Safe Zone," *Foreign Policy*, July 25, 2019.

55. Zeke Miller and Lolita C. Baldor, "US Pushes NATO Allies to Join Observer Force in Syria," *Associated Press*, February 23, 2019.

56. Bolton, *The Room Where It Happened*, 207.

57. Bolton, 210–12.

58. Carlotta Gall, "US and Turkey Avoid Conflict by Agreeing on Buffer Zone in Syria," *New York Times*, August 7, 2019.

59. Josh Rogin, "How Trump Just Destroyed His Own Syria Strategy," *Washington Post*, October 10, 2019.

60. "Turkey, US, Agree to Launch First Phase of Syria Safe-Zone Plan," Al Jazeera, August 22, 2019.

61. Daren Butler, "Turkey to Launch Own Syria Plan in Weeks Unless Has 'Safe Zone' Control: Erdogan," *Reuters*, September 1, 2019.

62. Sarah Dadouch, "Turkey to Launch Offensive in Kurdish Controlled Area of Northern Syria," *Reuters*, August 5, 2019.

63. Eric Schmitt, "US Poised to Send 150 Troops to Patrol Northeastern Syria," *New York Times*, September 12, 2019.

64. Ezgi Erkoyun and Tuvan Gumrukcu, "Turkey Says US Stalling on Syria 'Safe Zone,' Will Act Alone If Needed," *Reuters*, September 10, 2019.

65. "Turkish President Recep Tayyip Erdogan Speech at 74th UN General Assembly," UN TV, September 24, 2019.

66. Anna Getmansky, Toiga Sinmazdemir, and Thomas Zietzoff, "Most Turks Support the Syrian Invasion, Here's Why," *Washington Post*, October 25, 2019.

67. Eric Schmitt and Maggie Haberman, "Trump Endorses Turkish Military Operation in Syria, Shifting US Policy," *New York Times*, October 7, 2019.

68. Author's interview, February 23, 2020.

69. Uri Friedman, "What America's Allies Really Think About Trump's Syria Decision," *Atlantic*, December 14, 2019.

70. Rebecca Kheel, "House Passes Resolution Rebuking Trump Over Syria Pullout," *Hill*, October 16, 2019.

71. Friedman, "What America's Allies Really Think."

72. Letter from President Donald Trump to President Erdogan, White House, October 9, 2019.

73. "Turkey's Erdogan Threw Trump's Syria Letter in Bin," *BBC News*, October 17, 2019.

74. Lara Seligman, "Turkish-Backed Forces Are Freeing Islamic State Prisoners," *Foreign Policy*, October 14, 2019.

75. "Turkey Syria Offensive: 100,000 Flee Homes as Assault Continues," *BBC News*, October 11, 2019.

76. Liz Sly, "Turkish Led Forces Film Themselves Executing a Kurdish Captive in Syria," *Washington Post*, October 13, 2019.

77. Bethan McKernan, "Turkey-Syria Offensive: Kurds Reach Deal with Damascus to Stave Off Assault," *Guardian*, October 14, 2019.

78. "Syrian State Media Says Army Enters Town of Manbij in Northern Syria," *Reuters*, October 15, 2019.

79. "Pence Says Turkey, US Agree on Ceasefire in Northeast Turkey," *Reuters*, October 18, 2019.
80. Eric Schmitt and Maggie Haberman, "Trump Said to Favor Leaving a Few Hundred Troops in Eastern Syria," *New York Times*, October 20, 2019.
81. Bethan Mckernan and Julian Borger, "Turkey and Russia Agree on Deal Over Buffer Zone in Northern Syria," *Guardian*, October 23, 2019.
82. Bethan Mckernan, "Turkey Hails Erdogan as Hero as Death Toll Mounts in Border War," *Observer*, October 20, 2019.
83. Mazloum Abdi, "If We Have to Choose Between Compromise and Genocide, We Will Choose Our People," *Foreign Policy*, October 13, 2019.
84. See points expressed by Joshua Landis in Dominic Evans, Orhan Coskun, and Tom Perry, "Power Shift: Who Gains in the Battle for Syria's Northeast?," *Reuters*, October 16, 2019.
85. Isabella Nikolic and Reuters, "Russian Forces Take Over Abandoned US Air Base in Syria as Moscow Exerts Control Over War Torn Region," *Daily Mail*, November 15, 2019.
86. Kiril Semenov, "Russia Faces Dilemmas in Northeastern Syria," *Al-Monitor*, November 21, 2019.
87. S/PV.8645, October 24, 2019.
88. S/PV.8355, September 18, 2018.
89. Patrick Wintour, "Russia-Backed Syria Constitutional Talks Begin in Geneva," *Guardian*, October 31, 2019.
90. S/PV.8696, December 20, 2019
91. Kamal Alam, "In the Chaos of Syrian Geopolitics, Russia Remains Dominant," *RUSI Commentary*, May 15, 2020.
92. "Severe Message from Algeria: Syria Must Rejoin the Arab League," *Middle East Monitor*, March 3, 2020.
93. Bethan McKernan, "Idlib to Tripoli, Turkey Moves to Dominate Eastern Mediterranean," *Guardian*, May 26, 2020.
94. Edith M. Lederer, "UN Chief Says Cross-border Aid Into Syria Is Essential," *Associated Press*, December 17, 2019.
95. S/PV.8697, December 20, 2019.
96. S/PV. 8700, January 10, 2020.
97. Josh Rogin, "White House Worked Secretly to Delay Syria Sanctions Bill," *Washington Post*, September 21, 2016.

15. "NO MILITARY SOLUTIONS" AND OTHER ZOMBIES

1. S/PV.8715, February 6, 2020, 3.
2. Fabrice Balanche, "Assad Needs 'Useless Syria' Too," Washington Institute for Near East Policy, January 4, 2017.

3. Regis Le Sommier, "Bachar al-Assad: "Terrorists Are Terrorists: French or Not, They Must Abide by Syrian Law," *Paris Match*, November 28, 2019.
4. Ahmed Rasheed, "Exclusive: Baghdadi's Aide Was Key to His Capture—Iraqi Intelligence Sources," October 28, 2019.
5. Bethan McKernan, "Wife of Killed ISIS Leader Abu Bakr al-Baghdadi Captured, Says Turkey," *Guardian*, November 7, 2019.
6. Shawn Snow, "DIA Says ISIS Took Advantage of Turkish Invasion of Northern Syria, Baghdadi Death Did Not Degrade Jihadi Group," *Military Times*, February 4, 2020.
7. "Erdogan Says Astana Peace Talks Are 'Dead,'" *Enab Baladi*, February 2, 2020.
8. Emma Graham-Harrison and Hussein Akoush, "More than 235,000 People Have Fled Idlib Region in Syria, Says UN," *Guardian*, December 28, 2019.
9. Nabih Bulos, "As Syria's Army Advances Into Idlib, a Mass Exodus Is Underway," *Los Angeles Times*, December 26, 2019.
10. "Residents of Morthwestern Syria Flee from Government Forces' New Offensive," *Associated Press*, December 23, 2019.
11. "Russia, Turkey, and Iran Hold 14th Round of Talks on Syria War in Kazakhstan," *RFE/RL*, December 10, 2019.
12. "'Don't Do It': Trumps Warns Syria, Russia, and Iran Over Idlib Offensive," *Middle East Eye*, December 26, 2019.
13. Vladimir Soldatkin, "Russia Says Ceasefire Established in Syria's Idlib: TASS," January 10, 2020.
14. Nada Atieh, Alaa Nassar, and Walid al Nofal, "Aggression in Last De-escalation Zone Risks Fallout Between Turkey and Russia," *Syria Direct*, February 10, 2020.
15. "Erdogan Says Astana Peace Talks Are 'Dead,'" *Enab Baladi*, February 2, 2020.
16. "Syrian war: Government Troops Seize Part of Key Idlib Town Saraqeb," BBC News, February 7, 2020; and "Turkish Government Sets Third Observation Point Near Syria's Saraqib," *Daily Sabah*, February 1, 2020.
17. Atieh, Nassar, and al Nofal, "Aggression in Last De-escalation Zone."
18. International Crisis Group, "Deadly Clashes in Syria's Idlib Show Limits of Turkey's Options," February 29, 2020.
19. Bethan McKernan, "Turkish Soldiers Killed as Battle for Control of Idlib Escalates," *Guardian*, February 3, 2020.
20. "Erdogan Says Syrian Forces Must Pull Back from Idlib Posts," Al Jazeera, February 5, 2020.
21. "Syrian War: Government Troops Seize Part of Key Idlib Town Saraqeb," BBC News, February 7, 2020.
22. "Syrian Shellfire Kills Turkish Soldiers in Idlib," BBC News, February 10, 2020; and "Turkey Says It Hit 115 Syrian Government Targets, Destroyed 101 After Attacks on Soldiers," *Reuters*, February 11, 2020.
23. Quoted in Josie Ensor, "Assad Says Syria Regime Will See Victory 'Sooner or Later' as Hospitals and Refugee Camp Targeted," *Telegraph*, February 18, 2020.

24. "Security Summit Reiterates Turkey's Commitment to Retaliate to Assad's Attack in Idlib," *Daily Sabah*, February 11, 2020.
25. "Erdogan Threatens 'Imminent' Turkish Operation in Syria," Al Jazeera, February 19, 2020.
26. Jonathan Marcus, "How Russia's Putin Became the Go-to Man on Syria," BBC News, March 5, 2020.
27. Under-Secretary General for Humanitarian Relief Coordinator Mark Lowcock, briefing to UN Security Council on the humanitarian situation in Northwest Syria, February 19, 2020.
28. Jennifer Cafarella, John Dunford, Michael Land, and Blane Wallace, "Turkey Commits to Idlib," Institute for the Study of War, March 18, 2020.
29. Suzan Fraser and Vladimir Isachenkov, "Turkish Soldiers Killed in Syria Amidst Threat of Escalation," *Associated Press*, February 21, 2020.
30. "Turkey Rejects Russia's Idlib Plan Overlooking Region's People," *Daily Sabah*, February 19, 2020.
31. "Kremlin: Syria Talks with Erdogan, Macron, and Merkel Under Discussion," *Reuters*, February 21, 2020; and "Kremlin Says It Isn't Discussing a Syria Summit with Macron, Merkel," *Reuters*, February 25, 2020.
32. Orhan Coskun and Suleiman al-Khalidi, "Turkish-Backed Rebels Say They Seized Town in Syria's Idlib in First Advance," *Reuters*, February 25, 2020.
33. Bethan McKernan, "Syrian Rebels Retake Key Town in Idlib from Assad Forces," *Guardian*, February 28, 2020.
34. Simon Tisdall, "Erdogan Is Reaping What He Sowed: Turkey Is on the Brink of Disaster in Syria," *Guardian*, March 3, 2020.
35. Metin Gurcan, "Deciphering Turkey's Darkest Night in Syria," *AL-Monitor*, February 28, 2020.
36. Gurcan, "Deciphering Turkey's Darkest Night in Syria."
37. Tessa Fox, "Erdogan's Empty Threats," *Foreign Policy*, March 2, 2020.
38. Beth McKernan and Daniel Boffey, "Greece and Bulgaria Crack Down on Turkish Borders as Refugees Arrive," *Guardian*, February 29, 2020.
39. "Russia's Putin, Turkey's Erdogan Discuss Syria by Phone Amid Tensions," *Reuters*, February 28, 2020.
40. Edith M. Lederer, "UN Chief Urges Syria Ceasefire but Russia and China Oppose," *Associated Press*, February 29, 2020.
41. "Joint Turkish-Russian Patrols to Begin on March 15—Latest Updates," *TRT World*, March 7, 2020.
42. Sebastien Roblin, "Turkish Drones and Artillery Are Devastating Assad's Forces in Idlib Province—Here's Why," *Forbes*, March 2, 2020.
43. Mariya Petkova, "Turkish Drones—a 'Game Changer' in Idlib," Al Jazeera, March 3, 2020.
44. Jennifer Cafarella, John Dunford, Michael Land, and Blane Wallace, "Turkey Commits to Idlib," Institute for the Study of War, March 18, 2020.

45. Additional Protocol to the Memorandum on Stabilization of the Situation in the Idlib De-Escalation Area, Moscow, Russian Ministry of Foreign Affairs, March 6, 2020.

46. "Nearly 1,100 Military Units Cross Into NW Syria Since New Ceasefire Came Into Effect," *Syrian Observatory for Human Rights*, March 17, 2020.

47. Cafarella et al., "Turkey Commits to Idlib."

EPILOGUE

1. Several well-respected organizations have encouraged investment in Syrian reconstruction. The International Crisis Group, for example, suggested that investment be directed at the nonstate sector, as if "civil society" in government-held areas operated independently of government elites. It didn't in 2011, much less in 2020. Two key players in this space were Asma al-Assad and Rami Maklouf.

2. Jeremy Bowen, "Rami Maklouf: The Rift at the Heart of Syria's Ruling Family," BBC, May 20, 2020.

3. For example, International Crisis Group, "Prospects for a Deal to Stabilize Idlib," 2018, n. 34.

4. Bethan McKernan, "Syrian Protestors Call for Assad's Downfall as Economic Crisis Deepens," *Guardian*, June 13, 2020.

5. *Responsibility to Protect: Lessons Learned from Prevention. Report of the Secretary-General*, A/73/898-S/2019/463, June 10, 2019.

6. Charles Lister, "Assad Hasn't Won Anything," *Foreign Policy*, July 11, 2019.

7. Steven Simon, "Course Correction: Preventing State Collapse in Syria," Quincy Institute for Responsible Statecraft, *Quincy Paper* no. 3, August 2020.

8. Joseph Hincks, "In Solidarity and as a Symbol of Global Injustices, a Syrian Artist Painted a Mural to George Floyd on a Bombed Idlib Building," *Time*, June 6, 2020.

INDEX

CPSIA information can be obtained
at www.ICGtesting.com
Printed in the USA
LVHW111618160622
721144LV00005B/6/J